MANET
MANETTE

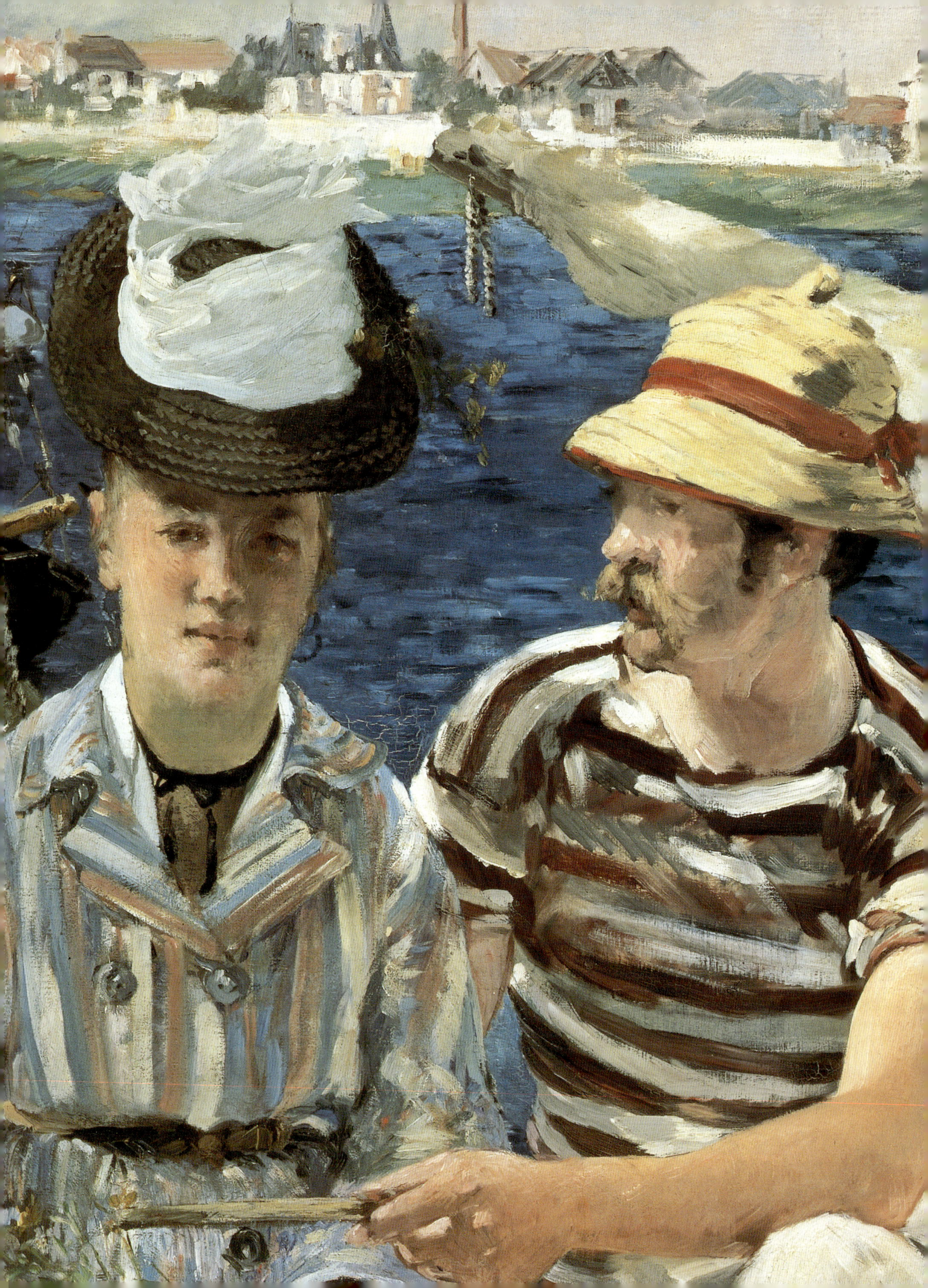

CAROL ARMSTRONG

MANET MANETTE

YALE UNIVERSITY PRESS

NEW HAVEN AND LONDON

Published with the assistance of
The Publications Committee, Department of Art and Archaeology,
Princeton University

Designed by Gillian Malpass

Printed in Singapore

Library of Congress Cataloging-in-Publication Data

Armstrong, Carol, 1955–
Manet Manette / by Carol Armstrong.
p.   cm.
Includes bibliographical references and index.
ISBN 0-300-09658-5 (hardback : alk. paper)
1. Manet, Edouard, 1832–1833 – Criticism and interpretation.   I. Title.
ND553.M3 A95   2002
759.4 – dc21   2002001582

A catalogue record for this book is available from
The British Library

Frontispiece   Edouard Manet, *Argenteuil* (detail of fig. 100)

To Ira, Aaron, and Zachary

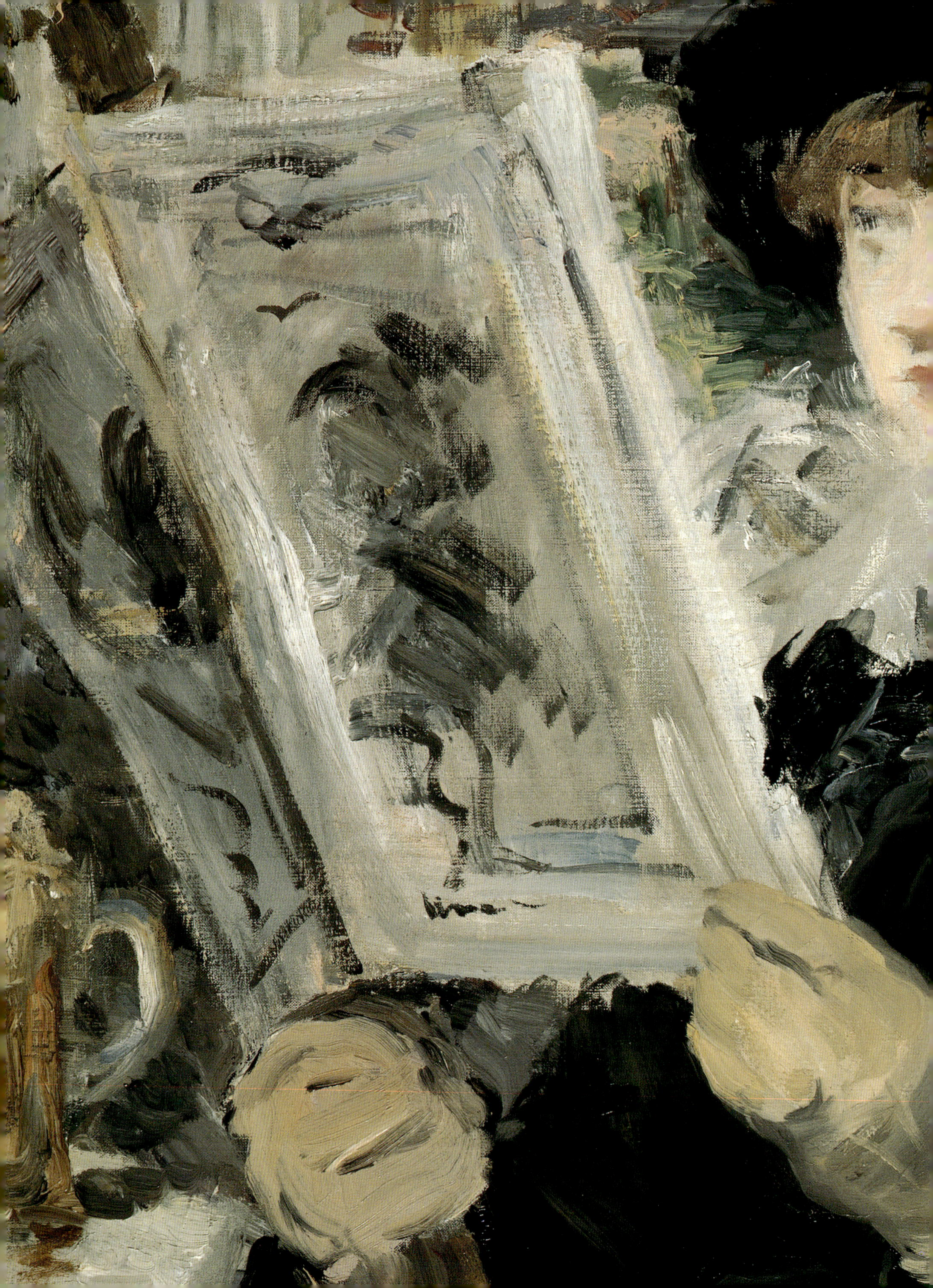

Contents

Detail of fig. 122.

Contents

Acknowledgments

I HAVE MANY TO THANK for their advice, input, and support or simply for the stimulus that their work provided me while I produced this book. The origin of *Manet Manette* lies in an article by that name that I published in the *Stanford Humanities Review* in 1992. But the seeds of it were sown earlier than that, during my years of teaching at the University of California at Berkeley. There the survey course that I taught each year with Svetlana Alpers first led me to pursue an interest in the pictures of Victorine Meurent painted by Edouard Manet in the 1860s: in an effort to understand Manet's complicated relationship to the museum of past art, and to comprehend how he did and did not fit into the standard narrative of modernism that led into Impressionism and out of it into abstraction, I began to think about the ways in which Manet picked up the threads of court painting in his representations of the female model, rather than rejecting them out-right. That thinking was spurred both by the narrative challenges of the introductory art-history survey, which once upon a time was so crucial to the discipline, and by the friendship and provocation of teaching with an art historian possessed of vivid, succinct intelligence about the art of Europe's Renaissance courts. Of particular significance to me were our discussions of Velasquez, who was vital to Manet: the relationship of Manet to Velasquez and the historically distinct eras that they represent have continued to be a site of productive argument between us and, indeed, were crucial to the completion of the manuscript, many of whose pieces Svetlana read and to which she responded use-fully and critically throughout.

I must also thank Jacqueline Lichtenstein, with whom I taught a graduate seminar on nineteenth-century art-writing at Berkeley. It was in the context of that early seminar that I first began to think in depth about the Goncourt brothers' novel *Manette Salomon*, which provides one of the meanings of the second half of my title, and more generally about the relationship between painting and literature. Jacqueline's ideas about color and the de-Pilsian rhetorial tradition, developed in *La Couleur Eloquente* (1989), continue to be an inspiration to me. The contributions of students in that seminar and in later courses at Berkeley, C.U.N.Y., and Princeton have been invaluable as well; here I think in particu-lar of Margaret Doyle, Melissa Hyde, Pamela Ivinski, Blake Koh, Neil Printz, Jeannene Pryzlbyski, Lora Rempel, Jennifer Shaw, and Marcus Verhagen. The combined efforts of the students in my seminars on formalism at C.U.N.Y. were fundamental – as was, in general, the liberating effect of teaching at the Graduate Center. And then there were the particular efforts of those students who helped me gather photographs and compile the index for the book: I am especially grateful for the work of Michelle Foa, Gordon Hughes, Lori Johnson, William McManus, and Lisa Schiff.

This book would not have been written without the goading of two very different books about Manet that I have used extensively in my teaching, which I admire immensely but with whose suppositions I ultimately disagree, and which are present in *Manet Manette* as both a necessary underpinning and a contrary undertow: Tim Clark's *The Painting of Modern Life: Paris in the Art of Manet and his Followers* of 1985 and more recently Michael Fried's *Manet's Modernism, or, The Face of Painting in the 1860s* of 1996. I am immediately indebted to Jim Rubin, for our discussions when he was at work on the final stages of *Manet's Silence and the Poetics of Bouquets* (1994) and I on beginning drafts of *Manet Manette*, and for his reading of the final manuscript and excellent suggestions for streamlining it. I have also been impelled throughout by the work of feminist historians of the nineteenth century – Hollis Clayson, Tamar Garb, Anne Higonnet, Linda Nochlin, Griselda Pollock, and Abigail Solomon-Godeau in particular – even, or especially, when I have ended up parting company with some of the main assumptions of that work too.

My thanks go as well to the editors of *October* magazine, and to Brad Collins and Paul Tucker, for their editorial advice, their support, and their help in the publication of essays that led to various chapters in this book. And I am indebted to the following individuals and institutions for inviting me to give papers that helped me work through many aspects of my thinking on Manet: the University of California at Berkeley; the Graduate Center of the City University of New York; Mark Gottlieb at Emory University; the School of the Art Institute of Chicago; Paul Tucker; the Department of French at Vassar College; the University of Delaware; Case Western Reserve University; the New York Society for Women in Philosophy; Duke University; Marcus Verhagen at Reed College; the N.Y.U. Institute of Fine Arts; David Joselit and Richard Meyer; Tom Crow at Yale University; Eduardo Cadava, Forbes College, and the Alumni Council at Princeton University; Sarah Rich at Pennsylvania State University; Norton Batkin and Martha Ward at the Bard College Center for Curatorial Studies.

I am grateful, too, to P.S.C.-C.U.N.Y. Research Foundation for the several grants it awarded me to conduct research and collect photographs for the book, to Princeton University for giving me an early research leave to complete the writing of the manuscript, and to the many museums and collections who have permitted me to reproduce their works in *Manet Manette*. And finally, without the editorial commitment and vision of Gillian Malpass, none of it would have been possible: I owe particular thanks to her, and to her assistant Sandy Chapman.

In the conventional order of acknowledgments, one's family generally comes last. But not least: for the affection, skepticism, and honesty that they provide, for their helping me to balance a professional with another identity, for being essential to my happiness, my sanity, and my insanity, my husband and two sons are most important of all. I thank them just for being there.

MANET'S "INCONSISTENCY"

ONE HUNDRED YEARS AFTER Edouard Manet's "exposition particulière" at the Place de l'Alma in Paris, on the periphery of the Universal Exposition of 1867, Clement Greenberg wrote about "the large Manet show" which traveled from the Philadelphia Museum of Art in November and December of 1966, to the Art Institute of Chicago in January and February of 1967. In that context, his estimation of Manet's painting was this:

> Manet is far from being the only master who doesn't develop in a straight line, with one step following the other in readily intelligible order. Nor is he the only master whose total body of work doesn't make a coherent impression. But he is exceptional in his *inconsistency*. I don't mean the inconsistency of his quality. He is uneven, but less so than Renoir or Monet. I mean the inconsistency of his approach and of his direction. This is what struck me particularly at the large Manet show in the Philadelphia Museum of Art.[1]

Thus begins a five-page essay on Manet, which treats his work more particularly and extensively than Greenberg had done in any of his other essays. More usually, Greenberg simply cited Manet as the figurehead of the nineteenth-century French beginnings of "modernism," such that the signification of the name "Manet" was the trajectory that it heralded: "[t]he evolution of modern painting from Manet on."[2] "Manet," in short, meant "painting since Manet."[3]

The judgments inscribed in Greenberg's telegraphic use of the name "Manet" were the ones that had currency, and continued to do so, in spite of the growing disaffection, in the 1970s, '80s, and '90s, with formalist criticism; and not his more particularized – and surprising – confrontation with Manet's "inconsistency" in 1967. Manet and Courbet; Manet and Monet and the Impressionists; Manet and Cézanne (and occasionally Gauguin); Manet and Matisse and Mondrian; Picasso and Braque; fauvism and cubism: coupled and uncoupled and recoupled again with the names of other modernist icons from the nineteenth and early twentieth centuries, standing at the head of a "line" leading from French "naturalism" to postwar American abstraction, representing not only freshness, novelty, and originality but also flatness and "optical" brushwork, the reversal of the Western tradition of the easel painting, the "radical" break with its illusionism, and in its place the frank and necessarily specialized declaration of "the physical nature of the medium," and the Kantian value of transcendent self-reflexivity, "Manet" was, for Greenberg (as well as for the rest of us coming after), nothing more or less than modernism's most often cited point of origin.[4] In many ways, this verdict depended upon its own cursoriness – but more on that in a moment.

This use of Manet's name was by no means unprecedented; it went back to the days of the Impressionist exhibitions, in which Manet never participated, though he was a friend of Degas, met the others at the Café Guerbois and the Nouvelle-Athènes, and in the 1870s began to associate with them at Argenteuil and to paint their subjects in something like their manner. But in the reviews of the Impressionist exhibitions his name came up repeatedly, signifying, though usually in a negative light, many of the same qualities that later added up to Greenberg's celebrated modernism: an *épater le bourgeois* attitude and a general radicality; a break with tradition, academic conventions, and illusionistic finish; *Epinal* flatness and the unabashed *tache*; the fathering of (and identity with) Impressionism.[5] Thus installed, his name was used in the same vein, in the short hindsight of, among others, Roger Fry's modernist updating of Berensonian formalism.[6] But it was with Greenberg's somewhat longer hindsight that "Manet" became the teleological origin of modernism in its most familiar incarnation.[7]

Most accounts of Manet's art since then have accepted Greenberg's condensed estimate of it, even when wrestling with the values of his model of formalist criticism, and attempting to substitute a socially and discursively contextualized reading of his imagery for Greenberg's exclusivist, evolutionary long view. To take just the two foremost examples in recent Manet scholarship, this is as true of T. J. Clark's *The Painting of Modern Life*, with its Marxian account of the "battle of representations" in which Manet and "his followers" participated in the 1860s and '70s,[8] as it is of Michael Fried's very different *Manet's Modernism*, with its phenomenologically informed understanding of Manet's art of the '60s.[9] *The Painting of Modern Life* assumes the heroic modernist lineage that Greenberg memorialized and with it its values of flatness and radical rupture with the illusionistic baggage of painting's representational past, not to mention Manet's more local position as the sire of Impressionism. Indeed, it constitutes an attempt to weave together the terms of Meyer Schapiro's and Greenberg's understanding of "modernism": to give a socio-historical, iconographically grounded account of "Manet's art as a turning point of culture," in which, in the "familiar form of words which we owe to Clement Greenberg . . . each art in the new age is thought obliged 'to determine, through the operations peculiar to itself, the effects peculiar and exclusive to itself'."[10]

For its part, Fried's book on Manet is introduced with a longer quote from Greenberg, from the same Kantian essay on "Modernist Painting" concerning the medium specifity, "purity," and flatness (and the Wölfflinian opticality) of modernist painting, describing Manet as the creator of the "first Modernist pictures," and placing him at the head of the "line" leading through Cézanne to the twentieth century.[11] Manet's "modernism," as Fried still names it, is still Greenberg's at root. Manet is still, in Fried's telling of the tale, at the head of a heroic tradition of radical, serious modern art – leading ultimately to the American moment from which Fried began writing in the 1960s, defending abstract painting against the incursions of the Minimalist object and looking back to the nineteenth and then to the eighteenth century to find a historical "line" simultaneously predicated on and in justification of that defense.[12] And the Greenbergian privileging of painting qua painting, of the transcendent value of "unity" – both pictorial and historical – and of a teleological art history are all still at work.

I too begin with Greenberg, but with a different Greenberg, who in 1967 wrote about Manet more specifically. That Greenberg claimed that, far from standing at the head of the modernist "line," Manet's own painting did not even "develop in a straight line"; that it did not submit well to the totalizing *coup d'oeil* of the connoisseur of the master-oeuvre; that it did not add up to one thing; that, more than merely incoherent or uneven, it was exceptionally inconsistent: indeed, as he proceeded to argue, its "inconsistency" was the mark of Manet's special genius, if not his very signature. Greenberg went on to assimilate his inconsistent Manet to the terms of heroic modernism, showing how "Manet's inconsistency can be attributed more to his plight as the first modernist painter than to his temperament"; how, for Manet, each new painting took nothing for granted, followed no formula, was a fresh new beginning and a whole world unto itself, utterly sincere and absolutely autonomous – "a one-time thing, a new start, and . . . completely individual" ("Manet in Philadelphia," pp. 241, 243). But in the meantime he also claimed that "Manet's best years were just those, the 1860s, in which he was the most inconsistent" (p. 241); that his worst were his more consistent ones, the Impressionist 1870s; and that his "inconsistency" separated his work from the day-to-day procedures of the Impressionists (as well as of other modernists like Cézanne, Van Gogh, and the Cubists). Manet, in other words, was most singularly himself when he was most plural; he was at his best when he was the least Impressionist; more than that, he was not Impressionist, he was not really even the forebear of Impressionism, if one considered his works up close, one by one, and in relation to one another.

To illustrate Manet's "inconsistency," Greenberg paired individual paintings by Manet that he felt were opposed in their effects:

> In one and the same year, 1862, Manet painted a picture like *Young Woman Reclining in Spanish Costume* and a picture like *Gypsy with a Cigarette*; the first, with its undulations of plum and silvery little gleams of bright color, is a masterpiece; the showy brushing and illustrativeness of the second anticipate present-day magazine art. ("Manet in Philadelphia," p. 240)

Speaking of two of Manet's somewhat lesser-known works (figs. 1, 2), Greenberg manages to convey that the founder of modernism was capable of both kitsch illustration ("banal and slick art," p. 241) and avant-garde masterpieces. At the same time, he describes two very different kinds of facture as equally characteristic of Manet's style of painting. Presently, he used two much more canonical works to binarize Manet's "inconsistency" more summarily:

> he so often changed his notion of what a picture should be: built-up, put-together, and "composed," or random and informal, studied or spontaneous, intimate and subdued, or grand and imposing. All through the 1860s he kept one eye on the Old Masters, but it was an eye that wavered. *Déjeuner sur l'herbe* (1863), though its layout *comes from Florence, goes toward Venice*; *Olympia* (likewise 1863), with an arrangement that *comes from Venice, goes toward Florence*. (p. 241)

(Greenberg then turned to the *Luncheon on the Grass* and read Manet's binary "inconsistency" into a single painting.[13])

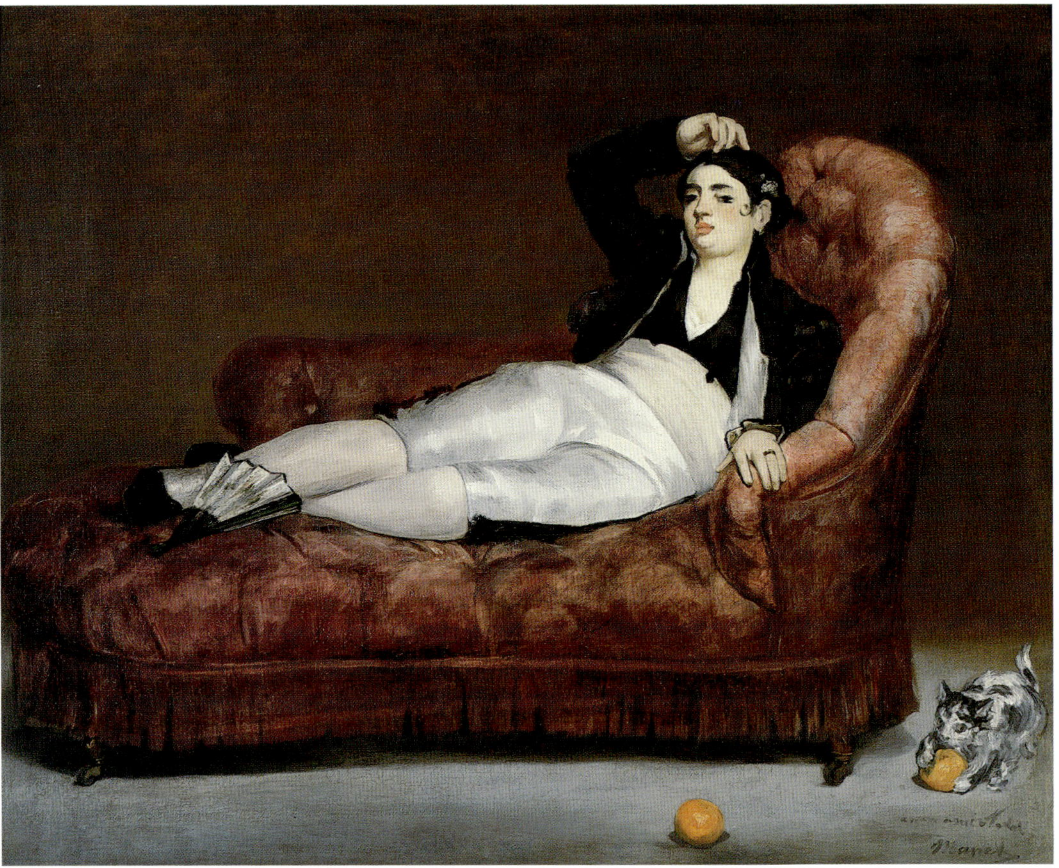

Here, then, is a Manet that does not fit. Here is a master-oeuvre that is not an oeuvre, if by "oeuvre" we mean a linear development, a coherent style, and a singular signature. Here is an author of great works with great ambitions who had no single voice, whose plurality cannot even be attributed to "his temperament" (only to his "orientation," whatever that might mean, exactly) (p. 241). And here is the source of Greenberg's great tradition of Kantian modernism: a painter who, though he strove to make each new painting a world unto itself, often failed to achieve the transcendent unity, the oneness, the self-consistency, self-identity, and self-mastery that every formalist system since the eighteenth century has privileged and desired. "Manet" is still "the first modernist painter" – but what a one he is: or rather, what a not-one, bringing to the fore all the dividedness-against-oneself that it has been the business of formalist aesthetics to repress.[14] And though he is still the "first modernist painter," he stands, off by himself, as an exception rather than the rule, inaugurating what looks more like a set of exceptional instances than a "line."

Famously, the German art-historical formalisms of the turn of the last century – those of Wölfflin and Riegl – traded in binary formulations: the linear versus the painterly, the optical versus the tactile – or haptic, the North versus the South, and so on.[15] In part, these were inherited from nineteenth-century positivist art history: for instance,

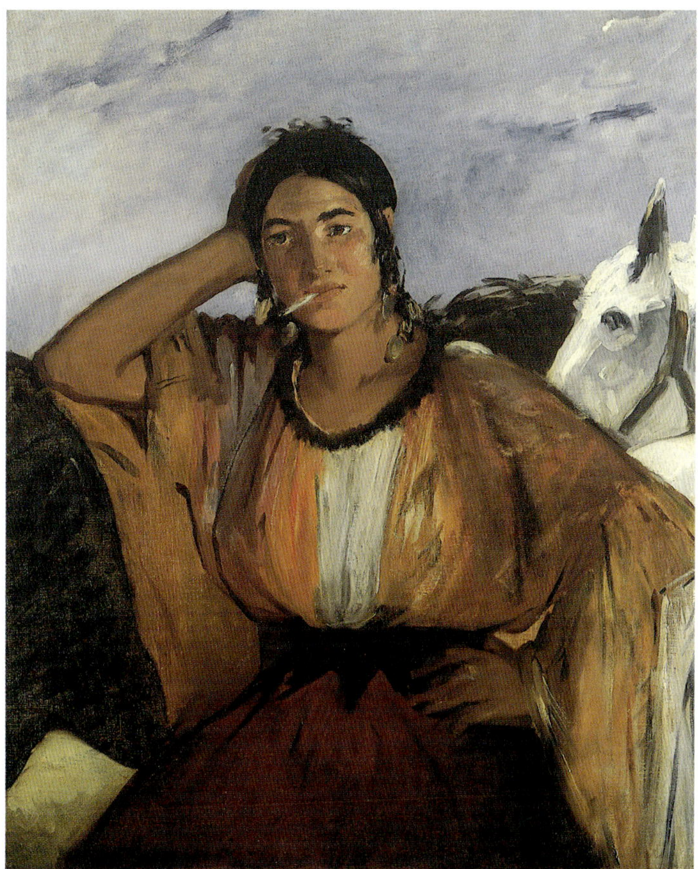

1 (*facing page*)　Edouard Manet, *Young Woman Reclining in Spanish Costume*, 1862, oil on canvas, 95 × 113 cm. Courtesy of Yale University Art Gallery, New Haven, Bequest of Stephen Carlton Clark, '03.

2　Edouard Manet, *Gypsy with a Cigarette*, 1862, oil on canvas, 92 × 73.5 cm. The Art Museum, Princeton University. Bequest of Archibald S. Alexander, Class of 1928.

Hippolyte Taine's *Philosophie de l'art* series of the 1860s, to which I will return, mobilizes most of these oppositions in the context of a nationalist, indeed racialist discourse on the history of art from the Renaissance to the seventeenth century. Greenberg's criticism had its own set of binaries, sometimes including the Wölfflinian. But here in "Manet in Philadelphia" his binary set describes a single artist, whose work is at once "masterpiece" and illustration, brushy and slick, composed and random, "from Florence, go[ing] toward Venice," and "from Venice, go[ing] toward Florence." And this dualistic Manet of Greenberg's is nothing like Riegl's exceptional Rembrandt, crossing and combining the modes of North and South: rather than a resolution, his art is an incoherence at the inception, and at the heart, of modernism.

There is an important paradox in all of this, and it turns on the singularity of Manet's doubleness – on the signature recognizability of Manet's one-of-a-kind plurality, but also on the relationship between single pictures and groups of pictures that make up oeuvres and retrospective exhibitions, like the ones held in Paris in 1867 and in Philadelphia and Chicago in 1966–67.[16] Greenberg declares:

Manet's case makes it quite clear that consistency is not an artistic virtue in itself. It did not keep him, any more than his prodigious skill with the brush did, from

creating great works of art that are not *tours de force* and have nothing to do with vir-
tuosity. Nevertheless, his inconsistency does seem to offer an obstacle to many people.
They find it difficult to get his art into clear focus. It's their own fault, of course, more
than it is Manet's. *One looks at one picture at a time, one looks at single works, not at a
whole oeuvre.* Or rather, one should. (p. 241)

Here Greenberg speaks of the difference it makes when one looks hard at "one picture
at a time," rather than taking in the "whole" – the "whole *oeuvre*" or the "whole" "line":
the closer, more individuated looking yields something other than the sweeping connoisseurial or historical gaze; the "single works" do not illustrate or represent the "whole,"
rather, they rupture it. Which, in addition to confronting something specific to Manet,
is a procedural comment: it is as much as to admit that the "line," whether that of the
single artist's work or of an entire lineage, and the "whole," whether that of an "oeuvre"
or of a tradition, are produced by the critic and the historian – and by a synthesizing,
surveying gaze that may or may not be supported by a more particularizing scrutiny.
(The "line" and the "whole" are two faces of the same value, which is related to the formalist criterion of pictorial "unity": the continuous, teleological chain and the coherent,
all-at-once *gestalt*, they both reduce to the unified shape of the One, to the unity and
self-identity of a historical, stylistic, and subjective totality.[17])

    Greenberg's remarks about "single works" and the "whole *oeuvre*" also put the singu-
lar and the plural into question with regard to exhibitions. It is true that Greenberg
recommends taking in Manet's paintings one at a time, suggesting that any difficulties
with Manet's "inconsistency" are the "fault" of those who seek to put them together
into a "whole," and thus resolving those difficulties for himself by privileging the unity
of the single work over the unity of the "oeuvre" or the "line." (Those single works,
like the *Luncheon on the Grass*, that do not cohere in themselves ought simply to be cut
down.) So Greenberg seems to be prescribing precisely that which is enacted by institutions exhibiting modern art, institutions such as the Museum of Modern Art in New
York but also the Philadelphia Museum of Art and the Art Institute of Chicago, the
Metropolitan Museum of Art, and the Grand Palais, Paris, which put on retrospectives
of single "oeuvres" and of modern "lines": namely, the repression of the exhibition
itself, of its ideological conditions and its serial presentation of works, in favor of the
isolated, autonomous realm of the single modern masterpiece. And yet, everything that
is of interest in "Manet in Philadelphia" proceeds from the fact that Greenberg looks at
works in an exhibition, and in relation to one another: *Young Woman Reclining in Spanish
Costume* in relation to *Gypsy with a Cigarette*; *Luncheon on the Grass* in relation to
Olympia; the works of the '60s in relation to the works of the '70s; the "still lifes and
seascapes" in relation to "paintings like *Olympia*, the *Déjeuner*, the *Luncheon* of 1868–69,
The Fifer of 1866, the *Bon Bock* of 1873, the *Bar at the Folies-Bergère* of 1882, and more
than a few others"; and those great "single works" in relation to the list of works, with
which Greenberg concludes, which "were to be seen in Philadelphia" (p. 244). Indeed,
it is as if Greenberg returns, in an uncharacteristic regression, to the "comparative" mode
of looking at works that had characterized the early museological order of the Ancien
Régime, rather than the taxonomic and teleological progression favored from the time
of the Revolution to our own day – applying that mode to different works by a single

artist rather than examples from different schools of art.[18] It is as if up-close confrontation with the "inconsistencies" of Manet's "oeuvre" necessitated such a regression.

Despite what Greenberg says to the contrary, then, "Manet in Philadelphia" is about looking at pictures in an exhibition; it proposes looking, one by one, at "single works" as they are exhibited in relation to one another – which is different, Greenberg makes clear, from looking at works produced and presented as a single series (as the Impressionists, Monet and Degas in particular, increasingly presented theirs[19]); it suggests that we ought to look at the differences between works that their exhibition puts on display. Greenberg's observation that Manet painted not in connected series but in large, ambitious singles – that like the old masters Manet "continued to believe . . . that a 'machine,' a picture big enough in size and complicated enough in subject and composition, was what a painter had to prove himself with" – is on target, as is his understanding that this made Manet fundamentally unlike most of the modernists who came after him. Throughout his career Manet surely did tend to paint big, single statements – such as *Olympia* and the *Luncheon*, those two icons of the Manet canon that Greenberg sees as emblematic of the differences within his oeuvre. At the most, he sometimes painted pairs of pictures that had something to do with one another – which might be considered rather complicated pendants (*Olympia* and the *Luncheon* make one such pair), but he hardly ever painted in series per se. And from 1861 all the way to 1882 he continued to exhibit in the mainstream forum that called for big, single statements – the Salon.

From the outset of his career, however, Manet also presented his works in privately organized retrospective exhibitions, and he did so over and over again, more repeatedly and insistently than most of his contemporaries: in his studio several times, at Martinet's in 1863, outside the Universal Exposition in 1867, at Charpentier's *La Vie Moderne* in 1880; and there are, in addition, the two portfolios of Manet's prints published by Cadart in 1862 and 1874, which like his retrospectives were also overviews of his work put before the public. It was as if Manet organized his practice around the exhibition – indeed, had an exhibition practice – and in it solicited the construction of his work as an oeuvre. But once again, what an oeuvre: rather than a unitary *gestalt* or a single "line," that oeuvre was constructed, just as Greenberg later proposed in response to the Philadelphia show, around a set of internal differences. That was what Manet's exhibition practice foregrounded fairly obsessively, despite the single "line" that supporters of his, Emile Zola most particularly, tried to make of it.[20] That is what the pursuance of Greenberg's suggestions in "Manet in Philadelphia" opens up.

This brings me to what I hope is the difference of my own interest in Manet. Among other things, I want to look at Manet's exhibition practice, with a view toward understanding his special mode of "inconsistency", which I believe is as good as any description of the strangeness of his oeuvre, of its unaccountability, its undecidability, and irreducibility – of what is not covered by normalizing "Manet" as the founding father of a heroic, Kantian modernism. Manet, of course, was not the only artist ever to have had a divided, differentiated style: looked at one way, all artists' oeuvres are marked by "inconsistency"; all artists' "consistency" is a selective construction of the critic, connoisseur, and art historian. But Greenberg was right, it seems to me, in seeing the special, signature "inconsistency" of Manet's art: his was an oeuvre that highlighted that inconsistency, showing how style itself was built on a fractured foundation, how the singularity of the artistic self was put together out of multiple personalities and many manners, borrowed from elsewhere, and set in new relation to one another – and if that was so of Manet's production of works, it was doubly underlined and all but thematized in his modes of exhibition.

It is that exhibited "inconsistency," not covered in any of the existing treatments of Manet's art which either stress or take its modernism for granted, that this account will address. Instead of the monologic principle of the "oeuvre" or the modernist series, it will suggest a dialogic paradigm for understanding the structure of relationships within and among Manet's works as they were exhibited in and outside of his studio, as well as between Manet's paintings, the museum of European art of the past, and the modernism of his Impressionist contemporaries.[21] Instead of the formula of a self-consistent modernist painting "hunted back to its medium" familiar from Greenberg's more canonical essays,[22] it will propose a view of Manet's art in line with Hegel's model of a disintegrative modern art – a late-coming romantic art that "falls to pieces," rather than a forerunning advance guard that paves the way to a unified modernism.[23] It will pursue that same conception of modern art as it was proposed in French novels of Manet's time about the plight of the modern artist, running from Honoré de Balzac's *Le Chef-d'oeuvre inconnu* of 1831/37, through the Goncourt brothers' *Manette Salomon* of 1867 (from which the Manette in "Manet Manette" partly derives), to Emile Zola's *L'Oeuvre* of 1886.

Manet Manette, moreover, will proceed according to a notion of the "difference," rather than the autonomy, of painting.[24] Dating back to the Ancien Régime, that idea of painting – as coloristic and cosmetic, "le beau fard" – opens onto the thematics of femininity that fascinated Manet so, as well as an erotics of painting other than that of the so-called "male gaze."[25] That idea of painting had its afterlife not only in the novels mentioned above but also in Charles Baudelaire's conception of the "painting of modern life," all of which applied directly or indirectly to Manet's art.[26] Thus, finally, this account of Manet's career will combine a feminist with a formalist perspective, reading the postulate of the "sex which is not one" into the form and facture, as well as the subject matter, of Manet's paintings: discovering the "Manette" in "Manet," in other words.[27] Clearly that takes us a very long way from Greenberg, but it is nevertheless an account of Manet's art opened up by Greenberg's close, inadvertently antiteleological encounter with the strangeness, doubleness, and unassimilability – the "inconsistency" – of the modernist configuration that goes by the name of "Manet."

Part One

1867

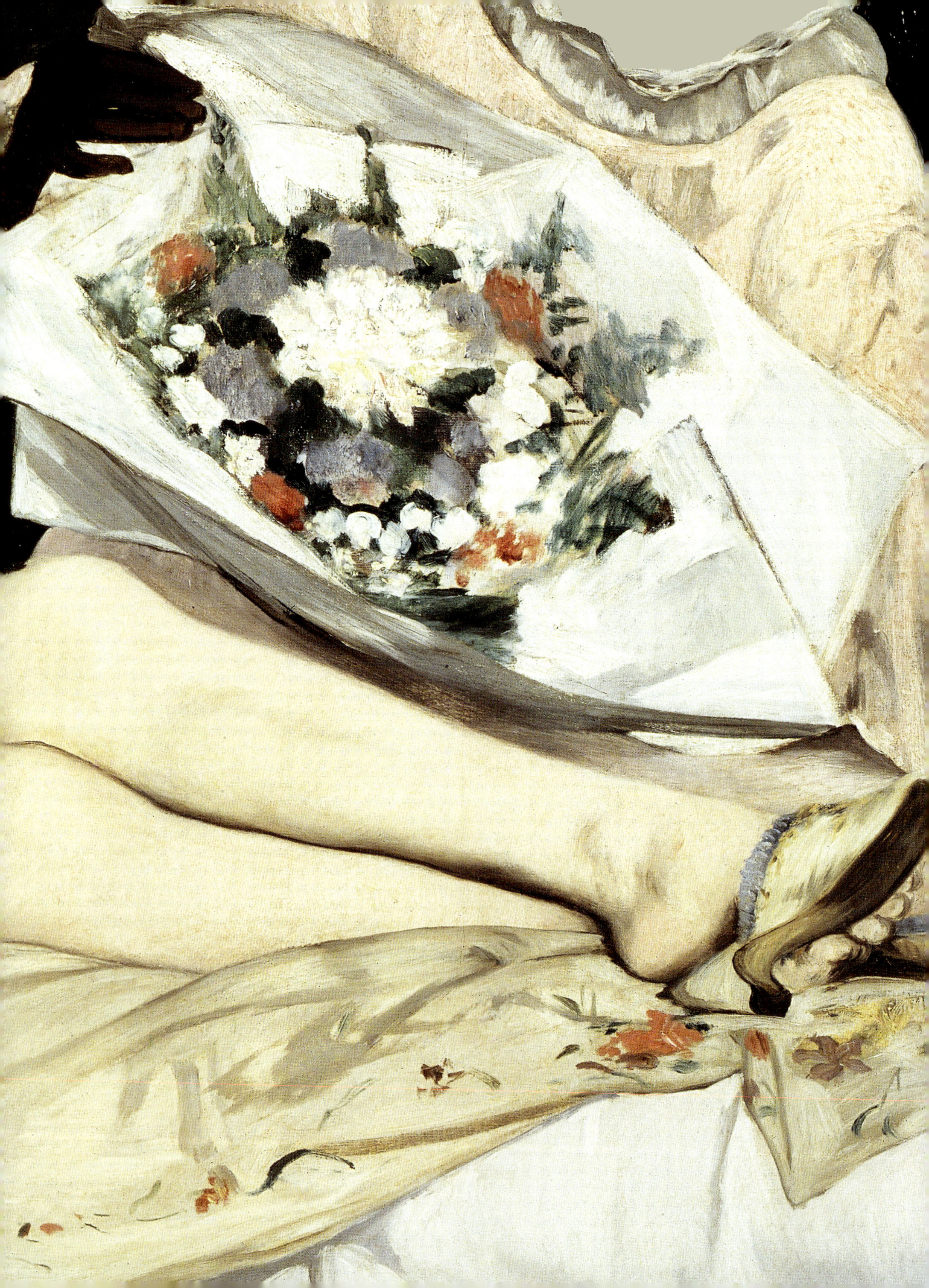

Chapter One

TWO RETROSPECTIVES:
COURBET IN 1855 AND MANET IN 1867

Part one is a tale of two exhibitions, one monograph, and one novel. The first of
the two exhibitions treated here in Chapter One is the retrospective mounted by Courbet
in Paris, at the time of the Universal Exposition of 1855. The second exhibition was
modeled on the first: it is Manet's retrospective of 1867, held, like Courbet's, in an independent pavilion on the threshold of the Universal Exposition of that year (during which
time Courbet mounted another, much larger retrospective of his own). The monograph,
to be addressed in Chapter Two, is Emile Zola's "Une nouvelle manière en peinture:
Edouard Manet," first published in the *Revue du dix-neuvième siècle* on January 1, 1867
and then republished in June as a brochure, after Manet had pondered and decided
against the essay as an introduction to the catalogue of his exhibition.[1] And the novel,
to be treated in Chapter Three, is *Manette Salomon* by the Goncourt brothers, set in the
years leading up to and culminating in 1855, the time of the first Universal Exposition
and the first of the two retrospectives, but published in 1867, the year of the second of
the two retrospectives, to coincide with the second of the two Universal Expositions held
in Second Empire Paris.[2]

Though the idea for the one came from the other, Courbet's retrospective of 1855 and
Manet's retrospective of 1867 ultimately proposed quite different views of modern art
and the modern oeuvre. Each was a response to the acceptances and refusals of the artist's
works, over the years and up to the moment, by the Salon juries. Each was a kind of
public studio exhibition mounted by a relatively young, upstart artist: Courbet was
thirty-six in 1855, had been kicking around Paris, on and off, since 1840, and had been
painting and submitting to the Salon – and getting some things accepted – since the
mid-1840s;[3] Manet was thirty-five in 1867, was Parisian born and bred, had left Couture's
studio in 1856 to begin his own career and, after having been rejected in 1859, had been
in his first Salon in 1861. And each was an overview of the artist's short career thus far:
Courbet had a total of fifty-six pictures on view in 1855, and Manet had the same amount
in his show of 1867, setting the "exposition particulière" in fairly explicit contrast to the
"Exposition Universelle," to the imperial presentation of the French patrimony and of
the relation between industry and the arts available within each of the two Universal
Expositions. There the resemblance ends, however: it is the difference between Courbet's
and Manet's conceptions of themselves, of their oeuvres, of modern art and its relation
to the retrospectives and hegemonic displays of national schools of art within the two
industrial Expositions that I wish to pursue in this first chapter.

Detail of fig. 9.

As for Zola's monograph and the Goncourts' novel, they represent two equally different views of the modern artist, the relationship between his life and his work, and the situation of modern art both within and outside of the embrace of the officially sanctioned institutions of art instruction, presentation, and advancement. Zola's monograph belongs to the biographical tradition of the *vie d'artiste* and addresses the life and work of a single, real-life artist, while the Goncourts' novel belongs to the fictional genre of the artist's "sentimental journey," and ranges rather diffusely across many different "lives" and "works," choosing not to center itself in any one artistic circle or limit itself to a recognizable, circumscribed set of references to the contemporary art scene. Yet both Zola and the Goncourts mythify their artists equally, treat their works, their careers, and their public reputations, and act as critics of the current art scene, particularly of the situation of painting at the time of the Universal Expositions. (Later, Edmond de Goncourt accused Zola of stealing the premise of his and Jules's story – and doing violence to it – when he made his final, revised judgments about Manet, and Monet and Cézanne and the rest of what was then modern art, in his artist novel of 1886, *L'Oeuvre*.) In short, "Une nouvelle manière en peinture" and *Manette Salomon* enter into the same discursive fray; literary counterparts to the relatively recently conceived device of the artist's retrospective,[4] they propose two alternative understandings of what artists like Courbet and Manet were about when they summarized their careers in exhibitions on the margins of the Second Empire's mammoth product displays of 1855 and 1867. It is in that light that I shall be concerned with them in Chapters Two and Three.

THE MODEL: COURBET'S RETROSPECTIVE WITHIN A RETROSPECTIVE

As the story goes, Courbet submitted fourteen paintings to the arts jury of the Universal Exposition, got eleven accepted and three rejected, and after maneuvering between Count de Nieuwerkerke and his private patron Alfred Bruyas, decided to keep the eleven accepted works within the Universal Exposition's Palais des Beaux-Arts and to mount a show of forty-five others, including the three rejected paintings, directly opposite the Palais des Beaux-Arts, in a temporary pavilion on the Avenue Montaigne, promoted in posters and in a manifesto written by him, "Le Réalisme," which formed the introduction to the catalogue of works accompanying the show. (The show opened at the end of June, about six weeks after the beginning of the Universal Exposition, but soon enough to coincide with it for a time.[5]) Thus Courbet was both in and outside of the Universal Exposition; he not only managed to rival the grand old men of the modern French patrimony – the Raphaelite Ingres and the Rubensian Delacroix, the orientalist genre painter Decamps and the battle painter Horace Vernet – who were honored with retrospectives of their own within the Universal Exposition, he did them one better by having two, one "particular," private, and rebellious, and one "universal," publicly endorsed, and governmentally sanctioned: one retrospective and one counter-retrospective, in short. Or, the two exhibitions could be thought of as bridging the spaces of artistic officialdom and insurrection in order to acheive one large, overarching retrospective such as was not permitted to Courbet otherwise, namely, on the order and of the size of the four formally recognized retrospectives of Ingres, Delacroix, Decamps, and Vernet. Either way, Courbet had his cake and ate it too, showing how he could belong to the great tradition, long before his elders and betters, and at the same time defy it, declaring himself a young "grand maître" and at the same time his own man, demonstrating the individuality of his work both when subsumed within and when pitted against the Empire.

Between the two venues, Courbet focused on his major specialties at that time: large-scale genre painting, portraiture, and landscape. In the Palais des Beaux-Arts, he had *The Stonebreakers*, *The Young Women of the Village*, *The Meeting*, *The Cornsifters*, and *The Spinner*, as well as two self-portraits, one portrait of a Spanishwoman, and three landscapes.[6] In his pavilion, he had *The Painter's Studio* and the *Burial at Ornans* (both rejected from the Palais des Beaux-Arts and numbered one and two in his catalogue), as well as the *Return from the Fair* (*The Peasants of Flagey*), the 1853 *Bathers*, the *Wrestlers*, a sketch for *The Young Women of the Village*, sixteen portraits (including *The Cellist*, *The Wounded Man*, *The Lovers*, and two other self-portraits, as well as portraits of Champfleury, Baudelaire, and others, plus a "rêverie" and a pirate), one other nude, sixteen landscapes, two "pastiches," and four drawings.

Among the paintings in Courbet's pavilion, there was just the odd picture here and there showing what his work had looked like at its inception, when it was most "inconsistent": these included four 1841–42 landscapes, one 1843 self-portrait, and the two "pastiches" (one Florentine look-alike of a head of a young girl and one Flemish knock-off of an "imaginary landscape") of the same year, and the 1844 picture of the pirate. Besides a few 1845 pictures in different genres, the rest were concentrated after 1847. They were not listed in chronological order – on the contrary, the roster begins with 1855 and with a focus on the '50s. But though the catalogue list does not keep utterly to its genre divisions, nonetheless all the large genre works come at the beginning, to be followed by a group of portraits, followed in turn by a long list of landscapes, interrupted here and there by a few portraits and some of the miscellaneous things, culminating with the four drawings and three afterthoughts.[7] (By the time of Courbet's much more comprehensive retrospective of 1867, which included well over one hundred works, the genre categorization of the first retrospective's catalogue had been solidified, much more rigorously and logically maintained, and even exaggerated, with works broken down not only into genres but also sub-genres: under a series of headings progressing downward in order of genre and medium importance, from "tableaux" through "paysages," "paysages de neige," "paysages de mer," "portraits," and "tableaux de fleurs," to culminate with "études et ésquisses," and a few drawings and sculptures.[8])

As both installations demonstrated, Courbet's manner was remarkably consistent from genre to genre and particularly over the previous seven to ten years of his career, from the late '40s to the mid-'50s, when he left his early "pastiches" and baroque-romantic gestures behind. It remained so, too, through 1867 and beyond, if anything becoming more and more uniform and more reduced, when he settled into a stable market and an established reputation, and moved with growing facility between the *pompier* nude and the "realist" genres.[9] His history-sized genre paintings, nudes, portraits, landscapes (and then later still lifes) – each had its own recurring formula, and each its limited and coherent set of art-historical references, ranging most often among the Dutch, the Spanish, the Caravaggesque, the Barbizon, and the *Epinal*, but whether brushed or troweled with the palette knife, all shared a mortar-like facture and a robust physicality increasingly conspicuous in their constancy. That is to say, Courbet made the most of his "consistency" – his unified individuality and the sameness of his signature across different subject matters – using his retrospectives to put it on display.

It would be redundant to look across Courbet's whole oeuvre as it was presented in the two settings of 1855. Rather, I shall take Greenberg's recommendation and attend to a single work, one painting in particular, which summarizes the rest – the recently painted and complexly titled *The Painter's Studio: A Real Allegory Summing Up Seven Years of My Life as a Painter* (fig. 3). The title of this painting spells out its function as a retrospective in and of itself, its status as a retrospective within a retrospective. This is so particularly of the second half of the title: "summing up seven years of my life as a painter" is what the immense, populous painting, with its array of portraits and its nucleus of landscape-and-nude-and-genre-figure-and-self-portrait, rather monomaniacally represents. The seven years that it designates, looking from 1855 back to 1848 – to the beginning of the short-lived Second Republic and the origin of Courbet's outsized identity as a revolutionary in both art and politics – predicates and qualifies the "painter's studio" which the title foregrounds. In other words, it proclaims the studio as a space of seven years' worth of production, as well as the display of that production – as if to define the alternative space of the pavilion in which *The Painter's Studio* was hung and of which it was the centerpiece as something like a personal, privately supported, in-studio exhibition (an exhibition convention with a revolutionary pedigree going back to David[10]), to be contrasted to the Fine Arts section of the Universal Exposition, with its official retrospectives and its epitomizing of the impersonal and eclectic warehouse mode of the Salons.

And it suggests a "real allegory" that is all about the retrospective – about defining an oeuvre retrospectively, and differently from the way oeuvres were being defined in the Palais des Beaux-Arts. That is to say, its "real allegory" concerns the definition of an "oeuvre" as much as a description of art's relation to the real world or to contemporary politics, and to the extent that the latter was also at issue, it was refracted through and defined as a property of the former. Courbet declared this in his manifesto "Le Réalisme," when he argued against belonging to a school or category called "Realism" and instead proclaimed "the reasoned and independent sentiment of my own individuality"[11] as the theme of his exhibition. The retrospectives within the Universal Exposition appear to have done the same – amounting to an apotheosis of artistic individuality, each one of the four contrary to the other. However, the retrospectives of Ingres, Delacroix, Decamps, and Vernet not only erased the particular historical circumstances and political meanings of individual works by each of the painters by subsuming them within the overviews of their oeuvres,[12] their contrary artistic individualities were also gathered under the universalizing embrace of the Empire and its triumphant demonstration of its patrimonial capacity to resolve all contraries within one all-inclusive national tradition.[13] It was emphatically otherwise with Courbet's counter-retrospective, and that is what *The Painter's Studio* allegorizes.

To start, *The Painter's Studio*, the headliner of Courbet's retrospective and the painted counterpart to his written manifesto, was a rejected painting, followed immediately by another rejected painting that had been produced during the Second Republic, the *Burial at Ornans*. Its title deliberately identified Courbet's "individuality" with 1848, thus refus-

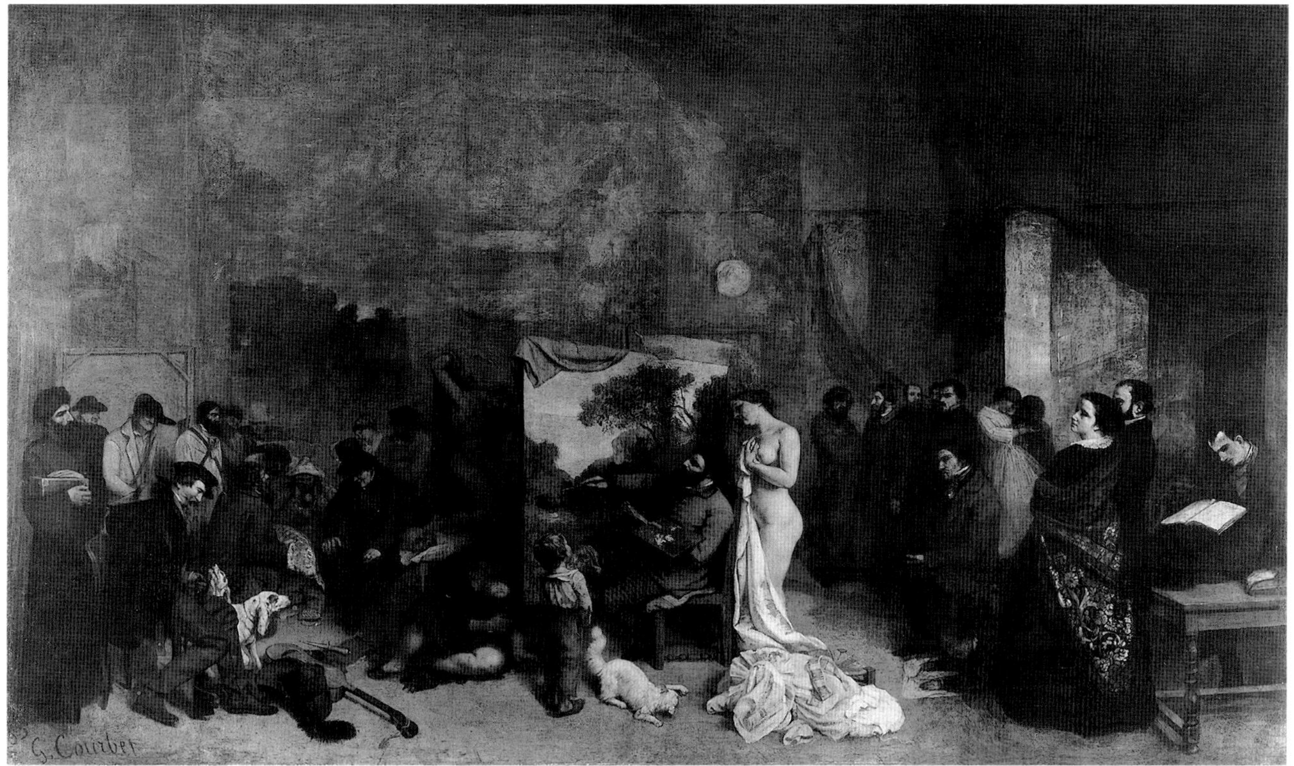

3　Gustave Courbet, *The Painter's Studio: A Real Allegory Summing Up Seven Years of My Life as a Painter*, 1855, oil on canvas, 359 × 598 cm. Musée d'Orsay, Paris.

ing to erase the political meaning of the works within his oeuvre. Instead the title insisted upon continuity – a continuity that was specifically Courbet's continuity – between 1855 and 1848; and it proposed that the "individuality" of Courbet's oeuvre be defined against the Empire rather than subsumed and collapsed within it. Rather than using the retrospective to depoliticize art, as the Empire did, Courbet's allegory, with its left-hand ticking-off of failed and betrayed revolutions (to be understood simultaneously as that which was and those who were antipathetic to Courbet) and its opposition between revolutionary failure and personal support and success (in the figures of Courbet's friends and patrons lined up on the right-hand side of the painting),[14] asserts a politicized reading of his retrospective, and defines that politicization as simultaneously contrary to the interests of the Empire and integral to the difference of Courbet's "individuality" from those interests.[15] But the politics of *The Painter's Studio* was self-referential rather more than outwardly referential: it referred not to art in general or to "Realism" at large as a subject matter, a movement, or a political stance but rather to the oppositional particularity of Courbet's own artistic identity – as against the "universality" of the Exposition and its retrospectives.[16]

The seven years named in the title were also the most coherent years in Courbet's production as displayed in his pavilion. Those years include work in portraiture and self-portraiture, the nude and genre, and landscape, all of which figure in *The Painter's Studio*. To the right are a series of portraits, many of them duplicates of individual portraits already painted by Courbet, some of which – those of Champfleury and Baudelaire – were included in the pavilion. Others were to be found already in other earlier works on display in Courbet's two shows – the portrait of Bruyas in *The Meeting* in the Palais des Beaux-Arts, that of Max Buchon in the *Burial at Ornans*, and the lovers in the *Sentiment of Youth*, numbered nine in the retrospective catalogue. The small boy standing in front of the painter's easel – the painting within the painting at the center of the composition – refers back to *The Stonebreakers*, on view in the Universal Exposition, while the nude to the right of the painter, though she does not repeat any earlier pose exactly, reminds one generally of the heavy-fleshed bourgeois woman with the discarded clothes in the *Bathers*, whose backside had been slapped by the Emperor in the Salon of 1853, now on view again in the pavilion of 1855.

Last but by no means least, of course, there is the image of Courbet himself at the center, a repeat of his *Self-Portrait with Striped Collar* of 1854, the most up-to-date of the several self-portraits going all the way back to 1841 on view in the pavilion, which in themselves added up to a summary of the development of Courbet's "life as a painter." And then the landscape on the easel that the painted painter paints in the teeth of the peopled interior surrounding him, as well as the *pentimento* dream of a landscape left hovering in the air and on the wall at the back of the composition, forcefully asserts Courbet's growing landscape practice, on display threefold in the Palais des Beaux-Arts and sixteenfold in his pavilion. Thus it demonstrates his special commitment to the genre that was newly prolific since 1848, nowhere more publicly so than in 1855, with the efflorescence of the Barbizon school in the arts section of the Universal Exposition. More than that, it displays that commitment to landscape as central to Courbet's identity as an artist.

The left-hand side of *The Painter's Studio* is a more complicated matter; certainly it is not as easy to read as an allegory of the retrospective. However, in among its references to mechanically reproduced images of public figures and other figurations not originally by Courbet is its appropriation of Ingres's *M. Bertin*, which was included that year in Ingres's retrospective in the Palais des Beaux-Arts. It is surely possible to understand that appropriated image as, among other things, a gesture to the retrospectives other than Courbet's that were officially blue-ribboned and imperially embraced.[17] And so, the point of the right–left opposition enacted in *The Painter's Studio* seems to be precisely a thesis–antithesis contrast between that which was integral and that which was inimical to Courbet's artistic "individuality." In short, the painting's "real allegory" might be summed up most persuasively as an allegory of what was inside and what was outside of Courbet's oeuvre – of what was and was not authentically "Courbet."

The thesis–antithesis of Courbet's painting has its dialectical resolution. For though the left side of the painting is slightly more jumbled and miscellaneous than the right, it is a matter of degree rather than of absolute contrast. And ultimately, Courbet organizes and absorbs the whole complex crowd of figures, left and right, into the single structure of his own vision, with himself at the center of it all, bringing it all into his own nucleic orbit and tying it all together. If his earlier large-scale compositions – in particular the Ornans triad – tended toward the aggregate and the spacially disjointed,

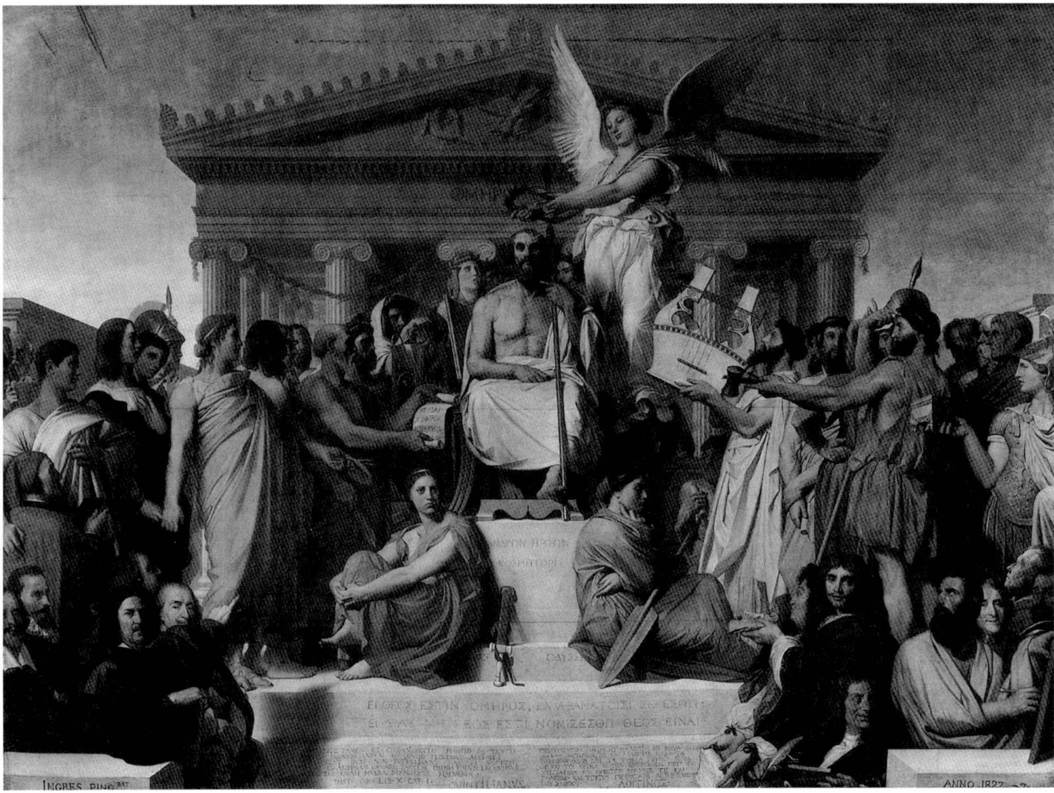

4   Jean-Auguste-Dominique Ingres, *The Apotheosis of Homer*, 1827, oil on canvas, 386 × 512 cm. Musée du Louvre, Paris.

The Painter's Studio, on the contrary, is remarkable in the way it gathers its large cast of characters into a spacially convincing arc, not unlike such overpopulated, insistently patrimonial works, exhibited in the Palais des Beaux-Arts, as François-Joseph Heim's *Charles X Distributing Awards to Artists at the End of the Exposition of 1824*, Jean-Léon Gérôme's *The Century of Augustus*, or Ingres's *Apotheosis of Homer* (fig. 4), to all of which Courbet's painting seems a pointedly individualistic rejoinder. Courbet, in other words, is at the center of a unity: the dualism of his composition is resolved into a singularity. Unlike the eclecticism of the Empire, with its colonizing and neutralizing of the differences among a plurality of names, styles, and art histories, his totality is presented as reducible to one – himself.

In *The Painter's Studio*, the singularity that is named "Courbet" is defined as organic, identified with a natural physicality, and literally placed under the sign of Nature. The painting on the easel is shown as the product of Courbet's hand and body, of an actively physical engagement with the materiality of painting.[18] And instead of depicting the social throng gathered around Courbet, that painting within a painting renders a bit of Nature. It organizes the paintings as a natural, organic whole. And the floating specter of a landscape to which it is connected is left in, presumably, to reinforce the point, to preside over *The Painter's Studio*, to define the painter's vision as a natural vision and his painting as a natural painting, and to reinforce the painter's transformation of society into Nature, redoubling precisely what Courbet is shown doing at the heart of the picture. Thus neither the landscape on the easel nor the *pentimento* landscape are anomalous or particularly mysterious intrusions into the represented social and vocational space of Courbet's studio. Rather, they are the key to *The Painter's Studio.*

This is another way in which the painting, along with the retrospective that it allegorizes, establishes Courbet's difference from the view of the arts that was promoted by the Universal Exposition. That difference is by no means just a matter of "Realist" naturalism versus academic classicism, as Courbet himself seemed to insist in his manifesto, by insisting upon his "individuality" rather than his belonging to a "Realist" school. Instead, it is a difference in the definition of painting as a product of work and a piece of property. For if the Palais des Beaux-Arts presented the works of art within it as the products and property of the Empire, and as the artistic counterparts to the products of industry on exhibit in the Palais de l'Industrie – even if the distinction between the fine arts and industry was maintained, this was surely the logic by which the diversified bounty of manner and iconography on display could be contained and shown off as imperial capital – Courbet's painting says nay to that logic quite emphatically. With it, and the rest of the retrospective to which it was the key, Courbet took back both the means and the ends of his painterly production.

Rather than the commodities of a multi-individual corporation, *The Painter's Studio* allegorizes his paintings as the products of the specific physical work of a specific physical worker – of his tools and materials, his hand and body, and his labor, all of which are presented as belonging to him, not to the Empire. Rather than erasing production in the interests of commodification, he insists upon his status as a physical producer, and asserts that his objects are physical products, rather than labor-transcended, physically sublimated items of exchange, handed over to the owner of the company and the buyer of the commodity. Not a machine-part in the industrial-imperial apparatus, he presents himself as an organic "individuality," bodily consuming Nature and bodily producing it in a natural round of intake and output, directly and without mediation, for buyers who wanted to buy his products (Bruyas, principally, figuring on the painting's "good" right side along with Courbet's other private consumers[19]), and then unifying those products organically, rather than cobbling and forcing them together as the Empire did.[20] This, finally, is where the politics of *The Painter's Studio* lay: in its oppositional allegory of the production and retrospective consumption of the *tout ensemble* of Courbet's oeuvre. And these are the politics of the retrospective to which he returned in 1867 in a more concerted fashion, honing them but also tidying their bumptious roughness – by then Courbet's art had lost much of its dissident edge. These are also the politics of the retrospective that Manet mimicked, mistook, and misread in 1867, and made over in his own quite different image.

MANET'S "EXPOSITION PARTICULIÈRE"

On May 24, 1867, about two months after the opening of the Universal Exposition of that year (and of the huge posthumous retrospective of Ingres's works at the Ecole des

Beaux-Arts), about six weeks after the opening of the contemporaneous Salon in which recent works were shown,[21] and five days before the opening of Courbet's new retrospective, Manet's "exposition particulière" opened at its site on the Place de l'Alma. Like Courbet's pavilion in 1855, Manet's show of 1867, mounted in an impermanent building large enough to contain it, was also a kind of out-of-studio variation on the tradition of throwing the artist's atelier open to the public – though not much of that public actually came to Manet's exhibit at the Place de l'Alma. After giving his "Motifs d'une exposition particulière," in which he claimed that he had "simply sought to be himself and not an other,"[22] Manet's catalogue went on to list the fifty-six works in the show as follows (see pp. 28–29 for a sampling of these works):[23]

1. *Le déjeuner sur l'herbe*
2. *Olympia*
3. *Le chanteur espagnol*
4. *L'enfant à l'épée*
5. *L'homme mort*
6. *Jésus insulté par les soldats*
7. *Le Christ mort et les anges*
8. *Portrait de M. et Mme M.*
9. *Les Gitanos*
10. *Le vieux musicien*
11. *Le fifre*
12. *Mlle V. en costume d'espada*
13. *Jeune homme en costume de majo*
14. *Portrait de Mme M.*
15. *Jeune dame en 1866*
16. *Un matador de taureaux*
17. *Lola de Valence*
18. *L'acteur tragique*
19. *La chanteuse des rues*
20. *Portrait de Mme B.*
21. *Un moine en prière*
22. *Le combat des navires américanes Kearsarge et Alabama*
23. *Le gamin*
24. *La musique aux Tuileries*
25. *Les courses au bois de Boulogne*
26. *La joueuse de guitare*
27. *Le liseur*
28. *Le ballet espagnol*
29. *Le buveur d'absinthe*
30. *Nymphe surprise*
31. *Philosophe*
32. *Philosophe*
33. *Une vase de fleurs*
34. *Le steam-boat (navire)*
35. *Jeune femme couchée en costume espagnol*
36. *Un déjeuner (nature morte)*
37. *Fruits*
38. *Poissons (nature morte)*
39. *Une dame à la fenêtre (étude)*
40. *Vue de mer, temps calme*
41. *Un panier de fruits*
42. *Un chien éspagnol*
43. *Portrait de Z. A.*
44. *Les étudiants de Salamanque*
45. *Bateau de pêche arrivant vent arrière*
46. *Tête d'étude*
47. *Fruits*
48. *Un lapin (nature morte)*
49. *Le fumeur*
50. *Paysage*
Copies: La Vierge au lapin, d'après Titien
    Portrait de Tintoret, d'après Tintoret
    Les petits Cavaliers, d'après Vélasquez
Eaux-fortes: Les Gitanos
    Portrait de Philippe IV, d'après Vélasquez
    Les petits Cavaliers, id.

(See *Le Journal Amusant*, figs. 5–7, for a contemporary view of Manet's exhibition.[24])

Unlike Courbet, Manet had no works at all within either the Salon or the Universal Exposition, having decided not to submit to the jury's judgment and to erect his pavilion instead of aiming for inclusion within the imperial display. (He had not been

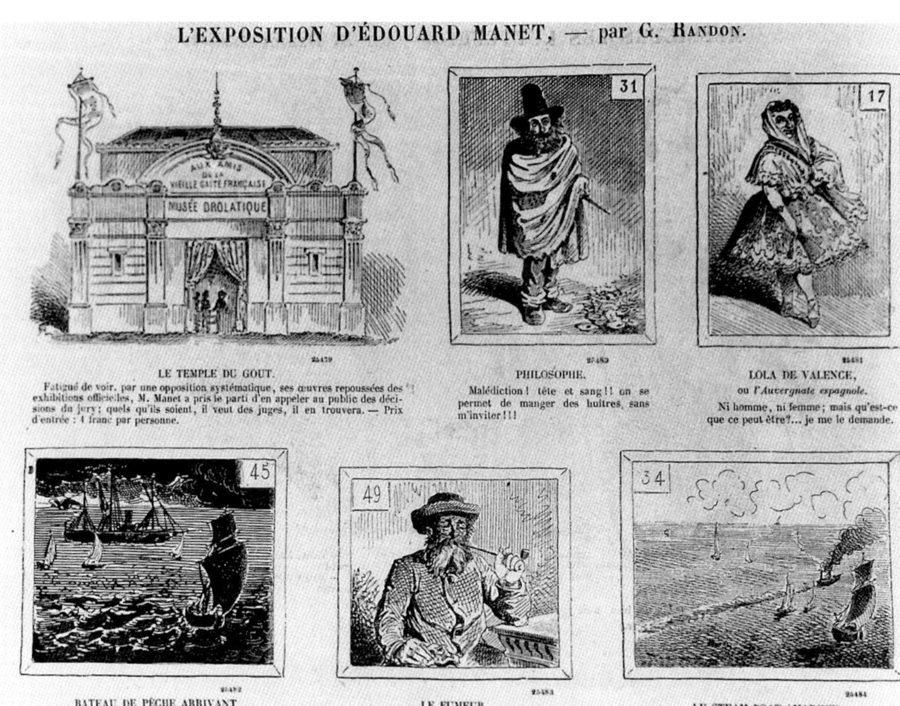

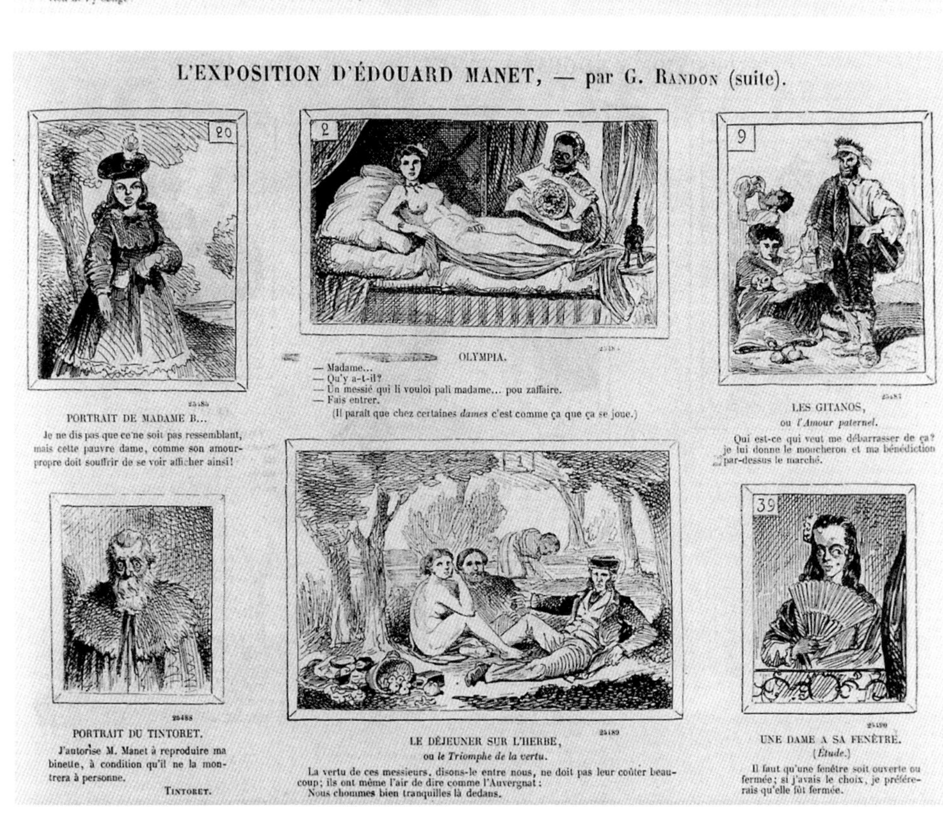

5–7 G. Randon, *Le Journal Amusant*, June 29, 1867 (no. 600), pp. 6–8.

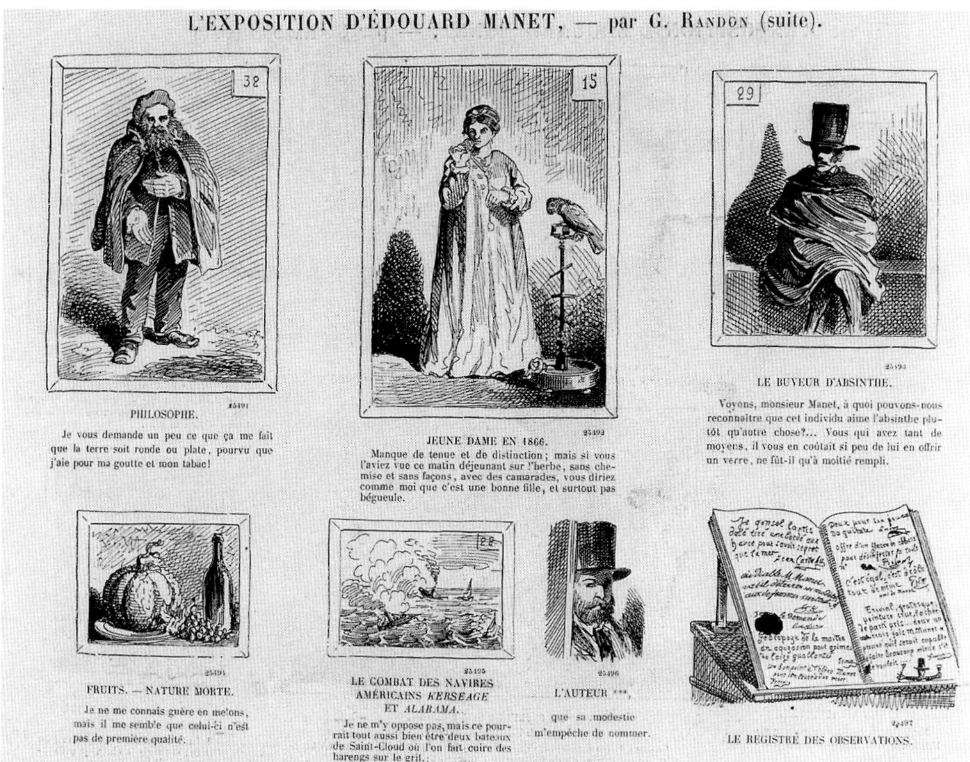

painting long enough to be in the Universal Exposition; like other artists he was not happy about being separated off from it in the Salon and anyway, he had not done well in the previous year's Salon; one way or the other, he could not have hoped for anything like Courbet's eleven works in the Palais des Beaux-Arts of 1855. Courbet himself had only four works in the Exposition of 1867.) Also unlike Courbet, there was no one painting that summed up the rest, or that could be viewed as the key to the retrospective: there could not have been, given the character of Manet's work. Numbering one and two in Manet's catalogue were his two most infamous works, both painted in 1863, both exhibited in earlier Salons (the Salon des Réfusés of 1863 and the Salon of 1865, respectively), both sporting the features of Manet's favorite model of the 1860s (Victorine Meurent), and both quoting from Italian Renaissance painting – the *Luncheon on the Grass* and *Olympia* (figs. 8, 9). That the first of these was a "Salon of the rejected" work, that the second of them was particularly notorious for its Salon reception – that they were both Salon scandals with which Manet's name was identified – suggests that, despite the artist's protestations, they served as headliners to his self-presentation as an intransigent *à la* Courbet. They also, however, headlined the fact that Manet was a different kind of "individuality" altogether from the one that Courbet had advocated for himself.[25]

To begin with the order of presentation in Manet's catalogue list. As disregarding of chronology as Courbet's list of works, Manet's roster jumps around rather more in terms of genre categories. It is true that it follows convention in the large emphases of its ordering, with portraits, nudes, religious works, genre paintings, and historical

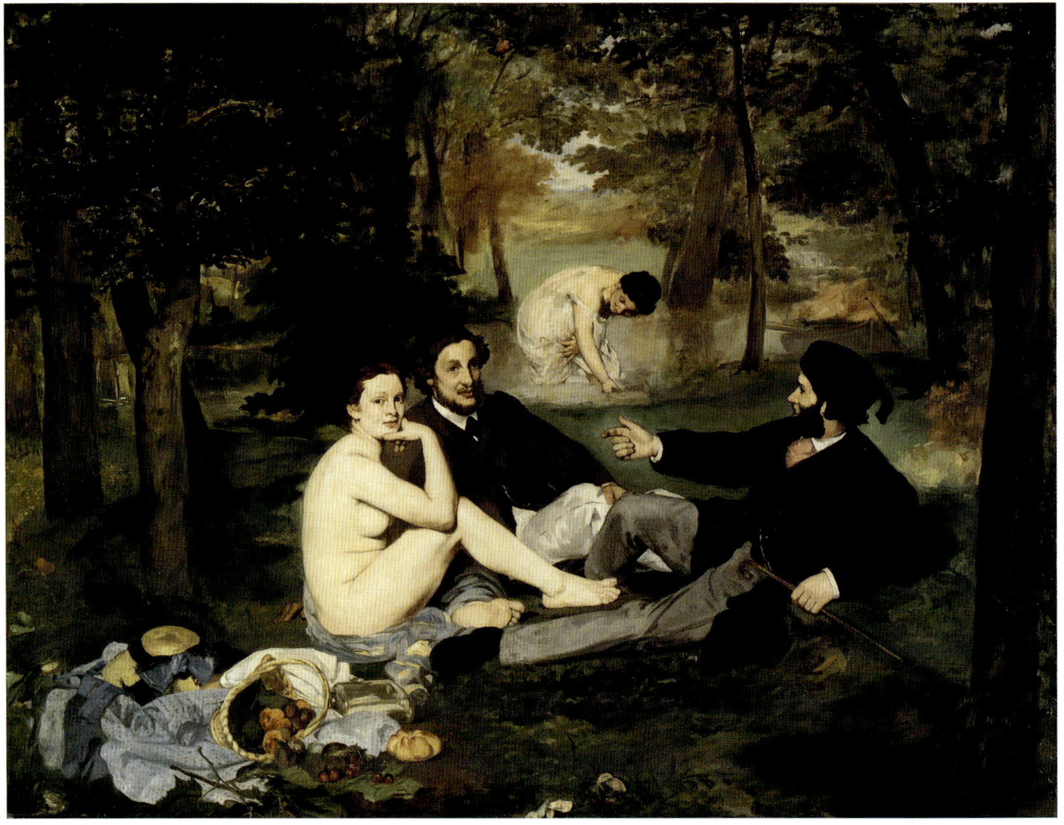

8 Edouard Manet, *Luncheon on the Grass*, 1863, oil on canvas, 208 × 264.5 cm. Musée d'Orsay, Paris.

quotations located mainly in the first half of the list, and landscapes and still lifes, as well as copies and etchings, found in the second half. But within this overall hierarchy, there are more anomalies, especially toward the end of the list: with the intrusion of the *Young Woman Reclining in Spanish Costume*, set adrift from the earlier concentration of similar Spanish-costume works, between a *Steamboat* and a still life, and the inclusion of the *Portrait of Zacharie Astruc* among the closing miscellanea of still lifes, landscapes, and other odds and ends. Earlier in the list, the marine battle painting of *The Kearsarge and the Alabama* is sandwiched between *Monk in Prayer* and *Boy with the Cherries*; and the early *Nymph Surprised*, separated from the only other nudes on the list, *Luncheon on the Grass* and *Olympia*, by some thirty works, is situated between the early *Absinthe Drinker* and the two later *Philosophers*. In fact, these intrusions are symptomatic of a larger principle of disorder in Manet's list: though his inventory of works is properly divided between "greater" and "lesser" genres, there is no concentration of landscapes or of portraits such as there was in Courbet's catalogue of 1855 (and especially in that of 1867).

Instead, there are scattershot pairings and groupings: two large Italianate works, a Spanish genre painting (one of Manet's two earliest Salon-accepted works), and two disparate, blank-backgrounded images with swords in them; then a pair of Christs, the por-

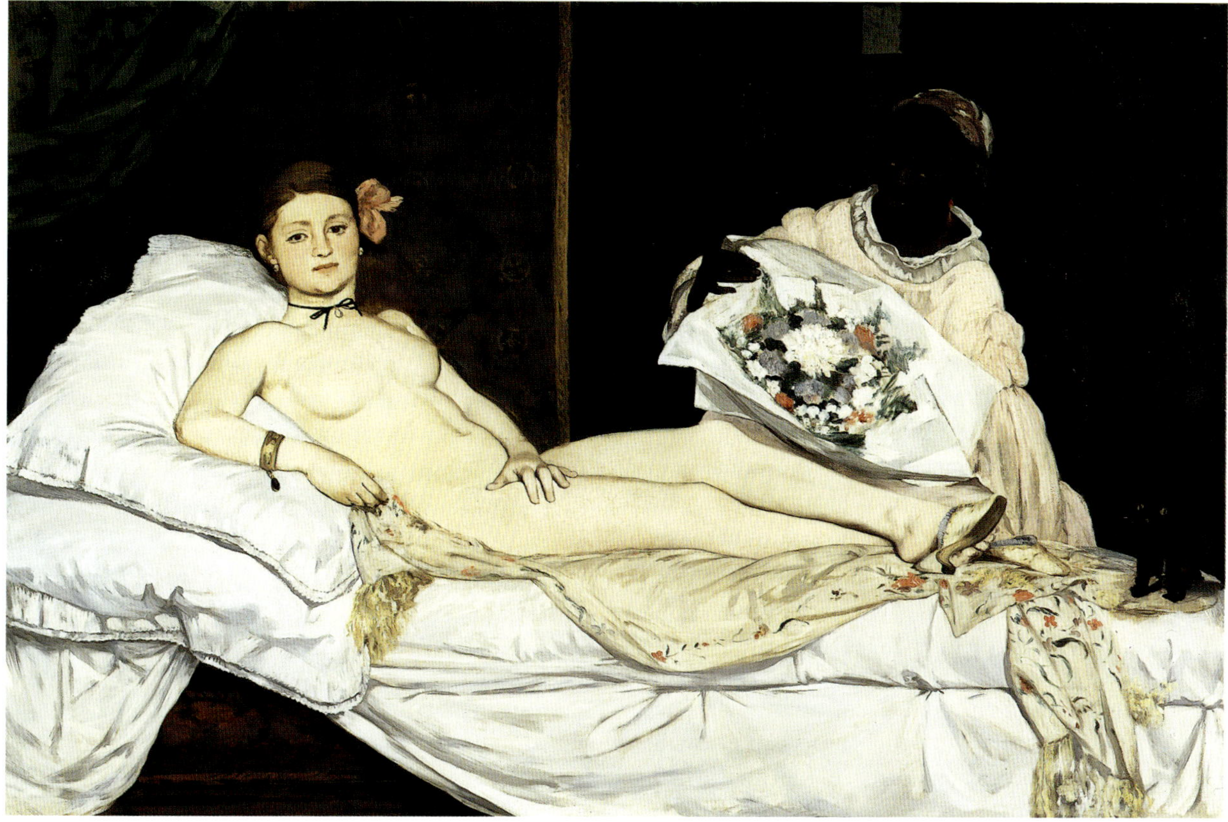

9   Edouard Manet, *Olympia*, 1863, oil on canvas, 130.5 × 190 cm. Musée d'Orsay, Paris.

trait of his parents (the other of the two works accepted into the Salon of 1861), and the thematically related *Gitanos* and *The Old Musician*; then the single-figure costume pieces, *The Fifer, Mlle V . . . in the Costume of an Espada* and the *Young Man in the Costume of a Majo*; then another portrait (of Manet's wife); followed by another series of single-figure pieces, the *Young Woman in 1866*, the *Matador, Lola de Valence, The Tragic Actor*, and *The Streetsinger*; then another portrait (that of Mme Brunet), the *Monk in Prayer*, the *Kearsarge and Alabama* and the *Boy with the Cherries*; followed by the sketchy modern-life pair of *Music at the Tuileries* and the *Racecourse at Longchamp* (in Manet's list as *Racecourse in the Bois de Boulogne*); followed in turn by the single-figure female pictures of *The Reader* and *The Guitar Player*; which are then succeeded by the little *Spanish Ballet*; which is succeeded in turn by the disparate single-figure group of *The Absinthe Drinker, The Nymph Surprised*, and the two *Philosopher*s; and then a stream of still lifes and landscapes, interrupted here and there by such miscellanea as *Young Woman Reclining in Spanish Costume*, a study of a woman at the window, the *Students of Salamanca*, the portrait of Zacharie Astruc and the *Smoker*; concluding with the odd little *Fishing* (which is dubbed a "*Paysage*"); and finally the copies and etchings, the latter of which, in two out of three instances, are duplicates of earlier items on the roster – of an original work (near the beginning of the list) and of a copy (nearby), respectively.

That is the pattern of Manet's list: a staccato rhythm of dispersal and interspersal, the miscellaneous and the extraneous, pairs and singles, and disparate suits of two or three. Rather than an occasionally interrupted pattern of genre divisions (as in Courbet's roster of 1855), it is the reverse – a pattern of interruptions, gathered occasionally into short sets. It is a pattern that increases one's awareness of the list's lack of chronological order, but more than anything else it is a pattern that disrupts the very logic of division by genres. For what there is of that logic is merely residual; otherwise, every set that might be thought of as a genre set is interrupted by adventitious items. With this list of works Manet does not describe any genre specialty or specialties as integral to *lui-même* (unlike Courbet, who had described himself as a genre painter, portraitist, and landscapist, with a growing emphasis upon the last as central to his career resumé). Manet's titles – and the works that go with them – also tend to escape genre categorization: for instance, what kind of work is his *Luncheon on the Grass*? Is the *Boy with the Sword* a genre picture, or some version of a theatrical portrait? And *Mlle V. . . . in the Costume of an Espada* (and the two or three similarly titled), is that a portrait or what? The same questions may be asked of the *Young Woman in 1866, Lola de Valence*, and *The Tragic Actor*, among others. (These paintings are bracketed a number of times by images with "Portrait" in their titles.) And then there are Manet's several "landscapes," odd hangers-on to the marine battle painting. (The conclusion of his series of original paintings with a *Paysage* which, though the title does not say so, is also a copy, a portrait, and a fantasy, dramatizes the genre confusions of Manet's catalogue.) In several cases (but not in others), Manet puts the genre classification of his still lifes in parentheses – "(nature morte)" – where that kind of identification seems least necessary, most self-evident. Was this to indicate a specialty? Or to index the hierarchy of genre divisions from which, precisely, he was departing? – from the bottom of that hierarchy, within the genre devoted to heterogeneity of the object world rather than the high humanist unities (and the one genre, besides history painting per se, that had not been on Courbet's list at all in 1855).

Rather than a hierarchy of the genres, then, what Manet's list proposes is the odd logic of the "single work," unassimilable to the genre group. And it is the logic of the "pastiche," too, as Courbet meant that word back in 1855, when it showed up twice in a row on his inventory of works, describing two early works (both painted in 1843). Indeed, it is as if Manet, in the dozen or so years of painting catalogued in his list, had isolated and homed in upon the principle of "inconsistency" that had described Courbet's earliest works, but which the rest of Courbet's oeuvre was shown to have surmounted by 1855. In Courbet's earlier retrospective, the "pastiche" was attached to immaturity, to such early things as pirates and reveries – the painter's efforts before his mature style had gelled into its signature consistency. The early "pastiche," in short, stood in contrast to the painter's up-to-date "individuality." It was otherwise with Manet. Although the word "pastiche" does not appear on his list, and though the only references to the non-native are found in the "Spanish" adjectives in several of Manet's titles[26] and in the "after" Titian, Tintoretto, and Velasquez found in the copies addendum at the end the list, nevertheless the hybridity and not-originality of the "pastiche" – the style(s) other than one's own that it implies – are definitive of Manet's view of *lui-même*, as exhibited in 1867.

The "Copies" at the end of Manet's list speak to something that is central to the list as a whole. Those three copies, in addition to the three etchings – one after himself and two "after" Velasquez – spell out the "pastiche" orientation of the entire list. (Neither in 1855 nor in 1867 did Courbet include either copies after other people's paintings or prints after his own works in his catalogue.) If we return once more to the list, we can see how Manet piles on his art-historical quotations and mixes up his manners. First there is the "from Florence . . . toward Venice," "from Venice . . . toward Florence" of the *Luncheon on the Grass* and *Olympia*, with their quotations "after" Raimondi/Raphael, Giorgione/Titian, and Titian, and their mix of harsh contrast, hard contours, and different kinds of painterliness. (Greenberg's turn of phrase suggests that we understand the "inconsistency" of these two works in terms of the old *disegno–colore* opposition. In fact, as I want to show, their "inconsistency" is much less conventionally binary than that, less reducible to such traditional aesthetic dualities.) After the somewhat different Spanishisms of the single-figure *The Spanish Singer*, the *Boy with the Sword*, and *The Dead Torero*, the pair of multi-figure Christ paintings picks up the theme of the dead body but now in the context of the sacred image, screened through Titian and Tintoretto. Then there is the native-tongued portrait of his own parents, with its properly modern, French apparel and acoutrements.

The Gitanos and *The Old Musician*, with their similarly bohemian groups of figures, mediate between the French and the Spanish, the native and the other, the quotidian and the quotational. *The Old Musician* (fig. 10), in particular, with its loosely strung band of waifs, urchins, and *chiffoniers* set flatly one next to the other in a manner not unlike such *Epinal*-evocative works of Courbet's as *The Return from the Fair*, condenses the dispersed, additive quality of the list on which it numbers ten, and feeds its depiction of the no-man's-land of the Parisian ramparts through a thick filter of art-historical references. In this way as well as in its style of rendering it is unlike the much simpler and more anecdotal *Gitanos* which it succeeds. The *Gypsy with a Cigarette* mentioned in the Introduction probably gives a good idea of the looser, "showy brushing and illustrativeness," and generally quite different appearance of *The Gitanos*.[27] Thus *The Gitanos* and *The Old Musician* together make a good example of Manet's often repeated habit of painting pairs of similar subjects in contrasting manners. *The Old Musician* was not the key to the rest of the oeuvre on exhibit in 1867 in the way that *The Painter's Studio* was for Courbet's retrospective in 1855. But insofar as Manet's strategies can be summarized in a single early work, *The Old Musician* does as good a job of it as any.

Michael Fried made *The Old Musician* the centerpiece of his 1969 essay, "Manet's Sources," and with good reason.[28] His discovery of Watteau's *Gilles* as the basis for the little urchin in white toward the left, the same painter's *L'Indifférent* for the top-hatted figure to the left (who is, of course, a repeat of Manet's own *Absinthe Drinker*, also in the retrospective of 1867, fig. 11), various works by the Le Nain brothers as the sources for the eponymous old musician as well as for the group at large, in addition to the acknowledged Murillo source for the little dark-haired boy (also a repeat of a work by Manet, *The Boy with the Dog*), and the accepted use of Velasquez's *The Drinkers* as a general palimpsest for the image, all seem to me compelling. However, whatever the prevailing discourse around the resuscitation of figures such as the Le Nains and Watteau, it does not seem plausible to read this layering of sources in nationalist, positivist, or universalist terms, or to resolve it in any one totalized direction.[29] On the contrary: what is precisely peculiar about this painting is the sheer excess of its art-historical quoting, its

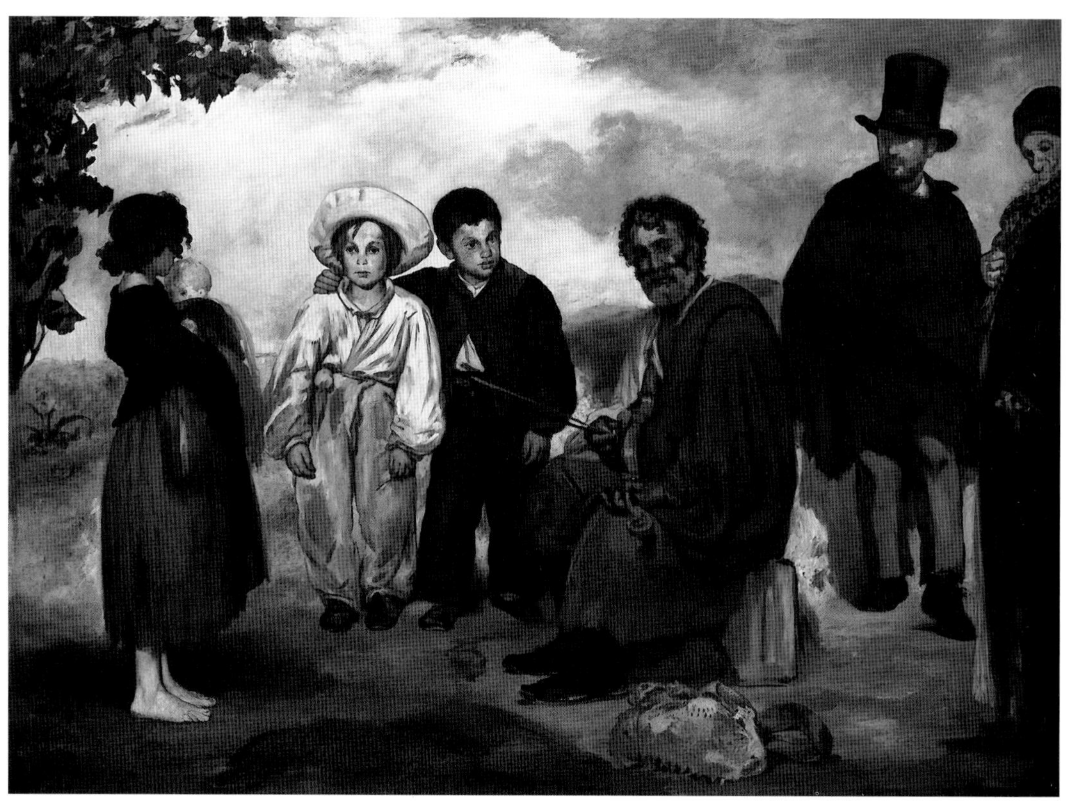

10   Edouard Manet, *The Old Musician*, 1862, oil on canvas, 187.4 × 248.2 cm. National Gallery of Art, Washington, D.C. Chester Dale Collection.

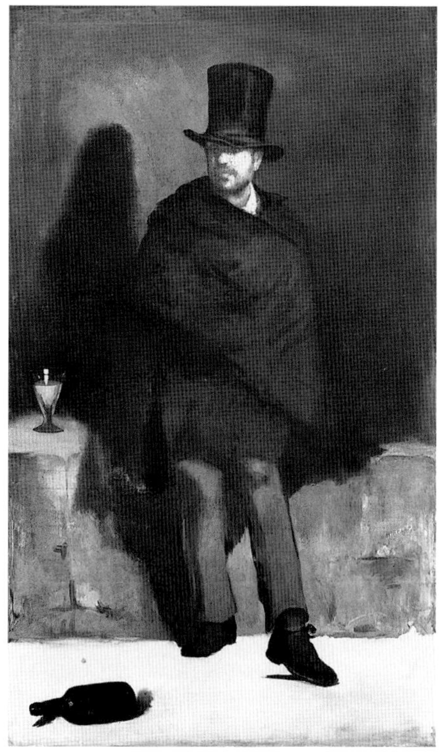

11   Edouard Manet, *The Absinthe Drinker*, 1859, oil on canvas, 117.5 × 103 cm. Ny Carlsberg Glyptotek, Copenhagen.

multiplication and refusal to add up its quotations, and its resistance to assimilating and naturalizing them, not to mention the singularly unresolvable meeting between the French and the Spanish that it enacts. This, indeed, is what is peculiar about Manet's art of the '60s more generally. It is also what his retrospective put on display.

That Manet relied upon sources from the great traditions of European painting in order to produce ambitious statements such as *The Old Musician* throughout the '60s put him in line with the *pompiers* and the old masters more than the new type of painting that relied on the motif itself instead of copying in the Louvre.[30] What was peculiar, however, was the way Manet left quotation marks around his quotations, and piled them one atop the other, nowhere more so than in *The Old Musician.* Just how many models did he really need, say, for the old musician who gives the composition its name? and how many for the composition as a whole? Was it really necessary to rely on both Velazquez and the Le Nains to produce the same figure, and the same group? Was it not just a bit too much to quote Velasquez and the Le Nains and Watteau and Murillo – and himself? And each several times over? And each spaced disjointedly across the surface of the painting like so many "afters" related to one another only through a string of commas and "ands?" – to form a painted phrase reading "'after Watteau,' 'after myself and Murillo,' 'after Le Nain and Velasquez,' and 'after myself again and Watteau again and Velasquez too, again.'" (And not "The old musician plays a song for a motley crew of beggars.")

It was thus that Manet made of "Realism" a repertoire of poses from the history of art, rather than a seemingly unmediated report on the look of life at the low end of things. (Not that "Realism" was ever actually unmediated, of course, but works like the one preceding *The Old Musician*, the *Gitanos*, proposed a spontaneous, anecdotal view of the motif, identified with "Realism," that pretended away its mediating conventions.) It was thus that early on in his career Manet made "Realism" a theater of the supplement,[31] using the staging devices of the *fête galante* (Watteau's stringing of his *faux*-rustic actors across the landscape in undulating clumps and clusters) to enunciate both the artificiality and the heterogeneity of the "Realist" panorama – to show how it was a pastiche pieced together out of oddments from the museum with and without walls.[32] It was thus that Manet used the French and the Spanish traditions, in particular, to articulate what one might call the gypsy principle of his own personal museum, and to state the terms of an uneasy alliance – between the native and the non-native, the *lui-même* and the *autre* – in which each term is mutually exchangeable, but neither dominates the other.

If Courbet had portrayed his own "individuality" as a gathering together of the world around him and of his own past production into his natural, bodily self, and then set that self in opposition to the patrimonial embrace of the Empire, Manet took that "Realist" "individuality" and dispersed it, among all the othernesses and artifices upon which its naturalism was founded. For instance, the difference between the way Courbet had quoted himself and the way Manet did could not be more pronounced. The figure of the absinthe drinker at the right of *The Old Musician* is representative of that difference: not a self-portrait but an oblique reference to himself as a Baudelairean *chiffonier*, clothed contrarily out of the mismatched odds and ends of top hat, tattered cloak, and gray trousers – and shoes in balletic third position – such that the ragpicker meets the dandy meets the courtier of old. The self-quotation of that off-center figure takes no precedence over the other quotations found throughout the painting, nor does he serve to organize them, as Courbet's centered self-portrait does in *The Painter's Studio*. He is, instead, just one among many, and he pronounces the disorganization of them all.

To continue with the roster of works shown at the "exposition particulière": after *The Old Musician* are listed *The Fifer, Mlle V. . . . in the Costume of an Espada*, the *Young Man in the Costume of a Majo*, the *Portrait of Mme M.*, the *Young Woman in 1866*, the *Saluting Matador, Lola de Valence, The Tragic Actor, The Streetsinger*, the *Portrait of Mme. B.*, and the *Monk in Prayer*. These are a series of similarly formatted compositions consisting of lone figures, most of them overtly dressed up in costume, some with blank backgrounds and some with theatrical and modern-life contexts brushed in. All of them, with the exception of the two images named as portraits, refer in one way or another to Spanish painting, and to Velasquez most consistently. The single-figure paintings shift among military, theatrical, quotidian, and religious costume, with the fact of their being costumed sometimes announced in their titles and sometimes not. Most of them are portraits of individuals known to the painter, and would be named and considered so were it not for the costuming of the sitters.

The two exceptions to the rule of titling them as other than portraits bear that out, for not only are the portraits of Mme Manet and Mme Brunet the only images other than full-length, their costumes are up-to-date ordinary wear, as detailed in their attention to sartorial design and decorative particulars as the others, but without the non-native glamor or theatrical function that accrue to most of the rest. Ultimately, the movement between pictures named as portraits and paintings characterized as costume-pieces has the effect of reading the theatrical constitution of the one onto the other, such that the line between the genre functions of the likeness and the costume-piece is blurred, as well as the related distinction between that which is innate to the person and that which the *poseur* puts on. Enhanced by the switching between everyday and exotic apparel, the blurring of that distinction is signaled most broadly in the oscillation between the French and the Spanish that runs through the entire series. (The identification of costuming with Spanishness is most clearly stated in the most theatrical of the series: *Mlle V. . . . in the Costume of an Espada, Young Man in the Costume of a Majo, Lola de Valence*, and *The Tragic Actor*, with his specific derivation in the portrait of a Spanish actor of Velasquez's day.)

The portrait of Manet's wife (fig. 12) also marks a stylistic difference from the set of which she is a part. For her loose, sketchy rendering, along with her bust-length, stands noticeably apart from the rest, until one begins to note incidents of similar looseness within the larger blocks of pigment and the usually more dense and pasty paint treatments of the other paintings, as in the partially revealed petticoat of *The Streetsinger*, or the dappled brushing of the face of the *Monk in Prayer*, at odds with the all-of-a-piece painting of the rest of him, to point to just two instances. This returns me to a broken thread running throughout the works in the "exposition particulière," for the difference between the *Portrait of Mme M.* and the rest of its set is no different from the obtrusive pieces of brushiness found from the beginning in, say, the *Luncheon on the Grass*, or from the contrasts in manner between works juxtaposed on Manet's list, such

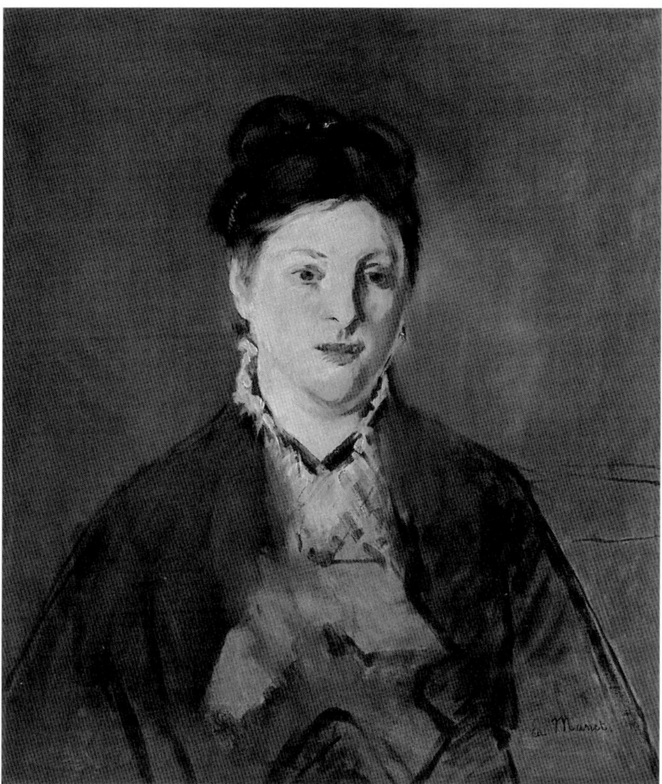

12   Edouard Manet, *Portrait of Madame Manet*, 1866, oil on canvas, 60.6 × 50.8 cm. Norton Simon Art Foundation, Pasadena, Calif. Gift of Mr. Norton Simon, 1973.

as *The Gitanos* and *The Old Musician*. But what that difference does now is to layer together Manet's signature "inconsistency" with his equally signature questioning of the boundary between the transparent naturalism of the (French) likeness (singled out in the face of his own – Dutch ex-patriot – wife) and the opaque artificiality of the (Spanish) costume-piece (multiplied in the figures of brothers, "son," model, dancer, and actor).

What follows on the heels of this single-figure set is especially hodge-podge. The interrupted Spanishisms of the preceding set become less persistent. More outstanding now is the particular kind of "inconsistency" inaugurated in *The Kearsarge and the Alabama*, an inconsistency both of genre and style, not to mention size and format. From one to the other, the abrupt shifts in manners of facture that characterize Manet's oeuvre are particularly in evidence – from *The Kearsarge and the Alabama*'s own mix of bounded areas, unmodulated opacity, and mottled brushwork to the more conventionally impastoed chiaroscuro of the Chardinesque *Boy with the Cherries*, to the dramatic, modern-life looseness of both *Music at the Tuileries* and the *Racecourse at Longchamp*, to the contrasting Velasquez-isms of *The Spanish Ballet* and the two *Philosophers* (once again summing up, in their different kinds of reference to Velasquez, the slipping between quick, patchy, multi-colored brushiness and large, slathered fields of buttery paint and nuanced single colors that is so often to be found in Manet's work), to the flattened Rubensian quality of *The Nymph Surprised*, and so on.

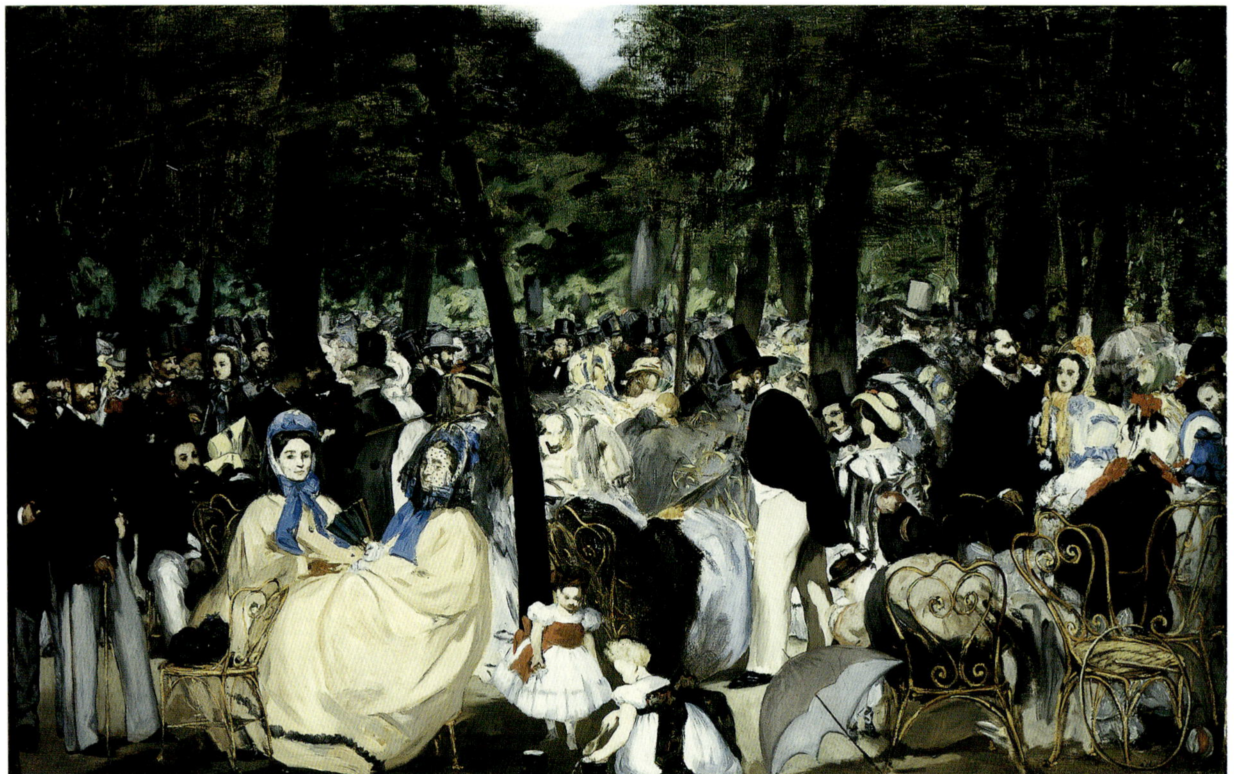

13　Edouard Manet, *Music at the Tuileries*, 1862, oil on canvas, 76.2 × 118.1 cm. National Gallery, London.

In the midst of this odd series, the *Music at the Tuileries* and the *Racecourse at Longchamp* (figs. 13, 14) make a pair, in terms of both their placement on the roster and their relationship to the rest of what was on display. Both paintings are depictions of the Parisian *haute-* and *demi-monde's* outdoor leisure activities, and both are painted in a rapid *esquisse* manner that is on first glance unlike anything else in the show, but which on further consideration turns up here and there, in bits and pieces, in other works whose overall manner and subject matter are other than that of either *Music at the Tuilieries* or the *Racecourse at Longchamp*. Both paintings look more like what was to be dubbed Impressionism in the next decade than anything else Manet did in the '60s. As such, they punctuate the rest of the "exposition particulière," marking it by their dissonance with the dominant note struck by Manet's work of that period. But it is not so much that they define what Manet's oeuvre is not as that they insert their discordance into it, making that discordance part and parcel of it.

Of the two paintings, *Music at the Tuileries* seems more definitive of Manet's view of *lui-même*: it depicts the painter, after all, and does so unusually – that is to say, directly rather than allusively – standing together with his old studio companion Albert de Balleroy at the left edge of the painting, partly cut off by it, so that he appears just barely and reluctantly squeezed into it. Reiterated in the similar, bearded, and top-hatted figure of de Balleroy, and in the masculine top hats, beards, and black coats found throughout

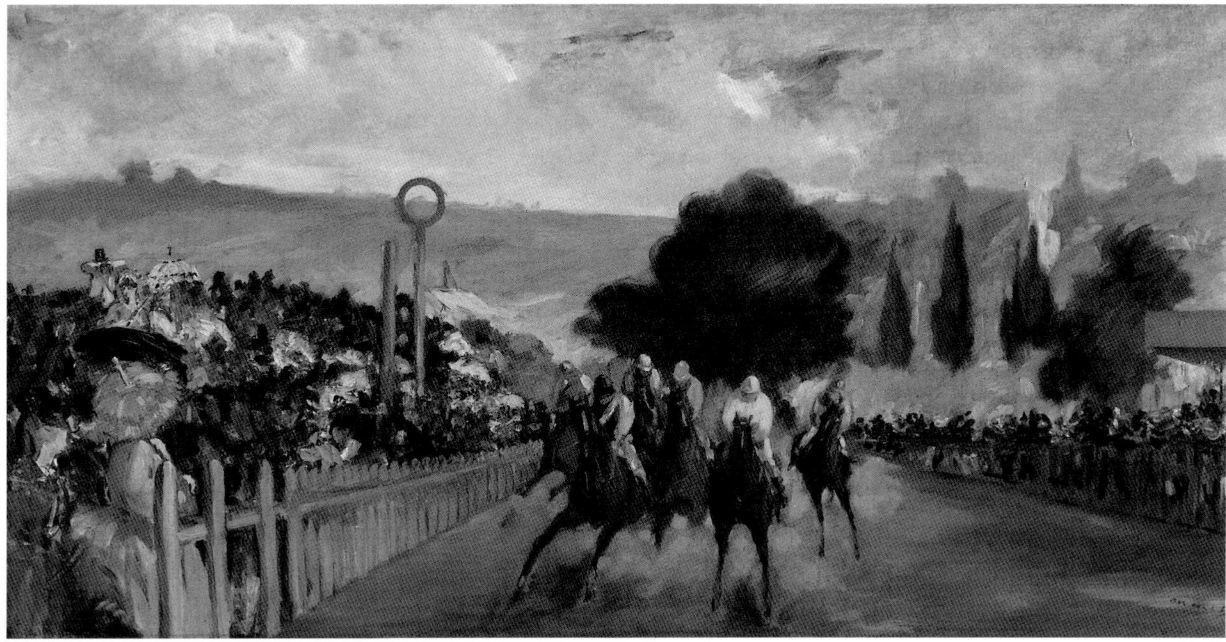

14   Edouard Manet, *Racecourse at Longchamp*, 1867, oil on canvas, 43.9 × 84.5 cm. The Art Institute of Chicago. Potter Palmer Collection, 1922. 424.

the painting, the dapper, urbane figure of Manet, marginalized as he is, could not be more different from the centered, rustic figure of Courbet in *The Painter's Studio*, playing the rough peasant to his Parisian audience. Shown in the urban landscape, to the side of it and thus almost out of it too, Manet positioned himself as if to look at the viewers in front of the painting as well as at the modish world within its frame, rather than to ignore or absorb them into himself. And thus, doubled by his monocled friend, the figure of Manet articulates a spectatorial rather than a producerly relationship to his world, and identifies *lui-même* with its frame rather its center, its edges and limits rather than its core.[33] That is, he locates himself at the very threshold between that which is interior and that which is exterior to the painting, thus articulating in another way what *The Old Musician* (with the self-alluding absinthe drinker at its opposite edge) had articulated as well, namely, the instability of the very boundary between *lui-même* and *autrui* that he drew in his "Motifs d'une exposition particulière." And rather than portraying himself as the beating heart of Nature, he disperses himself and his painter's interest in the visual world among a pageant of fashionable artifice – the scintillating finery of the black-suited dandy's feminine counterpart, the Parisienne, just as multiplied as he, but far more differentiated in her decor, her surfaces, and her colors. In that regard, *Music at the Tuileries* announced what came after 1867, when Manet shifted his attention away from the quotational strategies of his first decade or so of painting, handled at large in a Velasquez-like manner, toward the fashionability of the Parisienne, rendered in a *faux-*Impressionist mode. For the moment, however, the style and stylishness of *Music at the Tuileries* and its chic signaling of the stylistic pluralism of Manet's oeuvre stood out from the Spanishizing leanings and the *flânerie* through the museum signed and enacted almost everywhere else in his retrospective. And it marked the difference in Manet's conception of *lui-même* from that of Courbet.

The remainder of the retrospective's catalogue list concentrates on the two low genres that later were dear to Impressionism's heart – those of landscape and still life – with the intrusive exceptions noted above. Manet was hardly a landscape specialist, as Courbet was: indeed, in my opinion landscape was the very least of his talents, if not utterly out of tune with them. But still life was a specialty of Manet's: many critics at the time understood his entire production in still life terms, accounting either negatively or positively for his peculiar manner of rendering the human being, particularly the human face, by speaking to the still life appropriateness of his flat, blank – and I would add, singularly plural – way of painting. I shall expand upon Manet's still lifes in Chapter Ten, where I address them in the light of the countertop still life foregrounded in the *Bar at the Folies-Bergère*. For now, it is simply worth pointing to the way the still lifes gathered toward the end of Manet's list permitted him a particularly varied range of color and facture.

With its traditions of rough and fine painting, and its devotion to the differentiated textures of flowers, foodstuffs, domestic utensils, and luxury items, still life had always permitted and promoted such diversity – a diversity that defined both signifier and signified at once. And Manet made the most of that diversity, across a medley of still life spaces, laying out before the eyes, as on a counter or sideboard, the very relationship between painter's material and illusionistic effect that had always structured still life. Peonies, porcelain, linen, nuts, grapes, peaches, glass and silver, copper, oysters, salmon and eels, lemon, melon, and woodwork: a range of palette and a compass of opacity, translucency, and transparency, of the fringed, the folded, the shiny, smooth and reflective, the viscous and the slimy, the hard and bumpy and the fuzzy and soft, is offered up by the same hand to describe these different objects, their textures, and their tones. And yet – and here is the rub in Manet's "inconsistency," and what begins to differentiate it from the imperial eclecticism from which it set itself apart – these heterogeneous effects all sport what seems noticeably to be the same "handwriting."[34] It was in fact this central paradox that Manet's still lifes emblematized most of all: a remarkable singularity fashioned out of its opposite and alter ego, an extraordinary diversity. This too was what Manet's retrospective made manifest, across the board.

Manet's still lifes were more limited in their scope of reference to art-historical tradition. The rhetoric of Dutch still life, certainly, is recognizable in the pictures of meals about to be or already underway, with their plates of fish, diagonal swags of folded-back linen, glassware, and silver knife-handles. The traces of the Spanish *bodegone* are to be found in such items as the great, unopened circumference of melon dominating one of Manet's two *Fruits* pieces. But overall, the main reference is to the French tradition, in the figure of Chardin (filtered through Fantin-Latour). Thus, when Manet interrupted his list of landscapes, flowers, fruits, and fish with the overtly Spanish references of the *Young Woman Reclining in Spanish Costume*, the *Woman at the Window*, and the *Portrait of Zacharie Astruc*, not to mention *The Spanish Dog* and *The Students of Salamanca*, he interspersed his most obviously French productions with some of his most obviously Spanish ones, returning once more to the oscillation between the native and the non-

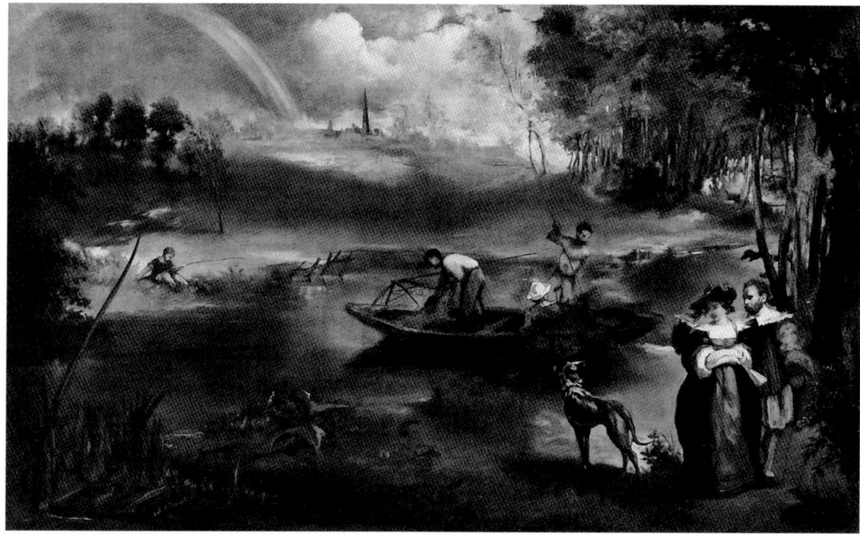

15 Edouard Manet, *Fishing*, 1861–63, oil on canvas, transferred from the original canvas, 76.8 × 123.2 cm. The Metropolitan Museum of Art, New York, Purchase, Mr. and Mrs. Richard J. Bernhard Gift, 1957. (57.10).

native signaled in the movement between the French and the Spanish. That interspersal, once again differentiated in its "Spanishicity" – here a matter of costuming, there a matter of the ethnic aspect of a face (as well as of prominent Spanish signifiers like mantilla, fan, and balcony, all of which may have been prompted by Manet's visit to Spain in 1865), and there again a matter of style and composition – also serves to theatricalize the naturalism of the landscapes and still lifes with which the Spanishizing pictures keep company on Manet's list of works. Since those paintings are all in their different ways transmuted copies of painting from the past (Goya, Titian, Velasquez), their interjections into the last part of Manet's list, with its emphasis upon landscape and still life, are also interjections of the artifice of the copy into the space of those genres most committed to the rendering of Nature. It is also to bring us up to Manet's odd last number, the "Paysage" which has become known as *Fishing*, and to the unnumbered painted and etched copies that follow.

Fishing (fig. 15), with its layering of quotations, this time of different paintings by Rubens, its return to the picnic-cum-museum thematics of the catalogue list's number one, the *Luncheon on the Grass*, and its consequent bracketing of Manet's roster with the two main terms of art-historical opposition, the Italian and the Netherlandish (the South and the North, as Wölfflin would put it) – such that everything else on the list literally falls between those two binary poles – also includes, at the very end of the inventory of the "exposition particulière," a more pointed address to the self-image, overtly articulated now in terms of pastiche.[35] As is known, *Fishing* includes the (diminutive) likenesses of Léon Leenhoff, Suzanne Leenhoff, and Manet himself, now at the right edge of the composition, and in the guise of Rubens together with his wife Hélène Fourment. His three copies, in turn, include Manet's painted reproduction of Tintoretto's self-

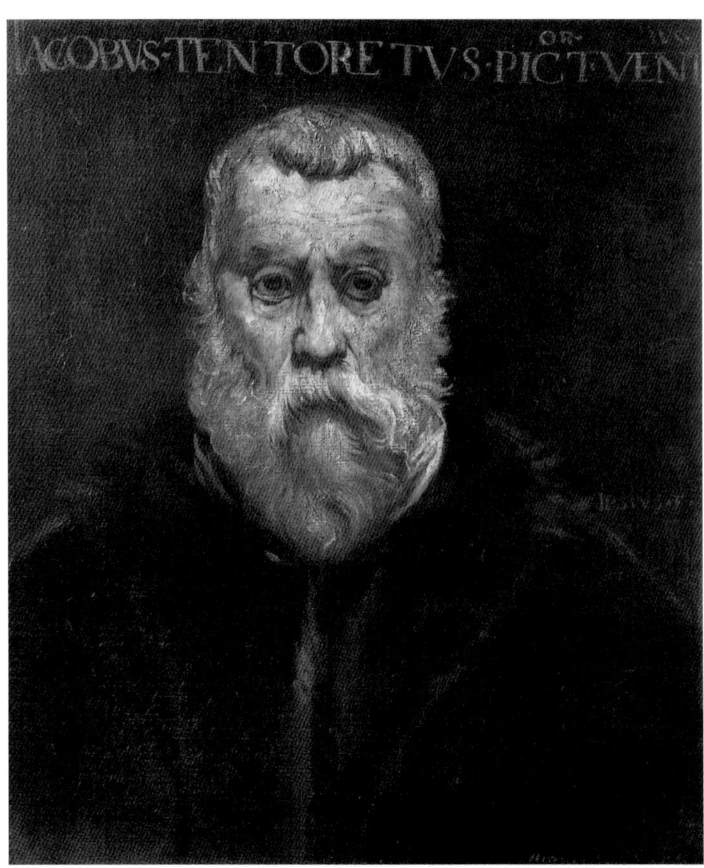

16   Edouard Manet, *Copy after Tintoretto's "Self Portrait,"* 1854, oil on canvas, 61 × 50 cm. Dijon, Musée des Beaux-Arts.

portrait as an old man, executed back in 1854 when Manet was still a student, with elderly features very much like Manet's youthful ones (fig. 16). (Coming right after *Fishing*, the first of the copies, that of Titian's *Virgin with the Rabbit*, immediately juxtaposes the Flemish with the Venetian strand of Italian art. Otherwise, the copies shift from the North/South dichotomy to emphasize the eccentric term that dominated Manet's retrospective, that is to say, the Spanish, in the name of Velasquez.)

Manet's list ends, in other words, not just with copies, but with images of *lui-même* as *autre*: ending with his beginnings, it parades a personal style made up out of Rubens, Tintoretto (and Titian), and Velasquez three times over – not to mention his own *Gitanos*, quintessential signifiers of the intrusion of the nomadic and the mobile within and at the edges of settled culture. Depicting himself as Rubens and Tintoretto, paired and solitary, young and old, at the outset and at the close of an artistic life, he draws a double line under the fact of his own pluralism, his own constitution out of multiple styles, his invention of his artistic self out of several lines of other artistic selves, his anti-linear presentation of his "individuality," and the derivation of his originality in the mechanical reproduction of the history of art. As much as it is a biographical gesture, the inclusion of the odd little figure of Léon Leenhoff, a portrait that because of its miniature dimensions is hardly a portrait, at the edge of the signature blue-green no-man's-land of the middle distance of *Fishing* signals the peculiarly unstable art lineage of Manet's retrospective. His paternity uncertain, his image repeated three times over in the retrospective – toward the beginning, in the *Boy with the Sword*, ambiguously in *The Fifer*, and barely at all in *Fishing* – the illegitimate child Léon Leenhoff points to the instability that lies at the very foundation of Manet's self-construction in the "exposition particulière" of 1867.[36]

In the end, Manet's restrospective constructs a view of *lui-même* that runs counter not only to the various imperial and official displays of 1867, but also to Courbet's presentation of his "individuality" back in 1855. Manet's retrospective kept his painterly self apart, just as Courbet's retrospective had done in 1855, only more so since he had nothing on view within the Exposition or the Salon; all of him and all of his oeuvre fell outside the embrace of the state. And Manet's manner, while it was evidently plural, was also, by the contrast that his separate pavilion enforced, utterly different from the diversity of what the Exposition and the Salon embraced. Picture by picture, it announced its unassimilability – its failure to be categorized by genre, style, or nationality. Picture by picture, it declared its "handwriting" openly and for all to see, as the work of a markedly individual hand. That frank handwriting (Manet called it "sincere") was precisely what the critics had derided; not wishing to "protest," nevertheless that handwriting was what Manet chose to exhibit, when he declared that "To exhibit is for the artist . . . the sine qua non"[37] and enacted that declaration with his fifty-odd works at the Place de l'Alma. Dramatically in contrast to the work of the nation, which drew as much as it could into its fold and yet differentiated between the schools of Europe, this was the signature work of one man, differentiated from the nation's differentiation of those schools as well as its colonization of them. Manet's retrospective was even less successful as a public event than Courbet's had been, but in the long view what it accomplished was indeed quintessentially modern: the utter individuation of the artist, and with it the substitution of the category of the individual for all the hierarchical divisions and categorical polarities that still obtained in the imperial system of the arts.

But Manet's "individuality" was as unlike the centered, natural one that Courbet had proposed in 1855 as it was other than the monographic overview of Ingres's retrospective, say, with its clearly categorizable identification with the linear, the Raphaelesque, and the *ancien* pole of the Ancients-and-Moderns dichotomy. Rather than identifying himself and his practice with the productive labor of the body, the physicality of Nature, the organic unity of a self centered in Nature and made in its image, or the progress of French art toward a universal naturalism, Manet's retrospective made a spectacle of a self made up out of others, a singularity that was as paradoxically multiple and as disordering of the accepted oppositions as it could possibly be, a *lui-même* formed out of artifice and the supplement rather than Nature's essence, an identity pastiched from the museum and its international array of poses rather than formed of the clay of the body and the earth of France. Jumping all over the historical and geographical map and ending with a youthful image of himself as an elderly Renaissance *autre*, it made a nonsense of the dream of progress toward an ever greater naturalism and a universalist resolution of differences, or of his own development out of the pluralism of the student's copy toward the unity of the mature artist's style. Signed through and through with the marked difference of his "handwriting" from all others, his was nonetheless an oeuvre divided: indeed, its

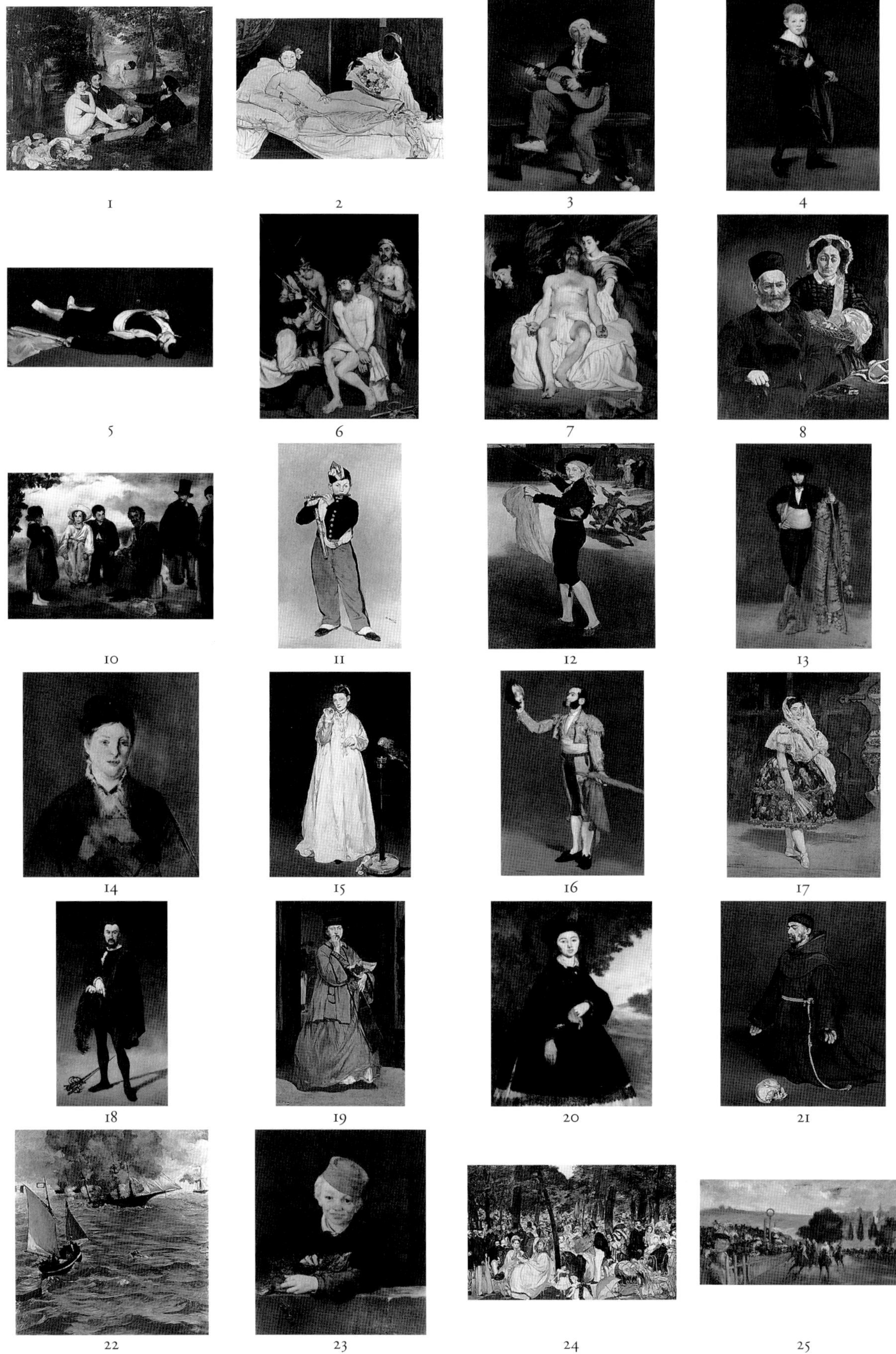

1

2

3

4

5

6

7

8

10

11

12

13

14

15

16

17

18

19

20

21

22

23

24

25

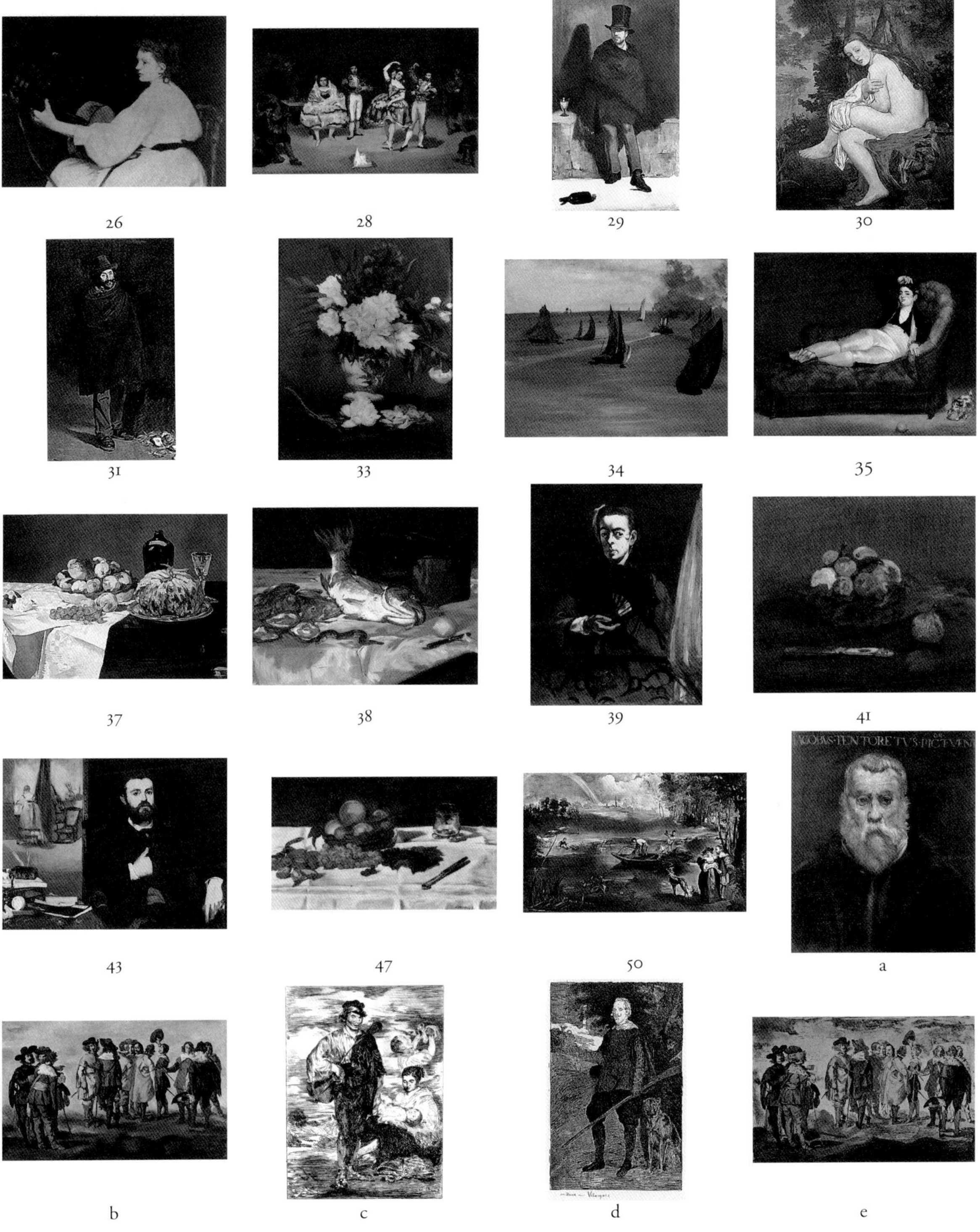

Manet's "exposition particulière" at the Place de l'Alma, 1867: a representative sample. For a listing of titles, see the Photograph Credits on page 382.

signature was its internal division – its difference not only from others but also from itself. And finally, if Courbet's "individuality" located its origin in the political moment of 1848, Manet's *lui-même* was much too disregarding of the linearity of historical progression, his own or any larger trajectory, to define any such point of origin.

Instead of Courbet's Republican robustness and natural frankness, Manet's *lui-même* was that of the urbane Second Empire dandy, for whom "sincerity" was a matter of distinction, a personal style crafted out of sharp wit and elegance, a divergence from others, and a mercurial freedom to differ from himself. Rather than grounded, mobile; rather than centered, kaleidoscopic; rather than muscularly natural, masked and costumed – a *soi-même*, to use the words of Baudelaire now, in the image of *autrui, la femme*. So much so that even Zola, the preeminent naturalist of Manet's moment, described the notorious *Olympia*, second on Manet's roster, as the face of Manet. He did so, however, by making her an image of the overall sameness of Manet's work, and an emblem of the organic constitution of his vision. And by disavowing her connection to the museum, and ignoring her relationship with her most immediate alter ego in the retrospective of 1867, the number one that she followed on the catalogue list, the *Luncheon on the Grass*.

Chapter Two

A NEW MANNER IN PAINTING:
EMILE ZOLA ON MANET

MANET COULD HAVE HAD Zola's early 1867 tract, "Une nouvelle manière en peinture: Edouard Manet," republished as his catalogue introduction. Zola's essay about Manet was as much a manifesto as Courbet's Realist declaration of 1855 had been: it is a vivid statement about Manet's "individuality" which sets that individuality in explicit contrast to the eclecticism of the Exposition's patrimonial display. In it, Zola announces that Manet's oeuvre is made of "his flesh and his blood," that in painting "he found *himself*," that his work tells of his "heart" and "flesh," as well as of his "civilization and his nation," that it has an individual point of view, and should be seen in contrast to the "vast sweets boutique" of the upcoming Exposition, where art has become "fragmented," "divided in pieces," "a crowd of little republics."[1] Zola implicitly contrasts what he had earlier described as Manet's manly style[2] to the effeminacy of the pictures of Cabanel and others, and describes many of the paintings that showed up in the pavilion on the Place de l'Alma. (He was, in fact, describing the contents of Manet's atelier in 1866, which he said Manet "had reunited there in order to judge the ensemble they would make at the Universal Exposition."[3])

Manet did not use Zola's essay, however, declining out of gentlemanly self-deprecation, because he did not wish to attach his already scandal-associated name to Zola's anti-state thematization of Manet's run-ins with the jury, the public, and the critics of the Salon – or perhaps because he did not see his retrospective and the *lui-même* it put on display in quite the same terms as Zola.[4] Whatever the reason, he chose the milder, less manifesto-like, almost pleading "Reasons for a Private Exhibition" as the introduction to his catalogue. But Zola went ahead and republished "Une nouvelle manière" as a brochure, including an etched portrait of Manet as its frontispiece (fig. 17) and interleaving a copy of Manet's etching after *Olympia* (fig. 18). And it is Zola's view of Manet that has held, in spite of the distance that grew between the writer's and the painter's views, and the rising disenchantment that Zola expressed with all manifestations of modern visual art. In many ways, it is Zola's view that underlies Greenberg's positioning of Manet as the father of modernism, as well as most subsequent, heroicizing treatments of Manet as the carrier of Courbet's intransigent torch and the advance scout of the avant-garde and its ever advancing movement into the future. It is as such that I want to take a closer look at it: it is worth following its logic in detail and in its order of presentation, from its prologue on the role of criticism, through its treatment of Manet's

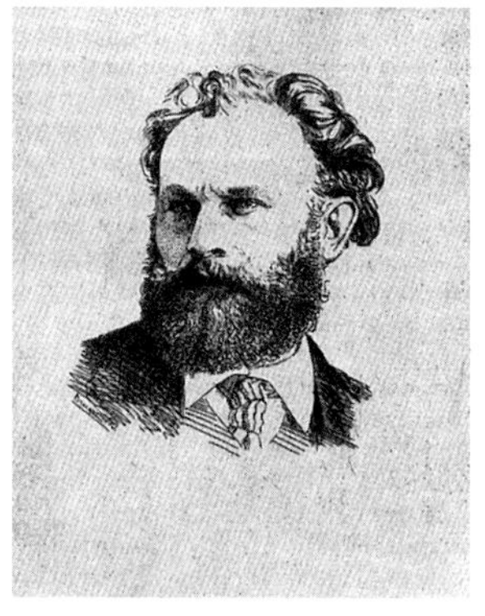

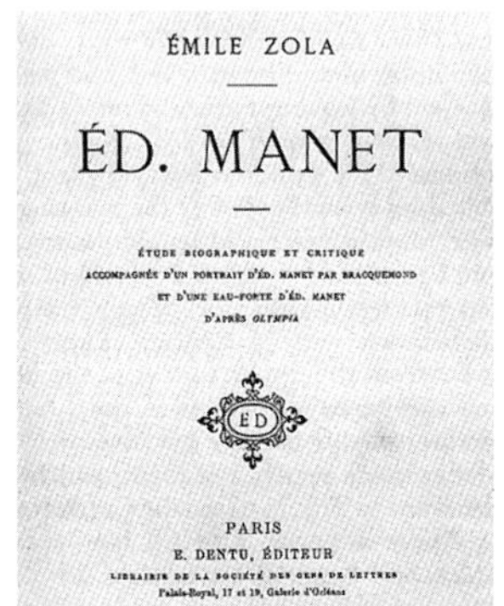

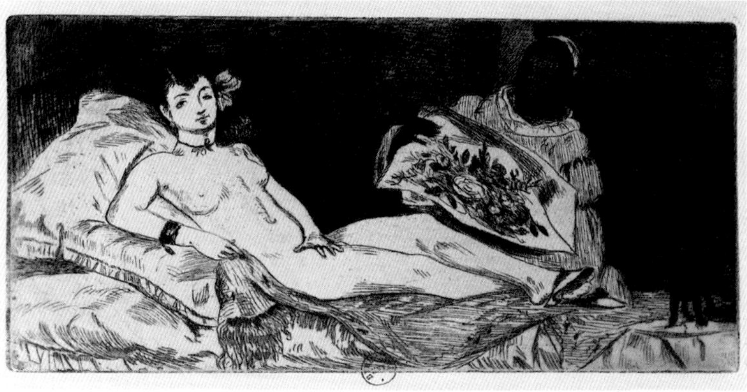

18 (*above*)   Edouard Manet, *Olympia*, 1867, etching. New York Public Library.

17   Bracquemond, *Portrait of Manet*, title page from Emile Zola, *Ed. Manet, Etude biographique et critique*, Paris: Dentu, 1867, etching. Bibliothèque Nationale, Paris.

life and personality, to its discussion of the works in the artist's oeuvre, which is followed by a concluding diatribe against the "Public."[5]

THE PRINCIPLES OF POSITIVIST CRITICISM

Zola's essay is a positivist fulfillment of his pronouncement of the year before regarding Manet: "That which I demand of the artist . . . is to deliver himself, heart and flesh, and to affirm out loud his powerful and particular spirit, his bitter and strong nature . . . it's a matter of being oneself, of showing one's naked heart, of energetically formulating an individuality . . . What I look for above all in a picture is a man and not a picture."[6] In other words, Zola conceives of Manet's paintings as organic products of the biographical body that was Manet, and seeks to discover the "nature" of that man directly reflected in them. Therefore, Zola commences with a thumbnail sketch of the artist's education and career, which includes a vivid description of the physical and personal presence of Manet, many of whose features are picked up in the ensuing discussion of works. He prefaces his treatment of Manet the man with an outline of his views on the critic's task and the ideal monograph. Speaking of the delicacy of the task of reconstructing the "personality of an artist," especially when that artist is young, has produced only a few years' worth of work, and thus has not yet come fully into his own or acheived what properly can be thought of as an oeuvre, Zola states the desideratum of being able to analyze "a complete ensemble," "all the faces of an entire genius," in order to produce an "exact and precise portrait" from which no features are missing."[7] Zola sums up what he sees as the critic's preeminent task:

> And there is, for the critic, a penetrating joy in being able to say to himself that he can dissect a being, that faced with the anatomy of a perfect organism, he then will be able to reconstruct, in all his living reality, a man with all his members, all his nerves and all his heart, all his dreams and all his flesh.[8]

This is the critic's version of the myth of Pygmalion, in which the critic dreams, rather paradoxically, of being able to bring the painter to life through the dissection of his oeuvre, his "body" of work. The pictorial model for the critic's task is the portrait, treated as the most transparent of genres, corresponding detail by detail to the face and physique of the individual. The scientific model for the critic's work is that of vivisection, in which the painter's paintings are treated, part by part – member by member – as his bodily remains, revivified by the knife of critical analysis, which simultaneously penetrates his flesh and breathes imaginative life back into it. On both counts, this is a positivist model of criticism, following the positivist emphasis upon the surgical gaze of the observer, the treatment of the human subject as an organism, and then proceeding from the small to the large, the part to the whole, the datum to the system. Even Zola's stressing of the future completion of the oeuvre and therefore of the picture of Manet conforms to the positivist accent on the progress of the individual sciences toward their future coming together in comprehension of the principle of totality.[9] All in all, Zola's ideal of criticism is an organic one, whose object is not the individual works of the artist but the organism of the artist, understood as a single entity and in its entirety – the "tout ensemble" of the body and soul of the painter, where paint is never paint per se but a fleshy epidermis beneath which one can see blood pulsing, heart beating, bones structuring, and nerves twitching, and where the materiality of the canvas gives immediately onto the living corpus of the man who once worked its surface. The concept of the artist's "genius" is an organic one too: the particular physical construction of the organism yields a particular way of seeing and painting, which eventually combines and realizes itself in an organic oeuvre.

Zola sets this critic's dream of the total picture in tension with what he sees as the partial development of Manet's art, revealing thus far only "a corner of his personality."[10] Nevertheless it is a sketch of the organism that was Manet that he seeks to describe in the rest of "Une nouvelle manière." And that sketch gains significance, Zola claims, because the organism of which it is a likeness is representative of "our artistic movement itself, of our contemporary opinions in the matter of aesthetics."[11] As partial as he felt Manet's work to be, in other words, Zola also felt it to be quintessentially modern – an instance of the modern artistic temperament and of the situation of the arts in modern France. Linking Manet's independence to his own,[12] he claims that independence, and the partial individuality of which it is an expression, for French modernity: it is Manet's specificity, and even his incompleteness, that is quintessentially modern. This too is a positivist principle, according to which the universal spirit of the "positive" age is inclined toward the specialized, the specific, and the individual: the most modern, most positive individuality will be precisely that which is the most individual. Moreover, the positivist quest after the general picture and the total summation is necessarily never complete: for future orientation is an essential component of the *a posteriori* mode of positivism, which makes incompletion a characteristically modern state of affairs.[13] So, though Manet is an imperfect object of organic criticism as Zola conceives of it, he is also, in his very imperfection, the perfect exemplar of Zola's positivist conception of modernism. (The eventual completion of the *tout ensemble* of Manet is assumed; indeed, at the end of his essay Zola claims to predict it, just as the positivist scientist might predict the outcome of his experiments. That that *tout ensemble* was never realized, in Zola's view, was the reason for his later disappointment in the artist and the artistic moment for which he stood.)

Before embarking on a description of his protagonist, Zola tells a familiar story about modern artists, their parents, and their teachers which he casts in mythic terms. Born into a tranquil bourgeois family, at a time when "Thank god!, the bohemian long-hairs of 1830 had all but disappeared,"[14] Manet finished his studies at the Collège Rollin, Zola tells us, only to fall headlong in love with a terrible, and for his family intolerable, mistress – painting, "the great *Impure*, the Courtesan ever hungry for fresh meat, who must drink the blood of their children and wring them all panting upon her insatiable breast."[15] This is the scarlet language that Zola later employed in his novels – already one sees that the line dividing criticism, biography, and literature is very thin. It is also the same topos that was picked up by Zola some two decades later, after Manet's demise, in *L'Oeuvre*, the novel with which Zola sounded the death-knell of his own championing of figures like Manet, and with them of modern art.

The figure of painting as a great Courtesan – an idol to whom sacrifices are made, who stands in place of a young man's healthier appetite for the real flesh of real women – underpins Zola's later enshrinement of the little street girl *Olympia* as the painted embodiment of Manet the man. Here the image of the Courtesan is sewn in with the "few biographical details"[16] that Zola admits to having on Manet. She floats before the eyes of the young artist-to-be when he sails off as a navy apprentice to Rio de Janeiro, becoming an all-consuming hallucination who informs every biographical event that follows in rapid succession on the heels of Manet's brief disciplinary exile, from his trips to Italy and Holland to his signing up at Thomas Couture's studio, his failed beginning as a Salon painter with *The Absinthe Drinker*, his entry into the public domain with his exhibition at Martinet's gallery, and his acceptances into the Salon des Refusés and the Salons of 1864 and 1865, climaxing abruptly with his apotheosis as the painter of *Olympia*. Over Manet's preliminary voyage hovers this mirage:

> Without a doubt *the great Impure, the Courtesan* ever hungry for fresh meat embarked with him and managed to seduce him in the midst of the luminous solitudes of the Ocean and the sky; she spoke to his flesh, she swayed before his eyes in the brilliant lines of the horizon, she spoke to him of passion with the sweet and vigorous language of colors. In return, Edouard Manet gave himself completely to *the Infamous One*.[17]

The fantasy function of the *grande Impure* is signaled in the repetition of the phrase – "the great Impure, the Courtesan ever hungry for fresh meat." She is phantasmatic, an all-consuming, imaginary femininity rather than a real female commodity. That is the reason for Zola's ambivalence about her, though she is as much a figure of his invention, his fantasy, as *Olympia* and her others were Manet's. The *grande Impure* stands as a vision of art made over in the image of flesh, her voluptuous curves blended with the waves of the sea and the "lines of the horizon" – as if to merge the disjunctive white body of *Olympia* with the hallucinatory blue-green sea of *The Kearsarge and the Alabama*. As an image of the femininity of art, then, here she inclines toward the old equation of Woman and Nature. Paradoxically, however, in her invocation of the corrupting influence of false idols, she is also a negative variation on the theme of Woman as Artifice. As she became in *L'Oeuvre*, therefore, she is already a condensation of Zola's mixed feelings about visual art and artists.

The Courtesan presides over Manet's inability to submit "his particular temperament" to the culture of Couture's studio, which was "contrary to his nature," and even over the production of his very first works after his departure from Couture's studio, which "already contained in germ the personal manner of the artist,"[18] to be more fully realized in works such as *Olympia*. And so, from the chimera of the great Courtesan, Zola proceeds to his likeness of Manet:

> Edouard Manet is of medium height, more small than large. His hair and beard are a light chestnut; his eyes, narrow and deep, have a youthful vivacity and fire; his mouth is characteristic, thin, mobile, a little mocking at the corners. The whole face, with its fine and intelligent irregularity, announces his suppleness and audacity, and his distrust of stupidity and banality. And if from his face we descend to the person, we will find in Edouard Manet a man of exquisite amiability and politeness, of distinguished attractions and sympathetic appearance.[19]

This is Manet the man, whom *Olympia* represents, having seduced him to art in the guise of *la grande Impure* and bound his soul to her body. From the sketch of facial details and coloring, to "the whole face" which expresses the personality underlying it on its surface, to the person, Zola attempts "to sketch the physiognomy" and "show the real personage,"[20] rather than the caricature accepted by the public, and to do so in a fully positivist manner: from the small to the large, the superficial to the deep, the part to the whole, the particulars betray the general principle of Manet's particularity, the *tout ensemble* of this very individual man.

There is a paradox in the constitution of this individual man that Zola cannot quite gloss over, however. An *homme du monde* living *en famille* with the young Dutch woman whom he had married three years before, so Zola informs the reader:

> He has confessed to me that he adores high society and that he finds a secret voluptuousness in the perfumed and luminous delicacies of the soirée. He is led to that, no doubt, by his love of bold and vivid colors; but there is also within him an innate need of distinction and elegance which I have become powerfully convinced is represented in his works.[21]

Evidently, the Courtesan still governs the soul of the domesticated young man, so that inside Manet the manly *bon bourgeois*, "walking straight ahead, obeying his nature," and enjoying "the calm joys of the modern bourgeoisie,"[22] there resides not only a dandy aristocrat but also a woman, with a feminine taste for delicacy, lightness, sinuosity, and color. And "in his interior"[23] there lurks a foreign element, *chez soi* a delight in the other, if not an identification with her. But having allowed this Baudelairean whiff of alterity to perfume his portrait of Manet, Zola steps hurriedly out of its range and then renounces it altogether (before returning to it again, compulsively).

Finally escaping "the precepts of a nature other than his own," and seeking to "see by himself,"[24] Manet, asserts Zola, belongs to those "whose masters do not recognize them as their children; they are a race apart, each one of them will contribute their word to the great sentence which humanity writes and which will never be complete, they are destined to be masters in their turn, egoists, distinct and decisive personalities."[25] Disowned by his artistic father (who, then, could better represent Manet than Léon Leenhoff, he who was both studio rat and child without father?), Manet defines his true self by expelling all that is alien to himself; by that very process he becomes a representative of a new race, quintessentially modern in its self-definition, and in its particular abilities to promote the forward march of humanity in general. Underlining the modernity of Manet's particularity, this is to make him the exemplar of the positivist principle of progress, but it is also to move away, with as much haste as possible, from the effeminate scent of Baudelairean synaesthesia, in which the fashionable effects of cologne and color are mingled.

And it is to move toward Zola's denial of the importance to Manet of Spanish art, of the museum more generally, and of Baudelaire, and to assert the physiological construction of Manet's particular eye as against those three influences. Remarking that, while the "rude and graceful" language that Manet spoke contained a few Spanish turns, nevertheless it was "a language that he had made his own,"[26] Zola launches into an opposition between the museum and the authentic self of this newborn artist:

> Sensing that he would come to nothing in copying the masters, in painting nature seen through individualities different from his own, he came to understand, all naively, one fine morning, that it remained for him to try to see nature as she is, without looking at her through the works and opinions of others. . . . he . . . set himself to reproducing it on a canvas, according to his faculties of vision . . . He made an effort to forget all that he had studied in the museums; he strove to remember no longer the painted works which he had looked at. There was no longer anything there but a particular intelligence, served by organs endowed with a certain way about them, face to face with nature, translating in his manner.
>
> Thus the artist obtained an oeuvre which was *his flesh and blood* . . . with a new flavor and a particular aspect . . . [which] was a face as yet unknown of human genius. . . . he had found himself: he saw with his own eyes, he had to give us in each of his canvases a translation of nature in that original language which he had just discovered deep within himself.[27]

We have already seen that Manet's retrospective of 1867 belied these observations of Zola's: Manet had not forgotten the museums; his language was precisely the language of others, of the old masters; his own very particular locution was full of foreign accents and speech in foreign tongues; the distinctiveness of his own way of seeing lay precisely in its filtering through other peoples' ways of seeing. So Zola's denials of these evident features of Manet's oeuvre to date have the status of disavowals. Moreover, directed at other critics' stated perception of Manet's works as much as at those works themselves (like Baudelaire and others, Zola enters into the discursive game of criticism by positioning himself relative to other players), Zola's opposition between Manet's nature and the culture of the museum was strategic, serving to define his practice as a critic as much as Manet's practice as an artist: "My aesthetic, or rather the science which I would call modern aesthetics" which differs from "the opinion of the crowd on art."[28] Making it quite plain that his definition of Manet's art is intertwined with his own self-definition as a critic, Zola states:

> One must proceed as the artist himself has proceeded: forget the treasures of the museums . . . chase away the memory of accumulated paintings by dead painters; no longer see anything but nature face to face, just as she is; in short search for nothing but a translation of nature particular to a temperament, alive with human interest, in the works of Edouard Manet.[29]

What could be clearer? Zola the critic proceeds as Manet the painter proceeds – his criticism is as transparent to Manet's art as that art is to whatever piece of nature it translates on canvas. But of course, what Zola actually does is to make Manet in his own image.

And that image is a positivist one, through and through. The emphasis upon the physiology of Manet's eye, its unmediated empiricism and even its unified way of seeing, as against the diverse, mediated manners of painting that the museum puts on view, flows right into Zola's own fantasy of a positivist repository of the advancing and ultimately unified history of human sight (as opposed to the view that "the large production of human genius" reduces to the "beautiful, absolute . . . immutable," in which the differences between "the pale, cold mornings of Holland, and the hot, voluptuous evenings of Italy and Spain" recede before the "simple blooming of Greek genius"[30]):

> Now here are my beliefs in the matter of art. In one glance I embrace the humanity that has lived and that, according to nature, in all moments, in all climates, in all circumstances, has felt the imperious need to create humanly, to reproduce objects and beings through the arts. Thus I have before me a vast spectacle whose every part interests and moves me profoundly. Every great artist has arrived on the scene to give us a new and personal translation of nature . . . I wish that the canvases of all the painters could be reunited in one great chamber, where we could go and read, page by page, the epic of human creation. And the theme would always be the same nature, the same reality, and the variations would be those particular and original ways in which artists have rendered the great creation of God . . . That which interests me, as a man, is humanity, my grandmother; that which touches me, which entrances me in human creations, in works of art, is to discover at the bottom of each of them an artist, a brother, who presents a new face of nature to me, with all the power or all the sweetness of his personality. Seen that way, that work tells me the story of *a heart and flesh*, it speaks to me of a civilization and a country. And when, in the center of the immense chamber in which are hung the pictures of all the painters of the world, I cast my eye over the vast ensemble, I have there the same poem in a thousand different languages, and I do not tire of rereading it in each picture, charmed by the delicacies and vigors of each dialect.

. . . And our creation extends from the past to the infinite future; every society will provide its artists who will contribute their personalities . . .[31]

In short, Zola dreams of a Universal Exposition of his own design – focusing on painting, bringing together all the national schools of Europe, demonstrating the historical progress and natural totality to which they all are subsumed, and culminating in the Gallic (and yet universal) modernity of an Edouard Manet. His *immense salle* is thus both in line with what the Empire envisioned, first in 1855 and then in 1867, in the arts sections of its Universal Expositions; and it revises the exhibition logic of the Empire in favor of a positivist vision of progress and unity, with a corollary accent upon modernity and the unified individual. That Zola closes his essay by setting the art of Manet, as seen in the retrospective at the Place de l'Alma, against the piecemeal "crowd of little republics" preferred by the public and presumably represented by the real Universal Exposition of 1867, underlines his commitment to an ultimately unified totality, as against an aimless eclecticism that in his Janus-figured view is merely the other face of the absolutism of classical aesthetics.

Where for those of the classicist persuasion (like Ingres) the *beau absolu* remains an *a priori* that governs all the dispersed and changing styles of European painting, from ancient Greece to the present day and from Holland to Italy and Spain, for Zola the artistic Tower of Babel grows historically, following an *a posteriori* trajectory toward a future that is simultaneously ever more diversified and individualized and ever more indicative of the grand evolutionary scheme and unfolding totality of Creation at large, in which visual styles proliferate like biological species moving in concert toward ever greater refinement and specialization. The diversity championed by Zola leads in one direction, that of science and the unmediated scientific fact.[32] That is also the direction of Manet's art, which Zola treats as at once analytical, like his own criticism,[33] and physiologically determined – which is to say at once engaged in a scientific way of seeing and a fit object of the scientific gaze. Says Zola, riding the crest of his description of the advancing tide of art: "I do not want to analyze anything but facts, and works of art are simple facts. /Therefore . . . I place myself before the pictures of Edouard Manet as before a set of new facts which I wish to explain . . ."[34] Those "new facts" are primarily represented objects – "fruits . . . placed on a table, are set off against a gray background . . . between [which] . . . the color values form a whole spectrum of shades":[35] like others, Zola understands Manet's art as governed by the terms of the *nature morte* and its object world, but he pitches that understanding toward an account of the unified, nature-based objectivity of the artist's way of seeing and its colored translation into the material "fact" of painting.

FLESH-AND-BLOOD PAINTINGS

Above all, the "new facts" of Manet's paintings represent a factual way of seeing, determined by the physical make-up of Manet; and the colored *taches* with which Manet paints are optical reflections not only of the objects before his eyes but also of his own physique – of the objecthood of his own subjectivity. Repeatedly Zola equates the palette of Manet's paintings with the palette of his eye, and the palette of his flesh, each the reflection and result of the other. Having already described Manet's complexion and hair color as "pale chestnut," his manner of working as "rough" (yet "gentle"), and the general flavor of his works as "strong and bitter,"[36] Zola proceeds to repeat and vary the adjectives *blonde* and *âpre* (bitter/biting/acrid/caustic/edgy – the French word translates very imprecisely) over and over again, with regard to both the artist's general way of seeing and individual works. Those instances of repetition are worth citing, beginning with Zola's characterization of Manet's tonal point of departure: "Ordinarily Edouard Manet departs from a lighter note than that existing in nature. His paintings are *blond* and luminous, of a solid and firm pallor. Light falls white and broad, illuminating objects in a gentle way."[37]

Then he elaborates:

> The artist . . . lets himself be guided by his eyes which perceive . . . in large tones . . . A head placed against a wall is no more than a more or less white spot against a more or less gray background; and the clothing juxtaposed to the figure becomes, for example, a more or less blue patch put next to a more or less white patch. . . . *The whole personality of the artist consists in the manner in which his eye is organized*: he sees *blond*, and he sees in masses.[38]

"The whole personality of the artist" is condensed in the way he sees, which in turn is registered in the way he paints. That "personality" is very much a matter of physique, the artist's "flesh and blood," of which his personality and his paintings, in that order, are both the products. And so, if the artist is blond (here "blond" indicates a light complexion together with a light hair color), his eye will see blond, and his paintings will also be blond: "The general aspect is . . . of a luminous *blond*"; "The new note which he contributes is that *blond* note which fills his canvas with light."[39] And if the artist's wit is sharp so will his works be: "The first impression that a canvas by Edouard Manet produces is a little *harsh and caustic* . . . render[ing] nature with a sweet brutality, if I may so express myself."[40]

This theme is continued in the opening generalities of the section on *Les oeuvres*: "There is both *bitter and sweet* in the first glance . . . And all those light colors, those elegant forms . . . have . . . a sweetness of an extreme simplicity and elegance."[41] In Manet's "whole personality," opposite flavors are conjoined and blended, with the result that the same dualistic effect is acheived in the paintings. This is proven true, again and again, with each of the painter's paintings, which Zola tends to organize in pairs, playing one off against the other several times over, but always in order to decide which is the privileged, dominant term, which strikes the stronger, truer note. Passing quickly over *The Absinthe Drinker* (which according to him does not yet have in it the true temperament of the artist), Zola contrasts the *Boy with the Sword* to *Olympia*, speaking of the sweetness, the modeling, and the Spanish parentage of the one, as against the "frank stiffness" and "powerful and accurate patches" of the other, which he prefers.[42] Following that pairing, Zola goes on to speak about the fourteen paintings shown at Martinet's in 1863, eight of which are also on view in 1867. Naming them all, he settles on *Lola de Valence* and *The Streetsinger* (before moving on to pair *The Spanish Ballet* with *Music at the Tuileries*):

But the picture that I prefer . . . is the *Streetsinger*. A young woman, well known on
the heights of the Pantheon hill, emerges from a brasserie while eating some cherries
which she holds in a paper wrapper. The whole work is of *a sweet and blond gray*, and
in it nature seems to me to have been analyzed with extreme sympathy and exactitude. Such a picture has, outside of its subject, *an austerity* . . . one senses in it the
harsh search after truth . . . of a man who wants, above all, to say frankly what he
sees.[43]

The comparison between *Lola de Valence* and *The Streetsinger* is implicit: the preferred
Streetsinger is a picture of a *Parisienne* rather than an *Espagnole*, and is treated as a straight-
forward representation of modern life just as Manet found it (rather than in relation to
a poem by Baudelaire).[44] And it is *The Streetsinger* that Zola claims to be the analytic,
factual, unmediated painting, and which he describes with his signature adjectives: *doux,
blond, âpre*, now with the addition of "austerity" thrown into the mix.

Following the list of works shown at Martinet's, Zola treats first those paintings shown
at the Salon des Refusés, then those at the Salons of 1864 and 1865, respectively, then
those refused by the Salon of 1866, culminating with those works of Manet's that are still
"barely dry," and a couple of still lifes included toward the bottom of the list of works
at Manet's retrospective at the Place de l'Alma. (Thus, as much as it is a history of paintings, treated one by one,[45] "Une nouvelle manière en peinture" is also very much a history
of Manet's exhibitions, acknowledging the importance of the *exposition*, and of the pairings and groupings set forth by this and that *exposition* to the story of Manet.) Out
of the three paintings at the Salon des Refusés, Zola selects the number one on Manet's
catalogue list, *Luncheon on the Grass*, which he treats at length and to which he returns
at the very end of his essay, making it the emblem of the public's misunderstanding of
Manet, of the advancing movement of *l'esprit français*,[46] and as such of Manet's eventual
inclusion in the Louvre, after Delacroix. Out of the two paintings exhibited at the
Salon of 1864, the *Christ and Angels* and *The Bullfight* (now cut down to the *Dead
Toreador*), he selects the former; the latter he finds similar, in its not yet fully Manet
effect, to the *Boy with the Sword*. Of the two paintings shown at the Salon of 1865, he
selects *Olympia* again, to which he devotes the lengthiest analysis of all, making it the
representative of Manet's signature way of seeing. Of the equally theatrical *Tragic Actor*
and *The Fifer*, both rejected in 1866, once again Zola prefers the latter, in the same
terms that he had preferred *Olympia* to the *Boy with the Sword*; while of the barely dry
works it is the *Young Woman in 1866* which he selects for a culminating, summary
analysis. Finally, the two still lifes with which he ends are paired together with *Olympia*
once more, the second of them in particular remaining juxtaposed to her in his memory,
as evidence of the inclination of the "mechanism" of Manet's "talent" toward the *nature
morte*.[47]

From one preferred painting to the next, whether treated in brief or at length, the
characteristics selected as quintessentially Manet, and the adjectives used to describe
them, remain the same. Describing the paintings with which the *Luncheon on the Grass*
was exhibited at the Salon des Refusés, *Mlle V. . . . in the Costume of an Espada* and *Young
Man in the Costume of a Majo*, as even more "colorist" than usual – "*blond* as always,
but of a wild and brilliant *blond*"[48] – Zola proceeds to tell his readers that the *Luncheon*

on the Grass should be looked at as a "whole landscape" rather than a luncheon on the grass, and that in it are disposed all of "the particular and rare elements which he had in himself."[49] Even more generally, in the *Christ and Angels* (as against *The Bullfight*) he finds "Edouard Manet whole-cloth, with the bias of his eye and the audacities of his hand."[50] *Olympia* is simply the *chef-d'oeuvre* of Manet's career thus far, the "flesh and blood of the painter. She is the complete expression of his temperament; she contains the whole of him, and contains nothing but him. She will remain the characteristic work of his talent, the highest mark of his power, the measure of his force. I have read in her the personality of Manet, and when I analyzed the artist himself, I had before my eyes this canvas alone, which contains all the others."[51] As such Zola devotes a page and half to her, to which I shall return.

Referring to a description of *The Fifer* as a "costumer's sign," he speaks of the 1866 work this way:

> Moreover I prefer the *Fifer*, a little gentleman, a child of a musical troupe who blows in his instrument with all his breath and all his heart . . . The yellow of his galloons, the black-blue of his tunic, the red of his breeches are here no more than large patches. And this simplication, produced by the clear and accurate eye of the artist, has made of the canvas a totally *blond* and utterly naive work, charming to the point of grace and real to the point of *harshness*.[52]

Finally, of the *Young Woman in 1866*, whom he titles the *Woman in Pink*, he writes:

> In conclusion, I find neatly characterized in the *Woman in Pink* that native elegance which Edouard Manet, man of the world, has at the heart of himself. A young woman, dressed in a long pink robe, is standing before us, her head graciously inclined, breathing the perfume of a bouquet of violets that she holds in her right hand; at her left, a parrot curves over on his perch. The robe is of an infinite grace, *gentle* on the eye, very ample and very rich; the movement of the young woman has an indescribable charm. This would be too pretty, if the temperament of the painter had not placed the imprint of its *austerity* on the ensemble.[53]

It happens that of the works exhibited at different times by Manet, which here are put in chronological order (as they were not in the retrospective), Zola selects most of those images in which Victorine Meurent's features show up. He does not say so, anymore than he acknowledges the presence of the illegitimate boy Léon in *The Fifer*, preferring instead to suggest that Manet happened upon *The Streetsinger* just as she emerged onto the street, that *The Fifer* was come upon throwing himself heart and soul into his music (in just the way that Manet throws himself into his painting), and that *Olympia* was "a young sixteen-year-old girl, no doubt a model that Edouard Manet has tranquilly copied just as she was,"[54] while at the same time denying any attempt at indecency, which is to say any engagement in the contemporary discourse on prostitution.

I shall take up this series of pictures of Victorine Meurent in much more depth in a later chapter, proposing a very different reading of them from the naturalizing one offered by Zola. Suffice it to say here that these are the images that for Zola best represent the physiological organization of Manet – from the lightness of his flesh and hair to the clear constitution of his eye and the bright signature of his hand, with its transparently direct transcription of his way of seeing. And besides the vividly formalist emphasis upon colored *taches*, repeated again and again, and the recurring accent on blondness, brusqueness, bitterness, and austerity, as well as gentleness and sweetness, there is in Zola's attention to these works a consistent focus on their duality. Even within the paintings of his preference, one will tend in one direction and another in the other direction – *The Fifer* in the direction of *âpreté*, the *Young Woman in 1866* in the direction of Manet's gentler side, his innate elegance – the one tied to the "fauve" aspect of the artist's nature, the other to his character as a refined "homme du monde." But whichever their inclination, they are the paintings that balance Manet's oppositions and resolve Manet's duality into a unity, a single vivid "personality." And so they are the paintings that, aside from representing whatever individual Manet happens to have come across in the world, best represent Manet himself; they embody his very essence as a physical, perceptual, and personal being. Zola is as plain about this in his culminating discussion of the *Young Woman in 1866* as he is in his longer discussion of *Olympia*: representing a young woman at home, she also represents Manet the man.

In these readings of Manet's individual works of art Zola was as fully positivist as he was in his more general statements about the specialization of modern art and its advancement toward universality, as well as in his call for the analytical transcription of "facts" on the part of both the artist and the critic. We have already seen that Zola sought to define his own practice through the screen of Manet's practice as a painter: in that regard, the etched copy after *Olympia* appearing in the pages of "Une nouvelle manière" was as much an emblem of his understanding of Manet's art – in opposition to the Baudelairean as well as the prevailing critical and caricatural view – as it was an image of Manet's "flesh and blood." In defining his own practice as much as Manet's – and doing so in explicit contradistinction from other views of Manet's work – Zola also identified his theory of criticism with an existing strain of positivist writing about art, that of the growing art historical discourse on European national schools of art, frequently reduced to the North/ South, Holland/Italy pair that now is such a familiar component of Wölfflinian art history.[55] (Although it has a longer history, as a major art historical trope that antinomy has its nineteenth-century ancestry in positivist thought, which I shall only excavate here as it relates to Zola's modernist updating of it: it is worth signaling, for one thing, that it resonates throughout his strategy of pairing individual works in antipodal sets.)

The side of the North/South opposition with which modern painting was identified was that of Dutch art.[56] (The French temperament, however, was often seen as a Southern one at heart, underlined by the alliance between French academic art and the Italian tradition.) Treated first and most extensively by Théophile Thoré (Wilhelm Bürger) in 1857, in his *Trésors d'art en Angleterre*, seventeenth-century Dutch art was also the focus of works published by Charles Blanc and Hippolyte Taine in 1861 and 1869 respectively, each following up earlier lectures and publications on other schools of art.[57] Overall, these treatments of Dutch art all took the Hegelian view of it and used Hegel's terms to describe it, but they changed Hegel's division of the history of art into the periods of the Symbolic (Egyptian temple art), the Classical (the sculptural art of ancient Greece and Rome), and the Romantic (everything after ancient Greece and Rome, with an emphasis among the visual arts upon painting), into the image of the narrower, nationalist opposition between Renaissance Italian art and seventeenth-century Dutch art, with the latter emerging as the more modern art form, by definition. (Like Hegel, these accounts did not pursue the history of pictorial art into the nineteenth century, so the national-historical representative of the modern temperament in painting remained that of Holland of two centuries earlier.[58]) Although it was published two years after Zola's essay on Manet, of the treatises on Dutch art Taine's *Philosophie de l'art dans les Pays Bas*, a sequel to his *Philosophie de l'art en Italie*, is the most germaine to "Une nouvelle manière."[59]

For Zola's "method" is precisely the same as that announced by Taine in "Les Causes Permanentes" of *Philosophie de l'art dans les Pays-Bas*, in which the first principle of positivist art history is declared to be that all great art must express its national character: "First I will show the seed, that is to say the race with its fundamental and indelible qualities . . . then the plant, that is to say the people itself with its qualities . . . transformed by its milieu and its history; and finally the flower, that is to say the art and most notably the painting, in which all this development results."[60] This too is the way Zola proceeds, defining his "method" at the outset according to proper positivist procedure,[61] and then applying the organic metaphor to the particularities of Manet's life and art – such that he proceeds from his portrait of the physical features of Manet (the "seed," in Taine's terms) to his brief account of the vicissitudes of Manet's life as a painter (the "plant"), to Manet's art (the "flower"), even describing the early works of Manet as containing "in germ" the artist's personality. Like Taine, Zola sees Manet's art as the direct outcome of his physical being – as physiologically if not racially determined. His chain of descriptions of Manet's light coloring, clear way of seeing and bright way of painting follows the same order and logic as Taine's descriptions of, first, the typical physique of the Northern person, second, the climate of the North and the culture that arises out of it, and last, the look of Northern art.

Taine's painterly description of the Northern complexion is as follows: "In their physique, we find a whiter and softer flesh, ordinarily blue eyes, often of a china blue, or pale eyes, increasingly pale to the degree that one moves north . . . The tint of the skin is a charming pink, infinitely delicate, in young girls, vivid and tinged with vermilion in young men, and sometimes even in old people."[62] Thus he begins by painting a portrait of the Germanic race, just as Zola began by painting a portrait of the modern French individual Manet. Taine goes on to describe the physical milieu of the North, speaking first of its foggy climate and the way it contributes to the phlegmatic constitution of Northerners, such that the Northern physiognomy is treated as if it were a Dutch landscape: "their sensory and expressive canals seem obstructed."[63] And the physique of the North begins to yield its personality: Taine describes the Northerner's love of domesticity and interiority – which is determined by Northern weather – and goes so far as to contrast the Northern devotion to the housewife to the Southern love of the "grisette." And what the Northerner lacks in quick wit, *éclat*, and elegant fashion (these are Sourthern traits), he makes up for in science, Protestant individualism, and "esprit positif":[64] it is in that sense that Northern culture is also modern culture (in contrast to the classical culture of the South), from the positivist point of view.[65]

Ultimately, these descriptions of body, landscape, and culture, all organized around the North/South, painterly/linear contrast, flow into the basic opposition between two ways of seeing, and the Northern preference for what Taine calls "le fond" over "la

                                    Manet Manette

forme."[66] Elaborating on that fundamental distinction, Taine speaks simultaneously of the Northern landscape and Northern painting, developing the theme of seeing in patches that so preoccupied Zola in the art of Manet:

> One of the principal merits of this painting is the excellence and delicacy of its coloring. That is because the education of the eye, in Flanders and in Holland, has been particular. The country is a humid delta . . . Here as in Venice, nature has made man a colorist . . . In dry countries, line predominates and draws attention first . . . Here the flat horizon holds no interest, and the contours of things are softened, blurred, blended by the imperceptible vapor which swims eternally in the air; that which predominates is the patch.[67]

Coming back repeatedly to the *tache*,[68] Taine states the same positivist principle that animates Zola's "Une nouvelle manière": "art has followed nature, and the hand has been led perforce by the sensation that the eye received."[69] And within Dutch art the most representative of this principle were Ruisdael and especially Rembrandt (a figure like "our Balzac" in his eccentricities), who have,

> according to the particular structure of the eye . . . pushed beyond their nation and their century to the common instincts which tie together the Germanic races and lead to modern sentiments . . . he has understood and followed this truth in all its consequences, that for the eye the complete essence of a visible thing is in the *patch*, that the simplest color is infinitely complex, that all visual sensation is a product of these elements and that besides its surroundings, every object in the visual field is naught but a *patch* modified by other *patches* . . .[70]

Representing the racialist principle of Northern seeing and Northern painting, an extraordinary figure like Rembrandt at the same time represents the universalist principle of modern seeing and modern painting – that of a purely optical visuality structured around the *tache*.[71] In the view of Zola, this was the modernist/universalist principle of Manet's painting as well, "led perforce by the sensation that the eye received" to paint in *taches*, and to join a Northern blondness and brusqueness to a Southern wit and elegance, to produce his signature mix of *douceur* and *âpreté*.

This was the principle, in short, that led to *Olympia* looking the way she does:

> Olympia, reclining on white linen, makes a great pale *patch* against a black ground; against that black ground is found the head of the negress who brings in a bouquet, and that famous cat who has so entertained the public. On first glance, one thus distinguishes only *two hues* in the picture, *two violent hues, each setting off the other*. Moreover, the details have disappeared. Look at the head of the young girl: her lips are *two thin pink lines*, her eyes are reduced to *a couple of black dashes*. Look now at the bouquet, and up close, I pray you: *yellow blotches, blue blotches, green blotches*. Everything simplifies itself, and if you want to reconstitute reality, you have to draw back a few steps. Then a strange thing happens: every object puts itself in its proper plane, the head of Olympia detaches itself from its background in strong relief, the bouquet becomes a marvel of brightness and freshness . . . the painter has proceeded as nature herself proceeds, *in clear masses and large splotches of light*, and his work has the some-

PROMENADE AU SALON DE 1865, — par BERTALL (suite)

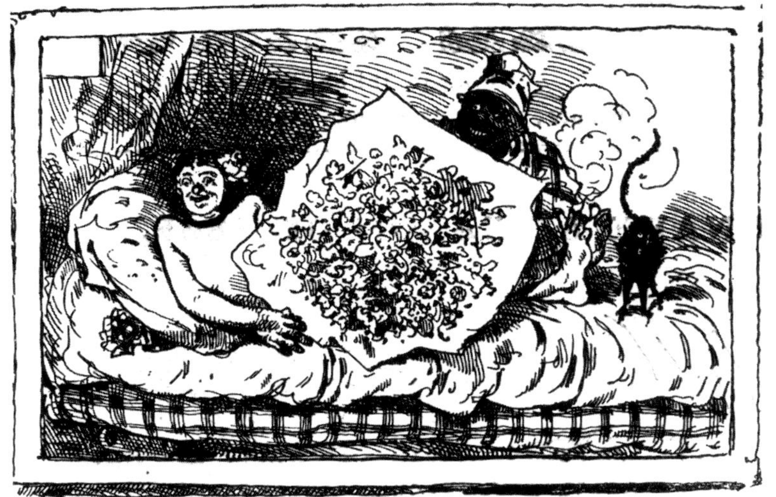

MANETTE, ou LA FEMME DE L'*ÉBÉNISTE*, par MANET.

Que c'est comme un bouquet de fleurs.
(*Air connu.*)

Ce tableau de M. Manet est le bouquet de l'Exposition. — M. Courbet est distancé de toute la longueur du célèbre chat noir. — Le moment choisi par le grand coloriste est celui où cette dame va prendre un bain qui nous semble impérieusement réclamé.

19   Bertall, "Manette, ou la femme de l'ébéniste," "Promenade au Salon de 1865," *Le Journal Amusant*, May 27, 1865.

what *rough and austere* aspect of nature. There are, moreover, biases . . . [which] are that *elegant curtness* and those violent transitions which I have signaled. That is the personal accent, the particular flavor of the work.[72]

If in 1865 one of the prominent caricaturists of the moment had seen *Olympia* not only as a prostitute (as was the norm)[73] but also as an image of Manet himself, dubbing her "Manette" (fig. 19), so did Zola in 1867. The terms in which he did so were all those of positivist criticism: his close-up formalist description of the spots and patches and dashes that make up the painting, from the large opposition of tones to the pink and black marks of the face of Olympia to the mosaic of *plaques* making up the bouquet, is a description utterly in line with the positivist understanding of the advanced opticality of "l'esprit positif," turning the Diderotian trope of the movement back and forth in front of illusionist paintings into the image of an analytical vision that proceeds just as nature proceeds, and that forces the viewer to do the same. And he makes over that trope in the image of Manet too: for, like Rembrandt, it was the "personal accent" of Manet's vision that made it analytical, and ultimately more universal than national, and which gained him such direct access to nature's self-analysis; it was the "personal accent" of paintings like *Olympia* that meant that "the future was for him."[74] *Olympia*, in brief, was a picture of the advanced, positivist state of Manet's eye – much more than she was a picture of a prostitute per se or of a Baudelairean *impure*. It was in that sense that Zola could "read in her the personality of Manet," using her, the distillate of "Les oeuvres," to transform the troubling figure and phantasmatic body of the great Courtesan who presides over the section on "L'homme et l'artiste" into an image of the physiology of the artist's gaze and the opticality of his "ésprit positif." (Significantly, however, *Olympia* also condenses Zola's various denials: in relation to her he dismisses Manet's interest not only in subject matter and subversion but also in the museum, asserting that this was simply how the artist found her, a little girl off the streets.)

Beyond its analytical disposition and its tendency to see in patches, the "personal accent" of Manet's vision also lay in its characteristic elegance, which betrayed his persona as an *homme du monde*: that aspect of Manet which Zola wrestled with on and off throughout his essay, and which he could barely tailor to his understanding of the artist's naturalism. He comes back to it at the end of his discussion of *Olympia*, just as he had struggled with it toward the close of his section on "L'homme et l'artiste," where he had explicitly taken the opportunity to deny the connection to Baudelaire:

> Edouard Manet is a man of the world, and there are in his pictures certain exquisite lines, certain slim and pretty attitudes which testify to his love of the elegances of the salons. That is the unconscious element, the very nature of the painter. And I profit from the occasion to protest against the parentage which has been established between Manet's pictures and Charles Baudelaire's verses. . . . if he assembles several objects or figures, he is only guided in his choice by the desire to obtain lovely *patches*, beautiful oppositions. It is ridiculous to want to make a mystical dreamer out of an artist who obeys such a temperament.[75]

Thus Zola asserts his view of Manet as against a Baudelairean understanding of the artist, and does so precisely in connection with that disconcerting dandyism of Manet's that was, he seems to have felt, some sort of optical "unconscious."[76] He never quite succeeds in smoothly assimilating that dandyism to his own unified, resolved view of Manet's "personality," but in various ways he attempts to define that trait as not-Baudelairean (which is to say in relation to, and against, Baudelaire's aesthetic position). Zola's Manet is not-Baudelaire's; Zola's understanding of modern criticism is not-Baudelaire's. (Zola defines Baudelaire as a "mystic," not a realist or naturalist, thus ignoring Baudelaire's *Le Peintre de la vie moderne* and associating the poet with an obsolete period of art, that of Romanticism, instead.) Zola, in other words, positioned himself as Baudelaire's opponent in the game of criticism; the modernism for which Manet stood was clearly a matter of critical contest.

In the rebuttal of Manet's Baudelairean connection, a question of "parentage" was involved, which gets me back to the racialist underpinnings of Zola's positivist discourse on Manet. And that is where I end this section: if, according to Zola, Manet was not the child of Baudelaire, neither was he the "bastard of Velasquez and Goya."[77] Zola could admit Epinal engravings and Japanese prints into his account of Manet's art, but not Titian and Raphael, and especially not that most obvious of "influences," Spanish painting, with which Manet had identified his practice ever since the acceptance of *The Spanish Singer* into the Salon of 1861. The Epinal print was an acceptable reference because of its established credentials as an indigenous tradition and a realist *point de repère*; and the influence of the Japanese print could be admitted because the *japoniste* craze was a new one,[78] and because its exoticism placed it outside the parameters and aesthetic oppositions of the European museum – enabling Zola to tie the Japanese print directly to the personalized modernism of Manet's vision: "It would be much more interesting to compare this simplified painting with Japanese engravings, which resemble it in their strange elegance and their magnificent *patches*."[79]

But what was inadmissible was the reference to Spain, admitted and yet undercut throughout "La nouvelle manière" – in Zola's comment about the lingering Spanish turns of phrase in Manet's otherwise personal locution, in his remark about the impurely Manetian qualities of works of Spanish parentage like the *Boy with the Sword*, and in the closing statement of the section on "L'homme et l'artiste" denying that Manet got his models from "au delà des Pyrénées" or that his painting was the misbegotten offspring of Spanish art.[80] Spain here stands for the impure, the illegitimate, and the inauthentic, for that which is not indigenous to Manet, not consistent with his Gallic temper, his modernism, or his universalism, and not assimilable to an organic, positive understanding of his oeuvre. Spain stands for that which is just the other side of the mountains (*tra los montes*, to use Gautier's phrase): of Europe but at the same time not of Europe, close to home but not home, and too much of a romantic fetish for Zola, as well. And Spain embodies the museum – the museum as a site of foreign elements, eclectic pastiche, and even plagiarism. As such, for Zola Spain represents that which Manet had thrown off, as the son throws off the authority of the father in coming into his own ("one is always the son of someone," admits Zola).[81] Like his Baudelairean dandyism, Manet's Hispanicism was an irritant to Zola, an alien element in his scheme, disorganizing its organicism, disrupting its picture of the *tout ensemble* of Manet "the man and the artist," and intruding upon its "ésprit positif." Spain, in short, made Manet's artistic bloodline impure, the paternity of his art suspect, his filiation uncertain, and the trajectory of his growth into universalist maturity unclear. It made him, like his "son" Léon, precisely what Zola did not want him to be – a bastard child of the European museum. And so Spain, like Baudelaire, and like the museum itself, had to be repudiated. Once, twice, and thrice acknowledged, it had to be once, twice, and thrice disowned.

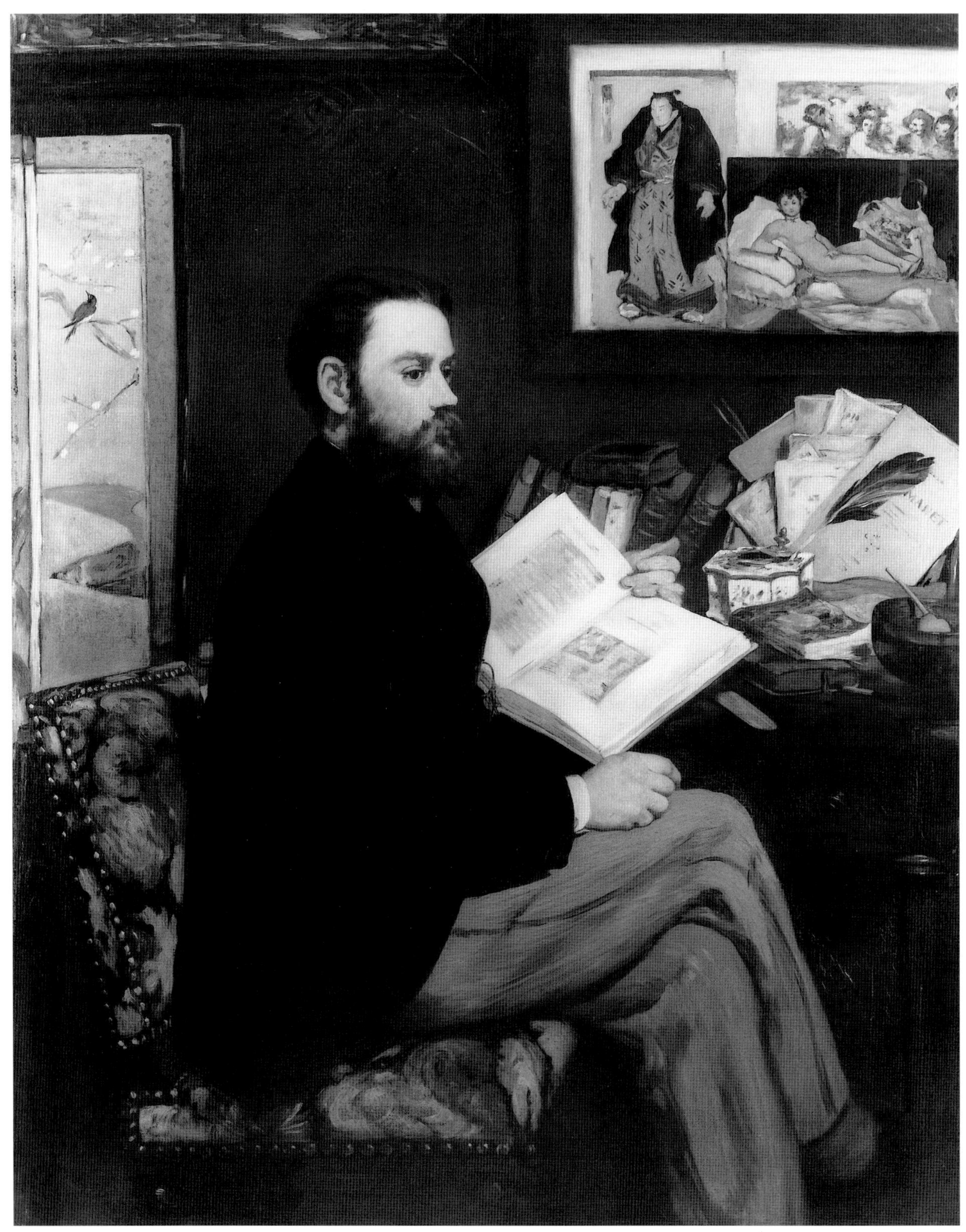

20　Edouard Manet, *Emile Zola*, 1868, oil on canvas, 146.5 × 114 cm. Musée d'Orsay, Paris.

Chapter Three

MANETTE SALOMON:
ANOTHER VIEW OF MODERN PAINTING

In 1883, three years before he published his artist novel *L'Oeuvre*, based partly on Manet and on the phantasmatic image of the great Courtesan already found in "Une nouvelle manière en peinture," Zola wrote the catalogue essay for the posthumous retrospective of Manet's oeuvre, in which he came back to the same themes as before and condensed them. That later "exposition personnelle" put everything in order: the catalogue listed Manet's works year by year, in chronological sequence, and consistently broke each year down into a hierarchy of "peintures," "acquarelles," "pastels," "eaux-fortes," "lithographes," and "dessins."[1] So the disorder of Manet's 1867 "exposition particulière" was swept away in favor of the image of rational development that underwrites the modern retrospective, and the disorganization inherent in his oeuvre – especially of the 1860s – was simply ignored. That had been Zola's effort already in 1867, when his essay on Manet put the artist's house in order, telling Manet's story chronologically, discovering the principle of organic unity in his work, and expelling or derogating those pictures and those views of Manet's production that did not jibe with that principle.

Back then it remained unclear what Manet felt about Zola's view of him. The artist shied away from "Une nouvelle manière" as a catalogue essay. And yet he continued to write to Zola in friendly, even grateful terms. Moreover, the year after his retrospective at the Place de l'Alma he painted a portrait of the writer that seemed to concur with the latter's statements; and, as if to make that concurrence public, he exhibited the portrait in the Salon of 1868, along with the *Young Woman in 1866*, with which Zola had finished his discussion of "Les oeuvres" in "Une nouvelle manière," describing the painting of the young woman in pink as a culminating characterization of Manet's temperament. In the portrait of Zola, just above the blue pamphlet on the writer's desk, on which Manet's name doubles as a signature and a title – as if to say that Zola's understanding of Manet was in accordance with Manet's understanding of himself, that painting and pamphlet could be equated and conflated, and the differences between them elided – three images are to be found painted on a bulletin board (fig. 20). The two most prominent of those images are a photograph of *Olympia* and a Japanese print: here the artist seems to agree with Zola's reading of *Olympia* as the emblem of Manet. He seems, furthermore, to acquiesce in Zola's equation of *japoniste* vision with his own opticality, going so far as to give the nod to Zola's suggestion that the Japanese print was a more interesting source to consider than the more commonly cited Epinal engraving.

And yet, tucked partly out of sight, behind the bolder duplicates of *Olympia* and the colored Japanese print, there is also a painted approximation of Goya's engraving after Velasquez's *The Drinkers,* upon which Manet's *Old Musician* was based. It is the least emphasized of the three prints painted on the bulletin board, it is true, as if perhaps to agree with Zola on one more point, that the Spanishisms of Manet's immaturity were behind him now, subsumed, subordinated, and surpassed. However, it is a deliberate and specific gesture to his quotational practice, and it is just as deliberate and specific in its reference to Spanish painting. It takes its place in Manet's triangulation of foreign and foreign-based traditions, and in his indexing of the role of the mechanically reproduced history of art in the production of the artist's modern, French originality. (It is important that the prints on Zola's wall form a triad, thus replacing the North/South binary with a more complex, three-pronged schema involving Spain, France, and Japan, none of which falls clearly on either side of the binary, and in which a tertiary term shifts the poles constantly between East-versus-West, one-South-versus-another-South, old-master-versus-modern, native-versus-exotic, and so on, so that all three points of the triangle are both neighbors and opposites of the other.) So, possibly Manet was disagreeing with Zola as well, contradicting both of the denials central to the writer's argument – Zola's discounting of the importance of Spanish art to Manet, and of the role of the museum quotation in the artist's work. The sly insertion of the Velasquez image into the prints on the wall insinuates that Zola was wrong on both counts: yes, the painter of *Olympia* was a museum-going quoter of tradition; and, yes, he was after all a "bastard of Velasquez and Goya."

Any ambivalence Manet may have felt about Zola's estimation of his work was no doubt partly strategic – he was willing enough, especially after the public failed to show up in force at his retrospective, to harness his reputation as an artist to Zola's reputation as a critic, and vice versa too: notoriety was better than no notice at all. But Zola's account of Manet goes so dead against the evidence of Manet's retrospective – at least in the matters of the museum and Spanish painting, not to mention the connection to Baudelaire – that one wonders if there might not have been some other view of modern painting on offer at the time that Manet might have preferred. There were a few other scattered accounts of Manet's retrospective, but none as thoroughgoing and celebratory as Zola's. Others, however, wrote about the Universal Exposition in relation to which Manet, like Courbet, meant his retrospective to be seen: both Hippolyte Taine and Charles Blanc, for instance, pegged their engagement in the national traditions of European art to the Universal Exposition's updated display of the same in one way or another.[2] But perhaps the most provocative address to the situation of modern art at the time of the Universal Exposition, and the one that was the most resonant with Manet's own strategies, was a fictional account – the artist novel, entitled *Manette Salomon,* published at the end of 1867 by Edmond and Jules de Goncourt, whose narrative climax is set at the time of the first of the two Universal Expositions held in Paris, but whose allegory of the invasion of the French national patrimony by artistic eclecticism and racial and sexual otherness clearly embraces the second of those Universal Expositions as well.[3]

Manet never remarked on this novel, nor did the Goncourts mention Manet in their journals before 1873.[4] But Antonin Proust tells us that the brothers visited Manet's studio some time in the mid-'60s in order to flesh out the figure of Coriolis, the main protagonist of *Manette Salomon*.[5] So it is possible that the feminized version of Manet's name given to the title character of the book, the Jewish artist's model and mistress of Coriolis, was in fact inspired by Manet himself, in the spirit of Bertall's caricature of 1865 referring to *Olympia* as "Manette." Whether or not that was so, *Manette Salomon* offers a dissenting view of modern art in the era of the Universal Expositions, a view much at odds with the positivist one espoused by Zola, proposing a radically decentered image of latecoming disintegration rather than a narrative of positivist advance and universalist resolution as its model of the "modernist" situation.[6] And *Manette Salomon* brings the question of race and racial pluralism into its equation, such that the racialism of the positivist understanding of art is also put on the table as a bone of contention. Finally, the novel is a rewriting of the (anti-) Pygmalion topos of the artist's mistress found in Balzac's *Le Chef-d'oeuvre inconnu* of 1831/37, such that the thematics of gender alterity is introduced into the mix as well, and the chimerical figure of Woman lurking in Zola's monographic essay on Manet is foregrounded and spotlit in *Manette Salomon*, in order to emblematize a different image of the state of the modern arts and the career trajectory of the modern artist. (This image was taken up in turn by Zola himself in *L'Oeuvre*, which Edmond de Goncourt explicitly challenged, claiming it was a vulgarizing plagiarism of *Manette Salomon*, and disagreeing with the common view that Zola's Claude Lantier resembled Manet.[7]) Thus there could be no better site for examining the contest over what the modern *exposition* put on view and what the modern art that Manet's name came to stand for meant – and seeing what other fantasies of cohesion and fears of dissolution were at stake in that debate.

Later, in a journal entry of August 2, 1885, Edmond de Goncourt quoted Zola's dismissal of *Manette Salomon* as nothing but a fragmentary series of sketches and mocked his ambition of creating a deeply researched psychological study. "Go on, my gigantic Zola, just try to make a psychology like that of the household of Coriolis and Manette!" he challenged.[8] For if *Manette Salomon* had diverged from the positivist discussion of the arts even in its choice of discursive mode – the novel rather than the monograph – it had undermined the linear, character-centered logic of the novel itself too, emphasizing instead the heteroglossia and polyvocal structure that are also integral to the form of the novel.[9] And that, in Goncourt's view, was the significance of *Manette Salomon's* contribution: to seek to rectify it with "une psychologie très fouillé" was to misunderstand its subversive undertaking, and to ignore its dissension with the positivist model of the novel by attempting to rewrite it in positivist terms.[10]

THREE ALLEGORIES: PAINTING FALLS TO PIECES

In order to understand *Manette Salomon*, or indeed *L'Oeuvre*, it is necessary to start with the novelette that begins the nineteenth-century chain of artist stories, *Le Chef-d'oeuvre inconnu*. Balzac's story is told as a de-Pilesian "dialogue" between two young seventeenth-century painters Porbus and "Poussin," concerning a late painting by the old Frenhofer, supposedly representing his mistress and model Catherine Lescault. The Rembrandt-like Frenhofer, whose name is a give-away that he represents the "Northern" pole of French seventeenth-century art, is convinced that his work, which he will not show to his young admirers until the conclusion of the story, is a masterpiece of illusionistic color that brings the image of his mistress to life.[11] But there is a modern twist to the tale: in the denouement, when Frenhofer's painting is finally made visible, it is discovered to be a mess and a chimera – a harbinger of the disintegrative destiny of Romantic art, which is to say of modern painting. The living flesh that Frenhofer claims to have rendered is naught but a smear of paint, the only remnant of successful illusionism being the fragment of foot that emerges, fetish-like (instead of the breast that Frenhofer believes he has brought into breathtaking being), from the confusion of swirling colors. Between the painting that Porbus and "Poussin" see and the one that Frenhofer hallucinates, there lies a chasm: Balzac divides the old illusionistic construct of *coloris* in two, and locates the dissipation of modern art precisely in that division.

In short succession, Balzac gives his readers three views of Frenhofer's invisible painting. The first goes this way:

Well! there it is! the old man said to them with his hair in disorder, his face enflamed with a supernatural ecstasy, his eyes sparkling, his breath coming short and fast as if he were a young man drunk with love. You expected a picture and you stand before a woman. There is so much depth on this canvas, the air is so true, that you can no longer distinguish it from the air which surrounds us. Where is the art? gone, disappeared! There before you are the very forms of a young girl. Have I not seized the color well, the life of the line which defines the edges of her body? Is it not the same phenomenon that presents objects in an atmosphere like fish in water? Do you not admire the way the contours detach themselves from the background? Does it not seem to you that you could pass your hand over her back? Thus for seven years have I studied the effects of light affixed to objects. And her hair, is it not suffused with light? . . . But she has taken a breath, I believe! . . . That breast, do you see it? Ah! who would not cast themselves on their knees and adore her? Her flesh palpitates. She is about to rise, just wait.[12]

Immediately after Balzac provides this description of the painting as it is finally made visible to Porbus and "Poussin":

In approaching, they perceived in a corner of the canvas the tip of a naked foot which emerged from a chaos of colors, tones, indecisive nuances, a kind of mist without form; but what a delicious foot, what a living foot! They remained petrified with admiration before this fragment which had escaped the incredible, slow, progressive destruction of the rest of the painting. That foot appeared there like the torso of some Venus in Parican marble rising up out of the debris of a city in flames.

– There is a woman underneath! cried Porbus while pointing out to Poussin the layers of color that the old painter had successively superimposed in the belief that he was perfecting his painting.[13]

And then Balzac returns to Frenhofer's view of the painting, before the old artist finally sees, in despair, what his young friends see, which is "Nothing, nothing!":

– Yes, my friend, replied the old man, coming awake, one must have faith, faith in art, and live with one's work a long time in order to produce such a creation. Some of those shadows have cost me much labor. Look, there on her cheek, beneath her eyes, there is a soft penumbra which, if you saw it in nature, you would swear was untranslatable. Oh! well, do you really believe that it did not cost me unheard-of pains to reproduce it? But my dear Porbus, look attentively at my work, and you will better understand what I have said to you about the manner of handling modeling and contours. Look at the light on her breast, and see how, by a series of touches and strongly impastoed enhancements, I have managed to attach veritable light to it and to combine it with the glistening white of limpid tones; and how, by a contrary process, in effacing the relief and grain of the paint, I have been able, by dint of caressing the contours of my figure, bathed in half-tones, to remove even the idea of drawing and of artificial means, and to give her the aspect and rounded volume of nature herself. Approach, you will see this work better. From a distance, it disappears. Do you see? There it is, and very remarkable it is, I think.

And with the tip of his brush, he indicated an area of light-colored impasto to the two painters.[14]

This is a painterly reversal of the Pygmalion legend: rather than coming to life, the woman represented in the painting dissolves from real flesh into paint (and marble) and becomes even less than lifeless, utterly formless, as formless as fire, chaos, ruin, rubble; moreover, it is the artist, not his creation, who is transformed, who becomes once again young and lively and vividly colored ("his face enflamed") when thinking of his painted woman.[15] And the creation that comes undone here is just as clearly constituted as feminine, but less as a female body, as in the Pygmalion myth, than as female painting – the cosmetic art of painting shadows and highlights on a face. (Although Frenhofer speaks of caressing a back, and of a palpitating breast, what he "seizes" with such erotic delight is color and line, and light-reflecting painter's materials, more than the body itself.) And though the painter plays masculine subject to his feminine object, what he loves is his own art, and its seduction of him. Furthermore, the object of his love and of his painting dissolves and slips through his fingers: so that the myth of the artist's mastery, the identification of the act of creation with sexual possession and the "male gaze," and even the opposition between lover and love object, maker and made, are undercut as well. What mad old Frenhofer most definitely is not is the young, virile, forward-looking hero of the "modernist" avant-garde; even so, he is a modern artist and his painting is modern art.

In the process of dividing Frenhofer's (nonexistent) painting in two, "showing" it to his readers only as it is seen differently by its different viewers, Balzac oscillates between the material surface of the painting – its "signifier" – and its ephemeral, illusionistic "signified." Between the first and the last of these three descriptions of the same fictional painting, he moves from the disappearance of art and the magical appearance of the woman herself ("You expected a picture and you stand before a woman . . . Where is the art? gone, disappeared!"), to the disappearance of the woman and the appearance of art ("a chaos of colors, tones, indecisive nuances, a kind of mist without form . . . the layers of color that the old painter had successively superimposed in the belief that he was perfecting his painting"), to a switching between the two ("Approach, you will see this work better. From a distance, it disappears . . . And with the tip of his brush, he indicated an area of light-colored impasto") that was already and remained a major trope of French criticism of modern painting, from Diderot on Chardin and others, to Leroy and his like writing on the illegibilities of Impressionist painting. This happens under the sign of *coloris* – for the impasto and loaded brushwork of Frenhofer's image, as well as the emphasis upon colors rather than forms and upon highlights and such that are at once paint and light itself, place it on the painterly side of the old de-Pilesian equation. But what was the indissoluble duality of painterly illusionism is now subject to disintegration and ultimately desublimation: the tip of a foot is replaced by the tip of a brush, which indicates what? No more than a patch of whitish impasto.

Thus here, in this prototype of the topos of the failed modern artist, Balzac addresses the binary structure of *coloris* – what de Piles in his *Dialogue sur le coloris* had defined as the "difference" of painting – and ties it to the declining destiny of modern art. (As he was wont to do, Balzac condenses a whole history of art in the single figure of the aging artist, whose biological and artistic decline stands for the decadent trends of an aging Europe.) This suggests a rather different understanding of the "modernist" "hunting back" of the art of painting to its medium. Here, it is in the nature, or rather the artifice, of painting to be divided between the literal and the illusionistic, rather than unified according to the abstract principle of the two-dimensionality of painting. And here, it is modern painting's fate to be split, and split again, according to a principle of internal division: so if modern painting ultimately yields abstraction, it is less because of its reduction to a single, unitary essence, than because of its two-faced, feminine constitution (as both nature and artifice, flesh and cosmetics, illusion and paint), which, when pulled apart, must inevitably lead to dissolution, as happens in the Hegelian account of the destiny of Romantic or modern art. The Goncourts, and then Zola, updated Balzac's scenario by making their artists nineteenth-century ones, but as differently as they evaluated it, Balzac's image of modern art – as coloristically disintegrative – was also theirs.[16]

*   *   *

The next in the chain of artist tales, *Manette Salomon* is a rambling, chatty story with a constantly shifting center and no real protagonist. Its action is set in the years between 1840 and 1855, and it circles around a group of artists of that previous generation, one of whom, Coriolis, now and then seems to be singled out from his friends, although others, like Anatole, are now and then singled out as well; indeed, the novel ends with Anatole rather than Coriolis, so that the baton of subjectivity is passed from one to the other. Early on, Coriolis is the most obvious candidate for a protagonist: his trials and triumphs at the Exposition are emphasized more than those of the others. And it is Coriolis's model, mistress, and then mother of his child, a mysterious Parisian Jewess by the name of Manette Salomon, who, though she does not make her appearance until about half way through the story, gives the novel its name. Were it not for her absence throughout the first half of the novel, and her shadowy presence as a figment of Coriolis's bigoted and misogynistic fascination throughout the second half, the eponymous Manette would be the obvious choice for the central character of the book: as a woman and a Jew, she is the main figure of otherness, of otherness within French art and culture, that is the topic of *Manette Salomon*.[17] But Manette is precisely just a figure and not a protagonist – a figure without a subjectivity or a point of view, a figure in an allegory. As for Coriolis, he is frontstage whenever he appears, mainly because of his alliance to the nonperson figure of Manette – which is really the only reason for his possession of a subjectivity, such as it is.

Beyond its lack of an identifiable protagonist and the nonperson status of its two most emphasized characters, *Manette Salomon* is decentered in a number of other ways. In fact, deracination is not only the subject of *Manette Salomon's* allegory of eclecticism but is also its main effect, littered as the story is with countless references to contemporary artists and old masters representing different factions, schools, and styles, and even nationalities and eras: Chassériau, Ary Scheffer, Delaroche, the Barbizon school, Decamps, Géricault, Delacroix and Ingres, David, Rembrandt, Boudin, Corot, Michelangelo, Houdon, de la Tour, Gavarni, and finally, Turner. There is no particular order, no historical rhyme or reason to the mention of these artists – though the book is encyclopedic in its references, it does not catalogue them in any way but mixes and scatters them about instead. Coriolis's friends are representative of different artists and styles: Garnotelle embodies a pure, David-descended Ingriste style; Anatole, a bohemian "saltimbanque" replete with grimacing, mimicking pet monkey, is gifted at caricature and is reminiscent in some ways of Daumier and in other ways of Decamps;[18] and Crescent, the Barbizon painter with whom Coriolis stays for a while, seems to be a sort of stand-in for Corot. Coriolis himself stands for Orientalist painting, and was modeled on Chassériau, the student of Ingres and representative of eclecticism, whose Orientalist nudes, some of them biblical Jewesses (fig. 21), were painted in a style that seemed to fuse the antagonistic, *dessin* and *coloris*, ancient and modern manners of Ingres and Delacroix.[19] (The most important of Coriolis's submissions to the Universal Exposition is a *Bain turc* which seems to have been a lightly veiled reference to Chassériau's *Tepidarium*, a painting that was actually shown at the Exposition of 1855; fig. 22.[20]) As such, Coriolis is a microcosm of the book's melange of artists, its "strange mix-up of talents and nonentities."[21] In that, he could not be more different from Zola's Claude Lantier, an amalgam of circumscribed references to a set of artists all belonging to the same "modernist" orbit, and the consistent center, for all its multitude of characters, of *L'Oeuvre*.

With his Shakespearean Roman name, his taste for foreign travel, and his obsession with the exotic, Coriolis is also a racial melange, a combination of colonizer and colonized, discovering in himself, "in the depths of the catholic man, the instincts of a Creole, that proud blood which is produced by the colonies"[22] once he becomes involved with Manette and uncovers the layer of exotic Jewishness hidden beneath her *parisienne* surface. (Even Coriolis's gender is a bit indeterminate, for his physiognomy apparently revealed a "temperament féminin."[23]) Thus Coriolis figures the racial hybridity of the Goncourts' novel as well, which from start to finish depicts Paris "à l'époque de l'Exposition"[24] as a chaos of classes and invading races (and colors too): it tells a tale of a Paris in which the colonialism of empire gives rise to a mixed, bastard world, and to its own disintegration, together with that of the unitary subjectivities that constitute it.[25]

The invasion of Paris is announced right from the novel's beginning, which is situated in the Jardin des Plantes, and which gives a taste of *Manette Salomon's pêle-mêle* effect as well:

21   Théodore Chassériau, *The Toilette of Esther*, 1841, oil on canvas, 45.5 × 35.5 cm. Musée du Louvre, Paris.

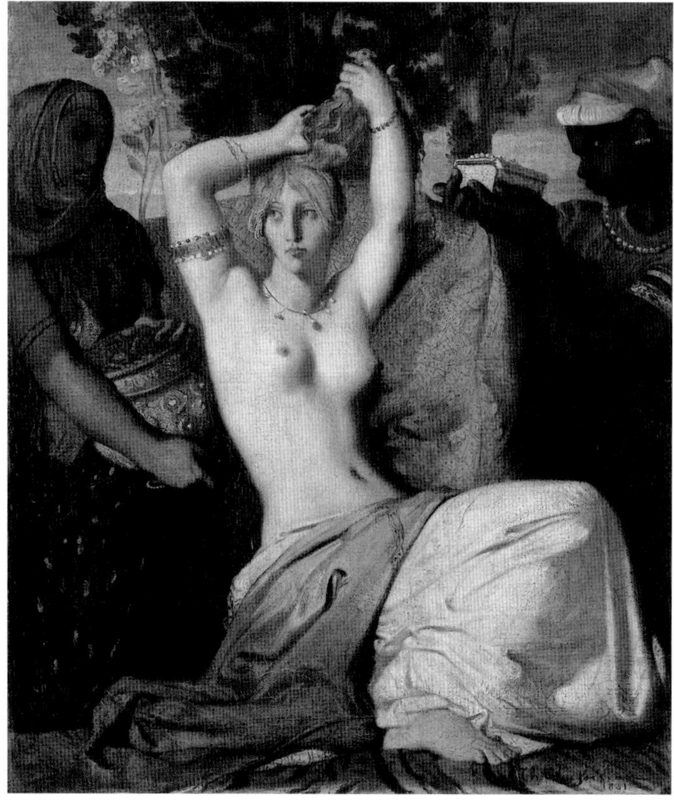

22 (*facing page*)   Théodore Chassériau, *The Tepidarium*, 1853, oil on canvas, 171 × 258 cm. Musée d'Orsay, Paris.

A crowd walked about in the Jardin des Plantes, and went up to its labyrinth, a distinctive crowd, mixed, cosmopolitan, composed of all sorts of people from Paris, from the provinces, and from abroad, which this popular meeting place brings together.

There was first of all a classic group of English men and women in *brown* veils and *blue* glasses.

. . .

Then there came: a militiaman . . . a *yellow* prince, freshly dressed by Dusautoy, accompanied by a species of Hussar with the features of a Turk, and the dolman sleeves of an Albanian; – an apprentice mason, a little wastrel just off the boat from the Limousin region.

A little further on, clambered an intern of the *Pitié* . . . And almost next to him, in the same line, a worker in his frock-coat . . .

A father with a rough *gray* moustache watched an attractive child run in front of him, in a Russian dress of *blue* velvet, with *silver* buttons, sleeves of *white* cloth, at whose neck there lay an *amber* collar.

. . .

And closing the procession, a lady's maid pulled and dragged a little *black* boy by the hand, embarassed in his shorts, and seemingly sad to have seen the monkeys in their cage.[26]

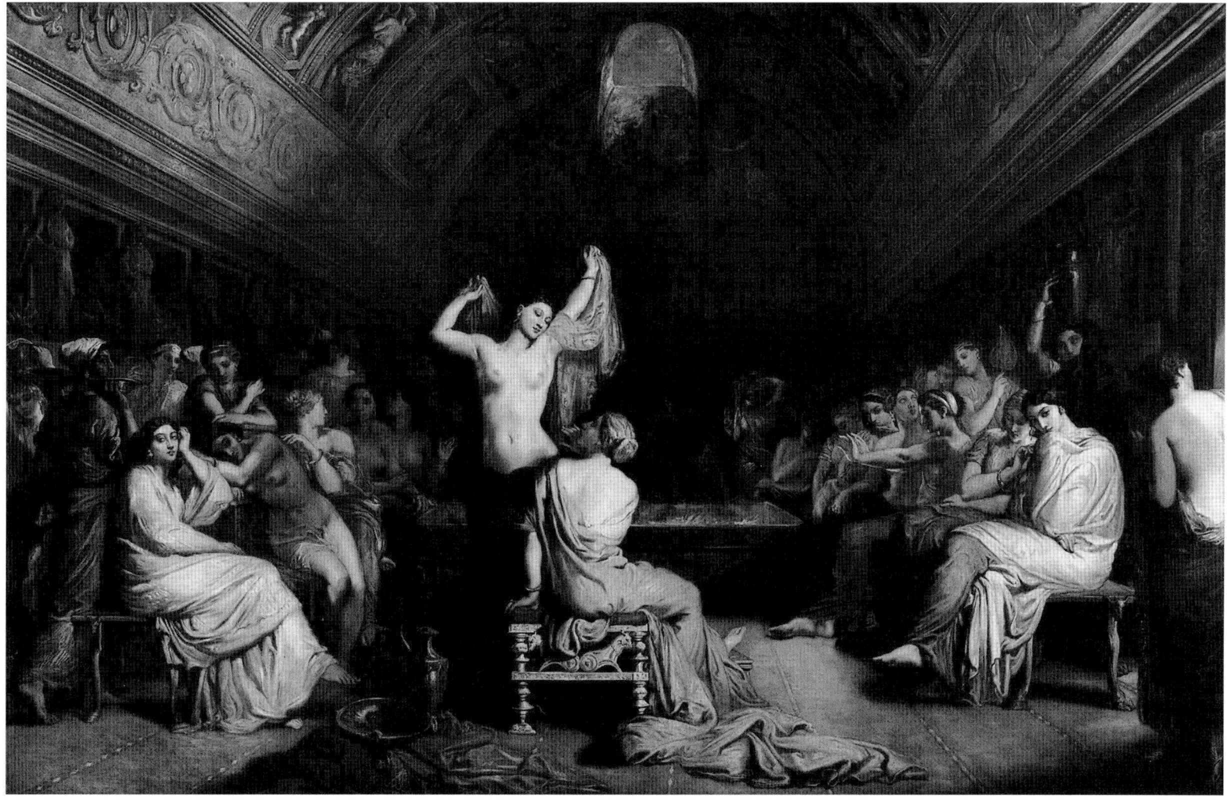

Having opened with a coloristic evocation of the multiracial human melange in the Jardin des Plantes (which immediately nullifies the racial unities of the positivist imagination), the first chapter of *Manette Salomon* continues with a description of the panoramic view of Paris to be had from the Jardin:

> Paris was beneath them, to the left, to the right, everywhere.
>
> Between the tips of the *green* trees, there where the curtain of pines opened a bit, pieces of the great city spread out, first some crowded roofs, with *brown* tiles, forming masses of a *burnt color*, darkened and subsumed in the *russet brown*, went down toward the quay. At the quay, the squares made by the *white* houses, with the *little black lines* in the middle of their windows, formed and developed like the front of a barracks of an *effaced and yellowed white*, on top of which gradually emerged, out of the mildewed stone, an older construction. Beyond this clean, clear line, one could see only a kind of *chaos* lost in the *leaden* night, a *jumble* of roofs, thousands of roofs from which the *black* chimneypipes sprang with the delicacy of needles, a *melee* of pinnacles and of copings enveloped by the *gray* obscurity of the distance, confused in the depths of the day's end; a *swarm* of dwellings, a *hash* of lines and structures, a *mass* of stones similar to a *sketch* and to the *disarray* of a quarry, above which soared the apse and dome of a church, whose cloudy solidity resembled condensed vapor.[27]

And so on – before the group of artists around whom the story revolves is introduced, the opening chapter continues with its impressionistic, color-laden description of the Parisian panorama, with a dash of foreign speech thrown in, as well as a brief, exclamatory map of the city's major monuments and points of touristic interest. And, added to the emphasis upon color and the equivalence of a variegated palette with the multiracialism of cosmopolis and empire, is an equation between color and chaos: with jumble, melee, confusion, swarm, hash, mass, sketchiness. In other words, the verbal equivalent of Impressionist color and facture is the writerly means by which the Goncourts make manifest the threat to the Empire's structures of identity and unity, right from the start.

It happens that Manet's painting of the Exposition of 1867 (fig. 23), which was finished too late to be shown in his retrospective, conforms almost exactly to the opening images of *Manette Salomon's* "suites d'aquarelles et d'eaux-fortes." For Manet's painting is a distant, panoramic view of Paris "at the time of the Exposition," from the multiple points of view of several groups of bourgeois and *demi-monde* figures at their leisure, succinctly differentiated according to clothing rendered in an abbreviated language of sketchy daubs and dashes reminiscent of the "acquarelles" of Constantin Guys: there are English tourists, *cocodottes, amazones, gamins, petits crevés,* Imperial guardsmen, and a laboring gardener.[28] Like the novel, this painting has no center, and its lack of a center is connected to its address to *flaneuriste* viewing – anything but centered, located, and native – emblematized in the floating balloon in the upper right corner. Painted in Manet's more Impressionist mode – the mode of the *Music at the Tuileries* and the *Racecourse at Longchamp* (which were shown in his retrospective) – the *View of the Universal Exposition* looks very much as the panoramic passages in *Manette Salomon* read: full of color, punctuated by scattered bits of attention to costume details and isolated monument profiles, constituted by a wandering vision and multiple viewpoints, without a fixed place or single self from which to view the chaotic spectacle in front of not one but many different viewers.

In *L'Oeuvre*, Zola too painted a verbal picture of Paris – in fact, he did so repeatedly, for apart from the image of Woman, it is above all else the painting of Paris that preoccupies both the author of *L'Oeuvre* and his painterly protagonist. And the pictorial means of evoking Paris in the later novel are often quite as vividly coloristic and painterly as these passages from the beginning of *Manette Salomon*. But Claude Lantier's vision of Paris is always an organic one, and its optics are always centered in the painter's subjectivity. Not so in *Manette Salomon*, whose colorism tends toward the inorganic rather than the organic, which rarely suggests that the pictures it paints are the result of anyone's looking, and which militates against the optics of any single subject. And if Manet's *View of the Universal Exposition* matches that optical decentering better than Zola's organic vision, the shape of his oeuvre, as exhibited in 1867, is also better provided for by the overall configuration and colorism of *Manette Salomon*.

There is no pattern at all to the novel's local movement from character to character and event to event, while the large shape of its movement from beginning to end is roughly circular, so that it is as resistant to the linear shape of time as it is to the linear development of a single subjectivity characteristic of the realist novel. At the end of the story, which focuses on the previously marginal figure of Anatole, the Goncourts cycle

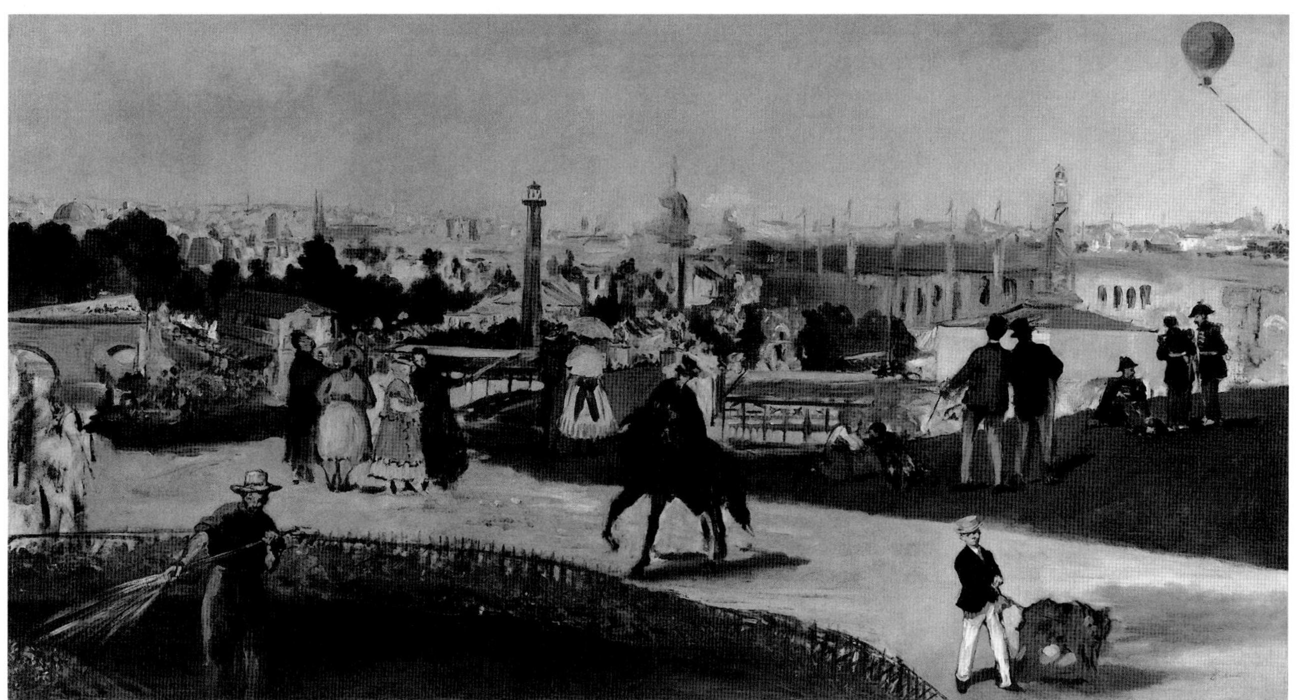

23   Edouard Manet, *View of the Universal Exposition*, 1867, oil on canvas, 108 × 196 cm. National Gallery, Oslo.

back to the site of their beginning, the Jardin des Plantes, in order to collapse Beginning and Ending, Paradise and Armageddon within a closing image of dissolution:

> Little by little, [Anatole] abandons himself to all these things. He forgets himself, he is lost to sight, to sound, to aspiration. That which is around him penetrates him by all his pores, and Nature embracing him by all the senses, he allows himself to run into her, and remains to soak in her. . . . He slides into the being of the beings that are there. It seems to him that he is a little in everything that flies, in everything that grows, in everything that runs. . . . the creature begins to dissolve into the living totality of creation.
>
> And sometimes, in this daylight of the day's beginning . . . the old Bohemian relives the joys of Eden, and he arises in himself, a little like the felicity of the first man in front of virgin Nature.[29]

In this concluding image a world of complete dissolution, which seems to suggest dusk, decadence, and last days, is joined to Eden, dawn, and the "day(light) of the beginning." The novel's claim throughout is that the invasion of the unified culture of national patrimony by eclecticism, diversity, and otherness, results in a decadent primitivism, and that the blending of the indigenous and the alien ends in the collapse of progressive history and culture, of structures of difference, and singular, unitary forms of subjectivity: it is that antiprogressivist logic of modernism that is condensed in the novel's closing image of the Beginning, and with it of Anatole's Edenic disintegration.

At the end Anatole dissolves into nothingness, but as a mimic, monkey, and *poseur* Anatole never had had any subjectivity or style of his own: "Anatole presented the curious psychological phenomenon of a man who is not in possession of his own individuality."[30] Coriolis, apparently, had possessed a self at the outset, but by the time of Anatole's ecstatic collapse in the Jardin des Plantes, Coriolis too had lost his "individuality" in the face of Manette's otherness: "It was like a long dispossession of himself, at the end of which he hardly belonged to himself anymore."[31] Like the Empire, in other words, Coriolis is invaded and dissolved by that which he colonizes and possesses – such that, taken together with its shifting locus of subjectivity, the rambling circularity of the book's time and plot structure is also a statement about artistic careers and characters, and the figures of chaos and amorphousness dispersed throughout it are also images of the shapelessness of the various artists' selves.

The final emblem of Coriolis's disintegration is indeed a circle – a circle of colors. Toward the end of the story, some dozen pages before the closing scene of Anatole in the Jardin des Plantes, there is this long passage on color, worth quoting at length, in which Turner's painting *Light and Color: The Morning after the Deluge* serves as the final icon of both the circular temporality of *Manette Salomon* and its preoccupation with disintegration:

> At the Louvre itself, in the Salon Carré, those four walls of masterpieces no longer seemed to him to shine. The Salon became somber, to the point that it no longer presented him with anything but a sort of mummification of colors beneath the paling and the yellowing of time . . .
>
> He came to the point of no longer being able to conceive of light, or to see it, except in its intensity, in its flaming glory, in its diffusion, in blinding brilliance, in the electricity of storms, the flamboyance of theatrical apotheoses, the fireworks of sleet, the blazing white of magnesium. During the day he no longer tried to paint anything but dazzle. Following the example of certain colorists who, the maturity of their talent achieved, lose the strength of their talent in excess, Coriolis . . . returned, in these last days, to his first manner, and little by little . . . he descended a little into that hallucination of the great Turner who, at the end of his life, wounded by the darkness of paintings, discontented even with the daylight of his time, tried to bring himself out, in a canvas, with the dream of colors, into a virgin, primordial daylight, into *The Light before the Deluge.*
>
> He searched everywhere for the stuff with which to strengthen his palette, heat up his colors, enflame and make them brilliant. In front of mineralogists' windows, attempting to steal from Nature, to ravish and carry off the multicolored fires of those petrifications and crystallizations of lightning, he stopped transfixed before the blue of azurite, the blue of chinese enamel, the feeble blues of oxidized copper, the celestial blue of lapis lazuli, all the way from royal blue to the blue of water. He sought the whole gamut of red, from sulfuric mercuries, carmine and bloody, to the black-red of haematite, and dreamed of *amatito,* the lost color of the sixteenth century, the cardinal color, the true purple of Rome. He sought the peacock golds and greens of diluvian pudding-stones, the greens of velvet, the changing, blue-tending greens of arsenic copper, the green of the lizard and of feldspar; the infinite variety of yellows,

from canary yellow to the honeyed yellow of crystallized yellow arsenic and of fluorins; the fiery colors of pyritic copper, the colors of pink or violet stones that make one think of crystal flowers.

From minerals, he turned to shells, to the colorations that give birth to tenderness and to the ideal, to all the variations of pink in a porcelain fount, from dusky purple to dying rose, to mother-of-pearl drowning the prism in its milk. He sought all the irisations and the opalizations of the rainbow, mirrored in old glass just come out of the earth, like pieces of buried sky. He visualized the azure of the sapphire, the blood of the ruby, the orient of the pearl, the water of the diamond. In order to paint, the painter believed he now had need of all that shone and all that burned in the Sky, in the Earth, and in the Sea.[32]

Coriolis's disintegration takes place not in Nature but in the museum. (At the very end of these passages, however, even the distinction between the natural and the artificial is undermined in the image of *coloris*.) Indeed, it is precisely within the context of the museum – more precisely the Salon Carré of the Louvre, that originary site of the modern Salon – that the artist circles back to his own beginnings (not to mention the beginning and ending of time itself, for the Creation, the Deluge, and the Apocalypse are collapsed in the circuit of these passages as well).

It is in the museum that Romantic painting, through its own excesses, spirals into coloristic chaos, and dissolves into an amorphous vortex of air, earth, water, and fire, figured in the rainbow-hued spin-cycle of Turner's painting. And it is there in the museum that the reader finds a peculiar variant on the topos of *Le Chef-d'oeuvre inconnu*: though it is again the artist's mistress who leads him to his decline, in the museum that is the site of Coriolis's apocalypse Balzac's image of painting disintegrated into pure color and facture is now detached from all chimerical intentions of figuring forth Woman and bringing her illusion to life. (Coriolis seeks to vivify his palette, not the represented body of a woman; and the "object" of his attempted ravishment is color itself.) Here chaos represents chaos, color represents color as such, simultaneously subject to petrification, liquefaction, and vaporization, and painting represents not a failed illusion but simply its own inbuilt, inexorable destruction. If Romanticism, from the Hegelian point of view, had always led inevitably to the disintegration of painting, the Goncourts' description of Coriolis's undoing within the space of the museum puts the period to that fate. Nothing, in short, could be further from the positivist understanding of the museum as the locus of the natural history of past art, and of modern art's linear progress into universality, than Coriolis's museum-situated regress into "his first manner."

That regress is figured this way: Coriolis's encounter with the museum leads directly to his fascination with "mineralogists' windows," where painter's pigments are ground, mixed, and sold, and where the museum's "mummification" of color gives way to a complementary mineralization of color – which is to say that the death and decay of color leads to its breaking down into its original mineral sources. But as much as color is literalized and petrified here – submitted to a kind of Medusa effect – it is also defined as fundamentally mutable: lacking a single essence, it is associated not with clearly delimited forms but with surfaces, substances, and materials: with hard stone, yes – frequently in the scintillating, translucent, light-refracting form of jewels – but also with the *informe* of liquid and ether, the alchemical combustibility of sulfur, the degenerative powers of poison (arsenic), and a host of other mercurial effects.[33] Color, moreover, is produced out of a seemingly infinite multiplication and diversification of adjectival language and unstable, endlessly insufficient descriptive qualifiers, signaled in the sheer excess of the listed gamut of different blues, reds, greens, and yellows associated with different substances and effects. Indeed, with their hectic melange of references to Byzantium and the Orient, the Italian Renaissance, and modern English painting, these fabulous passages treat the famous lability of color as the root and result, and certainly the surface effect, of eclecticism itself. Again, nothing could be further from the positive, biological function of the colored "tache" in Zola's writing about Manet's "new manner in painting" – set against the museum, according to Zola, rather than within it, and against the borrowing of manners and bastardization of personal and national styles promoted by the museum. Which is precisely what color is identified with in *Manette Salomon.*

The importance of color to *Manette Salomon* is emblematized in the name of the pet monkey, Vermilion (one of the brightest and most violent of hues), who, significantly, belongs first to Coriolis and then to Anatole. (As a monkey, Vermilion is also a figure of mimicry, which in its turn embodies the absence of indigenous identity, and the parroting of other styles characteristic of eclecticism, that are the novel's themes.) But as we have seen, color functions throughout, right from the start, in the opening passages evoking the diverse people and peoples of Paris with the assorted hues of their garments, and the panoply of colors constituting the dissolving, muddled panorama of Paris itself. Then, in addition to evoking the palette of race, the hectic scene of modernity, and the material rudiments of artifice, it is inevitable that color should figure the specter of femininity. That the passages above, concerning Coriolis's trajectory backward from museum to mineralogist's shop, are bedecked with jewels and all manner of ornament suggests that its color vocabulary bears the traces of the Baudelairean topos of ornamented and cosmeticized femininity.

This brings us back precisely to the woman, Manette, who is missing not only from the first half of the novel but also from its ending, and to the old de-Pilesian theme of the femininity of color in painting. For the descriptions of Manette as the object of Coriolis's (and her own) fascination earlier in the novel employ a language of color that is clearly Baudelairean in tone – and they contrast dramatically with Zola's vivid figurations of painted Woman at the close of his fictionalization of the story of modern art, *L'Oeuvre.* The following is one of the fullest descriptions of the appearance of the disappearing Manette:

> Beneath the warm palor of her complexion, shone through the pink of her blood, that blood which seems to flower and to smudge with carmine pastel the cheeks of Jewesses, that gleam of red at the summit of her cheekbones similar to the rubbed remains of the cosmetic powder which an actress has placed beneath her eye. All of that face, the forehead hollowed out to the beginning of the nose, the nose delicately arched, the nostrils indented and a little prominent, displayed a modeling incised with features. Her mouth . . . recalled the mouth . . . of those young boys in handsome Italian portraits.[34]

The Goncourts also indicate that Manette combines the features of different races in herself: "Above the Oriental, there was, in her person, a Parisian . . . there passed . . . over the pure and tranquil sculpture of her visage . . . the nasty smile of those naughty little heads of the poor quarters: one would have said . . . that the street rose up . . . in her face."[35] They emphasize her ability to exchange her race and also her age and gender – and her ability to masquerade as a boy, now an Italian Renaissance boy, now a little Parisian "gamin" with a musket: "a little cap on her head, smock on her back, her finger on the trigger of a hunting gun."[36] These descriptions, some of which are remarkably reminiscent of some of the paintings in Manet's retrospective – particularly those, such as *The Streetsinger* and *The Fifer*, featuring the changeable face of Victorine Meurent – stress the mobility of Manette's looks, their collapsing of differences between the "Oriental" and the "Parisienne," the boy and the woman, and their ability to move between identities. At the same time, they emphasize the artificed nature of the face and figure of Manette: a portrait and a sculpture, she is also a piece of face painting, worked in colors, as evanescent as the rubbed and powdered colors of which she is fashioned. Indeed, the "carmine pastel" of her cheeks shuttles between the effect of blood beneath the surface of skin and rouge upon that surface, as well as between pink and red, blush and blusher, such that it elides the difference between life and art, nature and paint – as both *coloris* and cosmetics do as well: that is their illusionism and their fascination. That elision, however, is all the effect of artifice, that of "modeling" with paint.

This is even clearer when, several pages later, the Goncourts describe Manette as herself a kind of artist, both her own maker and the narcissistic viewer of herself:

> Then she began to seek the beauties, the voluptuous poses, the nude grace of woman . . . And at the end, as if after a long period of artist's shaping work, emerged out of her undulating, flexible form, an admirable statue of the moment . . . For a minute Manette contemplated herself and possessed herself in the victory of her pose: she loved herself . . . And on the rim of her lips . . . the compliments that a woman murmurs beneath her breath to her own beauty appeared to rise and fall . . . in the living, speaking sketch of her mouth.
>
> " . . . there is only the mirror to watch me!"[37]

Here Manette makes herself up in the act of modeling – not, now, the act of "modeling" her features with paint but rather the act of taking up poses to be painted, through which she becomes first a "statue," and then, viewed in the mirror, a "sketch." (Thus the Goncourts do Balzac's reversal of the Pygmalion scenario one better: from "life" Manette is transformed into several, successively less dimensional degrees of lifelike art.) Indeed, the relations among posing, making, and viewing become a closed circle, all performed by the same figure, Manette, and excluding the male painter, Coriolis, from the circle. (Coriolis, once excluded, hies off on his own, attempting to "ravish" Nature's colors in lieu of Manette, before going into his decline and disappearing altogether.) What Manette constitutes, then, is a figure of the supplement and the principle of internal alterity: disrupting the boundaries between the native and the alien, the self and the other, the maker and the made, she stands in place of a Nature-made body and face, and instead of proper, heterosexual relations between male painter and female model. Split between herself and her mirror image, she not only personifies Nature as always-already

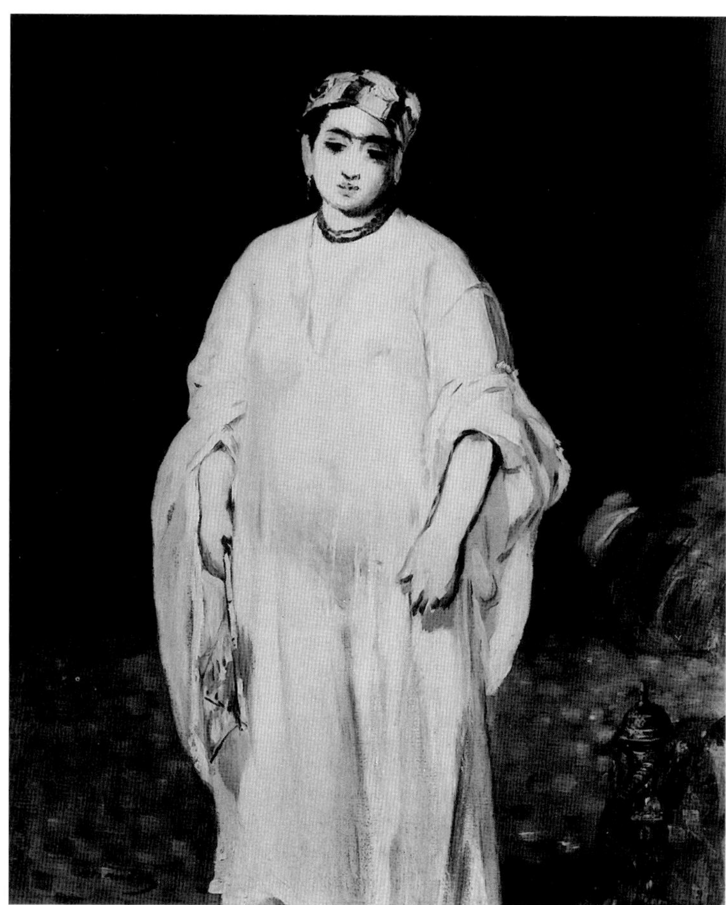

24 Edouard Manet, *Young Woman in Oriental Garb*, c.1870, oil on canvas, 96 × 74.5 cm. E. G. Bührle Collection, Zurich.

Art, she also figures the artist as a fundamentally split and doubled entity, and embodies the impossibility of neatly portioning the scene of art, Pygmalion-like, into the separate, opposed, clearly gendered spheres of the subject and object of art. Thus she represents a different conception of the artist's identity from that which we find in Zola's positivist "portrait" of Manet the man or in his characterization of *Olympia* as the "flesh and blood" of the painter: not a biological entity, a physiological image, or the mirror of Nature, she is, rather, the split, double figure of *coloris* itself. Was that the "Manette" Manet had in mind when he painted a single Oriental woman (fig. 24) some time after the conjunction of events in 1867?

*   *   *

Some two decades later, Zola sought to revise both Balzac's novelette and the Goncourts "'suite d'aquarelles et d'eaux fortes'" with his novel *L'Oeuvre*, published in 1886, during the year of the final Impressionist show, and based on the combined figures of Manet, Monet, and Cézanne, and perhaps Gustave Moreau as well.[38] *L'Oeuvre*, too, is the story of the decline of painting – or at least, the decline of Zola's faith in modern painting –

embodied in the disastrous project and death of its central character Claude Lantier. It too is a tale of the artist in love; as much as its forebears it upends the myth of Pygmalion; like them it hones in on the image of Woman as the cause of the failure of painting – indeed, it resuscitates the image of the "grande Impure" presiding over Zola's first treatise on the "new manner in painting," his essay on Manet, and puts her front and center stage, with no lingering ambivalences about her unhealthy effects on young painters and modern painting.

But *L'Oeuvre*, unlike its predecessors, is biography fictionalized. A portrait of the artist, like the essay on Manet, it focuses on the artist's "sentimental journey" and his domestic relationship with a flesh-and-blood woman, Christine. From beginning to end and unlike Manette, Christine is fully described and realized, an explicitly biological, corporeal, even reproductive entity with whom Claude has sex and who bears a child (this is the relatively minor feature of *Manette Salomon's* "plot" that Zola latches onto and elaborates as the main substance of his story, putting it in much more explicit terms than the Goncourts had done), and who turns out to be a veritable force of Nature. By the end, long after she has stopped functioning as artist's model, she forces a sort of Hercules' choice upon her lover, in which she represents the way of Nature as opposed to that of Art (that is, healthy, heterosexual, life-generating love as opposed to the death-drive of barren idolatry). Indeed, in the same journal entry of August 5, 1886 in which Edmond de Goncourt accused Zola of stealing the idea of Claude's painterly crisis from *Manette Salomon*, he also criticized Zola for making "that madness [which in my hands was] purely aesthetic" into an obscene genital obsession.[39] The following is the final scene, just before Claude's suicide, to which Goncourt seems to have been referring, and which underlines the difference between the Goncourts' and Zola's visions of the failed Pygmalionism of modern painting:

> Claude, obeying the domineering gesture with which she [Christine] showed him the picture, rose and looked . . . He finally awoke from his dream, and *the Woman*, seen thus from below, from several steps back, stupefied him. Who then had just painted *this idol* of an unknown religion? who had made her *of metal, marble, and gems, making the mystic rose of her sex bloom between the precious columns of her thighs, beneath the sacred vault of her belly*? Was it he who, without knowing it, had been the fashioner of this symbol of insatiable desire, of *this superhuman image of the flesh, made of gold and diamonds in his fingers, in his vain effort to make life of it*? And, gaping, he took fright of his work, trembling from this sudden leap into the beyond, well understanding that reality itself was not possible for him, at the end of his long battle to vanquish it and mold it, with his man's hands, until it was more real than real.[40]

On the next page, Zola contrasts this graven image – flesh petrified into glittering gold, hard, cold diamond, and architectural stonework, evocative of Moreau's *Apparition* of Salomé (fig. 25),[41] but also redolent of the Courtesan of his own essay on Manet, that "symbol of insatiable desire" with her barbaric lust for blood sacrifice – to the blood-ripened tumescence and sexual life force of her flesh-and-blood rival Christine, "the silky roundness of her haunches enlarged, her firm chest erect once more, swollen with the blood of her desire."[42] (This is a Christine, once shy, chaste, and cold, brought to life: the only object the Pygmalion effect works on, in *L'Oeuvre*, is a real

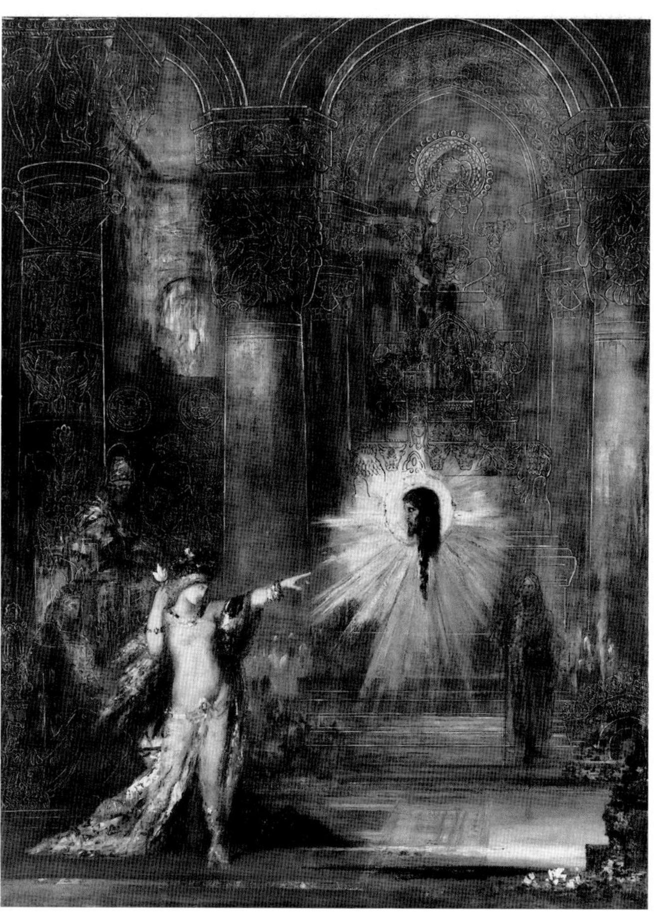

25   Gustave Moreau, *The Apparition*, 1874–6/1897, oil on canvas, 142 × 103 cm. Musée Gustave Moreau, Paris.

human body. It is not fortuitous – the rival effects of literature and painting had always been at issue in these artist stories – that it is literature, not painting, that brings her to life. Right from the beginning of the novel, before her awakening into sexuality, while she was still the object of the artist's gaze, the soft, Nature-made volumes of Christine's body had been described with this same literary liveliness. But where she had begun as all silk and golden-ness,[43] her Nature suggesting and indeed inducing Art, by the end she is cast as the libidinal, indeed phallic principle of Life itself, and as such the opposite of Art.) Here Christine takes up her model's pose of old, and demands that Claude compare her with the painted Woman on the altar, before seducing him back into her arms. In one last fit of life and libido, before he, like the bastard child Jacques before him, is killed off by his other mistress Art, Claude has lusty sex with Christine, thus dotting the i's, in the final climactic moments of *L'Oeuvre*'s lurid story, on the binary opposition that structures the novel as a whole – between the *femme vitale* of Nature and the *femme fatale* of Art.

Perhaps *L'Oeuvre* was Zola's revenge against such decadents as Goncourt and Huysmans, for betraying the cause of Naturalism from within its fold; against Manet, Cézanne, and the lot, for not realizing Zola's dream of a vital, fully realized, encyclopedic modern art to match his own literary project; and against Art in general, for not being understandable in the terms of either positivist criticism or naturalist literature. Certainly it was a verdict on modern art and as such it represented, like Zola's much shorter and more positive catalogue essay for the posthumous show of Manet's work of a few years before, the shutting down of Zola's engagement in contemporary painting and a repressive, retrospective response to his own earlier, future-minded enthusiasms. It contained many of the same ingredients as his 1867 piece on Manet's "nouvelle manière en peinture" – it was still a celebration of painting's organic attachment to the "heart and flesh" of the painter, but now, with all the earlier doubts about the phantasmatic femininity of art contracted into disapproval, its verdict was that painting had failed in its mission to render Nature in a virile, positive manner that was at once utterly individualistic and wholly universal. That is to say, Zola's view of the decline of modern art – which was finally less that of disintegration than of petrification, idolatry, and false religion – was argued in relation to the (failed) positivist value of Nature-ordained progress, the biological evolution of modern art toward the expression of the individual organism as the universal principle of Nature, promoted in "Une nouvelle manière en peinture: Edouard Manet" and elsewhere.

Such an understanding of modern art was not, and never had been, adequate to Manet's work: it surely did not correspond very well to the ensemble of fifty-odd works put on view by the artist in 1867. By contrast, *Manette Salomon*, whose understanding of the disintegration of modern art was not that of disappointed positivism, did provide a structure capable of encompassing what Manet was about. The adequacy of *Manette* to Manet, however, is not a matter of stylistic affinities between Manet's painting of the 1860s and the work of the various fictional artists sketched by the Goncourts; the Goncourts describe the generation previous to Manet's, after all. And Coriolis's Orientalism, which is in line with that earlier generation's Romantic manias, finds no stylistic match in Manet's flattened updating of Velasquez and others, of which, *tache* for *tache*, Zola's descriptions remain unsurpassed in their vividness. Nor is the fitness of *Manette* to Manet a matter of kinship between the latter's opinions and the Goncourts' overtly antisemitic and misogynistic sentiments: there is nothing to suggest that their racism and sexism were shared by Manet, quite the contrary.

Rather, the pertinence of *Manette* to Manet is a matter of structural suitability: it is the structure of eclecticism and *coloris*, the configuration of Coriolis's artistic identity and career, and even the logic of Manette's Orientalism, and her relationship as feminine object to Coriolis's masculine subject, that gives purchase on the shape of Manet's retrospective of 1867, his "oeuvre" thus far with its many styles of coloring and its many references to the museum, and his engagement in the constructs of femininity and Spanishness. (In this regard, Coriolis's obsession with a Jewish woman – the figure of otherness in the novel of her name – may be taken as parallel to Manet's fascination with things Spanish.) As an allegory, not an art-historical monograph or a Naturalist novel, *Manette Salomon* demands to be taken less as a story about several Romantic artists and one Jewish model than as a kind of treatise on the disintegration, alterity, and supplementarity of modern art, made available through the screen of the fragmented form and pluralist content of the story of Coriolis, Manette, and the others. And, since it was written in the same years that Manet was painting Victorine Meurent, Léon Leenhoff, and others, and published in 1867, the year of the second Universal Exposition and Manet's retrospective, it enters into the fray of 1867, directing its commentary at that moment and its representatives of modern art as much as at the earlier generation that is its apparent topic. In short, *Manette Salomon* may be understood as an allegory of modern art that corresponds to Manet's display of his own oeuvre, and his presentation of his own identity as a modern artist – as the museum's bastard son; as nonlinear, disunified, internally divided; as the yield of artifice rather than the mirror of Nature, identified with rather than against the coloristic figure of Woman and the values of artificiality, superficiality, mutability, and alterity that she represents.

This may sound like a deconstructive description of postmodernism, rather than that old familiar nineteenth century in which we locate the origins of modernism. But if it does, it is mainly because we are used to thinking, just as our positivist forebears did, in terms of an advancing movement from block to block of period style and period thought. It is because *Manette Salomon* not only represents the arena of modern art as a caco-phany of many different voices, but also because it constitutes one of the dissenting voices in the field of contestation that that era was: which is to say that it was one of those statements about modernity from those days that already implied something like what we now call deconstruction.[44] Thus *Manette Salomon* offers a way to think differently both about Manet's art and about the periodization of modern art at the head of which Manet's most famous pictures stand. And so, just as *Manette* may yield a different Manet and a different modern art, so too she may yield a different art history: a way, from the era of its origins, out of the model of the forward march of modernism from period to unified period.

Part Two

BEFORE 1867

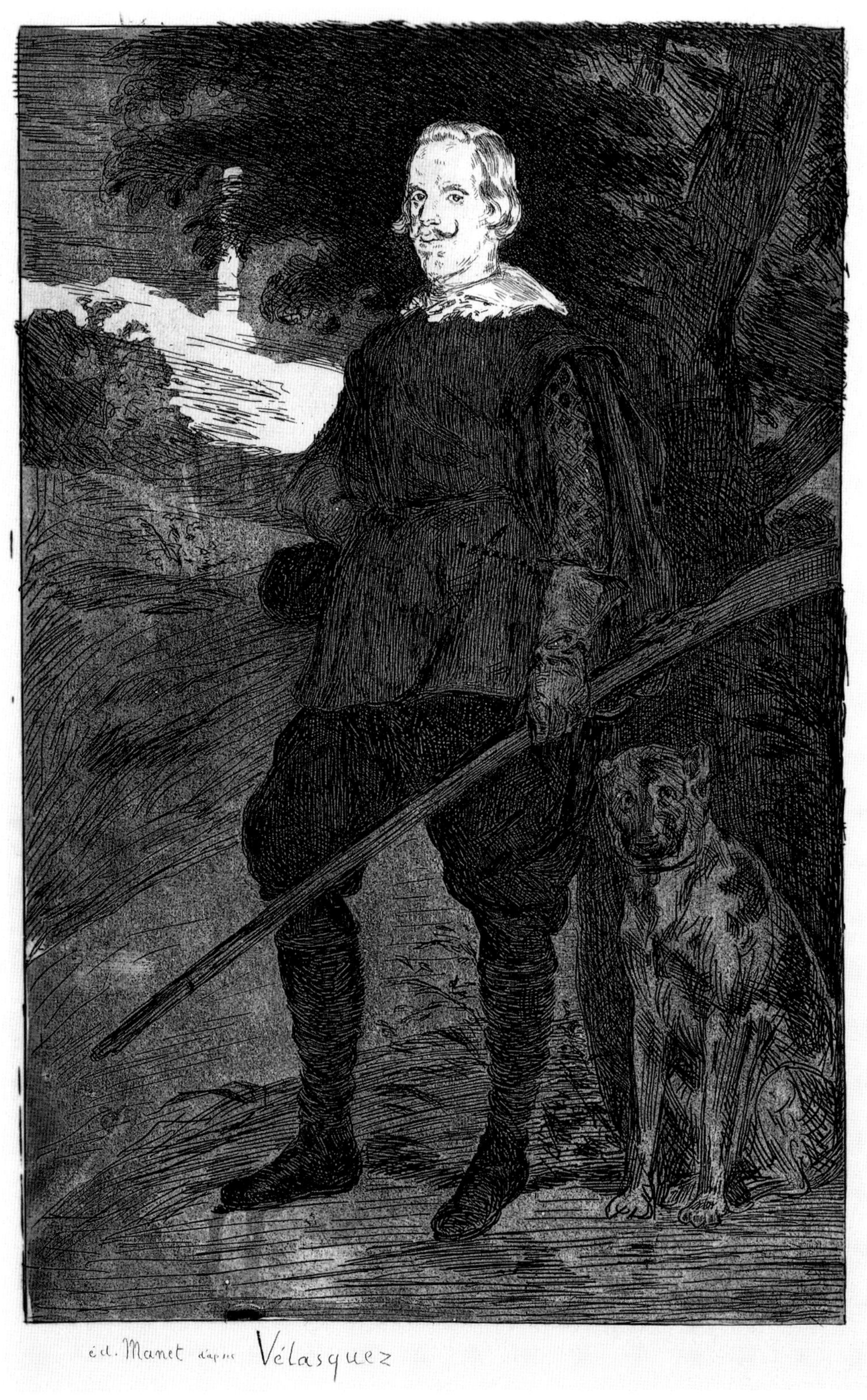

26 Edouard Manet, copy after Velasquez, *Portrait of Philip IV*, 1862, etching, drypoint and aquatint, 6th state, 32 × 19.9 cm.

Chapter Four

REPRODUCING ORIGINALITY:
THE CADART PORTFOLIO

IN 1862, WHEN MANET WAS ONLY THIRTY YEARS OLD and had been in his first Salon just the year before, he was already planning a retrospective, a summary of his oeuvre as it looked after no more than a few years of post-student practice. That first retrospective was mounted in March of the next year at Louis Martinet's newly reopened gallery on the Boulevard des Italiens, where both Dutch and Flemish painting and French art of the seventeenth through the nineteenth century was displayed, and which Martinet hoped to establish as an alternative to the Salon exhibitions.[1] Manet had already had a couple of paintings on view at Martinet's and exhibited more works there in the next few years, in group shows of the short-lived Cercle Artistique of the Société Nationale des Beaux-Arts, of which he became a member.[2] But in 1863 he had a one-man show, making it clear that he already felt that "To exhibit is for the artist . . . the sine qua non," and that summarizing his own oeuvre, even when he had barely begun and hardly had an oeuvre to speak of, was of particular importance to him. Having his say about who and what he was as an artist – in a forum in which he could single himself out, present the arch of his work in a way that he could control, and add up his paintings into some kind of concerted statement about his "individuality" as a painter – clearly already mattered to him.

This was part of the stated goals of Louis Martinet, that his gallery and with it the Société Nationale des Beaux-Arts, would provide a space for the young artist to show his work as an ensemble and determine its effect both on himself and on its audience: "we address ourselves as much to artists who begin as to artists of renown."[3] His gallery was not conceived as a replacement for the then biennial Salon, but rather as a complement and a kind of anteroom to it.[4] But Martinet did contrast the self-reliance of the artist that he wanted his gallery to represent to state sponsorship of the arts:

> In truth, one is too accustomed, in France, to counting on the support of the government, and one thinks too little about counting on oneself . . . of the government we ask a competition so universal, we interest ourselves in so many questions, we invoke a support on its part so continuous that the individual ends by annihilating himself . . .[5]

And Martinet also spoke of the difficulty that a *débutant* faced in singling himself out from the morass of works at the Salon: "It is almost impossible for a debutant to be noticed at the Salon . . . In an exhibition where the catalogue includes four thousand entries, and which one usually visits only once, the artist has nineteen times less of a chance to be seen than in a gallery with two hundred works."[6] And finally, he proclaimed the intention of expanding from the "isolated individual" to a group of "opposed" and "heterogeneous" temperaments, to an artist's association that would unify them all:

> That which the isolated individual would be powerless to produce, a society . . . would yield necessarily. In the arts above all, the spirit of association must change everything: then the most heterogeneous elements will support each other; those opposed temperaments, those diverse tendencies, and those hostile traditions will mix in an indestructible whole, and, all animated with a single thought, putting their multiple faculties at the service of a great idea truly useful to art, will be able to abolish the repugnances dictated by bias alone.[7]

Thus Martinet's was the place for Manet: for there the upstart, unfinished, individual talent could stand out, and the association of works and inviduals was to produce a totality from the ground up (rather than the state dictating an ensemble from the top down), all under the sign of a heterogeneity and pluralism that could be dialectically resolved.

Fourteen works were in Manet's show at Martinet's, among them *The Absinthe Drinker*, *The Boy with the Sword*, *The Urchin* (now known as *The Boy with the Dog*), *The Old Musician*, *The Gypsies* (both the "original" and its etched copy), *The Spanish Ballet*, *Lola de Valence*, the *Young Woman Reclining in Spanish Costume*, *The Streetsinger*, and the *Music at the Tuileries*.[8] A month and a half later, in May 1863, three paintings and three etchings of Manet's went on view at the Salon des Refusés – the infamous *Luncheon on the Grass*, *Mlle V. . . . in the Costume of an Espada*, the *Young Man in the Costume of a Majo*, and Manet's etched copies after Velasquez's *The Little Cavaliers* and *Portrait of Philip IV in Hunting Costume*, as well as after his own *Lola de Valence*, on view at Martinet's.[9] For Manet, then, 1863 already represented a mini-version of what Courbet had done in 1855: two successive exhibitions of work by an upstart young artist, one in and the other outside of the state's official venue. (Except that Manet was younger than Courbet had been, and did not yet have fifty works and more to show anywhere. Moreover, the official venue in question this time around was a Salon for the rejected, and Manet's inclusion in it rather than the Salon of the accepted was in part a consequence of his having elected to have his "exposition particulière" at Martinet's first.)

Manet had planned ahead, for many of the works at Martinet's and then at the Salon des Refusés had been announced and advertised in a portfolio of "autographic" prints published by the print publisher and dealer Alfred Cadart in 1862, giving advance notice of Manet's painting displays of 1863: the Cadart portfolio gives a good idea, among other things, of Manet's early focus on self-promotion and manifestion. Manet had had one print, his etched *Gitanos*, included in the first folio of modern etchings put out by Cadart's Société des Aquafortistes in September of 1862 (fig. 27). The next month Cadart put out a portfolio devoted to Manet alone, called "Huit gravures à l'eau-forte par Manet" and made up of the following plates (one of which included two images, so that the portfolio actually numbered nine etchings): *The Spanish Singer*, the copy of (Manet's painted copy of?) *The Little Cavaliers*, the copy after *Philip IV*, *The Espada*, *The Absinthe*

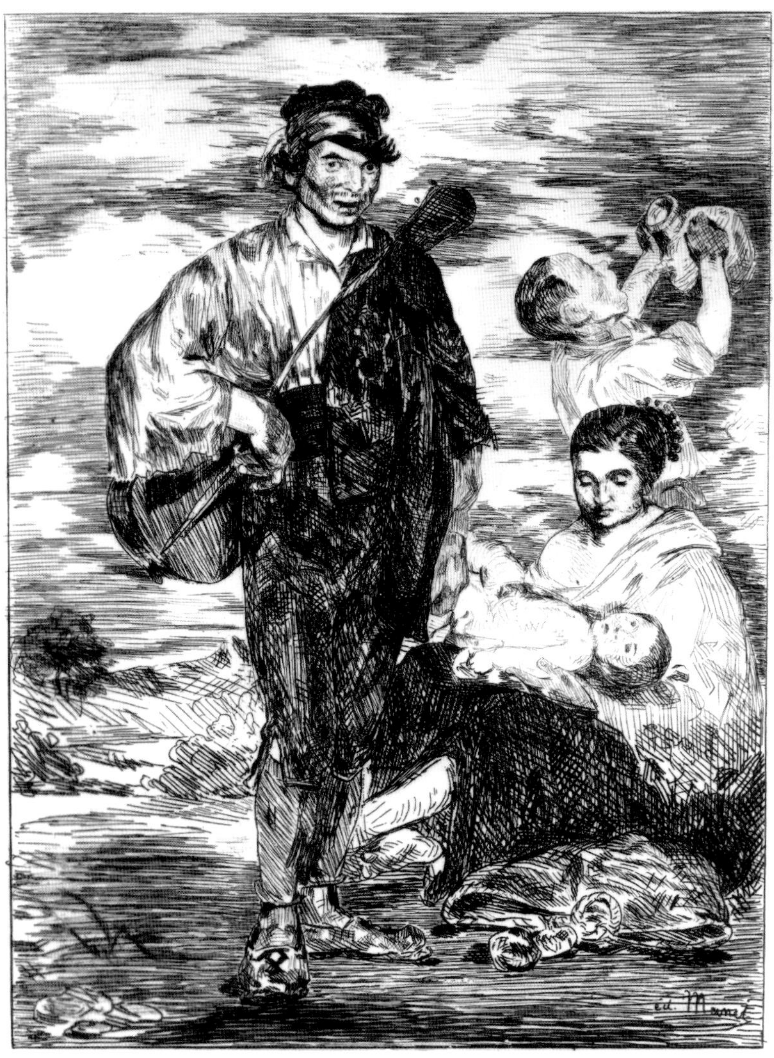

27   Edouard Manet, *The Gitanos*, 1862, etching, 3rd state. Bibliothèque Nationale, Paris.

Drinker, The Toilette, The Boy with the Dog, and *The Urchin/The Little Girl* (figs. 26, 28–32).[10] (Manet had planned to put in his portfolio the etched *Boy with the Sword* and *Lola de Valence* as well as *The Candle Seller* and *Mariano Camprubi* – his etched portrait of the male lead of the popular Spanish dance troupe of which Lola de Valence was a member – but then he left them out. His etched *Lola de Valence* (fig. 33) was included in Cadart's October 1863 Société des Aquafortistes edition of modern etchings, after the show at Martinet's and the Salon des Refusés.[11]) Of the etched images in Manet's portfolio, at least three appeared at Martinet's and three at the Salon des Refusés, either in the form of the "originals" of which they were copies, or in the form of "original prints" after "originals" by either Manet or Velasquez.

In fact, the Cadart portfolio was tied fairly directly to the show at Martinet's, through *Le Courrier artistique's* espousing of the Société des Aquafortistes, and its commitment

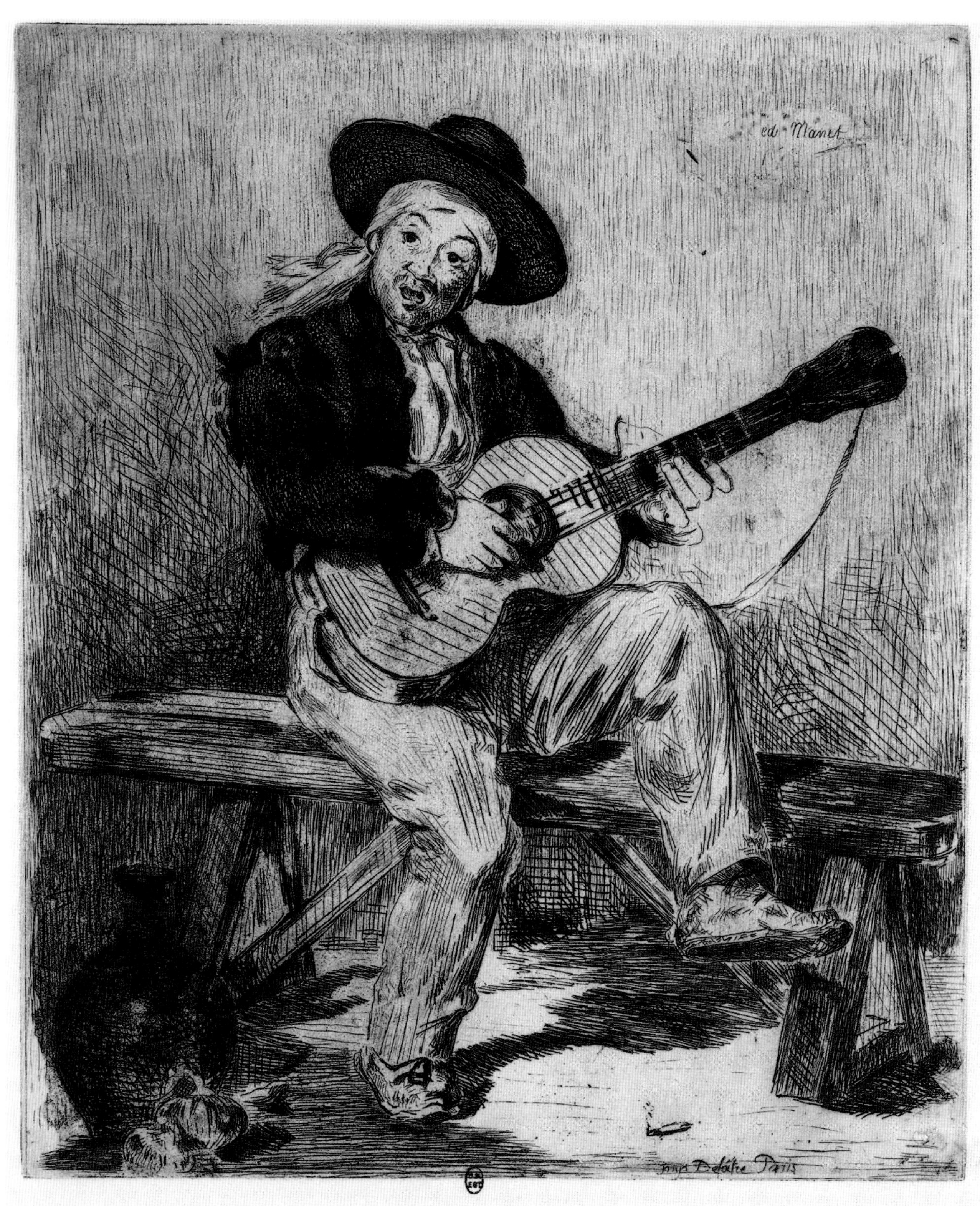

28 Edouard Manet, *The Spanish Singer*, 1861–62, etching, 5th state. Bibliothèque Nationale, Paris.

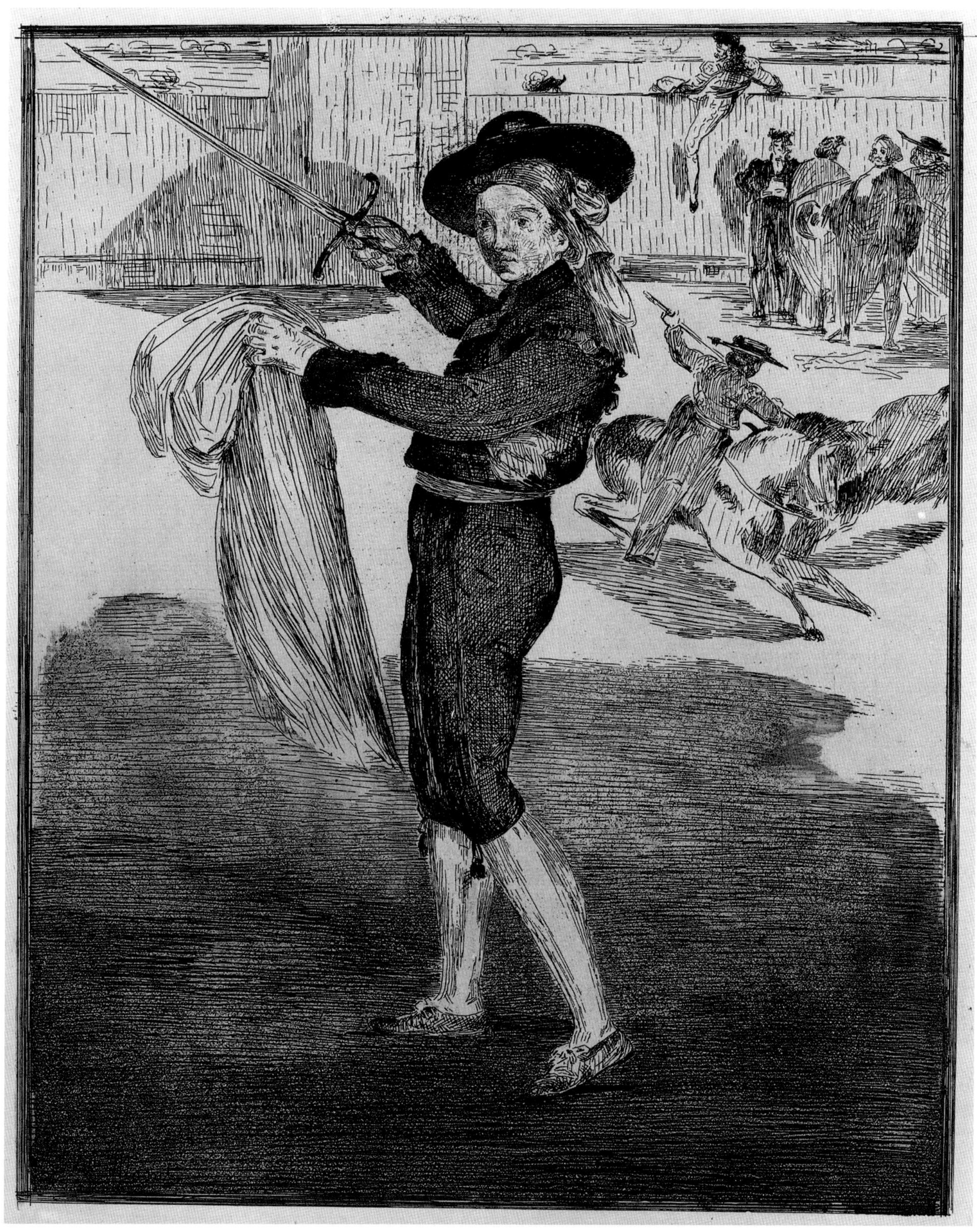

29   Edouard Manet, *Mlle V. . . . in the Costume of an Espada*, 1862, etching and aquatint, 3rd state. The Metropolitan Museum of Art, New York, Rogers Fund, 1969. (69.550).

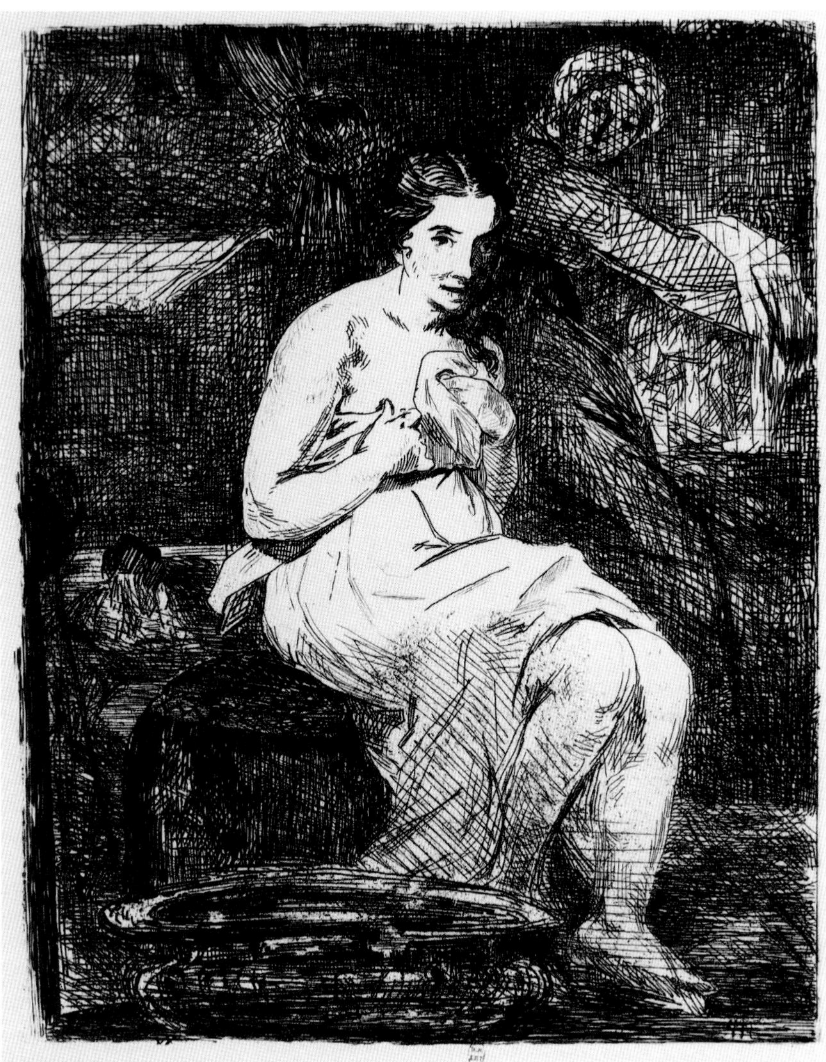

30   Edouard Manet, *The Toilette*, 1861, etching, 2nd state, Bibliothèque Nationale, Paris.

to artists' prints and reproductions more generally. In the very first number of his periodical, Martinet himself opened by announcing that "the *Courrier artistique . . .* wants above all to keep painters and amateurs abreast of all the remarkable reproductions that arise in the domain of the arts and in particular of those that each day enrich the exhibition at the Boulevard des Italiens."[12] Further, in the statutes of the Société Nationale des Beaux-Arts, which Martinet published in May 1862 in *Le Courrier artistique*, he declared one of the principal objects of the Société to be: "The sale, at the profit of the artists, of the reproductions of their works, thus constituting a special reproduction fund to which may then be attached everything that has to do with artistic property."[13] Finally, in October of 1862, the month in which Manet's portfolio came out, Martinet pointed directly to the Société des Aquafortistes, stating its shared commitment to quality printmaking that followed "the traditions of the masters."[14] Thus

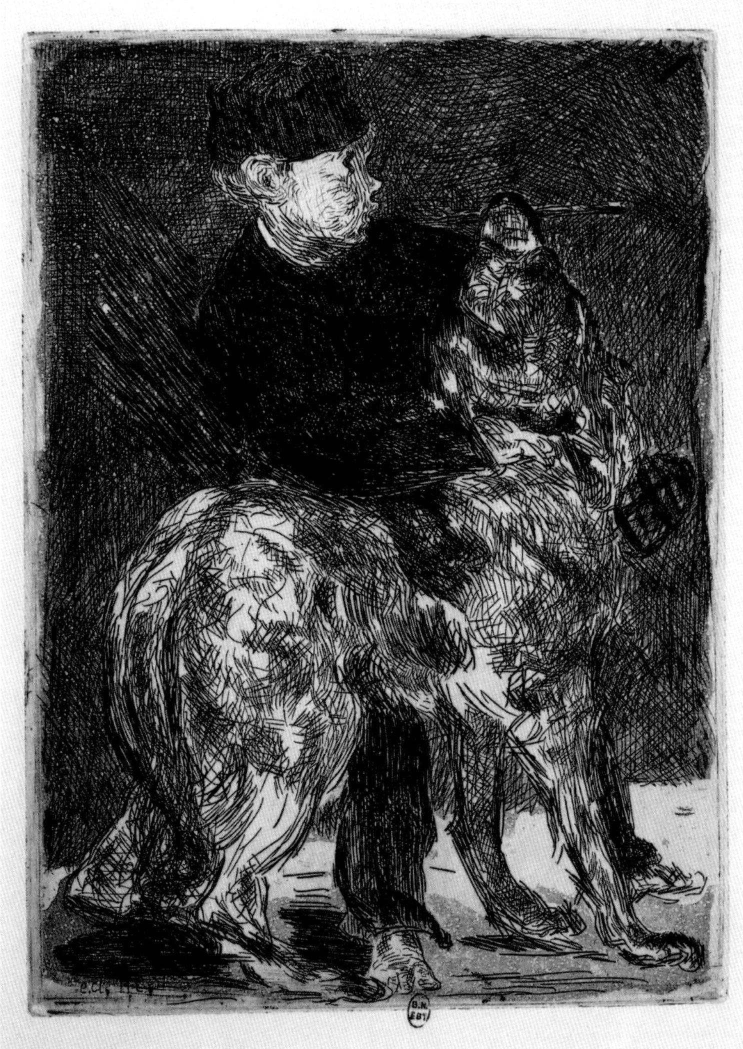

31　Edouard Manet, *The Boy with the Dog*, 1862, etching and aquatint, 1st state, 20.5 × 14.5 cm. New York Public Library.

Manet's "autographic reproductions" were very much part of a link forged between the association dedicated to the display of original works by promising young individualities at the outset of their careers and the society devoted to the renaissance of the artist's etching and the controlled reproduction of artists' works. That link hinged on the artist's right to represent and reproduce himself – to which Manet first laid claim in 1862.

REVERSING REPRODUCTIONS

Of the Cadart etchings, five were devoted to either Spanish themes or Spanish sources,[15] while of the paintings at Martinet's at least six were hispanicizing pictures, and of the six painted and etched works on view at the Salon des Refusés five had Spanish references.

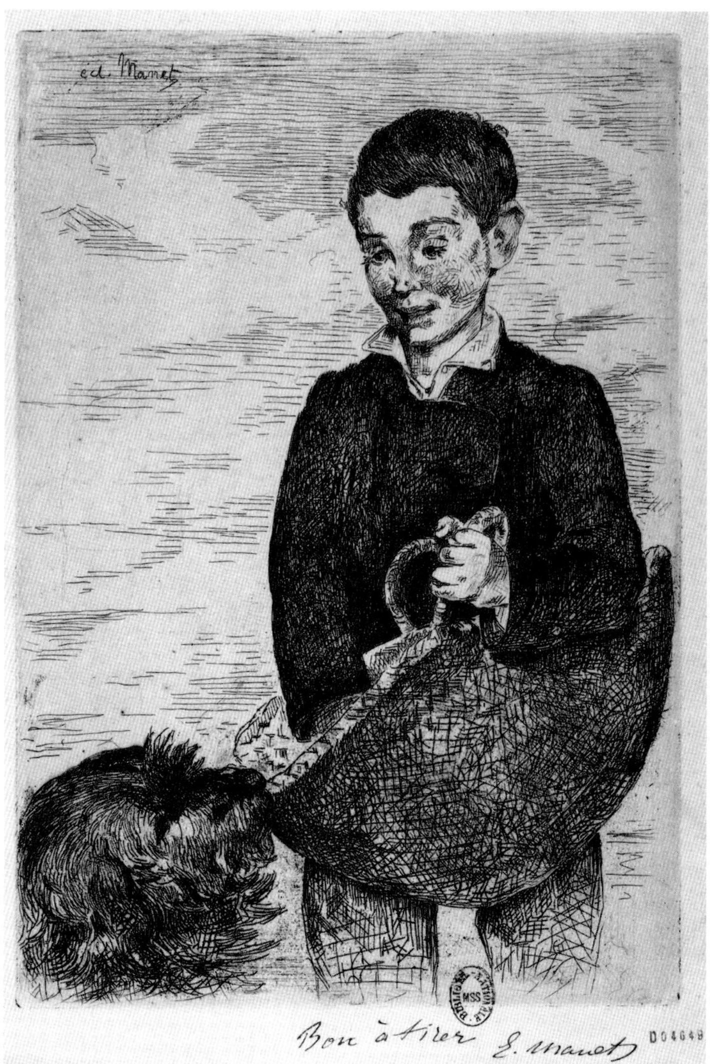

32   Edouard Manet, *The Urchin*, 1862, etching 20.9 × 14.8 cm. Bibliothèque Nationale, Paris.

I shall come back to the "Spanishicity" of Manet's portfolio and of his two sets of exhibited works in 1863.[16] For the present, it is worth attending to the curious mix of "originality" and the mechanically reproduced with which Manet introduced his work as a painter to his public: as an announcement of things to come and a piece of self-publication, the portfolio suggests that that mix was definitive of Manet's "oeuvre." Indeed, the oxymoron the "original print" had special resonance for Manet's work, as the portfolio demonstrated, locating Manet's authenticity – his "sincerity" and his signature style – within rather than against the practice of the museum copy, and aligning it with changeability and supplementarity, with manners and modes put on and taken off. Two of his proposed frontispieces for the portfolio (neither of which Cadart accepted) were emblematic of that brand of "originality" while also indexing the "Spanishicity" of the work – in the form of a pile of uninhabited studio properties, Spanish hat and Spanish

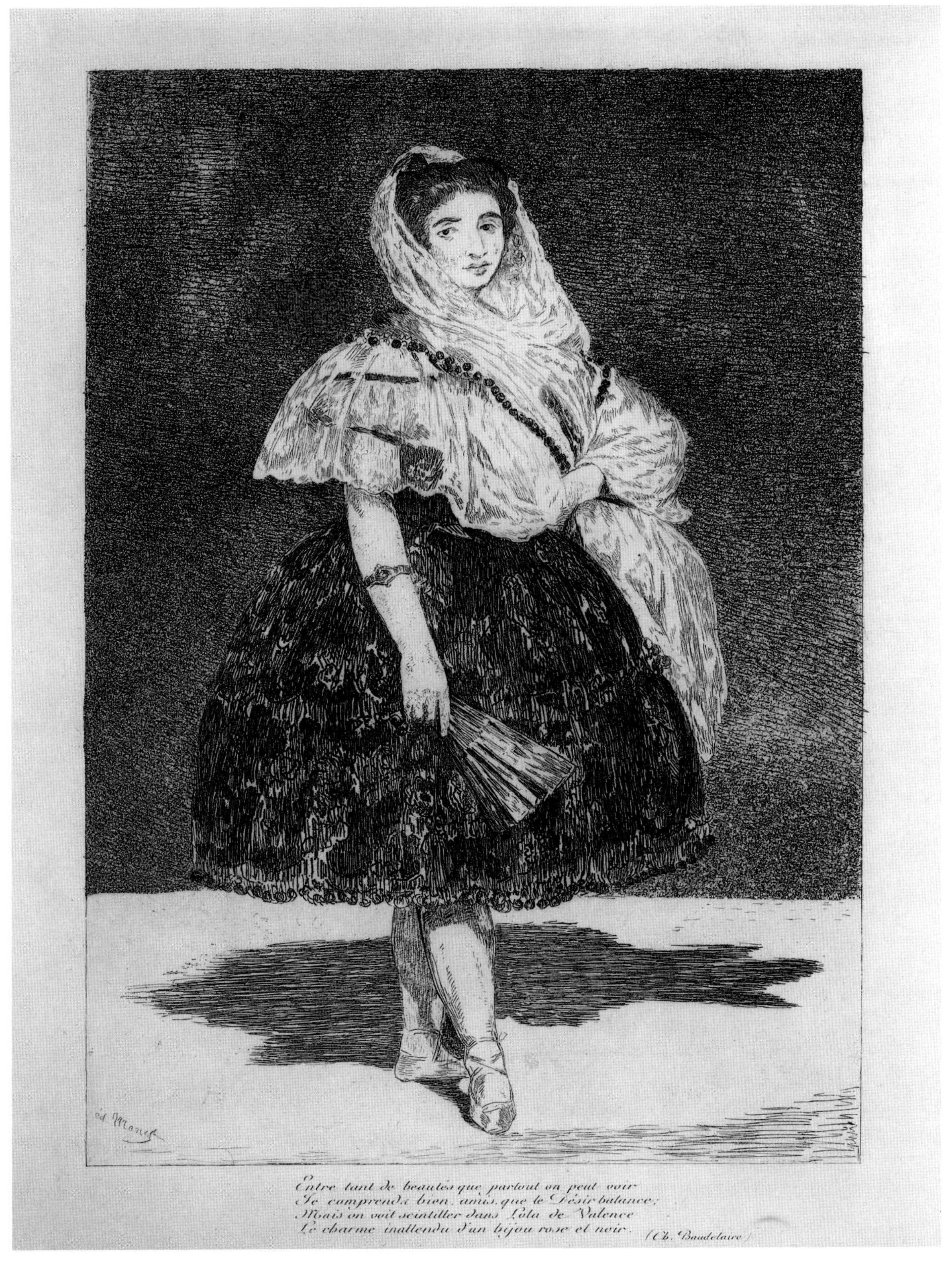

33   Edouard Manet, *Lola de Valence*, 1863, etching and aquatint, 5th state, 23.5 × 16.1 cm. Bibliothèque Nationale, Paris.

34   Edouard Manet,
*"Eaux-fortes par Edouard
Manet" avec chapeau et
guitare*, 1862–63/1874,
etching, drypoint and
aquatint, 2nd state,
23.1 × 21.9 cm. New York
Public Library, Astor,
Lenox and Tilden
Foundation.

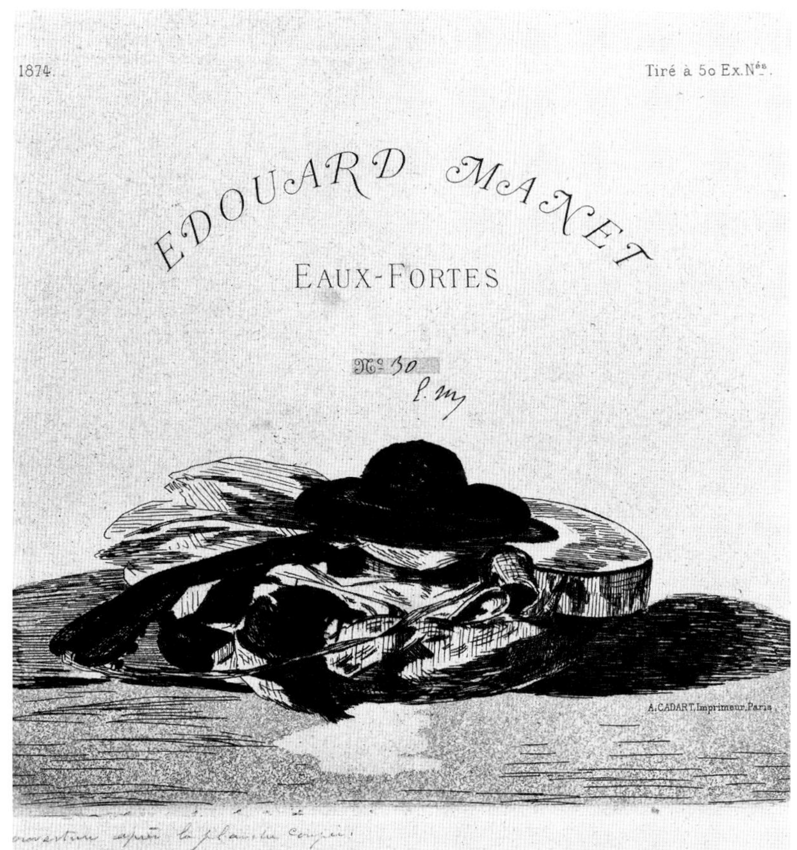

35 (*below*)   Edouard
Manet, *Hat and Guitar*,
1862, oil on canvas,
77 × 121 cm. Musée
Calvet, Avignon.

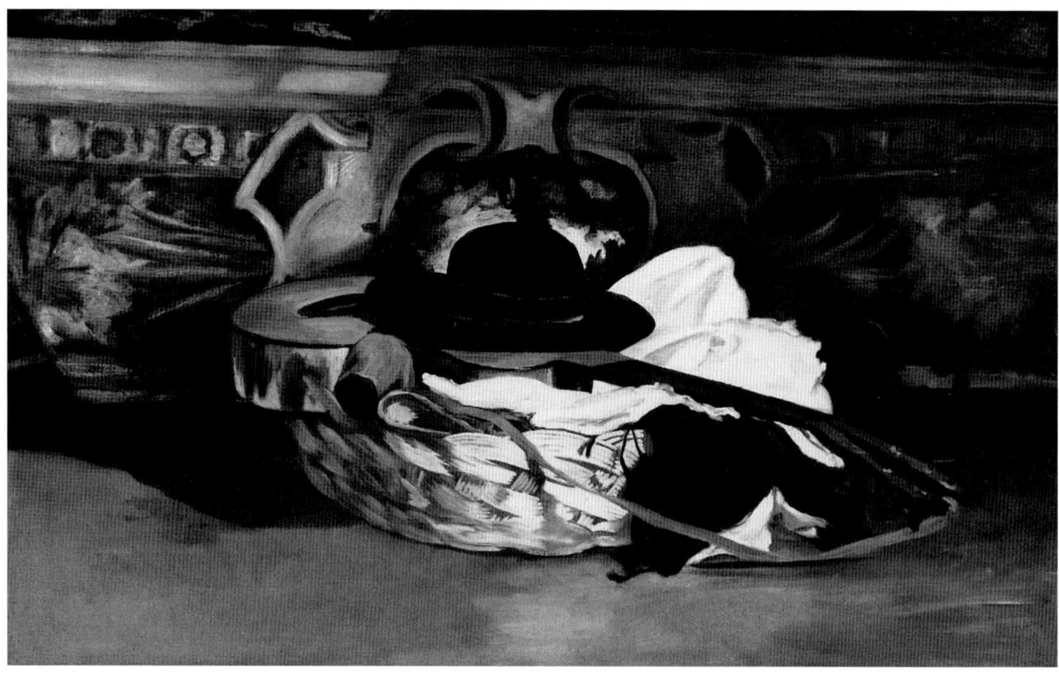

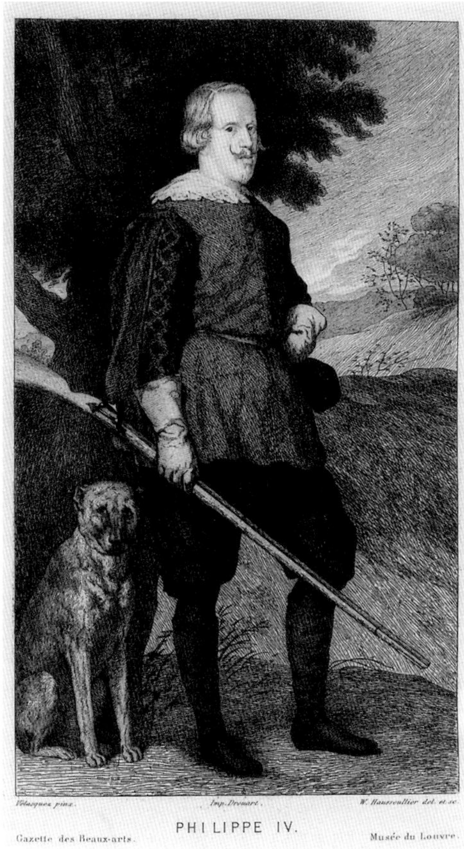

36   Haussoullier, copy after Velasquez, *Portrait of Philip IV in Hunting Costume*, *Gazette des Beaux-Arts*, July 1, 1863, Etching.

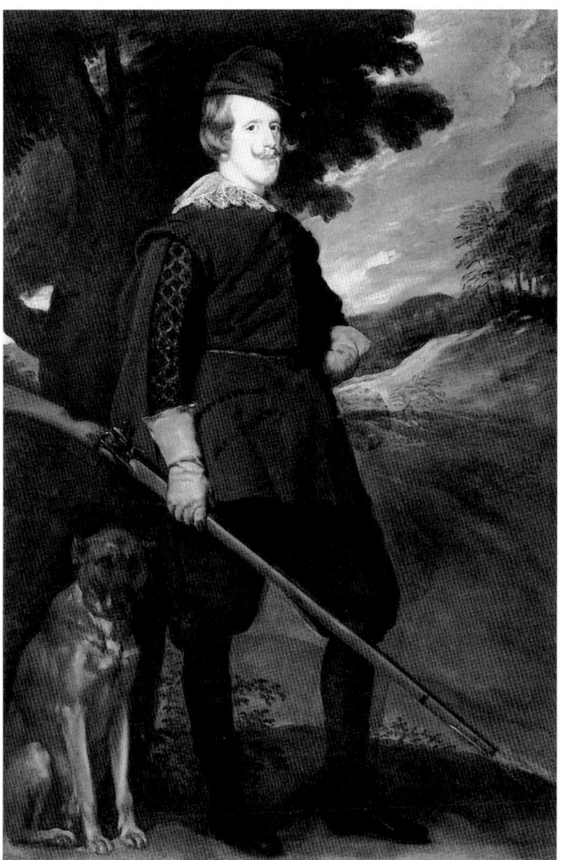

37   Diego Velasquez (now attrib. to Mazo), *Portrait of Philip IV in Hunting Costume*, oil on canvas, 189 × 124.5 cm. Museo del Prado, Madrid.

guitar prominent among them (fig. 34) and recognizable from his first Salon painting, *The Spanish Singer*, which came first in the portfolio's set of eight plates. (One of the two rejected frontispieces, which whittled down the composition from a more complicated image to just the list of etchings and the pile of props, did serve as the frontispiece to Manet's 1874 Cadart portfolio. Like the prints in the portfolio, that one was a duplicate, a copy of a painted "original" [fig. 35]. Or was the painting the copy and the print the "original"?)

Though it included reproductions of many of the works to be shown at Martinet's and the Salon des Refusés, the earlier Cadart portfolio did not so much predict the images to be shown in either venue as advertise Manet's general purpose; it pointed both to his intention to put himself on display and give his work an overview and to his concern to cultivate his reputation as simultaneously a modern master and a rival of the old masters whose works were reproduced in the *Gazette des Beaux-Arts* and in histories of European art such as Charles Blanc's *Histoire des peintres de toutes les écoles*. One such reproduction was Haussoullier's etching (fig. 36), published in the July 1, 1863 issue of the *Gazette des*

Beaux-Arts, after Velasquez's *Portrait of Philip IV in Hunting Costume*, bought by the Louvre in May 1862 (fig. 37). This appeared after the fact of Manet's portfolio with its distinctive, much looser rendering of Velasquez's portrait (and during the Salon des Refusés in which Manet's print of *Philip IV* was exhibited). But it does suggest the field of printmaking with which Manet entered into contest: which included both the romantic revival of interest in etching as an "original" art form replete with painterly gestures and Rembrandtesque tonal masses and the use of the medium as a detailed, more or less transparent means of reproduction of works from the history of art.[17] Manet tied his own engagement in modern etching back to earlier forms of art reproduction, such as Marc Antonio Raimondi's engravings after Raphael's paintings and other Renaissance works, which Manet quoted in two of the painted works shown in the Salon des Refusés, and to earlier figures, like Goya, who had worked with etching both as a medium of "originality" and as a means of mechanical reproduction.[18] Indeed, Manet seemed to put himself on a par with Goya, who had etched copies after many of Velasquez's paintings, such as the portrait of Philip IV itself as well as works like *The Drinkers* (one of the sources of *The Old Musician*), but who was also in vogue as the author of "original" series of etchings such as the *Tauromaquia*. That was a vogue in which Manet clearly shared, following the lead of Baudelaire.[19]

As in the case of the *Portrait of Philip IV*, Manet frequently copied after both "originals" and copies, conflating one with the other and layering them together with increasing complexity.[20] The year 1862 represented the beginning of a practice that accelerated over the next few years, and the portfolio of Manet's "eight etchings" spelled out the fact that the interweaving of the "original" and the reproduction was not merely a function of student copying but rather the signature feature of an oeuvre, the feature that Manet wished to advertise. The emblem of that wish was the set of multiple credits listed under the two copies after Velasquez – Manet's signature on one side vying with Velasquez's name on the other, and the "éd." of his first name shuttling between "Edouard" and "éditeur." (Beneath those dual signatures, the names of the "éditeurs" Cadart and Chevalier and the printer Delâtre are printed together with the larger, capitalized title of the "original" image, such as to suggest Manet's part in a larger apparatus of printerly collaboration, publication, and mechanical reproduction.) Thus Manet indicated that he was indeed both the plagiarizing "bastard" of Velasquez (and Goya), and that his "originality" was predicated on that plagiarism.

Two of the etchings in the portfolio were copies of works attributed to Velasquez (already copied by Goya and others), four were copies after his own works, and two, *The Toilette* and *The Boy with the Dog*, were "original" etchings with looser ties to "original" paintings by Manet as well as markedly looser handling than the other prints in the portfolio, themselves already rougher in treatment than was characteristic of the usual reproduction etching. In the case of the etchings "after" his own works, it is not always entirely evident which is to be understood as coming first, the drawing, the painting, or the etching, and so the order of "original" conception, sketch toward a work, the work itself, the copy after it, and the advertisement for it, is not clear either. For of course, most of the etchings were published before the works they reproduce were exhibited (*The Absinthe Drinker*, *The Espada*, *The Urchin/ The Little Girl*; only the copy of *The Spanish Singer* appeared after the painting was exhibited, at the Salon of 1861). Moreover, the two that were copies after Velasquez were then exhibited as "original" prints, mounted on the wall, signed as Manet's works and presented in the same forum as his "original" paintings (at the Salon des Refusés), while also keeping company with an "original"/copy print after another of his own recently exhibited paintings (*Lola de Valence*, at Martinet's). As if to underline that confusion, and to accent the imbricated relationship between "original" and museum copy upon which his work was increasingly based, Manet varied the amount of painterly gesture and blank paper from state to state of his portfolio etchings, running the gamut between fleshed-out reproduction of the "original" and "autographic" treatment replete with the artist's signature marks – playing around with the process of etching and printing so as to disturb further the boundary between the communication of authentic individuality and the function of reproduction.

Finally, some of the etchings in Manet's portfolio reversed the orientation of the "original" images of which they were copies (this is the case of *The Spanish Singer, Philip IV* and *The Urchin*); some did not (*The Espada, The Little Cavaliers*). In general, the failure to take into account the fact of image reversal with any consistency or to ensure that the print would reproduce the correct orientation of the original, where ordinary mechanical copyists took care to make certain of just that, speaks to Manet's privileging of the etching plate over and above the prints pulled from it – his devotion to the most "original" phase of printmaking, in which the hand of the author works physically to produce an image and leave its mark, over and above the mechanical part of the process, in which the printing press comes into play with its mechanism of reversal and reduplication. But paradoxically, this inconsistency on Manet's part also results in an acknowledgment of that very mechanism: rather than repressing it, as other mechanical reproductions did, it foregrounds the fact of reversal as a function of reproduction, adding to the opacity of Manet's copies in relation to their originals along the way. And Manet then made the fact of mechanical reversal integral to his mode of generating new images, underlined by his 1862 portfolio in relation to the two exhibitions of his works that followed in 1863.

To start, the printed reversal of *The Spanish Singer* (fig. 38) with which the portfolio began righted the left-handedness of the guitarist and, whether intentionally or not, addressed the problem of his bodily and instrument orientation by inscribing it within the process of printmaking.[21] In the Salon of 1861, that painting had been much admired and had gained notice, as well as an honorable mention, for Manet – as a painter of Spanish themes. That the etching after *The Spanish Singer* inaugurated the portfolio meant that Manet wished to capitalize on his first Salon success and market himself in the light of it as "the painter of the *Guitarist*,"[22] which Théophile Gautier, author of the 1843 *Voyage en Espagne (Tra los montes)*, had described as an absolutely authentic representation of Spanishness. From its costuming down to its coloring and brushwork, Gautier had declared that it spoke in a genuinely colloquial Spanish accent:

Caramba! Here is a *Guitarero* who hasn't stepped out of a comic opera, and who would cut a poor figure in a romantic lithograph. But Velasquez would have given him a friendly wink, and Goya would have asked him for a light for his *papelito*. How heartily he sings as he plucks away at his guitar! We can almost hear him. This bold Spaniard in his *sombrero calanes* and short southern jacket wears pants. Alas! Figaro's knee

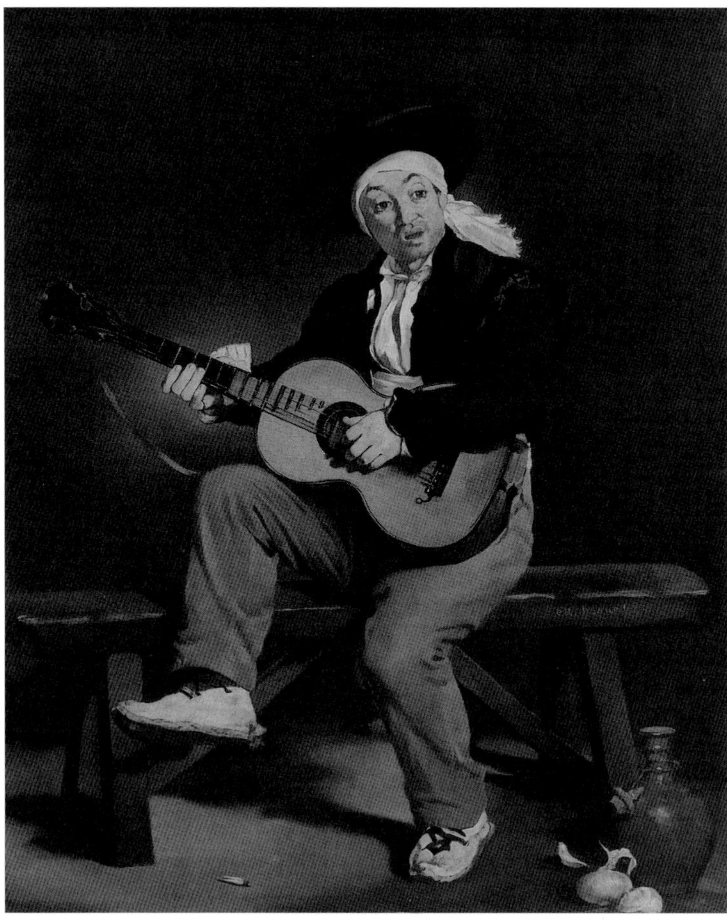

38 Edouard Manet, *The Spanish Singer*, 1860, oil on canvas, 147.3 × 114.3 cm. The Metropolitan Museum of Art, New York, Gift of William Church Osborn, 1949. (49.58.2).

breeches are now worn only by the *espadas* and *bandilleros,* but the *alpargates* atone for this concession to civilized fashions. There is a great deal of talent in this life-sized figure, broadly painted in true color and with a bold brush.[23]

That the print of *The Spanish Singer* corrected the problematic orientation of its "original" suggests that Manet might have counted on using his *avertissement* to enhance the authenticity for which the painting had already been praised – using his copy, in effect, to edit his original and promote a revised, polished version of the reputation that he had garnered with it. But it was not merely a case of cleaning up the one inaugural picture.

The flipping of *The Spanish Singer* was just one of a series of explorations of the relationship between the bodies of represented people and the orientation of pictures, the relay between bodiliness and mechanicalness embedded in the labor of the artist, that went on in various ways throughout Manet's career.[24] Indeed, the reorienting of his first Salon picture in his portfolio print of it seems to have proposed a particular mode of working between copy and conception, reference and further reference, one picture and another, that began to underwrite Manet's production, especially during the next

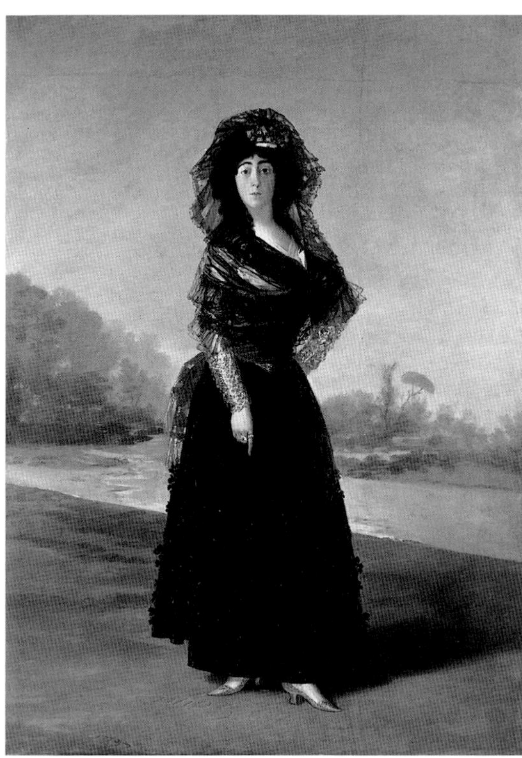

39 Francisco Goya, *Duchess of Alba*, 1799, oil on canvas, 201.2 × 149.3 cm. Courtesy of The Hispanic Society of America, New York.

year as he prepared for his exhibition at Martinet's and the Salon des Refusés. For even when he did not use his copies to correct his originals, he used the reversal inherent in printmaking to move from one composition to the next, to assert connections, not only between other people's paintings and his own but also within his own oeuvre, across exhibitions and exhibited works. The period was a time of discovery and concentrated work in and with that process.

It is fitting that it was Manet's copy after Velasquez's *Portrait of Philip IV* that seems to have set this process in motion. Again, in addition to translating the portrait into his own printerly "handwriting," Manet's print flipped the original painting. *The Gypsies*, in turn, which was shown at Martinet's, reversed the orientation of the print of *Philip IV*, so that the crooked arm of the standing gypsy is again the left arm, though the body of that figure is twisted in the opposite direction from that of the original figure of Philip IV, such that his elbow juts out toward, rather than inward away from, the viewer. His print of *The Gypsies*, with which he was represented in Cadart's first fascicule of modern etchings and which appeared with its original at Martinet's, re-reverses the left–right direction of the image, so that the print conforms to the orientation of the print after *Philip IV*, while retaining the difference in the bodily twist toward the viewer. *Lola de Valence*, one of the prominent pictures at Martinet's, then returns to the original orientation of Velasquez's painting, which is also that of Goya's *Duchess of Alba* to which the painting refers as well (fig. 39), while altering the stance of the feet to conform to contemporary photographs of dancers.[25] Meanwhile, another painting at Martinet's, *The*

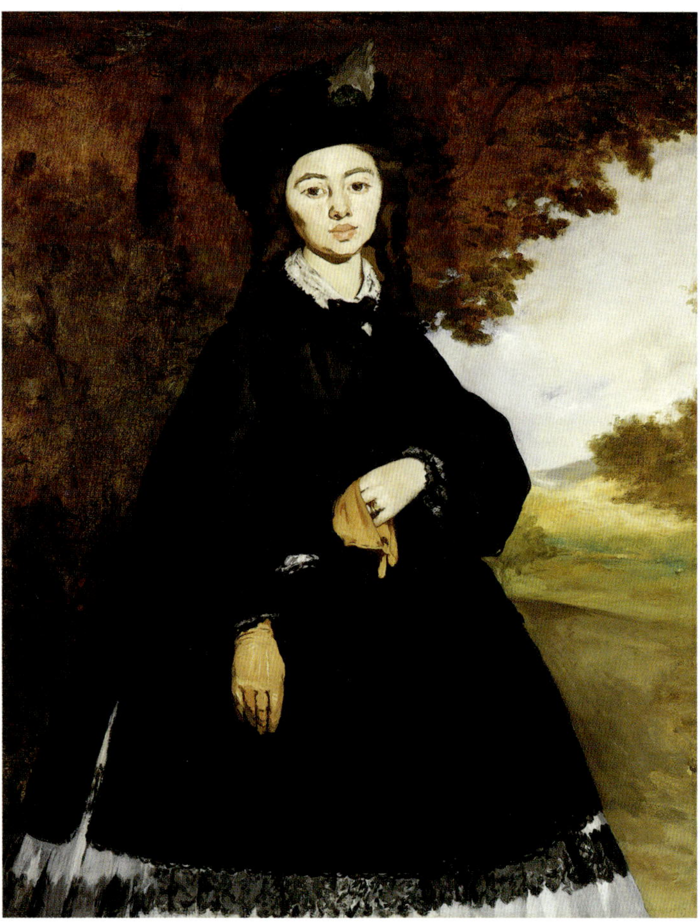

40　Edouard Manet, *Madame Brunet*, 1860, oil on canvas, 130 × 98 cm. Private collection, New York.

Streetsinger, also returns to the orientation of *Philip IV*, though it does so less obviously, altering the position of the left arm but retaining the crooked right arm, hiding the position of the legs beneath a long skirt, and like *Lola de Valence* giving over the whole stance to a female figure of the modern French *demi-monde*: so that the process of image reversal and re-reversal, already associated with the movement back and forward, left and right, of an otherwise frontal body, is attached to a play of gender reversal, class inversion, racial shifting, and modernization. At the same time, the *Young Man in the Costume of a Majo*, which was one of the three paintings to go on view at the Salon des Refusés, reverses the left–right orientation of *Philip IV* once again, giving the crooked elbow to the right side of the majo's body, which is to say, to the left side of the picture – while altering the stance of the legs and the position of the other arm, and shifting the hispanicism of the image to one of modern bullfight costuming. In addition, the portrait of Mme Brunet (fig. 40), another painting that possibly was shown at Martinet's in 1863, maintains the orientation of the original *Philip IV*, not to mention that of the *Duchess of Alba*.[26] Finally, the etching after *Lola de Valence*, which appeared both with the flipped copy of *Philip IV* at the Salon des Refusés and by itself in Cadart's October portfolio of the same year, stuck to the orientation of its original, while the lithograph

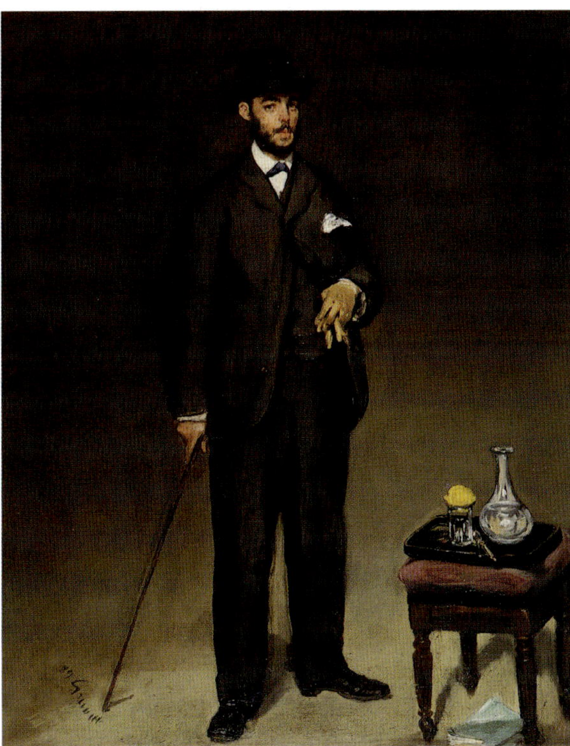

41　Edouard Manet, *Portrait of Théodore Duret*, 1868, oil on canvas, 46.5 × 35.5 cm. Musée du Petit Palais, Paris.

that had appeared earlier that year (in March, at the same time as the show at Martinet's), on the cover of Astruc's song "Lola de Valence," again reversed the image.[27]

I am not arguing for a chronological sequence of production here, though I do think that Manet's viewing of Velasquez's portrait in the Louvre was a critical moment in his early practice, and that his copy after it, to which he gave pride of place both in his "eight etchings" and at the Salon des Refusés, was seminal for his production of standing single-figure pictures, in theatrical costume and "native" clothing, over the next several years. (Manet's portrait of Théodore Duret, fig. 41, is a somewhat later example of this. But even Manet's other single-figure paintings which do not take up the crooked elbow and slack arm contrapposto of Velasquez's portrait and its reversal in the etched copy bear the deadpan, outward-facing traces of that first encounter.) Some time between the show at Martinet's and the retrospective of 1867, the *Portrait of Philip IV* seems to have yielded another one of those revisions suggested to Manet in the relay between painting, copying and printing, and exhibiting. This time it was a revision of an original oil painting: the original Velasquez-like blank background of *Lola de Valence*, as it was exhibited in 1863 and as it was retained in the etching of the dancer, was changed to include the back of some theater wings, whose contour echoes the line of the tree behind Philip IV, such that a landscape is made over in the image of the theater in the meeting between the two images.[28]

What is remarkable about all this printed and painted back-and-forth between left and right, and its tracing back to the "autographic" print after *Philip IV*, is the way

Manet's portfolio ties together exhibition value with the mechanical reproduction, showing how the aura of the original work of art depends upon the latter and locating Manet's "individuality" within the play of duplication, his "originality" within the performance of the copy. For it constitutes Manet's activity of troping, and even his portraitist's devotion to representing this individual and that, with all their class and gender differentiation and personal and historical specificity, on the ground of reproduction, explicitly identifying his (and his subjects') singularity with rather than against the duplicate, and defining his inventiveness in terms of the repetition and reversal of the mechanical template. Copying was still and always had been a formative part of the artist's apprenticeship, going toward the eventual production of a mature signature style, just as troping on the history of art was and remained common practice for all artists. But for Manet, copying was the very signature of his "originality": in his work the mechanical and the original were patently intertwined rather than implicitly opposed terms, and every "original" gesture was stamped with the mechanical while every mechanical repetition was marked with "originality." It was this production of an "original" modern "individuality" out of the mechanical mold of the reproduced museum piece that the portfolio of "eight etchings" advertised, and that found its emblem in the image of Philip IV.

THE SOCIÉTÉ DES AQUAFORTISTES AND THE AUTOGRAPHIC PRINT

In September 1862, Baudelaire reviewed Manet's portfolio and its place in the agenda of the Société des Aquafortistes in the *flaneuriste Le Boulevard*. Speaking briefly of Manet's Spanish subjects, his taste for modernity, and his "lively and broad, sensitive, audacious imagination" as the necessary "symptoms" of the authentic modern artist, Baudelaire went on to write more generally and at length about modern etching, its expression of the "personal character of the artist" and the espousing of the aquatint by the group of "young artists" gathered by Cadart.[29] The alliance between the goals of Cadart and those of Martinet is implicit in the emphasis upon youth. But more important is the stress laid on etching, particularly the aquatint, as the autographic medium of modernity: "the sharpest possible translation of the character of the artist."[30] Simultaneously remarking on its aristocracy and its economy – in the double sense of high speed and low cost[31] – Baudelaire cautioned against vulgarizing the aquatint by seeking too much popularity for it and warned that not all artists had temperaments fitted to the exigent immediacy of the medium. Manet was among those few who could "promenade the needle over the black plate that will reproduce all too faithfully all the arabesques of fantasy, all the hatchings of caprice!" whose aquatints would "glorify the individuality of the artist . . . describ[ing] on the plate his most intimate personality."[32] There are, said Baudelaire, "as many manners of cultivating aquatint as there are aquatint artists,"[33] thus underlining the same ties between individuality and pluralism that Martinet had proclaimed and that Manet represented within his own oeuvre.

The week before Baudelaire's article, Albert de la Fizelière had written about "La Société des Eau-fortistes" in the same journal:

Of all the procedures used to reproduce and multiply works of art by means of printing, there is none more lively, more spontaneous, and above all more sincere than the aquatint etching . . .

Accessible to all who know how to use the pen or the crayon, it offers the precious advantage of conserving the intimate character of the manner of the painter who employs it – either to reproduce his own painting, or to improvise a composition on the copper itself.

An aquatint print is always, to the same degree as a drawing, an original work. From that fact derives the value that certain celebrated plates have achieved, a value that is often equal to that of a unique work, because they carry in themselves the indelible seal of the master, and conserve for the eyes of the enlightened amateur the true pictorial qualities in which the thought of the author springs up beneath the cutting edge of the tool, in which his intention expresses itself . . .

It is not necessary to seek a name or a title imprinted at the base of a print in order to know how to attribute to any master of a vigorously individual temperament an aquatint that he will have treated to the complete expression of his independence and his talent.[34]

Unlike Baudelaire, de la Fizelière emphasized the aquatint as a reproductive medium, but in every other way his valuation of it was the same: it was the best reproducible means of gaining direct access to the artist's signature style, his work of the hand, his thought, his intentions. It was reproducible and it was original; it was a means of diffusion, but in this medium there was no substantial difference between the painting and the print, the source image on the copper plate and the reproductive proofs pulled from it, the imprint of the hand and temperament and the impression produced and reproduced by the printing press. For the aquatint represented that oxymoron the original copy, the autographic duplicate. De la Fizelière went on to suggest that the aquatint was the medium of replication that the connoisseur should prefer, for it was such a direct and authentic index of the artist's "handwriting" that it even dispensed with the need for a signature: "Thus one may say that the aquatint, in the estimation of someone given to the analysis of works of art, seeking to comprehend the principle and the means of execution of this or that school, this or that master, is the print medium par excellence, and the most intelligent and truthful agent of vulgarization."[35] There is a paradox here, of course, and in their different ways both Baudelaire and de la Fizelière were alive to it: in Baudelaire's essay, it emerges in his worries over the possible popularization of the medium he felt to be a properly aristocratic one; in de la Fizelière's article, it creeps in the form of the word vulgarisation – read mechanical reproduction and mass dissemination. Indeed, inasmuch as the aquatint stood for the paradoxical conflation of the original and the copy, it signaled the imbrication of authenticity and mechanicalness that was integral to the autographic print.

Some of that mechanical implication is felt in an 1863 piece on the Société des Aquafortistes and the renaissance of the aquatint by Paul de St. Victor, in the very language of temperamental immediacy that it deploys:

In the last two centuries, the aquatint was the caprice and recreation of the masters, they threw down on the plate in all its liveliness the idea or the conception that the brush would have slowed down; they drew on the varnished plate as they drew on paper. Their most intimate confidences are written in this free and rapid form, for the aquatint of a great painter always presupposes a burst of verve that he did not want to let cool. He was in a rush, inspiration came to him, the demon of verve nudged him, when instead of the brush he took up the point . . . He was in haste to fix that fugitive vision, to bite the copper plate with acid and retain on it the image that passed through his brain. His hand flew over the varnish and discovered the barely grazed metal beneath it; he threw the acid on it . . . the aquatint was made. – The aquatint is the sponge of Zeuxis falling upon the canvas, and there, in one spurt, forming the froth that his brush would not have been able to render.[36]

De St. Victor may have felt the aquatint to be an art of the old masters, but he also described it as a quintessentially modern medium. Indeed, it was as if it were some sort of subjective photograph: undertaken and produced with lightning speed, it rendered the imagination of the artist in terms of the automatism and reflexivity of photography – the "sponge of Zeuxis falling" like rays of light on photographic emulsion, registering an immediate impression. (At the same time, it was evidently comparable to a bodily emission, an ejaculation.)

Others put the problem more explicitly in terms of the invasion of photography. In his essay of support for the Société des Aquafortistes during the month of Manet's portfolio in 1862, Martinet himself wrote the following:

Etching in the black manner began to slow the zeal of the burin-etchers; photography seemed to have paralyzed their efforts, not that the latter replaced etching, but it invaded everything.

We are far from underestimating the services of photography; but everyone feels the necessity of a reaction against its incursions. From this idea was born the Société des aqua-fortistes.[37]

This was an "invasion" that clearly encompasssed both the original and the reproductive print, and not only etching but other print media as well, including engraving and lithography, the latter of which Manet also pursued. Just as, in this account, the *aqua-forte* meant not only the aquatint etching per se but also that end of the printerly spectrum that was attached to the hand and the temperament of the artist, eliding the distinction between copy and original in the direction of originality, so "photography" signified not only photography per se but also the mechanicalness of the mechanical reproduction – the lack of hand and temperament, the distance from originality, and the black-and-white opposition between the original and the mechanical copy. Accordingly, the twin discourses on the artist's reproduction and the renaissance of the artist's etching laid out a print field in which the reproduction and the autograph were simultaneously diametrically opposed, mutually implicated, and thoroughly intertwined – and in which the age of the decline of "aura," famously diagnosed by Walter Benjamin as a consequence of the mechanical reproduction, was at the same time the moment of the efflorescence and apogee of aura, predicated on the mechanical reproduction.[38]

The next year, in his preface to the first annual volume of the Société des Aquafortistes, Théophile Gautier sounded the same note more expansively than Martinet; indeed, he was explicit about the intertwining of the invasion of photography – read mechanical reproduction – and the rise of the "auratic" artist's print, even going so far as to declare that entanglement to be foundational to the Société des Aquafortistes:

> In these times in which photography charms the vulgar by the mechanical fidelity of its reproductions, it was inevitable that a tendency to the free caprice and the picturesque fantasy would declare itself in art. The need to react against the positivism of the instrument-mirror led more than one painter to take up the point of the aquatint etcher, and from the reunion of such artists' talents, tired of seeing walls covered with monotonous images from which the soul is absent, was born the Société des Aquafortistes . . .[39]

The "positivism of the instrument-mirror" was what the Société des Aquafortistes was founded to combat; its mission as an association of printmakers was, like that of Martinet's association of exhibiting individualities and young originals, to support and celebrate the signature of temperament – as against and in reaction to the mechanicalness of the photograph and its allied media. In short, the artist's etching, and with it the Société des Aquafortistes, was a printerly variation on a larger concern with protecting the soul of the artist against the "vulgar" fascination with transparency and mechanical reproducibility. Reversing both Benjamin's equation and the positivist art-historical teleology that puts "Romanticism" and "Realism" in a historical sequence, Gautier asserts a dialogic relation between the mechanical reproduction and the autographic imprint, as well as between the realist impulse and the romantic individual.[40]

Gautier proceeded to detail the relation between aquatint etching and the index of individuality at the technical level, stating that "No medium, in effect, is more simple, more direct, or more personal than the aquatint":[41]

> Once the mold is complete, the plate is made; one can pull it immediately, and right away have the very idea of the master, all sparkling with life and spontaneity, without the mediation of any translation. Every aquatint is an original drawing; how many charming motifs, how many exquisite intentions, how many impulsive movements has this rapid and easy method of etching conserved, which is capable of immortalizing drafts of which the original sheet of paper keeps no trace! But, to succeed with it requires a decision of the hand, a certainty of the feature, a prescience of effect, which not all honest and meticulous talents possess; aquatint does not suffer hesitation, retouching, or correction. Finish and finicky rendering do not suit it. But it will never betray naiveté of spirit; it understands understatement; in aquatint a few brusque hatchings are sufficient to comprehend and express your secret dream.[42]

Brusqueness and immediacy were not only the signs of the unmediated directness of the aquatint, they were also indices of the modernity in which the photograph and other mechanical reproductions shared. What was remarkable was that they simultaneously registered the hand and thought of the artist and the function of instantaneous reproducibility. It also happens that they were the signature of Manet the printmaker.

The Société des Aquafortistes had "no other code but individualism," stressed Gautier, and the artist's aquatint had "the authenticity of a signature, because the talent of he who practices it is signed in every cut."[43] And, excusing the extremity of certain "wild and truculent" practitioners, he again pitted the aquatint against the photograph, or against "photography, lithography, aquatint, etching whose crossed hatchings come to a point in the middle; in a word, regular, automatic work without inspiration, which denatures the very idea of the artist."[44] And like Martinet's gallery, he insisted that the Société des Aquafortistes wanted its plates to "speak directly to the public"[45] with as little mediation as possible. Along the way he emphasized heterogeneity as a necessary feature of the society's code of individualism, again much like Martinet and the Société Nationale des Beaux-Arts:

> Each artist must invent and etch for himself the subject that he brings to the collective oeuvre. No genre prevails, no manner is recommended; one is free to show all the originality that one possesses, and no one will find fault. This artist will strike his copperplate brutally as if with blows of the saber, and will content himself with a few rough and summary features, writing his thought only for those eyes that know how to read; that one will push toward effect, going over his hatchings, accumulating work; that other will seek a blond effect, while a fourth will risk brusque oppositions of black and white . . .[46]

One might contend that Manet sought all these effects in his artist's etchings which were at once copies and reproductions of the old masters and of himself – making his portfolio emblematic of the Société des Aquafortistes's signature combination of individuality, replicability, and heterogeneity, of the direct imprint of temperament and the "automatic" reproduction of the "traditions of the masters."

Other, slightly later writers for the Société des Aquafortistes said many of the same things that Gautier had said in 1863, but more than Gautier they emphasized the ambiguity of the relation between the autographic print and the mechanical reproduction. This was the case of Jules Janin, in his preface to the second annual volume of the Société. He began by stressing the opposition between the machine and the hand and genius of the artist, saying that the members of the society were:

> very hostile to the machine and full of respect for the hand that is full of flash and genius. They have resolved to conjure away invading photography with all their forces and to defend . . . the enchanted domain of the great masters. . . . they have opposed the burin, which etches imperishable works on copper and steel, to collodion, which evaporates with the slightest breath . . . the most fanatical supporters of photography have saluted etching . . .[47]

But very quickly photography began to trade places with the aquatint. In its evanescence photography seemed to take over the slightness of the aquatint (while aquatint acquired the gravity of tradition), and then aquatint became "as prompt as photography."[48] The next year, Thoré-Bürger reversed the equation, stating that "Relative to drawing, the aquatint is the analogue of the print shop and the press, which multiply written thought."[49] And finally, in 1866, Castagnary shifted the emphasis again, though he still insisted that the aquatint was "the expression of individual thought," that it was "personality itself," that the hand and the spirit were forged together in a form of pure originality that suppressed mere skill.[50] Yet Castagnary spoke also of aquatint's fashionability, and its potential return to its eighteenth-century status as a "charming pastime for a few women of the world."[51] Not quite photography then, but a chic print medium, a minor French art, in which volatility – the transient reproducibility of modernity – begins to jostle with originality as the dominant characteristic of the medium, and in which ephemerality competes with permanence in the same combination that Baudelaire had been ascribing to modern art from the beginning of his career as an art critic.

In the same year Philippe Burty shifted the focus to the aquatint still more. Writing for the *Gazette des Beaux-Arts*, with its trademark commitment to finish in its reproductions, and later stressing "a facility with the etcher's tool that could not be acquired at the first stroke,"[52] Burty praised the aquatint for its ability to render not so much the interior subjectivity of the artist as the exteriority of objects, in particular color and clothes:

> [it is] capable, more than any other procedure, of expressing coloration, the epidermis of objects . . . Where the modern burin tends only to reproduce the discrete coloration of the fresco, the general details of the picture, or the reserved expression of the portrait, the point, more lively, more alert, more passionate, excavates the shadows, burrows in the folds, brings out the angles, makes the planes reflect and the facets sparkle; it illuminates the gaze, it secures the gesture, it embroiders the garment of the prince with gold and cuts into tatters the old clothes of the poor man . . .[53]

The liveliness of the aquatint still registers the *anima* of the artist for Burty, but at the same time it is an animation put to the service of rendering princely raiment and pauper's rags. And it is an animation that is aligned with *coloris*, moreover, *coloris* as the "epidermis" – the fabric and ornament – of picture and world as much as the autograph of the artist.[54] This description brings to mind Velasquez's princes and paupers, and Manet's copies after them in the Cadart portfolio. It is also reminiscent of Charles Blanc's discussion of Velasquez in the *Gazette des Beaux-Arts* of 1863, illustrated with the reproductive etching of Velasquez's *Philip IV* by Haussoullier. As such it opens back onto the "Spanishicity" of Manet's etchings for the Société des Aquafortistes, not to mention his paintings at Martinet's.

"EAUX-FORTES ESPAGNOLES"

"Manet! his Spanish aquatints create the illusion of a painting, so colored are their patches; but why doesn't he etch his pretty Parisians for us?"[55] As much as Manet's *Philip IV* aquatint signaled his commitment to the autographic print that was also an old master copy, it emblematized the "Spanishicity" of the portfolio of which it was a part: it intertwined hispanicism with its presentation of Manet's "individuality" as a mechanical/"original" function of the "museum without walls." That is, where the print of *The Spanish Singer* advertised Manet as an authentically anecdotal painter of Spanishness, the etched copy after *Philip IV* revised that view to suggest that Manet's hispanicism was filtered through the museum in the figure of Velasquez, and that its authentic accent was a museum performance, put on for the purpose of making a modern exhibition of himself. The same thing was suggested by Manet's copy after *The Little*

Cavaliers, Velasquez's image of a gathering of thirteen seventeenth-century artists including himself, variants of which showed up again in Manet's "original" paintings of *The Spanish Ballet* and *Music at the Tuileries* at Martinet's, and in the background of *Mlle V. . . . in the Costume of an Espada* at the Salon des Refusés. (Manet is reported to have remarked that his *Absinthe Drinker*, among those early works included both in the Cadart portfolio and then at Martinet's, might have been accepted at the Salon of 1860 if only it had a Spanish theme like *The Spanish Singer*.[56] The prominent Spanish leanings of the Cadart portfolio, and then of the shows at Martinet's and the Salon des Refusés, seemed to make good that comment, deliberately casting Manet as the Spanishizing painter he thought the Salon wanted, while at the same time differentiating his "Spanishicity," characterizing it as a dramatic device and modern exhibition strategy, and setting it in relation to the Velasquez-accented French thematics of *The Absinthe Drinker*, the bohemian world of *The Gypsies*, and the Velasquez-based *Old Musician*.)

What did Spain and Spanish art represent to Manet? A possible answer is provided by Charles Blanc in an essay of 1863 that also appeared in 1869 as part of his encyclopedic series *Histoire des peintres de toutes les écoles*.[57] Like others, Blanc described Spain as "au-delà des Pyrenées," the Spanish people as a pure-blooded race which at least until recently and unlike other European cultures had retained its ancient character unmixed and untainted. Spanish culture, said Blanc, was one that had an Arab rather than a Greco-Roman cultural foundation, making it in some ways a closer relative of the Orient than of the Occident, and it combined in itself a courtly, Catholic, monarchic outward appearance with a fiercely republican spirit. The Spaniard had "a strongly marked physiognomy, a character of constantly preserving the color and truth of its locale, of being, in a word, above all and always Spanish" and of "following a path completely contrary to the tendencies of the other peoples of Europe."[58] Spain, in short, was at once racially pure and colonially invaded, both European and not-European, Western and non-Western, simultaneously close to France and the exotic other to France.

The school of painting associated with Spain stood in ambiguous relation to the North–South antinomies of nineteenth-century art-historical and critical writing: it was geographically southern, close to Africa and full of Moorish elements, but overtaken by the northern house of the Hapsburgs and raided by the French in the Napoleonic era, so that for a time much of it was housed in Paris in the Galerie Espagnole.[59] Spanish painting was dominated by the two figures of the courtly, painterly Velasquez, with his eclectic referencing of Raphael, Titian, and Rubens, and the dark, romantic Goya, with his brutally critical, anti-institutional print series and his eccentric "black paintings." Distinct in its tendencies from both Dutch and Florentine painting, Spanish art was neither decidedly northern nor purely southern. However, its tradition was a coloristic one, and according to Blanc and others, the best art of Spain betrayed its pure, primitive, not-quite-European character in its colorism. (Obviously, in spite of what was said about the colorism of the aquatint, paintings were needed to make any kind of point about color, and Manet took up that challenge in a concerted way in the paintings exhibited in 1863.) The colorism of Spanish art was thought to be most analogous to the Oriental colorism of Venice, that other liminal school to which Manet referred heavily in 1863. And interestingly – for its appositeness to the terms in which Manet's paintings were discussed throughout the '60s – Spanish colorism was also described as particularly attuned to the bottom-most rung of the genre ladder: still life.

I shall return to the claims about color, and the emphasis upon Spanish costuming found in nineteenth-century French discourse on Spanish art and culture, in the next chapter. For now, it must be said that it was Velasquez who represented the art of Spain to writers like Blanc. Velasquez was the most Spanish of Spanish painters, always paying in Spanish coin, as Blanc put it, and returning from his trip to Italy just as Spanish and just as Velasquez as he had ever been.[60] Velasquez was the colorist and costumist of the Spanish tradition; as the counterpart to the international Rubens, he was the representative of the Spanish court; and as the painter who had traveled elsewhere in Europe, he represented Spain's place in the European museum. Second to Velasquez, according to Blanc, was Goya, whom he viewed as a model of eccentric individuality, like no one else, and outside of all schools or general tendencies, at a time when Spain was being violently invaded by France: thus, in addition to representing the republican rather than the courtly side of Spanish character, Goya was simultaneously a model of the modern artist, the proud unassimilability of Spain, the traumatic encounter between modern France and ancient Spain, and modern Spain's post-Napoleonic decline. That is, Goya represented the dilemma and the romance of modern Spain much more than he represented the Spanish art tradition per se. And thus it was Goya rather than Velasquez whose name signified Spanishness for writers of the romantic persuasion, such as Baudelaire and Gautier.

Blanc also published an article on Velasquez in the *Gazette des Beaux-Arts* of July 1863, after the show at Martinet's. (This was the essay illustrated with Haussoullier's etching.) Blanc never mentioned Manet, but he did describe Velasquez's sober colorism in terms that are suggestive in relation to both Manet's caricatural colorism and Burty's (and others') discussion of the colorism of the aquatint:

> His palette, only very lightly loaded, is composed of two or three tones with which he combines all the variants of gray, which is the constant base of his color. Look at these full-length portraits; they are all colored on this theme: the tones of flesh and the black suit thrown into relief against a gray background; gray stockings thrown into relief against a black background. In Velasquez . . . the white is écru; the black is never matte . . . The merit of Velasquez . . . consists in uniting the charm of a colorist with an extreme sobriety of color. He is a gourmet . . . he is a virtuoso who executes excellent music with two or three notes, where Rubens or Veronese would take the occasion to play a piece with a full orchestra.[61]

Velasquez's paintings, in other words, were coloristic paradoxes; their colorism was a subtle, black, white, and gray colorism that might be expected to translate well into the black, white, and gray "colorism" and quasi-photographic tonality of the aquatint. Even when addressing Velasquez's brighter colors, Blanc described a high-contrast palette in which reds and blues are divided and opposed to one another like black and white, and internally split into nuances like the gray scale of the aquatint (or the photograph): "All the varieties of red play into it and are opposed to nuances of blue, it is true that this blue, very lightly glazed with yellow in the skirt of the spinner, turns to green; but the blues, more or less broken, are all on one side and all the reds are on another . . ."[62]

And yet Blanc also claimed that Velasquez's paintings were actually very difficult to reproduce in black and white:

> Thus nothing is more embarrassing for an etcher to have to transpose onto his plate than paintings of a coloration similar to that of Teniers or Velasquez, because where the painter was capable of distinguishing two tones of the same value, the etcher is led to confound them. He is therefore forced to make a free interpretation. Moreover, was not Velasquez reproduced beautifully by a painter, no doubt not so skilled, but full of temperament, intuition, extravagance, and genius, that's to say by Goya? Not fearing to invert the order of the values, Goya repainted the portraits of the master in aquatint, he even succeeded, by the manipulation of the paper and the freedom of his treatment of the plate, in giving them a spirit, an allure, a spiced savor that is not found in the original.[63]

One might say, then, that Manet was Velasquez (courtly, purist, *ancien régime* Spain) filtered through Goya (romantic, colonized, modern Spain) and then caricatured, and that in advance of his paintings, his portfolio of aquatints made that filtering and caricaturing his signature, while reversing the order of painting to print and replacing it with a logic of print to painting. If, according to Blanc, Goya was able to reproduce Velasquez successfully only by inverting the values of his paintings, freely interpreting them and making them into new original works of his own, all in the autographic, "coloristic" medium of aquatint, then Manet inverted the values once and twice more, freely interpreted them, and made them yet again into new original works of his own, at once at a second and third remove from the original originals and redoubled in their claims to a new originality, all under the autographic banner of the Société des Aquafortistes. In any case, it is evident that the Janus figure of Velasquez/Goya with which Manet associated himself placed the paradox of the artist's reproductive etching under the sign of a Spanishness that could not be comprehended within the standard polarities – whether North versus South, Occident versus Orient, drawing versus color, ancient versus modern, or original versus copy – of European art history and connoisseurship.

Blanc may not have mentioned Manet with regard to Spanish art, but many others did. Writing of the Cadart portfolio and describing Manet as "the painter of the *Guitarist* which caused such a lively stir at the recent Salon," Baudelaire spoke of Manet's intention to exhibit paintings at the next Salon "touched with the strongest Spanish savor, which leads us to believe that Spanish genius has taken refuge in France"; he also indicated that "Spanish savor" was intimately joined to "a decided taste for . . . modern reality."[64] Thus Baudelaire, with his own signature romantic taste for the modern Goya, not only suggested that Manet's obsession with Spanish art and culture, as promoted in the portfolio of 1862, was a peculiarly modern one but also that it was part of a French dialectic concerning the relationship between modern France and romantic Spain, in which Spain, the nearest exotic other to modern France, having been subject to the incursions of the Napoleonic armies and French imperial regime, was currently mounting a counter-invasion in the form of modern Spanish-flavored art, that is, in the work of Manet.

It seems, indeed, that the Cadart portfolio and the show at Martinet's that it advertised began to solidify Manet's reputation as a "Spanish genius taking refuge in France."

For the responses to both began a consistent trend in the critical reaction to Manet's work, which was to highlight the Spanishness of his French modernity, and which continued until the retrospective of 1867, when Jules Claretie proclaimed Manet "a Velasquez of the boulevards, or a Spaniard of Paris," and Hippolyte Babou remarked that Manet's "little personal museum" could serve as a boudoir and a chapel for a young Spanishwoman visiting Paris.[65] Back in 1863, Thoré wrote that Manet "adores Spain, and the master for whom he has the most affection seems to be Goya, whose vivid and clashing tones, whose free and impetuous touch, he imitates."[66] Paul Mantz wrote that "M. Manet . . . is a Parisian Spaniard" whose "mysterious parentage attaches him to the tradition of Goya," like Baudelaire identifying him as the painter of *The Guitarist* at the Salon of 1861. (He went on to describe Manet's paintings as caricatures of color.[67]) The same refrain is heard in de St. Victor's remarks about Manet's showing in 1863, which flow immediately out of his photographic-sounding discussion of the old master pedigree and temperamental verve of the aquatint, thus tying together the aquatint and "Spanishicity," the earlier print portfolio and the then current exhibition at Martinet's:[68]

> Imagine Goya gone to Mexico, become savage in the *pampas*, scribbling his canvases with the red juice of crushed Mexican beetles, and you will have M. Manet, the realist of the moment. His pictures at the exhibition on the Boulevard des Italiens are hullabaloos of the palette; never has anyone made lines grimace more frightfully or tones cry out so stridently. His *Toréros* would frighten off Spanish cattle . . . There is, nevertheless, a certain talent in his undigested sketches, but we doubt that M. Manet will ever apply himself to refining them. He was more successful with the aquatint than with the canvas: his *Gitanos* have the breeding and bearing of their race. I like above all the one that tips a pitcher into his open mouth with his head thrown back: the *Bevidores* of Velasquez would admit him into their brotherhood.[69]

Situating Manet between Goya and Velasquez, de St. Victor imagined him in Mexico, that site of French imperial domination of the Hispanic world which came to a crisis not many years later and which Manet painted in one of his last hispanicist paintings, *The Execution of Emperor Maximilian* (1868–69). In this context de St. Victor also treated Manet as a caricatural, if not primitivist, colorist. But most importantly, he identified Manet as an aquatint artist, whose etchings he preferred to his paintings because they escaped the latter's modern degeneracy, tied him back to the old masters (Velasquez – as reproduced by Goya, though de St. Victor does not say so), and allowed him to express the racial essence of Spanishness. (Or at least of Spanish gypsies, gypsies being like Jews a class of people identified with the principles of diaspora and exoticism, if not Orientalism: with not exactly European otherness within European France.[70])

In 1862 and then again in 1863 Manet put on view his own personal "galerie espagnole," first in the form of his portfolio of etchings and then in the show at Martinet's. That "galerie espagnole" embraced several of the Spains found in contemporary French writing on the subject, art historical and otherwise. There was Gautier's faux-authentic Spain, in the reversed and corrected orientation of the etched *Spanish Singer*. There was the Spain of Manet's *Philip IV* (and the *Little Cavaliers*), which was at once the Spain of the old court, the Louvre, and the *Gazette des Beaux-Arts*. That was a Spain reproduced and coopted, a Spain inside France. Then there was the Spain of the Velasquez and

Goya-filtered *Gypsies* and its related prints and paintings. That too was a Spain inside France – a migrant Spain, transported outside of itself, reproduced in the form of "eau-fortes espagnoles," remade in the image of the modern French individuality of Manet, and re-autographed in the modern aquatint. Mixing up the distinctions between original and copy, tradition and temperament, one side of the border and the other, the "galerie espagnole" of the Spanish aquatints also pointed to the question that Paul Mantz raised – the absence of Parisians, or rather Parisiennes, in Manet's portfolio. The next year, in the show at Martinet's, there were both Parisians and Parisiennes, painted ones, that is – paintings of Parisians mingling with paintings of Spaniards, mingling with paintings of Parisians dressed up as Spaniards; pictures of *gitanos* mingling with pictures of *demi-mondaines*; not to mention the modern colorist rendering of the Spanish enthusiasts Baudelaire and Gautier and Baron Taylor mingling beneath the Parisian trees of the Tuileries gardens. If there were no Parisians in 1862, it was only because Manet's "eau-fortes espagnoles" served so well to establish him as an "éd. Manet" original, inverting the tones of Velasquez–Goya in order to throw into relief his own imprimatur, and advertise himself as one of the most outstanding of Martinet's stable of young new Parisian talents.

Chapter Five

BETWEEN GAUTIER'S SPAIN AND BAUDELAIRE'S MODERN LIFE: MANET'S SHOW AT MARTINET'S

Before and after the show at Martinet's, Manet's hispanicizing tendencies took a variety of forms, ranging from the picturesque anecdotalism of *The Spanish Singer* (the *papelito, sombrero calanes,* and *alpargates* mentioned by Gautier) and the Murillo-like theme of the street urchin (*The Boy with the Dog, The Old Musician*) – both of which were common hispanicisms in Paris at the time – to the copies after Velasquez and other images referring to the court culture of the Spanish painter, to images celebrating the bullfight, the spectator event that already epitomized Spanish culture in the popular imagination: for example, *The Dead Torero* (fig. 42) from the year after Martinet's, cut down from a larger, *tauromaquia*-referring painting that was shown with the *Christ and Angels* at the Salon of 1864, and which was accused of being a Velasquez plagiarism.[1] Such images were neither novel nor idiosyncratic to Manet: other painters, such as Alfred Dehodencq, who had gone to Spain during the 1848 revolution, had long been submitting *Bullfight(s) in Spain* to the Salon (figs. 43, 44).

What was idiosyncratic to Manet was his emphasis on costuming, which was announced in the titles of the two Spanishizing paintings shown at the Salon des Refusés, together with the Italianizing *Luncheon on the Grass* (then called *Le Bain*), one month after Manet's fourteen paintings went on view at Martinet's: *Mlle V. . . . in the Costume of an Espada,*[2] *Young Man in the Costume of a Majo* (fig. 45). These were individuals who were not Spanish (Victorine Meurent and Manet's own brother Gustave, both of whose features were also to be seen in the *Luncheon on the Grass*) dressing up in Spanish clothing that was clearly not native to them, which was sometimes not even "native" to their sex (as in Victorine's cross-dressing in masculine costume) and which was signaled in sobriquets announcing that these were people dressing up, "in the costume of" Spain. Manet had announced the same theme of dressing up, and tied it more generically to his signature "Spanishicity," in one of the paintings shown at Martinet's – the Goya-based *Young Woman Reclining in Spanish Costume* of 1862 (see fig. 1). In both settings, in other words, Manet distinguished his offerings from the Spanish vogue of the day by underlining not their Spanish authenticity, as in *The Spanish Singer,* but their Spanish theatricality.

And theatricality was a theme to which Manet returned repeatedly, particularly in the context of his Spanishizing paintings, on either side of the show at Martinet's. In

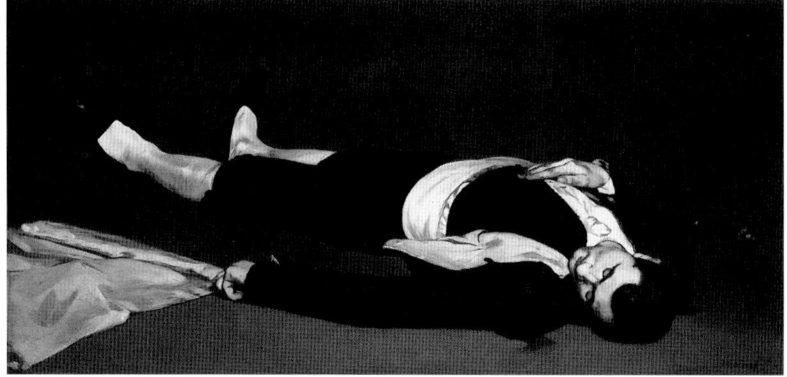

42   Edouard Manet, *The Dead Torero*, 1864–65, oil on canvas, 75.9 × 153.3 cm. National Gallery of Art, Washington, D.C. Widener Collection.

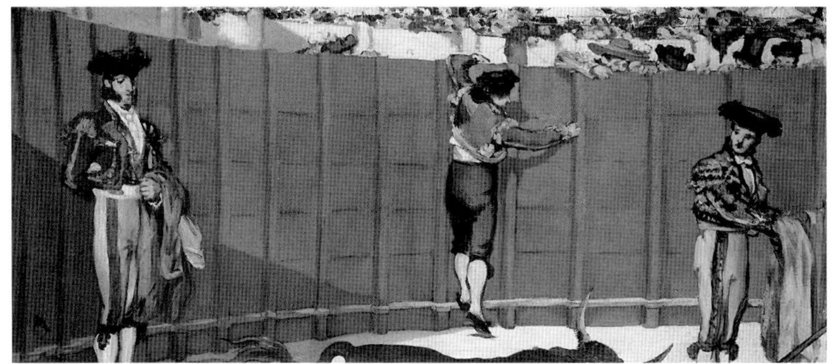

43   Edouard Manet, *The Bullfight*, 1864, oil on canvas, 47.9 × 108.9 cm. The Frick Collection, New York.

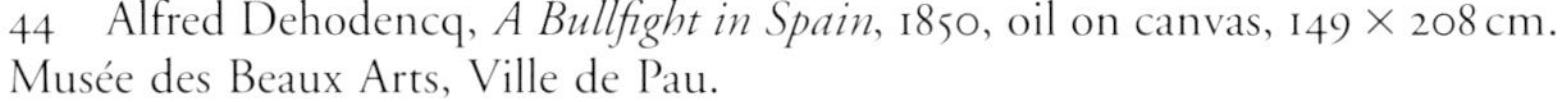

44   Alfred Dehodencq, *A Bullfight in Spain*, 1850, oil on canvas, 149 × 208 cm. Musée des Beaux Arts, Ville de Pau.

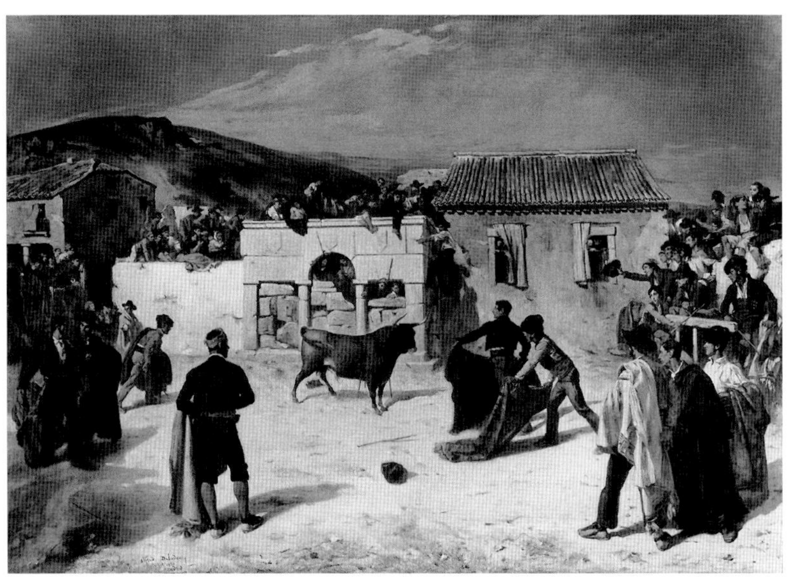

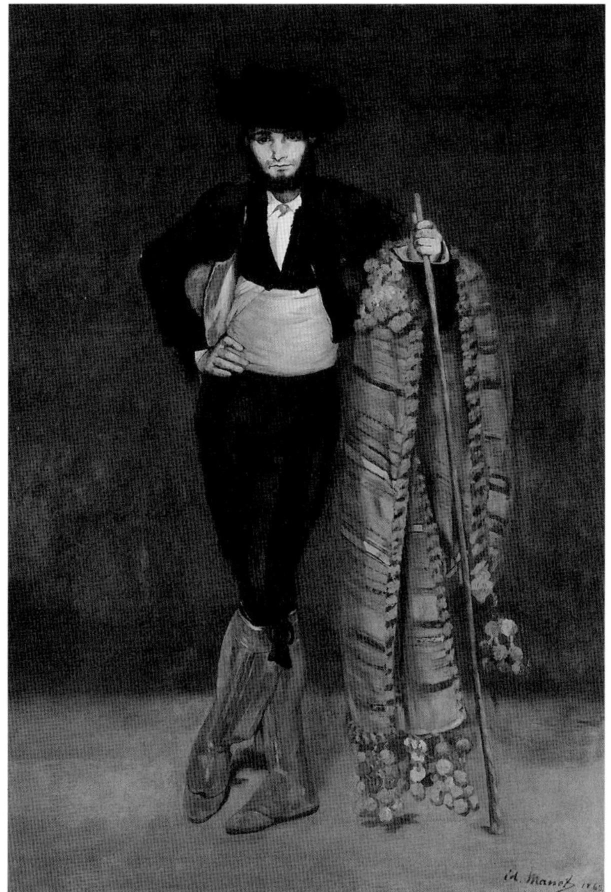

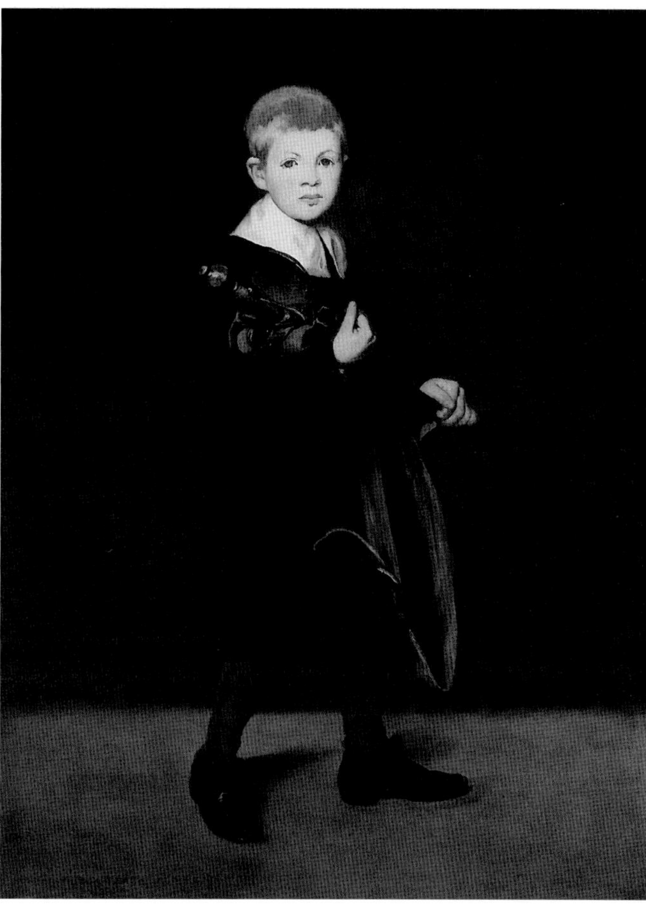

45 Edouard Manet, *Young Man in the Costume of a Majo*, 1863, oil on canvas, 188 × 124.8 cm. The Metropolitan Museum of Art, New York, H. O. Havemeyer Collection, Bequest of Mrs. H. O. Havemeyer, 1929. (29.100.54).

46 Edouard Manet, *Boy with a Sword*, 1861, oil on canvas, 131.1 × 93.4 cm. The Metropolitan Museum of Art, New York, Gift of Erwin Davis, 1889. (89.21.2).

addition to his Spanish copies and anecdotally Spanish paintings, he produced a series of single-figure paintings, which simultaneously declare their theatrical orientations and announce their connections to Velasquez in both specific and general ways. Among the earliest of these was the *Boy with a Sword* of 1861 (fig. 46), which appeared at Martinet's, in which Léon Leenhoff is dressed up in seventeenth-century courtier's costume and holds an outsized sword that is patently a prop. The background is characteristically vacant and undifferentiated, referring to Velasquez's pictures of royal children and court dwarves, and accenting the theatricality of the Spanish artist's way of painting.[3]

Sometimes Manet made the connection to Velasquez specifically theatrical, as in his mid-1860s portrait, called *The Tragic Actor*, of the painter turned actor Philippe Rouvière, famous for his erstwhile role as Hamlet, who in Manet's painting of him takes

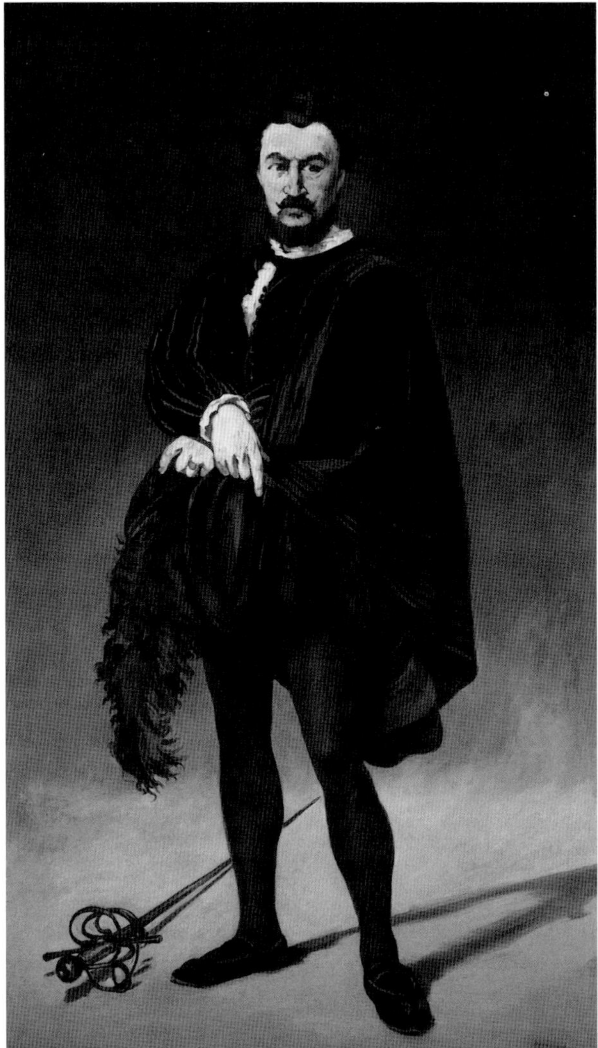

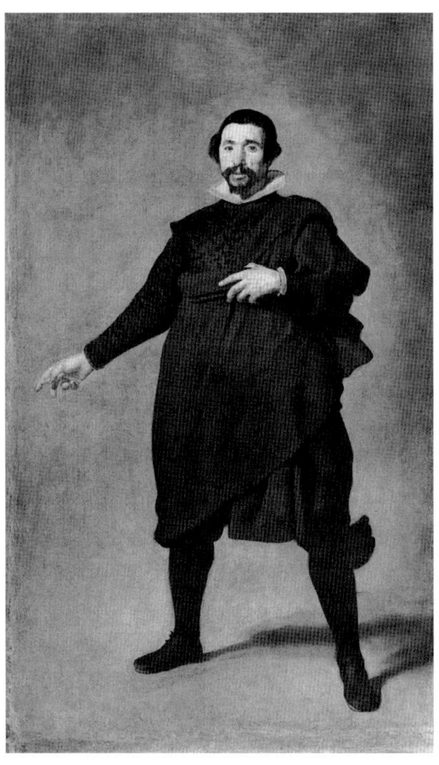

47 (*left*)   Edouard Manet, *The Tragic Actor* (*Rouvière as Hamlet*), 1866, oil on canvas, 187.2 × 108.1 cm. National Gallery of Art, Washington, D.C. Gift of Edith Stuyvesant Gerry.

up a revised version of the pose of a seventeenth-century Spanish actor, Pablo de Valladolid, as painted by Velasquez (figs. 47, 48). (When Manet saw the painting at the Prado during his visit to Spain in 1865, he called it "Portrait of a Famous Actor of the Time of Philip IV.") In Manet's version of the painting, the declamatory pose of *Pablo de Valladolid* is changed to a more static portrait pose, and Hamlet's sword-prop is discarded on the ground that is at once floor and painting, so that it is likened to the Velasquez-based shadow cast by Rouvière, defining that shadow as a painterly prop, equating the accouterments of the theatrical performer with the devices of the painter and claiming them for the space of painting, all under the Spanish sign of Velasquez.

Shortly after *The Tragic Actor*, Manet returned once more to the theme of the Spanish performer, using the combined features of his brother Eugène and a dancer from a Spanish troupe that visited Paris at the time of the 1867 Universal Exposition, to portray

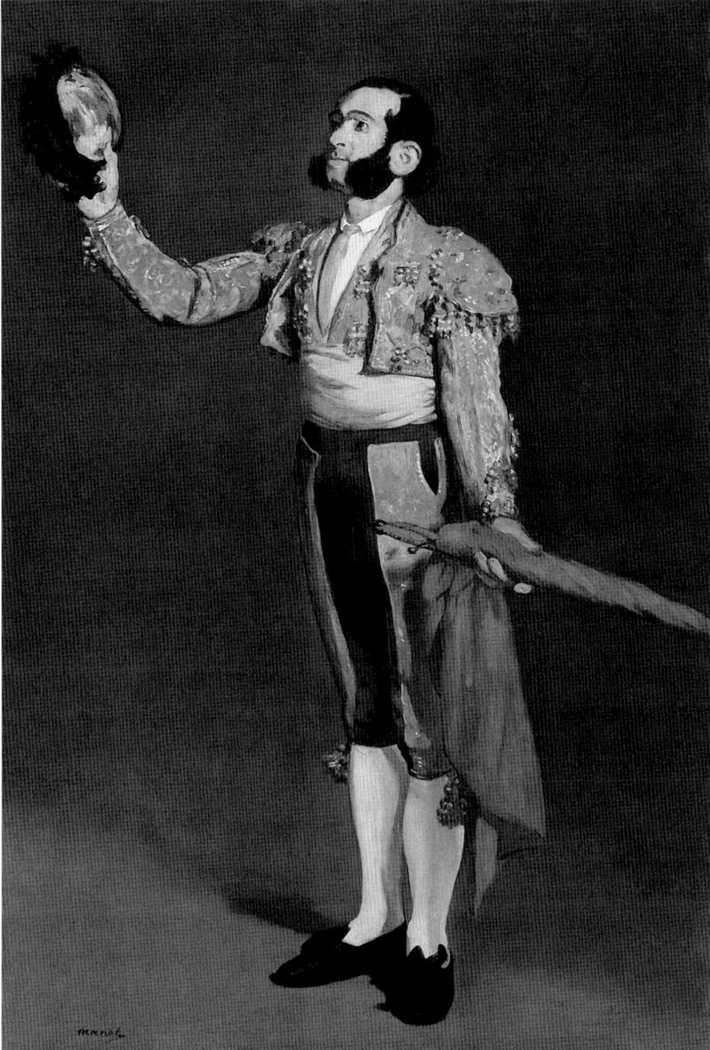

48 (*facing page right*)   Diego Velasquez, *Pablo de Valladolid*, c.1635, oil on canvas, 213.5 × 125 cm. Museo del Prado, Madrid.

49   Edouard Manet, *A Matador*, c.1865–67, oil on canvas, 171.1 × 113 cm. The Metropolitan Museum of Art, New York, H. O. Havemeyer Collection, Bequest of Mrs. H. O. Havemeyer, 1929. (29.100.52).

a matador in whose figure Spanish-style theatricality and Spanish-style painting could be united overtly (fig. 49).[4] But after his retrospective of 1867, there was a general shift in Manet's painting away from his practice of museum quotation, and his emphasis on Spanish painting, the example of Velasquez, and the theme of theatricality. The focus shifted to the more modern model of Goya, and the instances of "Spanishicity" were directed either at contemporary events, as in the Goya-based *Execution of Emperor Maximilian*, or at a more naturalized rendering of French modernity and the modern Frenchwoman, as in *The Balcony* of 1868, also Goya-based.[5] Only one last time after that did Manet turn back to the prototype of Velasquez: toward the end of his career, in one of his very rare self-portraits, which selects and reverses the figure of the painter in *Las Meniñas*. There Manet again pronounced the importance of Velasquez to his self-conception as a painter. But he also naturalized that persona in a way that he never had before, hiding the reference to Velasquez in a refusal of museum-enframed, backward-looking courtliness that was new to him in the 1870s. Back in the early '60s, as is witnessed in the Spanishizing works that he had on display in his "exposition particulière" at Martinet's, the tactic of naturalizing his art-historical references was not only one that Manet eschewed; it was one that his work argued against, repeatedly.

DRESSING UP *À L'ESPAGNOLE*:

BETWEEN SPANISH COSTUME AND FRENCH FASHION

Manet's commitment to the denaturing of the painted persona is even more evident in the *Young Woman Reclining in Spanish Costume* than in the earlier *Boy with a Sword* with which it kept company at Martinet's in 1863. Indeed, the later painting makes its denaturing argument explicit, by combining its overtly Spanish art-historical references with the artifice-embracing theme of costuming. *Young Woman Reclining in Spanish Costume*, for which Manet used the Spanish-looking features of a dark-haired and dark-browed young woman (reputedly the mistress of Nadar), is more singled-minded in its reference to Spanish art history, specifically Goya's pair of nude and clothed *Majas*. It chooses the clothed over the nude figure for its nineteenth-century French updating of Goya's duo, so that the theatrics of costuming are tied to those of coloristic painting. Against the theatrical brown of the background and the isolated props of the gray kitten and the orange oranges, the play of color generated by the young woman's clothing – narrowed to an arrangement of whites, blacks, and pinks that picks up and modifies the colors of the model's hair, skin, and lips, and mediates between those colors and the lusher red of the plump divan on which she reclines and to which her body is fitted – brings out the substituting of paint for cloth for flesh, and the standing-in of the artifices of costuming, furnishing, and painting for the body as Nature made it. Moreover, the clothing that Manet chooses for his young woman is simultaneously masculine and body-revealing, so that the indeterminacy of gender and the confusion between the categories of dressed and undressed in the painting's use of Goya underline the denaturing function of costuming and the reference to Spanish art history. Finally, in titling the painting as he did, and announcing that its model was dressed up in Spanish clothing, Manet equated Spanishness with masquerade and that which is supplementary – added, put on and taken off, rather than fixed, essential, and natural.[6]

Young Woman Reclining in Spanish Costume was the closest that Manet came, within the show at Martinet's and its address to costuming, to the genre of the female nude. Although he had had a nude in the Cadart portfolio, there were no nudes on view at Martinet's. But the *Young Woman Reclining in Spanish Costume* phrased the question of costuming in relation to that of nudity, suggesting that she was painted over the palimpsest of a nude body and making the genre of the nude hover behind her. Over the course of his career Manet painted the nude relatively infrequently, but in the early '60s the genre was one he addressed several times.[7] This began with *The Nymph Surprised* (fig. 50), his revision of the theme of Susannah and the Elders, reworked several times between 1859 and 1861, using the Dutch features of his wife-to-be, Suzanne Leenhoff, to recast a predominantly Northern, Rubensian view of the female nude, and

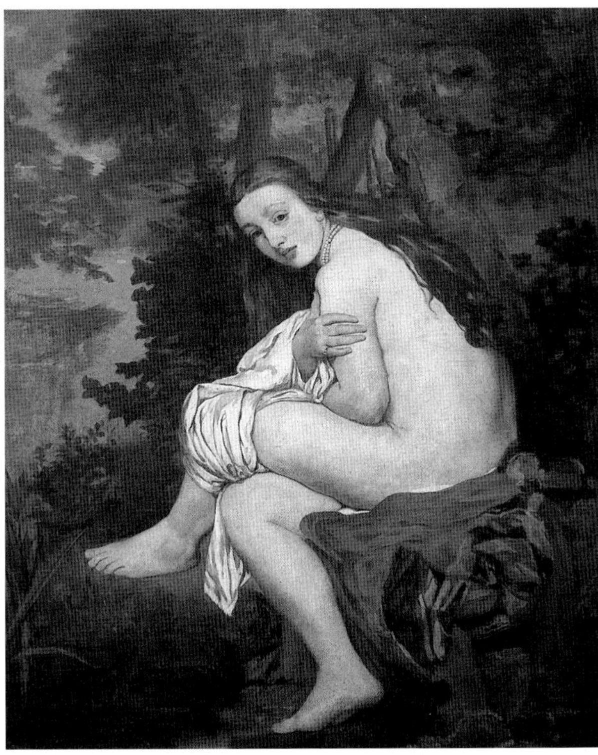

50　Edouard Manet, *The Nymph Surprised*, 1859–61, oil on canvas, 144.5 × 112.5 cm. National Gallery, Buenos Aires. Acquired 1914.

then revised again to be presented as a print in the Cadart portfolio.[8] It continued with his two most notorious images, the *Luncheon on the Grass* and *Olympia* of 1863, whose genesis could be traced back to Manet's copying of Titian's *Venus of Urbino* in the Uffizi upon his visit to Florence in 1856. Those paintings used the features of the Parisian *demi-mondaine* Victorine Meurent to link Manet's painting to the Italian tradition, again within the genre of the female nude, so that between them and the body of *The Surprised Nymph*, Manet ran the gamut of the standard art-historical antithesis between the national and racial schools of North and South.

Of course, there was another term in the racialist categories of nineteenth-century art history that fell outside the dominant polarities of the European tradition, namely the Orient, whose racial and sexual otherness was embodied in the reclining figure of the exotic odalisque. In the early to mid-1860s, Manet occasionally played around with that term as well.[9] His *Odalisque* (fig. 51) picked up the pose of the *Young Woman Reclining in Spanish Costume*, using the partially undressed harem woman as a mediating term between the costumed Spanishness of that painting and the Venetian nudity of *Olympia*, and twisting both away from the North–South physiogeography of Europe toward the colorism of the Orient. If nothing else, Manet's *Odalisque* announced the ties of the *Young Woman Reclining in Spanish Costume* to the painting of the nude, as well as the topic of Orientalism. For, without being even partly naked, the body of the *Young Woman Reclining in Spanish Costume* was the body of the Orientalist odalisque – dressed up *à l'espagnole*.

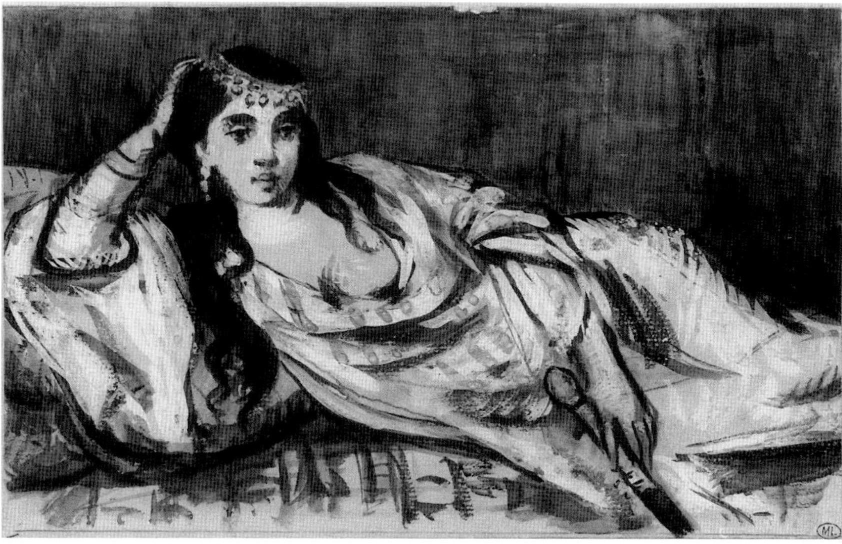

51   Edouard Manet, *Odalisque*, 1862–68, watercolor and ink and gouache, 13 × 20 cm.
Musée du Louvre, Paris.

This brings me to the Orientalism of the most elaborately costumed and visibly
Spanish figure in the exhibition at Martinet's – *Lola de Valence* (fig. 52), Manet's studio-
painted portrait of Lola Melea, the main dancer of Mariano Camprubi's royal Spanish
dance troupe, which visited Paris from Madrid and performed outdoors at the
Hippodrome between August and November 1862 to great popular acclaim. In the *Young
Woman Reclining in Spanish Costume* Manet defined his signature "Spanishicity" in terms
of the twin themes of costuming and color for which the art and culture of Orientalist
Spain were known in nineteenth-century French writing on the subject. In *Lola de
Valence* he increased that twinning of themes, more emphatically than ever shifting the
locus of the racial and sexual identity of the figure from the Nature of her body to the
Culture of her costuming and painterly color.

Around the time of the show at Martinet's, Manet's friend and fellow Spanish-
enthusiast, Zacharie Astruc, dedicated a song to Lola (for which Manet executed a lithographic version of his painting) that made her embody everything France thought
about Spain. Describing her as the object of "amorous desires," dark and voraciously
sexual, the "Rose Satan of Andalousia," and a "turbulent *Espagnole*" pounding the dirt
with her feet, equipped with guitar, fan, heavy skirt, cigarette, and castanets, Astruc's
song celebrates Lola as a Spanish *demi-mondaine*, which is to say as a double emblem of
exotic otherness and bohemian modernity, the alien and the close to home.[10] And it gives
an idea of her allure for French audiences of the day.

Yet Manet's painting leaves out many of the crucial, Spanish-signifying accouterments
found in Astruc's poem: it includes the fan, heavy skirt, and darkness (dark hair, at least),
but it omits the guitar, the cigarette, and the castanets, as well as the dancer's action of
dancing. In that regard, *Lola de Valence* differs also from the standard representations of
Spanish dancers of the day, showing the dancers swaying, pounding the ground, and
wielding castanets – as in a popular print from the 1840s, in which Lola's dance master

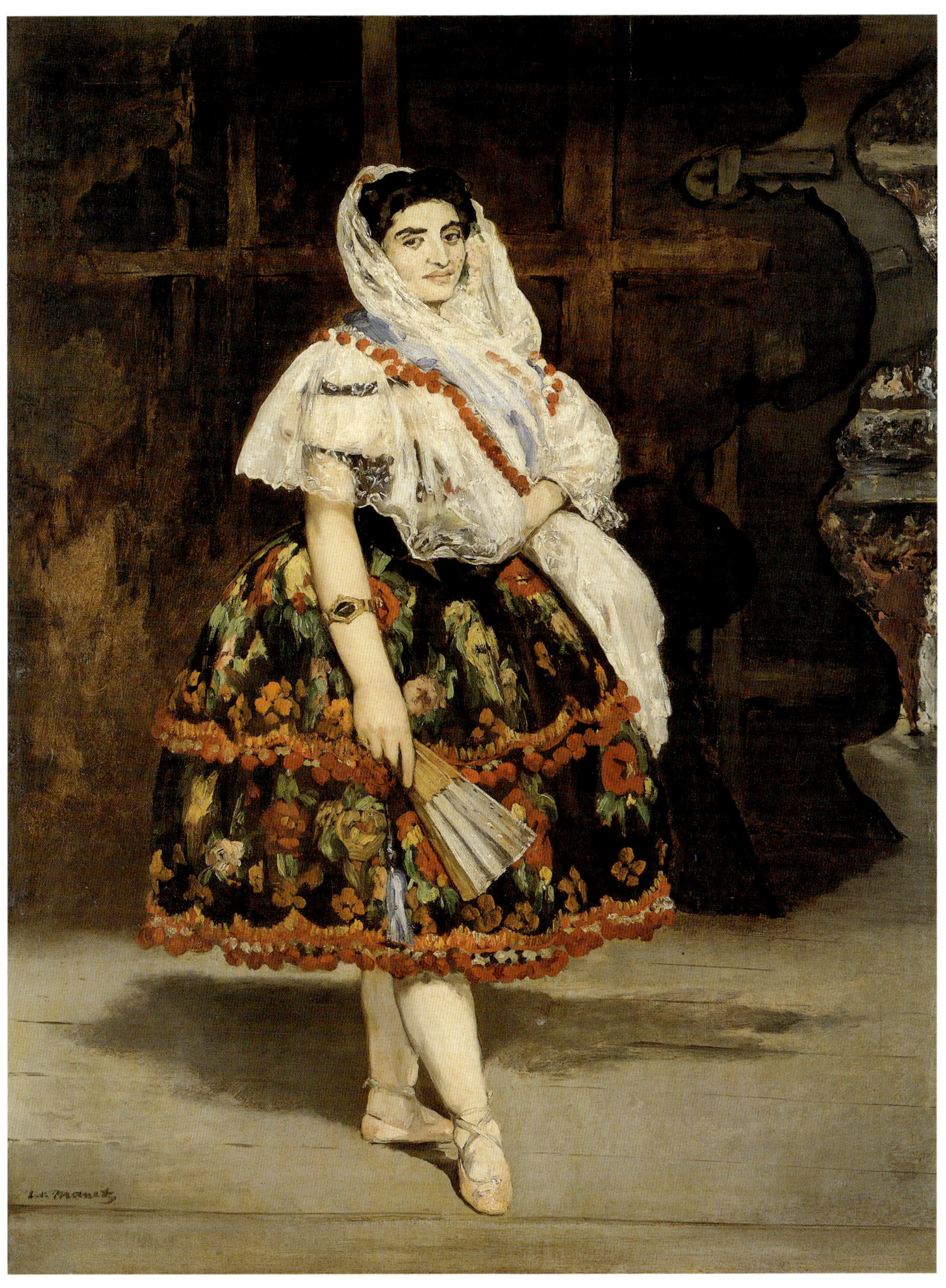

52   Edouard Manet, *Lola de Valence*, 1862, oil on canvas, 123 × 92 cm. Musée d'Orsay, Paris.

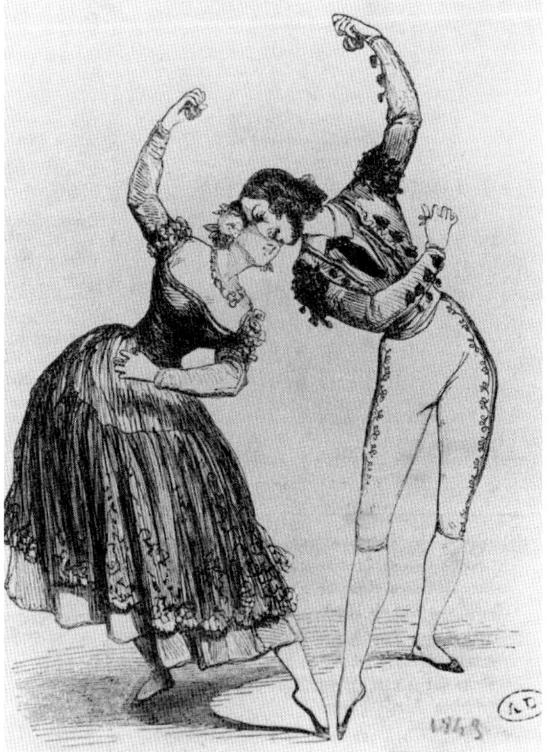

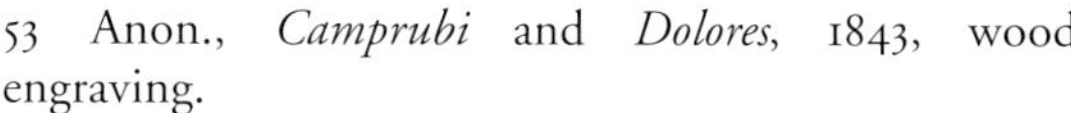

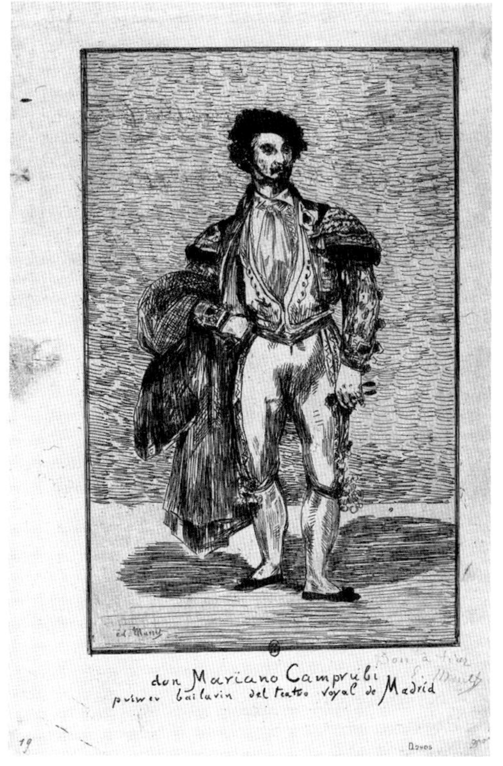

53 Anon., *Camprubi* and *Dolores*, 1843, wood engraving.

54 Edouard Manet, *Don Mariano Camprubi*, 1862–63, etching, 29.7 × 19 cm. Bibliothèque Nationale, Paris.

Mariano Camprubi is found with another female dancer, with whose features his bearded ones are conflated (fig. 53). The painting differs in the same way from *carte de visite* views of Lola dancing. Instead, Manet's Lola adopts the poses of Velasquez's *Philip IV* and Goya's *Duchess of Alba*, as well as of *carte de visite* presentations of contemporary Opéra ballet dancers, with their static ballet positions and frank acknowledgment of standing to have their portraits taken.

In other images of the same time, Manet did portray Lola's troupe as others did – in his painting and etching of Camprubi, whose stance the painted Lola's resembles more than it does most contemporary images of the dancer herself (fig. 54). And he did undertake to represent the whole troupe, who posed for him in his friend Alfred Stevens's studio, before he undertook the portrait of the lone figure of Lola. In the so-called *Spanish Ballet* (fig. 55), also exhibited at Martinet's, he showed Lola seated while to the right Camprubi and another female performer dance, represented as Spanish dancers more usually were. Situating the troupe between two guitar-players – the left one of whom is a quotation of his own first public success with a Spanish theme, *The Spanish Singer* – even here Manet did not show Lola dancing but rather as static as she is in the eponymous painting of her.[11] Despite his attaching her to Astruc's song, it is as if Manet

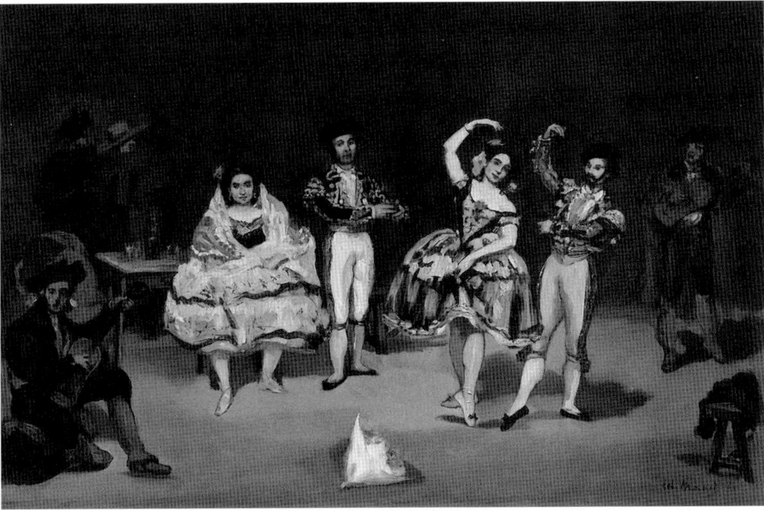

55   Edouard Manet, *Spanish Ballet*, 1862, oil on canvas, 61 × 91 cm. The Phillips Collection, Washington, D.C. Acquired 1928.

wished to call attention to the difference of his *Lola de Valence* from the "romantic lithograph," and to her status as a modern French mediation of Spanishness, combining the codes of the courtly and the bohemian, the French and the Spanish, the Goya and the Velasquez orientation, not to mention the masculine and the feminine. (In 1867 the caricaturist Charles Randon questioned *Lola*'s gender: "Neither man nor woman; what is this he/she?"[12])

In her colorful, highly ornamented dress, however, *Lola de Valence*, does correspond to written evocations of Spain going back to the 1820s, '30s, and '40s – such as those of two writers of the Romantic generation sketchily pictured with Baudelaire in another, very different work shown at Martinet's, the *Music at the Tuileries*, namely Baron Taylor and Théophile Gautier. Baron Taylor's historical, province-by-province narrative of 1826, *Voyage pittoresque en Espagne*, which begins at the border between France and Spain and with the series of treaties leading up to the sumptuous marriage of Louis XIV and Philip IV's daughter Maria-Theresa, emphasizes both Spain's bordering on and its difference from France, its ancient racial origins in the Iberian people – one half of which "stayed immobile in the Orient" while the other was "transplanted to the Occident" – its unchanging aspect, its colorism, and the quintessential Spanishness of the courtly Velasquez.[13] And Taylor stresses the colorfully decorative costumes of Spain, as in this description borrowed from a seventeenth-century French traveler to Spain, one Mme d'Aulnoy:

These girls are large, their figures fine, their complexions brown, their teeth admirable, their hair black and lustrous as jet . . . they wear on their heads a kind of light veil of muslin embroidered with golden flowers of silk which flows over and covers the bust; they wear earrings of gold and pearl and necklaces of coral . . . they [dress] . . . like our bohemians . . .[14]

Taylor goes on to remark that descriptions like this "of the seventeenth century are still true in our day."[15] While such a description does not fit *Lola de Valence* either in complexion or the details of costuming, her elaborate, decorative richness matches its terms in general, while her Velasquez-referring formality and immobility seem to echo Taylor's and d'Aulnoy's overlaying of the seventeenth upon the nineteenth century, the courtly upon the bohemian.

In 1843 Gautier proceeded in much the same manner as Baron Taylor, but in a decidedly more romantic vein and with rather less emphasis upon Spanish history and the old Spanish court – and with a definite preference for the romantic Goya to the courtly Velasquez. Gautier's *Voyage en Espagne* is the tale of a romantic journey *à la* Prosper Mérimée, whose 1830 trip to Spain ultimately resulted in the publication of the story of Carmen the Spanish gypsy and *femme fatale* two years after Gautier's travel memoir (not to mention the marriage of Napoleon III to Eugénie de Montijo and the ensuing craze for things Spanish).[16] Gautier's narrative is preoccupied, even more than Baron Taylor's, with descriptions of native costume, some of which – those devoted to Spanish *demimondaines*, Spanish dancers, and the inhabitants of Valencia – are relevant to *Lola de Valence*. For instance, Gautier's account of the *manola* of Madrid, the equivalent, he says, of the Parisian *grisette*, amounts to a discourse on the invasion of ancient Spain by modern France, which he condenses in his detailing of the confrontation between traditional Spanish costume and modern Parisian fashion. Remarking that of the traditional female garb of Spain only the mantilla and the fan remain, while the rest is "à la française," such that most Spanishwomen now resemble provincial French "merveilleuse[s]," aping "parisianisme" without getting it quite right, Gautier goes on to describe one particular *manola*, encountered in an out of the way district in Madrid:

> The *manolas* of Madrid have been much vaunted: the *manola* is a type, like the *grisette* of Paris or the Trasteverins of Rome, that has largely disappeared; she exists still, but stripped of her primitive character; she no longer wears the bold, picturesque costume of old; the ignoble chintz has replaced the brightly colored skirts embroidered with extravagant floral patterns; the frightful leather shoe has chased away the satin slipper, and, horrible thought, the dress has been lengthened. Once upon a time they varied the aspect of the Prado with their lively allure and their singular costume; today one can hardly tell them apart from the little bourgeoises and merchants' wives. I have sought the pure-blooded *manola* in all corners of Madrid . . . [finally] I found myself in a little deserted street, and there I saw, for the first and last time, the desired *manola*. She was a tall, well-built girl, of about twenty-four years, the oldest age attained by *manolas* and grisettes. She had a tanned complexion, a sad, firm gaze, a slightly thick mouth, and some hint of African in the construction of her mask. An enormous plait of blue-black hair, braided like a rush basket, was wound around her head and attached to a large comb; bunches of coral beads hung from her ears; her fawn's neck was decorated with a necklace of the same material; a black velvet mantilla enframed her head and shoulders; her dress, as short as that of the Swiss women of the canton of Berne, was of embroidered cloth, and allowed one to see her fine and sinewy legs tightly encased in black silk; a red fan trembled in her silver-beringed fingers like a cinnabar butterfly . . .[17]

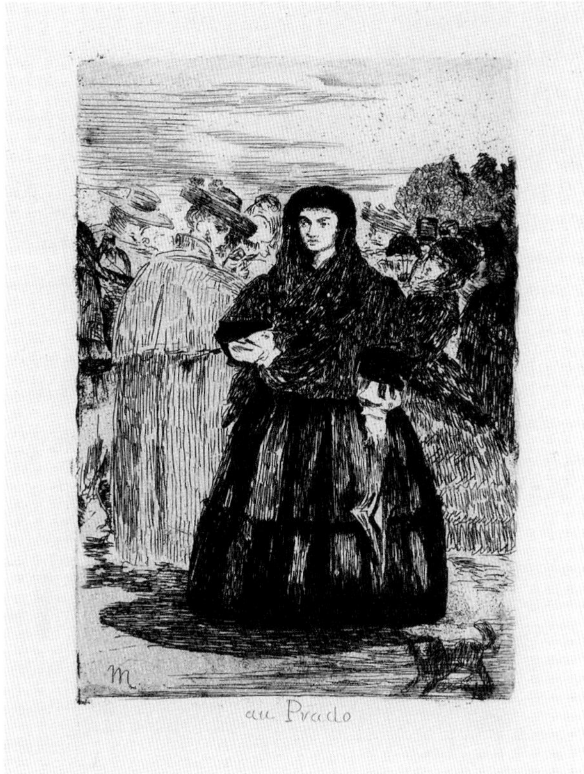

56 Edouard Manet, *At the Prado* (*Au Prado*), 1863, etching, aquatint, roulette, bittentone, 16.8 × 11.5 cm. The Detroit Institute of Arts. Founders Society Purchase, General Endowment Fund.

Colorful, decorated to the hilt, the extinct "pure-blood" *manola* condenses the difference of old Spain from modern France in her costuming and her aspect, or so Gautier would have it. (When Manet traveled to Spain in 1865, he remarked similarly on the charm of the women in mantillas that he saw in the Prado district. Earlier, around the time of his exhibition at Martinet's, he rendered such a scene from Goya-inspired imagination in the "coloristic" medium of aquatint, portraying his mantilla-clad Spanishwoman in the same pose as Lola de Valence; fig. 56.[18])

Gautier again thematizes the difference between Spain and France in an equally detailed contrast, of which the pose of *Lola de Valence* is redolent, between the sinuosity of Spanish dancing and the stiff, squared-off quality of the French classical ballet.[19] And in a closing section on Valencia, where he ended his journey, he represents the same difference – between old Spain and modern France, as well as between the Oriental and Occidental aspects of Spain – in the figure of the Valencian. There it is the male Valencian who represents the otherness of old, Oriental Spain, who wears a colorful, primitive costume hardly changed "since the invasion of the Arabs," little different from "the present costume of the Moors of Africa," with the "ferocious" "air of a Bedouin." By contrast, the female Valencian – "the women of these European *Kabiles*" – is pale, blonde, closer in aspect to the women of Venice, and dressed in modern clothes, in the "frightful Anglo-French costume . . . the dress with mutton-sleeves and other similar abominations."[20] (Gautier goes on to disparage further the modishness of the modern woman, while lauding the vividness of traditional costume: this is the view of modern fashion versus picturesque dress that Baudelaire later reversed in "Le Peintre de la vie moderne.")

What Gautier sets in place is a discourse on clothing, color, and ornamentation that is also a discourse on the indeterminacy of an otherness close to home, invaded by tourists like himself, and by the Frenchness and modernity they bring with them. (Thus his is also, as were most French discussions of Spain in the nineteenth century, a disquisition on purity versus racial and cultural mixture, which makes his *Espagnole* not unlike the figure of the Jewish woman in *Manette Salomon*.) As such, the discursive terms organizing Gautier's descriptions of colorful Spanish costumes are also those mobilized by *Lola de Valence*, with her ebony hair, dark brows, and beauty-marked (but not "tanned") complexion, her "well-built" (but shortish) figure, her jeweled bracelet (rather than coral earrings and silver-beringed fingers), her pompom decorated veil (rather than comb and "black velvet mantilla"), her short, colorfully embroidered skirt, her (white, not black) stockinged legs, her pink satin slippers, and her skirt-enfolded, color-surrounded fan (of a paler, more indeterminate color than cinnabar red). And when, at the end of *Voyage en Espagne*, Gautier introduces a note of gender reversal into the Spanish sartorial equation, so that after pages of female exoticism it is the male figure that is the object of the gaze and the bearer of all remaining marks of cultural difference, that too is dredged up by Manet's Valencian *hommasse*, with her gender-crossing pose.

Over in the Salon des Refusés, Manet had the print version of *Lola de Valence* mediating between the "original," Goya-esque, *torero* Spanishism of the painted pair of *Mlle V. . . . in the Costume of an Espada* and *Young Man in the Costume of a Majo* and the reproduced, reversed, Velasquez-based courtliness of *The Little Cavaliers* and *Philip IV* (to whom she is a kind of pendant) – but emphasizing the old-world, old-master, art-historical Spain of Baron Taylor and after him Charles Blanc. At Martinet's, by contrast, the painting *Lola de Valence* was more closely tied to Gautier's vision of Spain – to the *demi-mondaine* both French and Spanish, the *manola* both old and new, the bohemian both masculine and feminine, whose mixture was coded in his/her costume. That Lola represented a sartorial as much as an art-historical Spain. She also represented a Spain viewed through modern French eyes – Spain in relation to modern France, invaded by France, and now invading France in turn; Spain as a figment of the modern French imagination, fed through a "parisianiste" filter – the Spain of the urbane Parisian Manet, the good friend of Charles Baudelaire.

Some of this was underlined by the company that *Lola* kept in 1863. For besides his Spanish paintings, Manet also had a series of "bohemian" images at Martinet's: *The Absinthe Drinker*, *The Urchin*, *The Old Musician*, *The Gypsies* (two of which are simultaneously "bohemian" and Spanish-referring). This conjunction of themes matches the emphasis within romantic writing on Spain as Bohemia. And it provides a bridge between "Spanishicity" and the Baudelairean view of French modernity – condensed in the twice repeated image of *The Absinthe Drinker*, with his props, his Velasquez background, and Watteau pose, his mixed costume code of tophat and ragged cloak, simultaneously representing the Baudelairean figure of the *chiffonnier*, standing for the "bohemian" myth of the artist, and standing in for Manet himself.[21]

Apart from the "bohemian" series, there were also several pictures at Martinet's that fell in line with Baudelaire's more recent celebration of the costumes of "modern life": *The Streetsinger*, for one, in which Victorine Meurent's features are found, playing the role of a contemporary Parisienne, portrayed as if come upon as she emerges through the swinging doors of a bar or brasserie. Generally speaking, this painting still refers to Spanish art – to the facture, the interest in shades of gray, the engagement in costume, and the comportment of the single figure found in Velasquez's portraits which Manet so admired. But now the reference is very general, the background is sketched in so that the figure of the streetsinger has a modern-life context, and the bell-shaped, body-disguising dress she wears is patently modern. And thus, with *Lola de Valence, The Streetsinger* makes a Spanish–French, bright–drab pair of single-figure paintings at Martinet's – as opposed to the printed pendants of *Lola de Valence* and *Philip IV* at the Salon des Refusés. (In that *The Streetsinger* depicts the features of Victorine Meurent in a single-figure painting from around the same time, she also represents a modern-life alternative to the Spanish-costumed *Mlle V. . . . in the Costume of an Espada* at the Salon des Refusés: I shall return to that pair of alternative representations in Chapter Six.)

Of all the paintings at Martinet's, the one that was the most Baudelairean, and that stood out from the rest most obviously, was Manet's very modern, very specifically Parisian, very un-Spanish *Music at the Tuileries*, with its modernization and Frenchification of the artistic culture of *The Little Cavaliers*. Already at Martinet's, *Music at the Tuileries* announces the plurality of Manet's styles of painting, for its sketchy, *tachiste*, apparently instantaneous, "modern-life" look is markedly at odds with the more posed and formal, quotational, opaquely painted appearance of most of his other paintings, with their static, posed figures, their emphasis upon large areas of single colors, and their flat, pasty applications of paint. And as such, it looks to be a kind of pseudo-*plein air* alternative to what was the most notorious and overtly posed studio picture at the Salon des Refusés, the *Luncheon on the Grass*.

Both because of the style of its rendering and its modern Parisian subject matter, *Music at the Tuileries* appeared to diverge sharply from the other works on display; its intrusion into the predominantly Spanish mix at Martinet's meant the invasion of another kind of difference in a set of works already committed to the constant shifting and reversing of the terms of sameness and otherness, identity and alterity. In particular, it suggests a contrast, according to the terms of Gautier's sneering opposition between picturesque Spanish costume and prosaic modern fashion, with the static, oh-so Spanish *Lola de Valence*. But Gautier's polarization of colorful traditional Spanish costume and dull, colorless modern French costume corresponds complicatedly to Manet's apparent antithesis of two styles of painting, each as bright and sumptuous as the other. First, there is Gautier's own admission of the inflection of old-fashioned Spanishness by up-to-date demi-mondanity, which seems to be seconded in *Lola's* costume, and in her equivocation between courtliness and modern theatricality. And then, the antithetical styles of the two paintings are not all that antithetical after all, as exemplified in the broken up surface of Lola's dress, woven as it is with the same *taches* that fleck the surface of *Music at the Tuileries*, or the blue-marked, white veiling of her hair and upper body, which is not unlike the blue-ribboned, black-spotted veiling of one of the foreground women in the latter painting.

Perhaps this makes a kind of sense of a particular trio of *taches* in the *Music at the Tuileries,* representing Baudelaire, Gautier, and Baron Taylor: right at the heart of this quintessentially Parisian, modern painting (which is nevertheless a remaking of a copy of a seventeenth-century Spanish painting), Manet inserts two of the foremost representatives of the French discourse on the neighboring otherness of Spain, and places them in relation to the current representative of the discourse on modernism.[22] That is, there is an allegorical, and not just a transparently biographical, way of reading the conjunction of what an 1867 critic called the "tache-Gautier" and the "tache-Baudelaire" in the *Music at the Tuileries.*[23] together they index the complex dialectical movement between romantic "Spanishicity" and modern French fashionability enacted by Manet at Martinet's.

BAUDELAIRE ON COLOR: FROM DELACROIX TO THE PAINTER OF MODERN LIFE

The *Lola de Valence* painting was a Gautieresque image of the *Espagnole.* At the same time, it was a flashpoint of the interaction between Manet and Baudelaire, which even Zola had to admit.[24] For with *Lola de Valence,* Manet sought a connection with Baudelaire in the form of the slyly pornographic four-line verse by Baudelaire that he agreed to have attached to its frame, both in its painted incarnation at Martinet's and its printed copy at the Salon des Refusés, and then again when the painting was shown in the retrospective of 1867. This is the quatrain, a rewriting of an earlier poem that was part of Baudelaire's obscenity trial, that was appended to *Lola de Valence* three times:

> Among so many beauties which one may everywhere find
> I understand well, my friends, that Desire equivocates;
> But one sees scintillating in Lola of Valencia
> The unexpected charm of a jewel rose and black.[25]

The catalogue of the 1983 Manet retrospective exhibition at the Metropolitan Museum of Art and the Grand Palais puzzles over these lines, finding neither the "pink and black" colors nor the feminine attractions indicated by Baudelaire.[26] Yet, with the jewel on Lola's wrist, there are also several other conjoinings of rose and black – the black of her hair against the pink of the flower decorating it, the black of her brows against the pink of her lips, the glimpse of pink and black beneath the veiling of lace mantilla and shawl over her head and shoulders, the black of her dress against the pink of her slippers. The pink and black jewel, however, signifies more generally and elusively. It describes a series of color oppositions, and color and costume conjunctions, found elsewhere in Manet's oeuvre; pink and black, after all, is also the color scheme of the *Young Woman Reclining in Spanish Costume* at Martinet's. Additionally, one may find variations on that scheme in the *Boy with a Sword* and *The Streetsinger* at Martinet's, as well as in *Mlle V. . . . in the Costume of an Espada* at the Salon des Refusés, not to mention the naked flesh versus black suits of the *Luncheon on the Grass* and those pink cummerbunds binding the black-clad, Spanish-costumed waists of Manet's *majos* and *toreros.*

Moreover, Baudelaire's "bijou rose et noir" condenses the shifting of erotic interest from the body to its ornamentation to its rendering in paint – from signified to signifier – that Manet's painting may be said to thematize. The "jewel rose and black" is the emblem of that shift – from corporeality to supplementarity, the nominal to the adjectival, from single object to dualistic structure to plural "beauties," from the core of the body and the center of a jewel setting to the relational, lateral play of the surface. The shift is rendered visible in the painting in the setting of Lola's bejeweled wrist within and against – both constituted by and contrasted to – the fanning of colored *taches* across her skirt, which is at the same time the surface of the painting itself. Baudelaire's quatrain points to the way *Lola* the painting, as opposed to Lola Melea the Spanishwoman, thematizes the artistry that made her. By means of this artistry an elaborately embroidered and tasseled dress is built out of patches, or *taches*, of red, green, yellow, and black, a bracelet is fashioned out of daubs of brownish yellow and black, a fan is fabricated out of strokes of gray and brown, a transparent veil out of lightly scumbled veils of white over touches of blue, satin slippers out of a mix of gray and white and pink, and a Spanish face part feminine, part masculine, out of a palette of rose and black. She stresses the artifices of coloristic costuming and coloristic painting out of which the Valencian woman is made, and by means of which, "among so many beauties," she could stand for Manet's modern French painting as much as for her own racial "essence," which is simultaneously constructed and denatured by the painting of her. *Lola*, in other words, makes Spain the signified – which Baudelaire addresses not at all – into color the signifier – which Baudelaire addresses head on.

Sliding between several women, functioning at once as genital sign and coloristic *blason*, Baudelaire's "bijou rose et noir" serves to layer his own authorial history as poet and critic over Manet's, which Manet not merely allowed but encouraged.[27] For the "bijou" also condensed Baudelaire's own history from the 1840s up to the moment of 1863, as a perverse sort of Orientalist poet[28] and advocate of the pleasures of costume, cosmetics, and ornament, and also as a color-identified painting critic. When Baudelaire described *Lola de Valence* as he did, he not only called upon the Orientalism and "obscenity" of his *Fleurs du mal*, he also picked up the threads of his earlier art criticism and applied them to Manet's picture.[29] It is by no means new to suggest a relationship between the painter and the poet. Yet Baudelaire very rarely wrote anything about Manet's art and when he did his remarks were terse, as in his legendary quip to Manet about being "merely the first in the decrepitude of your art."[30] So in order to understand what was involved in Baudelaire's equally brief remarks about *Lola de Valence*, it is essential to investigate their resonance with Baudelaire's criticism, other than what little was directed at Manet himself.

Specifically, the colorism of the "jewel rose and black" refers back to Baudelaire's writing from 1845 to 1863 on Delacroix, who until Courbet, Manet, and the Impressionists, stood for modern art in France: "I do not know if he is proud of his title of 'romantic,' but . . . from his very first work . . . the majority of the public placed him at the head of the modern school."[31] Baudelaire had established himself as Delacroix's champion in his *Salons* of the 1840s and in his review of Delacroix's retrospective at the Universal Exposition of 1855. And then, at the time of Delacroix's death in 1863, he reprised those writings in "L'Oeuvre et la vie d'Eugène Delacroix," in which Delacroix is defined

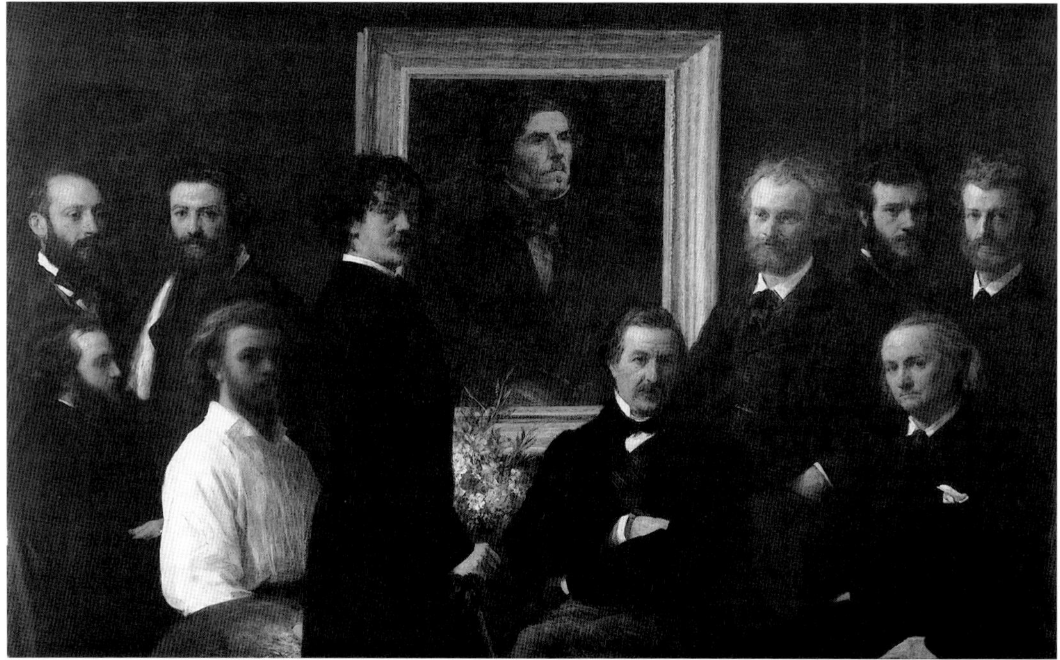

57   Henri Fantin-Latour, *Homage to Delacroix*, 1864, oil on canvas, 160 × 250 cm. Musée d'Orsay, Paris.

as the quintessentially Romantic artist, and therefore the most modern of the nineteenth-century moderns thus far. The year 1863, then, marks the confluence of Manet's show at Martinet's, Baudelaire's quatrain on *Lola de Valence*, the poet critic's last, summarizing essay on Delacroix, and the publication of "Le Peintre de la vie moderne."[32]

The following year, 1864, Manet's friend Fantin-Latour included Baudelaire's features as well as those of Manet in the cast of characters gathered to pay painted homage to Delacroix (fig. 57). (And some time in the next few years after that, Manet undertook an etched portrait of Baudelaire, in the temperamental medium of aquatint that Baudelaire celebrated, depicting him in a shadowed, starch-shirted, three-quarter view much as he is in Fantin-Latour's group portrait [fig. 58].) As Fantin-Latour's *Homage to Delacroix* suggests, Manet, like other later "moderns," learned an important part of his modernity at Delacroix's knee, copying his works (fig. 59), showing where Delacroix had shown (at Martinet's), and getting his name and face attached to the memory of the erstwhile Romantic.[33] Indeed, in associating Manet with Delacroix – placing him between the portrait of Delacroix and the seated figure of Baudelaire so that he appears as a middle term between the two and as a living, updated, out of the frame double of the memorialized artist – Fantin-Latour's *Homage* to the quintessential Romantic proposes that Manet might as usefully be considered a Romantic latecomer as an Impressionist or modernist forerunner: that in fact his being situated between the positions of latecoming and forerunning is what accounts for the peculiarity of his art.[34] Baudelaire is known to have described Manet as a "Romantic" too, which argues, I think, not so much for a stylistic or thematic relationship between the romanticism of Manet's and Delacroix's art, as a

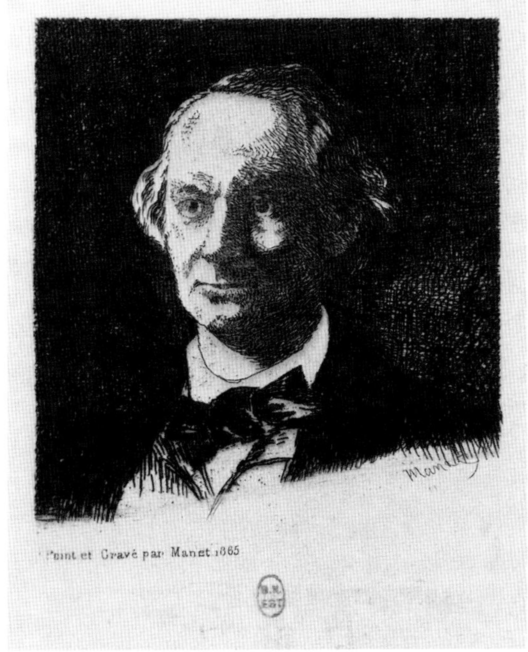

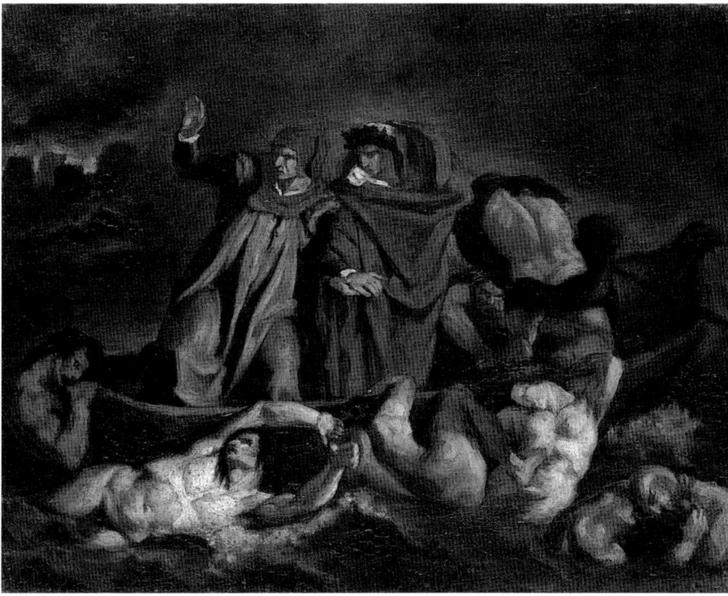

58 Edouard Manet, *Baudelaire*, etching and aquatint, 2nd state, 10.2 × 8.4 cm. Bibliothèque Nationale, Paris.

59 Edouard Manet, copy after Eugène Delacroix, *Barque of Dante*, c.1856, oil on canvas, 38 × 46 cm. Musée des Beaux-Arts, Lyon.

particular, antipositivist attitude toward the "modern" that Baudelaire must have believed was shared by Delacroix, himself, and Manet.[35]

Between his earliest *Salons* focusing on Delacroix and "Le Peintre de la vie moderne," Baudelaire's definition of the "modern" in art shifted; I believe Manet's art of the early 1860s can be located within that shift. But there were also some important continuities.[36] At the outset of his "Salon of 1846," directly following the poet critic's self-reflexive preface on modern criticism, romanticism is defined as neither a style nor a range of subject matter but as modernism itself: "To say the word Romanticism is to say modern art – that is, intimacy, spirituality, colour, aspiration toward the infinite, expressed by every means available to the arts."[37] Linking "romanticism" to color and defining it in eminently Hegelian terms – as "intimate" and "infinite," spiritual and material, and modern, which is to say, disintegrative by definition, internally bifurcated between signifier and signified, split between its subject and object modalities, and splintered into a thousand stylistic and iconographic options – he goes on to agree with Hegel in his view that "Romanticism is a child of the North, and the North is all for colour." ("The South, in return," he says in contrast, "is all for nature . . . The South is as brutal and positive as a sculptor . . ."[38]) Thus he updates the old de-Pilesian dichotomy of color and design into a modern contrast between the Italian Renaissance and Northern modernity, and identifies that modernity with color, producing this formula: Romanticism = modernism = colorism (= antipositivism).

From there, Baudelaire proceeds with a section "On Colour," before going on to make Delacroix the representative of his Hegelian modernity. And color, as he describes it, is a binary structure, as foundationally split as the modernity with which it is allied: flying the red and green flag of coloristic opposition ("red sings the glory of green"), Baudelaire defines nature as "infinitely divisible," a "spinning top," fracturing the world into the "gamut of tones." "Colour," says Baudelaire, "is thus the accord of two tones. Warmth and coldness of tone, in whose opposition all theory resides, cannot be defined in an absolute manner; they only exist in a relative sense."[39] The example he gives of this is "the detail within the detail" of "a woman's hand":

> you will see that there is perfect harmony between the green of the strong veins with which it is ridged and the ruby tints that mark the knuckles; pink nails stand out against the topmost joints, which are characterized by several grey and brown tones. As for the palm of the hand, the lifelines, which are pinker and more wine-coloured, are separated one from another by the system of green or blue veins that run across them. A study of the same object, carried out with a lens, will afford, within however small an area, a perfect harmony of grey, blue, brown, green, orange and white tones, warmed by a touch of yellow – a harmony which, when combined with shadows, produces the colourist's type of modelling, which is essentially different from that of the draughtsman, whose difficulties more or less boil down to the copying of a plaster cast.[40]

The system elaborated here reduces to two, to variations on red and green: the "fanfares of blood" produced by a setting sun, in which "green turns richly crimson";[41] the crude red and green stripes of the awning of the bar across the way from Baudelaire's own lodgings;[42] the "blood-soaked and savage desolation . . . offset by the sombre green of hope" of Delacroix's compositions;[43] or the green of veins against the "ruby tints" of "a woman's hand" – already suggesting the bejeweling of color that was condensed in the "bijou rose et noir." Color, in other words, is never one; it is always two and more: "for colourists . . . lines are never anything else but the intimate fusion of two colours, as in the rainbow."[44] The harmonic structure that Baudelaire elaborates was repeated by later color theorists, among them Paul Signac, rewriting the fragmentary color ruminations in Delacroix's own private journal as a wholesale piece of theory for public consumption and as the basis for his own Divisionism – as such, it belongs to an important thread of modern art theory.[45] But nowhere is it more clear than in Baudelaire's opening salvos of the "Salon of 1846" that this color theory, exemplified in a fragment of painted female flesh, treated as if examined "through a lens," is built upon a divided foundation. Relational, differential, oppositional, contrapuntal: color is as fundamentally split a structure as that of the sign itself. And though it reduces to two, Baudelaire's theory is elaborative, fanning out his red and green binary unit into a peacock tail of ruby, pink and wine, blue and green, "grey, blue, brown, green, orange, and white," and a "touch of yellow," and so on. If color is "infinitely divisible," it is also infinitely expandable – as it is in Manet's *Lola de Valence*, where the "pink and black" of Baudelaire's "bijou," together with the jewel on Lola's wrist and the fan in her pointing hand, indexes the binary gist of a fanned out matrix of many colors.

Baudelaire's early color theory is at the same time a theory of the authorial subject, of the subjective refraction of the objective world – the world refracted through the "lens [which] is the colourist's eye";[46] and of the subjective space created by modern coloristic painting such as Delacroix's – the space between "the spectator and the picture," which is other than that between "the spectator and nature," and which yields something "quite different from nature."[47] Says Baudelaire, differentiating between three kinds of art: "the physiognomic and the imaginative"; "the third . . . realizes another nature, analogous to the mind and temperament of the artist."[48] What is significant here is his definition of painting as not only "another nature," but another self as well: if colored nature is refracted through the eye of the seeing subject, the painting produced by the painting subject is, rather than the reflection of what the eye sees of nature, the construction of an alternative nature, split off from what it represents, altering it by means of the artifices of painting ("Falsifications are continually necessary"[49]), and thereby creating an "analogue" for the painter's "temperament." The metaphor for painting, here, is neither a window nor a mirror but a prism – a colored, faceted jewel, decorating a color-embroidered skirt, splintering nature into a thousand pieces, and turning it into something different from itself, an artificially achieved other world, which includes in its splintered images the altered figure of the artist himself. Or it is a kaleidoscopic surface, which is how Baudelaire described the art of the "painter of modern life" some fifteen years later.

The essay on Delacroix of 1846 contains descriptions of the painter's many representations of women, such as the *Women of Algiers*, which, "crammed with rich stuff and knick-knacks of the toilet, seems to exhale the heady scent of a bordello."[50] And it is immediately succeeded by a meditation on "Des sujets amoureux" in the form of a perversely dialectical celebration of pornographic prints and erotic subjects in art, in which the obscene is equated with the mystical and the universal, and Ingres, Watteau, Rubens, and Delacroix keep company: "The playful and elegant princesses of Watteau beside the grave and composed Venuses of M. Ingres, the resplendent pearls of Rubens and Jordaens and the sad beauties of Delacroix, just as one can imagine them – great, pale women, drowned in satin."[51] The binarism of Baudelaire's discussion of color structures this list of erotic-cum-aesthetic delights as well: Watteau opposite Ingres, Rubens and Jordaens opposite Delacroix, princesses opposite Venuses, pearls opposite satins. But, like the "low" of pornographic prints versus the "high" of the canon indicated here, these pairings are hardly the standard oppositions of aesthetic discourse, although they have something to do with them: Watteau opposite Ingres might be a twisted variant of the *colore–disegno* antithesis, while princesses opposite Venuses could be a peculiar spin on the old Moderns versus Ancients antinomy, but the pearls and satins of Rubens, Jordaens, and Delacroix, who are aligned on a coloristic continuum from the seventeenth to the nineteenth century more than they are opposed, complicate even those ends of the erotic-aesthetic spectrum with intermediate shades of opalescent gray.

Twisted and spun and elided, Baudelaire's pairings organize his hymn to the high erotic and the feminine around the figure of two – and three, and more.[52] And they propose a model of divided (and multiplied) form, painted in the image of Woman: a femininity that is never singular but always plural, never one with itself but always split into modes and manners at variance with one another, along lines of demarcation that are no longer black and white, no longer North versus South but Rococo and Neoclassical, Baroque and Romantic. Thus Baudelaire's perversely feminine art history is closer to Manet's combinations of the Venetian sixteenth century, the Dutch/Flemish and Spanish seventeenth century, and the French seventeenth and eighteenth centuries; or, as Greenberg put it (keeping to the more rational polarities of mainstream formalism, while narrowing them and underscoring their reversibility), to the "from Florence . . . towards Venice . . . from Venice . . . towards Florence" of Manet's *Olympia* and *Luncheon on the Grass.*

Baudelaire's trademark thematization of the pseudo-pornographic and the modern image of Woman was taken up again in a more concerted fashion in "Le Peintre de la vie moderne": there the *demi-mondaine*, with her ornaments and her cosmetics, serves as the counterpart and feminine face of the dandy-flaneur, with his lorgnette lens and his kaleidoscopic squint; and the attachment to the feminine artifice, over and above the nature, of color is unambiguous. And by 1863, in "L'Oeuvre et la vie d'Eugène Delacroix," his reprise of his earlier writings on Delacroix, he had updated the "Romantic" artist and made him into the image of the "painter of modern life":

> Eugène Delacroix was a strange mixture of scepticism, courtesy, dandyism, fiery will, guile, despotism, and withal, of a species of particular kindness and restrained tenderness that always accompanies genius . . .
>
> Eugène Delacroix always retained traces of this revolutionary background . . . Sceptical and aristocratic . . . A hater of the masses . . . Eugène Delacroix appeared simply as a man of the "Enlightenment" in the best sense of the word, a perfect gentleman without prejudices and without passions . . .
>
> There was something of the recluse in Eugène Delacroix; that was the most precious side of his nature, the side entirely dedicated to giving pictorial form to his dreams, and to the worship of his art. There was something in him of the society man; that part of him was destined to hide [veil] the other . . .
>
> . . . He had also, drawn from within himself much more than derived from his long experience of society . . . a self-confidence, a wonderful ease of manner, and with them a politeness that emitted, like a prism, every shade from the most cordial bonhomie to the most irreproachable brush-off . . .[53]

In 1846, Baudelaire had declared "the biography of Eugène Delacroix is poor in incident,"[54] thus taking a certain distance from the artist's life and suggesting that the task of criticism was other than biographical. A commemoration of the recently deceased painter, the 1863 piece retracts that in part, by attaching itself to the Vasarian genre of the "life of the artist." But true to Baudelaire's word, "L'Oeuvre et la vie d'Eugène Delacroix" is less a biography than it is a legend of the figure of the modern artist, representing Delacroix as "the man of fashion, the dandy, the scholar."[55] Part courtier, part recluse, and all Byronic bachelor, he prefers "woman as an object of art"[56] to the domestic reality. And he puts on a public face which, like bonnet netting or mantilla lace over a woman's cosmeticized visage, veils his private self, rather than reflecting or revealing it transparently.

"L'Oeuvre et la vie d'Eugène Delacroix" also retains traces of the 1846 essay's treatise on the art of "coloring": "let us imagine the case of a child destined to perfect that part of art called colour: it is from the collision or happy union of two tones and the pleasure he gets from it that he will derive the inexhaustible knowledge of tone combinations."[57] If color is two (and Woman is, too), so is the artist, in Baudelaire's account of Delacroix the Romantic dandy, for he is divided between his social and artistic selves. He plays one role in social intercourse and another in art, and those two roles are disjunctive and opaque to one another, each "another nature" to the other, each as prismatic and fractured, and as much a mask, as the other. It follows that, rather than flowing from the life, the work represents another life. Indeed, since the artist's social life is treated as a disguise for his aesthetic life, the biographical determinism of the "life of the artist" – particularly as critics like Zola would see it – is not only critiqued but also reversed and turned against itself. And "woman as an object of art" stands as the sign of the difference of art from life. Thus, between Baudelaire's theory of color and his account of the modern artist, there is a "harmony": the "spinning top" that is nature in all its divisibility, the piece of a woman's hand that is its exemplary fragment, the divisive "lens" that is the artist's eye, and the refractory "prism" that is his social self are all colored facets of Baudelaire's differential view of art and the artist, as articulated in his writings on Delacroix, reworked in "Le Peintre de la vie moderne," and applicable to the art of Manet as displayed in 1863.

*   *   *

As for "Le Peintre de la vie moderne" itself, it might well be understood as Baudelaire's manifesto of perverse criticism.[58] Therefore, it is worth unpacking, further than has been done so far, the complexities of "La Peinture de la vie moderne" as it applies to Manet's painting, as it plays on Baudelaire's own earlier writing, and as it distinguishes itself from other critical championings of modern painting, of the positivist and naturalist stripe. Sidestepping the nationalism of the positivist school of writing about modern art (he had once been quite caustic about such nationalism),[59] Baudelaire took up a little-known producer of "low" journalistic and sometimes pseudo-pornographic prints as his representative of the stance of the modern artist, in much the same spirit as his earlier celebration of the aesthetic experience of "spending long hours turning over a collection of bawdy prints," in which he had argued for the universality of that experience with tongue partly in cheek.[60] The choice of Guys as his subject, in other words, seems to have been in part a thumbing of his nose at established critical categories within both idealist and positivist strains of thought about art – as well as an effort to reinforce the resonances of his theory of the modern with his own history as a poet and art writer. Guys, about whom almost no biographical information can be given because of his excess of modesty (so Baudelaire tells us), thus comes to represent a deliberately marginal modernity traceable back to the "pastels, etchings and acquatints of the eighteenth century," and the "immense dictionary of modern life disseminated in libraries, in the cartons of print-collectors and behind the windows of the most vulgar boutiques";[61] a modernity that scrambles the oppositions of conventional aesthetic discourse, along the lines of that passage in the "Salon de 1846" concerning the "musée de l'amour" (in which Ingres,

Watteau, Rubens, and Delacroix are strung together like pearls on a necklace): "In this immense museum I envisage the beauty and the love of all climes, expressed by the leading artists – from the mad, scatter-brained *merveilleuses* that Watteau *fils* has bequeathed us in his fashion engravings, down to Rembrandt's Venuses who are having their nails done and their hair combed with great boxwood combs, just like simple mortals."[62]

Baudelaire's "museum" of "modern life" is an imaginary museum – a "museum" of the library and the printseller's boutique, rather than the "museum of the Louvre," with which his essay on the "painter of modern life" opens, negatively: "There are in the world, and even in the world of artists, people who go to the Louvre Museum, who pass rapidly in front of a crowd of very interesting pictures, although of *second order*, and who plant themselves to meditate in front of a Titian or a Raphael, one of those which have been popularized the most in prints; then they leave satisfied, more than one saying to himself: " 'I know my museum.' "[63] It is a "museum" of collapsed, scrambled styles and derogated images simultaneously made possible by the reproducibility of print culture and opposed to the reproduction's role in supporting a canon of high, auratic objects that can be located along a continuum of qualitative oppositions (such as that of Venice and Florence). And it is a "museum" not of national unity but of modish variety, a "museum" – or a "dictionary" – of feminine style, and styles of femininity, rather than of masculine style, or styles of art: of "those creatures which the dictionary of fashion has successively classed under the vulgar or trivial titles of the *impure*, the *kept woman*, the *lightskirt* and the *love*."[64] It is, in short, the "museum" of references (to Guys and to eighteenth-century prints) of Manet's *Music at the Tuileries* at Martinet's, as opposed to the "museum" of the *Luncheon on the Grass* (with its references to Titian and Raphael, through Raimondi) at the Salon des Refusés.

The "museum" advocated by Baudelaire is at once produced and consumed by "men of the world" like Guys, who are precisely not artists, in the sense of the Louvre-going artists mentioned above or the Titian and Raphael whom those artists admire: "I saw at once that I was not dealing with an *artist* precisely, but rather with a *man of the world* . . . *Man of the world*, that's to say a man of the entire world, a man who understands the world and the mysterious and legitimate reasons for all of its customs; *artist*, that's to say specialist, a man attached to his palette like a serf to his plot of earth. M. G. does not like to be called an artist."[65] And Baudelaire's hero, known throughout only as "M. G.," is not only not an artist, he is also not a person but a disappearing act, more a figment of the imagination than a flesh and blood character – or, to reverse Zola's terms of several years later when, with regard to Manet's pictures, he said he looked for "un homme et non pas un tableau," a painting and not a man. "M. G.," then, is a sort of anti-artist, as much an emptied out literary figure as Manette Salomon: he is less a real person than a representative of Baudelaire's anti-art conception of modern art. As much a blank, passive canvas as she, he also stands for the elision of the difference between the (masculine) subject and the (feminine) object of art.

That the "homme du monde," "homme des foules," or "flaneur" that "M. G." represents is also a cosmopolitan traveler, a "convalescent," a childlike creature and an aristocrat who bears some resemblance to the figure of the dandy is so thoroughly rehearsed by now as to be a cliché, as is Baudelaire's definition of "modernity" as "the transitory, the fugitive, the contingent, the half of art, whose other half is the eternal and unchanging."[66] But "M. G."'s union with that which he looks upon can bear some repeating, and some more unfolding in this context. Says Baudelaire, still within his description of his non-artist "Artiste": "Behind the window of a café, a convalescent, contemplating the crowd with pleasure, mingles with it in thought, with all the thoughts that churn around him . . . Finally, he precipitates himself through that crowd in search of an unknown whose glimpsed physiognomy had, in a blink of an eye, fascinated him."[67] Thus Baudelaire's "Artiste" gains pleasure – a feminine "jouissance" – from a kind of collapse (simultaneously active penetration and yielding immersion) into the undulating, scintillating, amorphous object of his gaze and desire. That collapse is the foundation of his art, "[h]is passion and his profession."[68]

Baudelaire describes this collapse over and over, elaborating it most extensively in his discussion of "L'Artiste":

> His passion and his profession is to *marry the crowd*. For the perfect ambler, for the passionate observer, it is an immense pleasure to choose a domicile in the numerous, in the undulating, in movement, in the fugitive and the infinite. To be outside of home and nevertheless to feel oneself everywhere at home; to see the world, be at the centre of the world and remain hidden from the world . . . The observer is a *prince* who everywhere partakes of his incognito. The lover of life makes the world his family, just as the lover of the beautiful sex composes his family of all the beauties . . . just as the lover of pictures lives in an enchanted society of dreams painted on canvas . . . One can also compare him to a mirror as large as that crowd; to a kaleidoscope endowed with consciousness, which, with each of its movements, represents the multiplicity and the moving grace of all the elements of life. He is a *me* insatiable for the *not-me*, who, at every instant, renders and expresses it in images more living than life itself, always unstable and fugitive. "Any man," said M. G. one day . . . "*who is bored within the breast of the multitude*, is an idiot!"[69]

Baudelaire proceeds to compare the eye of "M. G." with the "eye of an eagle" that can discern details from a great distance – particularly, fashionable details such as the slight transformation of the "cut of a garment," the replacement of ribbon knots and buckles by cockades, the enlargement of the bonnet and the descent of the chignon to the nape of the neck, the raising of the belt and the amplification of the skirt.[70] It is immediately following these remarks that Baudelaire's description of the spectacle before the specular eye of "M. G." – in this case a military regiment marching past – sounds remarkably like Manet's *Music at the Tuileries*, with its Guysian rendering, its "tache-Baudelaire" reminiscent of Manet's etched profile of the writer (figs. 60, 61), its musical alibi, and predominantly masculine crowd, mixed with the fashionable details of women's apparel: "Harnesses, scintillations, music, decided glances, heavy, serious mustaches, all this entered pell-mell in him."[71]

These passages indicate several important things about the eye of Baudelaire's modern artist, the self that it represents, and its symbiotic relation to the world it sees. Simultaneously a mirror, a kaleidoscope, and an eagle's eye – a sort of telephoto lens – that eye is at once general and sharply particular, reflective and refractive, passive and active, decentered, outside and at a distance from, and centered, inside and in the very midst

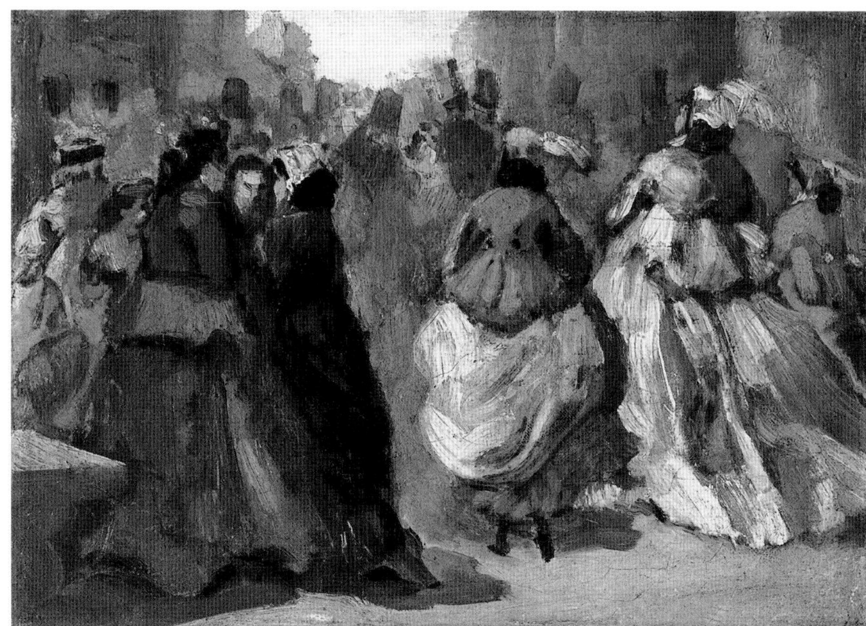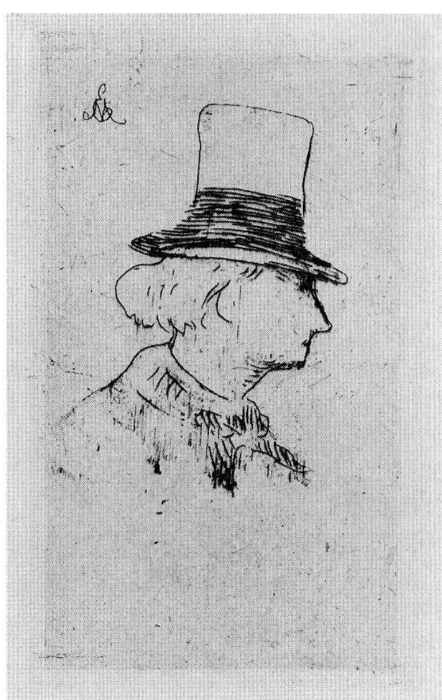

60 (*above left*)   Constantin Guys *Group of Men and Women*, n.d., gray wash and brown ink, 20.5 × 32.7 cm. Musée du Louvre, Département des Arts Graphiques, Paris.

61 (*above right*)   Edouard Manet, *Baudelaire* (*in profile*), aquatint, 2nd plate. The Metropolitan Museum of Art, New York, Rogers Fund, 1921. (21.76.23).

of the scene it sees. It is everywhere a voyeuristic eye, predicated on the invisibility and "incognito" – the *lack* of shape and flesh and blood presence – that is the trademark of Baudelaire's "Artiste": hence Manet's marginalization at the edge of *Music at the Tuileries* and the blurred shapelessness of the "tache-Baudelaire" in the midst of the painting; together the two figures represent the decentered/centered – or distantiated/immersed – vision of the "painter of modern life." It is also an eye that, while prismatically fragmenting the world it sees and thus turning it into "another nature" not identical to the objective world, nevertheless takes on the shape, size, and movement of the spectacle before it, such that the canvas of the "painter of modern life" comes to represent the conflation of eye with scene, and the elision of the boundaries between the two.[72] It is an eye, in short, that dissolves the distance between the "me" and the "not-me," the self and the not-self or the "other." (Rather later, describing the "dandy"'s search after originality, Baudelaire added, "It's a form of the cult of the self, that can survive the search for happiness to be found *in the other, in woman*."[73] This, in other words, is a model of the masculine self which depends simultaneously on othering and identifying with "autrui, la femme.")

"M. G."'s collapse with the "foule" is described in quasi-sexual terms, and the "foule" is feminized: when he plunges into the crowd, when he "marries the crowd," when he is clasped into the "breast" of the "multitude," the crowd is like the "undulating" body of a woman – or rather many women, for the femininity of the "multitude" is insistently, flickeringly plural – penetrated by her male lover.[74] But when "M. G." yields to an "immense jouissance," he becomes that body or bodies – those plural "beautés" to which he alludes both in the passage cited from "Le Peintre de la vie moderne" and in the quatrain dedicated to *Lola de Valence*. And when his visual "passion" is described primarily as a delight in clothes, fashion, *parure*, and color, its femininity becomes increasingly insistent, less a matter of objectification and othering than a kind of desiring identification that slips between gender positions. That passion, moreover, was first discovered as a child, at the scene of the father's, rather than the mother's, toilette:

> It is to that profound and joyous curiosity that we must attribute that fixed, animal ecstasy of the eye of the child in front of *novelty*, no matter what it is, face or landscape, light, gilt, colors, shimmering fabrics, the enchantment of beauty embellished by the toilette. One of my friends told me one day that when he was quite small he assisted at the toilette of his father, and that, in a delicious stupor, he contemplated the muscles of his [father's] arms, the degradation of the colors of the skin nuanced with rose and yellow, and the bluish network of veins. The picture of exterior life penetrated him already . . . Already form possessed and obsessed him . . . His *damnation* was accomplished. Do I need to add that that child is today a celebrated painter?[75]

(The child is not "M. G.," but along with the "convalescent" and the "dandy," who are also not always "M. G." either, he is nonetheless a figure of the modern artist – *à la* Delacroix, whom Baudelaire also compared with a child in love with color – making that figure as plural and shifting as the feminine "multitude" that is more often the field of his gaze.)

Evocative of Baudelaire's earlier description, in his discussion of Delacroix's colorism, of the color harmonies found in a woman's hand, this passage describes a child's vision of his father's naked flesh – in the context of the act of getting dressed, so that the delectation of the naked body, male or female, is always framed within the topic of clothes. This is a curious primal scene, a perversion of the Oedipal encounter, in which the gaze of the child is shifted to the body of the father and the androgynous delectation of color erases distinctions between male and female, as a prelude to the adult painter's calling, which is here constituted as a double delight in color and costume, rather than in the delimited *gestalt* of a body. And in this scene it is the male viewer – or rather, the child viewer who is not clearly male or female but undecidably both – who is reflexively "penetrated and possessed" by his own passion. In other words, Baudelaire's scenario of the origins of the *homme du monde* painter's fascination with color and costume is one in which the logic of the scopophilic gaze is perverted – turned aside from the "right" course, in terms both of its gendering and its structuring of subject–object relations, erotic and aesthetic. (Perhaps it was this perversion that Zola sensed both in his denial of the connection between Baudelaire and Manet and in his ambivalence about Manet the "homme du monde" obsessed with the "grande Impure" of painting.)

The specular, kaleidoscopic, telephoto eye of Baudelaire's "Artiste" is, thus, not the eye of Nature and neither is its collapse with the world seen a "natural" one. Authorized not by Nature but by the *toilette* – "beauty embellished" – its optics are decidedly not naturalist. The same may be said of Manet's *Music at the Tuileries*: as much as it appears to represent a *pleinairiste* alternative to the studio-posing, museum-referring scene of the

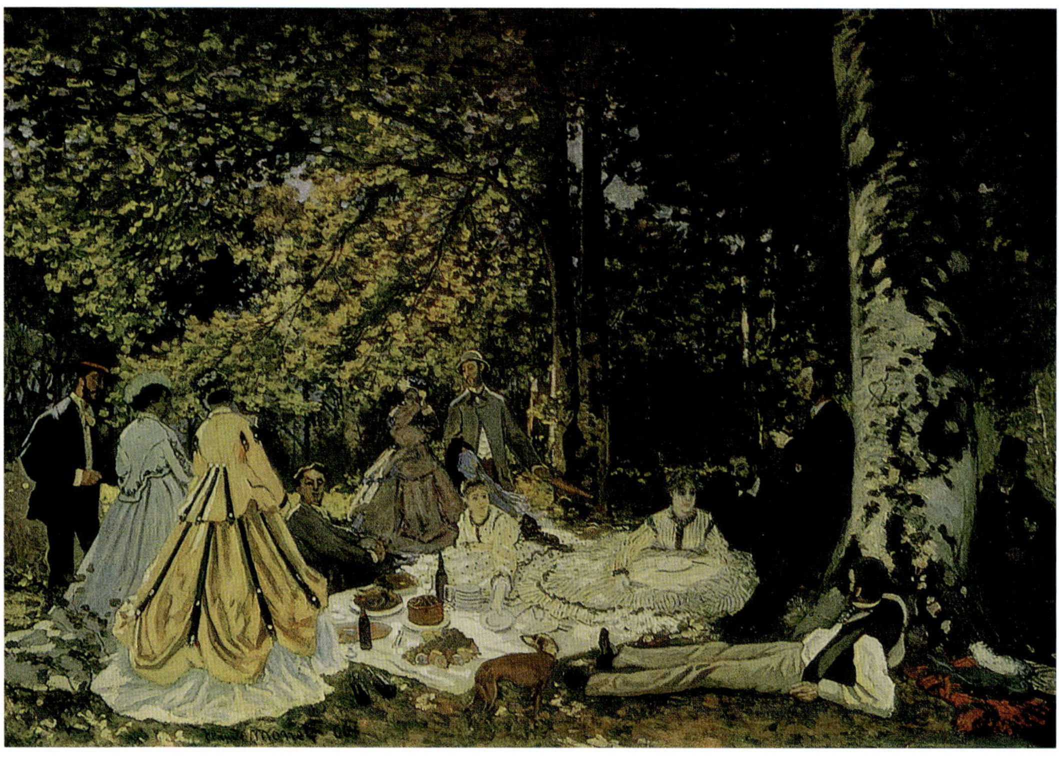

62   Claude Monet, *Luncheon on the Grass*, 1865–66, oil on canvas, 130 × 181 cm. Pushkin Museum, Moscow.

Luncheon on the Grass at the Salon des Refusés, it is actually no more "Impressionist" than the *Luncheon*.[76] That becomes clear, I think, in looking at Claude Monet's proto-Impressionist reference to both of Manet's pseudo-*plein-air* paintings of 1863. Monet's unfinished *Luncheon on the Grass* of 1865–66 (fig. 62) deploys its unmixed whites and bright tones across leaves, dresses, cuffs, dark jackets, flesh, parasol, picnic cloth, chicken, fruit, and cake to indicate the dappling of those surfaces by light. Manet's *Music at the Tuileries* does no such thing. Instead, Manet's painted world, whose "multitude" of inter-mingled men and women is much more numerously masculine than Monet's luminous universe of white dresses, is made up of black, blonde, blue, white, and red *taches* – with some green picking up the color of the canopy of trees overhead – signifying hat, frock-coat, skirt, dress trim, bonnet, veil, frock, sash, fan, parasol lining, but never light itself. Each of Manet's patches of paint corresponds to an item of apparel rather than a piece of reflected light, so that the scintillations of the surface of *Music at the Tuileries* are those of "gilt," not "light" (to select one of Baudelaire's set of binary terms – landscape/face, light/gilt, colors/shimmering fabrics – that turn from the natural to the artificial): the glitter of fashion, not the gold of sunlight, so to speak. And so, though Monet's paint-ing made over Manet's outdoor pictures in the image of what became known as Impres-sionism, the concerted Baudelaireanism of *Music at the Tuileries* kept it on a contrary path, quite apart from the positivist line of "optical" painting running from Dutch seventeenth-century art to French Impressionist painting of the Third Republic.[77]

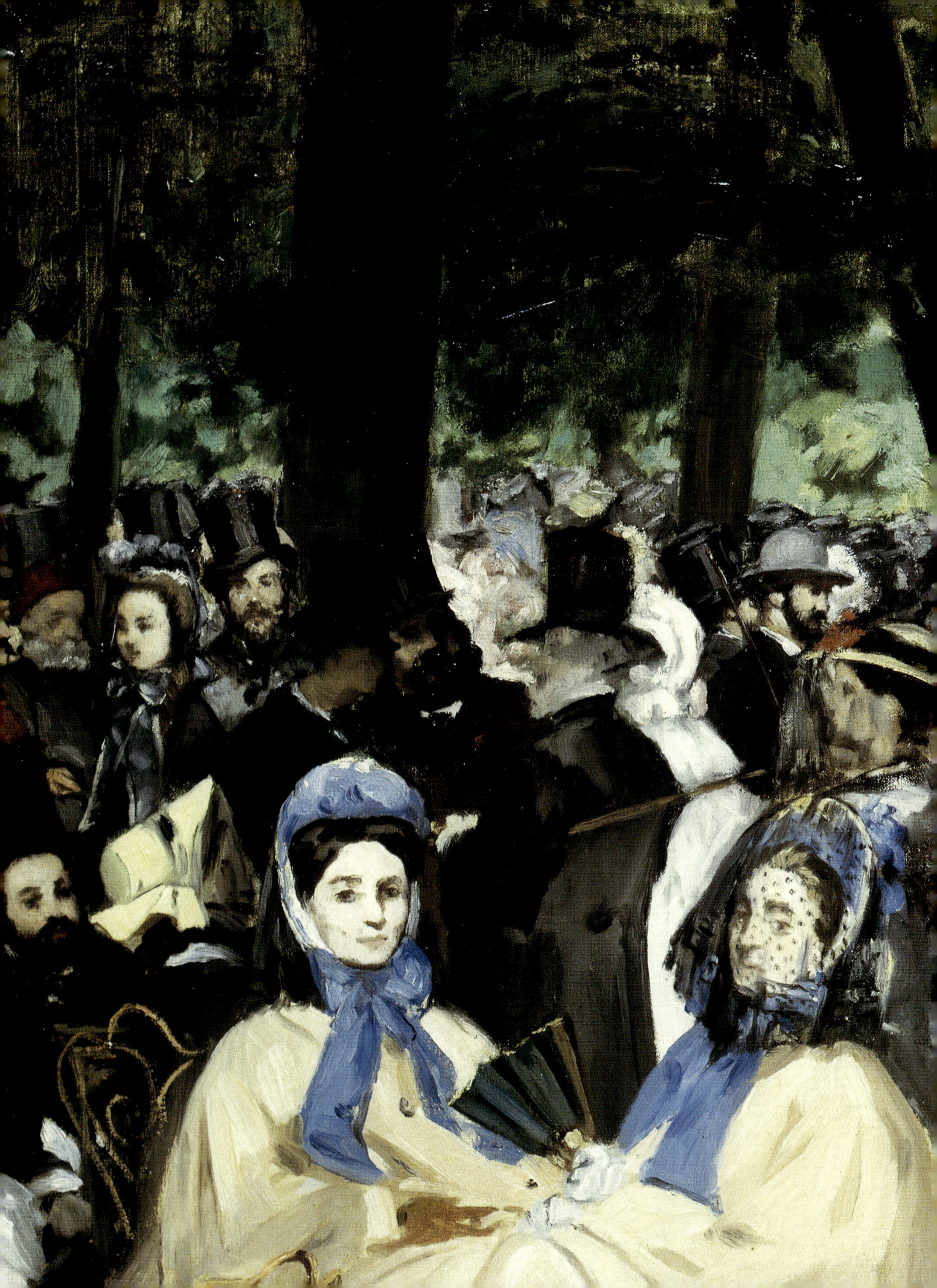

It is in the fact that most of its "*taches*" signify clothes that *Music at the Tuileries* approaches the declaredly sumptuary colorism of its Gautieresque "other" at Martinet's, *Lola de Valence*. This brings me back once more to the triadic grouping of the "tache-Baudelaire," the "tache-Gautier," and the "tache-Taylor" beneath the trees, within the sea of coats and hats, and directly above the bright pooling of bonnets, sashes, and veils in the foreground of *Music at the Tuileries*. For that group of "taches" gestures to Manet's grouping of works at Martinet's, his presentation of Gautieresque and Tayloresque works with the most programmatically Baudelairean of any of the paintings he ever had or ever did paint. It indexes the way Manet, like Baudelaire, addresses, revises, and perverts Gautier's opposition between the picturesque and the modern, ultimately promoting the latter over the former.[78] As such, it also points to what I take to be the most significant but least discussed portion of "Le Peintre de la vie moderne," the closing sections in which the old Romantic attachment to the Orient is intertwined with and transformed into an updated paean to modern femininity.

"Le Peintre de la vie moderne" retains the traces of Baudelaire's earlier interest in the Orient, particularly in his discussion of "M. G."'s imagistic reports on the Crimean War for the *Illustrated London News* and the related section on Turkish "Pompes et solennités."[79] But the Orientalist underpinnings of Baudelaire's celebration of the *Parisienne* are nowhere more evident – or more pertinent to Manet's grouping of Baudelaire with Gautier – than at the close of "Le Peintre de la vie moderne," after the sections on "Le Dandy," "La Femme," and "Eloge du maquillage." There Baudelaire arrives at his discussion of "Les femmes et les filles," which is "La Femme" made plural, as well as a gesture to the then prevalent discourse on prostitution. From bejeweled, expensive women enframed in theater loges to bourgeois women "in the alleys of public gardens," to the "inferior world" of actresses, dancers, clandestine prostitutes, and street whores – elsewhere catalogued as "impures," "filles entretenues," "lorettes," and "biches"[80] – Baudelaire details "M. G."'s encyclopedia of all the social orders of decorated and embellished womanhood,[81] wrapping up with this series of exotic images:

> Here, now . . . are the Valentinos, the Casinos, the *Prados* (at another time the Tivolis, the Idalies, the Folies, the Paphos), those capharnaüms where . . . Women who have exaggerated fashion to the point of altering its grace and destroying its intention, sweep the floors ostentatiously with the trains of their gowns and the tips of their shawls . . .
>
> Against a background of infernal light or of an aurora borealis, red, orange, sulfurous, rose . . . sometimes violet . . . against such magical backgrounds, imitating in various ways the fires of Bengal, arises the variegated image of illicit beauty. Here majestic, there light, sometimes svelte, even thin, sometimes cyclopian; sometimes small and sparkling, sometimes heavy and monumental. She has invented a barbarous and provocative elegance . . . She advances, glides, dances, sways with the weight of the embroidered skirts which serve at once as her pedestal and her pendulum; she darts glances beneath her hat, like a portait in its frame. She is the perfect representation of savagery within civilization . . .[82]

Baudelaire's seraglio of savage beauties is a modern French one, and just as its inhabitants are caricatures of modern modishness, so Baudelaire's inventory of the ranks of the lower orders of womanhood is a deliriously exaggerated variation on the physiognomic classification of the prostitute, popular at the time.[83] Mobilizing the lexicon of Orientalism to speak about "infernal" regions closer to home, Baudelaire fudges the differences among the bohemian, the *demi-mondaine*, and the "prolétariat de l'amour" – as well as between the Parisian geography to which they belong and that of the Oriental harem – in order to map the otherness of the Orient directly onto the otherness of class and sex back at home, "chez soi": the Orient is here and now, in "autrui, la femme." And, including the district of the Prado in its enumeration of modern "capharnäums," this passage brings the Orientalist Spain of Gautier's romantic imagination to mind as well: only to collapse Gautier's distinctions between picturesque and modish costume, and to regrade them such that it is modern French attire that takes precedence, shedding the drabness that Gautier had ascribed to it and stepping into the limelight to take on the palette and panoply of peacock colors associated with exotic costuming.

The passage, with its final delineation of a dancing, heavy-skirted, barbaric figure who condenses the many "beauties" of the *bas-monde* to become a painting – "a portrait in a frame" – is a vivid example of Baudelaire's colorism. It is also a prescient description of *Lola de Valence* and her reception. Indeed, it follows a section celebrating female "face-painting" whose color terms evoke Baudelaire's quatrain on that painting:

> *make-up* . . . so stupidly anathematized by the philosophers of candour, has as its aim and result to eradicate from the complexion all the spots that nature has outrageously sown upon it, and to make an abstract unity of the grain and color of the skin . . . As for the artificial *black* which rings the eye and the *red* which marks the upper part of the cheek . . . it is for satisfying a completely opposed need. *The red and the black* represent life, a supernatural and excessive life; *that black frame* renders the glance more profound and singular . . . the *red*, which enflames the cheekbone, further augments the clarity of the pupil . . .[84]

In this passage, the "frame" – here not the gilt frame of a portrait face and figure but the "black frame" of the kohl-lined eye, set within the rouge-"enflamed" face (such that the "frame" is brought within the purview of painting, rather than describing its outer edges)[85] – clearly designates the artificiality of cosmetics, its painterliness as well as its not-naturalness. The purpose of rice powder may be to unify the face, where the role of kohl and rouge together is to create an opposition – between the illusory depth of the eye and the enhanced surface of the cheek – but between them all, the function of "maquillage" is to make Nature in the image of artifice: to evoke Nature, to augment Nature, to remove blemishes – "taches" – from Nature, in short, to make up Nature but always to do so by the artificial means of *coloris*. Baudelaire has adopted the de-Pilesian concept of "le beau fard" and turned it around to refer back to the feminine signifier of "face-painting" from which the metaphor for coloristic painting had come in the first place. It is also to suggest that "le beau fard" of coloristic painting is finally the signified of Baudelaire's four-line salute to *Lola de Valence*, converting the "rouge-et-noir" of the "Eloge du maquillage" into the more ambiguous "rose et noir" of the Valencian "bijou," to reinforce the remaking of the body in the image of paint, and the displacement of attention from the fragment of "a woman's hand" (or the father's arm) to the jewel on that hand, the colors arrayed around it, the pigments constituting it – from the pink and black of vulva and pubic hair to pink and black paint. It is to provide the terms for showing how the *tachiste* realm of Manet's *Music at the Tuileries* is interwined with that of *Lola de Valence*, along the perverse, specular continuum of *maquillage* as paint/paint as *maquillage*.

To many, the crux of "Le Peintre de la vie moderne" is its definition of modernity as "the transitory, the fugitive, the contingent."[86] But in a reading of the essay emphasizing the painter part of "the painter of modern life," the crux of the matter has to be its eulogy to make-up, and thus the emblem of its celebration of the transient quality of modernity must be "la mode" – modern feminine apparel in all its colored artifice, its nuance, variation, changeability, and rapid obsolescence, more than the relatively unchanging black coat of modern masculinity. And indeed, it is in the section on "La Femme" – preceding the "Eloge du maquillage" and following "Le Dandy" – that the most important strands of Baudelaire's discourse on modern painting are all woven together, with twisted variations on some of the oldest themes of aesthetic discourse, images of idolatry that Zola picked up later and reviled, and jabs directed at other critics of Baudelaire's generation (Gautier among them, perhaps, although he goes unnamed). What I take to be the central passage of this section begins with the "bijou[x]" that showed up in Baudelaire's quatrain on *Lola de Valence*, here referring to the artifices of the artist, as much as those of feminine ornamentation:

> The being . . . for whom and above all by whom artists and poets compose their most delicate jewels . . . woman, in a word, is not only, for the artist in general and for M. G. in particular, the female of man. . . . She is a kind of idol . . . She is not . . . an animal whose limbs, correctly assembled, furnish the perfect example of harmony; she is not even the type of pure beauty such as might be dreamt by the sculptor in his most severe meditations . . . We are not speaking here of Winckelmann and Raphael; and I am quite sure that M. G. . . . would neglect a piece of antique sculpture, if it would cost him the chance of savoring a portrait by Reynolds or Lawrence. All that decorates woman . . . is a part of her . . . Woman is . . . above all a general harmony, not only in her allure and the movement of her limbs, but also in the muslins, the gauzes, the vast and shimmering clouds of material with which she envelops herself, and which are like the attributes and the pedestal of her divinity; in the metals and minerals that snake around her arms and her neck, which add their sparkle to the fire of her glance, or which fall gently from her ears. What poet would dare, in the painting of pleasure caused by the apparition of a beauty, separate woman from her costume? What man has not enjoyed, in the street, in the theater, in the glade . . . a toilette wisely composed, and has not taken away with him an inseparable image of beauty . . . thus making of the two, woman and gown, an indivisible totality? Here is the place, it seems to me . . . to come back to certain questions relative to fashion and ornament . . . and to avenge the art of the toilette from the inept calumnies that have been leveled at it by certain rather equivocal lovers of nature.[87]

Woman, here, is everywhere a work of art – a "bijou" composed by the artist, an "idol" made of "metal and mineral" and yards of diaphanous fabric, a harmony of the toilette, a colorist portrait (rather than an "antique sculpture" – now, instead of the colorist Titian, the name of Winckelmann, that avatar of modern classical aesthetics, is paired with that

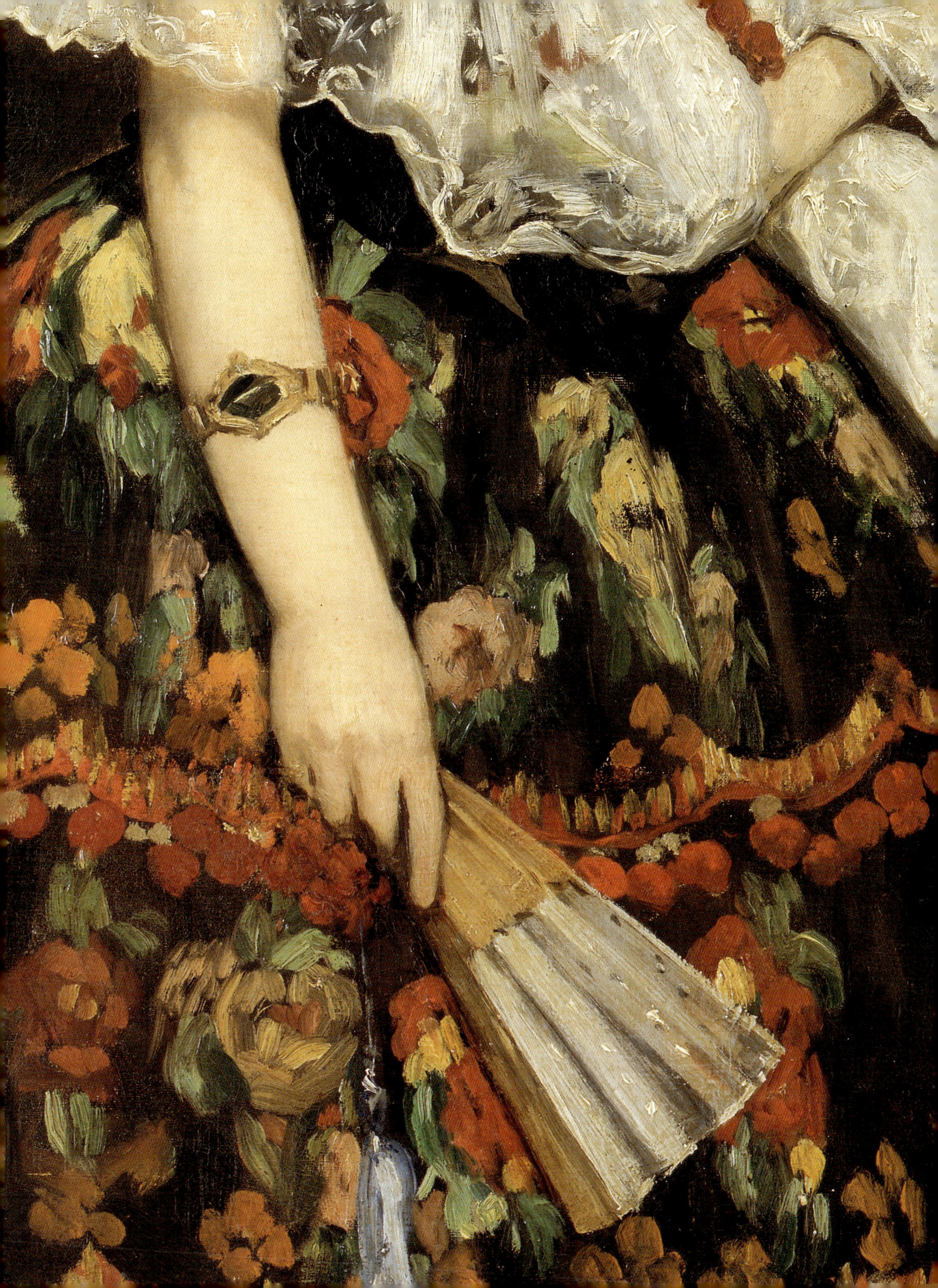

of Raphael). Woman, in this account, is never simply the female sex, the biological other of the male sex – she is not the "female of man"; neither is she an organic creature – an "animal" whose shape is copied by the sculptor. (Here as elsewhere, sculpture provides the counterpoint to painting, and is described as simultaneously a positivist and an idealist medium.) Instead, Woman is the image of Art, both muse and model; as the composer of her own toilette and the painter of her own face, she is an artist; as the composed result of her efforts, she is the figure of Art itself, at once its subject and its object. And in her doubled figure, colorist painting – the mode of Art that Woman represents – is placed under the anti-positivist, idolatrous sign of not-Nature, Art representing herself in a narcissistic relation that fundamentally complicates the subject–object opposition and the heterosexual structure of identity and alterity upon which the old sublimated equation between the erotic and the aesthetic is founded. From the beginning of "Le Peintre de la vie moderne" Baudelaire headlines the erotic/aesthetic equation, making the figure of the disinterested "amateur" of art in the image of the "amant," the lover of women, turning this metaphor, like that of "le beau fard," back on itself.

"La femme," in this extended passage, is also the figure of Baudelaire's perverse play on traditional aesthetic and contemporary critical discourse. For not only does he address himself to those "lovers of nature" who have heaped "calumnies" upon modern costume (Gautier?), throwing their aspersions back at them in order to deride the cults of Nature and the romantic-picturesque at one and the same time, not to mention that of antiquity. He also twists and turns his way through the lexicon of time-honored aesthetic values: "unity," "harmony," "beauty," "totality" (and elsewhere "universality" too). As a painted "idol" who is always "two" and never one, who is the snaky incarnation of modern evil, barbarity, emptiness, and lifelessness, who shuttles between the hard, serpentine fixity of stone and the ephemeral amorphousness of vapor,[88] the figure of "La Femme" can represent only the most twisted, doubled-back, undermining play on those values: the flipped, negative image of classical and positivist aesthetics, both at once.

More even than other critics of his time, Baudelaire proposes a model of dialogic criticism. As such, he provides a dialogic model for painting too: a model for thinking about the dialogue within and between paintings – paintings in an exhibition such as Manet's "exposition particulière" at Martinet's, for instance. Moreover, he offers a model for understanding Manet's "modernity" against the grain of positivist art discourse, and in the image of the feminine. This will be pursued in the chapters to come, both in relation to Manet's repeated depictions in the 1860s, across four or five years and several different exhibitions, of the figure of Victorine Meurent in various guises; and Manet's obsession, after 1867 and again across several exhibitions, with the fashionability of the feminine, in the figures of Berthe Morisot, Méry Laurent, Jeanne Demarsy, Mme Guillemet and other women of fiction and fact, such as "Nana" and "Suzon."

As laid out in "Le Peintre de la vie moderne," Baudelaire's definition of modernity attaches itself to the coloristic values of difference, alterity, and the splintered, multiplied pleasures of artifice as against the ideals of single essence, self-identity, and transcendent unity, and the authorizing laws of Nature. Rather than the heroic, evolutionary, monolithic "modernism" of Greenberg's Kantian tradition, with all its advancing forces gathered and honed and "hunted back," the "modernist" disposition that Baudelaire argued for was a deliberately perverse, contestatory, two-voiced one, constantly in dialogue with other critical positions, insistently eliding and reversing all the terms of aesthetic judgment and opposition. (As such, it might be said to contain some at least of the constellation of attitudes that came to be thought of as postmodernist, rather than standing in logical, historical opposition to them.[89]) With its coloristic *jouissance* in and fascinated attachment to the scintillating surface of *le beau fard*, the fashionable, and all that is feminized and spectacularized in the modern culture of the commodity, it proposes a modernism in the image of "la Femme." That is the modernism that applies to the group of paired, unpaired, and cross-paired paintings and prints shown at Martinet's in 1863, when Manet was thirty-one.

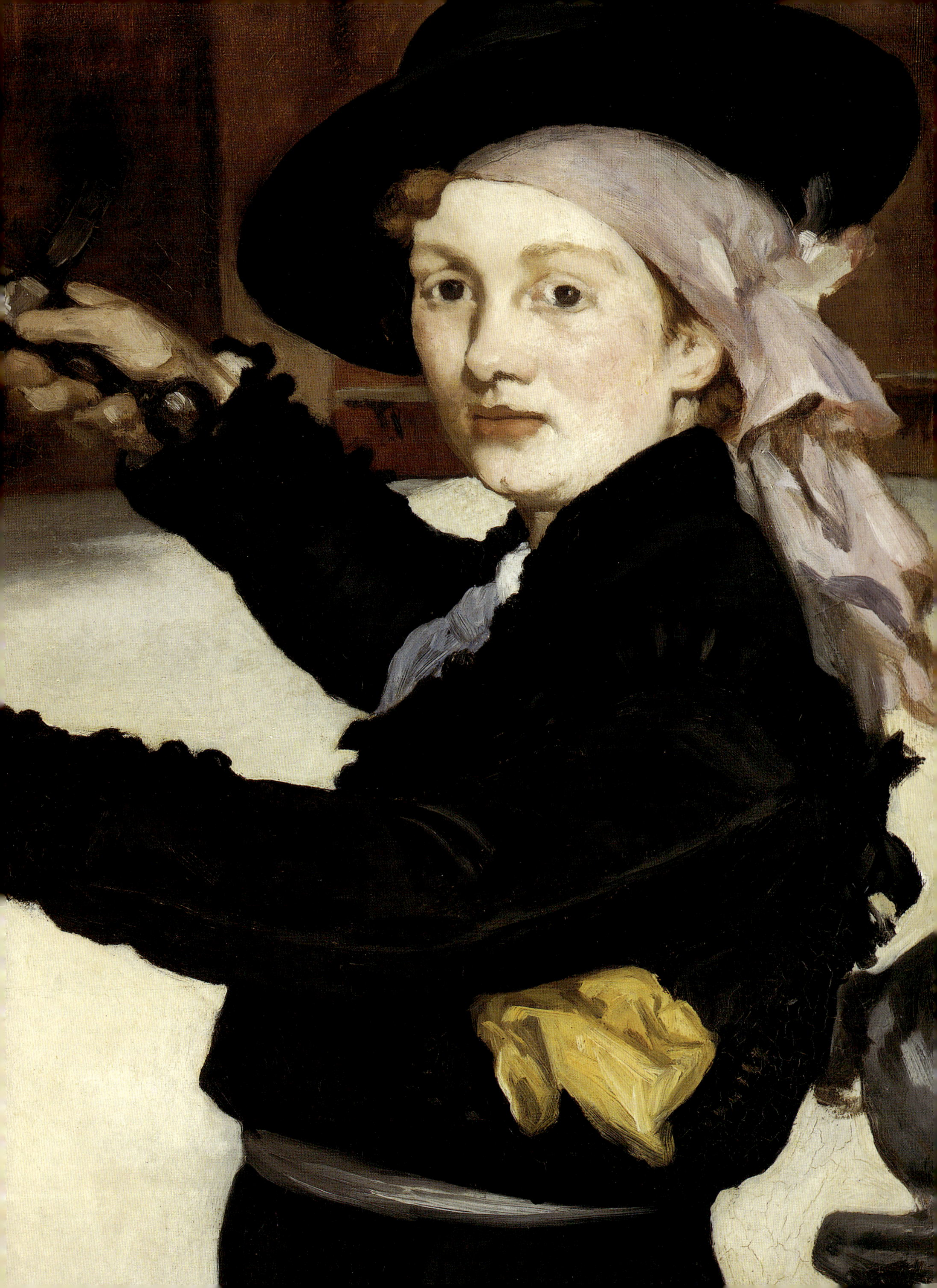

Chapter Six

MLLE V....IN THE COSTUME OF...:
PAINTING AND EXHIBITING VICTORINE
BETWEEN 1862 AND 1868

MANET PROBABLY PAINTED VICTORINE MEURENT for the first time in 1862. The earliest painting of her, which he never exhibited, was arguably the only time he painted her as "herself" (fig. 63). Of the large-scale, full-length paintings in which she later figured, some represented her in modern costume such as she might have worn herself either in the street or at home, while others represented her in male and/or Spanish costume or without clothes at all, adopting poses from the history of art, either juxtaposed to or elided with the features of other figures. But whether unclothed or wearing her own or other people's clothes, in all of those later paintings she was in masquerade, dressed up (or down) to be turned into painting, rather than simply having her portrait done. And like Manet's own style of painting, her features at once remain remarkably recognizable from one painting to the next and change noticeably, sometimes dramatically, as if to question the assumption of physical continuity and personal consistency that is the very foundation of the "likeness" (as it is of the "signature"). Victorine Meurent may or may not have been Manet's mistress during this period, but if she was Manet's paintings do not allude to their intimacy. Indeed, they forbear to reflect any biographical fact in a secure way or to suggest that painting could ever be counted on to mirror a prior reality. Instead, they seem to call into question what kind of knowledge painting provides about a person – about either its author or its referent. And this in spite of the fact that Victorine's features appear so often in conjunction or conflation with those of people who were family members of Manet's – his brothers, his brother-in-law, his wife's son. Personhood is founded in the biological and cultural circle of the family but what is that personhood? And what sort of thing is its painted "likeness"? Those are the queries that Manet's paintings of Victorine Meurent shown between 1862 and 1868 seem to address to their viewers.

There are a variety of stories about how Manet met Meurent – in or near a studio (she was registered as a model at Couture's studio), in a crowded street in the neighborhood of the Palais de Justice, or coming out of a bar-café. The last was Zola's preferred version, rendering *The Streetsinger* as a transparent record of the painter's first encounter with his favorite model of the 1860s: "A young woman, well known on the heights of the Pantheon hill, emerges from a brasserie while eating some cherries which she holds in a paper wrapper."[1] Antonin Proust revised that account somewhat, describing Manet

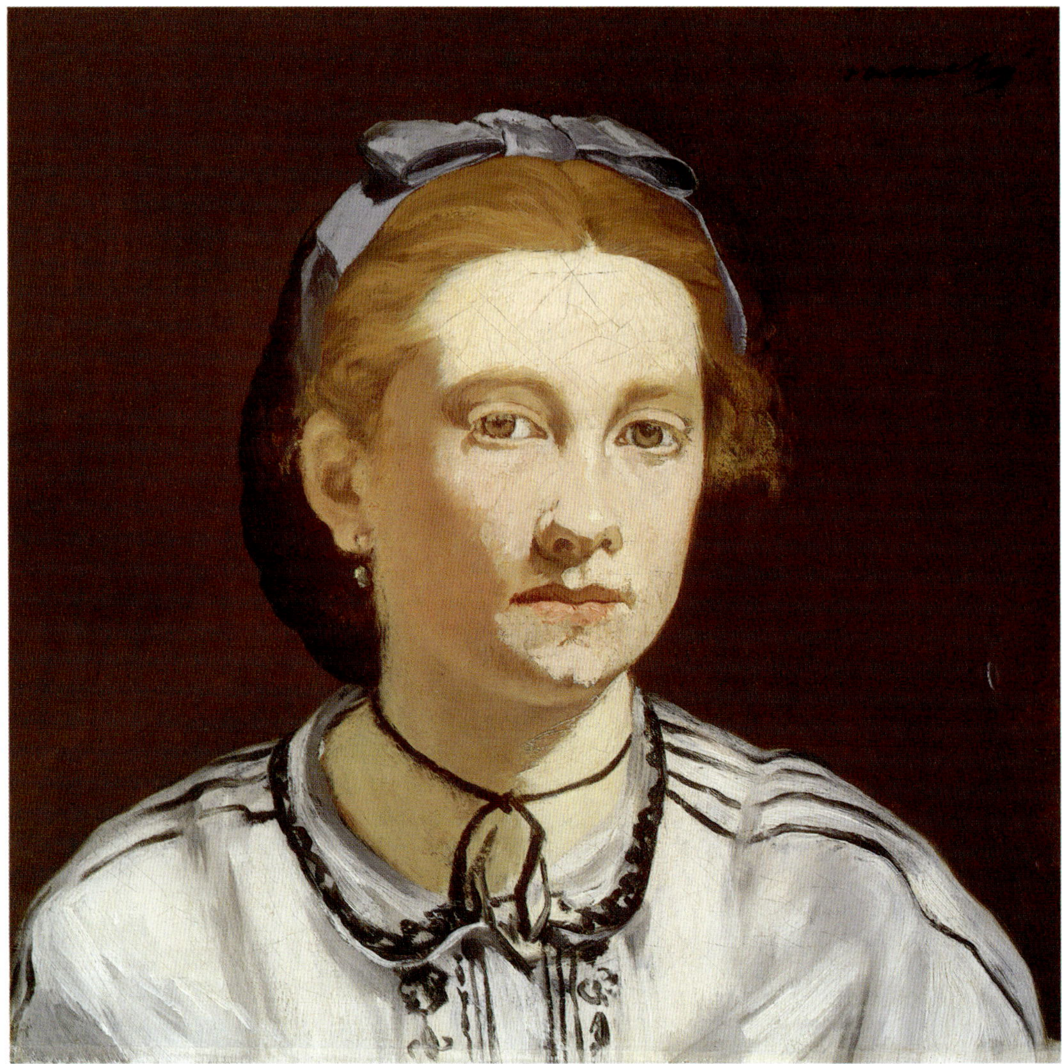

63   Edouard Manet, *Victorine Meurent*, c.1862, oil on canvas, 42.9 × 43.8 cm. Courtesy, Museum of Fine Arts, Boston. Gift of Richard C. Paine in memory of his father, Robert Treat Paine 2nd, 1946.

as a *flâneur* ambling along the newly cut Boulevard Malesherbes through what became the "quartier Monceau" and coming upon the following sight: "A woman came out of a sleazy cabaret, lifting up her skirt, clutching her guitar. He went straight up to her and asked her to come pose for him. She just laughed. 'I'll grab her again, he said, and then if she still doesn't want to come, I have Victorine.' Victorine Meurent, whose portait he had painted, was his favorite model. We went up to his studio . . ."[2] And later Tabarant filled in the blanks:

> Some time later a young woman arrived in the atelier to pose for the *Streetsinger*, who will play a considerable role in our story, because until 1875, though not without long

gaps, she will be Manet's reigning model: Victorine-Louise Meurent. She was barely twenty years old, in that year of sixty-two, but one would have said she was twenty-five, so marked with gravity were her features. It is true that if her profile was rather hard, her full face gave the lie to the impression of hardness, a face vivified by beautiful eyes and animated by a fresh and smiling mouth. In addition, she had the nervous body of the Parisienne, delicate in each of its details, remarkable for the harmonious lines of the hips and the graceful suppleness of the bust. Her chest was firmly and finely fleshed. Whence came this blond girl? We doubt that Manet encountered her, as Theodore Duret wishes us to believe, at the Palais de Justice, where he must have been "struck by her original aspect and her manner of standing out." She was not some unknown on the left bank. In his address book, which we have, Manet jotted this note: "Louise Meuran, rue Maître-Albert, 17." This certainly referred to her, for she called herself Louise as well as Victorine, and it is precisely on the Rue Maître-Albert, near Place Maubert, that Manet went to have his earliest aquatint plates etched. Very given to whimsy, she tried her hand at being an artist and strummed at the guitar. She even drew and later painted.

Manet represented her – in a canvas of 1m. 74 × 1m. 18 – just as she was, opening her eyes wide in her audacious, tired face. Toque, mantle, gray dress. Holding her guitar in her hand, she pressed beneath her arm some cherries wrapped in paper that she carried to her mouth. It would have been a genre portrait like many others, if Manet had not been shrewd enough to give his picture its background of a cabaret interior, where one glimpses drinkers at their tables, one of them sporting a top hat, and with his back turned, a waiter in a white apron. Signed below, at left, *ed. manet.*[3]

Tabarant gives us a vivid picture of Victorine in face, body, and spirit, informs us that she became a painter herself, corrects some of the stories that circulated (such as Duret's), and like Proust, makes it clear that she took up her pose in Manet's studio rather than encountering him in the street, thereby denaturing Zola's naturalist description of her.

Manet's first depiction of her, titled simply *Victorine Meurent*, does not pretend to sort through these alternatives. Unlike his other representations of her, this painting is a portrait head, without anecdotal detail or narrative implication. It is also an extraordinarily naked image and not because Victorine is undressed: quite the contrary, her wide, ice-blue hair ribbon, one visible earring, black neck ribbon, and demure white bodice with collar, pintucks, black piping, and black embroidery, have all been rendered with care. It is her face that is somehow stripped bare, with its (soon to be) trademark Titian hair parted and pulled back, escaping its confinement just a little on one side, its expanse of bleached forehead and blank stare (soon to become famously deadpan), its pale, almost nonexistent brows and strawberry-fringed eyes, its strongly shadowed nose with the highlit shine upon it, triangulating the whites of the eyes and rhyming with the highlit earring dangling from a single fleshy earlobe, its half-defined, half-indeterminate mouth and hesitant chin, and above all the starkness of its spotlighting against the unrelieved black of the background. It has about it something of a deer caught in the headlights, or a face frozen by flash light. It is a face without a role to play, one might say, what a face looks like without the cover of an expression or the mask of a persona – which is to say, blank. It gives the lie to the notion that the self resides within, behind the facade of the polite smile, underneath the clothing and outer lineaments of the flesh. If anything, *Victorine Meurent* reverses that equation, suggesting that the "soi-même" – here the "elle-même" – is the clothing, the outer, detachable layers of the person, and the flesh the layer "below."

As became clear in the later pictures of this "same" woman, however, even the flesh of a person is mutable. And as in those other pictures, in the portrait it is evident, if also diffident, that nothing except paint is "below" anything, and that both body and soul, flesh and person are constituted in paint – neither below nor above but in a set of side-by-side juxtapositions, oppositions, and elisions. Victorine is made of visible ear and earring versus their invisible counterparts; shadowed expanse of cheek at left versus the demarcated edge of the face at right; hair taut at left and hair a little loose at right, con-trasting smoother and tighter to slightly rougher and looser brushwork, and displaying the differences in ginger tonality that are produced by the shadowy range at left and the starker context of black and white at right; black on black rendering an almost unnoticed coil of hairnetted hair in barely differentiated degrees of ebony; and finally, a strong upper lip versus a weak under lip, all edge and shadowed russet rose versus a lighter hue of the same color, fudged and smudged underneath like the right corner of the mouth in contrast to the left, at once marked and blurred by a dab of shadow under it and underwritten by the uncertain double shape of the cleft of the chin below, which both mirrors and undermines the certainty of the double shape of the lip's indented bow above. These are indeterminate contrasts between left and right, top and bottom that were repeated, even thematized, in Manet's other, full-figure pictures of Victorine. They became integral to his manner of constituting people in paint; here, he begins to work them out, while also stripping the portrait down to them.

Victorine Meurent also introduces framing into the midst of the picture: the blue ribbon with its flat knot and bow is a frame for the head and the hair, as the hairline with its slight indentation is a frame for the face, the black neck ribbon a frame for the chin, its tie lined up with the bifurcating of the face above it – cleft chin, upper lip, bridge of the nose, part in the hair – its line doubled by the embroidered collar beneath it, while the bodice's black piping frames and reiterates, simultaneously accenting and blurring, making and unmaking the lines of Victorine's shoulders. And the white of the blouse, with its brushed layering of gray and rose at right, while it manages to suggest the crease of an arm and the fold of a sleeve, and to balance what might be the pull of a shawl at the bottom left corner, is also an exercise in demonstrating what "above" and "below" mean in paint – rather than profundity, the vertical and lateral scansion of the picture; rather than a hierarchy of inner substance and outer surface, the color on color, mark upon mark build-up of facture. It is at the same time a demonstration of how a pictorial illusion oscillates between painted fiction and material fact, maintaining the one while announcing the other. Here the equation of the thick and thin folding of cloth over skin and the pellucid brushing of pigment over pigment helps to make that point, parading as it does the dense superficiality of its effect of depth. Thus *Victorine Meurent* shows how a likeness is a framing, and how a person is fabricated in paint. But this making and unmaking of a person in paint was preliminary; in it Victorine performed nothing but the *tabula rasa* of personhood; and Manet did not exhibit the portrait.[4]

Manet painted Victorine twice more in 1862: as *The Streetsinger*, in which she is portrayed in modern Parisian clothes, and *Mlle V. . . . in the Costume of an Espada*, in which she is depicted wearing the knee-breeches of an *espada* (figs. 65, 66). Both were exhibited in 1863 but separately, one at Martinet's and the other at the Salon des Refusés. In 1863, he painted her twice again, this time in two multi-figured, Italian-based paintings, the *Luncheon on the Grass* and *Olympia*, in both of which Victorine appears naked, her clothes by her side in one and absent in the other. Again, Manet divided the pair, displaying *Luncheon on the Grass* with *Mlle V. . . . in the Costume of an Espada* and *Young Man in the Costume of a Majo* at the Salon des Refusés, while holding back *Olympia* until the Salon of 1865, when he showed her with *Christ Insulted*. Then in 1865 or 1866, Manet seems to have painted two other pictures using Victorine Meurent as the model, *The Reader* and *The Guitar Player* (fig. 64), an updating of the theme of *The Spanish Singer*. Neither of these paintings did Manet exhibit at the time, although one was shown in the retrospective of 1867.

64   Edouard Manet, *The Guitar Player*, c.1866, oil on canvas, 63.5 × 80 cm. Hill-Stead Museum, Farmington, Conn.

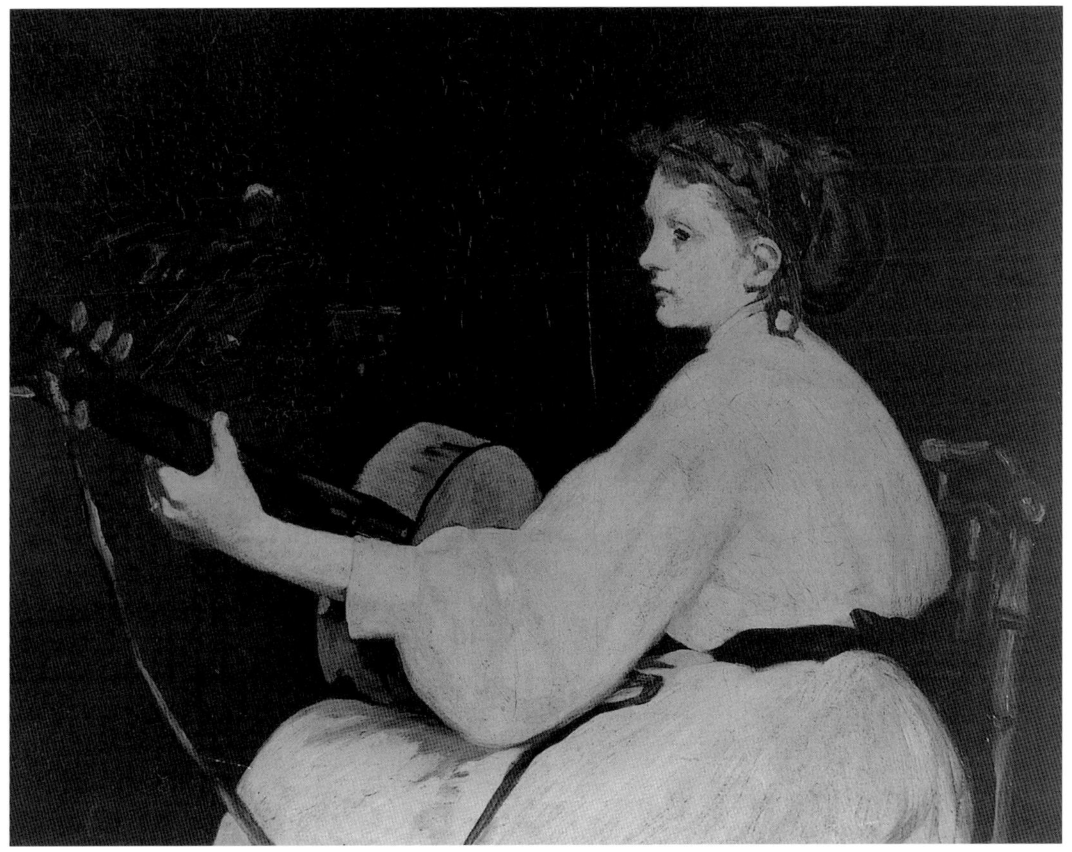

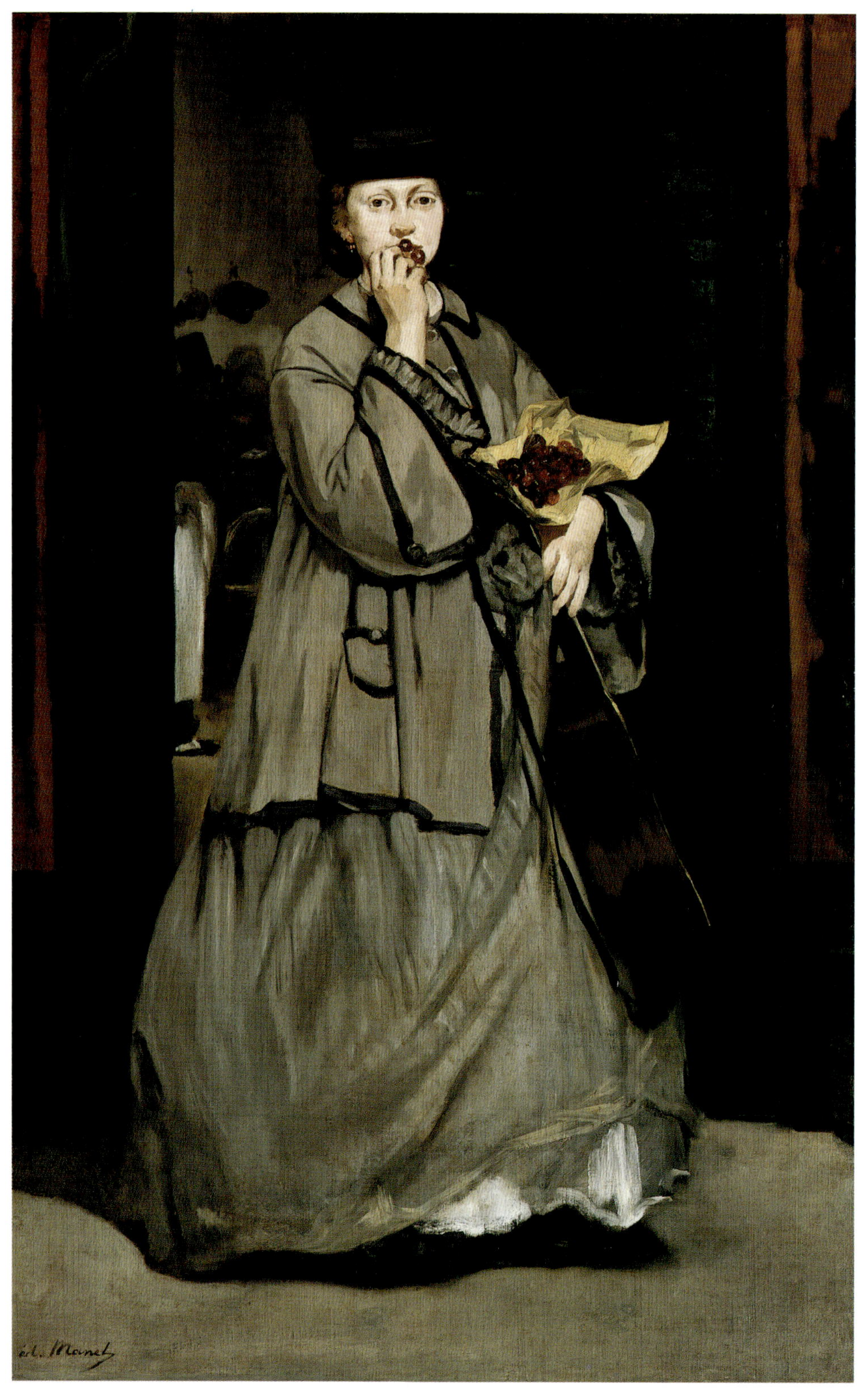

65　Edouard Manet, *The Streetsinger*, 1862, oil on canvas, 171.1 × 105.8 cm. Courtesy, Museum of Fine Arts, Boston. Bequest of Sarah Choate Sears in memory of her husband, Joshua Montgomery Sears, 66.304.

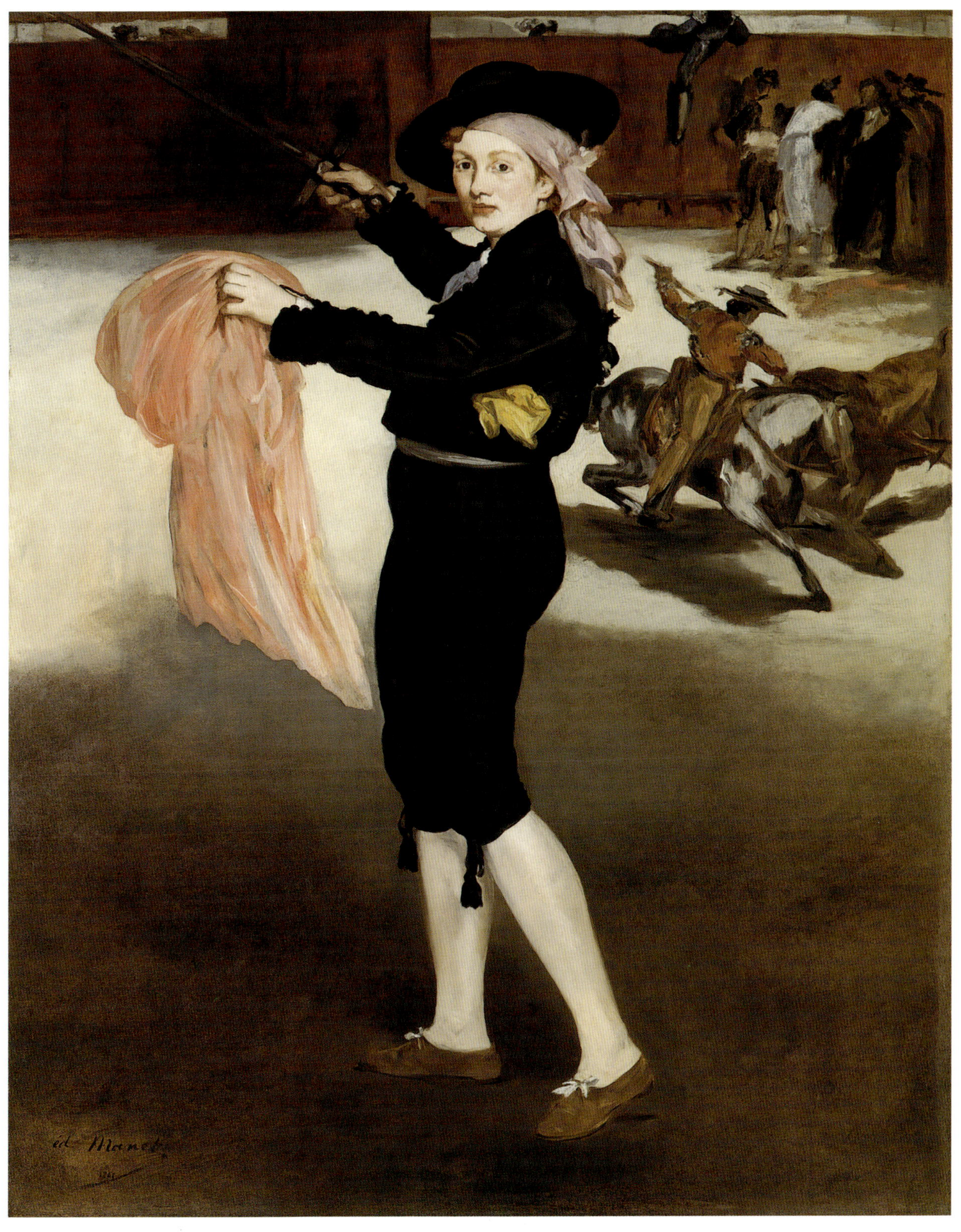

66   Edouard Manet, *Mlle V. . . . in the Costume of an Espada*, 1862, oil on canvas, 165.1 × 127.6 cm. The Metropolitan Museum of Art, New York, H. O. Havemeyer Collection, Bequest of Mrs. H. O. Havemeyer, 1929. (29.100.53).

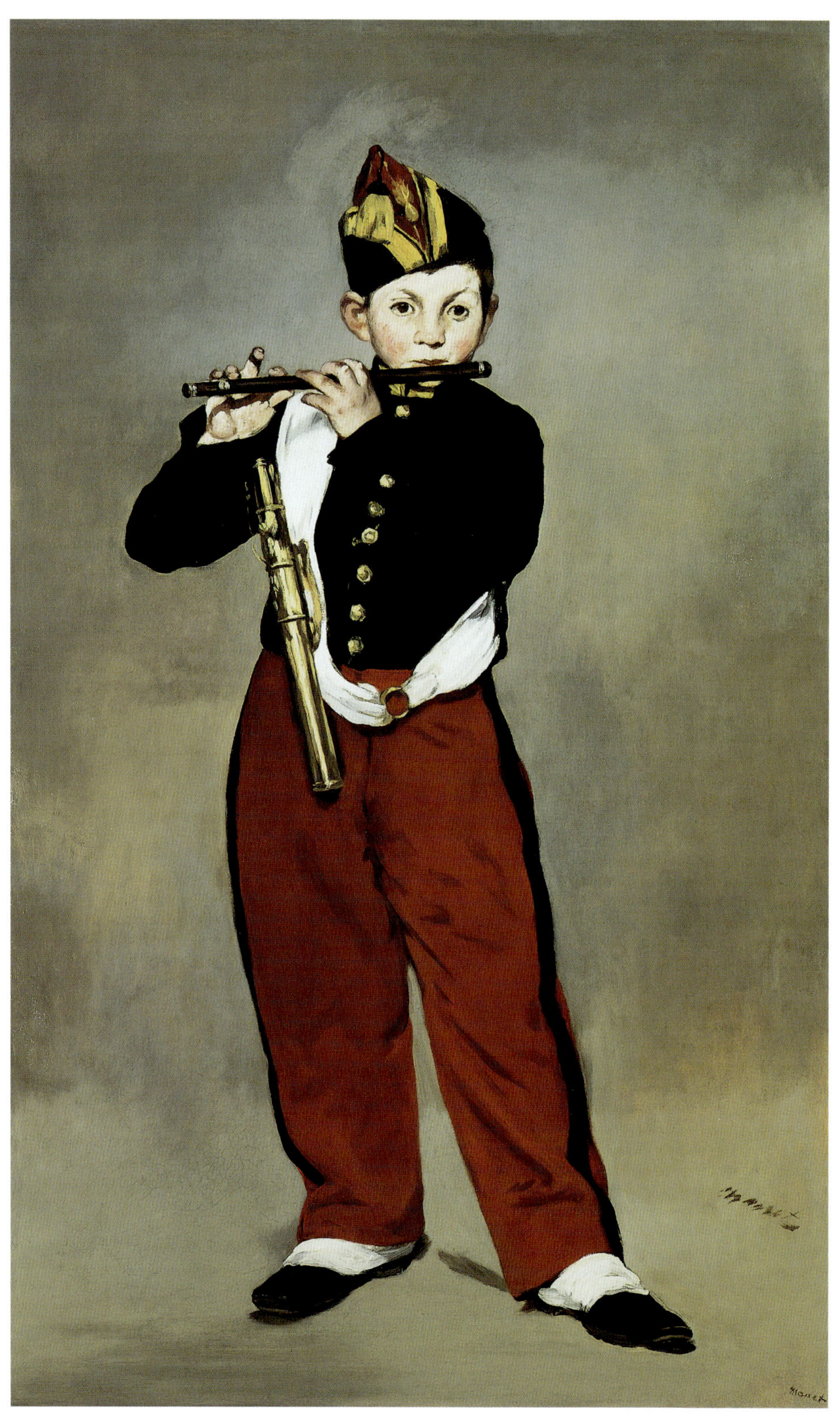

67   Edouard Manet, *The Fifer*, 1866, oil on canvas, 161 × 97 cm. Musée d'Orsay, Paris.

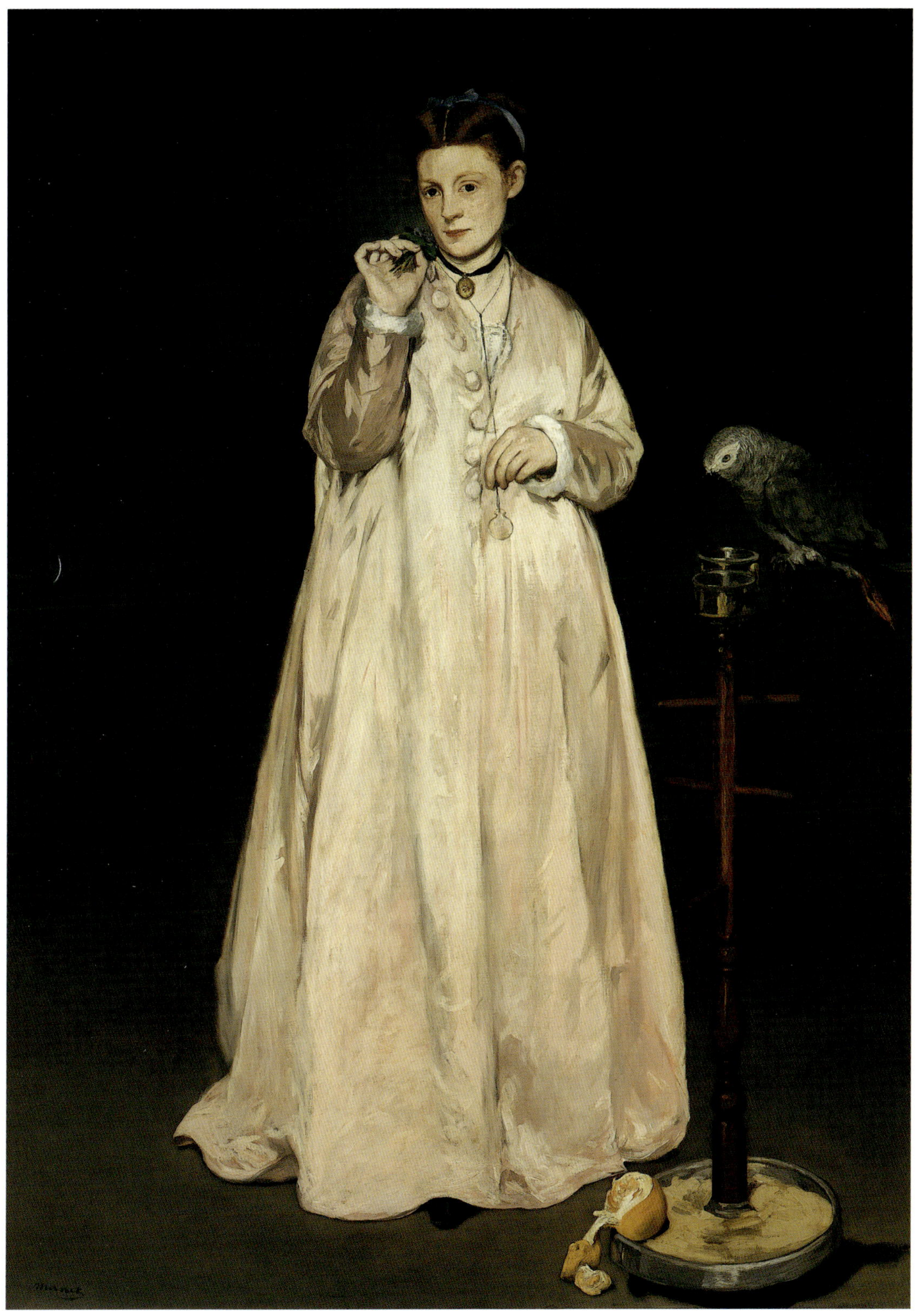

68   Edouard Manet, *Young Woman in 1866*, 1866, oil on canvas, 185.1 × 128.6 cm. The Metropolitan Museum of Art, New York, Gift of Erwin Davis, 1889. (89.21.3).

Then in 1866, Manet painted another pair of pictures in which Victorine figured, *The Fifer* (fig. 67), where her features were overlayed by those of Léon Leenhoff and another boy, and the so-called *Young Woman in 1866* (fig. 68). These Manet also divided, in the main because the *Young Woman in 1866* was not ready for the Salon of 1866, from which *The Fifer* was rejected. After the retrospective of 1867, in which all of these pictures appeared, Manet showed the *Young Woman in 1866* in the Salon of 1868, together with the portrait of Zola. The only other picture of Victorine Meurent that he produced was *The Railway*, which was painted, after a hiatus of some five years in which he had not painted her at all, on its own; like the inaugural portrait of Victorine of ten years before, it was not part of a pair. Manet showed this final depiction of Victorine, in many ways an anomaly in relation to his other pictures of her, in the Salon of 1874, the year of the first Impressionist exhibition – I shall return to it in Chapter Eight. For now, I wish to concentrate on the pairs of pictures of Victorine painted between 1862 and 1866, then divided and exhibited between 1863 and 1868. I shall focus on the pairings as they were painted and hung in Manet's studio (and then re-hung, all together, in the 1867 retrospective's monographic re-imagining of Manet's studio), and as they were separately partnered with other paintings from Salon to Salon, in order to see how Manet put the problem of personhood in paint, in private and in public, in the image of "Mlle V."

1862 (1863)

In the next painting that Manet did of Victorine, *The Streetsinger* (begun in 1862 and finished in time to be exhibited at Martinet's in 1863), she is painted in a "blond," "acrid," "austere" manner as a "young woman well known around the neighborhood of the Pantheon hill."[5] Here Victorine appears in contemporary women's clothes, in the guise of a profession that was close to hers – she was reputed to be a musical performer as well as an artist's model – and as a member of the class of the Parisian *demi-monde* to which she belonged. Her gender is clearly signaled in her clothing, even though the loose, trapeze cut of her jacket and the bell shape of her skirt completely hide the contours of her body. Her stance, as far as it can be made out, is not particularly theatrical: she seems to be caught, somewhat undecidably, between full frontality and a slight three-quarter turn. Indeed, she is depicted as if in a casual moment, apparently just emerging from a bar-café, trailing her guitar in one hand, snacking on some cherries, before, after, or in between performances. Thus the persona, pose, and costuming of *The Streetsinger* are all "native" to who and what Victorine herself was.

Victorine's features are rendered sharp and slim, chic and somehow urban, not unlike their rendering in the portrait, but now contextualized by the picture's full-figure presentation. Even though the countenance-defining contours of her lips and chin are obscured by the knuckles and cherry-wielding fingers of her right hand held up to the lower part of her face, one feels sure of the jawline, the contour of the lips, and the pointed chin – as given by the silhouette of her cheek on the right just before the chin is hidden by her hand, and the edges of her upper lip just barely visible along the line of her knuckle and between the round red gleams of the two cherries. One surmises the shape of her face and features from the hide-and-seek, "beholder's share" clues that are provided by the picture.[6] The broad, low baldness of her forehead, for instance, is both hidden and hinted at by the low, straight line of her hat. Her nose is barely distinguishable from her cheeks, marked only by the shadow beneath it, and her eyebrows are hardly indicated at all, suggested by the two parentheses-shaped shadows between her eyes, marking the beginnings of two winging lines, but one is led to fill in the line of the nose and the arcs of the eyebrows, to arrive at something like the face given in the portrait. (When the painting was shown at Martinet's in 1863, Paul Mantz remarked on the eyebrows, saying: "All form is lost in his great portraits of women, and notably in that of the *Singer*, where, by a singularity which troubles us profoundly, the eyebrows renounce their horizontal position in order to be placed vertically alongside the nose, like two shadowy commas; there is no longer anything there but the loud battle of chalky tones with black tones."[7])

So in *The Streetsinger* Victorine is recognizable as Victorine. And yet those characteristics that seem to make her more "herself" in *The Streetsinger* than in the other full-figure renderings of her are also those that are the most tied up in a series of odd color relationships and factural variations. For all the picture's appearance of graphic and coloristic boldness, its palette is peculiarly narrow, inspired by Velasquez's subtle colorism: the white of the waiter's apron in the background and Victorine's petticoat in the foreground tying together near and far, background and underneath, underpainting and highlight; the flesh tones of Victorine's strangely bald face, her shadowed and delineated left hand, and her limp and brushier right hand; the russet of Victorine's hair and the highlit, sonorous wood of the guitar, and the lighter brown of the ground upon which Victorine stands; the variegated red of the mass of cherries framed by the yellow wrapper and the flesh of the hand, underscoring the red tinge of the guitar's highlight, which in turn leads one to notice the pinkish quality of the gray of the loosely painted skirt; the red of the two highlit cherries held up to Victorine's lips, picking out the reddish cast of her skin, hair, gleaming earring, and even the slightly dead black-brown of her eyes; and the red of the two vertical strips of wall next to the swinging doors of the café.

The enframing red of the strips of wall marks and emphasizes the reddish range of the entire painting, and serves to join and elide the painting's outermost edge to its innermost contents, its "support" and frame to its literal surface and its illusionistic representation of a woman. Interrupting that connection between edge and interior of the painting is the dark bottle green, barely distinguishable from black, of the swinging doors – it stands in stark contrast to the red tendencies of the rest of the painting. Yet it also enhances the enframedness, as well as the connectedness of edge and surface, that characterizes the painting in its entirety. For it too is echoed elsewhere in the work. Its contrast function, blackness, and virtual absence of color are all picked up in the manifold edges and limits of the surfaces of Victorine's person and costume: the black piping of her jacket, the black strap of her guitar, the black shadow cast by the guitar, the shadows inside her right sleeve, marking off outer from inner sleeve and emerging hand, the black of her hat at the apex of her figure, the black of the shadow beneath her skirt at the base of her figure, and the lower part of the swinging doors themselves, where they turn most to black and silhouette Victorine's figure. These blacks are tonally related to the light gray of Victorine's costume, the dark gray of the waiter's suit, and the range of light and dark gray of the upper part of the background. At the same time, because of the pinkish cast of the gray skirt, and the fading of the background into the pinkish brown of the floor both fore and aft of Victorine, what begins as strong coloristic contrast ends as a close, subtly dissonant harmony of colors, while color saturation and virtual absence of color begin to lose their difference, and framing edge, literal surface, and painted illusion begin to lose theirs.

The instance of strongest contrast is the yellow wrapper, which joins edge to surface in its contact with the thin line of yellow of the guitar string (or glimpsed guitar front – here the same yellow pigment convincingly does double duty as cheap rustling paper and either stretched metallic wire or gleaming laminated wood). The wrapper stands out from the ensemble, announcing its paintedness, and by extension the paintedness of the whole, while also insinuating the undecidability of the relationship between the literal and illusionistic dimensions of the painting of which it is the very heart. It is situated between the two hands, the one articulated and volumetric, the other flat and peculiarly shapeless, and between the opaque, flat slickness of the painting of the *pelisse*, a kind of quick caricature of traditional finish, and the increasing looseness and brushiness of the painting of the skirt, with the greater tonal variation of its more complicated folds, its hint of transparency and coloristic variation (there is the barest whisper of stripes in or beneath the skirt), its definite suggestion of lift, drape, and buoyancy, and the sketchy glimpse of petticoat beneath it. As the eye moves down Victorine's dress, the descent from layered overclothing to glimpsed underclothing is matched to a slide from *fini* to *non-fini* effect. So the yellow wrapper serves also as a kind of juncture between different factures, the different illusionisms they enact, the different clothing surfaces they represent, with the different kinds of concealment and exposure they provide for the figure of Victorine.

The wrapper in *The Streetsinger* is the crux of the picture's painted assertion that the inherently undecidable illusionisms of facture and color are precisely what constitute the persona of Victorine. They are what constitute her stance, her appearance of casual naturalness as well as professional posedness, her accouterments and costume, her model's involvement in dress and undress, her *demi-mondaine* doubling of identity. They are, in short, what constitute the painting's fundamentally ambiguous effect of "Victorine herself." This painting sends us searching for the line dividing frame, form, and content, the boundary between the literal and illusionistic, the frontier between the "natural" and the artificial, the threshold between what is "native" and what is foreign to a person. And what that search yields is the realization that while these oppositions are all of a piece, cut from the same cloth, made from the same substance – oil paint – their double nature and elusive color shifts are absolutely essential to the constitution of a person in painting.

The other painting of the 1862 pair, *Mlle V. . . . in the Costume of an Espada*, begun in the spring of 1862, was probably not finished to Manet's satisfaction in time for the exhibition at Martinet's the next March. In this full-length view of "Mlle V." in Spanish, masculine costume, with its screen of references to a Raimondi print and Goya's *tauromaquia* images, Victorine's salient features are presented to the viewer – red hair, milky skin, and expressionless gaze. Her red hair, however, is almost all hidden by her dusty pink bandana, peeking out beneath her black Spanish hat in one fat curl, glimpsed behind her ear and beneath the bandana. Victorine's face, still somehow recognizable, is

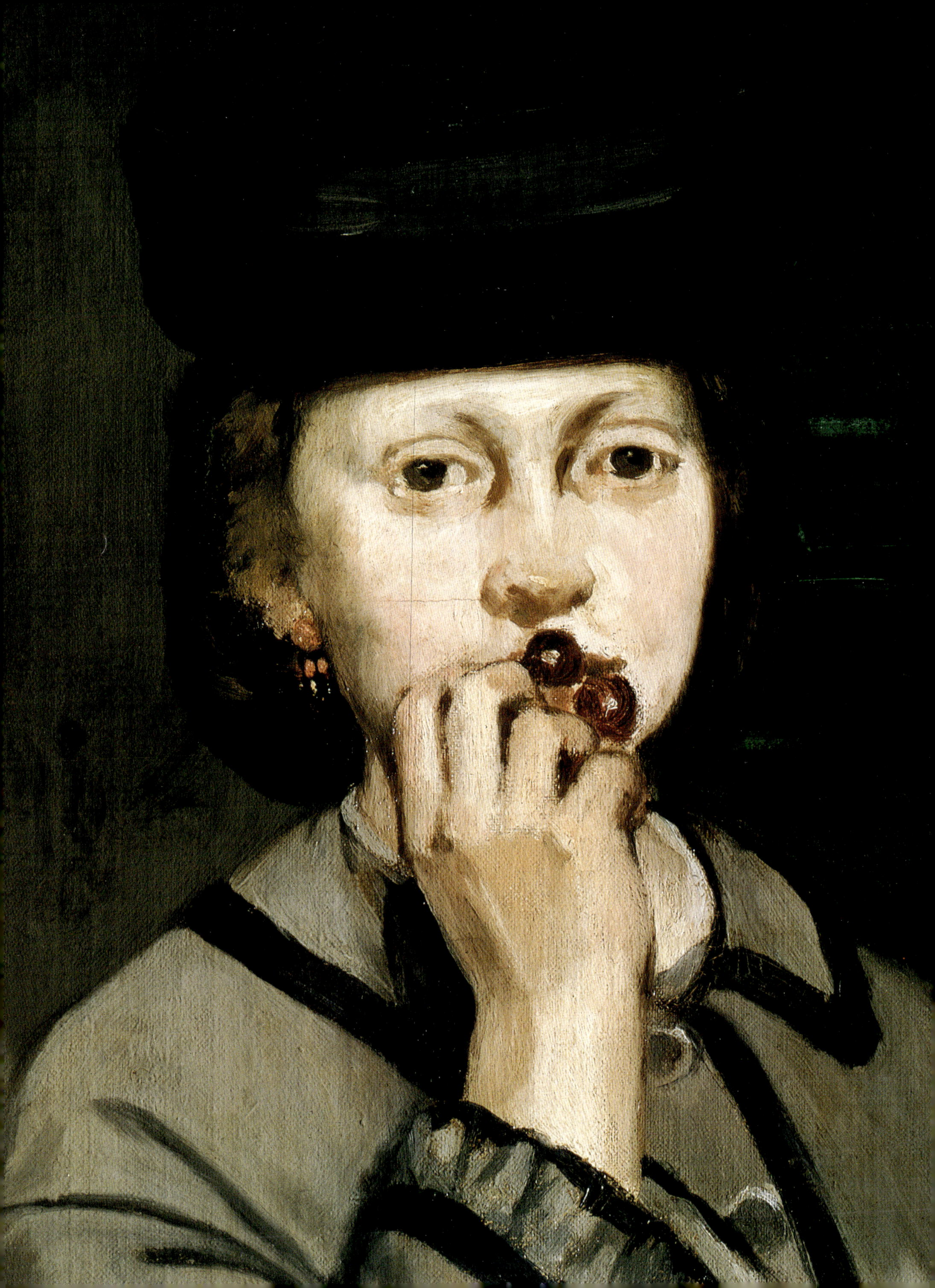

very different from the way it was depicted in *The Streetsinger*: plump and Rubensian, with the suggestion of a double chin, fleshy nose, appley left cheek, and on that side of her face, very little hint of bone beneath the padding of her fatty skin. (The right side of her face, by contrast, is more defined: even the brow and bone above her eye socket are more articulated, in sharp though subtle distinction from the flatness of her left brow. It is almost as if two different faces had been joined at the nose, as if the three-quarter view were interesting because of its potential for ambiguous differentiation between sides and views of the same face.)

Victorine's body is also more ample and female than it seems to be in *The Streetsinger's* body-concealing dress, and its theatrical presentation in male drag emphasizes that. Although her bolero jacket and the crossing of her left arm across her chest both succeed in hiding the curve of her breast, the profile view of her skin-tight pantaloons emphasizes the female line of her belly and slope of her buttock, and the plump, unmuscled curve of her thighs. The shiny white of her stockings, in stark contrast to the flat black pantaloons above them, emphasizes the plumpness of her calves, while at the same time echoing the flesh tones of her plump face, and declaring the paintedness of both, since hosiery and naked skin are both of the same pigment, deriving, one sees, from the same palette. This blatant, painted artificiality is enhanced by the coloristic sameness of Victorine's left hand and stockinged calves, and punctuated by the contrast between her two hands, the one white with the suggestion of linear detail, the other yellow-ish, as if gloved, picking up the hue of the brighter yellow slash of cloth beneath her arm.

And that loop of cloak held in her left hand, framing its whiteness and detail with a swatch of salmon-pink paint, is no cloak but blatantly paint, an odd, brushy shape which sits atop the canvas like a blob of off-color icing,[8] edged by the cloudy bluishness beneath it, in flat profile on the whitish ground. As the right hand almost picks up the color of the underarm slash, the face and left hand almost pick up the color of the legs, the eyes almost pick up the flat black of the hat, jacket, and tasseled pantaloons, the russet curl almost picks up the colors of the wall, one of the horses, the horseman's jacket and his trousers, Victorine's shoes, and even parts of the thin, Davidian lower part of the ground, so this piece of salmon paint is almost picked up in the stroke of paint beneath the feet of the group of spectators in the upper right-hand corner of the painting. And as the russet, flesh, and rose tones in and around Victorine's face almost clash with one another, so that salmon patch of paint clashes in turn, almost, with that ensemble of pigments forming and framing the face. Finally, that slightly gauche pairing of rose and russet is picked up and emphasized behind Victorine, in the mahogany color of the wall, and set off by the meeting between the pink of her bandana and flesh tone of her face, with its cheek's hint of a different rose tint, turning the bandana, by association, into a more purplish hue.

What begins to become clear about this painting, then, is the close association between the play with pigment and the exploration of the ambiguities of identity; between the changeability of colors and the instability of a model's personality and physicality; between the declared literalness of paint and the enactedness of gender, professional role, and self-presentation, of personhood in short. As Thoré said about this picture: "to the right, a young Parisian woman in the costume of a *matador*, agitating her purple coat in the bullfight ring . . . There are some astonishing fabrics . . . but, beneath these brilliant costumes, the person herself is a bit lacking; heads should be painted differently from drapery . . ."[9] Thus it was possible at the time to point directly to the bold but ambiguous colorism – a pink can be called a purple – as well as the paintedness, quotational quality, costumed character – *parisianisme* dressed up as Spanishicity – and the central absence of the model's self from this picture, or at least the equation of her selfhood with color, paint, quotation, and costume. The salmon swatch of paint is the sign – and again the crux – of that correlation between the ambiguities and artificialities of pigment and personality. It also announces that confounding the eye of the viewer, as the "red" cape is meant to confound the eye of the bull, is the way illusionism works, and that the indeterminacies of color and the deliberate confusions of optical illusionism are as inseparable from one another as they are from the illusionistic constitution of a "person."

In sum, between *The Streetsinger* and *Mlle V.*, Victorine is rendered very differently, in two paintings that present her as alternately close to and far from who she was in life. In the one, she wears the streetclothes of a *demi-mondaine* performer, those clothes are appropriately feminine and French, and as a "streetsinger" she is identified as a modern vocational type in the tradition of the physiognomic print. In the other, she is rendered not "after life" but after the art of Goya and others, she wears the theatrical costume of another kind of performer, and that costume is masculine and Spanish – as distant from who Victorine "really was" as the streetclothes are proximate to it. And yet it is the latter picture that has her own (abbreviated) name in the title, while at the same time announcing that she is appearing in costume and playing a role, that she is precisely not herself. In the one, Victorine's body is covered and indistinguishable; in the other it is revealed (as feminine) by her (masculine) attire. In the one she is shown against a more or less convincing contemporary background; in the other she appears pasted onto a tipped up, spatially unconvincing ground, demonstrably lifted from mechanically reproduced images: for all the figure's roundedness of face and figure, *Mlle V.* is curiously flat, in contrast to the illusionism of ballooning, layered bulk and the hint of a volumetric underneath offered in *The Streetsinger's* dress. Together *The Streetsinger* and *Mlle V.* form an odd couple, pairing several sets of terms – female/male, slim/plump, Parisian/Spanish, clothed/costumed, concealed/revealed, street/hippodrome, from "life"/from art, volumetric/flat, and so on – disordering the binary logic of those terms somewhat so that they cannot quite be neatly aligned on clearly opposed continuums. And the same unstable binaries operate throughout these mismatched pendants, in Manet's exploration of the two-sidedness of the human face and figure, and the possibilities for internal division and lateral differentiation that it offers: it is condensed in the contrasts between hands worked out in almost all of these paintings.

Thus the coupling of *The Streetsinger* and *Mlle V. . . . in the Costume of an Espada* pursues the problematics of personhood in paint that the stripped-down face of the *Portrait of Victorine Meurent* had begun to open up. But *The Streetsinger* and *Mlle V.* were uncoupled when Manet showed them in 1863 and were brought together again only in 1867, as numbers 19 and 12 in Manet's retrospective, gathered with all the other Victorine "pendants" toward the beginning of the catalogue list. In 1863, *The Streetsinger* kept company at Martinet's with *The Gypsies, The Old Musician,* the *Young Woman Reclining in Spanish Costume, Lola de Valence, Music at the Tuileries,* and the rest. In that context, she served as a kind of shifter between the genres of the physiognomic type and the costume piece, the subjects of the *chiffonnier,* street musician, and exotic performer, the "pretty Parisian" and the *Espagnole,* and the themes of bohemianism and demi-mondanity, Velasquez-style courtliness and Baudelairean modernity organizing the other paintings on view at Martinet's, where the problematics of painting personhood were more diffusely presented than they were in Manet's own studio.

In May of 1863 *Mlle V.* went on view separately at the Salon des Refusés, re-paired in two directions, with her male companion, the *Young Man in the Costume of a Majo,* and her alter ego in the *Luncheon on the Grass,* such that she served as a middle term between the Spanishicity of the one and the quotational Italianicity of the other, between cos-tuming and nudity, masculinity and femininity, contextlessness and context, tight and loose facture, the single-figure and multiple-figure composition, the family member that the *Young Man* portrays and the circle of alterity and familiarity that the *Luncheon* rep-resents. I shall come to the Salon des Refusés positioning of *Mlle V.* and the *Luncheon on the Grass* as two points of the triangle made by that trio of paintings. But first I turn to the next of Manet's studio pairings of the face and figure of Victorine, that of 1863, in which, prior to being exhibited, the *Luncheon on the Grass* was the pendant of the soon-to-be notorious *Olympia* (figs. 8, 9).

1863 (AND 1865)

The 1863 pair of paintings in which Victorine Meurent's features appear is distinguished by two facts: Victorine is rendered naked in both (all the other paintings of her show her clothed) and she appears in company; whereas all the other images of her are essen-tially single-figure pictures, both of these are multi-figure compositions. Moreover, the 1863 duo is the most dramatically quotational of all of the pairs; each is a direct citation from Venetian painting, the one of Giorgione/Titian's *Fête champêtre* in the Louvre, layered together with other quotes, and the other of Titian's *Venus of Urbino,* which Manet had copied in the Uffizi on an early trip to Italy. Because of the furor that developed around them when they were exhibited in 1863 and 1865, the *Luncheon on the Grass* and *Olympia* quickly became the best-known of Manet's paintings of Victorine, the ones with whom his reputation as a *succès de scandale* was most identified. Yet they are anomalous in these regards.

At the same time, in *Luncheon on the Grass* and *Olympia,* Victorine's face and figure undergo the same subtle changes as found in the 1862 pair of *The Streetsinger* and *Mlle V. . . . in the Costume of an Espada.* As in those paintings, Victorine's Titian hair and the quality of her stare continue to suggest that it is the same model in each. In this pair of pictures, that sameness is both asserted and questioned, this time by matching a certain indeterminacy in the rendering of Victorine to a movement between different factural manners. In the *Luncheon* we find those different manners assigned to two separate renderings of the female figure, one smooth, hard, and unmodulated, rendering Victorine large-bodied and whitely naked in the front plane, the other soft, light-handed, and loosely sketched, depicting a smaller, more recessive female figure in her chemise in

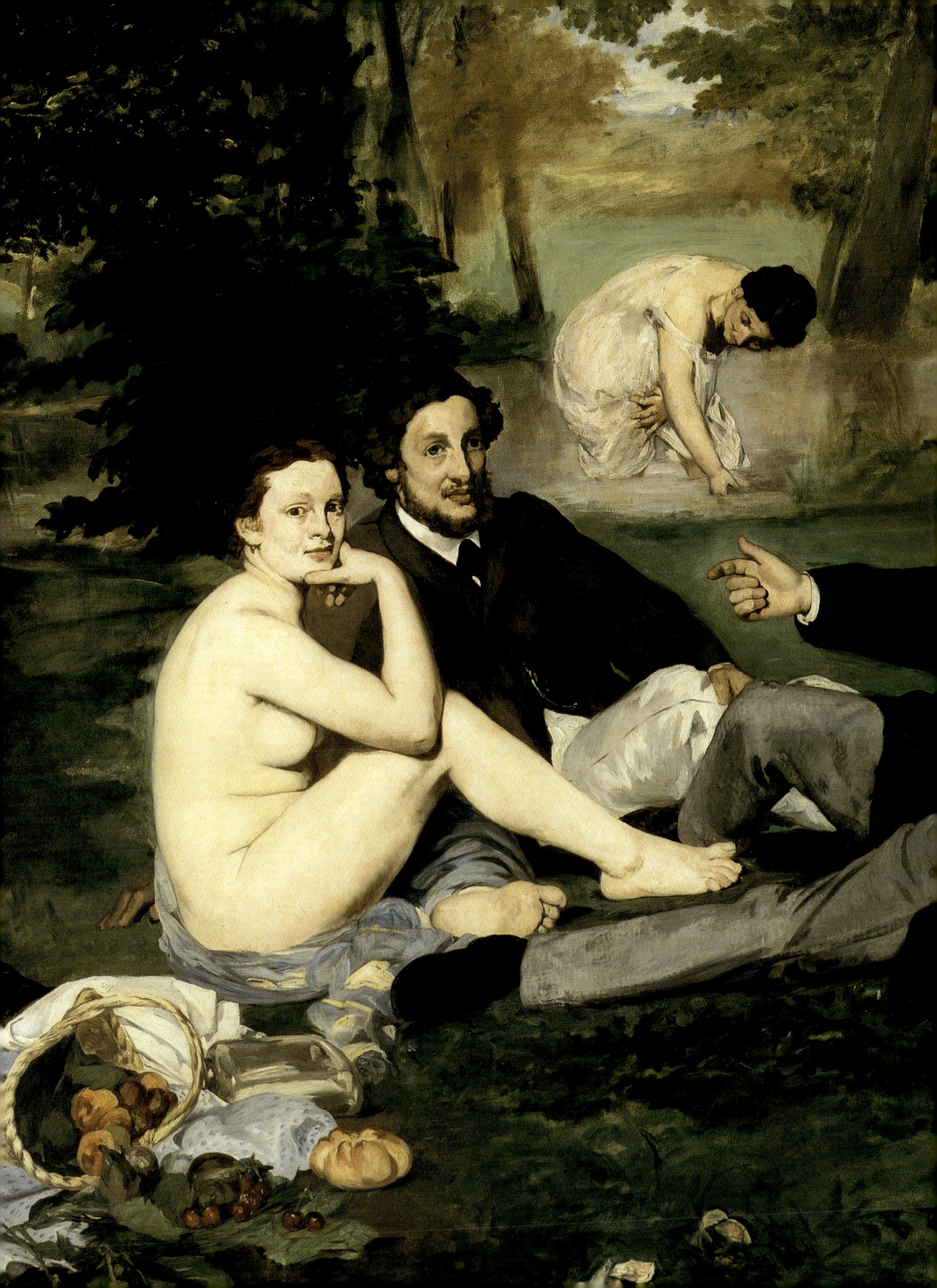

the middle distance, whose folded over posture is a tilted variant of the foreground C-shape of Victorine. These two renderings have the air of two views of the same woman (although my guess is that Victorine did not pose for both: the sketchy Watteau-derived figure is clearly lifted from art rather than life). In *Olympia*, on the other hand, those two manners are collapsed into the single rendering of her face, distinguishable only when one moves back and forth in front of the painting, from the hard, slicked back, resistant flatness of Olympia-Victorine's face from a medium distance, to the softer, more yielding painterliness of her mouth, chin, and loosened hair up close.[10] Thus *Olympia*, which extends the hard–soft, determinate–indeterminate contrasts, and even the tight–loose rendering of the hair of the little portrait of Victorine of the year before, is a bit like the two women of the *Luncheon* collapsed into one – one, however, who is also two.

Between the *Luncheon* and *Olympia*, it is not only the identity of the model's face but also the rendering of her body that is brought into question. For in these two paintings the body takes part in Manet's play with painted personhood, and in running the gamut between large, heavy, and inert, at once flattened and rounded on the one hand, and small, pert, and recalcitrantly angular on the other hand, the two pictures, taken together, seem to tread the line between the body's essential anonymity and its taking part in a person's personality – or in this case, multiple personalities. Moreover, that the locus of pictorial interest and painterly pleasure is not the female body per se – is everywhere but the female body – is observable in both paintings. It is clear that the sensuous rendering of naked female flesh was neither Manet's forte nor his fascination. In each painting a stark, unmodulated body is framed by and contrasted with a deliciously and variously painted world, including a rich assortment of colored accessories.[11] Given the traditional function of the female nude as the object of the "male gaze," which naturalized the gendered splitting of visuality into the to-be-looked-at-ness of (unclothed) femininity and the (clothed) masculinity of the bearer of the "look," a reading begins to suggest itself of Victorine's twice-painted body as a meditation on the gendering of subject–object relations and the differentation between self and other so fundamental to the construct of the "person."

With her frank stare, the bouquet of flowers from a client, and her play on the *Venus of Urbino* as well as on seductive contemporary nudes like Cabanel's *Birth of Venus*, *Olympia* has always been understood as unmasking the logic of the gaze at work in the tradition of the female nude. To a lesser extent, and for similar reasons, the *Luncheon on the Grass* has been understood in the same way.[12] Put together, the two paintings go to work on the problem in a more complicated fashion. Where the *Luncheon* shows two white women, one large and the other small, in different states of undress, *Olympia* poses the small white body of the nude next to the more ample, clothed figure of a black servant, both differentiating between their otherncesses and the classed services they perform, and associating, doubling, and underscoring the alterity of femininity with that of negritude, thereby reiterating a longstanding tradition.[13] On the one hand, the *Luncheon*'s odd sociability groups two views of the same Other – two women of the same culture, race, and class – in a familial circle made up Manet's male familiars – Ferdinand Leenhoff, the sculptor brother of his soon-to-be wife, posed for the clothed male figure looking out at us, while both of Manet's brothers are said to have taken turns posing for

Detail of fig. 9.

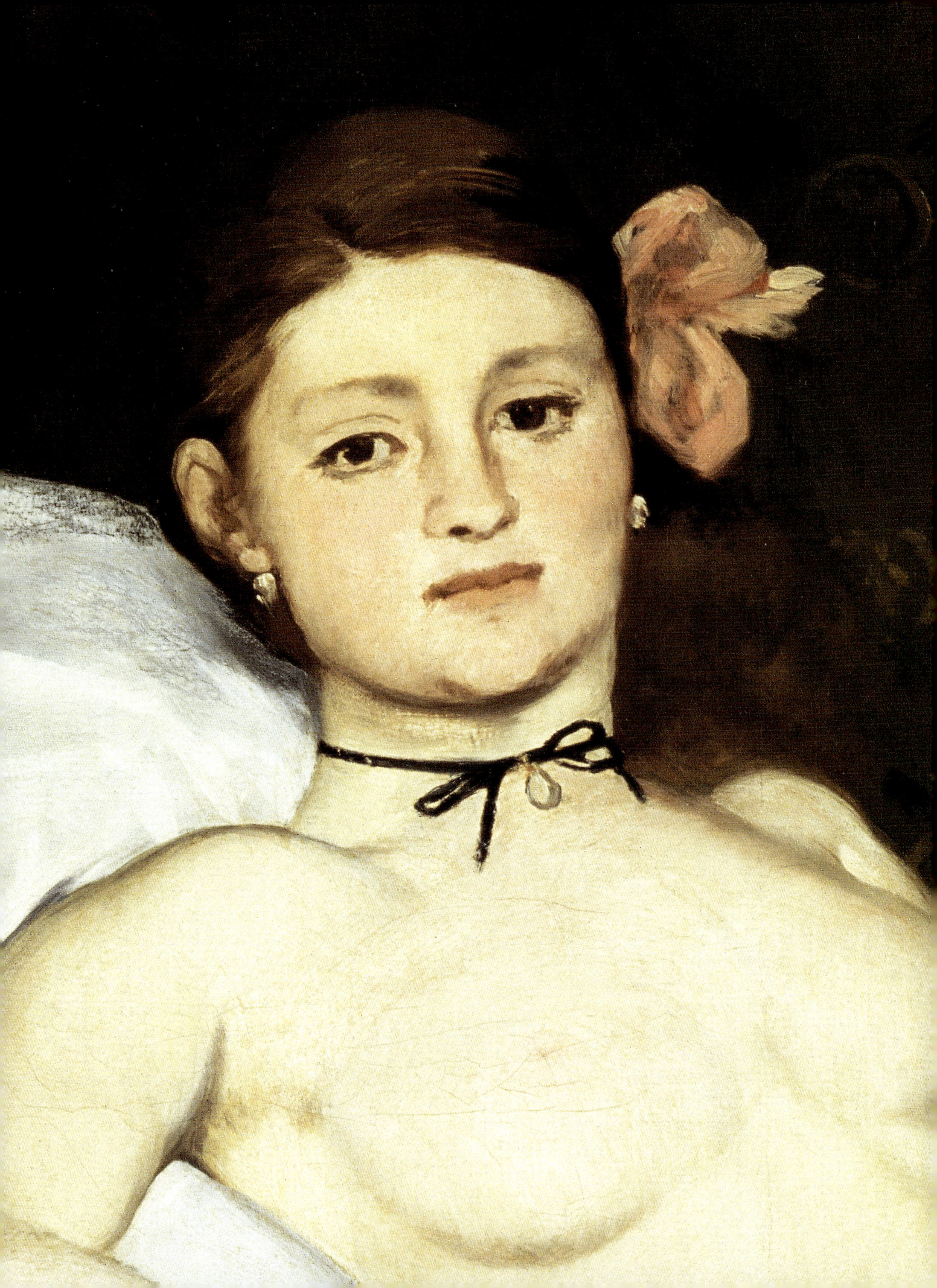

the gesturing male figure at right. On the other hand, *Olympia*'s alienated little *fille* keeps company with an Other who others her more completely.[14] And while the *Luncheon* includes the implied (and doubled) male consumer of the female body within its frame, *Olympia* excludes him, at the same time implicating and addressing him as the viewer of the painting. Thus in the latter, same and other, subject and object, male and female, are clearly opposed terms, while in the former they are linked and combined, found together on the same side of the pictorial divide.

In *Luncheon on the Grass*, Eugène/Gustave's index finger points our gaze to the way Victorine Meurent and Ferdinand Leenhoff are as much alternates as they are opposites: which is underlined by the close pairing of their two heads, feminine and masculine, smooth and bearded, *roussâtre* and *brunâtre*; and their two bodies, unclothed and clothed, white and black, the line of Ferdinand's arm duplicating that of Victorine's leg, while his oddly painted white trouser-knee joins with the opposite gray knee of Eugène/Gustave. Male and female are twice opposed, but they are also twice twinned, to form a double Janus figure. The same pointing gesture also indexes some other things concerning the same and the other, *soi-même* and *autrui*. For in the *Luncheon* alterity intrudes into the family circle: Manet sets his favorite model and two or three family members next to one another, folding them out, side to front to side, so that female model and male family members together form a closed, self-referential circle, broken only by Victorine's white body and the loose facture of the bent over figure in the middle distance between the two men. Thus, in the *Luncheon on the Grass*, gendered identity functions much like the gravure – in a series of varied replications and reversals, dark to light, left to right, masculine to feminine, intimate to other. In short, the *Luncheon* proposes a system in which the female body mirrors and partners the "male gaze," rather than being opposed to it. Victorine's outward stare (matched by Ferdinand's similarly directed but more inward-feeling look) is the emblem of that system.

As she appears in the *Luncheon* Victorine is a two-fold figure of the gaze itself, as well as of its object. She untidies the neat old binarisms of gender and the gaze; rendering them together, she alters them. The same may be said of *Olympia*, in that Victorine's deadpan look, at once bold and blank, dominating and affectless, reciprocal and unreceptive to the viewer's ogling glance, and yet sensuously vulnerable up close under the touch of the painter, may be understood as at once subverting and combining the subject and object terms of the gaze. And in *Olympia*, Victorine is stared at by her other Other, from within the picture, whose visible black hand is so oddly similar to the pubic hand of her mistress, and who brings her the bouquet that is simultaneously the sign of her prostitution, the flower of her femininity (if we are to believe those caricaturists who blew up the bouquet to outsized proportions and collapsed it with her body, in close juxtaposition to the equally exaggerated pussy-cat, transforming *Olympia* into an extended play on genital substitution and signification *à la* Baudelaire), and the emblem of her constitution in paint, her displacement of erotic and aesthetic pleasure from the body to its painted surrounds, to all that frames, complements, attends, attributes, and responds to it.

Yet, if Victorine refuses to submit to the gaze in *Olympia*, she seems also to be more clearly its object and opposite term than she is in the *Luncheon*. She is much more single than she is in the *Luncheon*, where she is circled by companions in relation to whom

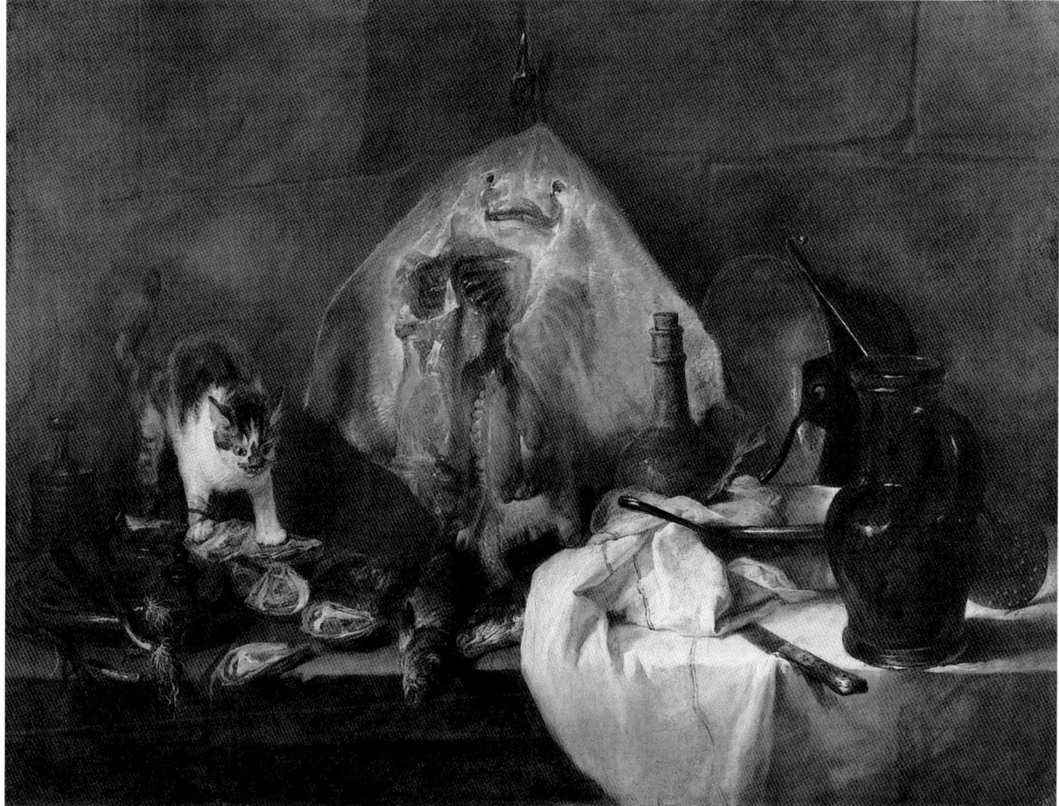

69　Jean-Baptiste-Siméon Chardin, *The Ray*, c.1727, oil on canvas, 114.5 × 146 cm. Musée du Louvre, Paris.

her disruptive separateness is defined and diffused. And, as Zola remarked, she is a still life. Where in the *Luncheon* she is seated next to an array of objects that form a still life in its own right, in *Olympia* it is the ensemble of Victorine's body, accouterments, and setting that is the *nature morte*: the vaginal-pink bloom in her hair; the bunch of flowers with its white chrysanthemum at the center, its white wrapping similar to the white sheet on which she rests; her gold bangle; the shawl that she fingers with its scattered, embroidered blossoms and bit of fringe echoing the fall of the locket from her bangle, in turn echoing the locket hanging from her neck ribbon; her blue-edged satin slippers, one off and one on (like the gloves in other pictures); her white bedlinen suggesting the ubiquitous white napkin of the still life genre; and even the black cat, irresistibly recalling the rearing, rigidified cat at the left of Chardin's 1728 reception piece, *The Ray*, then in the La Caze collection (fig. 69).[15]

Thus in *Olympia*, Victorine figures another conflation of terms – corporeal substance and decorative supplement, predicate and attribute, the genres of nude and still life, the categories of human figure, animal life, and inanimate object.[16] The genre of the female nude, from Titian's *Venus of Urbino* to Cabanel's *Birth of Venus*, had always made a still life of the human body – a luxury commodity, an object of appetite, exchange, and imaginary consumption, rather than a bearer of narrative value, or a sign for human subjecthood. The female nude, that is, had always played still life to the history painting function of the male body. But *Olympia*'s novelty lies in her confronting of that fact, and in her locating of subjective effect in her obdurate, impassive objectness. Indeed, this seems to have been a consistent disturbance for Manet's critics, in that they all, almost to a man, spoke of Manet's treatment of people (mostly female people) as objects; *Olympia* was simply the public focus and flashpoint of that disturbance.

If we imagine the *Luncheon* and *Olympia* side by side in Manet's studio, then, the two paintings enter into dialogue with one another on the subject of the otherness and objecthood of the female person. And each riffs contrapuntally on Baudelaire's observation that "for the artist woman is not . . . the female of man . . . everything that adorns woman . . . is a part of herself . . ."[17] For the two paintings' conversation on the subject of femininity points directly to Baudelaire's tract on "l'autrui, la femme," in which he opposed the representation of contemporary woman to the image of the female body mediated by the museum and the print. Twice Baudelaire spoke of precisely those old masters most prominently cited in Manet's two paintings, Titian (*Olympia*) and Raphael (the *Luncheon*).[18] Although it might seem that he was castigating his friend Manet (in advance) for aping the past masters of art in the *Luncheon* and *Olympia*, at the same time the oppositions between contemporaneity and art history found in his essay match the tensions built into Manet's 1863 quotations from the Louvre and the Uffizi. Titian and Raphael versus the modern *impure*, the museum versus the chic *fille entretenue*, the old master gravure versus the up-to-the-minute *lorette* and state of the art *biche*: these were exactly the oppositions mobilized by Manet in his two pictures of Victorine dating from 1863. Except that Manet collapsed the oppositions, pictorially demonstrating that the old masterpieces of Titian and Raphael were enacted by an *impure* whose modern job it was to do such acting, and that the museum and the gravure, rather than the boudoir and the forest, were the habitat of his *fille entretenue*. For Manet it was in the artificial habitat of the studio museum, with all its costume changes (nudity was just another one of those), that Baudelairian femininity could best be performed in painting.[19]

The *Luncheon* disputes its own alibis in contemporary culture and *plein-air* nature more obviously than *Olympia* does. As in the other pictures of Victorine, the *Luncheon*'s assertion of the artificiality of its own fiction seems to reside most of all in the obstinate opacity of Victorine's gaze. But to that gaze it adds also the manifest illogic of its naked women and clothed men and their patently false updating of the Renaissance court pastorale and mythological beauty contest, the implausibility of the quickly brushed in background, the narrative emptiness of the one man's pointing gesture, and the plethora of art historical images to which that gesture seems to refer while also directing us to Victorine. Moreover, added to the *Luncheon*'s equation is the fact of mechanical reproduction, most prominently found in the central gesture of Eugène/Gustave's arm, lifted from Raimondi's engraving after Raphael's *Judgment of Paris* (and then copied again by Manet himself in an ink and watercolor version of his painting).

Olympia, for her part, was not only a variation on Manet's painted reproduction of the *Venus of Urbino*, a redoing of the *Young Woman Reclining in Spanish Costume*, and the end product of a fairly traditional series of studies, she was also reproduced as an etching (it was thus that she figured in Zola's pamphlet) and as a painted photograph hung on the wall in his portrait of Zola of 1868.[20] Thus both the *Luncheon on the Grass* and *Olympia* added Manet's already well established problematic of the reproduction of originality to their dialogic investigation of the Baudelairean dialectic of femininity, in which authentic modernity is mediated by reference and reproduction. Although Manet seemed to go against Baudelaire's censuring of the academic habit of "separat[ing] woman from her costume," at the same time he followed Baudelaire's dictum in both paintings of 1863, proposing that femininity is costuming, and that "the painting of pleasure" lies in everything that frames and supplements the female body, rather than in that body itself – in its artifice rather than its "nature," its fashionability rather than its animal corporeality, its changeability rather than its stable essence. In other words, in the 1863 pair Victorine is yet again *Mlle V. in the Costume of . . .* , twice over. Seen together, the *Luncheon* and *Olympia* inflect each other with their different statements to this effect: that the woman they depict plays several characters from the history of art and that, rather than the street or the boudoir, her real context can only be the studio in which her persona is variously constructed, through the screen of the museum and the print.[21]

The couple formed by the two Victorines in 1863 was again divorced when the time came to exhibit them – and this time the separation was more pronounced, with two years and one Salon coming between them. In the Salon des Refusés, Manet's trio of pictures positioned Victorine in a related but different way from the studio pair in which her features appeared in 1863. As in that pair, her features appeared twice, but in the Salon des Refusés, the anomaly of her nude, Italianizing presence in the *Luncheon on the Grass* (or *Le Bain*, as it was then titled) was highlighted, while the fact of her identity as the studio model "Mlle V." seemed to be underlined, both by the doubling of her features and the similarity of her face and body in the two pictures in which she appeared. The related fact of her costuming was also stressed, by the "in the costume of" found in the titles of both *Mlle V.* and the picture of Gustave Manet as a *majo*. The etchings were displayed separately, in the prints section of the Salon des Refusés, but with the inclusion of the print after Velasquez's *Philip IV*, the print after Velasquez's *Little Cavaliers*, and the print after Manet's *Lola de Valence*, the quotational quality of both of the Victorine pictures in the painting section was redoubled, if anyone chose to notice. Finally, *Mlle V. . . . in the Costume of an Espada* and the *Young Man in the Costume of a Majo*, sharing their featured models with those of the *Luncheon on the Grass*, slyly pointed to the latter's mixing and matching of otherness and the family circle, and its refusal to describe the functions of alterity and identity as opposite terms. Thus, if the studio pair of 1863 was parted, the dialogue on the model's personhood in which it engaged was nevertheless maintained, in the company that Victorine kept in the Salon des Refusés, both in the already conversational picture *Luncheon on the Grass* and in its companions.

It was otherwise in 1865, when Manet gave Victorine a partner altogether different from herself, and thus removed her completely from the studio thematics in which her features seemed to be involved. We can only speculate as to why Manet decided to hold *Olympia* back rather than submitting her with her alter ego to the Salon in 1863. Perhaps he did not feel that *Olympia* was finished to his complete satisfaction, and therefore was not sure that he was ready to put it on public display. By 1864, with the painting of *The Dead Christ and the Angels* (fig. 70), it may have occurred to him that, if he held *Olympia*

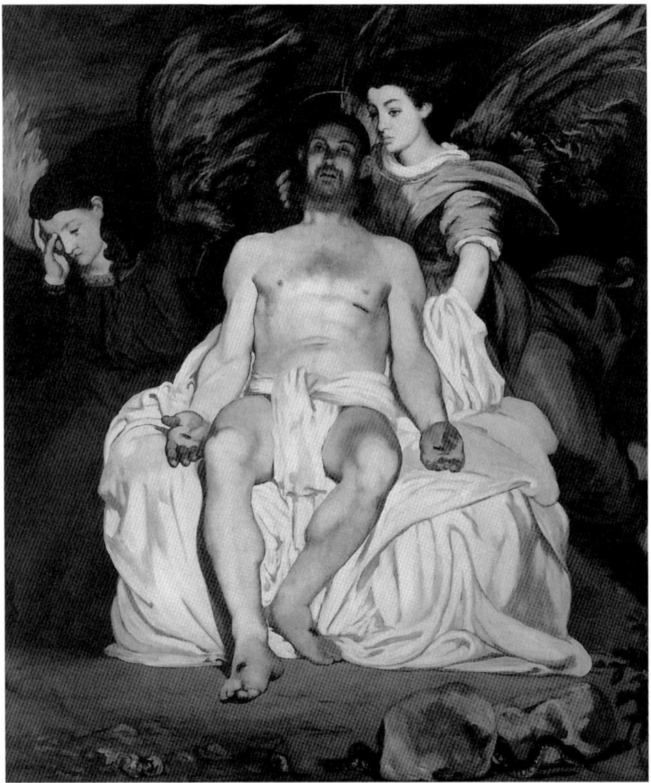

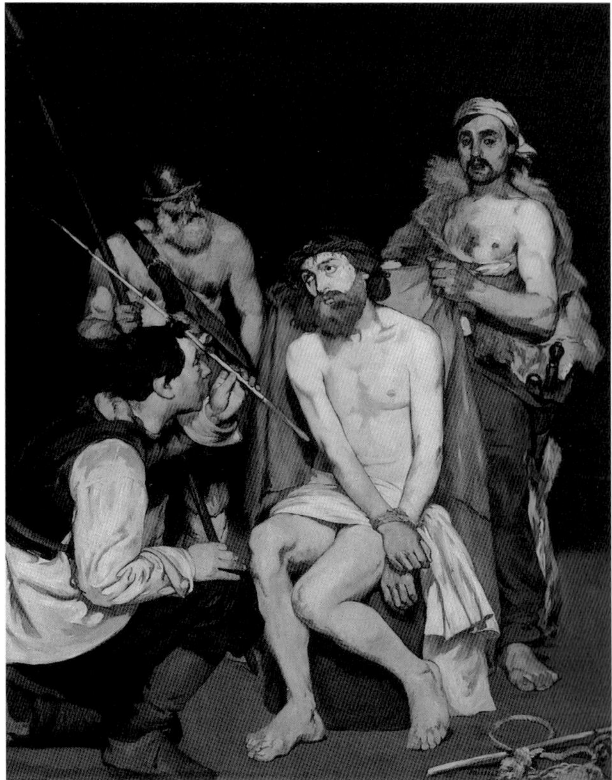

70   Edouard Manet, *The Dead Christ and the Angels*, 1864, oil on canvas, 179.4 × 149.9 cm. The Metropolitan Museum of Art, New York, H. O. Havemeyer Collection, Bequest of Mrs. H. O. Havemeyer, 1929. (29.100.51).

71   Edouard Manet, *The Mocking of Christ*, 1865, oil on canvas, 190.3 × 148.3 cm. The Art Institute of Chicago. Gift of James Deering, 1925.703.

back one more year, he could finish another religious picture that was a more overt Titian quotation and present them together, thus underlining his bid to be considered Titian's descendent, a kind of latter-day court painter working in two of the most ambitious and traditional genres associated with the Venetian school. Perhaps by that time, after the fact of the Salon des Refusés, he was disappointed in the critics' failure to understand the *Luncheon on the Grass* as a great picture in the tradition of the old masters, and then wished to stress the quotational dimension of his practice in a more consistent way. If so, the ploy did not work, for *Olympia's* reference to the *Venus of Urbino* went largely unnoticed and, even more insistently than the *Luncheon on the Grass*, it came to be situated within contemporary discourse on the female body – that of the prostitute.[22]

Indeed, the exhibiting of *Olympia* together with *The Mocking of Christ* (fig. 71), with its address to the abused male body, seemed to reinforce the critics' understanding of her within a contemporary thematics of the body, articulated in terms of references to the corpse and the morgue. Visually speaking, however, of the two religious pictures with which she could have been associated, the *Christ with the Angels*, with its similar presentation of the body to the viewer by retainers (the angels), and its similar still life arrangement of that body against a sheet in such a way as to emphasize the coloristic meeting of blue-ish white and dirty flesh, makes a better companion for *Olympia,* underlining the pairing of male and female bodies, the gendered alibis for making those bodies objects of the gaze, and the mortified aspect of *Olympia*'s flesh. His pairing of *Olympia* with *The Mocking of Christ* instead of *Christ with Angels* suggests that his references to the museum were more important to him than any reading of the body as corpse, or woman as "the female of man."[23]

It suggests also that, after 1863, Manet no longer thought the Salon was an appropriate venue for putting his studio meditation on the personhood of the model on view. It was the place, not to question the structure of his own persona as a painter, but to garner and bolster a reputation by claiming an updated version of old master status for himself, and by reinforcing his own consistency rather than his inconsistency. *Olympia,* at the same time, is the prime example of Manet's constant misunderstanding of the audience whose admiration he courted, and of the mismatch between his interests as a painter and its expectations and discursive limitations. For the dialogue that Manet worked out between paintings in his studio was simply unavailable to most of his audience in his time. As in 1864, so in 1865: Manet's critics selected one painting for their incomprehension and ridicule, focusing on *Olympia* by herself rather than her pairing with *The Mocking of Christ,* not only ignoring her updating of Titian, but insisting on reading her, against the visual evidence of her setting and her accouterments, as the poorest and meanest of prostitutes. It was a case of misreading on both sides: Manet of his public and his public of his paintings.

The proper place to put the thematics associated with Victorine was not the Salon but the studio – to which Manet returned all of his Victorine pictures after exhibiting them in the various Salons in which they showed up. It was in the studio that he assembled them for display, and in that context that Zola and others saw them in 1867, before the Universal Exposition. It was in the studio that he rehearsed his retrospective, and then out of the studio, in the Place de l'Alma site, that he reassembled his Victorine pictures, producing what amounted to an off-site studio display for the same wrong public that frequented the Salons, and headlining it with the re-paired Victorine duo of *Luncheon on the Grass* and *Olympia.* This time the public was more indifferent than indignant. No matter; all the other Victorine pictures were gathered too, after the 1863 pair and toward the beginning of the retrospective list, to stand for the experimentation in multiple personal styles and self-presentations that the rest of the monographic "exposition particulière" enacted across its disordered spectrum of genres and art-historical references. And by 1867, the list of Victorine pictures had grown to include another pair, painted in 1866 and included among those on view in the retrospective – *The Fifer* and the *Young Woman in 1866.*

*　　*　　*

1866 (AND 1868)

After the 1862 and 1863 pairs of Victorine pictures and their divided exhibition in 1863 and 1865 came another pair sporting Victorine's features, *The Reader* and the *Woman Playing the Guitar*. Executed between 1865 and 1866, *The Reader* was not exhibited at all and the *Woman Playing the Guitar* only at the 1867 retrospective, where it was number 26. Each represents Victorine in profile, in modern clothing, engaged in an activity – reading or guitar playing. In that they naturalize their model, they fall outside the logic of the Victorine series so I shall not address them, except to point out that they conform to the pattern of pairing pictures in which Victorine's face appeared. (And to remark that Manet's 1869–70 portrait of his acolyte Eva Gonzalès returned to the guitar playing pose of his favorite model of the first half of the 1860s, substituting a paintbrush for the guitar, and that he also returned to the theme of the female reader several times. Thus this unusual Victorine pair pointed the way toward, and resurfaced in, the shift in Manet's pictorial preoccupations that occurred after the retrospective of 1867.) I close this chapter, instead, with the last pair of Victorine pictures painted by Manet. In 1866, between *The Fifer* and the *Young Woman in 1866*, he returned to Victorine's alternation between performing someone else and performing herself – Victorine even further from herself than she was in *Mlle V. . . . in the Costume of an Espada*, playing at being a little boy with whose features her own are merged; Victorine *chez elle, en déshabille* in a pink *peignoir*, playing herself even more intimately than in *The Streetsinger*.

The first painting of the pair to be completed, *The Fifer* (see fig. 67), was rejected from the Salon of 1866 before Manet showed it the next year, first in his studio and then at the Place de l'Alma as number 11 (immediately followed by *Mlle V. . . . in the Costume of an Espada*). I begin with its conflation of Victorine and Léon Leenhoff.[24] Although Zola mentioned Léon's mother in the biographical section of his essay, stating that she and Manet were married in 1863, he specified Léon's identity even less than he did Victorine's, which is to say not at all. It goes without saying that Zola also avoided mentioning the indeterminacy of Léon's paternity: the fact that he might have been the illegitimate son of Manet himself, of Manet's father, or of Manet's brother, does not arise. But Léon's identity was as indissoluble from Manet's obsession with the studio masquerade as Victorine was. His features are recognizable in pictures shown in the retrospective, such as the *Boy with the Sword*, whose modeling and "narrow, contrived delicacies" Zola contrasted unfavorably to the "frank stiffness, the accurately and powerfully painted patches of the *Olympia*"[25] (thereby contrasting Léon to Victorine). Léon's features are present as well, diminutively and therefore less readably, in another picture shown in the retrospective, listed as number 50 – the little pastiched *Paysage*, in which Léon, Manet, and Suzanne are fantasized together in domestic harmony, seventeenth-century style. (And yet even there Léon is set apart, on the farther shore.) And the same features are recognizable in pictures painted after the retrospective, as in *Soap Bubbles* of the same year (fig. 72), and the *Luncheon in the Studio* of a year later, to which I shall turn in the next chapter.

Where Victorine's features change a bit inconsistently from picture to picture – from the plump, rosy contours of the *Espada*, the thinner, flatter face, and slightly winged brows of *The Streetsinger*, the straight brows, pointed chin, slight insolence, and subtle

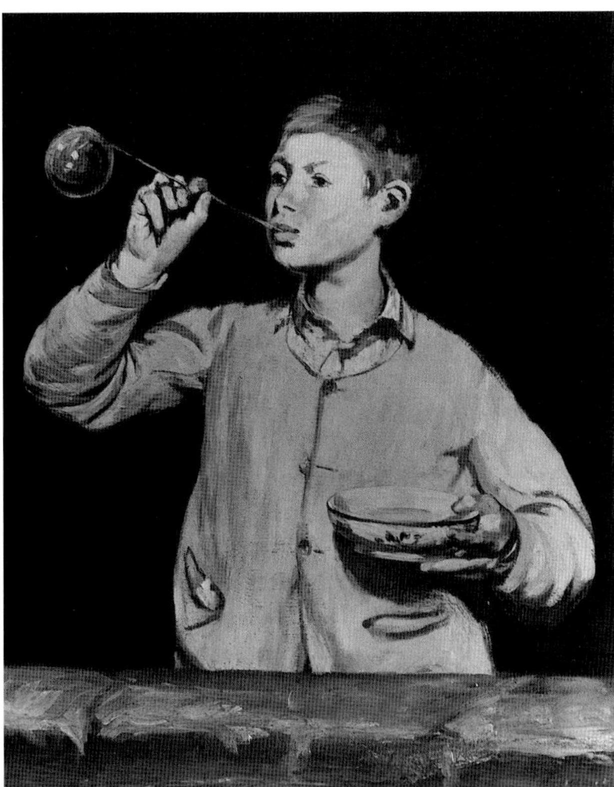

72   Edouard Manet, *Soap Bubbles*, 1867, oil on canvas, 100 × 81 cm. Calouste Gulbenkian Foundation, Lisbon.

undecidability of the *Olympia*, to the slimmer face of the *Young Woman in 1866* – and where her physiognomy is often half obscured by an object held up to her mouth or the line of a hat across her forehead, Léon's usually unobstructed features are shown to progress in a more linear way, maturing from those of a child to those of an adolescent and young man. It is these two, the Parisian *demi-mondaine* model (and perhaps mistress), and the half-French, half-Dutch son, nephew, or half-brother, who keep cropping up in Manet's paintings, and it is their features that are blended in the squat, boyish face, winging brows, snub nose, blank gaze, rose-tinted, milky skin, prominent ears, and short body of *The Fifer*. (Curiously, in addition to the quality of the gaze and the parenthesis-shaped brows – criticized earlier in *The Streetsinger* – it is the occluded parts of the face – the obscuring of the mouth by the fife, and the low framing of the forehead by the cap – that most evoke the Victorine of several years before.) For here Manet increases the ambiguities of personhood that preoccupied him throughout the 1860s, particularly underlined in his picturing of Victorine.

In *The Fifer*, Manet conflates the woman of changing identity and the child of uncertain origins in a manner that calls to mind the layering together of musket-toting *gamin*, Renaissance youth, and exotic woman in Manette Salomon's face and figure, in the Goncourts' novel of a year later.[26] Thus he underlines his celebration of the indeterminacy and mutability fundamental to personhood – to a woman whose job it is to play roles, adopt poses, and assume guises, and to a child as he grows – and also fundamental to paternity, and to the constitution of a gentleman painter's signature style. For the conflation of the features of Léon and Victorine, and the simultaneous maintenance of their individual recognizability (not unlike the way parents' separate features can remain recognizable in a child in their altered, because combined, state; or the way an infant's face, when a fleeting expression passes over it, will remind one briefly but vividly of one relative and then of another), joins the chameleon qualities of Victorine the model, Léon the child, and Manet the painter. At the same time, that elision seems to be a demonstration of the fine line trod by age, sex, and individual differences – the way those differences verge on sameness, the way sameness hedges on differences, and the way indeterminacy is fundamental to the very distinction between sameness and difference. And finally, when *The Fifer* is linked to the other pictures of Victorine and Léon, the linear development of a (masculine) individuality is intermixed with and undermined by the "inconsistency" of the (feminine) masquerade.

The painterly vehicle of *The Fifer's* elision of different genders, ages, and selves with different relations to Manet is the doubling of liveliness and flatness, illusionistic subjecthood and flat-out objecthood that is suggested in Zola's oscillation between the evocation of "a child of a musical troupe who blows in his instrument with all his breath and all his heart" and the "costumer's sign" description of "[t]he yellow of his galloons, the black-blue of his tunic, the red of his breeches . . . here no more than large patches."[27] It was the signboard aspect of Zola's description that held sway, such that *The Fifer* came to stand as a pattern card of modernist flatness. Later, when Manet's first posthumous retrospective was mounted, Paul Mantz wrote about *The Fifer* in similar terms, describing the "young musician" as "a playing card" "pasted on monochrome gray background," "glued to a chimerical wall," "a Jack of Diamonds posted on a door," with "no terrain, no air, no perspective" and no "positive atmosphere" behind and around "bodies," as, in short, adhering to "the system of the cutout."[28] Although Mantz's vocabulary was by then predictable, recycled from some twenty years' of Manet criticism, its collage-like account of the gluing, affixing, and posting of crudely readymade popular images to flat surfaces underwrites later Greenbergian accounts of Manet's modernist flatness.

Mantz's posthumous review of *The Fifer* speaks of it as one of an 1866 series of gray-background paintings, of which the *Young Woman in 1866* is another example. It is in that grayish ground, shared by the Victorine pair of 1866, in which the manner of Velasquez is referred to, and the efforts at contextualization found in the earlier Victorine pairs are relinquished. According to Mantz, it is that blank ground that is responsible for *The Fifer's* cutout look. And indeed, as if to underline its elided illusionism, there is that little joke of a shadow cast by the fifer's foot, similar to the shadow cast by Victorine's foot in *Mlle V.*[29] *The Fifer* is more of a flat shape and silhouette against a wall of gray than the *Young Woman in 1866*, whose fade from the light gray of the floor to the dark gray of the background is more coherently shaded. Nevertheless, with his/her black pant stripes, here and there confounded with the outer contour of the trousers, the flat black shoes run together with the flat black shadows beneath them and sharply contrasted with the stark white of the spats, and the dead-black cap not quite distinguishable from the brown-black of the short hair beneath and contrasted with the red of the cap's apex, there is an oscillation between elision and clear separation in the

Detail of fig. 67.

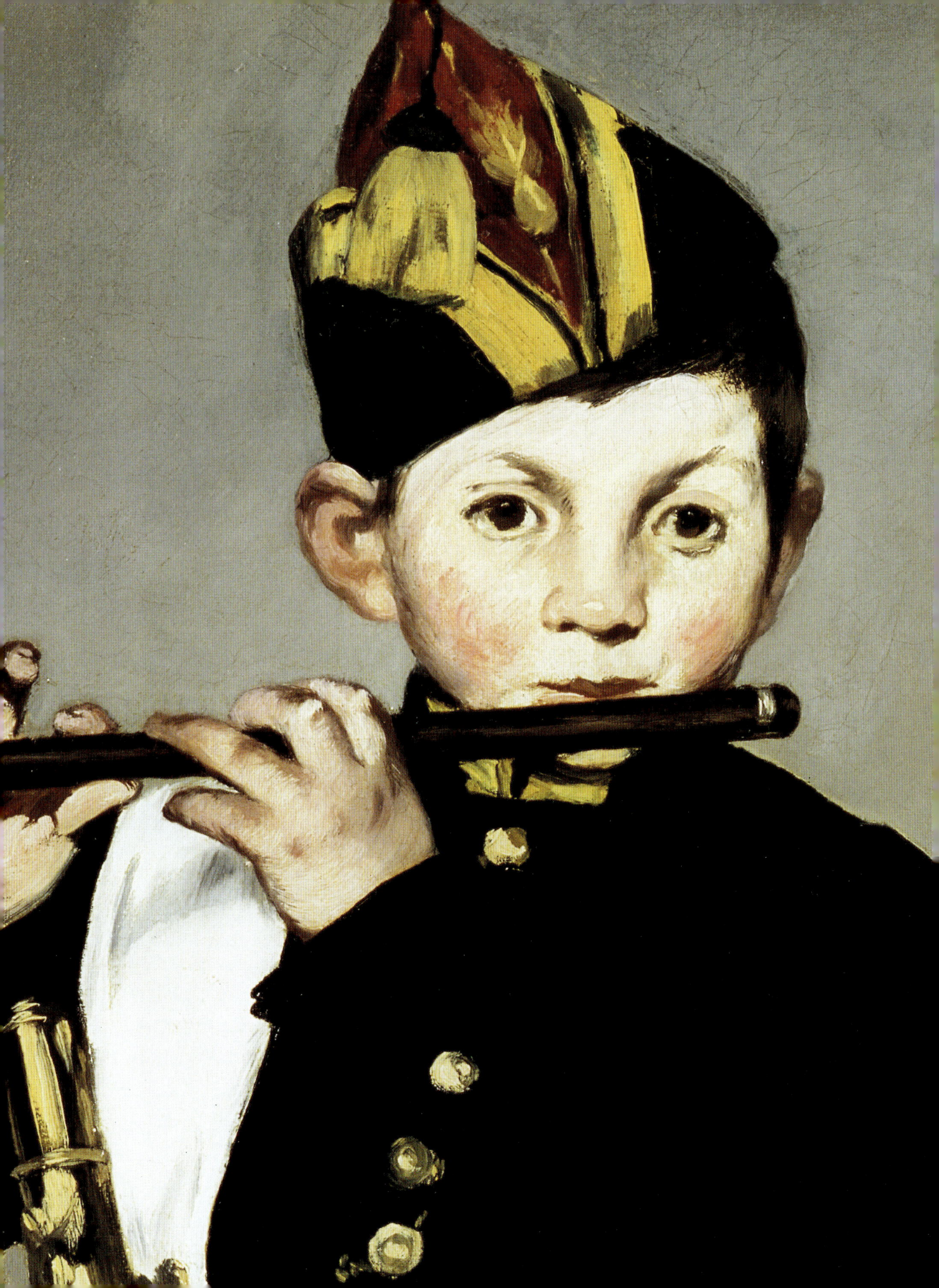

fifer's figure, and the ground against which it is silhouetted fluctuates between the effects of optical "atmosphere" and flat "chimerical wall." Perhaps it was that that Zola hinted at when he described the simultaneous liveliness and flatness of the picture, its vivid coming to life and frank status as an image. For it is precisely this illusionistic ambivalence, together with the "beholder's share" elements of the fife that cuts off the chin and the hat that cuts into the forehead, that constitutes the "chimerical" personhood of *The Fifer*.[30]

The relationship between the somewhat confounded flatness of *The Fifer* and the indeterminately constitutive illusionism of the *Young Woman in 1866* (see fig. 68) is complementary: together the two pictures assert the reciprocity of the founding and undermining of Manet's brand of coloristic illusionism, which together "constitutes all his talent," as Zola put it.[31] In "*La Femme en rose*," as he called it, Zola saw "that native elegance that Edouard Manet, man of the world, has at the heart of himself." He described her "breathing the perfume of a bouquet of violets," and claimed that "the temperament of the painter [had] placed the imprint of its austerity on the ensemble."[32] Mixed into Zola's characteristic treatment of a painting by Manet as a picture of Manet, in which the charming *demi-mondaine* serves as a representation of the austerely elegant *homme du monde*, there is an accent upon apparel and attributes, as well as on the illusionism of movement. But Zola paid unusually scant attention to the colorism of the *Young Woman in 1866*. Thoré, by contrast, when he saw the painting in Manet's studio prior to its exhibition at the Place de l'Alma, did attend to its *coloris*:

> There was . . . a study of a young girl in a pink dress . . . These rose tones against a gray background would defy the finest colorists. It is a sketch, it is true, as is, at the Louvre, the *Island of Cythera*, by Watteau. Watteau would have been able to push his sketch to perfection. Manet still struggles against the extreme difficulty of painting, which is to finish certain parts of a picture in order to give the whole its real worth . . . One hardly pays attention to the head, even though it is frontal and in the same light as the pink cloth; it is lost in the modulation of the coloring.[33]

Thoré noted the Rococo, Watteau-like qualities of the "study of a young woman in a pink dress," its subtle color harmonies, its leveling of costume and visage and the coloristic tailoring of one to the other. Writing in response to the picture when it was exhibited later in the Salon of 1868, other critics also concentrated on its colorism and criticized its rendering of Victorine's facial character. In 1868 Gautier wrote, "This young woman has been painted, they say, after a model whose head is fine, pretty and witty, and adorned by the richest Venetian hair that a colorist could wish . . . The ugly head which he presents to us has surely been subjected to reverse flattery."[34] And Mantz wrote, "The intention of Manet was, one must suppose, to engage in a symphonic dialogue, a sort of duo beween the young woman and the rose tints of her face. He has not succeeded at all, because he does not know how to paint flesh."[35] Whether attributing it to an inability to paint flesh, a sort of "devenustation,"[36] or a failure to pick out the head, all the critics were agreed that Manet had somehow failed to render Victorine's face properly, and all were agreed in their assessment of his status as a (failed) Venetian colorist. Their judgments nonetheless pointed to the coloristic ambivalence of Manet's project of constituting a persona, and Gautier, at least, was alive to the "young woman"'s status as painter's

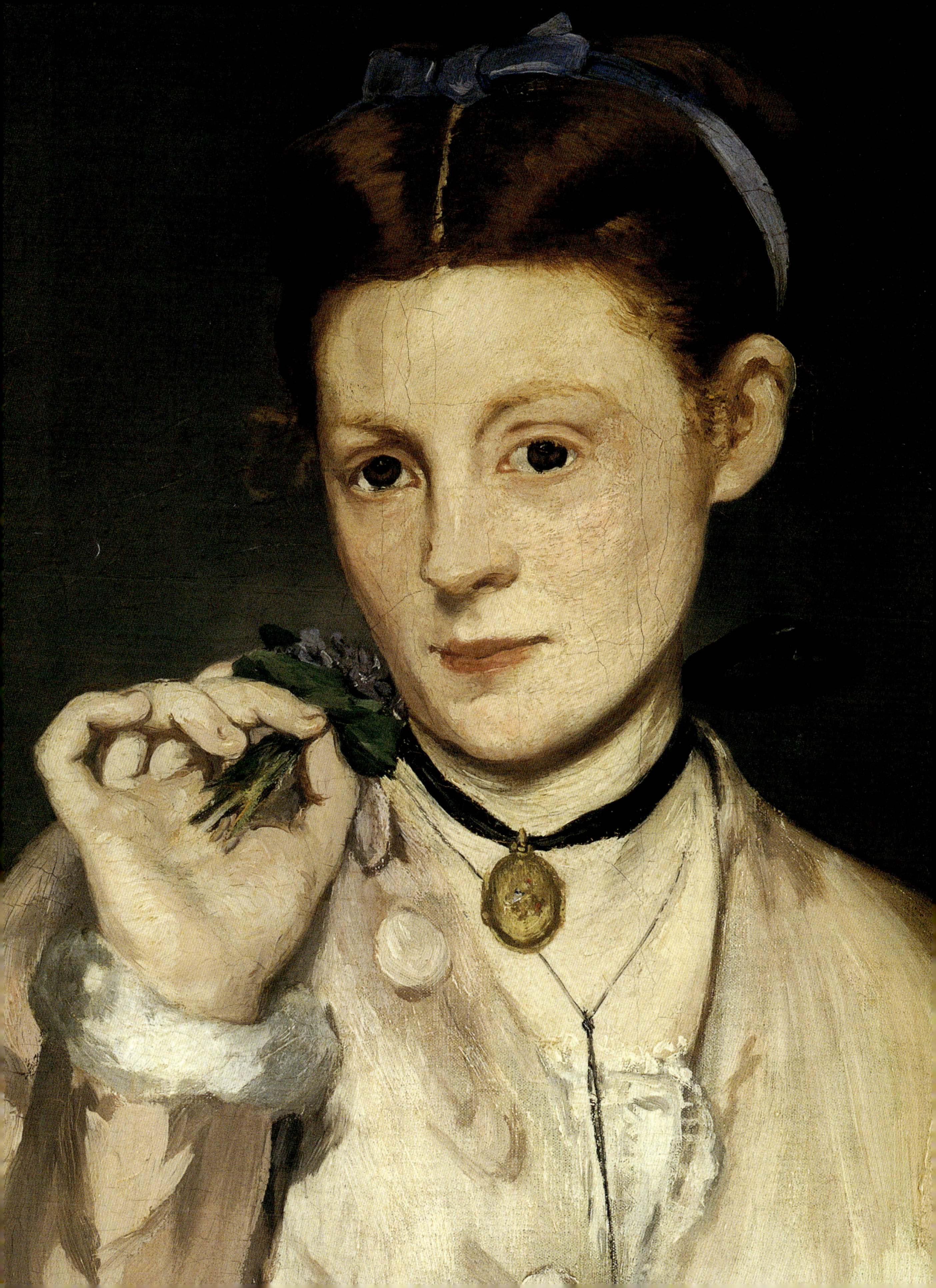

model, and the vexed relationship between painting and model, painted and "real" persona.

The coloristic gambits of the *Young Woman in 1866* are both more obvious and subtle than those of the other Victorine paintings: the critics were right, they are what the picture is about. At the center of the colorism of the *Young Woman in 1866* is the gown. And what is most noteworthy about the *peignoir*, beyond its status as a piece of undress and its paradoxical hiding of Victorine's figure in a shapeless mass of pink paint, is the way it combines the colors adjunct to it within its illusionism of shadow and highlight and Watteau-like satin material, bringing together the red of Victorine's lips, the white of the lace at her neck and cuffs, the gray of the background, the gold of the locket, the similar gold of the sand at the base of the bird-stand with the neighboring and slightly differing orange of the orange, the almost "titian" brown of the stand itself, highlit with pink and similar to Victorine's hair, and so on: in the *peignoir* these colors are joined and arrayed, announcing the color constituency of the Rococo effects of flesh, fashionable fabric, and femininity too. Indeed, with the tip of her slipper emerging from the bottom edge of the mass of intermixed pink paint of which she is made, this Victorine is reminiscent of Frenhofer's "chef-d'oeuvre," in which "they perceived in a corner of the canvas the tip of a naked foot which emerged from a chaos of colors, tones, indecisive nuances, a kind of mist without form . . . There is a woman underneath . . . the layers of color that the . . . painter had successively superimposed in the belief that he was perfecting his painting."[37]

As in *The Streetsinger*, here is a series of carefully calibrated color indeterminacies. First, there is the violet hair-ribbon, compared with the nosegay of violets held up to Victorine's face, harmonized oddly with Victorine's "titian" hair, mediating closely between the gray of the background and the rose of Victorine's robe. The nosegay with which it is compared is linked to the lorgnette, through the similar though differentiated gestures of the two hands – the one palm up and more open, the other back-of-the-hand and more closed. The formal relationship between the two hands, set in play by a neighboring color comparison and enhanced by another sequence of formal relationships – hair-ribbon, neck band with locket, and pendant lorgnette (opacity converted into transparency and back again) – is strongly reminiscent of *The Streetsinger*. Indeed, the whole pose is virtually the same, along with the bell-shaped gown and the hand holding something colored up to the mouth, suggesting that we might want to recall the earlier picture of Victorine as "herself." Certainly Manet's retrospective would have reinforced the relationship between the two pictures, as well as among all of the Victorine series (in which the differentiation between hands and sides of the face and body is reiterated).

In addition to the series of coloristic ambiguities established by the nosegay of violets and the rose *peignoir* (whose color name is also a flower name), there is another series of important relationships indexed by what became the titular accessory, the parrot. And again, color plays a constitutive role in the play of indeterminacy, so that the supplementary (namely, both the parrot accessory and color itself, which still in the nineteenth century was thought to be superficial and differential, not to mention feminine, in relation to the masculine essentialism of drawing) becomes foundational.[38] Most obviously, the parrot's range of grays mimics the range of grays found in the painterly elision of background and floor: an elision that is both outwardly referential – to Velasquez, as is

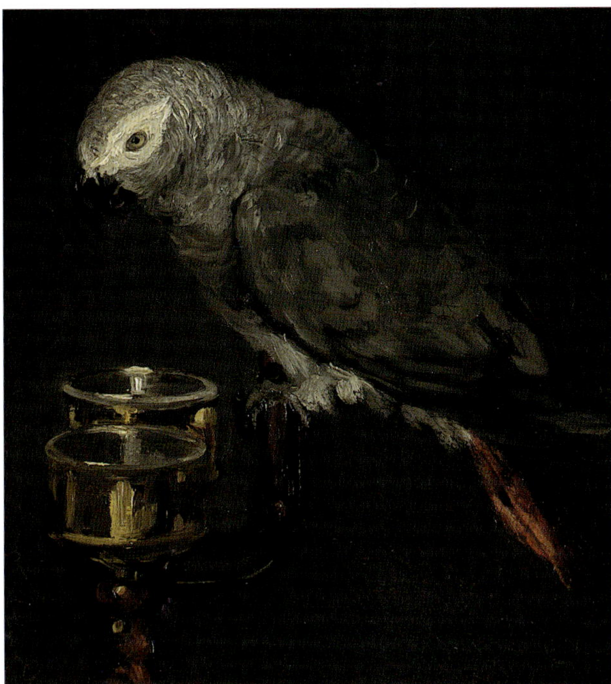

Detail of fig. 68.

the subtle colorism of the painting more generally – and self-referential – referring to what was by then a signature of Manet's oeuvre, and to the flat surface of painting, as constitutive of painterly illusionism as it is undermining of it. The simultaneity of flatness and illusionism is all but emblematized in the parrot stand, with its three perches, the top oriented to match the picture's flat plane, the bottom turned in space and foreshortened. The parrot stand then points to the half-unpeeled orange, with its general reference to Dutch still-life painting and generic Spanishness and to the orange in Manet's earlier *Young Woman Reclining in Spanish Costume*.[39] As for that orange (another color-named object, or vice versa), it suggests a simultaneous connection between the pink and white painterliness of Victorine and the demonstrable paintedness of its own orange outer surface and white inner pith, between her state of undress and its own half unpeeled condition, such that the clothing of a body in layers of fabric and the building up of an object in layers of pigment is linked and rhymed, while the oscillation among surface, substance, and depth effect is reiterated and renewed.

To return to the parrot, its differential play of grays is picked up in the grays rendering the reflective silver edge of the base, just as that edge picks up the orange of the orange in its reflection, just as the water glass, similarly constituted out of whites and grays, similarly picks up the gold of the sand at the base in its reflection, at the same time differentiating the transparency of its reflective surface from the opacity of that of the base, and announcing the unitary constitution of the illusionisms of transparency, reflection, and opacity in yellow-orange paint. So the parrot's pink tail, mimicked in the pink of the stand, also mimics the pink of Victorine's *peignoir*, and at the same time declares its constitution in pink paint through its double existence as parrot's tail and stroke of pigment. In short, the gray and pink of the parrot are a condensation of the constitutive colors of the painting in its entirety. They drive one to notice the only bit of color that falls, though only barely, outside of that color range: the violet of the nosegay and hair ribbon. Barely, because the color violet (yet another flower-named color or color-named flower) is not so distant, after all, from the color rose. That violet is different from the rest of the color scheme only because of its blueness, a blueness, however, that is not so distant from the green of the nosegay's leaves and stems, or from the gray of the parrot, the background, and the edge of the base. Again the color game turns in a circle. A mediating point in the triangulation of color-named surfaces and objects – violet, rose, and orange – the parrot stands as a sign of the constitutive game of colors played out in the *Young Woman in 1866*, alias the *Woman in Pink*, alias the *Woman with the Parrot*.

Victorine's accessories always point back to their own referential, indexical function, their job of pointing, framing, and referring both inward to the painting itself and outward to other paintings. Such was very evidently the case of the *Young Woman in 1866*, especially when she was dubbed *Woman with the Parrot* by another critic in 1868:

> The *Woman with the Parrot* was much attacked: M. Manet, who was not able to forget the panic caused several years ago by his black cat in the picture of *Ophelia* [sic], has borrowed the parrot of his friend Courbet, and placed it on a perch next to a young woman in a pink *peignoir*. These realists are capable of anything! The trouble is that this parrot is not stuffed like the portraits of M. Cabanel, and that the pink *peignoir* is of a too rich tone. The accessories even keep us from remarking the countenance; but one does not lose anything by that.[40]

Chaumelin links Victorine through her title attribute to three other paintings: to *Olympia* (whom he calls "Ophelia"), Courbet's painting of a nude with a parrot of 1866 (fig. 73), shown in Courbet's pavilion of 1867, and Cabanel's clothed portraits. Thus he implies a connection to another, more famous image of Victorine. (If the painting itself makes any reference to *Olympia*, it is through another accessory, the nosegay, which, with its attachment to the domain of gentlemanly compliments, gallant gifts, and elegant dalliance, echoes in much diminished form the great, profuse bouquet, that calling card of the client, in the earlier picture.[41]) Chaumelin proposes a different order of quotation from that of *Olympia*, this time from current painting, in the form of an accouterment, directly announcing Manet's rivalry with his model Courbet and indirectly pointing to the relationship between the two men's retrospectives. And by referring to other paintings, the critic inserts the *Young Woman in a Pink Peignoir* (as he might also have called her) into a dialectics of dress and undress, in which color continues to play its part.

Olympia's quotation from Venetian Renaissance painting was a matter both of accessories and the pose of her body, pulled up short out of the voluptuous languor of Titian's *Venus*. The *Young Woman in 1866*, by contrast, is a quotation only by accessory: located completely in the accouterment of the parrot and nowhere in her body, which despite the *peignoir*'s suggestion of undress, is lost in its morass of pink paint. Indeed, hers is more a gesture to another painting than a quotation of it. For the two paintings do not resemble one another at all: Manet's figure is upright and the painting vertical where

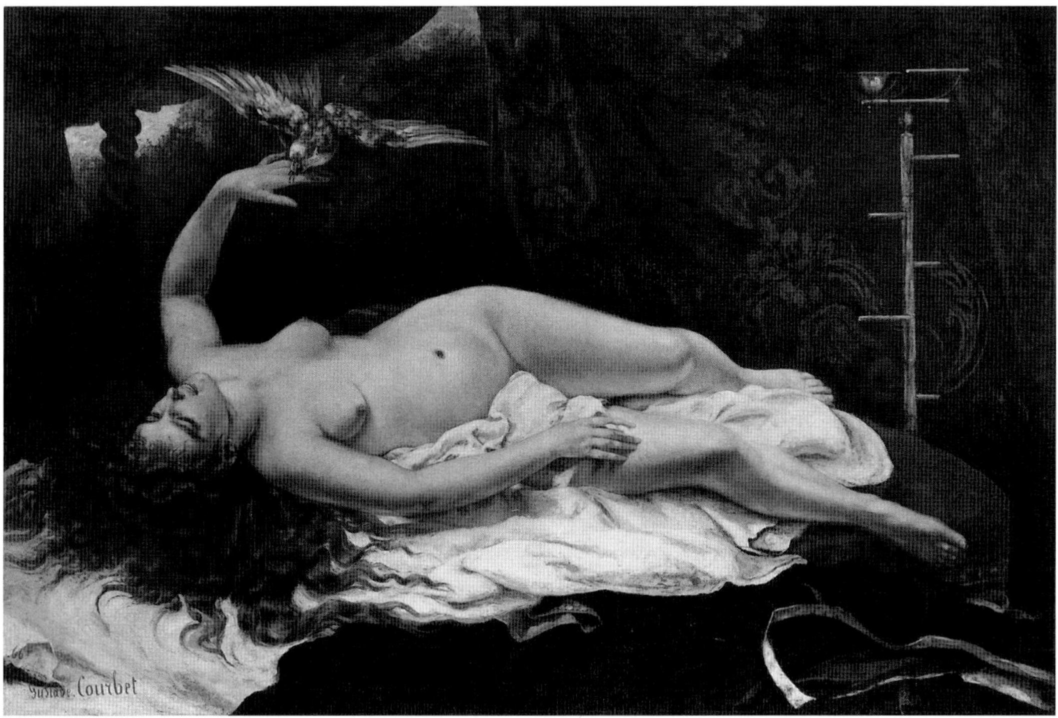

73　Gustave Courbet, *Woman with a Parrot*, 1866, oil on canvas, 129.5 × 195.6 cm. The Metropolitan Museum of Art, New York, H. O. Havemeyer Collection, Bequest of Mrs. H. O. Havemeyer, 1929. (29.100.57).

Courbet's reclines within a horizontal space; Manet's "young woman" is draped from neck to toe while Courbet's abandons herself to ecstatic nudity; Manet's "femme" is pointedly contemporary (so declares her original title) and, despite her blank background, evidently *chez elle*, while Courbet's nude is perfumed with the remote odor of the Orient; and even the parrots of the two pictures differ markedly, the one primly, drably, and vertically perched to the side of its vertical mistress, the other brilliant green, with wings dramatically outstretched, alighting on the beckoning finger of its equally outstretched owner. Finally, for all the grayness of its parrot and surrounding gray tonality, Manet's painting is vividly colored and factured, where Courbet's is a dark, licked-surface *grande machine*. In every way, the *Young Woman in 1866* departs from the painting she refers to; in every way she constitutes a dialectical response to both its thematics and its appearance, defining Courbet's nude as a *pompier* production in relation to the new *nouveauté* of Manet's *jeune dame*. And with its equation of color, femininity, and supplementarity, its response to Courbet's painting substitutes a demonstration of the painter's coloristic vocation and the location of the painter's *jouissance* in the pleasures of paint for Courbet's turning of the "male gaze" on the depicted body of woman, the "female of man," as Baudelaire put it, replacing the baroque Orientalism of Courbet's painting with a more subtle, identificatory otherness.

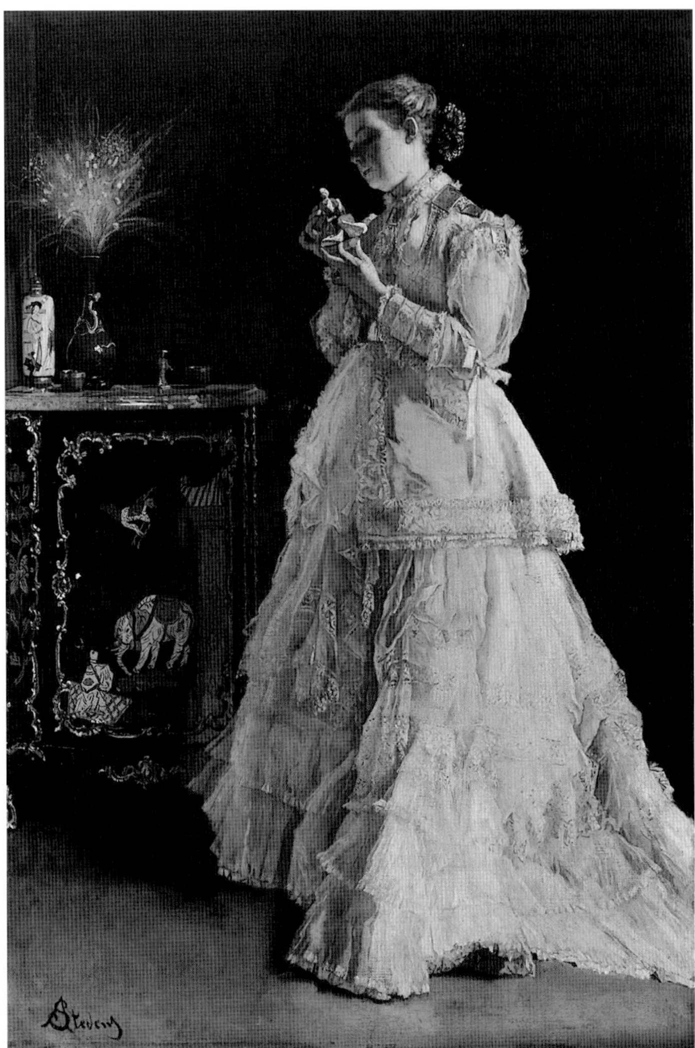

74   Alfred Stevens, *Young Lady in Pink*, 1866, oil on canvas, 87 × 57 cm. Musées Royaux des Beaux-Arts de Belgique, Brussels.

There was another painting besides *Olympia* and the *Woman with the Parrot* with which Manet's *Young Woman in 1866* entered into dialogue. That was an alternative rendering of Victorine, the *Young Lady in Pink* (fig. 74) by Manet's friend Alfred Stevens. Painted likewise in 1866, it had been a hit first in Belgium and then in the Belgian section of the Exposition, where it was shown as part of a series of eighteen "femmes de qualité" extensively described by Thoré, just before Manet showed his painting at his *exposition particulière* and then in the Salon of 1868.[42] In 1866, when Stevens's painting showed up too late to be hung in the Paris Salon, Thoré quoted a Belgian critic at length:

The *Lady in Pink* is another young woman, standing, in an elegant interior. Her hair, of a chestnut blond, is thick, rebellious to the comb, with the light curls that distinguish the beautiful Venetian women of Paul Veronese; the face is full, with delicate and witty lineaments, and it breathes that familiar grace by which the Parisian woman is recognized; her long, plump, tapering hands are marvels; her toilette is a deshabille of the most fantastic and charming taste. A pink dress, loose and yet flirtatious, like that of Watteau's women; atop it lots of gauze and lace . . . The type is so well rendered that it succeeds in being the expression of a character. One can see, as if through a transparent medium, the situation, the habits, the tastes, the life of the person represented; one discerns all the refinements of a century mad for luxury, all the liberty inherent to elevated social circles, all the natural amiability of a country where woman is queen. Each feature stirs up a whole little world of thoughts.[43]

The next year, Thoré wrote about the painting himself, more briefly, together with the seventeen other color and clothing-identified paintings in Stevens's series, one of which he compared with "the colorist Velasquez." After describing the paintings in detail, Thoré concluded with a curious physiognomic paean to the painted "woman of quality": "You can see very well that what they do is fairly indifferent. Theirs is the life of "women of quality." Smelling flowers, amusing themselves with knick-knacks, putting on their gloves or taking off their jewelry, reading or writing a note, reclining on a divan, looking at the color of the sky, growing restless or dreaming, that is the existence of these lovely ladies. The insignificance of the subjects in these pictures by Alfred Stevens has, therefore, its signification, it is perfectly expressive of aristocratic and even bourgeois society." Thoré, the champion of Dutch painting, cited Dutch painters of the seventeenth century, such as "Terburg, Metsu, Frans Mieris, Pieter de Hooch, Vermeer," as other examples of painters who painted women doing nothing, where the insignificance of their activities was physiognomically signicant, and claimed that "no one paints better than he the fresh and rich fabrics, the cashmeres, the carpets and all the little objects of luxury dwellings . . ."[44]

Stevens's *dame en rose* is much closer than Courbet's *Woman with a Parrot* to Manet's picture in its verticality, its presentation of a figure fashionably clothed in pink, and its presentation of the features of the same female model. Yet it is also different from Manet's painting in its finicky, hyper-detailed rendering of the frills and frippery decorating Victorine's gown, its anecdotal elaboration of luxury and idleness, and its effect of transparency, thus lending itself to the specificities of Thoré's descriptions and his physiognomical emphasis – his theorization of a paradoxical, *l'art pour l'art* physiognomics, in which the Baudelairean aesthetic of modern femininity meets the positivist theory of the *milieu*, and of which the *femme de qualité*, in all her modern uselessness, meaninglessness, and superficiality, and her willingness to turn herself into a luxury commodity like those she handles, is emblematic. But however much the thematization of modern woman, the references to Watteau, Velasquez, Terborch, and others, and the celebration of the colorism of costume tie Stevens's paintings to Manet's, it was impossible for Thoré to describe Manet's painting in the same physiognomic way. Rather, in a much briefer treatment, he located Manet in the camp of the colorists, and complained of the diminishing of the importance of the physiognomy of the *Young Woman in 1866* in the face of the pink facture of her dress, repeating much the same complaint in 1868, when the painting was shown again in the Salon. And indeed Manet distinguished his painterly *tons brisés*, his painterly Velasquez gray and Watteau pink, from Stevens's minute precision, his constitution of a person in paint from Stevens's reportage. He also distinguished his equation of color and costume from that of Stevens – specifically, his loosely handled "peignoir" for Stevens's "loose and flirtatious" morning dressing gown.[45] The *Young Woman in 1866*'s answer to Stevens's picture, in other words, substituted caricatured Velasquez colorism and overt paintedness for the transparent reproduction, anecdotal repleteness, and stable, readable physiognomics that Thoré so treasured.

And thus Manet differentiated his painting doubly, from two pictures, one of a clothed and heavily accessorized *femme de qualité*, and the other of a naked and barely accessorized odalisque, and from two kinds of finicky, *pompier* colorism. In that way he positioned himself and his painting in a complex field of reference to other paintings, stressing the differentiality of the singularity he put on display in 1867. That within his *exposition particulière* he differentiated also between the *Young Woman in 1866*, the *Fifer*, his other Victorine paintings, and all his other various productions too meant that his singularity came in many different guises, and that it was achieved through differentiation, not just from Courbet's and other people's paintings and painting styles, but also within and between his own. The connection between the latest and one of the earlier of them – the *Young Woman in 1866* and the *Luncheon on the Grass* – was noted at least once more (by the caricaturist Randon in *Le Journal Amusant*).[46]

Too few came to the retrospective, however, and few were the comments about it. Perhaps Manet regretted his refusal to attach his name to Zola's then, for the next year he showed the *Young Woman in 1866* with his portrait of the art critic and naturalist writer.[47] Once again removed from her studio context of differentiation among many pictures of her variable but always recognizable features, the 1866 Victorine who appeared in 1868 now seemed to give the nod to Zola, and agree to his positive view of Manet's singularity. This face of Victorine was selected from the rest in the post-Exposition Salon; according to Zola, this was the feminine face of Manet. But if this face was Manet's *Manette*, in its singular presentation it reduced to one the many Manettes that the Goncourts had allegorized and the many Manets that Manet had displayed the year before. Even the split double style evident in such works as the *Luncheon on the Grass* was woven back together. And after that, the Victorine of many faces, guises, and manners disappeared, to reappear one last time as a nanny (or mother) minding her childish charge in front of the Gare Saint-Lazare,[48] and then to be replaced many times by the image of Berthe Morisot, several up-to-date, but slightly frowsy suburban *demoiselles*, and a series of elegant Third-Republic *demi-mondaines*. It was a turning point: the end of Manet's pitting himself against the museum over and over again, the end of such artist-individuating, Salon-alternative organizations as the Société des Aqua-fortistes and the Société Nationale des Beaux-Arts, and soon the end of the Second Empire as well. It was also, for a while, the end of Manet's efforts to represent himself monographically.

Part Three

AFTER 1867

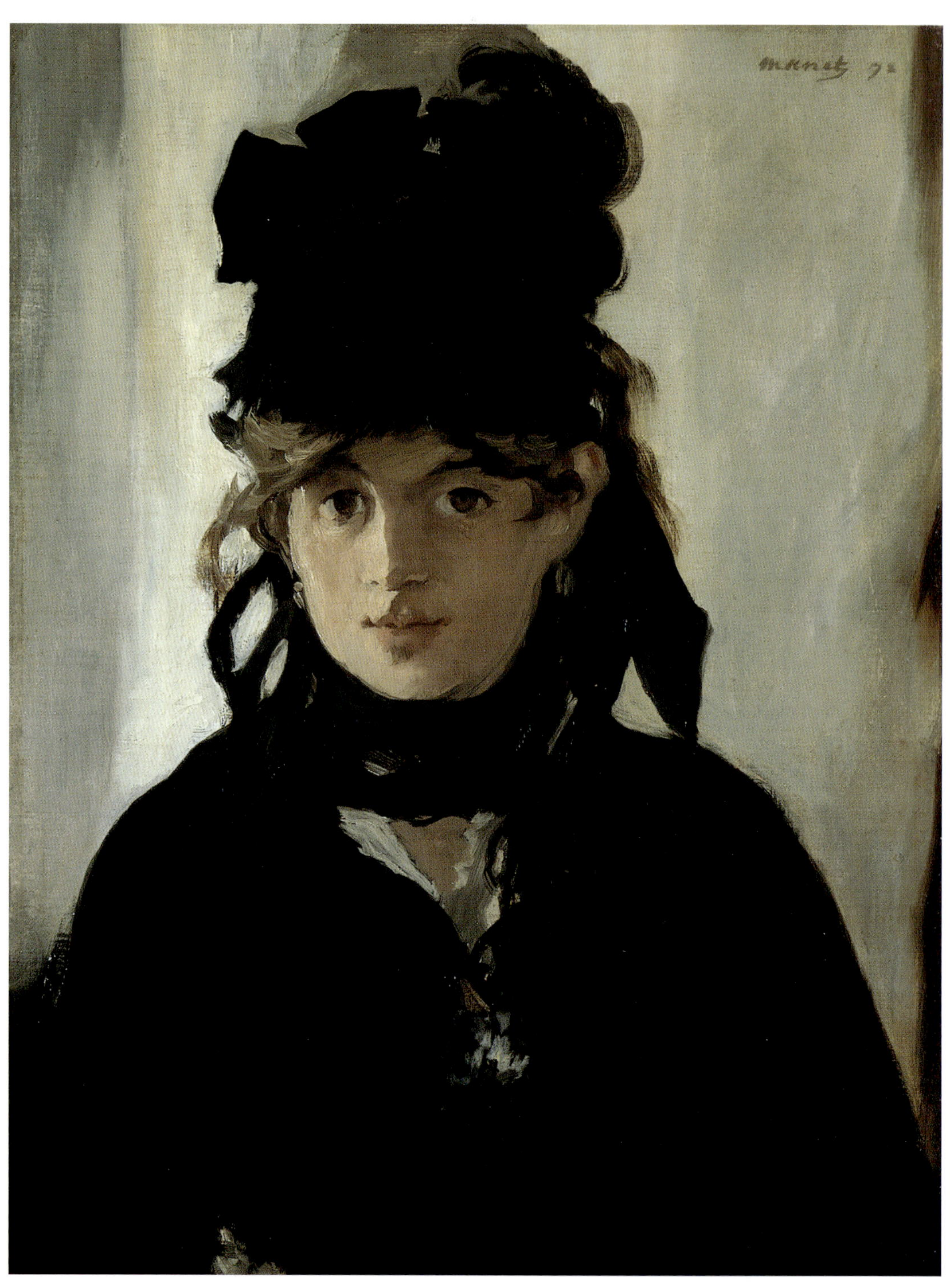

75   Edouard Manet, *Berthe Morisot with a Bouquet of Violets*, 1872, oil on canvas, 55 × 38 cm. Musée d'Orsay, Paris.

Chapter Seven

MANET, MORISOT, AND THE GONZALÈS AFFAIR: THE SALONS OF 1869, 1870, AND 1873

IN 1932, ON THE OCCASION OF THE CENTENARY OF Manet's birth and his retrospective at the Orangerie, Paul Valéry wrote the following about one of the several portraits of his aunt Berthe Morisot done by Manet between 1868 and 1874 (fig. 75):

> What struck me before all else was the *black* – the absolute black of a little mourning hat, along with its tie strings as they mingle among the locks of chestnut hair with rosy gleams of light on them; it is a black that could only be Manet's.
>
> Attached to the hat is a wide fold of black ribbon, coming over the left ear, then surrounding and sitting oddly on the neck; a short black mantle round the shoulders parts to reveal slightly the clear skin in the opening of a white linen collar.
>
> . . . What with those overpowering blacks, the cool simplicity of the background, the pale or rosy luminosity of the flesh, the odd silhouette of the hat, which was "young" and "the latest fashion," the confusion of curls, tie strings and ribbon to each side of the face; the face itself with its great eyes whose vague fixity suggests the profoundest abstraction, a sort of *presence in absence* – the total effect adds up to a singular impression of . . . *poetry* . . .
>
> . . . He has matched the physical likeness of his sitter with the one and only harmony that might convey a singular personality, thus boldly transfixing the distinct and abstract charm of Berthe Morisot.[1]

Valéry addresses Manet's diverse handling and its capturing of the singularity of Morisot and the details of her apparel. He celebrates a Baudelairean modernity that consists in speed and the ephemera of fashion, in which a face is "framed," constituted, and intermixed with the facture and color of costuming, and in which the funerary black of the modern masculine *habit noir* so famously celebrated by Baudelaire is translated into the mourning apparel worn by Morisot. And he articulates a theory of the "poetry" of painting as residing in its "strange color harmonies." Earlier in the same essay, in what was by then a common understanding, Valéry tied Manet's art directly to Baudelaire. He referred first to the green and red of Baudelaire's Delacroix essays ("the eye replies with a 'green' to a too prolonged and insistent 'red' . . ."),[2] and then addressed what he saw as the Baudelairean hispanicism of Manet's early work:

> Manet, with his fondness for the picturesque exotic, still paying tribute to the toreador, the guitar, and the mantilla, though already half won over to everyday objects,

to models found in the street, must have seemed to Baudelaire a close reflection of his own problem: the crucial condition, for an artist, of being subject to several opposing temptations and actually capable of expressing himself in a variety of admirable styles.

. . . I recall the delicious line – a line that seemed equivocal to the evil-minded, and a scandal to the Law – the famous *bijou rose et noir* which was Baudelaire's tribute to *Lola de Valence*.[3]

Valéry also identified his views with those of Mallarmé, and in the intervening pages he went on explicitly to oppose Zola's views to Mallarmé's, before settling into his praise of Manet's Morisot (and then after that of Morisot herself, whom he describes as a Mallarméan exception to the Impressionst rule). Effectively, he treats the 1872 portrait of Morisot as an updated, fashionable condensation not only of Manet's Baudelaireanism in general, but more specifically of the *bijou rose et noir* that *Lola de Valence* had been. Going on to speak of Morisot's work in much the same way – in terms of its colorism, "presence in absence," feeling of foreignness, and effect of estrangement – and mingling his address to Morisot's painting with a continuing celebration of Manet's portraits of Morisot, Valéry made Morisot, at once fashionable woman, artist, and object of Manet's aesthetic regard, into the emblem of Manet's Baudelairean colorism and of his translation of the erotics of the flesh into the erotics of paint, in which the *rose et noir* of old resonates anew in the closely described pink and black harmonies of Manet's *Berthe Morisot*. At the same time, Valéry made his own portrait of Morisot into the sign of Manet's shift from "the toreador, the guitar, and the mantilla" to the Baudelairean modernity of "'the latest fashion'." Morisot's hat, with its "wide fold of black ribbon," and the resulting intermingling of "curls, tie strings and ribbon" enframing her face, along with the "short black mantle round the shoulders part[ing] to reveal slightly the clear skin in the opening of a white linen collar," replace the *maja*'s mantilla and rework the *bijou rose et noir* into a "harmony" of modern black clothing and the "rosy luminosity" of flesh glimpsed through it.

Indeed, that was just how the image of Morisot functioned for Manet – as the site of his shift from the Spanish museum to fashionable French modernity. Manet first met Morisot in 1868, when he began work on his first portrait of her, in company with Fanny Claus and Antoine Guillemet, in the painting known as *The Balcony* (fig. 81). This was shown with the *Luncheon in the Studio* (fig. 80), his last real depiction of Léon Leenhoff, in company with Auguste Rousselin and a female servant, in the Salon of 1869. Like the *Execution of Emperor Maximilian* of 1867, *The Balcony* was a redoing and updating of a Goya composition, in this case a scene with two *majas*. But unlike the *Execution of Emperor Maximilian*, an extremely rare foray into modern history painting with little precedent and not much follow-up in Manet's art, *The Balcony* spawned a series of paintings of Morisot, in white dress and black, bearing a muff, wearing a plumed hat or a black mourning bonnet, holding a fan (fig. 76), extending a rose-shod foot, often half reclining, sometimes fully upright, but never painting. He painted other fashionable women of his acquaintance as well, they too sporting various hats, gowns, and accouterments, all rendered with a fashion hound's feel for fabric, facture, line, and color.[4]

A "harmony" in green, black, and white, *The Balcony* was a first instance of Manet's changing of the museum-borrowed hispanicism of his early work into the feminine *vie*

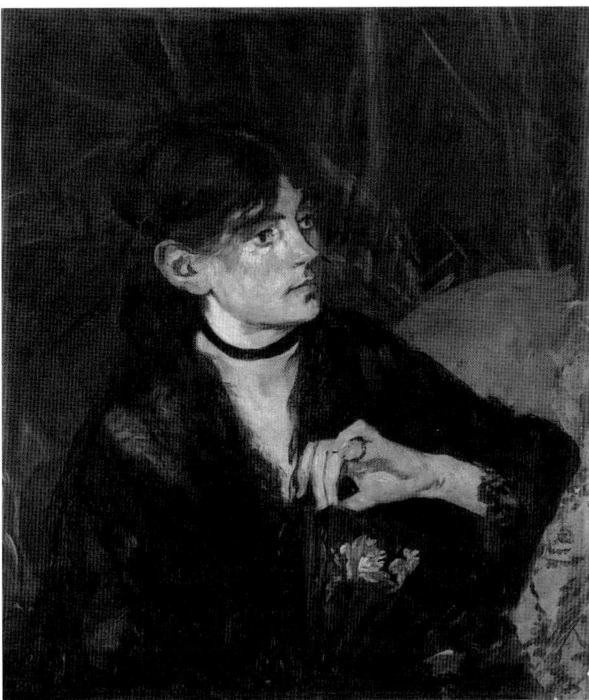

76   Edouard Manet, *Berthe Morisot with a Fan*, 1874, oil on canvas, 61 × 50 cm. Musée des Beaux-Arts, Lille.

moderne of his second decade. It was painted a few years after his trip to Spain and his subsequent hispanicizing portrait of the dark, spit-curled "Angelina" (fig. 77), who sports a fan and mantilla and addresses the viewer from an iron grillwork balcony that could just as easily indicate Madrid as Paris. *The Balcony*, with its up-to-date French clothing, revises that earlier painting and explicitly resituates Manet's interest in femininity in the French "capital of the nineteenth century."[5] (At the same time, it is inflected by some of the flavor of "Angelina.") In the Salons of 1870 and 1873, *The Balcony* was followed by the portrait of Morisot's competitor Eva Gonzalès painting at her easel, dressed to the nines in a beautiful white dress (fig. 85), and by the painting known as *Repose* (fig. 90), perhaps the most famous of Manet's portraits of Morisot, also featuring a summery white gown.[6] Then in the Salons of 1874, 1875, and 1879, Manet showed paintings with Impressionist subject matter featuring other women, with close attention paid to both hats and dresses, mediated by the painter's art and equated with the pigments of his palette.

At the close of the 1870s, Manet returned to the hispanicism of the previous decade, with a portrait of the opera singer Emilie Ambre dressed as Carmen, adopting a Carmen pose that went all the way back to the stance of Lola de Valence (fig. 78). In following the vogue for Bizet's opera (1875) on the theme of Merimée's romantic novelette, Manet was again very much of his moment.[7] But the painting was a conventional theater portrait of an actress in role. And it represented a very brief resurgence of Manet's old enthusiasm for Spain. Otherwise he committed himself to the figure of the Parisienne. What better way was there to usher in that new enthusiasm than by substituting the darkly elegant *parisianisme* of Berthe Morisot for the Spanishicity of the *maja*, the *espada*, and the Spanish dancer?

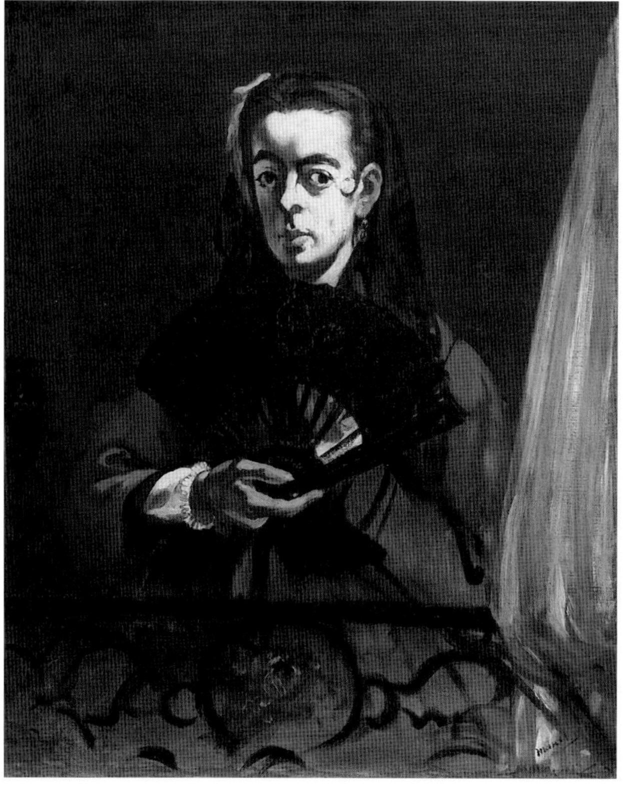

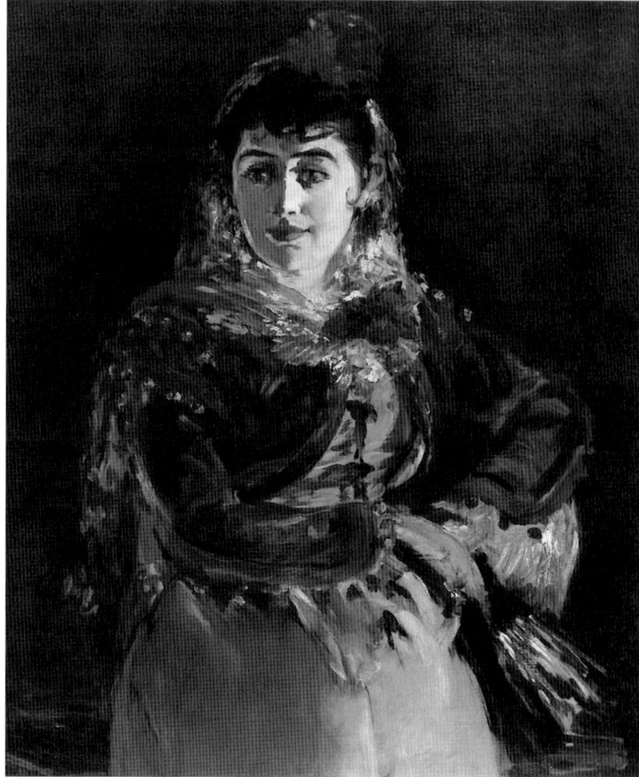

77 Edouard Manet, *Angelina*, 1865, oil on canvas, 92 × 73 cm. Musée d'Orsay, Paris.

78 Edouard Manet, *Emilie Ambre in the Role of Carmen*, 1879–80, 91.5 × 73.5 cm. Philadelphia Museum of Art: Given by Edgar Scott.

CHANGING COURSE: PRELUDE TO AN INTERLUDE

The Salon of 1869 was the Salon in which Manet switched strategies, moving from his signature obsession with the styles of the museum to a new fascination that became his trademark preoccupation of the '70s, with the image of modern woman. The two paintings that Manet showed that year, *The Balcony* and the *Luncheon in the Studio*, chart that change. Simply put, the *Luncheon in the Studio* represents the museum, and *The Balcony* the modern-life half of the pair. In the first, the studio properties to the left – helmet, sword, gun, cat – reprise elements of several of Manet's earlier paintings, including his pile of Spanish accouterments from the early '60s, the outsized accessory of the *Boy with a Sword*, and the infamous black cat of *Olympia*, here represented among objects in a more docile crouch. This armchair still life, by alluding to Manet's habit of using props and evoking the eclectic paraphernalia of the historicist painter's studio, signals the artifice of Manet's old costume paintings. With the Vermeer-quoting servant, it also refers to Manet's devotion to the theater of art history and the museum. The same may be said, more subtly, of the other half of the composition, with its complementary tabletop still life: it is much more quotidian – like a naturalist alternative to the artificial pile on the left – but it too quotes from the museum. The projecting knife handle, white damask cloth, the lemon with its coil of skin, and the oysters all belong to the historical repertoire of still life, and had already shown up in Manet's earlier still lifes. Indeed, the right side of this painting may be understood as a self-quoting resumé of Manet's still-life practice to date. In answer to the left side of the painting, the realist right side includes itself within the museum of still-life painting too, folding studio and luncheon, Manet's costume pieces and still lifes, into the same interior space of one man's art history.

For its part, *The Balcony* replaces all of that with an open air scene – critics spoke of housepainting and thus tied it to the contemporary scene of the Haussmannized city.[8] Switching from inside to outside, the shutters of the studio are opened to the street (though that street is only implied, as the object of several differently directed gazes represented within the painting). *The Balcony* moves the potted plant half outdoors and substitutes a lapdog for the black cat, a stool that serves as a modern person's seat for the chair that houses history-painting studio properties, and a sea of modern white dress for the standard still-life tablecloth of its Salon companion. And if *The Balcony* recalls any of Manet's earlier works, it is those with modern-life accouterments: the green shutters of *The Streetsinger*, the fan of *Lola de Valence*, the locket of the *Young Woman in 1866*, the Velasquez-based challenge of the street dress in shades of gray and the *peignoir* in tones of pink and rose, not to mention the Titian-based game of nude flesh against white sheet, transferred to the white-on-white of two summer dresses screened through a latticework of housepainter's green, signifying the out-of-doors modernity of the new Paris – as distinct from old Madrid and its Prado.

Of course it is not as simple as that. For *The Balcony* is as quotational as the *Luncheon in the Studio*. And it is not just Goya's depiction of Spanish *lorettes* that it quotes and updates. In the tenebrous background behind Berthe is the glimmer of Léon Leenhoff's younger tray-bearing self from the Velasquez-quoting *Spanish Cavaliers* of 1859 (fig. 79), here serving as a masculine counterpart to the pitcher-bearing female servant in the *Luncheon in the Studio*.[9] Contrasting one hispanicism with the other in the figures of Léon and Berthe – the courtly, museum Spain of Velasquez and the dark

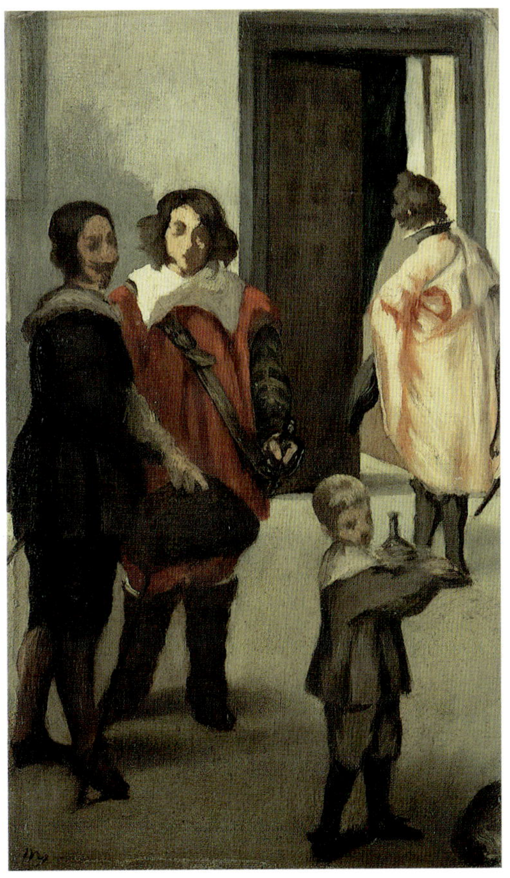

79   Edouard Manet, *Spanish Cavaliers*, 1859, oil on canvas, 45 × 26 cm. Musée des Beaux-Arts, Lyon.

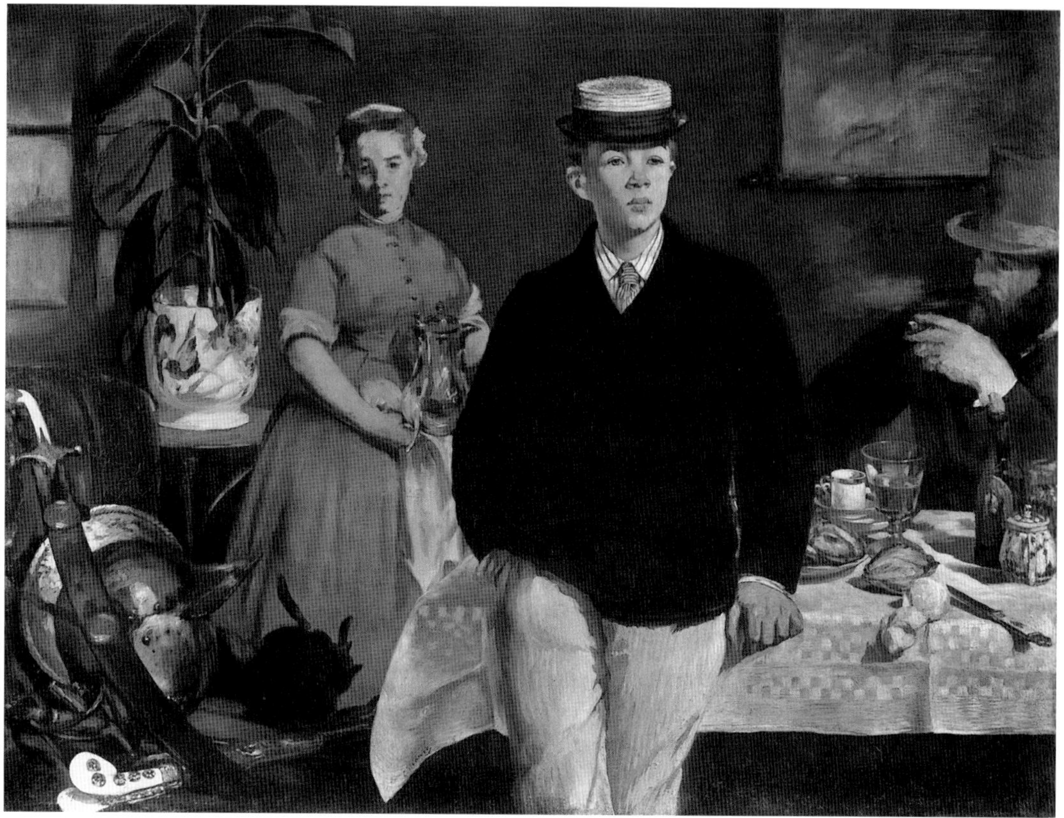

80   Edouard Manet, *Luncheon in the Studio*, 1868, oil on canvas, 118 × 154 cm. Neue Pinakothek, Munich.

modernity of Goya – *The Balcony* relegates the first to the shadows, little more than a
dim recollection of Manet's early museum-referenced career, and transports the second
into the broad daylight of the here and now, so that the single painting constitutes a
chiaroscuro of past and present. And then, taken together with the fresh, foregrounded,
up-to-date portrayal of Léon in summer whites in the *Luncheon in the Studio*, the two
pictures on view at the 1869 Salon give us two versions, dark and light, then and now,
of the son of Manet's wife, whose features had vied with those of Victorine Meurent in
the first decade of Manet's career and who was equally associated with Manet's art-
historical masquerade.[10] The contrasting presentation of Léon in *The Balcony* and the
Luncheon in the Studio speaks to Manet's change in direction quite as much as the *pleinairiste* presentation of Berthe Morisot, updating the *maja* as a modern *parisienne* wearing
a modern Parisian dress.

Indeed, the two pictures are equally concerned with modern clothes. Perhaps, for the
binary pair of museum and modern life, one might substitute that of modern male clothing and contemporary female fashion: Léon with his straw boater, carefully matched pin-
striped shirt and inversely black-and-white striped cravat, black pea-coat, and white,
faintly striped summer trousers, versus Berthe with her own faintly striped, translucent
white gown, replete with fichu, wide, ruffle-edge bell sleeves and long, ruffle-edged sash,

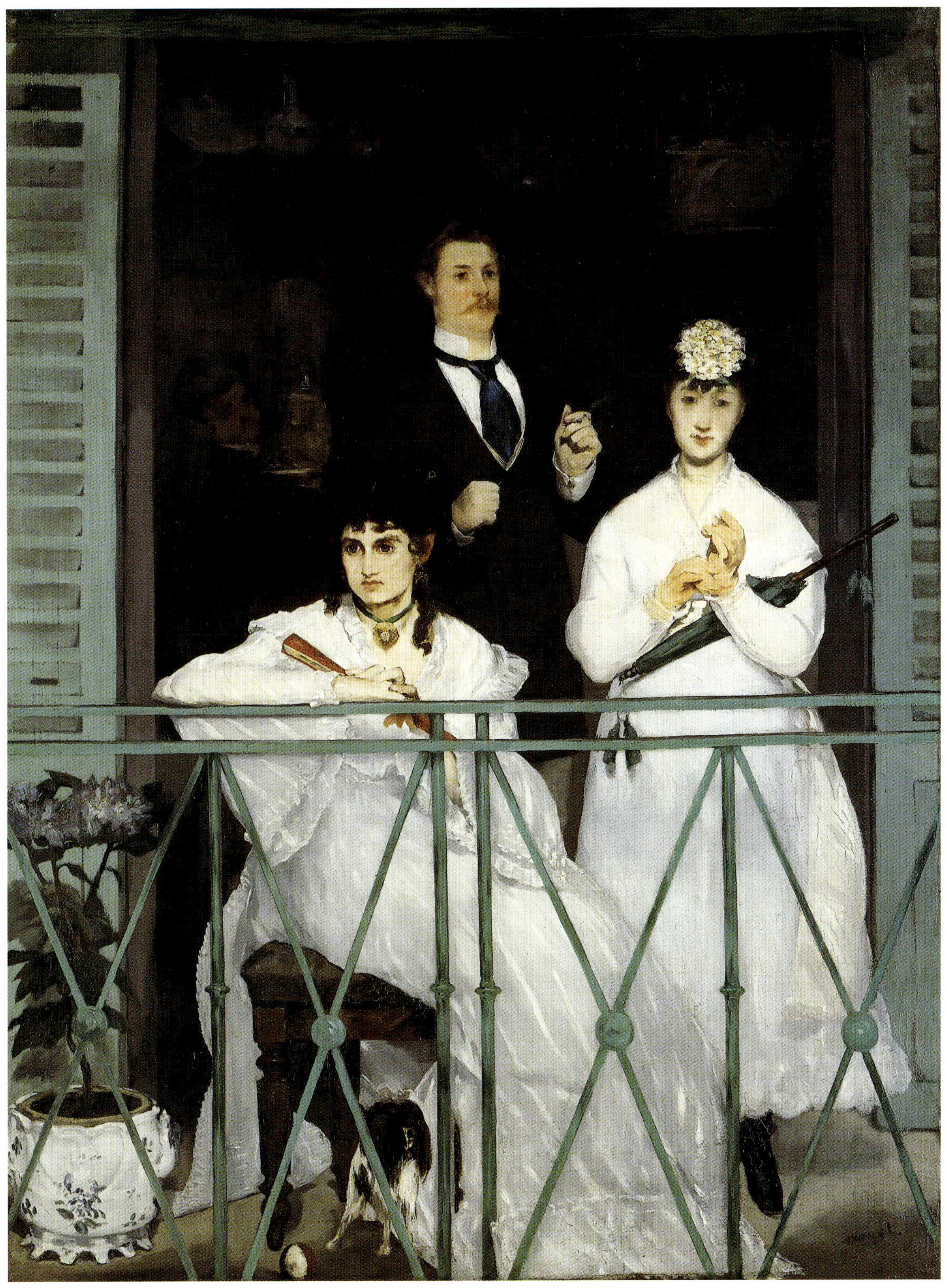

81   Edouard Manet, *The Balcony*, 1868–69, oil on canvas, 170 × 124.5 cm. Musée d'Orsay, Paris.

her "cinnabar" fan and her locket, its green ribbon harmonized with the balcony railing and window shutters. And next to her, Fanny seems to provide the female counterpart to Léon's youthful elegance: she stands in a short-hemmed walking dress beneath which is glimpsed a trim black boot, another matching slant of green provided by the closed parasol clutched in the crook of her arm, one yellow-gloved hand adjusting the other, linked and contrasted to Berthe's bare hands, folded over each other on the balcony rail.[11] In short, each painting is as carefully specific as the other in its observation of modern clothing.

Come to think of it, even the gender breakdown just suggested is too simple: Antoine Guillemet with his cravat and cheroot intrudes between Berthe and Fanny in *The Balcony*, his cobalt cravat harmonized with the potted blue hydrangea in the foreground, his bare hands mimicking the gloved hands of Fanny, one upraised like hers, reversed and cigar-bearing in contrast to her tucked parasol, the other fisted like her adjusting hand, the two flesh spots mediating between the white shapes of the two female figures, just as the white wedge of his shirtfront intrudes between their two whitenesses. Guillemet forms a contrapuntal middle term, the masculinity of his clothing, coloring, and accessorizing contrasting as well as shifting, echoing, and adjusting the femininity of theirs. Placed next to the overshadowed, nearly obliterated figure of Léon as a child, he stands between two unmarried women whose maturity is differentiated according to their dress (despite the fact that Mlle Claus, aged twenty-three at the time of the Salon of 1869, was past girlhood – indeed, she was just one year younger than Morisot). Thus, shown in concert with another view of Léon, this time as a sixteen or seventeen-year-old young man, the figure of Guillemet reinforces a thematics of the age specificity of modern costume, male and female, shared by the two paintings of 1869. So the relationship between the *Luncheon in the Studio* and *The Balcony* cannot quite be formulated as an opposition. It might, finally, be better to say that each is concerned in its way with Manet's own coming of age as a painter after the retrospective of 1867: each marks his move to a fascination with modern fashion and its indexing not only of sex but also of generation, era, and temporality.

As was so often the case, Manet did not paint himself into either of these compositions. And yet each presents the furnishings and familiars of the painter's life, not to mention surrogates for the painter himself, in the figures of Auguste Rousselin and Antoine Guillemet, both painter compatriots of Manet's. (Rousselin had been in the studios of Couture and Gleyre, where Manet met him, while Guillemet was a painter of Parisian landscapes and a friend of the Impressionists-to-be.[12] Thus Rousselin and Guillemet match the studio and street thematics of the two paintings they inhabit, and as such they too mark Manet's shift in attention.) The *Luncheon in the Studio* is obviously self-reflexive; it was, moreover, a response to paintings like Courbet's *After Dinner at Ornans* and, more recently, Renoir's *The Inn of Mère Antoine*,[13] except that it persisted in its attachment to the interior life of the studio, and in its pointing to the studio property status of everything within it.

Stepping out into the light of modern day, *The Balcony* is less obviously self-reflexive. Instead it presents an ambiguous set of urban relations between a man of the world and two unmarried women, one a painter and the other a musician, arranged in a bouquet of hands, accouterments, and outward gazes reminiscent of earlier groupings of hands and faces such as the *Luncheon on the Grass*. Indeed, *The Balcony* continues in the vein of that earlier painting's notoriously ambiguous relations between men and women, removing them from the domain of the museum studio. Notably lacking from the 1869 arrangement, however, is a gaze with the quality of Victorine's. This brings me to the other shift in attention marked by *The Balcony*: the changing of the guard from Victorine Meurent to the "presence in absence" of Berthe Morisot and others. With that shift the character of Manet's plural individuality became less *âpre*, less sharply concentrated and more diffuse, scattered in the cut and diaphanous fabric of dresses, sewn in the floral decorations of hats and bonnets, rather than filtered through museum references and honed in the steady, deadpan gaze of a model. It is hard to know exactly how to account for this turn, except to say that the relationship between Manet and Meurent must have shifted, and that the failure of the painter's retrospective to gain him an audience or a reputation outside of the one he already had as a provocateur and figure of fun must have caused him some confusion, and a desire to make a change. One could also speculate that this new loosening was Manet's response to the work of a female painter whose painting had a marked impact upon him, though he never really acknowledged it. Certainly this moment of shift from the museum to modern fashion was also a moment in which Manet suddenly became involved in the work and lives of two female painters with developing reputations.

AN EPISTOLARY ROMANCE

At least until Morisot married Manet's brother Eugène in 1874, her relationship with Manet was a mixture of painter-to-painter friendship and chivalrous flirtation, in which he paid court to her with paintings, posies, and charming, if barbed, compliments, and she responded with worries about his opinion of her painting, and the waxing and waning of his attention. It was a period, after her sister Edma married in 1869, in which Morisot seemed particularly fretful about her work, and her uncertain position as a woman who chose to try to carve out an artistic identity for herself rather than marry; her letters are full of bouts of depression and failures of confidence, with the name Manet sprinkled everywhere through them. (It is not that Manet had no such lapses in assurance himself, but in the letters between the Morisot women the public ebullience of Manet's anxieties about the reception of his paintings at the Salon stands in marked contrast to the private fluctuations of Morisot's self-doubt.) There is a string of incidents in the Morisot letters, reported from several sides, that has some bearing on the relationship between the two painters, and in particular on Manet's representation of Morisot at the Salon. They are well-known incidents, but they are worth following in detail here, for they form an epistolary romance that strongly suggests both the dialogism of the two painters' relation to each other and the function of the figure of woman as the site of dialogue.

   The first incident concerns Morisot's response to *The Balcony* and its reception at the Salon: "I am more strange than ugly. It seems the epithet of *femme fatale* has been circulating among the curious."[14] A week later a letter follows in which Morisot claims to be nauseated by the sight of her own painting,[15] and a week and a half after that, a letter from her mother reporting that Manet was making overtures to Jeanne and Eva

Gonzalès. (At the same time, her mother reported that he had been asked the price of *The Balcony* and felt that Berthe was bringing him luck.) Then, in the summer, upon a visit to Manet's studio, Cornélie Morisot remarked that he was in ecstasies over Gonzalès, and went on: "His mother made me touch her daughter-in-law's hands, saying that she was feverish; the latter [Suzanne] forced a smile and reminded me that you had promised to write to her. As for Manet, he did not move from his stool. He asked how you were, and I answered that I was going to report to you how unfeeling he is. He has forgotten about you for the time being. Mlle G. has all the virtues, all the charms, she is an accomplished woman . . ."[16]

In August, Berthe wrote to her sister: "Manet lectures me, and holds up that eternal Mlle Gonzalès as an example; she has poise, perserverance, she is able to carry an undertaking to a successful issue, whereas I am not capable of anything. In the meantime he has begun her portrait over again for the twenty-fifth time. She poses every day, and every night the head is washed out with soft soap. This will scarcely encourage anyone to pose for him."[17] To that jealous remark, Edma wrote in reply, "The thought of Mlle Gonzalès irritates me, I do not know why. I imagine that Manet greatly overestimates her, and that we, or rather you, have as much talent as she . . ."[18] In September, the saga continued, still centering around the portrait of Eva Gonzalès that Manet showed in the Salon that year:[19] "We spent Thursday evening at Manet's," wrote Berthe to Edma. "He was bubbling over with good spirits, spinning a hundred nonsensical yarns, one funnier than another. As of now, all his admiration is concentrated on Mlle Gonzalès, but her portrait does not progress; he says that he is at the fortieth sitting and that the head is again effaced . . ."[20] The next Tuesday evening Manet and Suzanne paid a visit to Berthe and looked in on her studio, and Manet surprised her with praise; "it seems," she told her sister, "that what I do is decidedly better than Eva Gonzalès."[21]

Eva Gonzalès made it clear that she was Manet's student and follower; in the same Salon of 1870 in which Manet showed his portrait of her, she displayed *The Little Soldier*, clearly a tribute to Manet's rejected *Fifer* of a few years back.[22] Morisot, by contrast, refused to set herself up as Manet's pupil in any such direct way. Manet nonetheless took it upon himself to act as Morisot's teacher, dispensing advice and judgment, and going so far as to interfere in Morisot's painting. Wrote Berthe to Edma, in the same letter in which she reported Manet's favorable comparison of her painting with that of Gonzalès, "Manet exhorted me so strongly to do a little retouching on my painting of you, that when you come here I shall ask you to let me draw the head again and add some touches at the bottom of the dress, and that is all. He says that the success of my exhibition is assured and that I do not need to worry; the next instant he adds that I shall be rejected. I wish I were not concerned with all this."[23] And then later that winter, Berthe wrote to Edma again, recounting at length the most notorious of Manet's interventions, his reworking of her portrait of her mother and her sister Edma (fig. 83), which she showed either with *The Harbor at Lorient* (fig. 84) or the *The Artist's Sister at a Window* (fig. 82) at the Salon of 1870:

> Tired, unnerved, I went to Manet's studio on Saturday. He asked me how I was getting on, and seeing that I felt dubious, he said to me enthusiastically: "Tomorrow, after I have sent off my pictures, I shall come to see yours, and you may put yourself in my hands. I shall tell you what needs to be done!"

The next day, which was yesterday, he came at about one o'clock; he found it very good, except for the lower part of the dress. He took the brushes and put in a few accents that looked very well; mother was in ecstasies. That is where my misfortune began. Once started, nothing could stop him; from the skirt he went to the bust, from the bust to the head, from the head to the background. He cracked a thousand jokes, laughed like a madman, handed me the palette, took it back, finally by five o'clock in the afternoon we had made the prettiest caricature that was ever seen. The carter was waiting to take it away; he made me put it in the hand-cart, willy-nilly. And now I am left confounded. My only hope is that I shall be rejected. My mother thinks this episode is funny, but I find it agonizing.

I put in with it the painting I did of you at Lorient. I hope they take only that.[24]

Later in the same second-guessing letter, Berthe changed her mind about the portrait of Gonzalès: "Manet has never done anything as good as his portrait of Mlle Gonzalès; it is perhaps even more charming now than when you saw it."[25]

Evidently Berthe's mother saw the episode a little differently. She wrote to Edma of Berthe's morbid overworking of herself, speaking with some exasperation about "your nervous and febrile dispositions," and reporting that she had tried unsuccessfully to get the portrait with Manet's "atrocious" "improvements" returned (while worrying herself over whether Manet would be offended).[26] In May Mme Morisot reported to Edma that Berthe was feeling better about her painting, having gotten some compliments at the Salon, and Berthe confirmed it, adding that Manet was bothered at the placement of his painting. While her confidence was on the increase she changed her mind yet again, saying that while his paintings looked well, that of Gonzalès was nothing but mediocre.[27] When Edma wrote that she had heard Manet had spoiled his portrait of Gonzalès, Berthe replied, "I cannot say that Manet has spoiled his paintings. Indeed I saw them in his studio the day before the exhibition, and they enchanted me, but I do not know how to account for the washed-out effect of the portrait of Mlle Gonzalès: the proximity of the other paintings, although execrable, is enormously detrimental. The delicacies of tone, the subtleties that charmed me in the studio, disappear in this full daylight. The head remains weak and not pretty at all."[28]

It is significant that this epistolary soap opera commences with Morisot's understanding Manet's portrait of her in the 1869 Salon not as a painting per se but as a perception of her as a woman – neither conventionally pretty nor downright ugly, but a strange *femme fatale* – as if Manet's picture of her, bare-headed on a public balcony with a man present, had started a rumor that weighed her beauty in the balance and called her standing as a young unmarried woman of good reputation into question. Between social calls and engagements, Morisot's doubts alternate with Manet's, and when the competition between Morisot and other women concentrates itself in the painterly-cum-romantic rivalry with Gonzalès, both as a painting hand and a painted face, the oscillation between Morisot's and Manet's hesitations over their paintings is intensified to the point that they become thoroughly – and literally – intermingled. Until the carting away of the portrait of Edma and Cornélie, it is not clear which painting was the bone of contention, the single portrait in profile of Edma at the window that Morisot painted during the same period and possibly showed at the Salon, or the more famous double portrait of her mother and sister.[29] But it is clear that Manet's repainting of Gonzalès's face became entangled with his repainting of the dress that Morisot had painted. It is also clear that the portrayal of faces ultimately receded before the picturing of dresses, which became the crux of a painted competition.

Thus the *Portrait of Eva Gonzalès* was at the uneasy center of an uneven exchange between Manet and Morisot, in which the ups and downs of painting and flirting were not clearly distinguished, and in which the symbiotic ties linking mothers, daughters and sisters, wives, friends, and romantic rivals knot themselves around the painters' duet. It is evident that Eva, whose image replaced Berthe's in 1870, functioned as a weapon in Manet's duel with Morisot. After the Commune, Manet returned to painting and exhibiting Berthe at the Salon again. But where he had posed Gonzalès to show her as a painter, even when Berthe took up posing for him again, he never showed her painting: it was as if Manet wished to keep her in her place as the object of his attentions, and show her, in her own image, how a dress should be painted. Entwined in this to and fro between Manet and Morisot, this redoing of faces and frocks, this sitting-in of figures and substituting of hands, was an air of two-mindedness about painting – Morisot's, but also Manet's. For there was more to the story that unfolds in the Morisot womens' letters than a woman's double awareness of herself as subject and object of masculine scrutiny, although that is certainly an important part of the mix. For Manet's part, a sort of feminine indecision began to take the place of his more pointed undecidability of the preceding decade, such that he began to usurp Morisot's female double consciousness for himself.[30] His was always a duet with himself as well as with others: at this moment of sea-change in his career, his dialogue with Morisot was a crucial catalyst for altering the terms of the dialogue with himself.[31] And between the two of them stood a third, the face and dress of Eva Gonzalès.

PAS DE DEUX: A PAINTERLY TRIANGLE

The Balcony was the curtain opener to the play. Another portrait by Morisot of her sister Edma followed Manet's painting, revising *The Balcony* by showing her sister, equally in white, equally bare-headed, seated by a balcony with a fan but safely interiorized, unaccompanied, and completely absorbed in herself — rather than betwixt inside and outside, indeterminately accompanied by a man and a younger woman who was neither chaperone nor chaperoned, and poised between her interior thoughts and the exterior spectacle of the street.[32] The double portrait of her sister and mother that Morisot showed at the Salon continued the game, showing Edma once more in white and once more inside, looking, despite the fact that she was the married older sister, as young and girlish in her high-necked morning gown as Fanny Claus had looked the year before in her short walking dress, now properly accompanied by and distinguished from the mature, black-gowned figure of her mother, lost in a book.[33] *The Harbor at Lorient*, by contrast, shows Edma, ever in a white summer dress, as unequivocally outside as the portraits show her inside, serving now as decorative staffage for a summer landscape, in the context of an appropriately looser, less furbelow-specific manner that soon aligned Morisot with the Impressionists. (Both paintings were exhibited again in the first Impressionist show.) Between them, Morisot's paintings served as ripostes to Manet's dubious *femme fatale*,

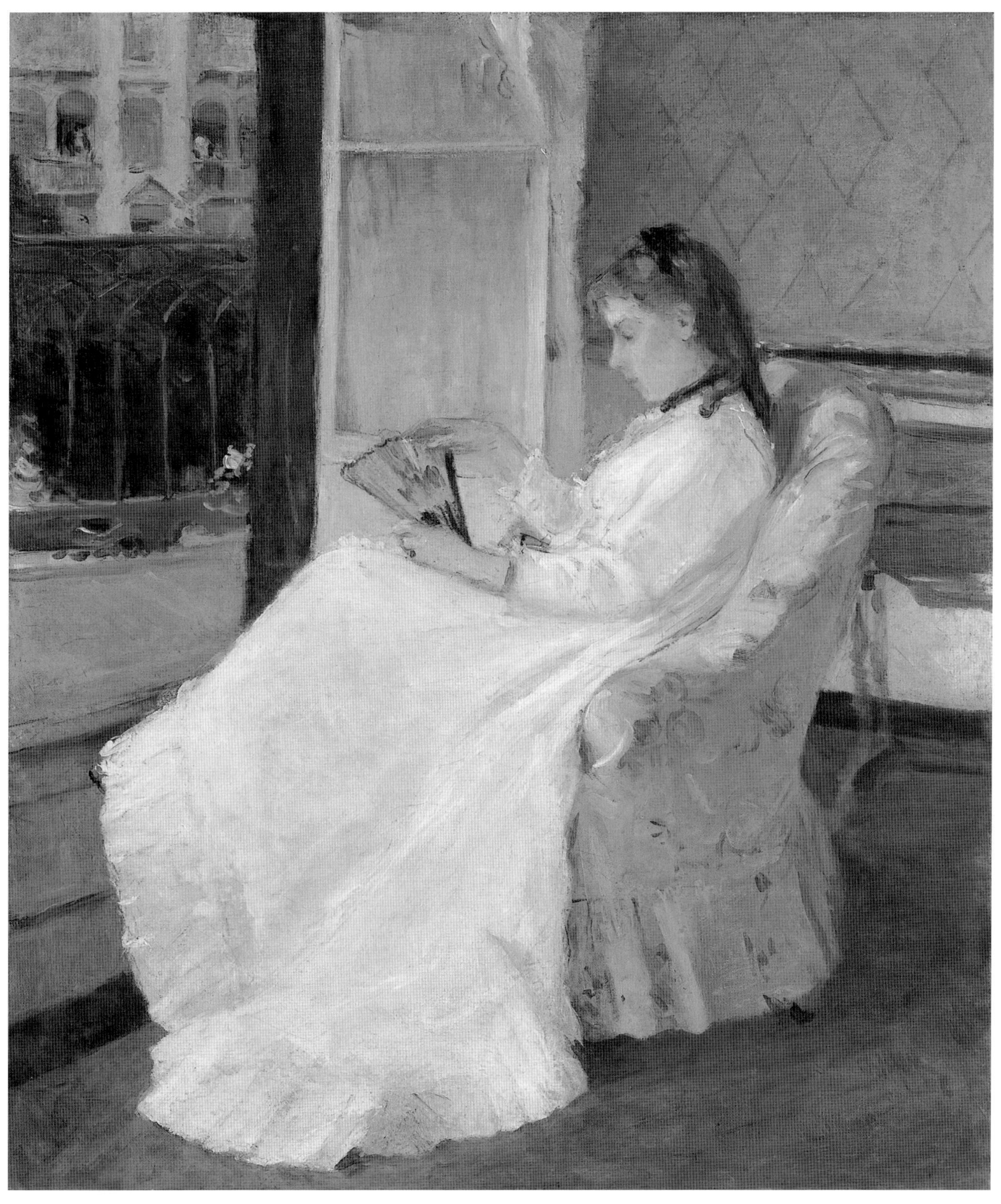

82   Berthe Morisot, *The Artist's Sister at a Window*, 1869, oil on canvas, 54.8 × 46.3 cm. National Gallery of Art, Washington, D.C. Ailsa Mellon Bruce Collection.

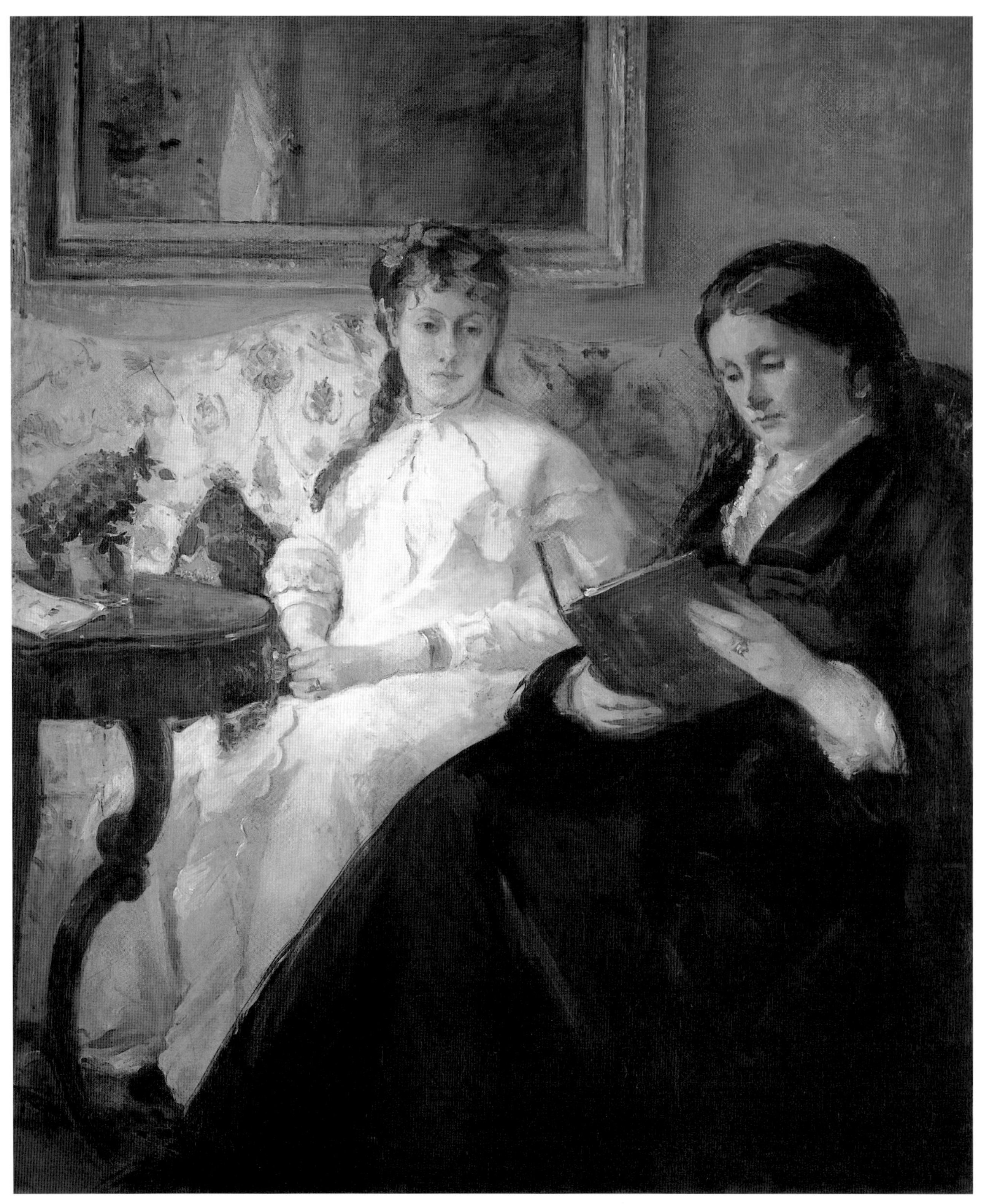

83 Berthe Morisot, *The Mother and Sister of the Artist*, 1869/70, oil on canvas, 101 × 81.8 cm. National Gallery of Art, Washington, D.C. Chester Dale Collection.

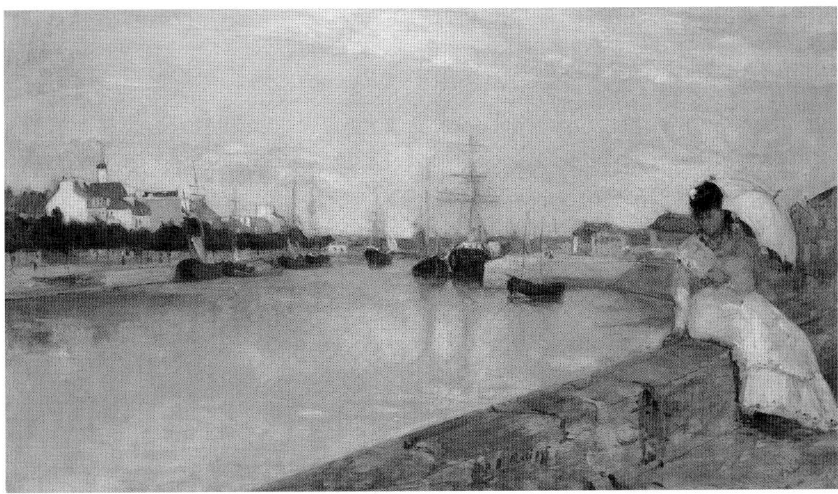

84   Berthe Morisot, *The Harbor at Lorient*, 1869, oil on canvas, 43.5 × 73 cm. National Gallery of Art, Washington, D.C. Ailsa Mellon Bruce Collection.

securing the reputations and boundaries of the Morisot women, if not quite finding a single-minded space for them.

When Morisot first wrote about Manet's advising her to retouch her painting of Edma's dress in 1870, it could well have been the single portrait of her sister that she meant, rather than the double portrait. In the single portrait, Edma's profile is much less the center of attention than the pleated ruffle at the edge of her skirt, which is even more fashion specific than Manet's rendering of Berthe's dress the year before. Manet's forceful depiction of Berthe's dark-haired, dark-browed, dark-eyed face vied with his frothy rendering of her white frock, viewed more complicatedly from the front and side and through a balcony railing that casts its green upon the white of the dress, with close attention to the fabric of the gown and the differential effect that sleeve edges, sash, and petticoat-billowed skirt have here and there upon its hint of stripe and translucence. By contrast, Morisot's rendering of her sister is more clear in its fashion-plate presentation of Edma in profile, and careful in its attention to the pleating of the edge of her skirt, which is echoed in the dust-ruffle of the plump, flowered chair on which she sits, and then fitted, as often was the case in fashion plates, to the decorative geometries of the room. Already the broadness of Morisot's cake-icing handling separated it from the mechanical fussiness of the fashion prints to which she looked, and in her alternative, landscape presentation of Edma at Lorient, she was even broader: in comparison with the stylistic dividedness of Manet's first decade, it was not so much two distinct styles as degrees of departure from a licked-surface norm that distinguished Morisot's several views of her sister.[34] But what is clear in the portrait was that Berthe's head of Edma lost any war it might have waged with Edma's dress. Thus when Manet stepped in to correct Morisot's rendition of dress and face in the double portrait of Edma with her mother, aiding and abetting Morisot in her apprehensions, he reinforced Morisot's already divided attention to head and hem with his own dividedness.

If Morisot's paintings of her sister alone and with her mother were rejoinders to Manet's painting of her, Manet's portrait of Gonzalès was an answer in return. It is impossible to know which was started first, Manet's portrait of Gonzalès or Morisot's portrait of Edma; the Morisot letters mention the former first in 1869, but it sounds as if the latter was all but complete when Manet suggested retouching it. Finally finished, according to Morisot, the day before her own double portrait received Manet's finishing touches, the one does not have clear priority over the other. But whichever was started earliest, and whoever reached the finish line first, one has only to look at the positions of the bodies, the white of the two dresses, and in particular the hem of both skirts, to see how entwined the two paintings were. As much as Manet's *Portrait of Eva Gonzalès* is a revisiting of the white-dressed, guitar-bearing pose of Victorine Meurent of a few years before, it shares the seated-in-profile, crooked-elbow pose of Edma as well. More significantly, given Manet's suggested repainting of Edma's gown (and his beginning at the hem of Morisot's double portrait), the line of the lower edge of Eva's dress is almost exactly the same, down to the knee- and toe-lifted drape of skirt to the left, the extended fold of fabric beneath it, and the wide, thinly fluted border trimming it all around. That border is fashioned and painted somewhat differently by Manet, just as above it the slightly deflated ballooning of the dress, the dark-belted waist, and the short sleeves and low-necked bodice all differentiate themselves from Edma's loose, long-sleeved morning *peignoir* in their style and their handling. So when Manet intervened in the painting of Edma's or Cornélie's flounce, he was continuing a competition already begun in which facture is equated with fashion and the closely observed patterning of one dress after another distinguishes one hand finely from another – and then blends the two together until they are indistinguishable.

It was otherwise with the head of Eva, not to mention her painting arm, the floral study that she appears to paint, and the accessory of the flower painted at the right of her hem. Perhaps one of the reasons Manet was attracted to the Gonzalès girls was because of their Spanish name. But in Eva's head, turned toward the viewer and away from the profile orientation of her body – unlike either the "prett[y] caricature" of Edma's profile or her fully frontal view in the double portrait – there is no trace of the brooding darkness that was ethnically and art historically stereotypical of Spanish representation, which was evoked in *The Balcony* and continued to suggest itself in Manet's later, mantilla-evoking heads of Morisot. Morisot had it right in the end: Gonzalès's likeness is uncompelling, an utterly conventional presentation portrait, the face bearing the indefinable traces of Manet's indecision, the extended painting arm and delicate-fingered, palette-holding hand unconvincing, and the flowerpiece upon which she appears to work little more than a decorative Rococo escutcheon of the standard province of the female painter, bearing little resemblance to either the flower paintings that Manet had produced earlier in the decade and continued to turn out later on, or to Gonzalès's own work in that genre.[35]

Gonzalès's flowerpiece alludes to paintings such as Manet's *Vase of Peonies* (1864; fig. 86), perhaps, but only so as to differentiate itself from them; its light-handedness, signaled in the way that Gonzalès wields her painter's tools, her palette like a teacup, her paintbrush barely making contact with the canvas (as if only to retouch it), could not be more different from Manet's usual manner of thickly laying on paint. By contrast, the

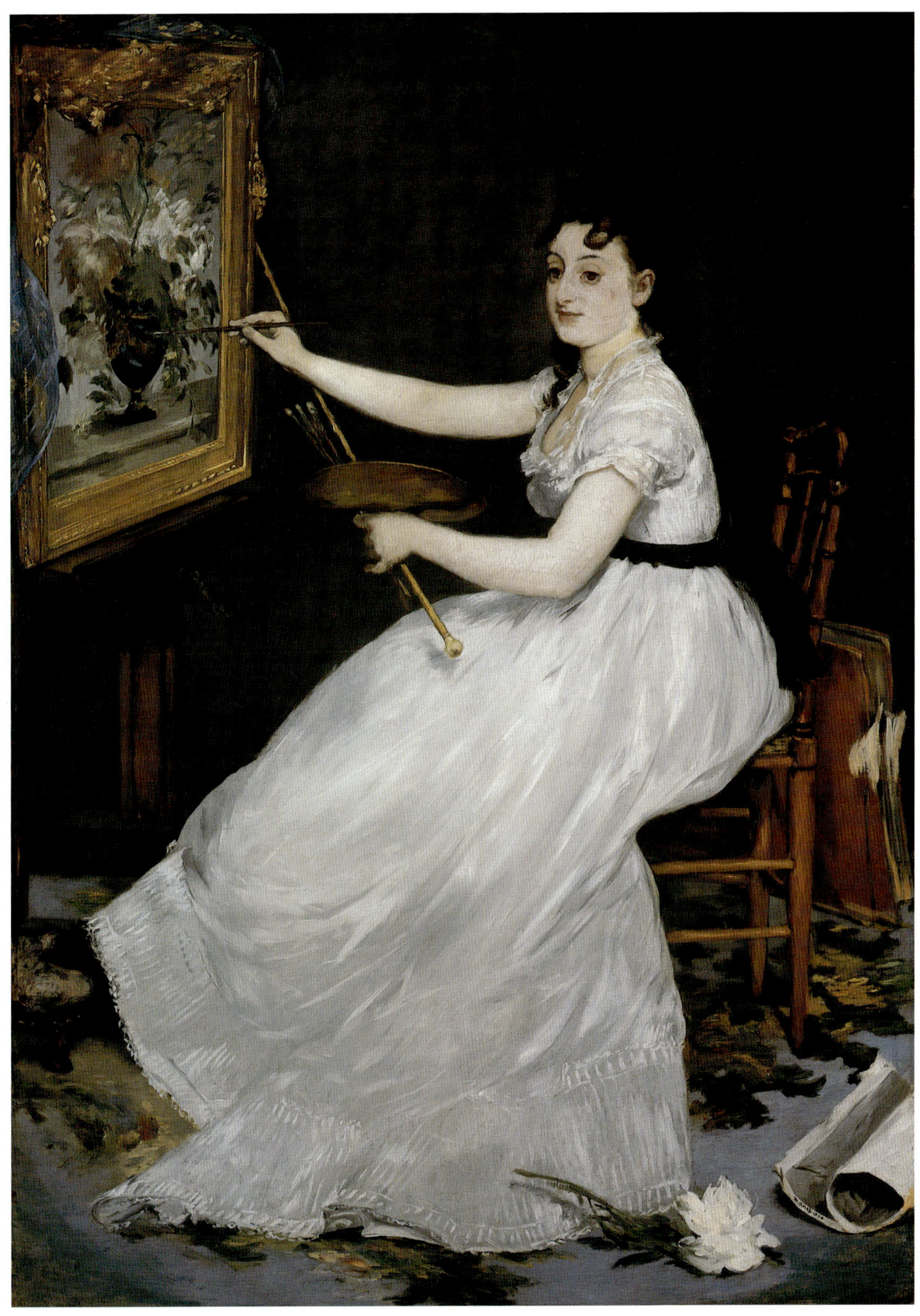

85   Edouard Manet, *Portrait of Eva Gonzalès*, 1870, oil on canvas, 191.1 × 133.4 cm. National Gallery, London.

87 (*facing page left*)
Edouard Manet, *Stem of Peonies with Shears*, 1864, oil on canvas, 31 × 46.5 cm. Musée d'Orsay, Paris.

88 (*facing page right*)
Edouard Manet, *Bouquet of Violets*, 1872, oil on canvas, 22 × 27 cm. Private collection.

86 (*right*)   Edouard Manet, *Vase of Peonies*, 1864, oil on canvas, 93.2 × 70.2 cm. Musée d'Orsay, Paris.

flower at her hem almost exactly repeats the shape and creamy facture of the loose peony at the base of Manet's earlier flower piece, already reiterated in one of his fruit desserts, not to mention his sketch of *Stem of Peonies with Shears* (fig. 87), in which he had managed to link his painter's art to that of the female gardener, cutting flowers from her garden to arrange in a bouquet. That loose flower signs the bottom of the painting and the hem of Gonzalès's skirt with a self-referential flourish that is as evidently the insignia of Manet's painting hand as the painting on the represented easel is not. To underscore the point, the peony is neighbored by a rolled-up painting that has Manet's name diminutively printed on its edge, curling in a line that follows the swag of curving stem and rounded flower.

Thus several things happen at once in Manet's painting of Gonzalès painting. He displays two manners of painting – one stereotypically feminine and not his, the other demonstrably his own signature style. In one way he claims them both, shows them both

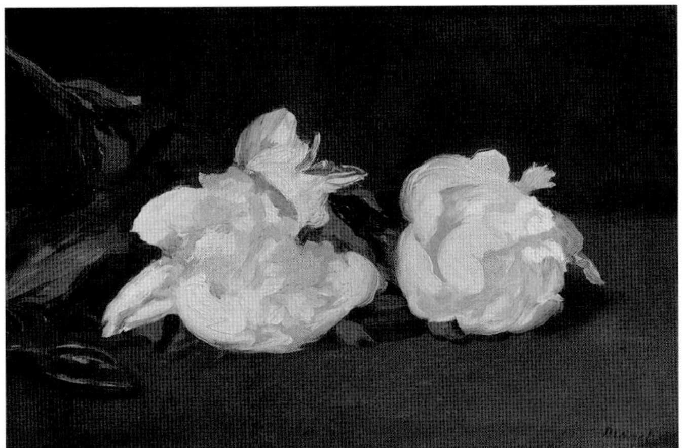 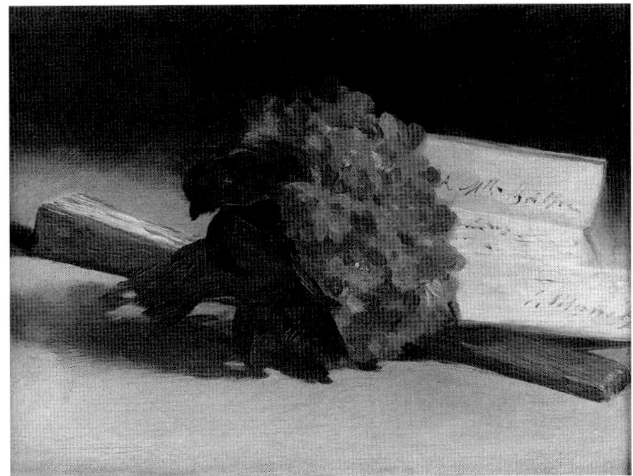

to be the product of his painting hand – Gonzalès, after all, is herself a painting by Manet, so that even the painting she paints is painted by Manet. In another way, Manet divides the regions of her painting and his into top and bottom, head and hem, bouquet-producing arm and blossom-franchised skirt, and with them separates the space of her painting subjecthood (her washed-out face and feathery floral) from that of her painted objecthood (her gorgeously factured frock and flower). The *Portrait of Eva Gonzalès* seeks to answer the question of whose painting is whose, by having it both ways: at once asserting, as he had before in relation to the museum but now more narrowly in relation to the work of female contemporaries, that everybody's painting could be Manet's painting, and differentiating his painting from that of the women with whom he mingled. The *Portrait of Eva Gonzalès* was a painting divided, as no painting by Morisot was. Yet it was also a painting that staked claims more vigorously than Morisot did to Morisot's own psychic world of feminine double consciousness.

Manet decked Morisot out with painted flowers too. Indeed, in a famous later gesture he sent her a painted bouquet (fig. 88). Representing a posy of violets larger than the nosegay held by Victorine in the *Young Woman of 1866*, a folded fan of the same color as the one carried in *The Balcony*, and an unfolded letter illegible save for its address to "Mlle Berthe . . ." and its signature "E. Manet," this little still life doubles as a gallant offering and a painter's double entendre, wittily standing in for a real bouquet and a real note, thus playing on the transparency of the painting to its referent (which in its manner of facture it undercuts), while continuing and participating in the epistolary romance begun in the late '60s, and underlining the intermingling of painting and courtship that characterized the two painters' relationship until Berthe married Eugène instead of Edouard two years later.[36] That same year Manet painted Berthe holding her fan up to her face flirtatiously so as to veil it, having received her violets, though the posy is dimished to the size of the nosegay held earlier by Victorine, and now functions as part of the color scheme of the portrait, effectively turning posy back into painting. Evidently, if no-one else would pose for Manet anymore after Eva Gonzalès's forty-odd sittings, Berthe would, taking up her rightful place as object of Manet's painted attentions once more.

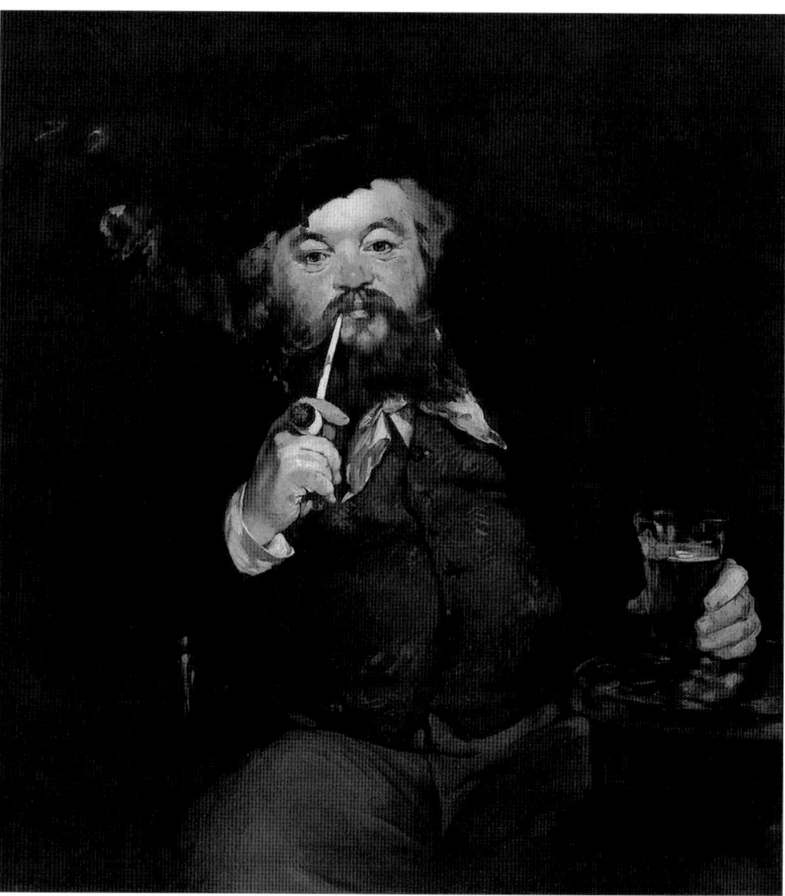

89   Edouard Manet, *Bon Bock*, 1873, oil on canvas, 94 × 83 cm. Philadelphia Museum of Art: Mr. and Mrs. Carroll S. Tyson, Jr. Collection.

The next year Manet showed *Repose* at the Salon, together with *Bon Bock* (fig. 89).[37] This pairing of extraneous works again underscores Manet's straddling of the worlds of museum and modern life, although this time it is to the naturalist school of Dutch genre painting, in the figure of Frans Hals, to which his museum-reference painting gestures. (In a general way, the coarse, heavy figure of the printmaker Bellot and his dark surrounds refer to Courbet as well, once more including the Realism of the previous generation within the museum embraced by Manet.) To the gray-backgrounded, pot-bellied, and leg-spread masculinity of the *Bon Bock*, whose public beerhall surroundings are only to be inferred from the painting's subject matter, *Repose* opposes the slim, white-frocked, feminine elegance of Berthe in a fully contextualized salon interior, deploying the fan and extending the slipper that appear as well in other portraits of her, once more sporting a flounce, this time with cream-petaled, green-leafed flowers (peonies or roses) strewn around it in the hinted, submerged pattern of the dress fabric itself. Overall, the beer-quaffing, pipe-smoking, grossly masculine *Bon Bock*, to be replaced at the end of the decade by male and female beer-drinkers and cigarette-smokers in modern dress situated in the solidly modern-life milieus of Parisian brasseries and café-concerts, looks back again. Meanwhile, *Repose* looks forward, to a world of fashionable femininity.

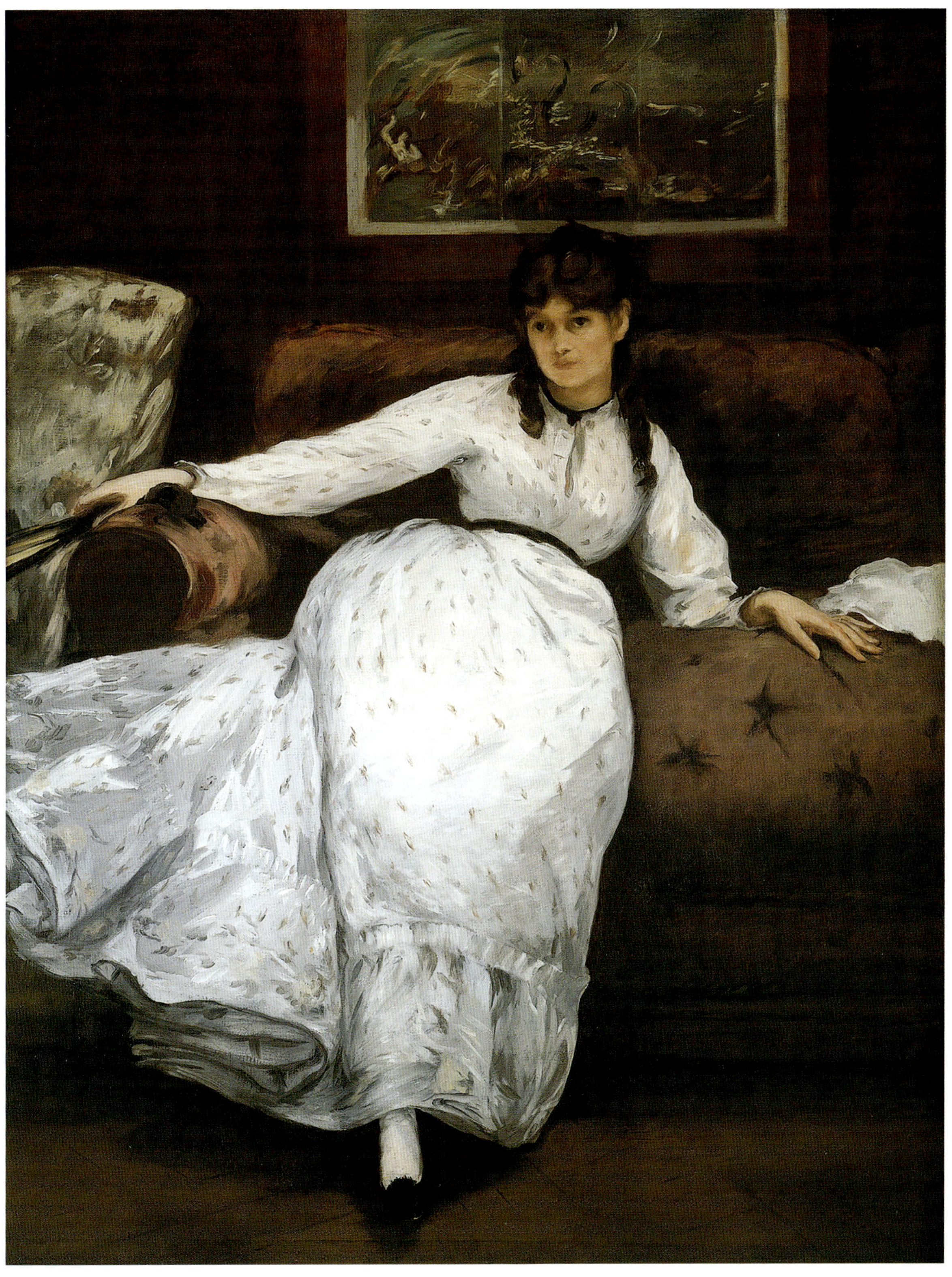

90   Edouard Manet, *Repose*, c.1870, oil on canvas, 143 × 113 cm. Museum of Art, Rhode Island School of Design, Providence, R.I. Bequest of Edith Stuyvesant Vanderbilt Gerry.

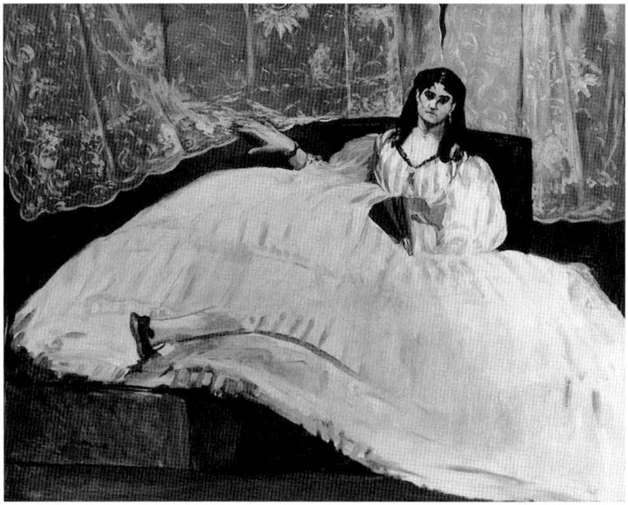

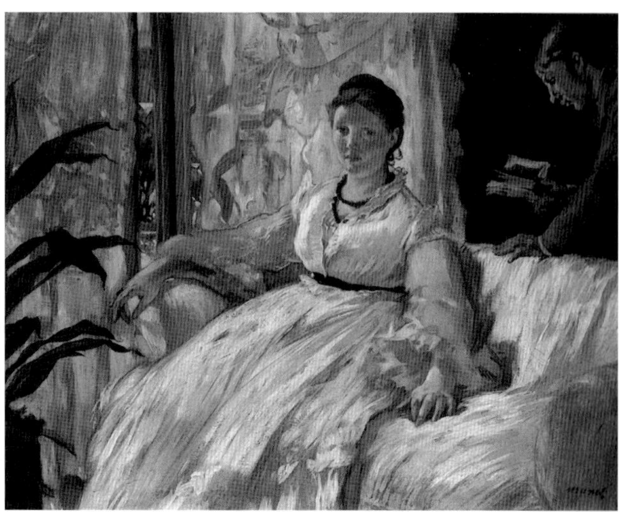

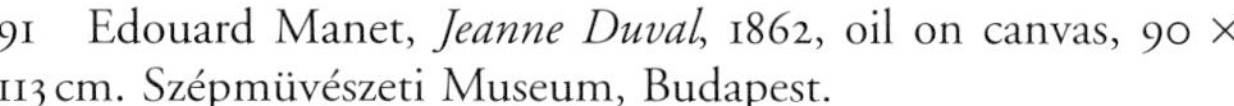

91   Edouard Manet, *Jeanne Duval*, 1862, oil on canvas, 90 ×
113 cm. Szépmüvészeti Museum, Budapest.

92   Edouard Manet, *Reading*, 1865–73, oil on canvas, 61 ×
74 cm. Musée d'Orsay, Paris.

More immediately, *Repose* looks around itself, to a burgeoning throng of white dresses.
The white dress was already and remained an Impressionist stock in trade, perfectly suited
to brightening the palette from dark register to light, the open-air competition between
dappled sunlight and delicately patterned fabric, and the self-referentiality of a blank
surface primed for optical effects. For Manet it was some of that, and it began to give
him purchase on the same contemporary world outside the museum that it did for Monet
and Renoir. But for Manet, most of whose white dresses were ensconced indoors, it was
also more specifically suited to taking up Baudelaire's challenge of the painting of modern
femininity, while at the same time vying with Morisot. Indeed, Manet's first white dress
had been that of Jeanne Duval, Baudelaire's mistress (fig. 91), back in the days of *Music
at the Tuileries. Repose* repeats the pose of that "portrait," from the ballooning white dress,
to the semi-reclining body lost within it, down to the slippered foot emerging from
beneath it. But *Repose* also demonstrates how far Manet had come since then, for the
farouche little head, awkwardy proportioned and fragmented body, and rapidly sketched
in stripes of the exaggeratedly massive skirt of Duval, together suggesting a caricature *à
la* Constantin Guys, are replaced by the accomplished head of Berthe, the elegant disposition of her hands, foot, and body, clearly indicated beneath the billowing of her
dress, and the superbly rendered translucence and petticoat-layering of her faintly dotted
white dress.[38] And Berthe, of course, was not the Creole invalid mistress of Baudelaire;
she was the poised daughter of the wealthy bourgoisie of Paris, as the portrait
demonstrates.[39]

Manet's second white dress was that worn by his wife Suzanne in the portrait known
as *Reading* (fig. 92), taken up in the mid-1860s but not put aside until some time in the
early '70s.[40] That picture shows the plump Suzanne in a white dress with a black belt,
seated on a white-draped settee, against another transparent, white-curtained window,
with her son Léon, this time in a swiftly caricatured profile, here, as before in *The Balcony,*

relegated to obscurity. Berthe's pose in *Repose*, with its counterpoised arms, one extended and the other at rest on the divan, repeats that of Suzanne as well, while also awarding higher marks to the gracefulness of Morisot, whose similar black neckband and belt prove the greater slenderness of her neck and waist: if these two paintings also represent some sort of symbiotic competition between the women that they render, Morisot is clearly the victor.[41] (That said, there is an intimacy and gentleness to the portrait of Suzanne that suggests a private knowledge and domestic sympathy with her that is lacking in the parlor presentation of Morisot.) Morisot's victory, such as it is, is as an object. The title of the painting signals her passivity; her extended arm replaces Eva Gonzalès's painting gesture with a resting one; and the paradoxical combination of dividedness and unity that her pose achieves is one of body and above all dress: she is at once divided into upper and lower body by her twisted, half seated, half reclining position on the sofa, and unified by the long, almost vertical sweep of her cloth-covered leg and the opposing, horizontally inclined diagonal of the fanned out flounce at left, mimicking the line of the fan-bearing arm above it, just as the line of the leg mimicks that of the arm to the right.

Flattering Morisot above her female competitors, *Repose* also demonstrates Manet's increased mastery as a painter relative even to *Reading*, particularly in the rendering of the white frock. Where *Reading* shows off his capacities in the differential rendering of transparent, translucent, and opaque whites – window, sleeves, bodice, skirt, and sheeted sofa – *Repose* again does it one better, differentiating more narrowly between whites, all in the single terrain of the skirt. Berthe's dress does not have the transparent sleeves or the skimming of sheer over opaque of the bodice of Suzanne's ruffle-edged confection. Instead it displays the slightly different effects of translucency, opacity, and buoyancy that result from the bunching and pouffing of the skirt at the waist, the creasing and billowing of the overskirt above several layers of cloth underneath it, the tucked gathering and extra fullness of the flounce, the catching of an extended leg in a long, thickened stretch of cloth, and especially the inflated folding of a petticoated hem under and over itself, there where the floral pattern is sown so as to increase the complexity of the flounce's gathering, as well as the indeterminacy of its transparency and opacity and the undecidability of its upper and lower layers: all achieved by varying suggestions of blue in the field of white, and by the scattering and veiling of brushmarks, white, cream, green, gray, and pale plue, of different lengths, areas, and directions, over that field. As before, Manet shows himself especially adept at conveying the design and differential heft and feel of a dress, substituting vivid painting for fine sewing, and equating both with the materialities and the illusionisms of facture and fabric. Overall, *Repose* represents the triumph of the hem.

That Manet's attention is especially focused on the hem of Berthe's dress is significant – particularly given the dialogue between head and hem in the pictures by Manet and Morisot coming before it, and the blossom functioning as a signature at the bottom of Gonzalès's skirt. That same blossom is multiplied and woven into the painted field of the skirt's edge in *Repose*, subtly signaling the identification of Manet's signature brand of painting with clothes, accessories, and supplements, and with the field of femininity: florals and folds, petals, crimps and creases, surfaces and layers at once gathered and scattered, the diaphanous, diffuse, and dispersed, the indeterminate, doubled, and

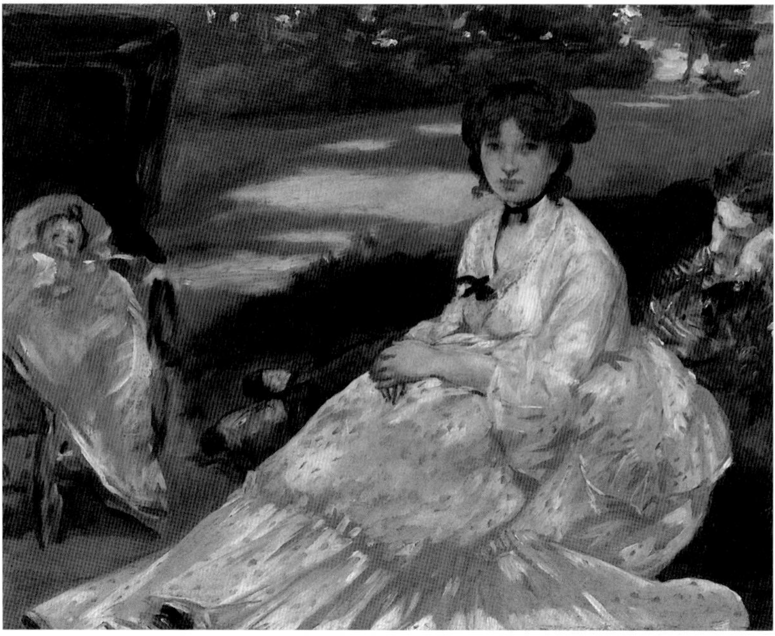

93   Edouard Manet, *In the Garden*, 1870, oil on canvas, 44 × 54 cm. Shelburne Museum of Art, Vermont.

undecided. Moreover, while spelling the overtaking of all references to the painting of others by self-reference, it continues the Manet–Morisot contest begun with *The Balcony*: game, set, match. For *Repose* is as much a retort to Morisot's paintings as the portrait of Gonzalès had been, taking up the double portrait of Edma and Cornélie in particular, using its arrangement of space and furniture and trumping its aura of domestic respectability with Berthe's single, unchaperoned unattachment, her *je ne sais quoi* of salon-hostess elegance, and her command of the art of arranging herself into complex positions.[42] The room corner and arrangement of framed painting over sofa are much the same, but the fussy table is gone; the contrast between chaperoning maturity and chaperoned youth, and with it the claustrophobic hemming in of the latter by the former, is missing (instead there is an empty white chair next to Morisot); the floral-patterned Rococo curves of Morisot's divan are replaced by the flower-flounced skirt and plushly pink sofa, into which Berthe's body sinks so luxuriously, and which, like the painting within a painting above it, is so much more vividly painted than in the earlier picture. In *Repose*, the erotic displacement of bourgeois furnishings is displaced again, in signature paintwork at once aligning itself with the feminine and differentiating itself from that of the female painter whom it represents.

After *Repose*, the next (and last) of Manet's white dresses was that worn first by the Valentine Carré mentioned by Morisot at the end of the *affaire* Gonzalès and then by Edma, seated in *In the Garden* (fig. 93) together with Edma's baby daughter and Morisot's brother Tiburce.[43] In this painting Manet produced another white muslin dress, also dotted, flounced, and superbly characterized in its ruffled mix of flesh-tinged trans-

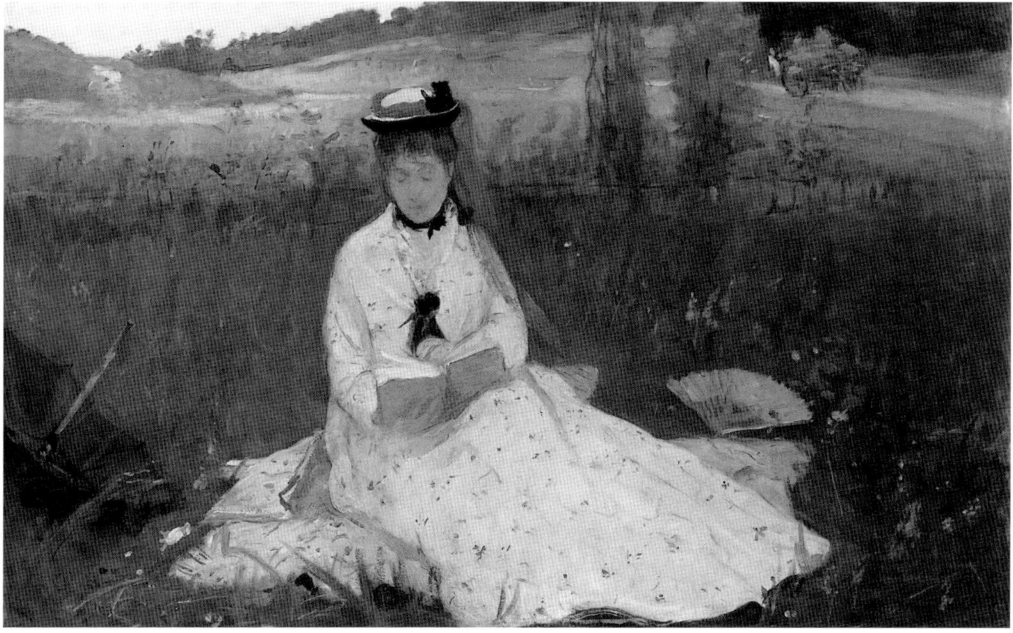

94   Berthe Morisot, *Reading*, 1873, oil on canvas, 46 × 71.8 cm. The Cleveland Museum of Art. Gift of the Hanna Fund, 1950.89.

parency and opaque whiteness. And he yielded another overpainted, unsuccessfully rendered face, no doubt because of the changing of models. But this time the white dress is arranged out of doors, in the Morisot garden rather than the Morisot salon. And on this occasion, by the time Valentine's mother had forbidden her unmarried daughter to sit for Manet and Morisot's married sister had replaced her, the white dress was surrounded by a secure, unambiguous domestic arrangement: woman, man, and baby, the perfect nuclear family. (The man was a brother in actuality, lounging just as Manet's brothers had lounged less than a decade ago in the *Luncheon on the Grass*. But the innuendos attached to that picnicking arrangement are safely neutralized in *In the Garden*.) Here, now, as a postscript to the Manet–Morisot saga of 1869–70, are all the ingredients of the Impressionist picture: *plein air*, enclosed garden path dappled with sunlight, the domestic unit naturalized. Morisot replied in 1873, the year of the Salon in which *Repose* appeared, with her own outdoors picture of Edma in a white dress sewn with blossoms (fig. 94), shown reading (like her mother, back in the double portrait of that title), alone as she had been in the portrait at the window, with the fan from that earlier portrait half open and discarded next to her, her face quite as vague and washed out as Manet's undecided portrayal of her features doubled with those of Valentine. Here the chapter ended, and this particular conversation about women in white dresses came to a close. But the dialogue between Manet and Morisot was far from over. And Manet's engagement with the clarity or ambiguity, the propriety or impropriety of painted relationships that that dialogue had raised continued apace, in the context of his own Salon variations on Impressionist painting of the next few years.

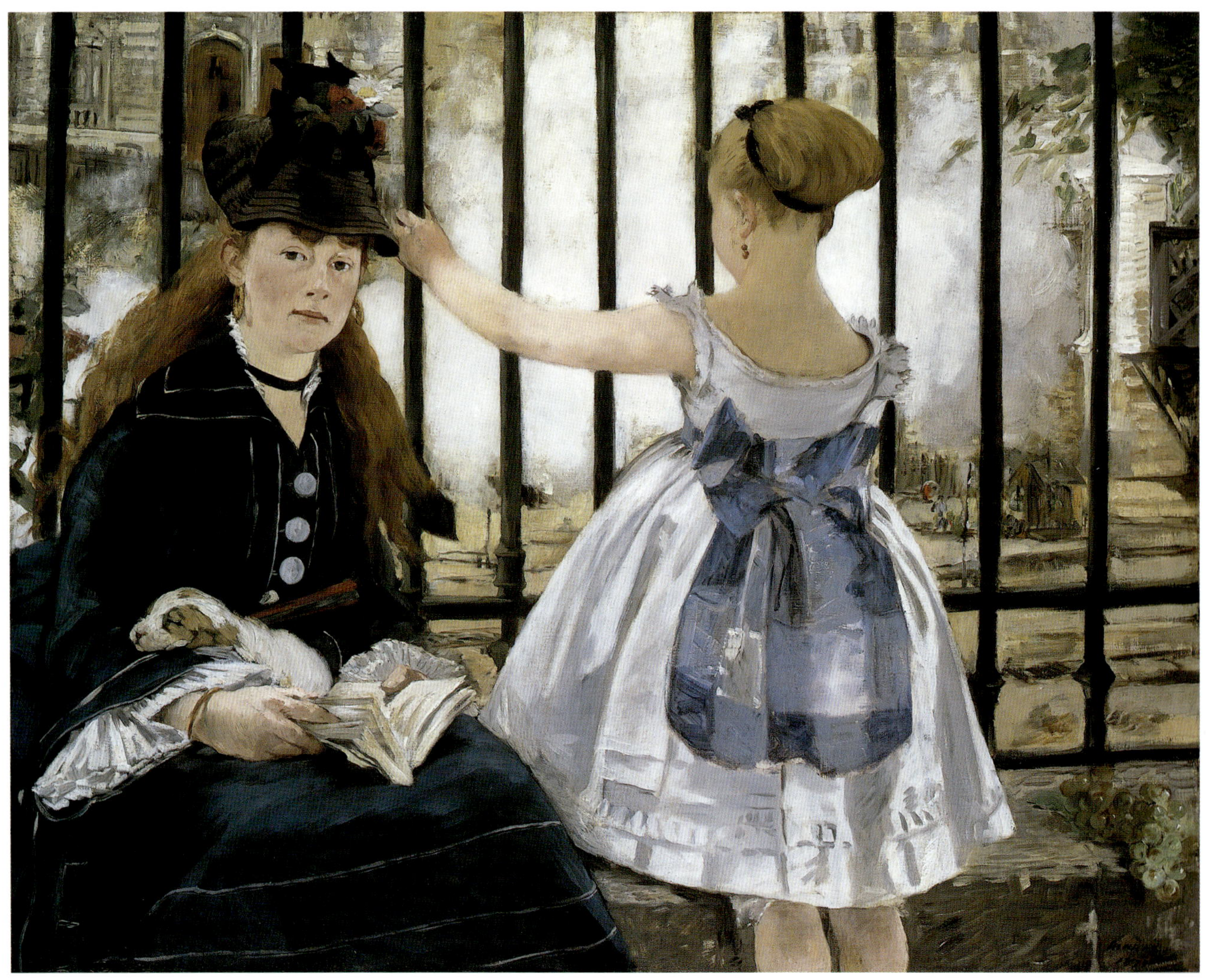

95   Edouard Manet, *The Railway*, 1873, oil on canvas, 93.3 × 111.5 cm. National Gallery of Art, Washington, D.C. Gift of Horace Havemeyer in memory of his mother, Louisine W. Havemeyer.

Chapter Eight

MODERNITY ACCORDING TO MANET: IMPRESSIONISM AT THE SALON, 1874 TO 1879

THE GARDEN WAS NOT A SALON PAINTING. The only white dress to show up in Manet's next Salon was worn by a child, in *The Railway* (fig. 95). In the Salon of 1874, Manet showed this painting and a little watercolor of Punchinello with a poem by Théodore de Banville appended to it. He had submitted *Swallows*, showing his wife and mother reclining in a field in a caricature of Morisot's loose new style, and the *Masked Ball at the Opera*, countering the indistinctly rendered domesticity of *Swallows* with a crowd of *demi-monde* encounters whose manner was somewhat reminiscent of *Music at the Tuileries* of a decade before. But neither of these paintings were accepted. *The Railway*, in which Victorine Meurent posed one last time next to the daughter of Manet's painter friend Alphonse Hirsch, had its usual impact, while the watercolor went more or less unnoticed.

Between the paintings of 1869 and 1870 and the Salon of 1874, much had happened. In 1870, in the same Salon in which Manet showed his portrait of Gonzalès and Morisot showed her two differently painted and conceived images of Edma, Fantin-Latour had exhibited the *Studio at the Batignolles* (fig. 96), presenting Manet as the head of the new school of painting. It shows Manet painting Astruc (who was featured in Manet's *Music Lesson* at the same Salon), with Zola standing directly over Astruc at the edge of an empty frame; the *Studio at the Batignolles* positions Manet anew in relation to these writers (instead of Baudelaire, with whom Fantin-Latour had associated him in the *Homage to Delacroix*, and who had died in 1867). It places Renoir, who had two paintings accepted at the Salon of 1870, at the center of things, even going so far as to frame his head much in the manner that Delacroix had been framed in the 1864 painting – except that Renoir also breaks the closure of the frame to stand in the world in front of it. Bazille, meanwhile, who had one entry accepted into the Salon, unmistakably dominates the right side of the painting because of his height, while Monet, with all of his submissions rejected, is all but squeezed out of the picture. For his part, Manet paints with the gesture of Velasquez in *Las Meniñas* and is differentiated from his painter *confrères* by his seated position and his location next to the bright red tablecloth on the left, with its array of *objets d'art*. And the internally differentiated gathering not only comes together in a studio that is more Fantin-Latour's than Manet's, it is painted in a unified, formal, finished manner that is distinct from the style of the new group – Fantin-Latour's manner rather than theirs. Thus with this Salon painting Fantin-Latour accomplished several things at once: he located himself as an associate of the adherents of advanced painting,

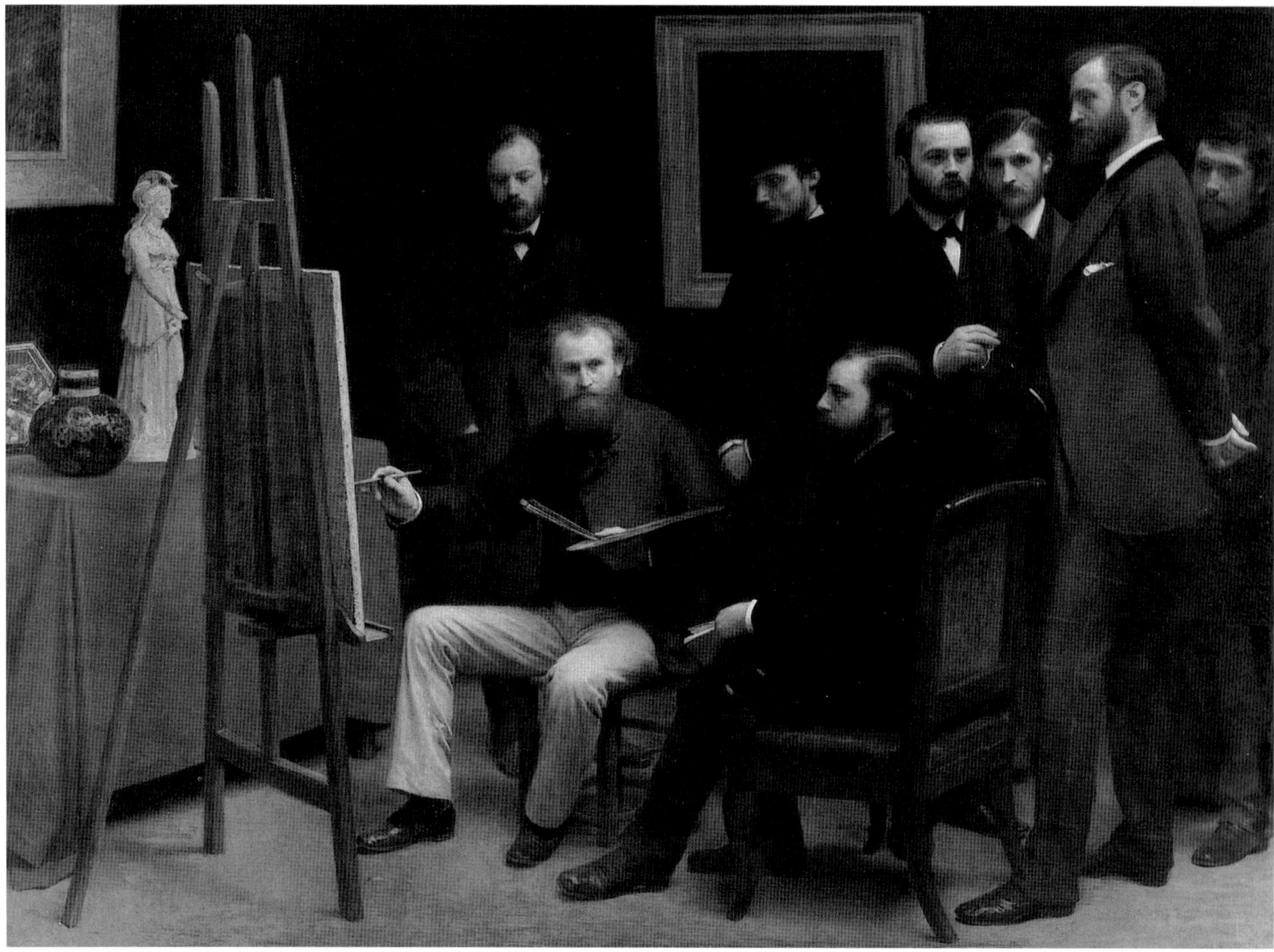

96   Henri Fantin-Latour, *A Studio at the Batignolles*, 1870, oil on canvas, 204 × 273.5 cm. Musée d'Orsay, Paris.

while also making sure that it would be noted that he was not of the group (this time he did not represent himself within it); he differentiated between its members according to how far "in" or "out" (of the Salon that he was in) they were; and most importantly, he simultaneously characterized Manet as a new Velasquez and the *chef d'école* of the new painting.[1]

This was a reputation with which Manet had already been contending.[2] In 1874, when he sent *The Railway* to the Salon, the first Impressionist exhibition was underway, but Manet was not in it and ever after declined to join up, preferring to remain a Salon painter with private shows of his own on the side. Nonetheless, he was regarded as the founder of Impressionism, and in the 1870s took up its prime subjects one by one – the railroad, sailing in the suburbs, the café – sometimes ahead of the game, sometimes slightly behind it. But he took up these subjects to dispute them, not to fall in with them.

Between the Salon of 1870, in which Fantin-Latour's painting was shown, and the Salon of 1874, in which Manet first wrestled with his relationship to the Impressionist group, first the siege and then the Commune had occurred, Manet had joined the artillery of the National Guard, he had recycled his Goya-based *Execution of Maximilian* in order to represent the civil war in Paris, and he had sent Suzanne and Léon to the Pyrenees where he later joined them.[3] During that time, he got himself a new studio in the heart of Haussmannized Paris, on the rue de Saint-Petersbourg, near the Gare Saint-Lazare, and two years later proceeded to paint that locale rather obliquely, while sending an old marine painting, the *Battle of the Kearsarge and the Alabama*, to the Salon of 1872.[4] For a while during this period, Manet stepped up the pace of his painting of Morisot, without sending any of the paintings of her produced around this time to the Salon. (He sent *Repose*, painted just before the siege and the Commune, instead.) The year 1874 was the culmination of Manet's painting of Morisot; it was also a turning point for Morisot herself.[5]

PAINTING THE GARE SAINT-LAZARE

What did it mean, in the context of these events, for Manet to paint first *The Railway* (several years before Monet adopted that subject) and then *Argenteuil* and *Boating* (shortly after Monet's most concentrated work in that area), and present them at the Salon rather than within the Impressionist exhibitions? In the first instance, the question is best answered by returning to some of the issues raised in the contest between Manet and Morisot of the preceding years. For *The Railway* still engages elements from the 1869–70 relay of images, adding to them ingredients from an 1872 series of paintings by Morisot, while also taking up a new and more determinedly modern-life subject than ever before.[6] Its view through railings recalls *The Balcony*, although white steam has replaced the white dress as the screened object of the viewer's regard, and the painting's protagonists now stand in front of the railing: they appear to have moved fully outside (rather than posing on the brink of a street that is not only out of frame but a figment of the painted gaze, an imaginary site corresponding to the viewer's place before the picture, which must actually be indoors). Its contrast between a darkly dressed woman reading and a white-dressed child takes up the composition of Morisot's painting of Cornélie and Edma once more in order to reverse and complicate it, and locate it outdoors. And, following Morisot's efforts and Manet's own trial run in *The Garden*, *The Railway* begins a policy of trying to secure and domesticate the ambiguous modern relationships between urban people in which he specialized and of which *The Balcony* had been emblematic.

More particularly, *The Railway* takes up the theme of the mother–daughter pictures that Morisot was producing contemporaneously, featuring her other sister Yves Gobillard with her daughter Bichette, including *Interior*, *Paris seen from the Trocadero*, and most importantly, *On the Balcony* (fig. 97).[7] It has been remarked that Morisot's Trocadero painting depends upon Manet's *View of the Universal Exposition*; it is equally the case that *On the Balcony* looks back to the balcony picture by Manet that marked the inception of the dialogue between the two painters.[8] At the same time, Manet surely

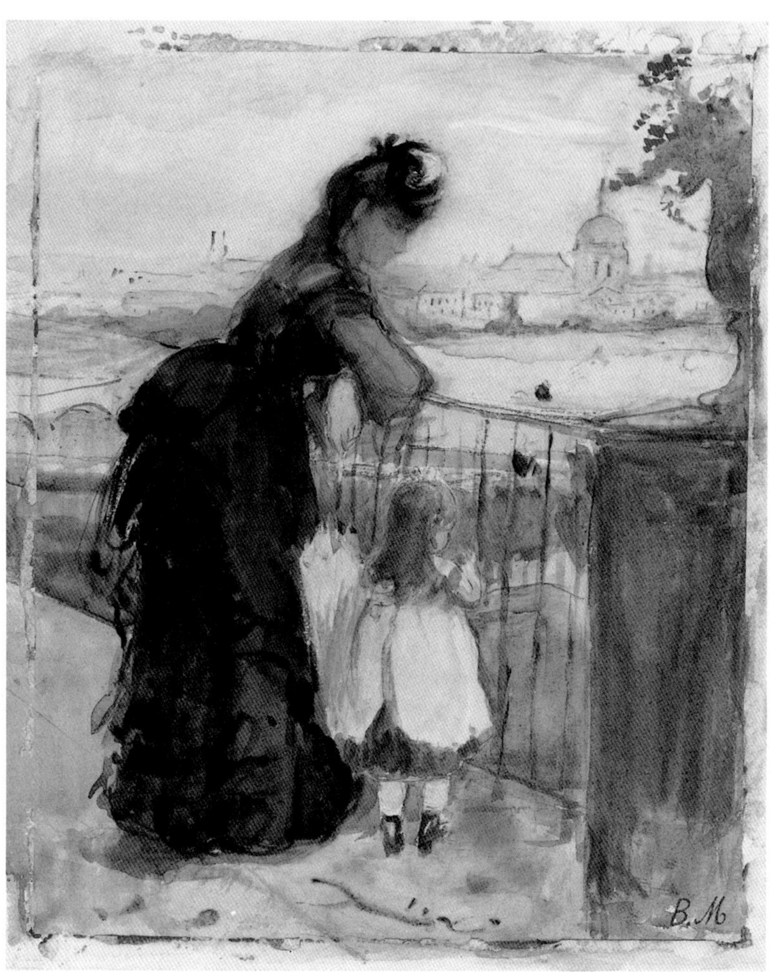

97   Berthe Morisot, *On the Balcony*, 1872, watercolor, 20 × 17 cm. The Art Institute of Chicago. Gift of Mrs. Charles Netcher in memory of Charles Netcher II, 1933.1.

relied in return on Morisot's *On the Balcony*, with its representation of a dark-gowned woman and a child in a white pinafore seen from behind peering through railings in the Bois de Boulogne, responding to it in his view of a woman and a child with her back turned, posed in front of the bars of an iron fence near the railway station. Manet closes in on the scene, cutting off the ground on which the figures stand and placing the viewer almost on a level with, or just slightly above, the child's view through the bars, as if cutting off the adult panorama, and giving us instead something like what Morisot's little girl in the pinafore sees. But where Morisot's mother and child look in tandem at the same view, thus uniting them, Manet's woman and child, one seen head-on from the front, and the other from the rear in *profil perdu*, look in opposed directions, one out at us and the other away, with the result that it is much less clear what their relationship to one another is supposed to be, whether mother and daughter or governess and ward, or some other even less determinate arrangement, like that of two models unknown and unrelated to each other. This led one critic, who felt that Manet was "an essentially bourgeois painter," to puzzle over the painting's genre: "Is Manet's *Railway* a double portrait or a subject picture? . . . We lack information to solve this problem; we hesitate all the more concerning the young girl which at least might be a portrait seen from the rear . . ."[9]

On the one hand, then, *The Railway* seeks to rectify the instability of the relationships given in *The Balcony*, by taking up Morisot's domesticating responses to that painting and using them as the basis of his own attempt at *embourgeoisement*: a duenna and her charge, replete with faithful lapdog, rather than unmarried men and and single women consorting together, and the promiscuous black cat of Victorine's earlier days as a model.[10] On the other hand, the two figures are so divided from one another, their relationship so unexplained, and as usual Victorine's gaze so deadpan, that their patently borrowed domesticity is compromised. And instead of the family unit that Morisot gives us, Manet again focuses all his attention on fashion. Again he trumps Morisot, for characteristically, Morisot too was concerned with fashion in *On the Balcony*. But in place of Morisot's caricature of a fashion plate, with its quickly notated profile view, Manet supplies a detailed rendition of an (almost) up to date, *matelot*-style dress in navy blue duck cloth with white buttons, white trim, neck edging, and undersleeve ruffles, with a backfold of pelisse or overdress and the suggestion of a bustle in the bunching of cloth to the left, and an even more detailed rendering of Victorine's equally up to date black straw bonnet, replete with pleating, topknot of black velvet ribbons and red flowers, and the pulling in of the whole confection at the sides by the band threaded through it, implying the back-tie that was current.[11] (It is worth noting the intensiveness of Manet's attention to the hat, the way it not only obscures Victorine's forehead as earlier headgear had done but also actively competes with her face, for the first time mitigating the old, compelling *punctum* of her gaze.[12] That the tipped forward design of the hat suits it to the flat plane of the picture partly explains Manet's new interest in it; indeed, hats of various styles preoccupied him, over and above the design of dresses, in the years to come.) Manet had always been a painter of costume pieces; now his shift from art-historical costume to modern fashion was complete.

In addition, Manet produced just as detailed a treatment of the child's formal, sleeveless dress, with its stiff pressing into wide, white tablelinen folds and its huge, blue sash of variegated translucency, along with the bandeau in her hair and the dainty garnet earring dangling from her ear in contrast to the large gold hoops in her putative chaperone's ears. If, despite the near-currency of her outfit, Victorine manages to look frumpy next to the starchily dressed child, her trademark Titian hair at long, loose ends in contrast not only to the way she had been presented in the 1860s but also to the sleek, tightly banded coiffure of the girl next to her, that is simply to reverse the formal–informal logic of mother–daughter wear suggested in Morisot's painting.[13] It is also to increase the unsettling effect of Manet's painting, for that reversal adds to the indeterminacy of the figures' association with one another. Certainly it underscores the divided field that the painting both represents within itself and produces in the optical psychological space inhabited by the viewer – front/back, before/behind, out/in, with/against, here/there, screened/unscreened, diffuse/sharp, loose/tight. And then/now, for *The Railway* continues Manet's 1869 meditation in *The Balcony* and *Luncheon in the Studio* on the indexing of youth, age, and temporality, both in clothes and in paint, in relation to previous paintings, and in the representational context of ambiguous human relations. That use of fashion and facture, along with divergent gazes, to fissure the fabric of space and time was Manet's peculiar contribution to the defining of modernity in painting. And it was distinct from the way the Impressionists, for all the differences among them, defined modernity in their paintings.

The informality of the daughter's clothes in *On the Balcony* is matched by the sketchy informality of Morisot's facture; instead of Morisot's loose handling and apparently unposed, impromptu scene, Manet uses a differentiated facture whose greatest looseness is relegated to its backdrop – between or on the other side of the bars through which the girl looks – while in parts of the foreground, especially in Victorine's bonnet, it is tight, precise, and finished, almost *léché*, in order to render a situation which, for all that Victorine appears to have been interrupted in the act of reading, is obviously a posed one. As a woman Morisot was allowed her light touch in the Salon, and was encouraged in it in the Impressionist shows; by contrast, Manet either assumed or was learning that there were distinctions to be made, even within his outrageous style of painting, between a formality that was appropriate for the Salon and an informality that was not, that in his case was refused.[14] Thus his portrait painter's focus on posed faces, bodies, and clothes, and the manner of painting that occupies the foreground of *The Railway*, spell out his self-conception as a Salon painter as opposed to an Impressionist landscape exhibitor.[15] If anything, that is, *The Railway* marks Manet as not an Impressionist.

As for the modernity of the subject matter, where is the railway of the painting's title? Nowhere but in the obscuring cloud of steam and a series of screened details, such as the bit of ironwork at the upper right edge of the painting, the suggestion of tracks glimpsed through the lower horizontal bars of the railing, and the tiny guardhouse and signal that upon close scrutiny are to be found between the first and third vertical bars on the right. That railing, whose vertical–horizontal structure is picked up in the tracks and guardhouse and in the buttons, sash, and trim of the two figures' dresses, is indeterminate in its relation to the railway station. Are we to know from the painting that the figures were posed, not on the street or the bridge overlooking the station, but in Hirsch's private garden, which must have had a view of a bit of the Gare Saint-Lazare? And thus, that the railing that takes up so much of the painting, aligning itself with the support and plane of the picture and dividing it narrowly into what is before and behind it, actually separates a private enclosure from the public urban domain? Not from the uncertain domestic duo of woman and child, but perhaps from the still-life detail of the grapes spilling over the bench at the lower right corner, a scrap of private space that contrasts with the piece of public space in the form of the fragment of Haussmannized facade glimpsed at the upper left-hand corner.[16] Together the grapes, whose projection over the the edge of the bench matches Victorine's forward-looking gaze and projecting, cut-off skirt, and the facade, whose shuttered blankness somehow corresponds to the little girl's lost profile and the rendering of the bottom of her dress, speak to the Impressionist project of rooting the spectacle of city and suburbs in the enclosed world of house and garden (of which Monet's paintings of his family from this period are the best examples). But they do so obliquely and complexly, in the form of supplementary fragments that serve as framing decorations: the grapes are manifestly that, and by association they make the facade type that was the emblem of the new city into the same kind of thing – a corner filler and painter's prop.

Detail of fig. 95.

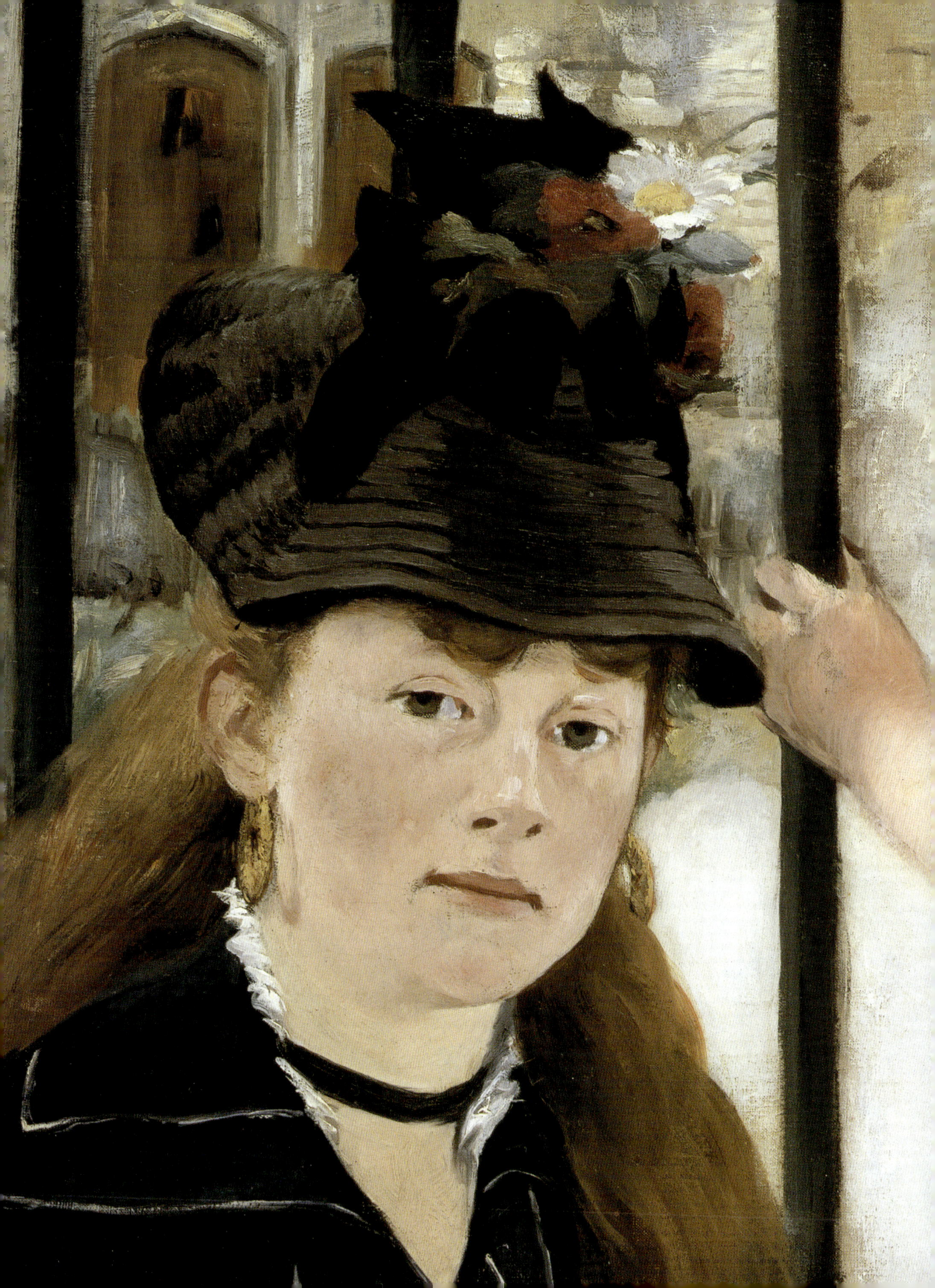

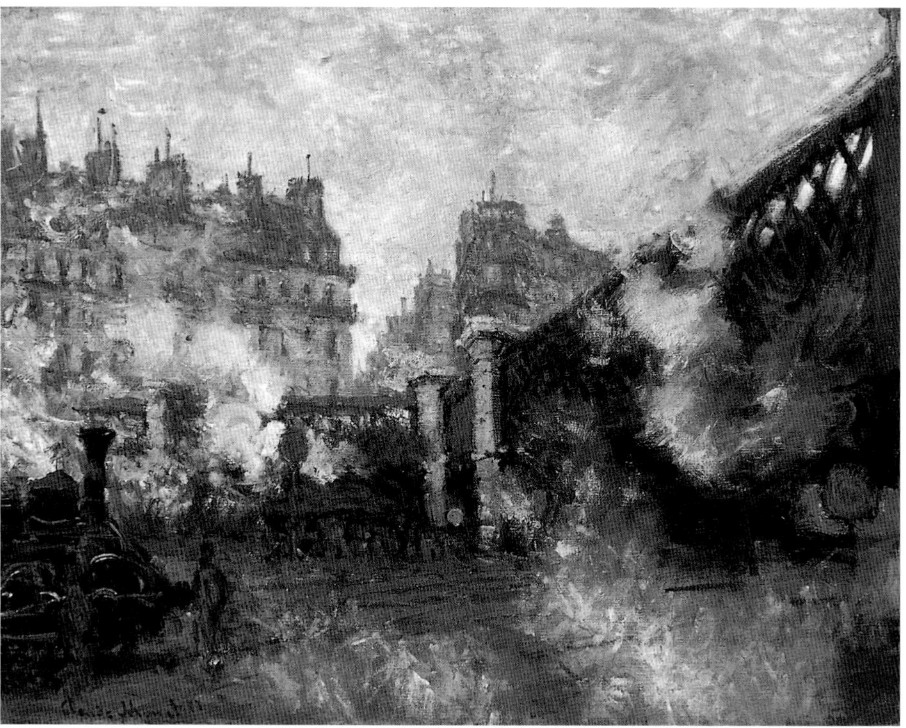

98   Claude Monet, *The Pont d l'Europe* (*Gare Saint-Lazare*) 1877, oil on canvas, 64 × 80 cm. Musée Marmottan, Paris.

Three years later similar elements functioned very much otherwise in Monet's and Caillebotte's renderings of the Gare Saint-Lazare, which were centerpieces of the third Impressionist exhibition in 1877.[17] In Monet's series of six paintings shown that year, the station is seen from inside and out. In one exceptional view (fig. 98), the iron grillwork of the Pont de l'Europe, a red signal, and the new uniform facades of Haussmann's city, with their top-floor balconies, slate roofs, and red clay chimney pots, are visible through the ubiquitous steam of the railway station, together with that central element, the loco-motive, which was missing from Manet's painting. The locomotive and some aspect of the industrial structure of the station were common to all six paintings by Monet, but the steam was what unified each and every one of them; it was an urban landscape effect that screened and dissolved solid structure in the pure play of ephemeral atmosphere. Underscored by the serialized variations on the railway station theme, that spectacular evanescence was modernity, according to Monet's lights.

Caillebotte saw it differently, in his famous depiction of the Place de l'Europe in the district of the Gare Saint-Lazare, the *Paris Street in Rainy Weather*, and in *The Pont de l'Europe* (fig. 99), both of which were in the 1877 Impressionist exhibition with Monet's series. Both attend to a physiognomics of modern costume, the anonymity, alienation, and vertiginous effect of modern urban space, the uniform facade apartment building, and more generally to industrial replication – in the form of umbrellas, hats, coats, and facades in the *Paris Street in Rainy Weather* and in the bolting and riveting of the repeated

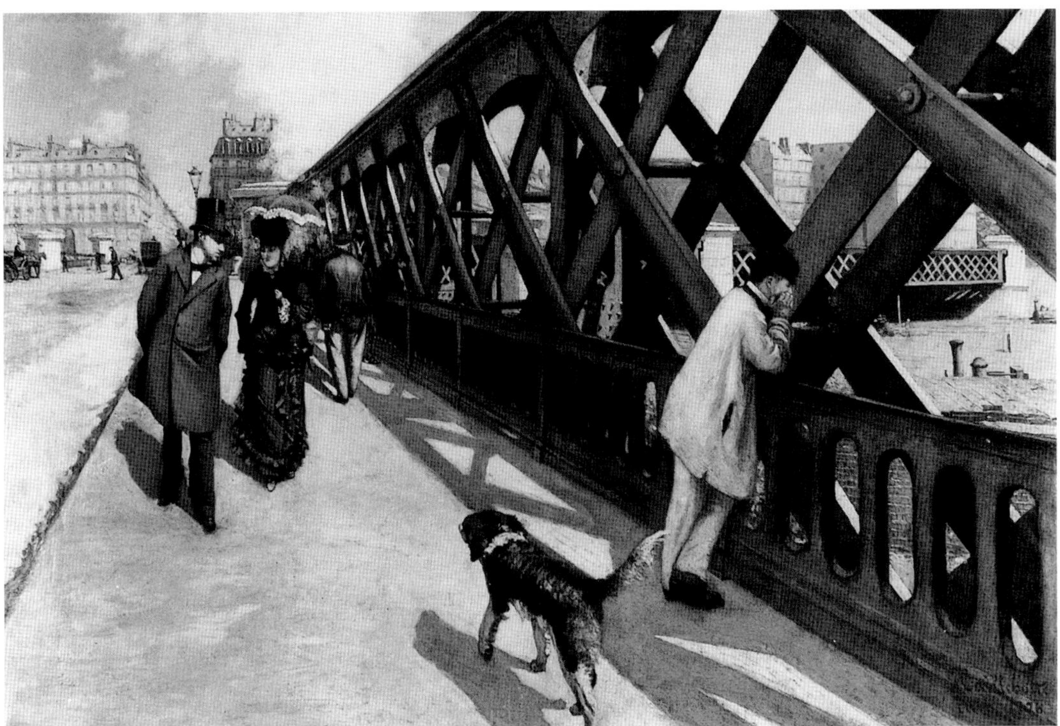

99   Gustave Caillebotte, *The Pont de l'Europe*, 1876, oil on canvas, 124.8 × 180.7 cm. Musée du Petit Palais, Geneva.

iron crossbraces and the stamped, prefabricated bridge railing in the *Pont de l'Europe*. The latter also adds its share of rising steam into the equation, and a screened glimpse of the station below, viewed by the worker at right whose smock and cap provide a class counterpoint to the bourgeois apparel of the couple walking toward the viewer. But in *The Pont de l'Europe*, the steam and indeed everything else is dominated by the industrial ironwork of the bridge, whose very fashioning out of replicated parts is foregrounded. No delightful dissolution here (nor, for that matter, any of Manet's carefully worked out indecision about iron and vapor, the detailed and the dissolute); instead the dreadful one-thing-after-another of industrial (re)production is the order of the day, at once inscribed into every detail and aspect of the depicted scene – space, architecture, people, clothes, accouterments – and underwritten by the slick, everywhere the same, hard-surfaced manufacture characteristic of Caillebotte's style of painting, very much in contrast to Monet's amorphously scumbled facture and its equivalence with ephemera. It is tempting to understand Caillebotte, the wealthiest and most technocratic of the Impressionist coterie, as the group's most perspicacious critic of the capitalist edifice that Haussmann's city was, in which class and technology worked together as parts of a total configuration.[18] At the very least, it is fair to say that in these two pictures he conceived of industrial replication as the very system of modernity. Far from being inchoate, as Monet would have had it, Caillebotte's modernity was a structure, a mode of production rather than an optical spectacle.[19]

It is easy to see that the Impressionist exhibitions did not represent anything like a single, cohesive picture of modern life, any more than they offered uniformity in modern painting. Indeed, it would be much more to the point to understand them as putting on display divergent definitions of the modern, as the concentrated but contested thematics of the railway station suggested in 1877. But *The Railway* by Manet, which must have helped to suggest that subject matter to Monet and Caillebotte, enfolded that divergence within itself, so that it structures the painting from the inside. Moreover, Manet's version of the Gare Saint-Lazare, which was the urban point of origin of the Impressionist journey out to suburbs like Argenteuil and Gennevilliers and beyond to the Normandy coast, did not address itself to the question of what was the most significant feature of modernity – although certainly the painting situates modern clothes and fashionability in the foreground and relegates smoke and ironwork to the figures' backdrop. Instead, Manet's depiction of the railway station differs fundamentally from those of his Impressionist friends in proposing that modern painting is the question at hand, that his is a painter's (not an engineer's or streetworker's) fabrication, a figment of the pictorial gaze and a function of the relationship between picture and viewer, more than a reflection of modern life per se; and that modern painting is a matter of the *parergon*, the frame that separates and differentiates painting from the world around and beyond it.[20] *The Railway's* bifurcation of facture, space, and psyche and its divided address to the viewer continue tendencies in Manet's painting that went all the way back to the art-historical picnic of the *Luncheon on the Grass*; in the updated context of a rendering of a feature of the modern city; those characteristics of *The Railway* predict the famously fissured *Bar at the Folies-Bergère*. Unlike Monet's and Caillebotte's leanings in the matter of modernity, Manet's inclinations had an internal history in painting, and although they fared badly in the Salon, they were nevertheless dependent on the formal display values of that venue, and its ties to the portrait, costume-piece, and museum of past art, as well as the single work rather than the series.[21]

"MANET AND MANETTE": *FAUX*-IMPRESSIONIST COUPLES

In 1875, Manet broke with his usual practice and submitted only one painting to the Salon. That painting was *Argenteuil* (fig. 100) and, although it was accepted, it was met with the mock horror that was by now habitual. Beneath his caricature in *Le Journal Amusant* of May 22, Stop wrote, " 'Good Lord! What's that?' 'That's Manet and Manette,'" affecting uncertainty about the boat the pair was supposed to be in, and going on to describe the Seine behind them as a "blue wall."[22] On this occasion "Manet and Manette" were posed by Manet's brother-in-law Rudolph Leenhoff and an unknown woman – or perhaps a combination of women including his wife Suzanne – when Manet was staying at the family house in Gennevilliers. An adult heterosexual couple this time, "Manet and Manette" is Manet's Salon painting answer to Monet's depictions of boating on the Seine, which were concentrated between 1872 and 1874, when Monet lived in a rented house in Argenteuil.[23]

This painted couple continues the preoccupation with domestic relationships and the issue of respectability that marked Manet's duel with Morisot. In *Argenteuil* Manet at

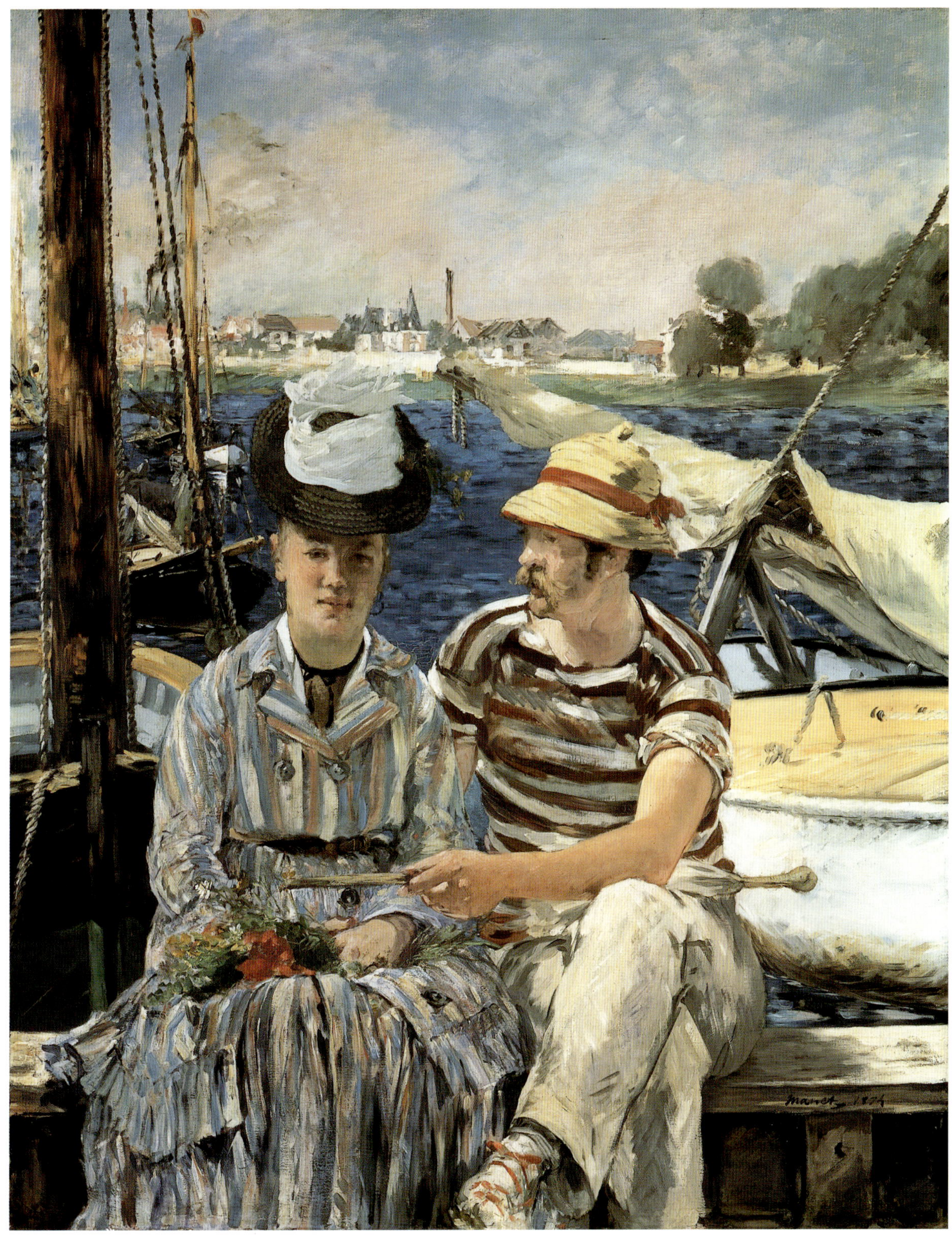

100   Edouard Manet, *Argenteuil*, 1874, oil on canvas, 149 × 115 cm. Musée des Beaux-Arts, Tournai.

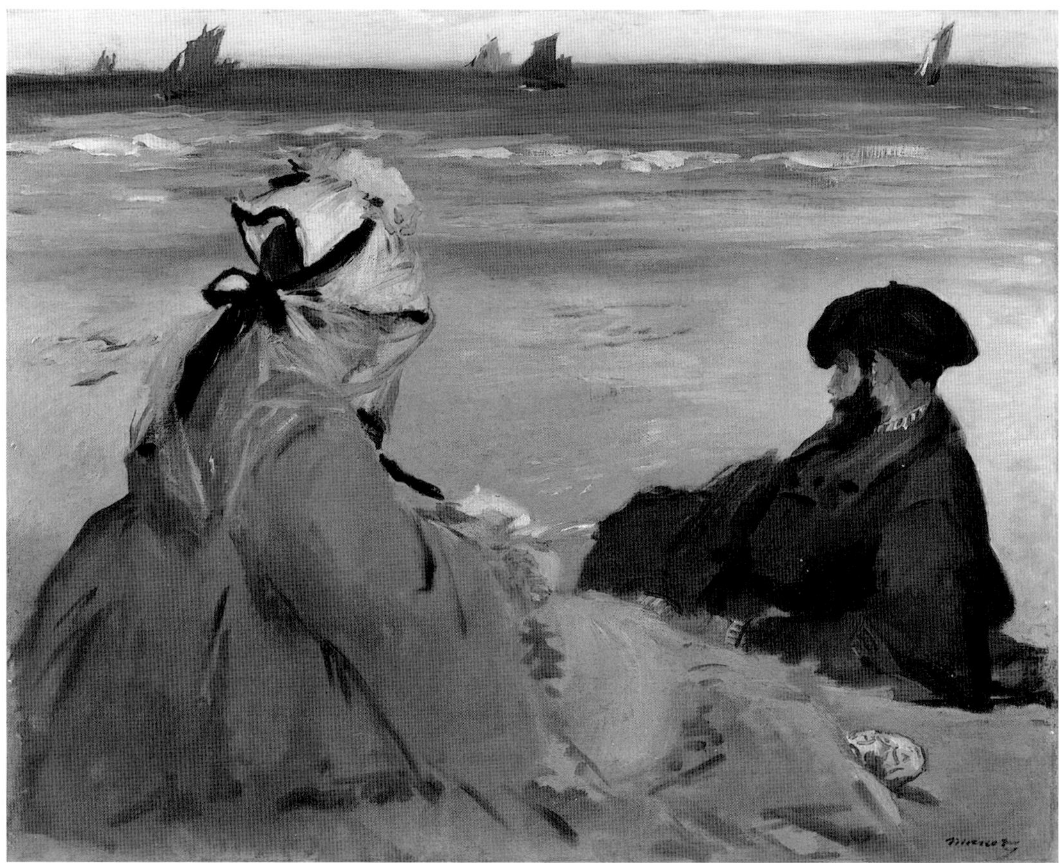

101   Edouard Manet, *On the Beach*, 1873, oil on canvas, 59.6 × 73.2 cm. Musée d'Orsay, Paris.

once makes the couple the structural mainstay of the painting and anecdotalizes the association between man and woman, attempting thereby both to fix and determine that relationship and describe it as fundamental to the Impressionist ethos. In the period between the Commune and 1874, when *Argenteuil* and its companion *Boating* were painted, Manet painted a variety of couple pictures, such as the *Interior at Arcachon* of 1871, featuring Suzanne and a grown-up Léon in exile from Paris, and *On the Beach* of 1873, with Suzanne and Manet's brother Eugène, soon to be Morisot's husband (fig. 101). (It is characteristic that, although they may sometimes look it, these couples are not actually husband and wife pairs.)

More than the sketchy little *Interior at Arcachon* with its indoors setting and quiet domesticity, *On the Beach* sports Morisot's outdoors style of painting; like *The Garden* before it, it also recycles the pictorial concept of the *Luncheon on the Grass*, using Eugène for the reclining male figure just as in 1863. But *On the Beach* dispenses with the unquiet of that earlier painting (produced by its combination of art-historical quotation, female nudity and male clothing, and outward stare) in favor of inwardly facing absorption, an indolent calm, and an easily explained relationship between clothed figures. It is punctuated at top by vertically inclined dashes of a murky color rendering sailboats in the manner of Manet's Boulogne paintings, and embellished at bottom by the splash of red representing the embroidery on the tip of a shoe.[24] In between, the veiled, topknotted, back-tied bonnet handled *à la* Morisot crowns the triangular mass of Suzanne, and evokes the sailboats just above it in its black strokes and diagonal movement.[25] In spite of their indistinct painting, the veiling of Suzanne's face, the ornamentation of her shoe, and the detailing of Eugène's neck and wrist with a striped shirt are all admirably suggested. For a change, the picture is unified both facturally and psychologically; it is as if Manet used the combination of Morisot's manner and the theme of the couple to settle his painting.

Around the time of the painting of *Argenteuil*, Manet also painted Monet in couple and *en famille*. In *The Monet Family in Their Garden at Argenteuil* (fig. 102), he painted Claude, Camille, and Jean Monet together in their garden. A happy family unit replete with a matching family of cock, hen, and chick, lounging about in front of flowerbeds that Monet seems to be tending, they appear more contentedly together than in Monet's contemporaneous pictures of his own family in the garden. Their relationship is fully anecdotalized – indeed, Manet seems to joke about pictorial anecdote in the family of poultry in the left foreground. Sartorial details are given with Manet's usual flair, including Monet's blue shirt, Jean's blue suit and straw hat, and Camille's red fan, picking up the red of the flowers behind and to the left of her, as well as her cap, with its topknot of ribbons and pink flowers blending with the flower garden to either side of her head, thus uniting fashion and Nature, her, her child, and their garden, with the *pater familias* appropriately occupied off to the side. All this happens in a manner of facture that is very much Morisot's, as in recent pictures shown in the 1874 Impressionist exhibition, such as her *Hide and Seek* (1873), also blending mother, child, and Nature. And, of course, it picks up a refrain begun with *The Garden* and continued in Morisot's *Reading* of 1873, with its half-open pink fan discarded in the grass.

It was not until Manet's Argenteuil paintings, however, that the family, or rather the couple, served to structure the very canvas that it inhabits. That was so in *Monet and His Wife in His Floating Studio* (fig. 103), also painted in 1874, with the self-reflexive theme of the painter painting that Manet shared with Monet and Renoir during this period. For Monet and Renoir it served to underwrite and authenticate their painting the same motif side by side and to stress their solidarity as a pair of Impressionist painters. But in Manet's case, while the depicted painter paints the river, the painter of the painting paints the other painter's wife. Camille is shown at Monet's side, his other half, yet at the same time divided from him, facing outward as the object of Manet's portrait gaze, and framed within the cabin of the boat like a picture within a picture, much as the mast on which Monet is shown leaning functions like a frame within a frame. Camille, that is, serves the function of at once joining a domestic to a painterly relationship, distinguishing Manet's painterly interest from Monet's, and announcing the self-reflexive structure of the painting. And if that was so in the floating studio picture, with its reiteration and exaggeration of Morisot's loose, light style, it was even more so in *Argenteuil*, which was painted rather more formally, for all its Impressionist-looking factural fireworks and its purported painting outdoors.[26]

In the second Impressionist exhibition of 1876, the year after the Salon in which Manet's *Argenteuil* appeared, Monet showed at least six paintings of Argenteuil, mostly painted between 1872 and 1874, with the earlier *Beach at Sainte-Adresse* and *La*

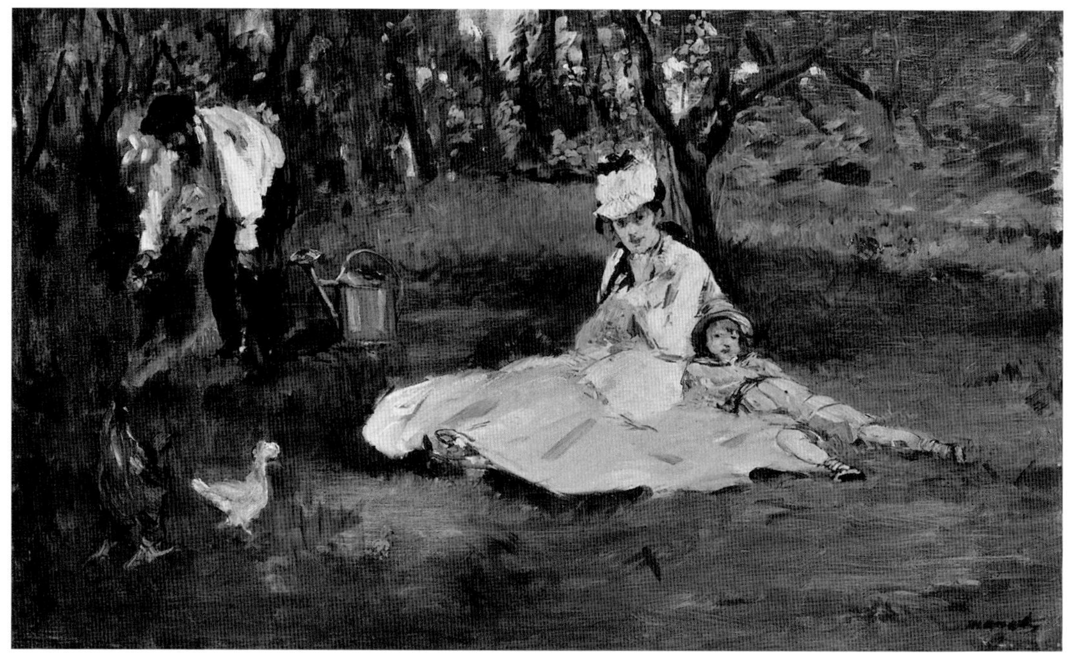

102   Edouard Manet, *The Monet Family in Their Garden at Argenteuil*, 1874, oil on canvas, 61 × 99.7 cm. The Metropolitan Museum of Art, New York, Bequest of Joan Whitney Payson, 1975. (1976.201.14).

103   Edouard Manet, *Monet and His Wife in His Floating Studio*, 1874, oil on canvas, 80 × 98 cm. Bayerische Staatsgemaldesammlungen, Munich.

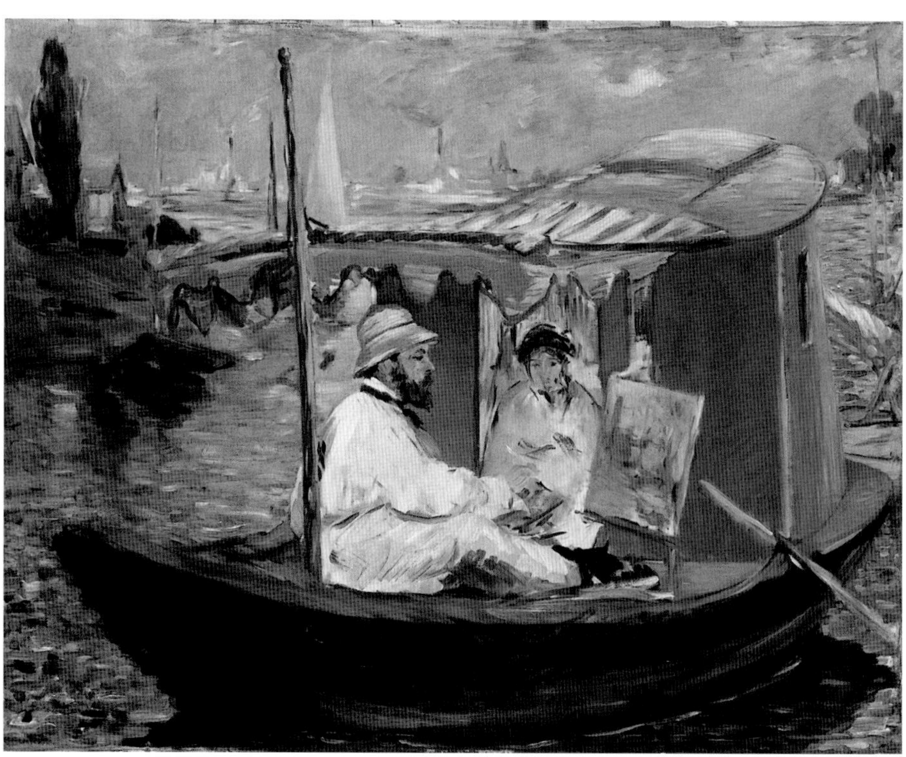

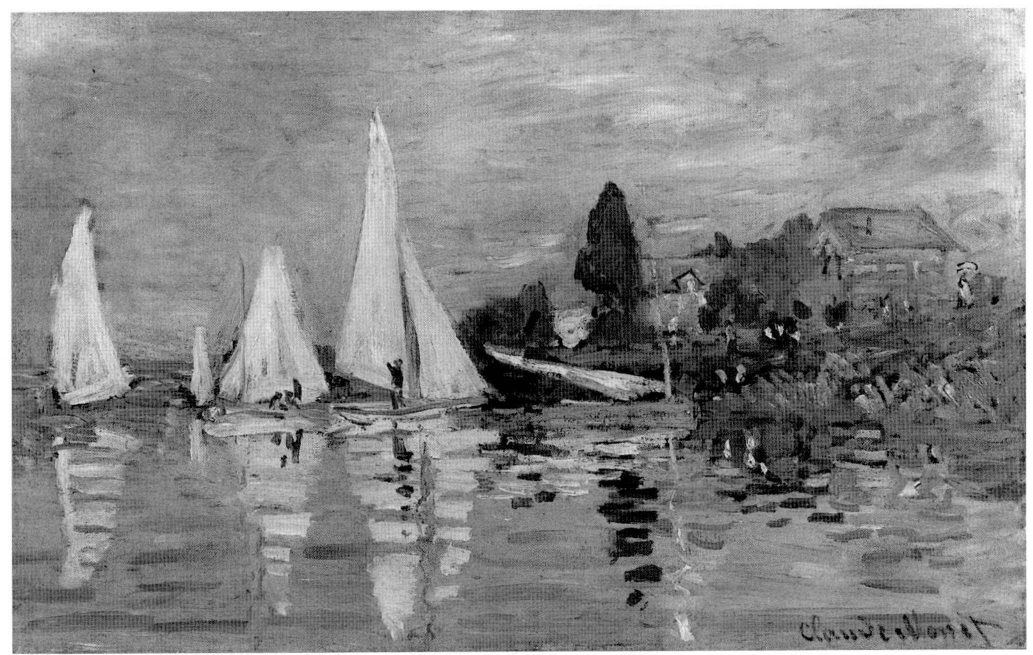

104   Claude Monet, *Regatta at Argenteuil*, 1872, oil on canvas, 48 × 75 cm. Musée d'Orsay, Paris.

105   Claude Monet, *The Bridge at Argenteuil*, 1874, oil on canvas, 60 × 79.7 cm. National Gallery of Art, Washington, D.C. Collection of Mr. And Mrs. Paul Mellon.

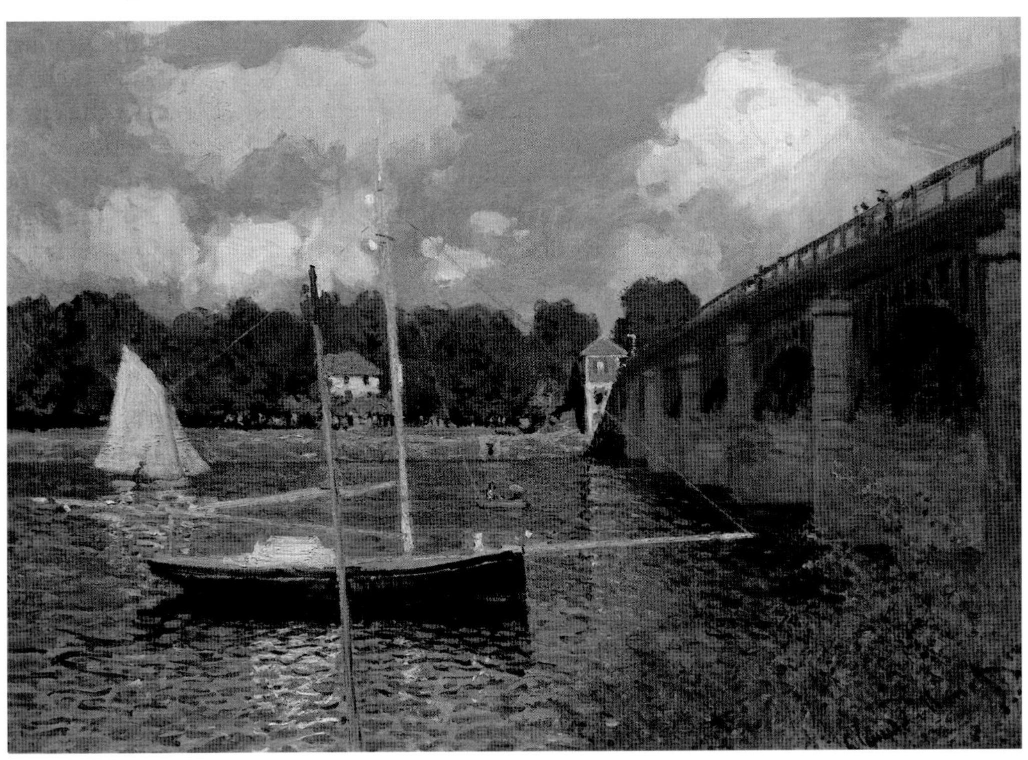

Grenouillère. One such painting might have been the *Regatta at Argenteuil* of 1872 (fig. 104); another almost certainly was one of the several paintings called *The Bridge at Argenteuil* that Monet did in 1874 (fig. 105). These do not quite form a sustained series as the Gare Saint-Lazare paintings did soon after (although Monet obviously waited until he had a sizable sampling of Argenteuil paintings in order to show them as a group), but together they contain all the ingredients of that *ne plus ultra* of Impressionist subject matter, sailboats in the suburbs, to which Manet responded in his painting of Argenteuil. The *Regatta at Argenteuil* constitutes one of Monet's most consolidated studies of the relationship between objects and their reflections: divided into two horizontal strips, the painting displays a row of sailboats above the horizon and below it a set of broken, upside-down stacks of orange, red, cream, and blue brushstrokes, such as to deconstruct on the bottom the constituent marks that make up the sailboats on the top, while also demonstrating, above and below the waterline, the range of marks of which a *plein air* illusion is made.[27] It is as if the *Regatta at Argenteuil* reproduces on its surface and in reverse that spectatorial action of moving back and forth in front of a painting to watch paint turn into illusion that Diderot had described more than a century before vis-à-vis Chardin's paintings, and that journalistic critics of the nineteenth century like Louis Leroy reiterated sarcastically in their reviews of the Impressionist exhibitions, when they feigned puzzlement at what brushstokes and palette scrapings were meant to represent.[28] *Regatta at Argenteuil* naturalizes that procedure, proposing that the facture out of which a painting is fabricated is the equivalent of Nature's own optical process of reflection — that the canvas is to the world what reflecting water is. The same may be said of the leisurely world of Impressionist painting: it comes as naturally and lightly as the wind moving cloud, sail, and sunlit river.[29]

Paintings like *The Bridge at Argenteuil* more seamlessly show off another, fuller range of facture. Cloud-strewn sky, distant rivershore, bridge and buildings, tiny staffage, foliage, smooth and choppy water, rowboat afloat and sailboats at anchor: each are handled somewhat differently, with the brushwork appropriate to the object or the effect, and again as if this diversity of handling is the natural result of Nature's optics, of the perceptual relay between eye and scene, reflecting retina and recording hand. (In other paintings from the Argenteuil series, contrasting kinds of movement — that of the wind, the sailboat, the pedestrian, and the locomotive — are added to the equation, such that the perceptual experience of temporality is included in Monet's simultaneous spectacularization of Nature and naturalization of painting as pure sensation.) At the same time, *The Bridge at Argenteuil* demonstrates the concern for structure that distinguishes Monet's paintings from Renoir's, for example: the masts of the moored sailboats also serve to moor the painting itself at left, while the bridge secures the right edge in a solid construction and then bridges the fore- and background of the picture, engineering its unity as a spatial composition. For Monet, evanescence had its own natural order and self-reflexive logic.

Manet no doubt took some of that from Monet in his *Argenteuil.* Indeed, his response to Monet's Argenteuil paintings is signed in the Monet sky that hovers over the high horizon in *Argenteuil.* As for the rest, Manet's *Argenteuil* exaggerates Monet's interest in pictorial structure, to the point that the boat in which "Manet and Manette" are seated is not only the painting's content but its frame as well (though Stop was right, qua boat it is a very uncertain vessel). Moving inside the craft that Monet depicts from the outside, Manet has its mast, seat, mooring, and rigging repeat the vertical and horizontal framework of the picture within and on the canvas surface, so that its armature spells out the painting's support: depicted wood, rope, and canvas fold back onto literal canvas and wood. And then the boat provides the scaffolding on which to build the rest of the painting's structure. The vertical and horizontal chassis of the boat and canvas is picked up everywhere; indeed, it is the structural foundation of the anecdotal meeting between the sexes that unfolds in the painting. For the vertical of the mast at left is repeated in the large vertical of "Manette"'s frontal figure as well as the smaller verticals of the striping of her holiday dress, while the horizontal of the wooden boatseat on which the two sit is echoed not only in the horizon above, but also in the arm, cane, T-shirt stripes, and hatband, as well as the profile orientation, of "Manet." The diagonal of his shoulder, upper arm, and leg, moreover, continues the diagonal of the rigging behind him, joining his espadrilled foot, reminiscent of Suzanne's protruding slipper in *On the Beach*, to his partner's skirt at the base of the composition. The line of his gaze as well as his cane, which intrudes upon the striped belly of his female companion (in this context it is not farfetched to consider it a phallic jest), is picked up in her belted waist and the bouquet of flowers resting in her lap (another below the belt quip?), marking her seated position – a gift, no doubt, from him. In short, the sexuality of their encounter (easily readable, although whether their relation is respectable is not) is supported by the self-reflexivity of the picture's support. The one turns into the other, and back again.

T. J. Clark has described the series of jokes that *Argenteuil* makes about its own illusionism, beginning with the bit of rope hanging from the diagonal of furled sail, which meets the shoreline and doubles as the upside-down reflection of a factory chimney. Aside from the reflection/rigging gag that intervenes between "Manet and Manette" is another set of pranks. Next to it is the equally jokey swish of wind-ruffled white tulle on the upturned hat, the top of which merges with and becomes all but indistinguishable from the white wall of the town above the shore, and mimics the grey whiff of wafting smoke to the left, curling between and behind the boat's rigging and then blending almost imperceptibly with the clouds of the painted sky. That flourish of white paint is matched below it by some white marks on the left notating a distant rowboat and its reflection, wittily collapsing near and far, and some quick strokes of pink on the right denoting artificial hat flowers and finishing off the mirage of a chimney reflection begun by the tongue-in-cheek tie of rope.[30] Together they point to the fact that the "blue wall" between "Manet and Manette" is thick blue pigment, not the reflecting blue of the river. The sum effect of all of this, as has been remarked, is to flatten the picture out. Monet's paintings also flatten out, and do so with their share of self-reflexivity – the *Regatta at Argenteuil* is an excellent example. The difference between Manet's and Monet's versions of Argenteuil, however, is spelled out in "Manette"'s hat: a painter's inside joke, it announces the illusionist's smoke and mirrors, and along with it, the utter artificiality of this utterly fake world: its not-naturalism, its *faux*-Impressionism, its self-definition as everywhere *parergon*, its identification with *parure*.

It is almost needless to say that the focus on posed people and their clothes is the most obvious difference between Manet's and Monet's Argenteuils. But some comments on the meaning of that difference are requisite, vis-à-vis that factured, flattening hat and its vicinity. We have seen a hat like that before, in *The Railway*, a hat tipped forward to join itself to the plane of the canvas. The black straw of this hat is painted much like the black straw of that: as slick-surfaced, detailed, and finished looking as everything around it is not – especially as the white sash of paint decorating it and the man's limp-brimmed straw skimmer next to it are not. It is thus a concentrated declaration not only of the equation between clothing and painting but also of the doubleness of Manet's facture. As one scans around it, one begins to see how everything else in the canvas is fabricated out of different kinds of paintwork, from the soft blurring of the *faux*-Monet sky and riverbank, the short horizontal strokes of blue rendering water as wall, the broad white and cream of the inside and outside of a boat at right, the differently directed and diversely broken marks equating shirt and dress stripes, the light handling and variegated colors of the bouquet in the lap, to the loose, Morisot-like gray and white hatching of the trousers and red dashes of the espadrille at the bottom of the painting.

At first, *Argenteuil* appears more facturally unified than others of Manet's Salon paintings – it has none of the obvious internal fissuring of *Luncheon on the Grass, The Railway*, or later, *The Bar at the Folies-Bergère*. On second glance, its factural diversity seems none other than that deployed by Monet in the rendering of Nature's different effects. Except that, on third consideration, it is absolutely other than that: in fact, it disputes the perceptual alibi and natural underwriting of Monet's Impressionist brushwork. Not the natural datum, but the *trompe l'oeil* of vestimentary handiwork: that is what the lady's hat emblematizes, lying between false reflections, seaming together the extreme ends of tight and loose facture, fixing the windblown, and joining the illusionism of distance to the plane of the painting. It also signals *Argenteuil*'s setting side by side a man and woman, together forming a structural unit, whose anecdotal relationship to one another is evidently posed, plotted, and carefully produced by the inward repetition of the picture's frame, and who are nothing but a pair of painted alternatives (emblematized in their two hats): front/profile, vertical/horizontal, formal/casual, artificial/natural, fashioned/spontaneous, feminine/masculine. And between those alternatives, the painting is at least somewhat more particular about that which falls under the sign of the feminine.

In their holiday apparel, "Manet and Manette" pose as a *plein air* Impressionist couple, in order to spell out the "vestimentary code" less of class and gender than of Impressionism per se.[31] That is to say, *Argenteuil* is a costume piece, a picture dressed up as Impressionism, addressing the Salon in order to announce its own masquerade. Two other pictures of couples addressed the Salon, this time as a pair, at the end of the '70s. One was *Boating* (fig. 106), painted in 1874 as a kind of alternative to *Argenteuil*. The other was *In the Conservatory* (fig. 107), painted closer to the time of its showing in the Salon of 1879, as an indoors response to *Argenteuil*, among other things. *Boating* keeps the couple (Rudolphe Leenhoff and unidentified companion once more) and a much looser version of *Argenteuil*'s equation of boat wood-and-canvas with picture wood-and-canvas, complete with a reversal of the diagonal of sail rigging at right. But at the same time it sets the boat asail in its watery wall of pigment, and reverses many of the oppositions of *Argenteuil*, declaring the dialogism of the formal binaries of which each is made: the woman is seen in profile and the man from the front, her hat is lumpen (a return to the veiled hat of *On the Beach*) while his is stiff-brimmed and more precisely

Detail of fig. 100.

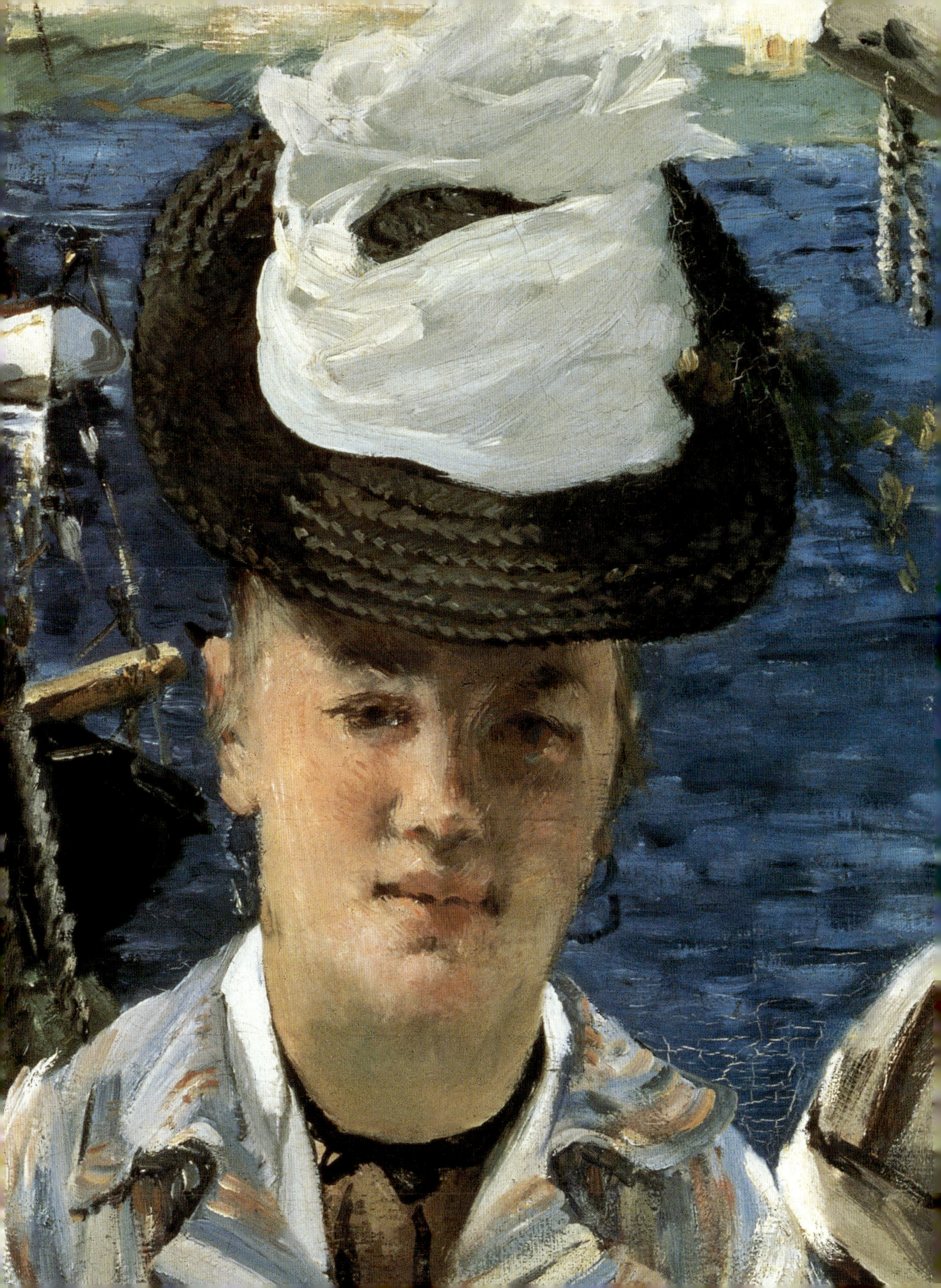

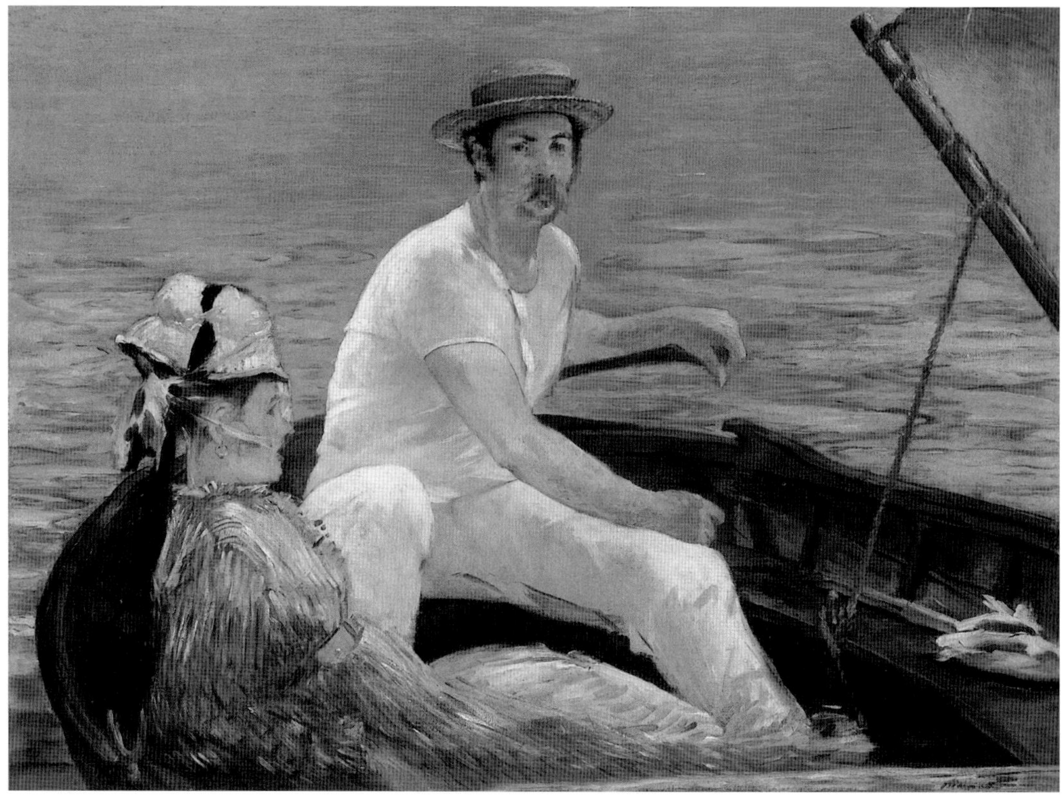

106   Edouard Manet, *Boating*, 1874, oil on canvas, 97.2 × 130.2 cm. The Metropolitan Museum of Art, New York, H. O. Havemeyer Collection, Bequest of Mrs. H. O. Havemeyer, 1929. (29.100.115).

painted, and in general she is softly indistinct and rounded (not to mention Morisot-like) in the feathered blue wateriness of her dress, while he is broader, flatter, and certainly more angular (that is to say, somewhat more Manet-like) in his masculine whites. And overall, *Boating* chooses what had been the masculine side of *Argenteuil* to emphasize as its keynote.

For its part *In the Conservatory* has been given a thorough treatment as an exemplar of the cloven subjective structure of modern visuality.[32] It may be that, but it is also part of a more specific painter's dialogue – mostly between Manet and himself. Harking all the way back to *The Balcony* of a decade earlier, it resuscitates that painting's potted plant(s), its green "house paint," formal wear, cheroot and parasol equipment, and the screened field common to it and *The Railway*. *In the Conservatory* represents a married couple, Jules Guillemet and his American wife, who as owners of a fashionable clothes boutique on the rue de Faubourg Saint-Honoré, were more tied up in fashion, in life as well as in art, than any of Manet's other well-dressed sitters so far.[33] This "Manet and Manette" (it was remarked that Jules Guillemet bore some resemblance to Manet himself) picks up many features of the earlier "Manet and Manette" too: the bench on which Mme Guillemet sits, the line of M. Guillemet's arm as his body leans attentively in toward hers, and the echoing line of the parasol in her lap, which replaces both the masculine cane and the feminine flowers of *Argenteuil*. And of course the hat – though this one is of a different design and does not tip forward or flatten out. It does, however, foam with yellow paint in much the way that the *Argenteuil* hat swirls with white. Matching the off and on yellow gloves and the yellow-frothed parasol, it points to the painting's insistent fashioning out of the height of fashion, and a facture quite different from the overall field of *Argenteuil* (not to mention *Boating*, *The Conservatory*'s casualwear counterpart at the Salon) but similar to that of *Argenteuil*'s flattened black straw hat: slickly finished, relatively speaking, and finicky in its attention to fashionable detail.

Around the same time, Manet used the same conservatory setting to produce several dress and hat pictures, including a loose rendition of a matronly, bare-headed Suzanne in a smooth chignon and a much ribboned bodice and an even looser pastel of a hatted and demi-caped Jeanne Demarsy in profile, trying out various degrees of looseness, informality, and fashion-print evocation against the hothouse background, that is, against an artificially natural background that in its loosest incarnation suggests floral wallpaper. But the Salon version of this set of images represents the other end of the factural and sartorial spectrum, its relative finish matching its formality of dress, not to mention the respectability of its married couple, whose closely paired wedding bands finally resolve the unfixed relationships of *The Balcony* and all the others. The taking off of a glove and the coupling of hands were old devices in Manet's art, but the placement of a carefully wrought detail at the center of the composition was a newly anecdotal solution. With that detail, the equally careful handling and arranging of the rest comes into focus: the matching of parasol, gloves, and hat, the exquisitely detailed tailoring of the tight, ribboned, corset-molded dress with its pleated train upfolded once more (as in *Repose*) so that it can be seen, neatly echoed in the decorative fringing of the palms and the regular beat of the bench bars, and tidily contrasted to the black frock coat and buff trousers next to it, and finally the dispersal of pink flowers, picking up the pink note of a single ear (*Olympia*'s overblown, ear-tucked hibiscus, delicately multiplied and discreetly moved aside?) and running it through the flat, claustrophobic wall of densely detailed greenery. With the suffocating density of the bourgeois hothouse providing a model for the *horror vacui* of quasi-*pompier* painting, all that detailing contributes to the subtly insistent propriety of this painted couple, and its revision of the *faux*-Impressionist couple of five years before.

The next year, in 1880, Manet got another couple picture accepted into the Salon, *Chez la Père Lathuille* (fig. 108). In it he returned to a loose style, *plein air* setting, and a relationship not so much indeterminate as openly illicit – what appears to be a pick-up scene at an open-air café – thereby suggesting the narrative instability and dialogic reversibility of the theme of the heterosexual couple, not to mention the importance of the parts played by facture, setting, and detail. That year his gesture to respectability came in the form of his accompanying slick-surfaced, blank-grounded, sartorially detailed, suited-up portrait of Antonin Proust, institutional *bourgeois gentilhomme*, to which I shall return. Meanwhile, Morisot replied to Manet's Argenteuil pictures with her own boating scene of 1879, *Summer's Day* (fig. 109). Setting her boat afloat closer to home in the Bois de Boulogne, she displayed two fashionable ladies together in innocent, bucolic companionship, once more correcting the connotations of leisurely

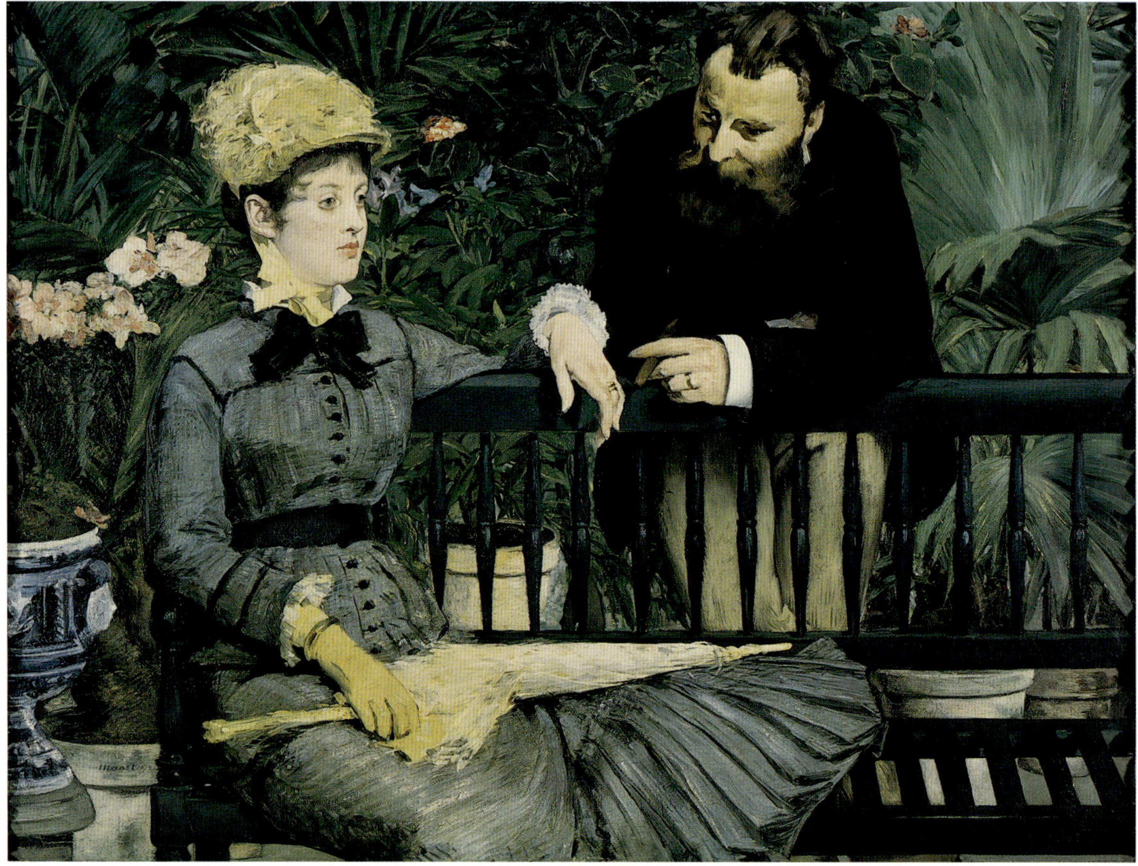

107   Edouard Manet, *In the Conservatory*, 1879, oil on canvas, 115 × 150 cm. Nationalgalerie, Berlin.

dalliance on a summer's day. But Morisot showed no particular interest in the internal relay between anecdote and pictorial structure – between the dialogism of painted relationships and the binarisms of painterly form – or in Manet's refutation of the naturalness of modern leisure. For Manet that was essential, and he could not let the matter drop.

A MALLARMÉAN POSTSCRIPT

It came with some "new painting" touches but *In the Conservatory* was fully a Salon painting. As such, Jules Castagnary approved it:

> Manet brings us back to the elegance of fashionable life and to the pastimes of the sporting world. Of his two pictures, *Boating* and the *Conservatory*, the latter is the better, and positively entrancing. On a garden bench, sheltered by palms and exotic plants, a young woman sits, a parasol in her hand. Leaning on his elbows on the

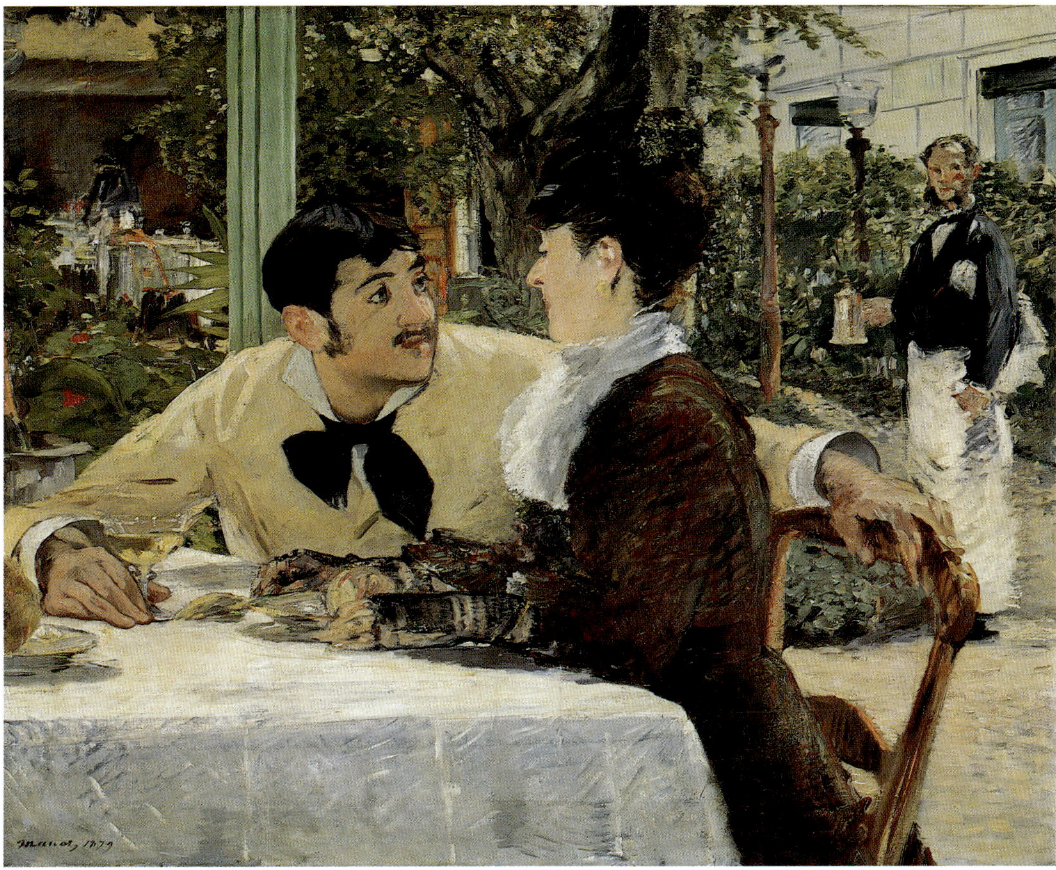

108   Edouard Manet, *Chez la Père Lathuille*, 1879, oil on canvas, 93 × 112 cm. Musée des Beaux-Arts, Tournai.

back of the bench and bending over her to speak to her is a middle-aged man who resembles the painter himself. Nothing could be simpler than the composition, nothing more natural than the attitudes. One thing, however, deserves even more praise: that is the freshness of the hues and the harmony of all the colors. But what is this! Faces and hands are more carefully drawn than usual: is Manet making concessions to the public?[34]

An anecdotal picture rendering "the elegance of fashionable life," in which the "middle-aged man" admiring the modish young woman stands in for Manet, this painting finally shows that Manet could depict faces as well as dresses, heads as well as hems, and thus, according to Castagnary, it suits the Salon public. Although he does not say so directly, the "carefully drawn," more or less finished facture of the painting makes all the difference.

Joris-Karl Huysmans, speaking in favor of modern painting, was obliged to judge the picture a little differently. After a comparison between modern painting and modern couture, in which he likened the productions of most Salon painters to those of the house

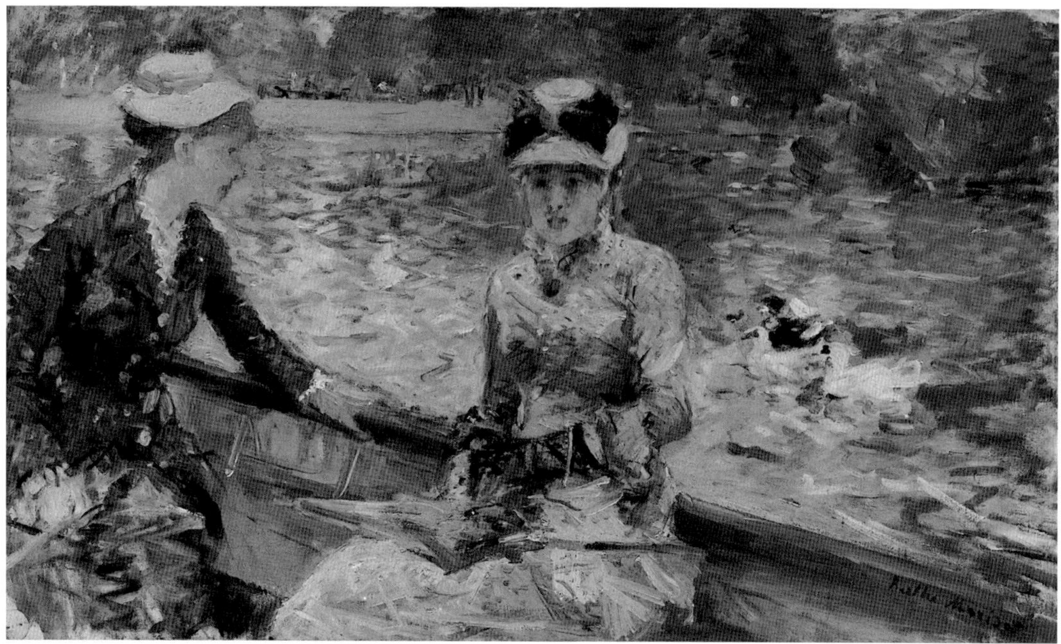

109   Berthe Morisot, *Summer's Day*, c.1879, oil on canvas, 45.7 × 75.2 cm. National Gallery, London.

of Worth, he too praised *In the Conservatory* as a modern conversation piece but saw its facture as broad:

> *In the Conservatory,* represents a woman seated on a green bench, listening to a gentleman who leans over the back of the bench; on all sides are tall plants, and on the left some red flowers. The woman, a bit awkward and thoughtful, is dressed in a gown which seems made with great strokes, rapidly . . . and superbly executed; the man, bareheaded, the light playing over his forehead, sparkling here and there, touching the hands boldly drawn in a few strokes, holds a cigar. Posed this way, in a casual conversation, the woman is truly beautiful; she is a lively flirt . . .[35]

This is signature Manet, as his contemporary supporters saw him: the father of Impressionism rendering the fall of light "*à grands coups*" so that its "touching" of forehead and hands underscores the anecdotes of masculine glance and almost-touching fingers at the center of the picture. Huysmans's remarks also point to the fact that, relative to other Salon paintings, Manet's facture was still noticeably vigorous; indeed, that it was always a twofold facture, and remains a facture that can be seen in divergent ways. For the density of detail of *In the Conservatory* is everywhere a density of painted matter as well: thick areas of gray, black, yellow, and white, equally thick pink and blue dabs, and above all a thicket of green pigment. Huysmans evidently felt nothing but contempt for the licked-surface couturier painting that was everywhere to be seen at the Salon; the difference of Manet the painter couturier was that his dress was "made with great strokes." His clotheshorse was made very evidently of paint.

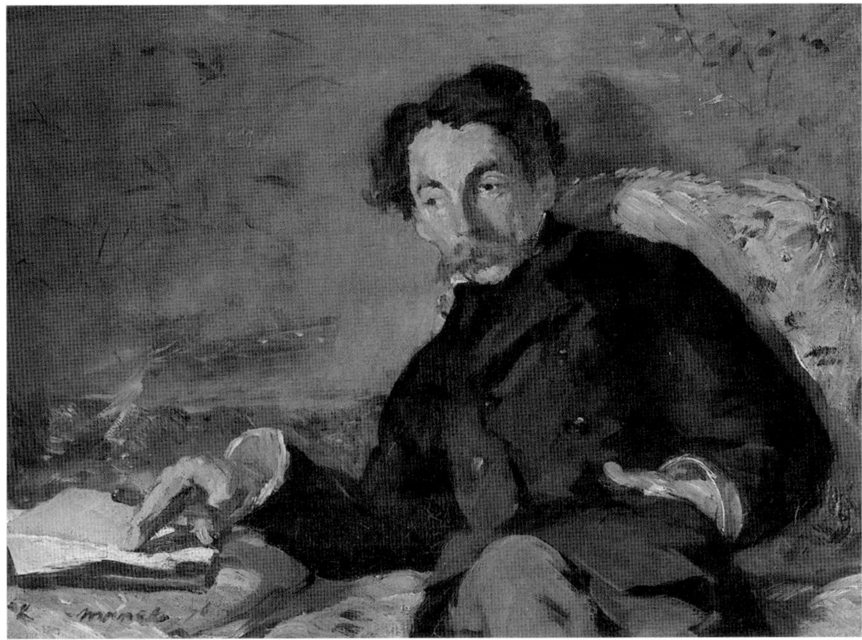

110   Edouard Manet, *Stéphane Mallarmé*, 1876, oil on canvas, 27.5 × 36 cm. Musée d'Orsay, Paris.

Neither Castagnary nor Huysmans were clear about the narrative tone of the painting, although for all their differences in point of view, their anecdotalized treatments of it share an aura of elegance combined with the staid and middle-aged, light flirtation safely domesticated by the indoors and the everyday. But in their different ways both Castagnary and Huysmans emphasized fashionability. And together their responses to Manet's painting suggest the way it doubled as Salon painting and Impressionism: for Huysmans it was Salon painting turned into Impressionism, for Castagnary something like the reverse. That is to say, they attempted to locate Manet on the spectrum running from Salon painting to not-Salon painting, Impressionism to not-Impressionism. Castagnary represented the older generation of ambivalently sympathetic critics, Huysmans the new generation of avant-garde champions, joining the likes of Mallarmé in his appraisal of Manet's place in the history of modern art.

Mallarmé, who had met Manet in 1873, had written "The Impressionists and Edouard Manet" for a London magazine in 1876, sealing Manet's reputation as the founder of Impressionism.[36] One of the two paintings by Manet that Mallarmé addressed specifically in that essay was *Repose*, which Manet had revisited, reversed, and revised in the pose of his portrait of Mallarmé of the same year (fig. 110). The writer is shown indoors, cheroot rather than fan in hand, in a manner that was again close to Morisot's, replete with a lightly handled floral background spelling an "elegance . . . become artless" (Mallarmé's words about Morisot).[37] The other painting that Mallarmé addressed was one of Manet's most Impressionist both in its look and its subject: *Washing*, a mother and daughter picture *à la* Morisot turned down by the jury of the 1876 Salon, thus permitting Mallarmé to develop his theme – by then the main theme of avant-garde criticism – of Manet's unfair treatment at the hands of the Salon jury.[38] The other principal theme of Mallarmé's essay was the factural equivalence to open-air effects common, he felt, to the painting of Manet and the Impressionists, making it the "representative art" of the period, "marking a general phase of art . . . particularly in France," because it "steeped" painting "again in its cause, and its relation to nature." He closed by stating that this was the province of painting: "that which I preserve through the power of Impressionism is not the material portion which already exists, superior to any mere representation of it, but the delight of having recreated nature touch by touch. I leave the massive and tangible solidity to its fitter exponent, sculpture. I content myself with reflecting on the clear and durable mirror of painting, that which perpetually lives yet dies every moment . . . [and] constitutes in my domain the only authentic and certain merit of nature – the Aspect."[39]

The advancing self-reflexivity special to modern painting, in short; this was later Greenberg's point about Manet and the Impressionists too, making Mallarmé's obscure little essay, which brought together Baudelaire's modern artist with Zola's positivist outlook ("our last great poet" and "the then coming novelist"),[40] one of the earliest sources of the classic view of late nineteenth-century modernism in France.[41] There is a difficulty, however, signaled in several places in "The Impressionists and Edouard Manet": Manet does not reduce to Impressionism any more than the "perverse . . . tendency" of Baudelaire is reconcilable with Zola's "insight into the future."[42] For Mallarmé's essay divides into two, the first half constituting a Baudelairean paean to Manet, whose remarkable singularity is stressed, the second half devoted to the *plein air* optics of the Impressionists, who "paint wondrously alike."[43] Mallarmé enumerates the different Impressionists and their specialties, but it is in the headlining section about Manet that the note of difference is sounded, within and between Manet's paintings: "One of his habitual aphorisms then is that no one should paint a landscape and a figure by the same process, with the same knowledge, or in the same fashion; nor what is more, even two landscapes or two figures. Each work should be a new creation of the mind. The hand, it is true, will conserve some of its acquired secrets of manipulation, but the eye should forget all else it has seen . . ."[44] Mallarmé thus predicts Greenberg here as well, the Greenberg of the 1967 Manet essay, who spoke to both the singularity of Manet and the internal differentiation of his oeuvre, and did not, in that one instance, subsume him within the advance toward Impressionism.

Significantly, Mallarmé used the figure of modern woman as the seam between the two sections of his essay, transforming Baudelaire's celebration of the feminine artifice of cosmetics into a hymn to the natural "complexion," lit by "bright gleam[s]," veiled by "diaphanous shadow[s]": "painting, which concerns itself more about this flesh-pollen than any other human attraction."[45] Shifting Mallarmé's terms a little, we might say that the figure of the modern *parisienne*, with her elaborately confected gowns and hats and her many, differently factured "flesh pollen[s]," represents the false complexion of Impressionism. Produced for the Salon, posed and paired with "Manet" indoors and outdoors, "Manette" stands in the breach between Manet and Impressionism. With and without her male companion, she continued to do so in the few remaining years of Manet's career.

Chapter Nine

FACTURING FEMININITY, FASHIONING THE COMMODITY: BETWEEN *NANA* AND *LA VIE MODERNE*

EVEN AFTER A NUMBER OF SALON REFUSALS in the second half of the 1870s, Manet still declined to participate in the Impressionist exhibitions. Instead, he looked to other arrangements, among them throwing his own studio open to the public, showing a rejected painting in the window of a *bibelot* shop, returning to the idea of an *exposition particulière* that would give an overview of his career, and exhibiting a range of recent works that he had not bothered to submit to the Salon in the gallery of a publisher devoted to "modern life." In 1876, when both *Laundry* and *The Artist* were rejected, Manet made his studio into a one-man Salon des Refusés, showing those and other works there during the last two weeks in April. In May 1877, after *Faure in the Costume of Hamlet*[1] had been accepted and *Nana* rejected, Manet decided to show the latter in the window of Giroux's boutique on the Boulevard des Capucines, which as well as pictures also exhibited fans and diverse accessories, decoratives items, and other commodities – "bimbeloteries, tableaux, éventails" – for sale. Like Courbet in 1867, in 1878, at the time of the Universal Exposition, he planned another, more ambitious retrospective of one hundred paintings, pastels, and prints, double the amount of works of his first retrospective. It was to be headlined "Il faut être mille ou seul," declaring Manet's resolution either to be officially accepted or remain apart, keeping the exhibition of his individuality separate from the group presentation of his Impressionist friends. The 1878 retrospective never happened, but that did not keep Manet from stepping up his ambitions; the next year he proposed a decorative program for the Municipal Council's *salle de séances* in the new Hotel de Ville, on the model of Delacroix but with new modern subject matter: a ceiling pantheon of modern Parisian greats and an encyclopedic wall program illustrating Manet's version of Zola's *Le Ventre de Paris*, to consist of depictions of Les Halles, the railroad, port, underground sewer system, racetracks, and public gardens. That did not happen either but it does testify to a number of things: Manet's aspirations to be the painter of modernity that critics like Duranty, Zola, and Huysmans continued to call for; his unflagging desire to be an officially sanctioned public painter; and his stubborn failure to understand his audience.

Manet's unrealized project for the Hotel de Ville also reveals a discrepancy within his own self-conception as a painter of modernity that is important to understand in relation to the works he actually did execute and exhibit during these years: while he clearly fancied himself as a large-scale, Zola-esque summarizer of the representative scenes and spaces of modern Parisian life, most of them muscular and masculine, what he in fact undertook was a much less grand series thematizing the frivolities of fashion and the commodification of femininity. That series, which began with the anecdotal *Nana* and culminated with the antinarrative *Bar at the Folies-Bergère*, needs to be seen against the backdrop of his fantasized role as a Zola in paint. For the disparity between the fantasy and actuality of Manet's modernism structured the exhibition strategies of the last few years of his life.

In April 1880, instead of the Hotel de Ville project, Manet put together a small show of recent works including two *nanas* at their toilettes, several café scenes focusing increasingly on women, and a variety of pastels (one of which was a portrait of Zola's wife) at the gallery of the illustrated journal *La Vie Moderne*, owned by Zola's publisher Georges Charpentier.[2] Meanwhile, the next few years found him showing odd, miscellaneous pairs at the Salon: in 1880, he exhibited a very official portrait of his illustrious friend Antonin Proust with the outdoors café scene *Chez le Père Lathuille*; in 1881, the year he received his Legion of Honor, he exhibited a peculiar masculine pair, a portrait of Henri de Rochefort with the curious, patently posed *Pertuiset the Lion Hunter*; and then in 1882, he paired the *Bar at the Folies-Bergère* with *Jeanne*, the springtime member of the seasons quartet of fashionplate images done at Proust's behest.[3] The Salon of 1882 was his last and the *Bar at the Folies-Bergère* was a last stand, returning to themes that had preoccupied Manet since the beginning of his career, placing them in a modern-life context, working out a thematics of the mirror that tied it to both *Nana* and one of the paintings at La Vie Moderne, and building into it a carefully plotted, self-reflexive relationship between the surface of painting, the fashionably dressed figure of woman, and the sumptuary regime of the commodity. At the same time, the *Bar* was the product of the same discordance between a public and private, a masculine and feminine, an essential and a supplemental modernism that structured *Nana* and the others.

SHOPWINDOW NANA

Nana (fig. 111) returns us to the *cocotterie* of *Olympia*. In her association with a male patron – the seated figure of the top-hatted, cane-bearing gentleman cropped at the right, who adopts and revises the pose of the male figure in *Argenteuil* – she is involved in an internal relationship that mirrors her exchange of glances with the external spectator, thus drawing a connection between the consumption of bodies and paintings, the sexual and aesthetic gaze. Except that the actress Henriette Hauser, who posed for *Nana*, has none of the refractory quality of Victorine Meurent, her *grande cocotte* none of the insolence of *Olympia*. She offers what *Olympia* withheld; indeed, her plump flirtatiousness and froufrou delicacy would have done a Boucher proud, and translated very easily into the salaciously exaggerated daintiness of the visual language of illustrated journals such as *La Vie parisienne*, where she was caricatured.[4] And the parallel between internal and external acts of consumption that she proposes reverses that of *Olympia*: instead of replacing the internal narrative relationship between prostitute and client with the external relationship between picture and spectator, thereby confronting the viewer with his complicity in the sexual scenario of the painting and forcing on him an awareness of the anything but sublimated character of his pictorial contemplation, Nana turns around and uses that contemplation to further the descriptive and narrative illusions of the picture she inhabits.

The painting's commodification is declared in order to promote the delectation of the commodities represented within the space of Nana's boudoir. Displayed in a vitrine, she is a self-advertising object for sale who is at the same time, like a bathing beauty on the hood of a car, an advertisement for a whole array of other objects for sale, for her sexual come-on is also a solicitation to shop, inciting the shopper's desire by throwing a dose of titillation into the account.[5] Although Manet painted her for the Salon,[6] he must have recognized her shopwindow suitability, not to mention the advertising advantage of his own notoriety, which must have resonated loud and clear in *Nana*'s evocation of *Olympia*. Whether the critics responded or not, people would come and stare, and even – or especially – if they were scandalized, they might enter the boutique and buy Giroux's wares. And, in the circular logic of advertisement, there would be benefit in this for Manet as well.[7]

A whole world of *bibeloterie* is offered in *Nana*. This was carefully devised by Manet, who set up a complex *mise-en-scène* of furnishings and objects in his studio in order to paint *Nana*, making his atelier into both boutique and boudoir. That *mise-en-scène* includes a plush wine velvet sofa whose neo-Louis XVI curves mimic those of Nana herself seat for seat and leg for leg, while also horizontalizing her verticality, evoking the sinuosity of a reclining body, and drawing a serpentine line between her backside and the glance of her male companion; two plumped, greenish white tapestry pillows on either side of Nana, together emphasizing her roundedness front and back; an elaborate mirror mounted with candles probably bought especially for the occasion and later given to Eva Gonzalès's sister by Manet's wife; a gilt-edged piece of Second Empire *ébénisterie* in the form of an inlaid, ormolu side-table bearing a turquoise, gilt-edged potted plant; and a *japoniste* piece of tapestry whose decorative stork, *la grue*, famously signifying prostitute in the slang parlance of the day, picks up the curves of Nana's crooked arm, sway back, and thrust out stomach. Nana rounds out the *boutiquiste* inventory of knick-knacks with her hair circlet, earring, ring, gilt bangle, powder puff, and rouge stick, not to mention her ruffle-strapped, ice-blue corset, sheer-hemmed bloomers, clocked, powder-blue stockings, embroidery-toed, high-heeled slippers, and the piece of blue-and-white ruffled garment flung over a spindly legged chair to the left, completing the ensemble of blue and white harmonies that links Nana to tapestry and chachke-laden surroundings. At the same time, it implies the temporal finish to the picture's account of Nana's toilette. Thus an inventory of *Nana*'s painted contents supports a narrative reading of her; and in this way the painting of her painting herself for the pleasure of a male observer encourages consumption.

According to Huysmans, the first to publish in the spate of stories about prostitutes that flowed from the pens of naturalist writers between 1876 and 1881,[8] *Nana* was an expert rendering of luxury undergarments, including not only her corset and pantaloons but also her London-made silk stockings, which he testified were authentic. "The aristocracy of vice," he intoned, "is recognized by its underwear," silk being "the trademark of courtesans who rent out at a high price." In his article for the Brussels weekly *L'Artiste*, Huysmans undertook an elaborate description of the underwear of Nana the quintessential *fille*, and claimed that "Nana has thus arrived, in the painter's tableau, at the summit envied by others of her trade, and, savvy and corrupt as she is, she has understood that the elegance of stockings and slippers is surely one of the most precious instruments that expensive whores have devised for overthrowing men."[9] It was also Huysmans who told his readers that the subject of the painting was "the Nana of *L'Assommoir*, powdering her face with rice powder, while a gentleman watches: Manet was absolutely right to present us, in his Nana, with one of the most perfect samples of that type of prostitute that his friend and our dear master, Emile Zola, is about to depict for us in one of his next novels. Manet has made her appear such as she will be forced to be, with her complicated, knowing vice, her extravagance, and her debauchee's luxury."[10]

Thus Huysmans, a specialist himself in such matters, made it clear that in *Nana* the excess of depicted commodities was physiognomically significant, and that the inventory of those commodities was integral to the telling of her story, such that here description and narration are one. He tied the painting specifically to Zola's writing as well – to the Nana who already existed in *L'Assommoir*, but also the Nana of the eponymous novel serialized in *Le Voltaire* beginning in 1879 and published by Charpentier in February of 1880, two months before Manet's show at La Vie Moderne opened.[11] Ever since *Nana* was displayed in Giroux's window there has been argument about her relationship to Zola's story of the same name. But Huysmans was unambiguous: in his view, as a member of Zola's *cénacle*, it was very definitely a picture of Zola's "heroine." Indeed, it was an index of Manet's insider status in relation to Zola's enterprise; giving advance notice of what Zola had in mind next, the painting was a literary *annonce* as much as a boutique commercial. However, since the Nana of the painting bears little resemblance to the Nana of *L'Assommoir*, and the earliest notes Zola appears to have made on the subject of his new novel date from the summer of 1878, the current of influence must have run both ways: Zola's Nana must have been suggested at least in part by Manet's.

The painted Nana of 1877 was positioned between one novelistic Nana and the other, according to Huysmans: the trace of the gin-mill daughter of *L'Assommoir* and the harbinger of the gilded courtesan of *Nana*, she represented the making of one into the other. And she was an *avertissement* of the finale of a story that was an allegorical summation of modern urban culture as Zola saw it. This was how Zola described his projected heroine in 1878:

> Blonde, pink, Parisian face, very wide-awake, her nose slightly turned up, her mouth small and laughing, a dimple on her chin, her eyes blue and very bright, with golden lashes. A few freckles which come back every summer, but very few, five or six on each temple like flecks of gold. The nape of her neck an amber colour, with a tangle of little hairs. Smells of woman, very much a woman. Light down on the cheeks.
>
> Must tell the story of her previous life. See *L'Assommoir* for all the first period: played as a child in the Goutte-d'Or district, served her apprenticeship as a flower-girl at Titreville's in the Rue du Caire, ran away to live with an old man . . . left her old man to run around; ups and downs; returned to her parents' home several times, ran away again, finally didn't reappear. That's where I left her . . .

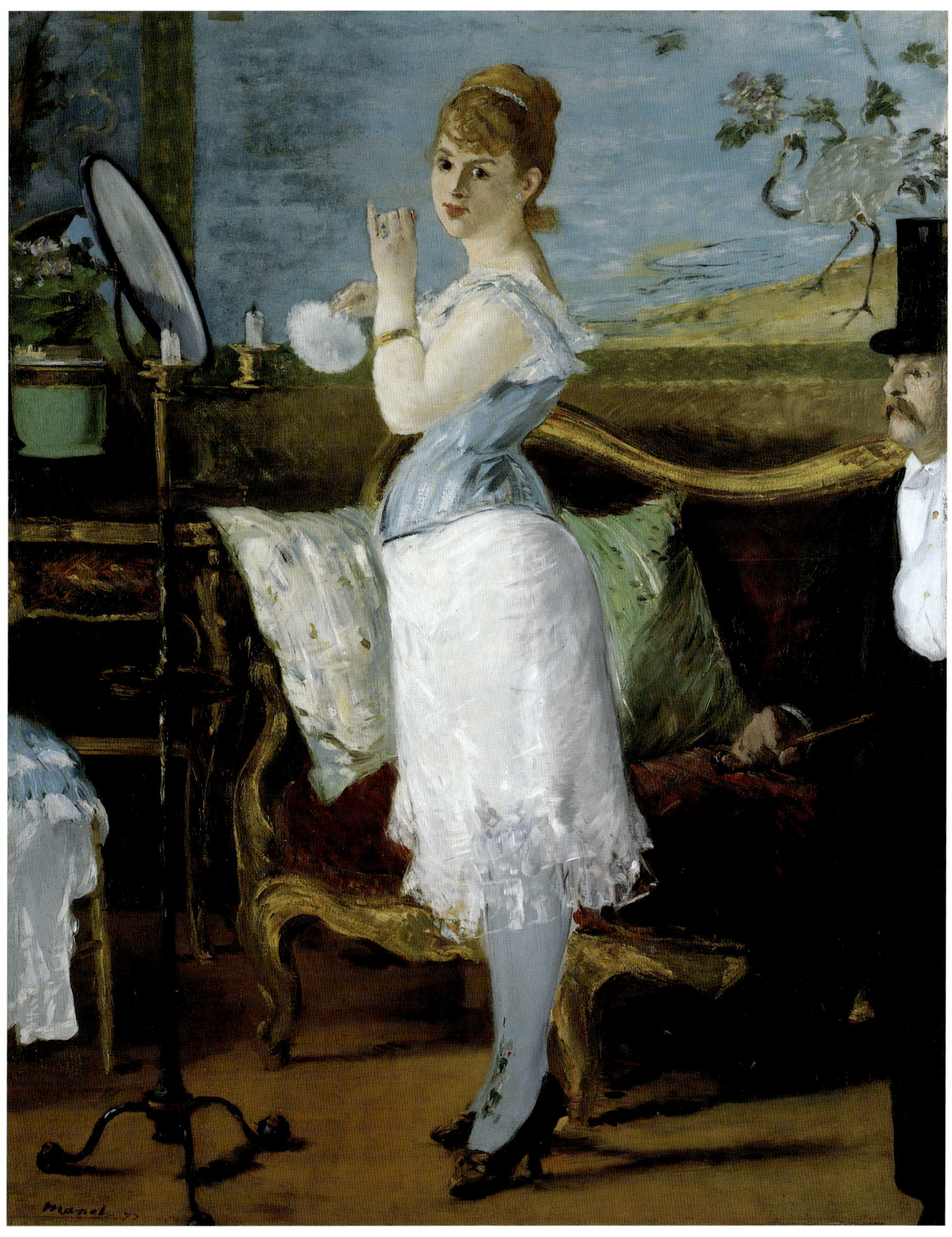

111 Edouard Manet, *Nana*, 1877, oil on canvas, 154 × 115 cm. Kunsthalle, Hamburg.

. . . At first very slovenly, vulgar; then plays the lady and watches herself closely. – With that, ends up regarding man as a material to exploit, becoming a force of Nature, a ferment of destruction, but without meaning to, simply by means of her sex and her strong female odour, destroying everything she approaches, and turning society sour just as women having a period turn milk sour. The cunt in all its power, the cunt on an altar, with all the men offering sacrifices to it. The book has to be the poem of the cunt, and the moral will lie in the cunt turning everything sour. As early as Chapter One I show the whole audience captivated and worshipping; study the women and the men in front of that supreme apparition of the cunt. – On top of all that, Nana eats up gold, swallows up every sort of wealth; the most extravagant tastes, the most frightful waste. She instinctively makes a rush for pleasures and possessions. Everything she devours; she eats up what people are earning around her in industry, on the stock exchange, in high positions, in everything that pays. And she leaves nothing but ashes. In short a real whore. – Don't make her witty, which would be a mistake; she is nothing but flesh, but flesh in all its beauty. And, I repeat, a good-natured girl.

Ups and downs. In the end she has to die at the height of her youth, at the height of her triumph.

The question of heredity in Nana. An extreme case of the Rougon-Macquarts. The product of Gervaise and an alcoholic, Coupeau.[12]

These notes connect the two novels between which Manet's *Nana* was sandwiched, making it clear that Zola's *Nana* was part of the larger Rougon-Macquarts project. But their description of Nana's physical appearance is also a description of Henriette Hauser as she appears in Manet's painting, from the alert, pink and blond face with its milk-maid features down to the amber "tangle of little hairs" at her nape. Only her freckles are missing from the painting – those "flecks of gold," which surely are the physical expression both of Nana's hunger for gold and her function as a golden idol, are part of Zola's apparatus of allegorical description. Zola underlines what Nana stands for: with her milk-curdling menstrual odor, she represents the raw power of sex – what Zola calls the cunt – combined and equated with pure greed and wastefulness; she is the sexpot of gold at the end of capitalism's rainbow.[13] As much as his Nana loves artificial things and turns herself into a "lady who watches herself closely," she also represents Nature in society, Nature run amuck – the natural force of capital with its inbuilt tendency to excess, which makes the prostitute its perfect representative.[14] In this she is pure Zola, and very little Manet, who was no spinner of Naturalist allegories. But though Manet may not have painted his *Nana* to represent the principle of money or excess spending per se, it may very well have been all the knick-knacks painted into his painting that suggested to Zola the idea of Nana's innate "rush for pleasures and possessions."

The scene in Zola's novel that seems to depend most directly on Manet's *Nana* is the boudoir chronicle of Nana's toilette, her process of putting on her stage makeup while three of her admirers, the Prince, the Marquis de Chouard, and the haplesss Count Muffat, look on.[15] I shall return to that scene shortly; at present I want to address some of Zola's descriptions of Nana's furniture and clothing later on in the novel, once she has "arrived." The first of these to concern me is a lengthy account of Nana's upstairs chambers, which are contrasted to the "somewhat too sumptuous Louis Seize" public rooms downstairs, only visited by Nana, somewhat reluctantly, upon "gala occasions." To those stately surrounds Nana prefers her own private domain, whose eclectic, overstuffed luxury has strong overtones of the bordello:

Nana . . . lived on the first floor, in three rooms, her bedroom, her dressing-room, and a small drawing-room. Twice already she had redecorated the bedroom, the first time in mauve satin, the second in blue silk under lace; but she was not satisfied, considering the lace appliqué insipid and still looking in vain for something better. On the lavishly upholstered bed, which was as low as a sofa, there were twenty thousand francs' worth of Venetian point lace. The furniture was lacquered blue and white with silver filigree patterns; and everywhere there were scattered so many white bearskins that they completely covered the carpet – a luxurious caprice on Nana's part, for she had never been able to break herself of the habit of sitting on the floor to take off her stockings. Next door to the bedroom the little drawing-room was full of an amazing medley of exquisitely artistic objects. Against the pink silk hangings – a faded Turkish pink, embroidered with gold thread – were outlined a host of knick-knacks from every possible country and of every possible style: Italian cabinets, Spanish and Portuguese coffers, models of Chinese pagodas, a Japanese screen of delicate workmanship, together with china, bronzes, embroidered silks and needlepoint hangings, while armchairs as wide as beds, and sofas as deep as alcoves, suggested voluptuous idleness and the somnolent life of a seraglio. The keynote of the room was again old gold, blended with green and red, and nothing it contained indicated the courtesan too obviously, apart from the luxuriousness of the seats. Only two porcelain statuettes, a woman in her chemise hunting for fleas, and another stark naked, walking on her hands with her legs in the air, sufficed to sully the room with a note of basic stupidity.

Through a door which was nearly always open the dressing-room was visible, all in marble and glass, with a white bath, silver jugs and basins, and crystal and ivory appointments. A drawn curtain admitted a pale white light which seemed to slumber in a warm scent of violets, that disturbing perfume peculiar to Nana which filled the whole house from the attic to the courtyard.[16]

Later, Zola repeated his conceit of armchairs as wide as beds and sofas as deep as alcoves, compulsively underlining the erotic possibilities of those pieces of furniture by adding that "they invited the visitor to slumbers . . . and to gay, affectionate, whispered conversations in shadowy corners." He described the drawing-room again, "where a couple of lamps shed a soft glow over the pink hangings and the lacquer and old gold of the knick-knacks . . . played discretely over coffers, bronzes and china, lighting up silver and ivory inlaid work, picking out the shining contours of a carved stick, and covering a panel with the shimmering gleams of watered silk," and remarked that the "room was full of Nana's intimate life: a pair of her gloves, a fallen handkerchief, an open book lay scattered about, evoking an impression of their owner en déshabille, in the midst of her scent of violets and that happy-go-lucky untidiness which created such a charming effect in these surroundings."[17] Nana's violet perfume is mentioned again – Zola was not one to shy away from reiteration – and the point is driven home: her apartments reek of her half-undressed body, her "intimate life," her living off her sexuality.

Description is so fully physiognomic that its logic of expression, as usual with Zola, becomes a mode of allegory. More than that, it participates in the consumerly excess that it inventories in such obsessive detail.

Of this catalogue of Nana's furnishings, what did Zola get from Manet's painting? Very little that is specifically derived from the decor depicted in the painter's *Nana*, except perhaps for the Japanese screen, the low sofa, and the general blue-and-white scheme (of the bedroom, not the boudoir). But the general effect of *déshabillé*, an object-crowded space, and the irresistible invitation offered by things might well have been prompted by the painting, just as the listing of a "pair of her gloves, a fallen handkerchief, an open book" could have been suggested by the painting's association with just such *bibelots* in the window of Giroux's boutique.[18] Likewise, the wealth of description, which both produces and is supported by the wealth of objects described (the more objects one invents to describe, the more description is yielded), and the use of that description to advance the narrative may have been encouraged by the painting's simultaneous pleasure in its own material devices and the diversity of objects created by those devices, as well as its use of that pleasure to assist narrative illusion and urge consumption of real objects in the real world of Giroux's shop.[19] In short, whether Manet's *Nana* suggested it or not, description as excess consumption is shared by painting and novel.[20]

In the foregoing passages, Zola dwells upon the color schemes of Nana's apartments, addressing her indecision about the palette of her rooms as integral to her pattern of surplus consumption, but also pointing to her artistry and aesthetic sensibility. A color scheme is also at issue in Zola's description of one of Nana's outfits, the confection she put together for the Grand Prix race at Longchamp in the Bois de Boulogne:

> She was wearing the blue and white colours of the Vandeuvres stable in a remarkable outfit. This consisted of a little blue silk bodice and tunic, which fitted closely to her body and bulged out enormously over the small of her back, outlining her thighs in a very bold fashion for this period of ballooning skirts. Then there was a white satin dress with white satin sleeves, and a white satin sash worn crosswise, the whole decorated with silver point-lace which shone in the sun. In addition to this, in order to be still more like a jockey, she had jauntily stuck a blue toque with a white feather on her chignon, from which her golden locks flowed down to the middle of her back like a huge russet horse's tail.[21]

The elaborate toilette of blue, silver, and white matches the temporarily settled upon "keynote" of Nana's bedroom. Just as the wine-colored settee and blue tapestry in Manet's painting may have suggested to Zola the rejected mauve silk and current blue of Nana's room, so the blue and white underwear and piece of dress featured in the painting may have proposed the colors of the riding costume described in this passage. Those colors are an important feature of Nana's very evident fashion consciousness, linked by color to her concern with interior design, and in Zola's hands a crucial index of her function as an allegorical figure of capitalist excess and consumption as waste. Since along with sex, fashion and interior design are also Nana's principal means of upward social mobility, the coloristic sensibility that informs both is, in addition, a signifier of her self-construction.

Feminine self-construction is an important theme of Manet's painting. Indeed, self-construction is self-reflexively allied with pictorial composition, through the carefully worked out matches and mismatches of its painterly palette. From head to toe, Nana is coordinated by color with her surroundings, her gold bangle picking up the gilt edge of the sofa, her blue corset the blue of the tapestry behind her, her stocking, and the piece of dress flung over the chair at left, the green border and floral decoration of that tapestry the green of the plant, pillow, and ankle embroidery. Meanwhile, the wine of the sofa stands out from the blues, just as Nana's pink and russet head is set off against the blue background. The fluffy white powder puff triangulates white mirror and candles, white pillow and drawers, white ruffles and underdress. And between the back of the opaquely painted mirror and the potted plant, whose turquoise color mediates between the room's greens and blues, an odd piece of non-referential blue attaches the fictive back plane to the literal front face of the canvas, sliding one surface into the other. Thus, Nana's act of making herself up is situated in the midst of the picture's color harmonies, her self-painting with powder and rouge allied with its coloristically organized self-reflexivity as a painting.

The following is Zola's version of the same cosmetic scene, from earlier in the novel:

> After rubbing cold cream over her arms and face, she laid on the grease-paint with the corner of a towel. For a moment she stopped looking at her reflection in the glass, and glanced smilingly at the Prince, but without putting down the grease-paint.
>
> . . .
>
> This time Nana did not turn around. She had picked up the hare's-foot, and was lightly dabbing at her face, giving all her attention to this operation. She was bending forward over the dressing-table so far that the white curves of her drawers stood out below the edge of her chemise. . . .
>
> . . . she laughed amiably, and turned around for a moment with her left cheek very white, in the midst of a cloud of powder. Then she suddenly turned serious, for it was time for her to put on her rouge. With her face once again close to the mirror, she dipped her fingers in a jar and began applying the rouge below her eyes, gently spreading it back towards her temples. The gentlemen maintained a respectful silence.
>
> The Comte Muffat indeed had not yet opened his lips. His thoughts had returned willy-nilly to his younger days. His bedroom as a child . . . And now, all of a sudden, he was thrown into this actress's dressing-room, into the presence of this naked courtesan. He, who had never seen the Comtesse Muffat putting on her garters, was witnessing the intimate details of a woman's toilet, in a chaotic disarray of jars, in the midst of that powerful perfume which he found so sweet . . .
>
> . . .
>
> She had dipped her paint-brush in a pot of kohl; then, putting her nose close to the glass, and closing her left eye, she passed it delicately between her eye-lashes. Muffat stood behind her, watching. He saw her reflection in the mirror, with her round shoulders and her breasts half hidden in a rosy shadow. . . . When she shut her right eye and passed the brush along it, he realized that he belonged to her.
>
> . . .

Her face and arms were finished now, and with her finger she put two broad strokes of carmine on her lips. The Comte Muffat felt more disturbed than ever. He was fascinated by the perverse attraction of Nana's powders and paints, and filled with a frantic longing for the young woman's painted charms, the unnaturally red mouth in the unnaturally white face, and the exaggerated eyes, ringed with black . . . Meanwhile Nana went behind the curtain for a moment to take off her drawers and slip on Venus's tights. Then, with calm immodesty, she came out and unbuttoned her little cambric bodice, holding out her arms to Madame Jules, who pulled the short sleeves of the tunic over them.[22]

Zola's account of Nana's getting dressed and putting on her makeup provides much that is missing from the outward-gazing painting, including much more of Nana's body, more detail about her cosmetics, and her mirror image. But overall it reproduces the painting's emphasis upon feminine self-construction. And in its suggestion that Nana's erotic appeal lay as much in her art of making herself up as in her corporeal charms, it follows Manet's address to Nana's artifice. Except that for Zola, that artifice spells falsity, and the attraction to it leads to the downfall not only of Nana's lover, the Comte Muffat, but also the whole culture that he represents, both its old class order and its involvement in the new regime of the stock exchange. Whether he condemned the Nana of his creation or not, Zola clearly did condemn the economic system she allegorized.

As much as Manet may have wanted to undertake an encylopedic project *à la* Zola, he did not partake of Zola's cultural criticism.[23] His *Nana*, with its unctuous reversal of the sexual politics of *Olympia*, is nothing if not a celebration of the scenario of cosmeticized and commodified femininity that it depicts, and the opportunities for self-reflexivity in painting that it offers. Despite the anecdotalism of *Nana*, Manet was not a literary painter, and despite the connection between *Nana* the book and *Nana* the painting, this episode ultimately demonstrates the divergence in media between novelist and painter – the difference between the allegorical direction of naturalist literature and the material self-reflexivity of painting. That difference was underlined in the episode that followed, the exhibition at La Vie Moderne, in which Manet showed an antinarrative, fully self-referential alternative to the descriptive and anecdotal surplus of *Nana*.

MODERN LIFE AT LA VIE MODERNE

When Manet exhibited twenty-five new paintings and pastels at La Vie Moderne in April of 1880, he associated himself with Zola's publisher Charpentier, the owner of the gallery and illustrated newspaper of the same name.[24] Manet had already had some objects in group shows at La Vie Moderne: significantly, they were *bibelots*, a painted tambourine and a decorated ostrich egg.[25] Now it offered another exhibition option for Manet, one that fell between those of the Salon, the Impressionist shows, and boutique vitrines like Giroux's, which had fewer aesthetic affectations and more direct ties to commodity culture than other zones of art display: La Vie Moderne bridged those spaces.

The devotion of La Vie Moderne to "modern life" was spelled out in its name. It was also given in the pages of the "journal hebdomadaire illustré litteraire et artistique" that had begun a year earlier, on April 10, 1879, both in the list of names that decorated its articles and *feuilletons* – Emile Zola, Armand Silvestre, Théodore de Banville, Alphonse Daudet, Ludovic Halévy, Emile Bergerat, Edmond Duranty, the Goncourts, Antoine Vollon, Gustave Flaubert, among others – and in the form of the illustrations that graced them each week. In his description of the journal's "program" in its first issue, Bergerat made it clear that *La Vie Moderne* was both an art journal and a newspaper devoted to "actualités," and that its novelty lay in its images as well as its text, which the reader was meant to take in together: "A journal that by this double mode of information, text and drawings, allows one to participate in all the events of modern life, initiates the reader in all the progress of art, interests him in all the phases of his evolution, gives him in his armchair the spectacle of all the discoveries of science, as well as that of the fluctuation of habits and customs, and which leaves out only the discordant world of politics from its universal exploration."[26] Dedicated to the rejuvenation of France and the celebration of family life – in case "some philosopher of the Folies-Bergère tells us again that the family is dead" – the task of *La Vie Moderne*, said Bergerat, was to bring men and women together by addressing both of their interests. To that end, "Perhaps it is also time to show that not all elegant women are necessarily adventuresses, not all great ladies trollops, and that the love of the interior is not the exclusive attribute of the poor classes."[27] Finally, again in the interests of bringing the bourgeois sexes together, Bergerat announced the journal's devotion to the "industrial" arts:

> I know there are people who would like it to be possible to show a dress, a carpet, a piece of furniture at the Salon, and for the jury to award medals to such items. Therefore, we will act on that given, and we will faithfully follow the movement of industrial art on the trajectory of progress that the Universal Exposition seems to have launched.
>
> *La Vie Moderne* would give the lie to its name, I think, if it neglected to converse regularly with its readers on the subject of the extension of that characteristic passion for trinckets and bric-a-brac that is one of the signs of our times . . .[28]

True to its word, *La Vie Moderne* proceeded to cover displays of feminine "industrial art" along with Salons and other painting exhibitions. In the early months of the journal, the Vicomte Georges de Létorière offered several "Voyage[s] autour des Parisiennes." (For instance, on July 3, 1879, in the thirteenth issue of *La Vie Moderne*, he addressed "what one says at the dressmaker's.") The next year, Ernest d'Hervilly covered a fashion show while Manet's exhibition was up,[29] and later "d'Orsay" offered a number of "Gazette[s] du Chic," counseling women on what was appropriate to wear when, and guiding them to fashion, fabric, and fan "exposition[s]."[30] On October 2, 1880, in the fortieth number of the journal, d'Orsay advised his readers as follows:

> It is the season of intimate soirées and family dances, preludes to the great winter balls. One is at home with one's family and ballgowns are strictly forbidden; at the very most, the half-gown is tolerated. For these occasions, Ladies, I counsel an apparel of charming taste, of perfect grace, which partakes at once of the summer that is departing and of the winter that threatens. It is a dress of Indian muslin, supple, strong, and light at the same time, picked out with knots of white satin ribbon. It is with this material, moreover, that the prettiest bridal dresses are currently made. – White indian

muslin goes marvelously well with lace and serves to bring out its transparency and lightness; a few knots of satin, throwing their lively sparkles here and there against the matte tone of this toilette, completes it admirably.

For your winter purchases, Ladies, I note at the *Comptoir des Indes*, maison Bizé, 45, ave. de l'Opéra, a series of new fabrics that are all that one can imagine of the most charming: *Cloth of Tibet*, for example, woven in five different shades, whose ensemble produces a material of a curious and seductive fantasy, strong, supple, and warm; *Pastou*, with silk Grecian panes on a wool background, whose bright embroidery, picked out against the matte tone of the wool, has an incomparable brilliance; gold-spangled fabrics of great richness, covered with gold or silver Chinese designs in silk, with which one can fashion corsages, dress, and ballgown garnishings, as one chooses; new and innumerable variations of *Indian Cashmere* brought together, and a fabric of a new kind, called *Hungarian Plush*, which resembles otter enough to be mistaken for it and which one could use as fur for corsages, coats, or mantles and as dress decoration . . .[31]

Addressing himself to female members of *La Vie Moderne*'s audience, d'Orsay set his fashion advice in the context of quiet bourgeois family life, fulfilling the journal's mission of making such modern sentiments as fashion consciousness respectable, disassociating it from its taint of Nana-style license and licentiousness and removing it from the odor of the "Folies-Bergère," as Bergerat had recommended. (No doubt the influential Mme Charpentier, whom Renoir painted in a dress by Worth together with her young son and daughter at home in her *bibelot*-furnished "Japanese salon" (fig. 112), thus showing her to be both good mother and fashionable *grande dame*, was behind this charge, and in general behind the journal's attention to what were supposed to be female needs and interests in the way of material culture.) At the same time, d'Orsay addressed his "ladies" as fashioners of their own garments and styles, rather than as clients of fashion houses like that of Worth. His readers were not necessarily the seamstresses of their own dresses – no doubt they had their dressmakers put them together out of fabric they purchased – but they were being asked to choose the conjunction of fabrics and garnishings that would go into the making of their gowns. And it is worth noting that, while attention is paid to pattern, color, decorative detail, and the "seductive" opticality of gold, silver, and other forms of glitter and sheen, d'Orsay's description appeals equally to a tactile imagination – to the fingering as well as eyeing of cloth, the meeting of different textures, the playing off one another of the heavy and light, the solid and gossamer, and the material illusioning of insubstantiality by substantial means. "Mesdames" were expected to concern themselves with fantasizing the facture of their fashionable wear.

Several issues later, d'Orsay counseled the ladies to visit an "exposition" at the Printemps department store, and study it in detail:

This year, as in the past, there is a stock of marvels at the *Printemps* department store, and on Monday next, November 8, there will be an exhibition of dresses and coats for women and children that will surpass everything that is the most attractive of its kind that one has seen, and will bring together the most varied and charming samples that fashion has ever dreamed up.

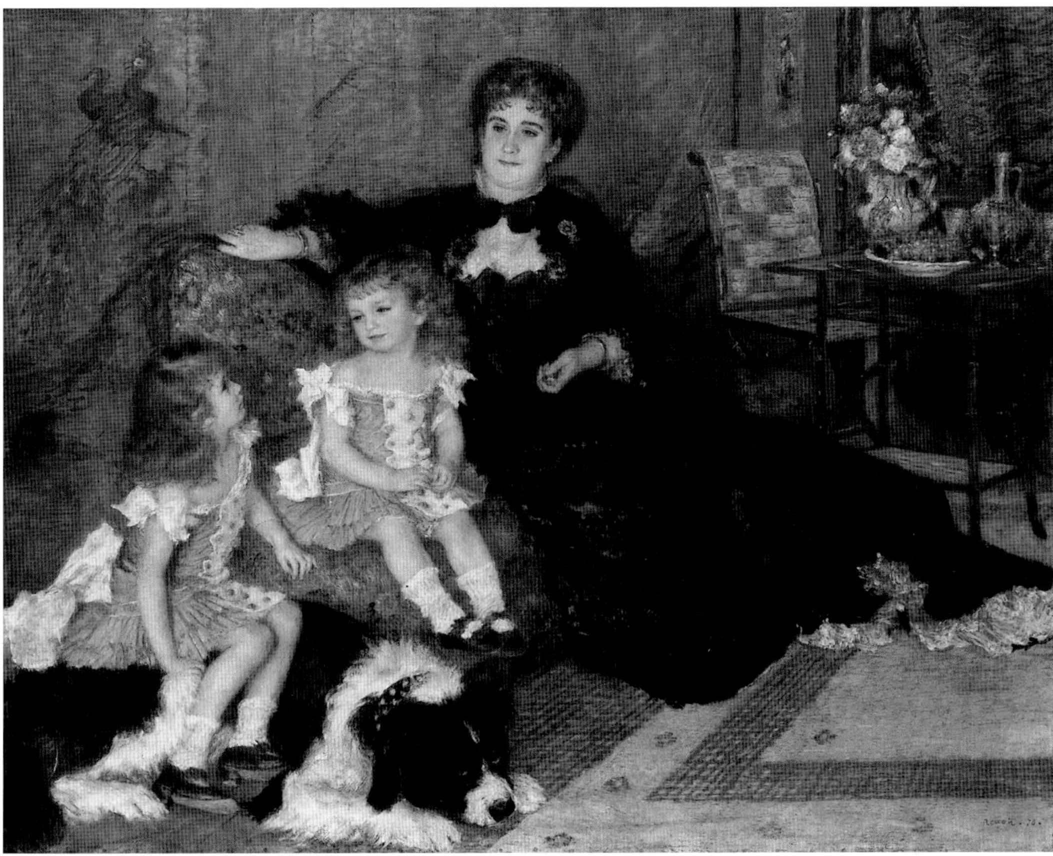

112   Pierre-Auguste Renoir, *Madame Georges Charpentier and Her Children, Georgette-Berthe and Paul-Émile-Charles*, 1878, oil on canvas, 153.7 × 190.2 cm. The Metropolitan Museum of Art, New York, Catharine Lorillard Wolfe Collection, Wolf Fund, 1907. (07.122).

One is well aware that, for the elegance of its designs, the richness, variety, and strength of its fabrics, the *Printemps* has long been almost without rival. Yesterday I saw on its shelves fabrics of silk and velvet whose high quality and low price seemed incommensurable. Our charming readers will be satisfied customers, finding there all the most seductive things that their imagination could conjure, yet at a price that will certainly please the most parsimonious and the most prudent . . .[32]

Again, "Mesdames" are treated both as fashion consumers and guardians of their households, defying the pattern of excess spending described in *Nana* as well as the current perception that fashion-preoccupied wives were the ruination of their husbands' hard-earned fortunes and with them of French family life.[33] And again, they are assumed to be the imaginative designers of their own costumes, going to fashion displays in order to study them closely toward the production of their own dresses and coats out of fabrics they would purchase at the same department store. Finally, windows with mannequins and display shelves with bolts of material are treated as "expositions" fully as much as

Salons and other smaller art exhibitions, effectively realizing Bergerat's suggestion "to show a dress, a carpet, a piece of furniture" in the same manner, with as much high dignity, as a painting or a piece of sculpture – but in this case to an explicitly female audience. Displays at the Comptoir des Indes and the Printemps could be thought of as the distaff-side counterparts to exhibitions at the Louvre, the Ecole des Beaux-Arts, the Rue des Pyramides (the Impressionist exhibition of 1880), the Boulevard des Italiens (*La Vie Moderne*), and elsewhere.

To accompany such fashion advertisements and admonitions, *La Vie Moderne* displayed a wide variety of its own special kind of "industrial art": mechanical reproductions of fashion illustrations and other visual material, including paintings at the Salon and in its own and other gallery spaces. Those images included conjunctions such as the detailed full-length "Etude de Femme" by Stewart (fig. 113) and the sketchy, three-quarter-length "Parisienne" by Kaemmerer that accompanied the July 3, 1879 "Voyage autour des Parisiennes" (fig. 114); half-page illustrations of Parisian hats and coiffures (fig. 117); full-page reproductions of paintings, such as the lithographic reproduction of Fantin-Latour's 1867 portrait of Manet (fig. 115) that accompanied Gustave Goetschy's

113   Stewart, "Etude de Femme," *La Vie Moderne*, July 3, 1879, no. 13.

114   Kaemmerer, "Parisienne," *La Vie Moderne*, July 3, 1879, no. 13.

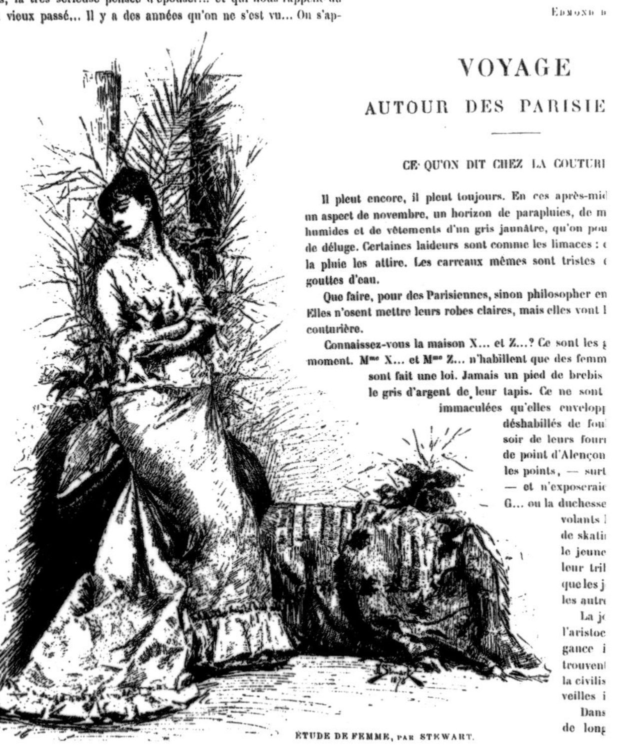

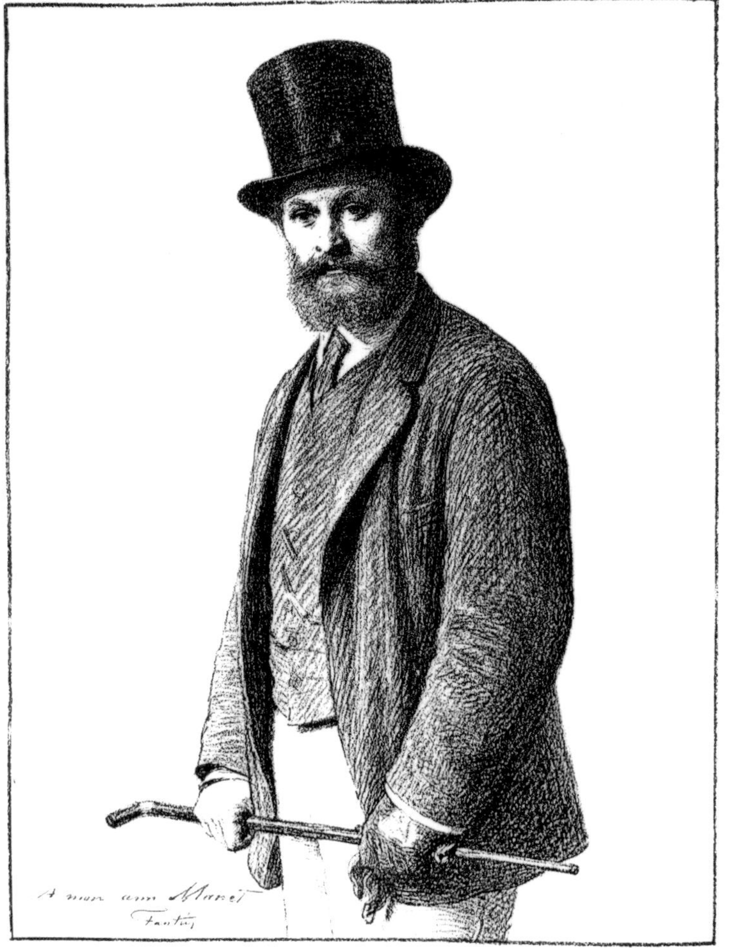

EDOUARD MANET, par FANTIN-LATOUR.

115 Lithograph of Fantin-Latour's "Portrait of Manet," *La Vie Moderne*, April 17, 1880, no. 17.

116 a and b (*below*) "Croquis par Edouard Manet," *La Vie Moderne*, April 17, 1880, no. 17.

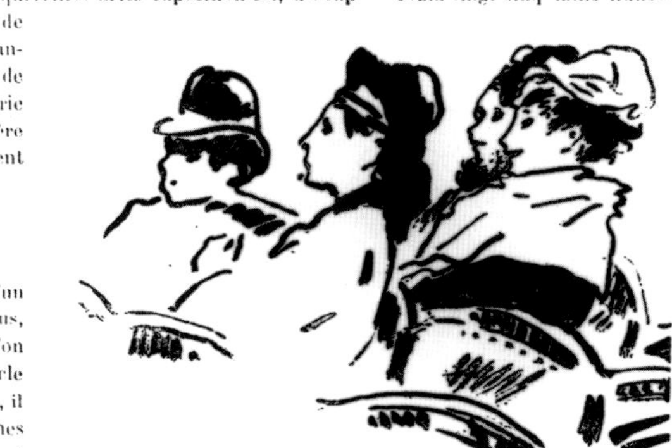

118 (*right*)   Jeanniot, *Vernissage, La Vie Moderne*, May 1, 1880, no. 18.

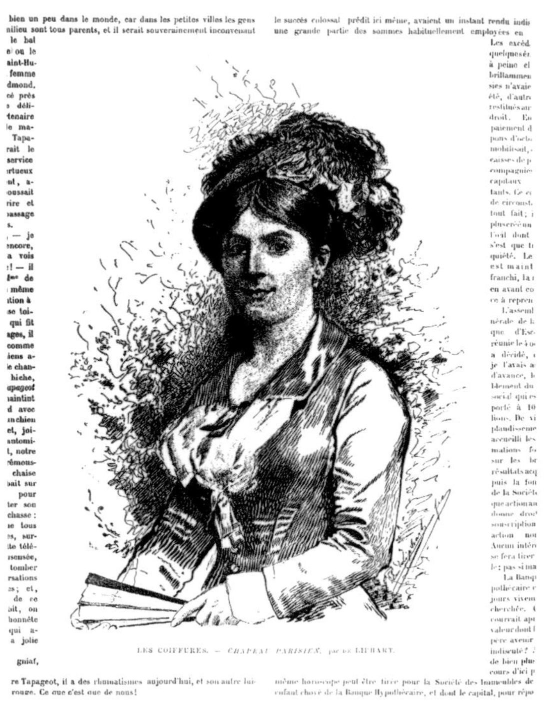

117   Liphart, "Les Coiffures: Chapeau Parisienne," *La Vie Moderne*, October 11, 1879, no. 27.

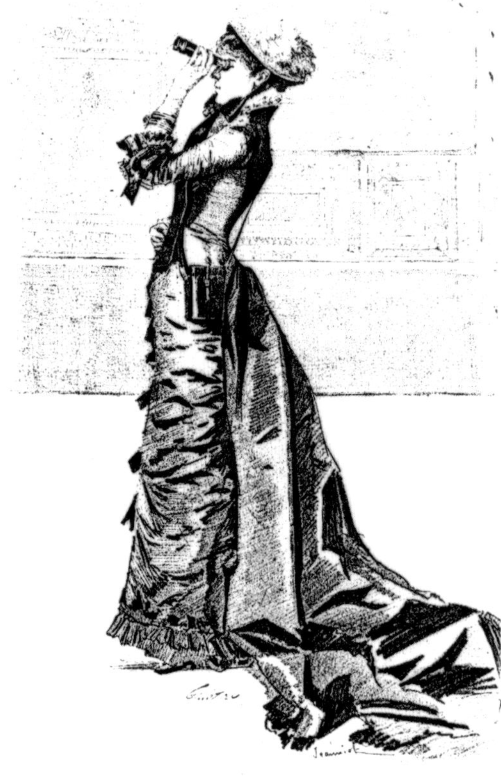

report on his show at La Vie Moderne; as well as reproductions of Manet's own pen-and-ink sketches of spectators (fig. 116);[34] a "Vernissage" by Jeanniot accompanying a May 1, 1880 article, showing a fashionably dressed woman at the Salon (thus combining fashion display with art exhibition; fig. 118); on May 8, a final-page reproduction of one of the café-concerts that Manet showed at La Vie Moderne (fig. 119); and on June 12, a full-page "Toilette d'Eté" by Worth rendered by Jeanniot (fig. 120).

This sampling of *La Vie Moderne*'s range of mechanical reproductions gives an idea of its attachment to both art and fashion, as well as its variety of styles and graphic codes, some tight and finicky, with the high density of detail characteristic of steel engraving (though they are mostly lithographs), others open and loosely handled, with the lithographic reproduction of drawn mark-making superseding detail.[35] Because of that variety of codes, *La Vie Moderne* embraced a graphic spectrum whose two poles were represented

120 (*right*)   Jeanniot, "Toilette d'Eté: Juin 1880," *La Vie Moderne*, June 12, 1880, no. 24, p. 381.

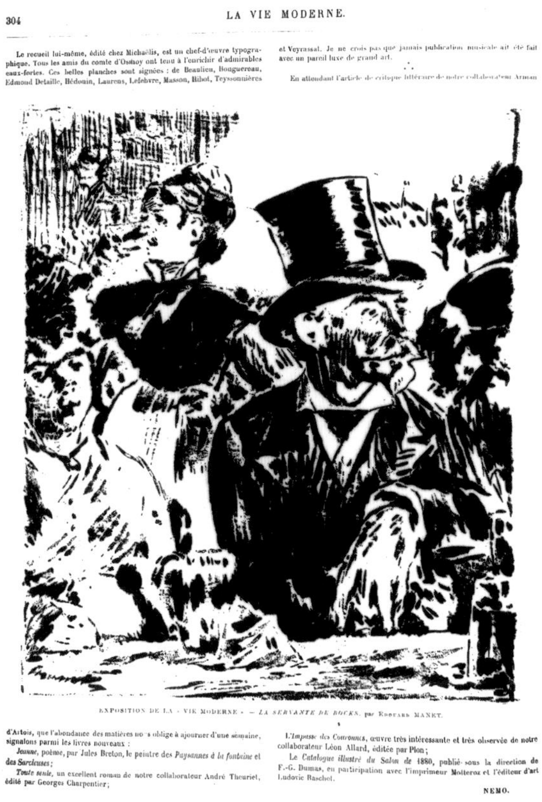

119 (*above*)   After Manet, "La Servante de Bocks," *La Vie Moderne*, May 8, 1880, no. 19.

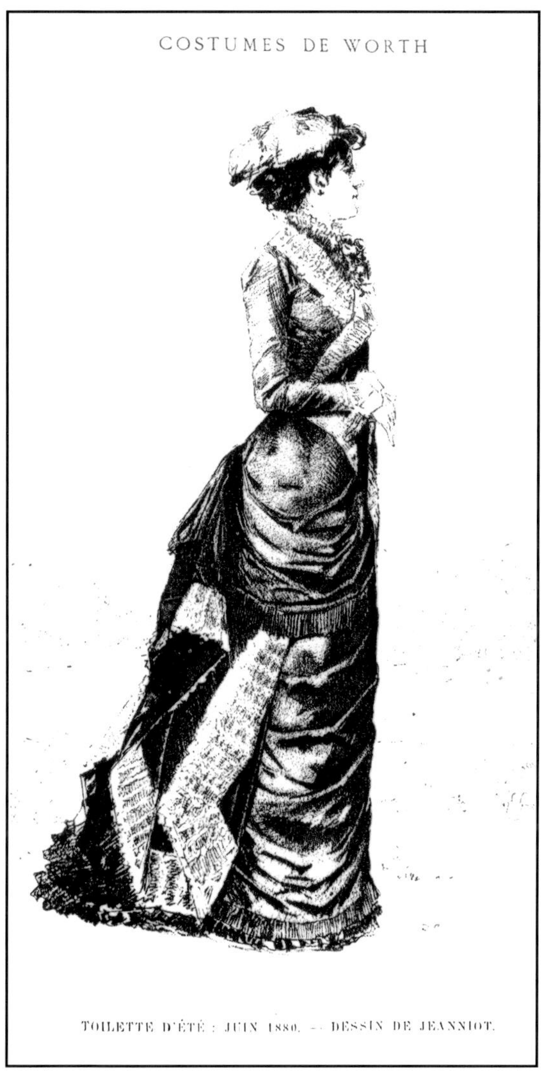

by contemporary illustrated journals like the somewhat staid *L'Illustration*, with its hallmark density of engraved images, and the libertine *La Vie parisienne*, with its exaggeratedly Guysian manner of mechanical facture.[36] Indeed, just as emporia like the Printemps and the Comptoir des Indes put on lavish, eclectic displays of designs and fabrics that vied with one another for the attention of the eye, so *La Vie Moderne* put on its own display of competing modes of textural representation and factural reproduction, with all their contesting patterns and registers of detail density, and the visual dexterity that they demanded from the viewer. This range was *La Vie Moderne*'s graphic code, its trademark, particularly concentrated in the depiction of fashion and fabric, and it was integral to its presentation of modernity. Illustration, after all, was the "industrial art" proper to a modern journal like *La Vie Moderne*, which addressed itself self-reflexively and encyclopedically to the state of illustrated journalism in France and elsewhere.[37]

In among Manet's list of works at the gallery of *La Vie Moderne* were two images of women at cafés that, while hardly supportive of the pro-family, anti-Folies-Bergère program announced the year before by Bergerat, seem to pick up on the magazine's simultaneous devotion to facture and fashion: *Plum Brandy* and *Woman Reading (Reading the Illustrated Magazine)* (figs. 121, 122).[38] Indeed, together they offer a contrast in modes of painterly mark-making that is reminiscent of *La Vie Moderne's* own range of printerly codes; they display their various manners of facture in the rendering of fashionable clothes; and in the case of *Woman Reading*, there is even an articulation of the relationship among fashion, facture, and the illustrated journal framed within the image itself.

Both images show women, no doubt of dubious virtue, seated alone at café tables, viewed from a close vantage-point, framed by moldings and window divisions that repeat the pictures' frames internally, wearing hats and elaborate dresses, and shown with café *consommations*.[39] In every other way they are different, however. The woman of *Plum Brandy* is clearly seated indoors, she is shown slumped in a posture of supreme lassitude (borrowed from Degas's *Absinthe Drinker*), and the keynote of her color scheme, as given by her dress, is pink. *Woman Reading*, on the other hand, is ambiguously placed, either outdoors, just this side of a window giving onto a café garden, or before a mirror reflecting waiter and foliage; she is shown in an upright, more alert attitude, perusing an illustrated magazine; and the dominant color note, if there is one, is the black of her street costume, which vies with the bright colors around her.[40]

The biggest difference between the two paintings is one of facture. Broadly speaking, *Plum Brandy* and *Woman Reading* present a contrast between relatively tight handling, replete with the illusionistic rendering of differently textured surfaces, and a markedly loose, gestural facture, superseding illusionism. That contrast is evident in the treatment of the surroundings of each woman: the smooth, flat presentation of gilded wall mouldings and olive-green grillwork framing the head of the woman in *Plum Brandy*, the lighter handling of the wine-colored seat on which she sits, overlaid with white touches to soften it, and the finished gray and white variegation producing the marble table on which she leans, complete with a highlit front edge; as opposed to the turbulent field of broken red, green, flesh, black and light blue marks framing the head of the woman in *Woman Reading*, the dashes of gold-brown, white, and scumbled buff rendering the frothing mug of beer and its reflection on the table next to her, and the black scribble on a gray, yellow, and blue-tinged ground signifying the illustrated front cover of the mounted, wooden-handled newspaper that she reads. In both pictures the mark-making used to produce different effects is internally differentiated, but at the same time each belongs to a system of marks that noticeably distinguishes one from the other, such that the differentiated handling in each is shown to go toward divergent ends: the illusionistic adaptation to a variety of represented surfaces, versus a self-reflexively varied notation that calls attention to the painterly hand that produced it. To put it schematically, on one side the weight of differentiation falls on the signified, on the other it falls on the signifier, a distinction foregrounded in the gray and white contrast between the marble table of *Plum Brandy* and the illustrated newspaper of *Woman Reading*.[41]

The disparity in treatment between the two paintings is concentrated in the rendering of the women's clothes. In *Plum Brandy*, the woman's pink dress is shown to have starched white shirtpoints and cravat at its throat, red embroidery, pleated ruffles and possibly lace at its sleeve edges, while above a lace band is deftly rendered around her hat, and beneath the table a dark red bow is glimpsed at the picture's bottom edge, such that it is both cut off by and identified with the *parergon* of the frame. The painter's palette harmonizes the interior in which she sits with the dress that she wears, and his facture is used variously – precision here, feathering and scumbling there, streaks of white and overlays of gray elsewhere – to render starched linen, lace, pleating, fabric folds, decorative edging, and dress garnishing. Like *La Vie Moderne, Plum Brandy* identifies fashion with facture.

Woman Reading does the same, but with more explicit means at variance with *Plum Brandy's* dependence on harmonized areas of local color. *Woman Reading* is mostly a matter of varied black picked out by contrasting colors: the lumpy edges and gray strokes in the hat producing the effect of plush velvet; the bits of bluish gray at the bottom edge of the painting suggesting the inner lining of sleeves, just beneath the contrasting yellow of the kid or suede gloves, where light dashes of gray and a lighter yellow produce an abbreviation of fingers and bent knuckles; the scribble of black intervening between ruff and newspaper to suggest a black tie or bow; and of course, the scrawl of white, gray, and black touched with bits of blue and russet edging the flat black of the dress or coat and linking ruff to illustrated newspaper page. While the marks that refer to beer glass, reflective table top, and background foliage fail to cohere into an illusion of those things, those that render hat, ruff, sleeves, and gloves do at least produce a legible semblance of their referents. This is truest of the marks rendering the woman's face: the fringed amber and black yielding her bangs, the slight, horizontal dashes of black signifying her eyes, the finely edged, differently hued lines of coral producing her mouth, the roseate hatching that factures her complexion. But the signified of these marks turns out to be less flesh and blood per se than rouge, kohl, and powder, less skin than cosmetics, so that the gap between signifier and signified is closed, and paint of one kind equates paint of another. So, in line with Baudelaire's discourse on the painting of modern life, *Woman Reading* identifies painterly facture not only with fashion but also with "le beau fard" of feminine face-painting.

And so, where *Plum Brandy* lies closer to the *Illustration* end of the mechanical reproduction spectrum of *La Vie Moderne, Woman Reading* falls at the other, libertine end of illustrated journals such as *La Vie parisienne*. Which brings me to *Woman Reading's* inclusion within its frame of a mounted illustrated magazine of the type represented by the periodical in whose gallery Manet showed the painting, and the fact that, as illegible as they are, nonetheless the scribbles marking the front and back pages clearly signify illustration. Thus *Woman Reading* distinguishes between specific legibility and the basic recognition of a graphic code, between the kind of reading required by letterpress and the form of perusal solicited by illustration, to which the viewer's consumption of the painting of this woman is evidently linked. So the decoding of Manet's painterly marks is identified with the deciphering of the graphic code of illustrated journalism. It is also identified with female visual culture, as it was constructed in *La Vie Moderne* itself: the claim of *La Vie Moderne* to cover both male and female interests in modern life enters into *Woman Reading's* relay between the graphic codes of modern fashion and those of modern illustration.

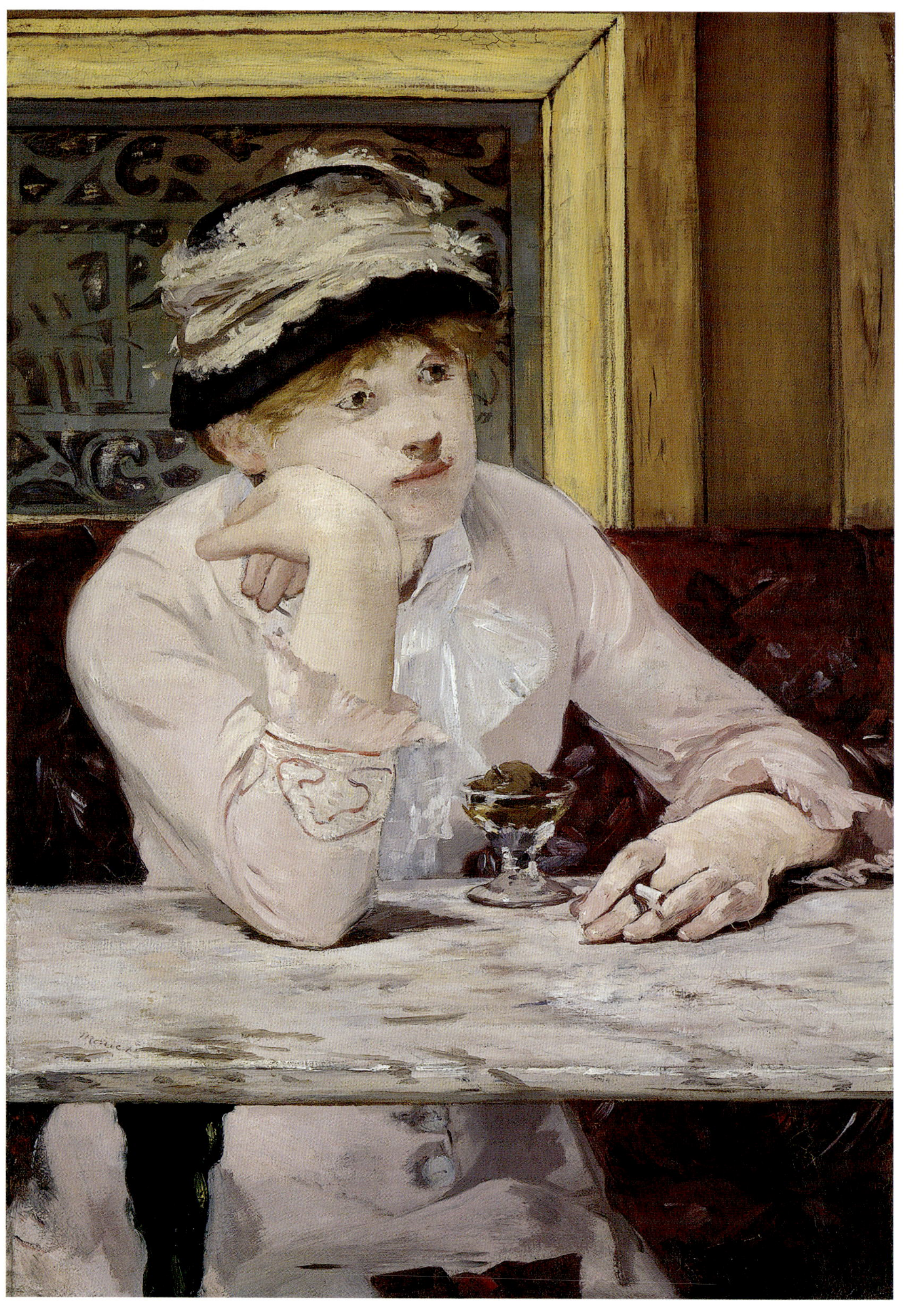

121 Edouard Manet, *Plum Brandy*, c.1877, oil on canvas, 73.6 × 50.2 cm. National Gallery of Art, Washington, D.C. Collection of Mr. And Mrs. Paul Mellon.

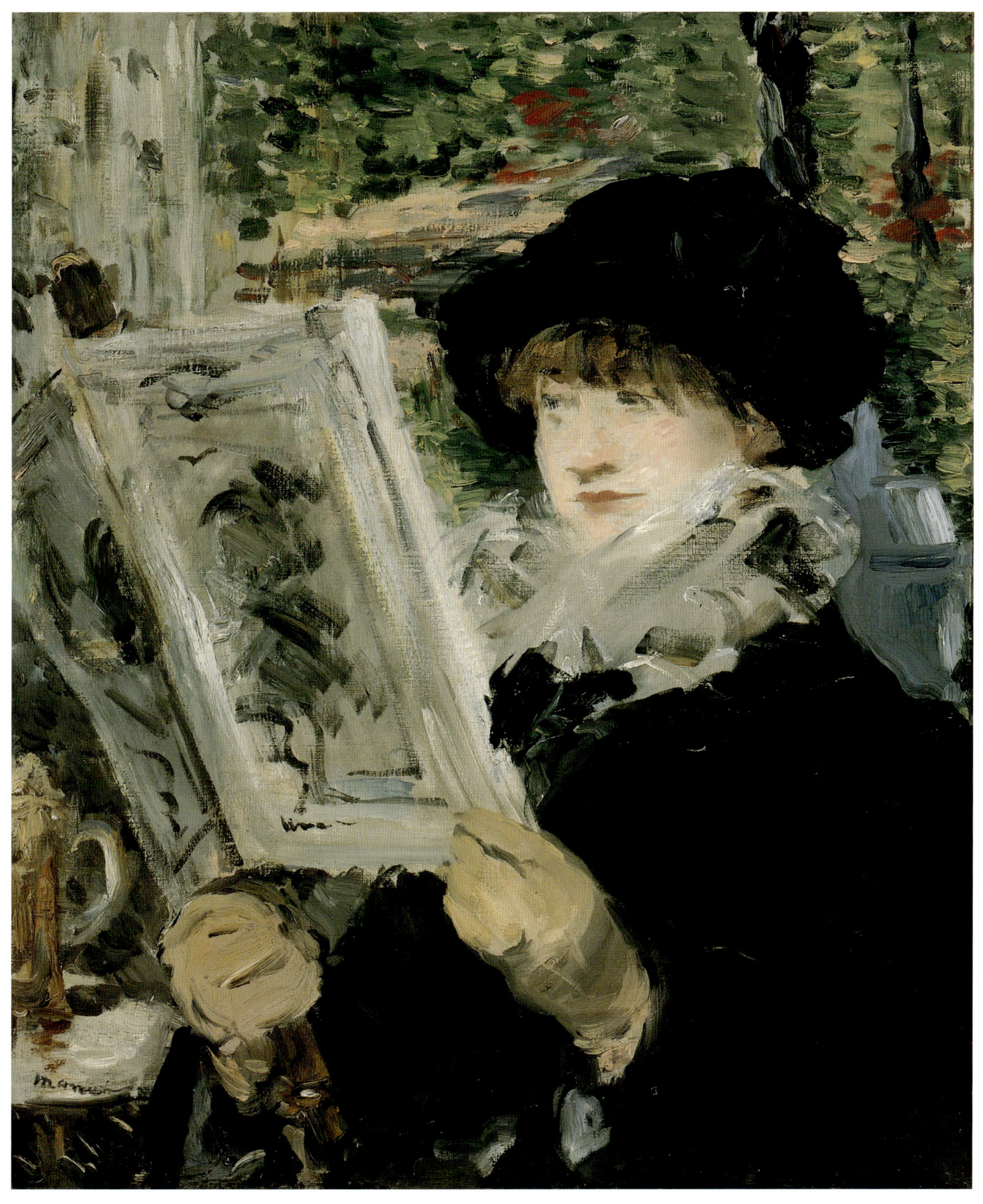

122   Edouard Manet, *Woman Reading (Reading the Illustrated Magazine)*, 1878/79, oil on canvas, 61.2 × 50.7 cm. The Art Institute of Chicago. Mr. and Mrs. Lewis Larned Coburn Memorial Collection, 1933.435.

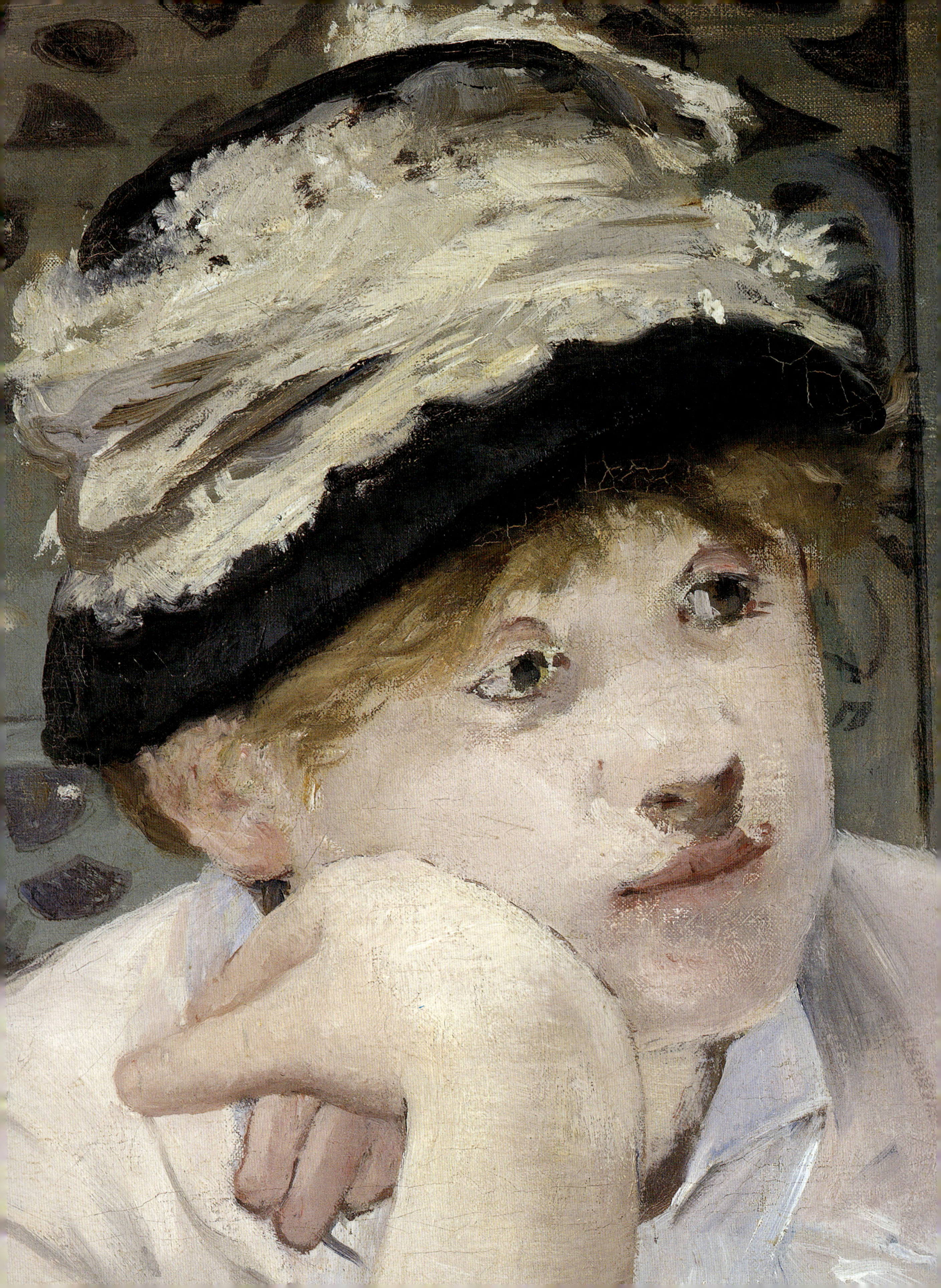

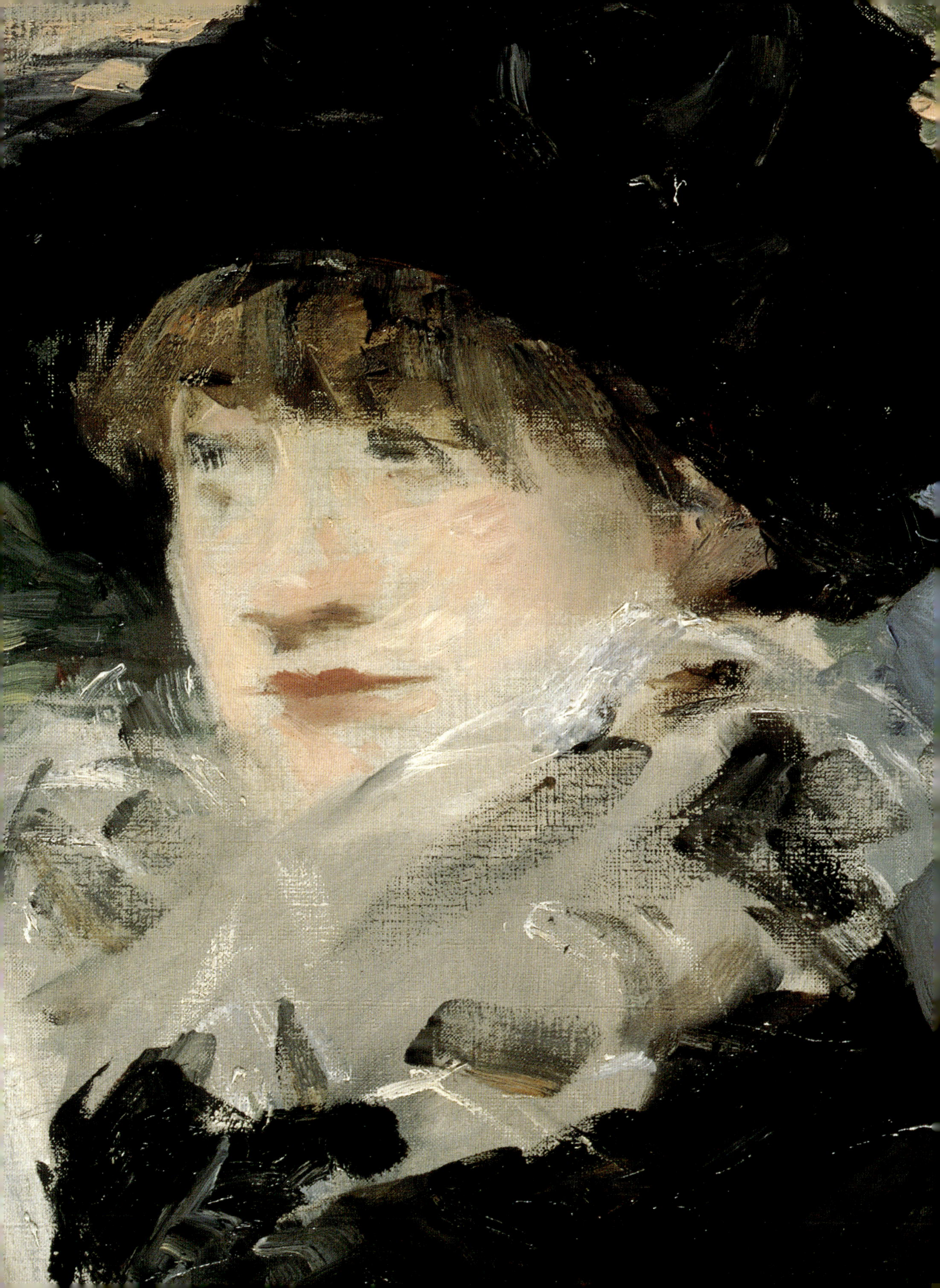

Much as writers like d'Orsay did, but without following up his magazine's sponsorship of bourgeois family values, *Woman Reading* thematizes female consumerism. Although the beer on the table beside her and her presence alone at a café seem to mark her, like the woman with the cigarette in *Plum Brandy*, as something other than a *femme honnête*, the painting does not offer any transaction with her.[42] Rather, it focuses on her own consumerly acts of buying and drinking a beer at a café, and reading an illustrated paper. It is obvious as well that her consumerism includes the clothes she wears and the garnishings decorating those clothes, both of which were advertised in illustrated journals such as the one she reads: the link between the two is made graphically, in the similarly pigmented loose marks that tie ruff to newspaper. In sum, *Woman Reading* draws a tight circle around modern fashion's production of modern femininity, the graphic codes of modern journalism represented in *La Vie Moderne*, and the brand of modern painting that Manet exhibited at La Vie Moderne, all in the image of the modern female consumer to which *La Vie Moderne* purported to speak. At the same time, the loose, libertine graphic code that constitutes *Woman Reading* replaces the tighter codes of the fashion illustration, substitutes the gentleman flaneur's sophisticated decipherment of graphic codes *à la* Guys for the female reader's simpler consumption of her illustrated newspaper, and suggests the rapid, *flaneuriste* consumption of her consumerism, from a "Folies-Bergère" point of view.

AN ALTERNATIVE TO *NANA*

It is evident from the pages of *La Vie Moderne* (and from publications like *Nana* promoted by Charpentier and his magazine) that the image of the female fashion consumer was a contested one, with *grandes dames* like Mme Charpentier and *bonnes bourgeoises* such as the ones addressed by Bergerat and d'Orsay weighing in on one side, representatives of the Folies-Bergère persuasion on the other side, and a large gray zone in between. Had Manet also included his other, earlier picture of a female reader in the show at La Vie Moderne, the image of his own fashionably dressed wife being read to at home by her son, it might have argued for his presentation of differing views of women and female consumption. One could say the same of the oil *Skating* (fig. 123), with its loose but detailed rendition of a fashionably dressed woman made respectable by the sketchy indication of an accompanying child, along with the pastel sketch *Knitting*, the pastel portrait of Mme Charpentier's sister Isabelle Lemonnier, and the very conventional pastel bust of the good wife Mme Gabrielle Zola, all shown at La Vie Moderne too, countered by other, looser portraits, such as those of George Moore, man about town, and Constantin Guys, Baudelaire's old "painter of modern life," shown there as well. (Together these portraits and the variety of other studies that accompanied them, including an oil floral and a portrait of Monet in his studio, and pastel studies of unnamed female heads and male drinkers, also put on display the variable codes of pastel, as opposed to oil painting.)

The overwhelming majority of Manet's display at La Vie Moderne, however, was committed to the Folies-Bergère side of things, as represented by café culture. His *Café-concert* and *Corner of the Café-concert* (figs. 124, 125) depict male and female, bourgeois and

Previous pages Details of figs. 121, 122.

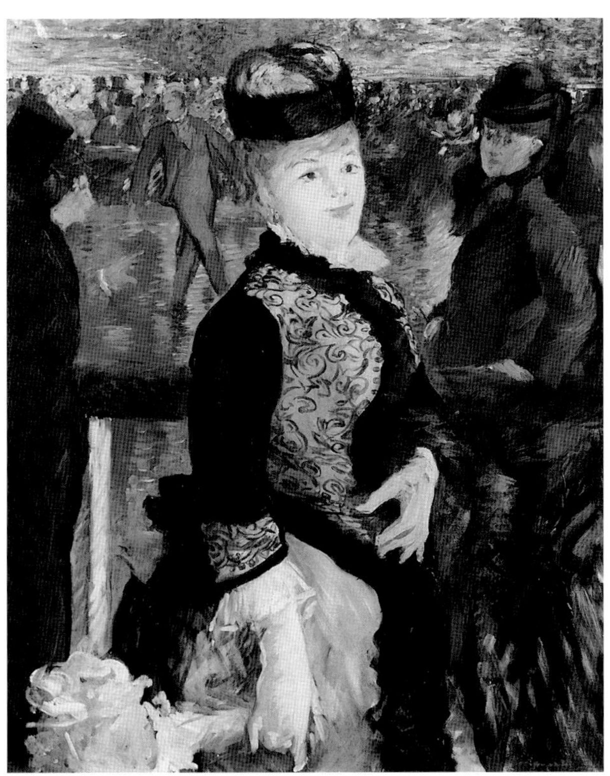

123 Edouard Manet, *Skating*, 1877, oil on canvas, 92.5 × 72 cm. Courtesy of the Fogg Art Museum, Harvard University Art Museums, Cambridge, Mass. Bequest of Collection of Maurice Wertheim, Class of 1906.

124 (*below left*) Edouard Manet, *The Café-concert*, 1879, oil on canvas, 47.5 × 39.2 cm. The Walters Art Museum, Baltimore. Acquired by Henry Walters, 1909. 37.893.

125 (*below right*) Edouard Manet, *Corner of the Café-concert*, probably 1878–80, oil on canvas, 97.1 × 77.5 cm. National Gallery, London.

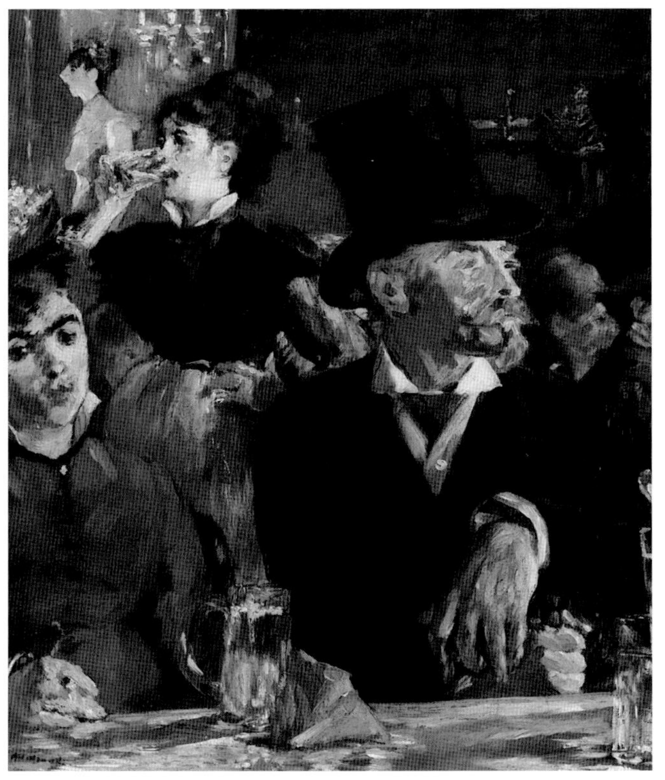

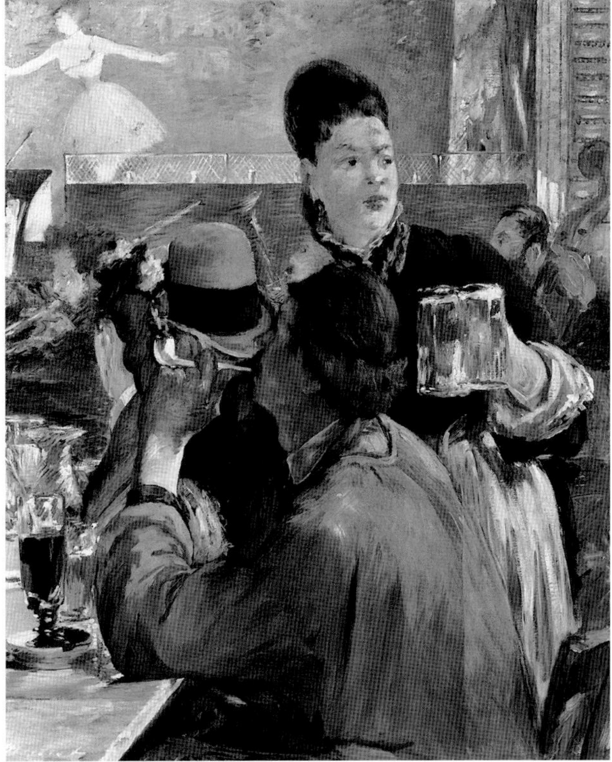

working-class consumers side by side, combining the cigarette of *Plum Brandy* and the beer of *Woman Reading*, exaggerating the frowsy female sloth of *Plum Brandy* in the one, contrasting its top-hatted gentleman with the blue-smocked, pipe-smoking figure and bowler-hatted head in the other, and tilting them both downmarket with the increasing focus on the female beer-server, who quaffs a mug of beer in the first image and serves it in the second. Thus many of the pictures in Manet's show at La Vie Moderne seem to have emphasized the trollops and poor classes that Bergerat had wanted to de-emphasize.

Nowhere was this more the case than in another pair of related pictures shown at La Vie Moderne: the oil *Before the Mirror* (fig. 126) and the pastel *Woman Fastening Her Garter* (listed as *La Toilette*, fig. 127). These images, showing one woman tightening her corset and another putting on her stockings, return to the libertine topic of the toilette that had been *Nana's* theme; indeed, in the few existing reviews of Manet's show at La Vie Moderne, the two paintings were either implicitly or explicitly referred back to *Nana*.[43] Huysmans was among those who concentrated on *Woman Fastening Her Garter* in a manner that evoked *Nana's* thematic world – not surprisingly, since he had written at such length about stockings (and other pieces of underwear) as the most coveted commodity and true mark of the prostitute in his description of *Nana* in 1877. In 1880, he wrote thus:

> One of them, the *Toilette*, representing a woman in her décolletage, the top of a chignon and the tip of a nose advancing on the summit of her chest, as she attaches a garter to a blue stocking, reeks of the prostitute who is so dear to us. Enveloping his characters in the odor of the world to which they belong has been one of the constant preoccupations of M. Manet.
>
> His bright work, from which have been scrubbed the mummified mud and tobacco juices which have mucked up canvases for so long, is possessed of a coaxing touch, beneath its swaggering appearance, a brief and concise but somewhat hesitant drawing, a bouquet of vivid marks within paintwork that is both silvery and blond.[44]

It is likely that this description refers to both pictures, run together as if they were one. Indeed, the two images suggest alternate views, if not of the same woman, certainly of the same theme of the toilette – various stages of getting dressed in the privacy of a woman's boudoir, from the tightening of the lacings of a corset to the lifting of petticoats to fasten a garter. The one presents a blond woman from the back, standing upright, looking at herself in a mirror, in which we can see a fragmentary reflection of her. The other presents a woman from the front, bending over to provide not only a view of one of her stockinged legs but also of her breasts, pushed up and overflowing her corset, such that the viewer is offered a glimpse of one of her nipples. The two women seem to be proportioned similarly: the plump, sloping shoulders, dimpled arms, and wide backside of *Before the Mirror* suggest the same amplitude as that of the *Woman Fastening Her Garter*, though what passes for her mirror image gives little information as to how buxom she is. Each has her hair dressed in a chignon or coronet, and each one picks up the blues of the erstwhile *Nana*, in the form of a blue corset on the one hand and a blue stocking on the other.

However, in their different views of a similar female body, *Before the Mirror* and *Woman Fastening Her Garter* present a contrast as well. That contrast has much to do with what is given to the gaze – a lot in the case of the latter, quite a bit less in the case of *Before the Mirror*, in spite of its provision of a mirror image. The mirror, of course, is a familiar accouterment of pictorial thematizations of boudoir femininity, but here it does not properly serve its usual function in such scenes, which is not only to double a face or body but also to present the viewer with the other side of it, so as to reward the gaze with more, and further the visual fiction of possession.[45] All the spectator is given in this mirror, however, is some indication of the function of such specular doubling – in the briefest suggestion of an hourglass shape rendered in a curving dash of blue. But because of the odd point of view onto the mirror image and the abbreviated style of notation that characterizes it, the reflection is almost entirely elided. So what is given to the gaze in *Before the Mirror* is given entirely in the form of suggestive but insufficient glimpses, and mediated prominently through self-announcing facture. In the *Woman Fastening Her Garter*, on the other hand, much of what one would want to see of the woman's body is given directly and frontally to the gaze, is swiftly and broadly caricatured in the graphic rendering of her contours, and, in a visual joke about upholstery-like fashions in clothing and bodies that was common currency at the time, doubled in the plump, overstuffed piece of furniture seen in the lower right corner. In short, facture in the *Woman Fastening Her Garter* produces bodily exaggeration and salacious directness, whereas in *Before the Mirror* it yields only bodily occlusion and erotic indirectness. In the one, facture serves the representation of a body and its delivery to the gaze; in the other, it strains a little against both.

Thus the contrast between *Before the Mirror* and *Woman Fastening Her Garter* resides as much in their different means of producing their views of a female body as in the aspects of the body that they put on offer, and nowhere is that difference in means more clearly marked than in their graphic codes of oil paint and pastel. Huysmans's review registers that difference. In running the two images together, his two short paragraphs on Manet's show also produce a description that is riven between a somewhat hackneyed description of what is represented that obviously refers to *Woman Fastening Her Garter*, and a glowing account of how it is represented that corresponds rather better to *Before the Mirror*, thus dividing "content" from "form," insisting on a tension between the two, and assigning each to different pictures.

In describing a woman's *pif* and *poitraille*, not to mention her garter and blue stocking, Huysmans could only have been referring to *Woman Fastening Her Garter*. Not only do those words index the bodily and sartorial contents of the pastel, their slanginess is also more appropriate to the quality of caricature that is found in it. Because of her evocation of popular-press imagery, and the bawdiness of her bodily rendering in the graphic language of pastel, therefore, *Woman Fastening Her Garter* lent itself more easily to allusions to the discourse on prostitution in which Huysmans himself had specialized. But Huysmans's description of facture in his second paragraph suggests the domain of oil painting rather more than that of pastel: the contrast between canvases "mucked up" by "mummified mud and tobacco juices" and a "bright work" whose facture is both "silvery and blond" points to a conventional contrast between styles of oil painting. Its

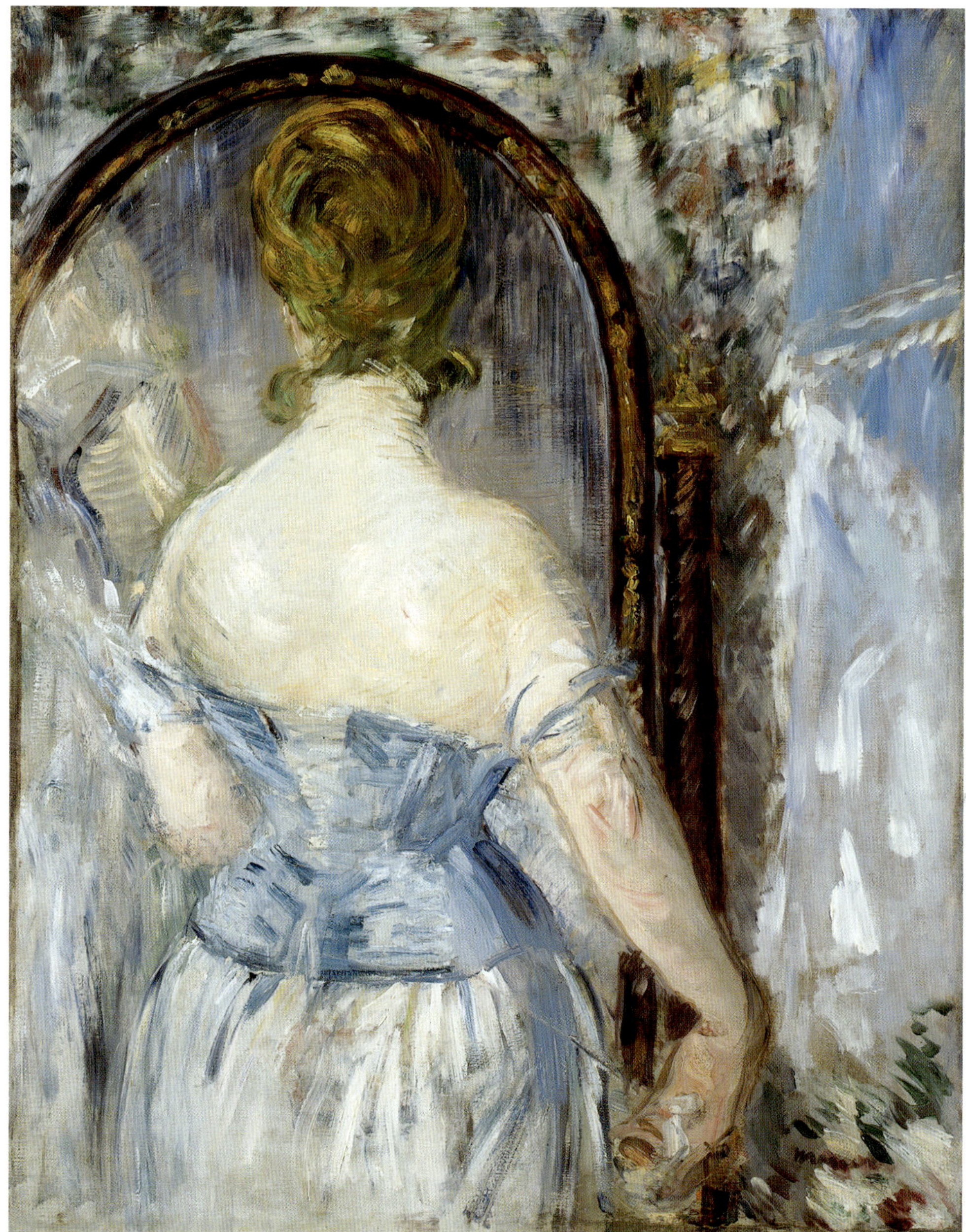

126 Edouard Manet, *Before the Mirror*, 1876, oil on canvas, 92.1 × 71.4 cm. Solomon R. Guggenheim Museum, New York. Thannhauser Collection, Gift, Justin K. Thannhauser, 1978.

celebration of the "blondness" of Manet's painting is taken straight from Zola's criticism of the '60s in reference to the palette of Manet's oil paintings of those years. In other words, Huysmans's second paragraph refers the reader to the domain of high-art oil painting that is suited to *Before the Mirror*, as opposed to the world of caricature and

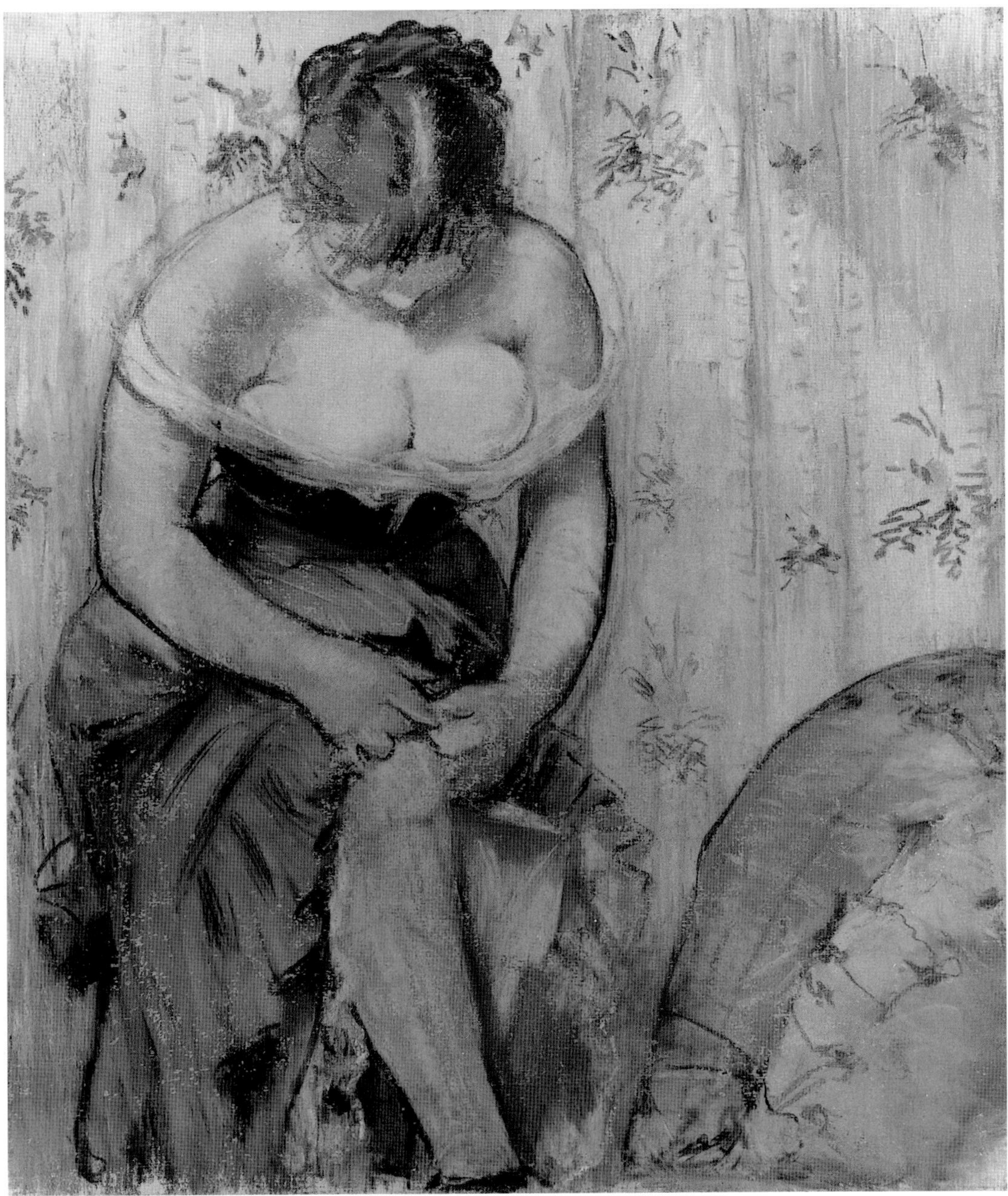

127 Edouard Manet, *Woman Fastening Her Garter*, 1878–79, pastel on canvas, 55 × 46 cm. Ordrupgaard, Copenhagen.

popular-press imagery that the *Woman Fastening Her Garter* evokes. Of course, the facture of *Before the Mirror* also aligns it with *Woman Reading*, and refers to popular-press imagery of the libertine variety – erotic lithographs of women at their toilettes, either alone or attended by lovers, tightening their corset laces, that went back to

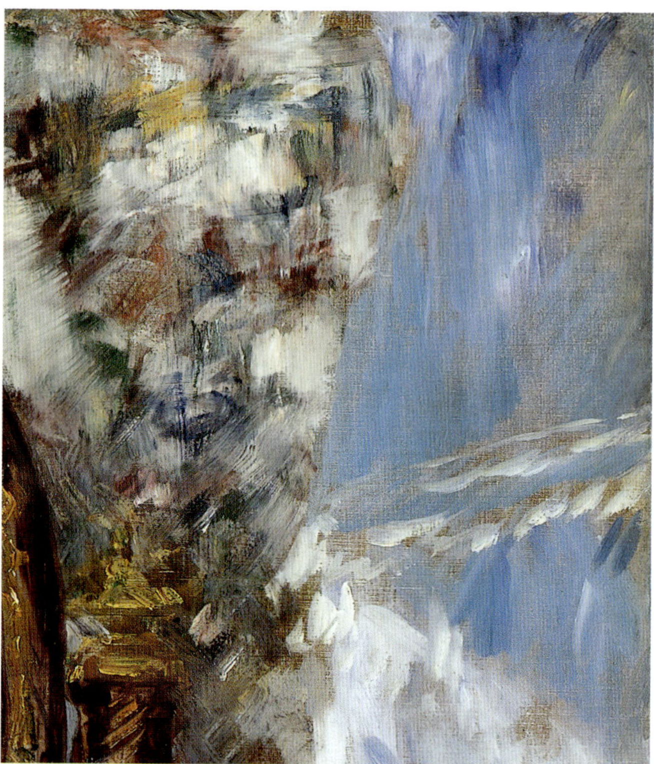

Detail of fig. 126.

the early decades of the nineteenth century. But *Before the Mirror* complicates that reference, as *Woman Fastening Her Garter* does not, by a handling that threatens to tear its bodily referent apart at the seams, and make the familiar corset lacing gesture almost illegible.

Huysmans's "silvery and blond" is a good description of the palette of *Before the Mirror*: it evokes the brushy, golden rendering of the woman's hair and the gilt frame of the standing mirror, and the equally brushy, silver-suggesting, white and blue rendering of corset, shift, and glazed mirror surface, the white flesh of the woman's back and the fabric hanging from the upper right-hand corner of the painting. And Huysmans's references to "paintwork," Manet's "coaxing touch," his "swaggering," "brief," and "concise" but "hesitant drawing" and "vivid marks" evoke the foregrounding of brushwork per se that is everywhere evident in *Before the Mirror*. For the painting contains a virtual catalogue of possible kinds of brushmarks and their relationship to the business of representation at hand, ranging from the variegated array of short, thick hatchmarks rendering the wallpaper, to the swirling, circular marks suggesting the woman's chignon and escaping neck-curls, the horizontal strokes indicating the lacings of the corset, the longer vertical strokes of blue and white calling forth the transparency of the shift, the thinner paint application evoking the mirror's surface and bit of an image caught upon it, the combination of thick and thin, opaque and translucent marks that characterizes the blue and white fabric in the upper right-hand corner, the swift dashes rendering arm, elbow, and hand, the overlay of yellow on brown that represents the mirror frame; and so on.

Consider that cataloguing of marks together with the contrast between the woman's back and mirror image, constituted by marks that successfully coalesce into an image versus more dispersed marks that more or less fail to do so: *Before the Mirror* begins to read as a kind of self-reflexive meditation on its own constitution out of paint. And then, there is the insistent comparison between two areas of blue above white, rendering corset and shift versus one does not quite know what, one serving the representation of a semi-clothed three-dimensional body, the other flattening out into a declaration of palette, pigment, and paintedness associated with the enframing edge of the picture just as the blue and white corset is enframed by the edge of the mirror. What that comparison suggests is a sort of deconstruction of the transparency of representation, the illusion of content, and hence the imagistic thematics of female body and boudoir, dress and undress, and their contemporary erotic associations – in short, all that is on more direct, frontal offer in the titillating, similarly coiffed, and semi-clothed buxomness of *Woman Fastening Her Garter.*

Of these two *Nana*-recalling images, *Before the Mirror* is actually closer to *Nana*, in spite of the fact that it was to her garter-fixing companion that most critics looked for reminiscences of *Nana*. For not only does the female figure in *Before the Mirror* stand in front of a mirror just as Nana had done, wearing the same blue corset and white shift or bloomers, and sporting a coloration close to that of *Nana*, the same bit of blue and white fabric is also to be found in both paintings. In the *Nana* context, that smaller piece of blue and white fabric more clearly signals a dress about to be donned, and hence the next step in the narrative sequence of the toilette, whereas in *Before the Mirror* that piece of fabric is representationally much more ambiguous, more clearly declaring itself to be just what it literally is, a piece of painting. Thus *Before the Mirror* seems to be an alternative version of *Nana*, whether an earlier, less resolved attempt, a later revision, or simply two variants worked on simultaneously, it is hard to say.

One way or the other, *Before the Mirror*'s emphasis on a disappearing mirror image, a face and body virtually replaced by paint and brushwork, the factural process rather than the illusioned product of the toilette, conjures up the erotic adoration of facture found in the toilette scene in Zola's novel even better than the painting *Nana* does. Zola's *Nana*, written after the painting of both pictures, published just before the exhibition of *Before the Mirror*, and very much on the minds of Huysmans and other critics, itself contains some of the tension between the forward-moving erotics of narrative content and the narrative-stopping erotics of facture, the thematics of sexual possession and that of eroticized unpossessability, that is suggested in the contrast between Manet's two *Nana*-alternatives, *Nana* and *Before the Mirror*.[46] As such, it points to some of what was at stake in the dialogue between Manet's oil and pastel at La Vie Moderne (as well as between other pictures, such as *Plum Brandy* and *Woman Reading*).

Before the Mirror represents a kind of painterly argument with *Nana*. The narrative of feminine artifice, the male gaze and sexual consumerism that *Nana* enacts so fully in paint is de-narrativized and somewhat undermined in *Before the Mirror*, though that narrative is indexed and abbreviated in the mirror, corset, shift, and blue and white fabric hanging from the upper right corner. Not only are all the well-known puns and anecdotes of *Nana* lacking, the triangulation of gazes and glances linking Nana herself, her gentleman caller, and us, the viewers of the picture, is also absent from *Before the Mirror*, though it is suggested only to be refuted in the mirror image that the viewer is and is not given. *Before the Mirror* sets out to be *Nana* from behind, as if the viewpoint of the gentleman in *Nana* had been swiveled around and aligned with the viewer's, with the aim of seeing the mirror image that is hidden from our gaze in *Nana*. But with the viewpoint swiveled around and a piece of mirror image given, one ends up seeing nothing but a lot of paint. Add to that its undercutting of facture's complicity in manufacturing the narrative illusion of *Nana: Before the Mirror* stands as a factural alternative to the other's narrativity, substituting "le beau fard" of painting for the "debauchee's luxury" of silk stockings, "armchairs as wide as beds," and all the rest.

It is in this way that *Nana*'s equation of different kinds of commodity becomes rather strained in *Before the Mirror:* the equivalence is undermined between the various commodities that are the represented subject matter of *Nana* and the commodity that the painting of *Nana* literally is, while the union of woman as object of the consuming gaze and painting as object of that same gaze is countermanded. Instead, the one stands in the way of the other, reinforcing the either/or-ness of painterly illusionism, in which the illusion and the paint that produces the illusion can be absorbed in quick succession, flickering between the two in an on–off alternation, but cannot be comprehended simultaneously.[47] In *Before the Mirror*, one can have the paint but not the woman too, which stands in contradiction of what *Nana*, that shop-window ware of 1877, had proposed. Ultimately, *Before the Mirror* thematizes a conflict between two levels of commodity, two kinds of exhibitionism, not to mention two kinds of erotic spectacle, establishing a tension between the fact that as a painting it is a commodity and the fact that as a representation it also depicts a commodity, or a related series of commodities, the woman, her corset, her femininity.

At the time of the show at La Vie Moderne Manet had both *Nana* and *Before the Mirror* in his possession and could have exhibited either or both.[48] That he chose to exhibit *Before the Mirror* suggests that he wanted to put an alternative to *Nana* on view rather than the painting that had caused a stir when it was shown in Giroux's window. Perhaps he did not want to be as closely associated with Zola's novel as he would have been had he shown *Nana* again in 1880 (the association was made nevertheless). Perhaps he had continued to work on *Before the Mirror* and thus it was the more up to date of the two works; it was the one he had not yet shown. Perhaps he wanted it on view at a time when Morisot was putting together her own related showing at the Impressionist exhibition of that year. And perhaps its brand of facture was one he wanted to accentuate at La Vie Moderne, in relationship to its emphasis upon the graphic codes of modern life. But whichever the reason for his choice of *Before the Mirror*, what its contradiction of *Nana* made clear was the way in which the "Folies-Bergères" perspective enabled the dismantling of itself, as well as a fundamental doubleness with regard to the gendering of the libertine gentleman's point of view and the graphics with which it was conjured up.[49]

*   *   *

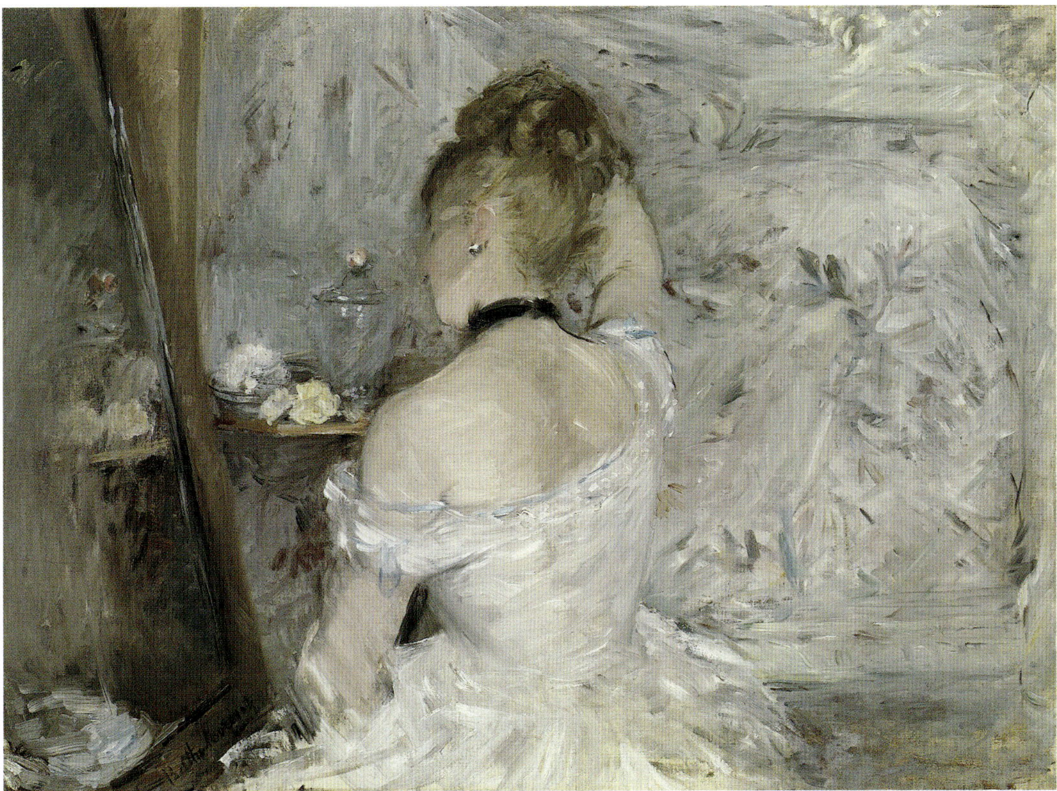

128   Berthe Morisot, *Woman at Her Toilette*, c.1875, oil on canvas, 60.3 × 80.4 cm. The Art Institute of Chicago. The Stickney Fund, 1924.127.

FEMINIZING FACTURE

Before the Mirror was part of a larger conversation about how to represent the fashion-conscious modern woman in general, and the topic of the toilette in particular. It had a dialogic relationship with another painting that went on view in 1880 as well: Berthe Morisot's *Woman at Her Toilette* (fig. 128), painted some time between 1875 and 1880 and exhibited at the Impressionist show of that year.[50] Given the Morisot–Manet friendship and family connection, it is quite possible that Morisot saw Manet's painting in his studio before it was exhibited at La Vie Moderne. Or perhaps it was the other way around, and Manet saw the *Woman at Her Toilette* in Morisot's studio and then took to painting his own version. Whichever way it went, the two paintings exhibited in rival exhibitions continued the Manet–Morisot dance begun in 1869. (In 1876 Morisot had painted *The Cheval Glass*, whose depiction of a woman in her shift in front of a mirror relates to both *Nana* and *Before the Mirror*, and could well have had a role in Manet's painting of either or both. In 1880, Morisot continued the dialogue, painting the *Woman Putting on Her Stocking*, which surely had something to do with Manet's *Woman Fastening Her Garter*.)

Morisot's meditations on the theme of the toilette argue against the libertinism of Manet's contributions to the topic, situating themselves closer to the bourgeois

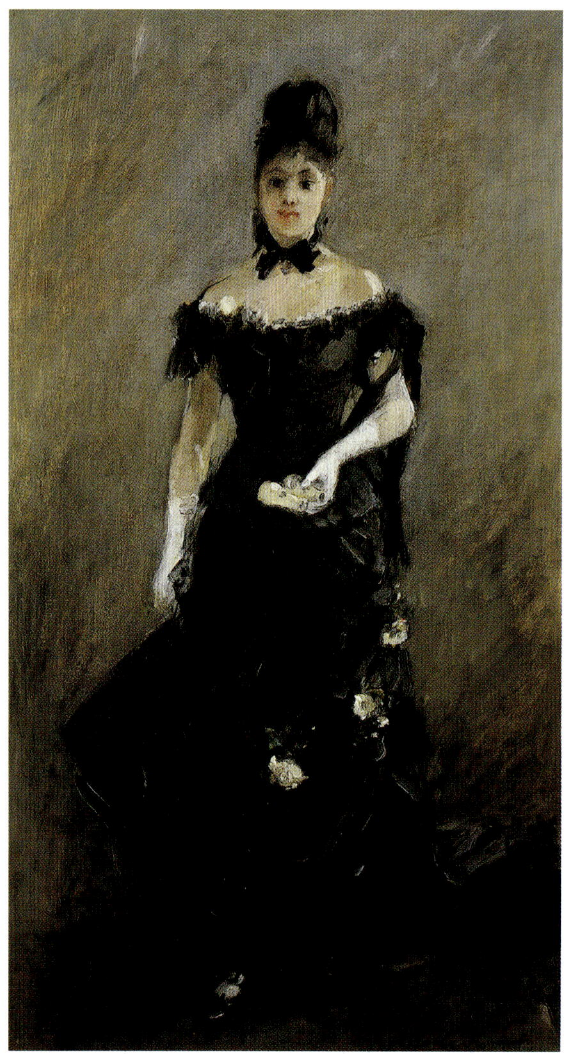

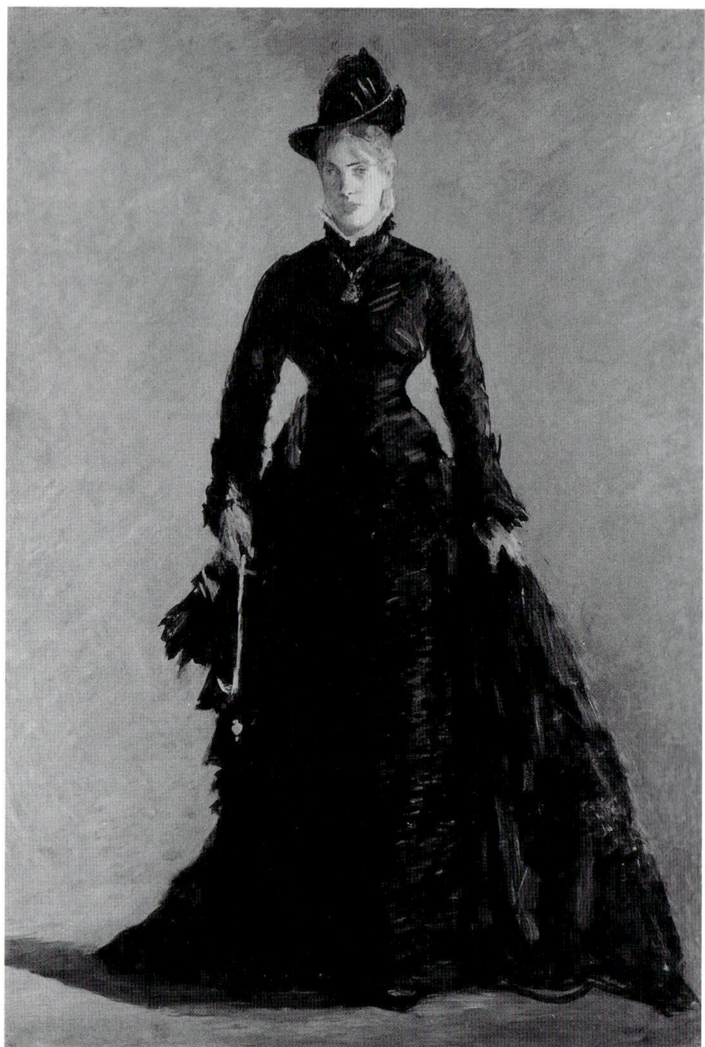

129   Berthe Morisot, *Before the Theater*, 1875–76, oil on canvas, 57 × 31 cm. Galerie Schröder und Leisewitz, Kunsthandel, Bremen.

130   Edouard Manet, *Parisienne (Ellen Andrée in a Dress with a Train)*, 1875, oil on canvas, 193 × 125 cm. Nationalmuseum, Stockholm.

respectability promoted in *La Vie Moderne*. Her women getting dressed in front of mirrors are not *nanas*; rather, they suggest Morisot's own act of dressing and self-preparation. In particular, *Woman at Her Toilette*, with her earring, black neckband, and white ballgown, seems to be at the end rather than the beginning of getting dressed, evidently preparing herself for a society ball rather than a stage performance or the titillation of present or future lovers. Back in 1875 or '76, when she began work on the theme of the toilette, Morisot had painted a young woman in a black ballgown (fig. 129), based perhaps on an 1875 depiction of a *parisienne* in a black dress with a long train by Manet (fig. 130), and replete with three Manet-referring white blossoms strewn around the

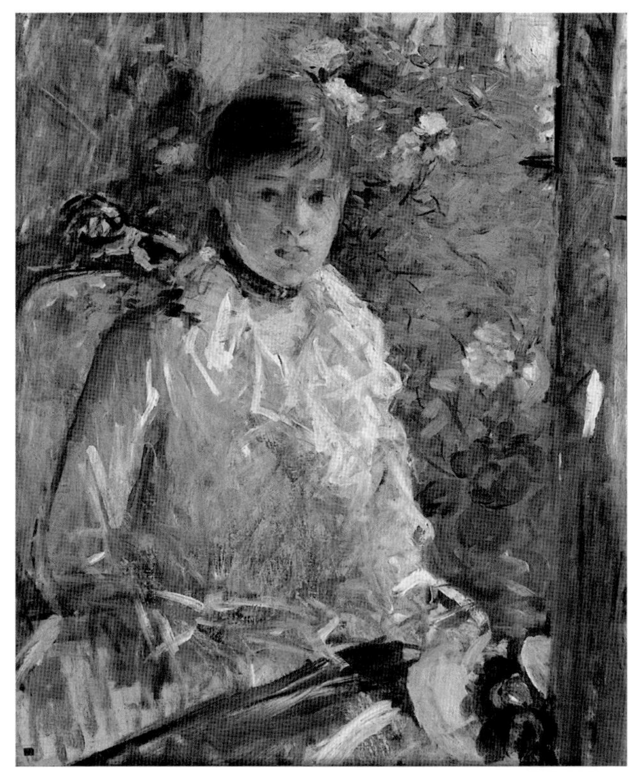

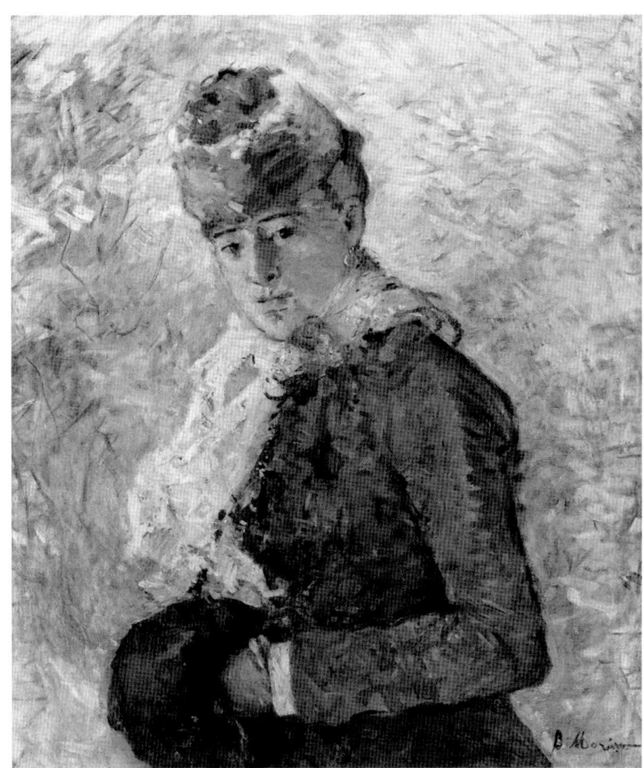

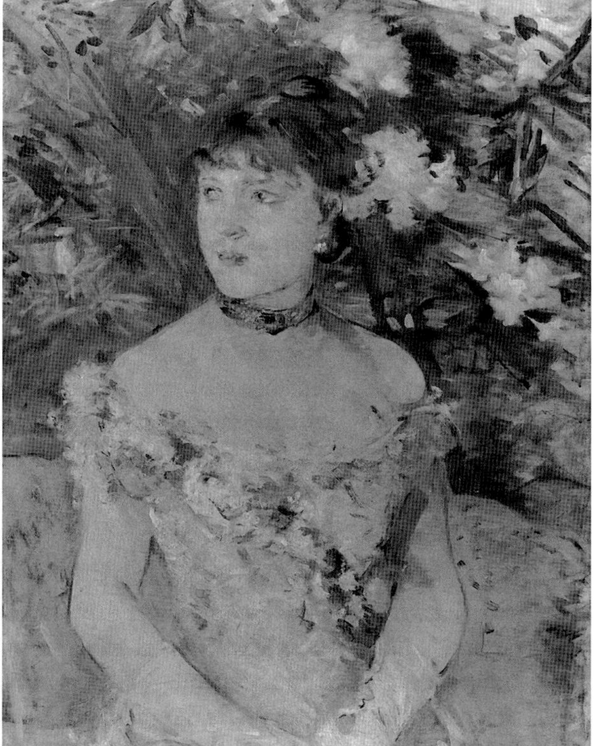

131 (*above left*)   Berthe Morisot, *Summer*, 1878, oil on canvas, 76 × 61 cm. Musée Fabre, Montpellier.

132 (*above right*)   Berthe Morisot, *Winter*, 1880, oil on canvas, 73.5 × 58.5 cm. Museum of Art, Dallas. Gift of the Meadows Foundation, Inc.

133   Berthe Morisot, *Woman Dressed for the Ball*, 1879, oil on canvas, 71 × 54 cm. Musée d'Orsay, Paris.

bunched front of the overskirt at thigh level – which Manet in his turn picked up more loosely and complicatedly in an 1878 *Woman in an Evening Dress*. As far as the viewer can see, Morisot's *Woman at Her Toilette* seems to be situated in a boudoir of upper-class distinction and propriety; given its factural and thematic association with Morisot's other female (self?) portraits on exhibition in 1880, *Summer*, *Winter*, and *Woman Dressed for the Ball* (figs. 131–33), she declares herself to belong to Morisot's class.

Despite its Watteau-like *profil perdu* and its curious blending with the background, more is given of the young woman in Morisot's image than in Manet's *Before the Mirror*. But even less is given of her image in the mirror; indeed, it is not seen at all. Instead, there is a reflection of the flowers, powder puff, and cosmetic glassware on the shelf beside her, and at the bottom edge of the mirror a drift of white and powder-blue strokes indicates a reflected glimpse of the edge of her gown, picking up the pale blue ribbon of paint threaded delicately around the back-viewed décolleté of her bodice, which in turn picks up on the painterly dissemination of floral marks throughout the background. Like her body, the mirror is oriented at an angle intersecting the foliate plane of background wall, while the glassy mirror edge and mirror frame with Morisot's signature upon it divide the spaces of body and mirror into separate, demarcated domains, which are, however, equally amorphous in their scattered fields of paintwork.

In the relay between glassware and glassy mirror surface, and among the floral patterning of wall surface, flowers, and powder puff and their reflection in the mirror is to be found a play on the relationship between cosmetic and painterly artifice. In the smudged separation between the flowers and powder puff this and that side of the mirror, in the sharply highlit mirror edge, and in the triangulation of three other highlights – the glimmering white earring on the pink earlobe, the pink and white floral top to the lid of the glass jar and its pink and white reflection in the mirror – Morisot condenses her evocation of *maquillage*, with its combination of blending, veiling, and hinted articulation, at once self-effacing and self-announcing in its application of pigment, simultaneously distinct and indistinct, literal and illusionist. As Charles Ephrussi put it:

> Berthe Morisot is French in her distinction, elegance, gaiety, and nonchalance; she likes her painting festive and spirited; she grinds flower petals onto her palette, in order to spread them later on her canvas with witty, airy touches, thrown down a little haphazardly, which harmonize, blend, and finish by producing something fine, lively and charming that you do not see so much as guess at . . . Young women cradled in a boat . . . another at her toilette, are all seen through fine gray tones, matte white, and light pink, with no shadows, set off with little multicolored daubs, the whole giving the impression of vague and uncertain opaline tints. This fugitive lightness, this amiable, sparkling, and frivolous vivacity recalls Fragonard, though not so much the profound science, the solidity of facture, and the diffuse light which gives so much homogeneity to the master's painting.[51]

In other words, the *Woman at Her Toilette* is a thoroughly "feminine" painting, as feminine as Fragonard's Rococo (minus the solidity and unity of the masculine master); and its cosmetic topos is matched by an evanescent, self-effacing facture that evokes the layered, veiled effects of cosmetics on female flesh.

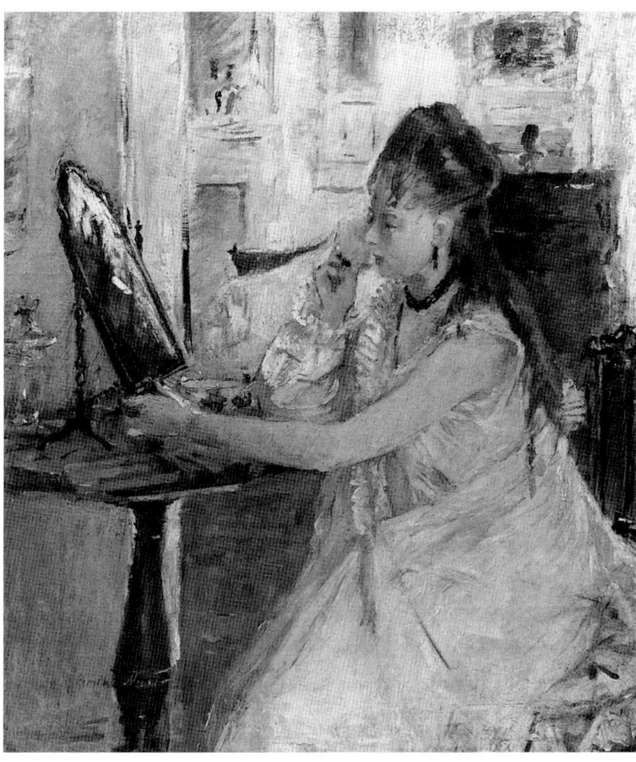

134   Berthe Morisot, *Woman Powdering Herself*, 1877, oil on canvas, 46 × 39 cm. Musée d'Orsay, Paris.

The blossoms on the shelf of the *Woman at Her Toilette*, which refer to Manet (*Eva Gonzalès*), together with the powder puff, which does the same (*Nana*), are the signature and sign of the dialogue between Morisot's *peinture maquillée* and Manet's factural fireworks at La Vie Moderne. This was, of course, merely the latest and most intense moment of the two painters' conversation on the entwined subjects of facture and femininity; indeed, the series to which Morisot's *Woman at Her Toilette* belonged included another image that tied the dialogue between herself and Manet on the subject of the toilette back to their earlier duel at the time of the Gonzalès affair. Her *Woman Powdering Herself* of 1877 (fig. 134) picked up the painting gesture of Manet's portrait of Eva Gonzalès and, refracting it through the theme inaugurated by *Nana*, used it to depict a self-painting gesture that not only toned down the libertinism of the topic of *Nana* but also tied facture to cosmetics explicitly, eliding her vocation as a painter with her creation of herself and her own femininity. This was a reply to Manet that reclaimed her manner of painting and her image of herself simultaneously. And it spoke directly to the critics' repeated address to the "femininity" of her style of "palette and brush" – which they said was "pretty," "delicate," "subtle," charming and seductive, refined and amorphous, and very eighteenth century. The concentration on brushwork was a signature of Morisot criticism, nowhere more acute than in her exhibition of 1880, with her series of Rococo bouquets on the subject of the toilette.

This was also a moment of specifically focused dialogue between two exhibitions, in which Manet and Morisot marked him/herself as distinct from the other within the same topos and handling. In both *Before the Mirror* and *Woman Reading* Manet's manner of facture is strikingly like Morisot's, especially close to the handling of *Summer, Winter,* and *Woman Dressed for the Ball* at the Impressionist exhibition. But the cataloguing of different kinds of painterly gesture that goes on in Manet's *Before the Mirror* is not evident in Morisot's *Woman at Her Toilette.* Instead, Morisot's airy, light-handed facture retreats from objecthood along with the body it portrays; it flees the glance it solicits, dissolving and disembodying itself before the eyes, marking itself and the world of *bibeloterie* it represents with the signs of fragility, incorporeality, and unpossessability, seeking to situate itself in a private world of eroticized decorative effects apart from the domain of the sexual commodity. In spite of its taking its place in a public exhibition space, it implies an intensely private, self-enclosed vantage-point on the themes of *maquillage* and the toilette, a refuge from rather than a confrontation with the libertine "male gaze."

It was otherwise with Manet's paintings, both at La Vie Moderne and afterwards. Sewn with Morisot's floral facture, equally self-reflexive in their deconstruction of their femininity effects, equally in argument with the commodified *cocotterie* of his own *Nana,* nonetheless both his female fashion-consumer (*Woman Reading*) and his female self-fashioner (*Before the Mirror*) produce themselves before the eyes of a consuming audience that they simultaneously implicate and frustrate. They do so to different degrees, the one situating itself in public and the other in the private space of the boudoir, but both are inscribed with the graphic codes of illustrated magazines produced for the consumption of men and women alike, and both engage the voyeuristic perusal that Morisot's paintings exclude. One later painting, the so-called *Modiste* of 1881 (fig. 135), picks up Morisot's blossom-strewn brushwork again (it was only one of many to do so), while also speaking directly to the ambiguity of Manet's position(s) on the topics of trollop and toilette, sexual commodity and fashion consumerism, and the double valence of his facture.

The Modiste was never exhibited during Manet's lifetime. But had Manet finished it in time for his exhibition at La Vie Moderne, it surely would have qualified as an entry in the show. It was a continuation of the theme of *Nana, Before the Mirror* and the *Woman Fastening Her Garter,* belonging, with the pastel *Woman in the Tub* (fig. 136), to a sequence cataloguing the important moments in a woman's toilette, in which a woman fashions herself and produces her femininity, either implicitly or explicitly under the gaze of a man. Built into *The Modiste,* however, was the possibility of a double reading that was not available in other pictures of the series. The woman in the painting is labeled a milliner because of the hats and hat stands before her and the black bonnet nearest her, removed from its stand, into which her hand is sunk, as if to shape its crown from within its satin-lined interior.[52] But at the same time, she is in a state of deshabille that suggests a boudoir and a hat-buyer or hat-owner, as much as a shop and a hat-maker. Behind and around her stretches a flower-vined wallpaper ground reminiscent of Morisot's boudoir-ensconced *Woman at Her Toilette.* Through her black lace shawl the icing-pink edge of a corset is glimpsed; above it is an expanse of neck and chest reminiscent of *Before the Mirror,* with one pentimentoed patch of pink and cream skin extending over the black *barbouillage* of the shawl, reversing the order of flesh and cloth, and recalling Baudelaire's *"bijou rose et noir"* of eighteen years before; below is an indeterminately sketched in skirt that looks to be a petticoat. If *The Modiste* is a modiste, she is a remarkably undressed one.

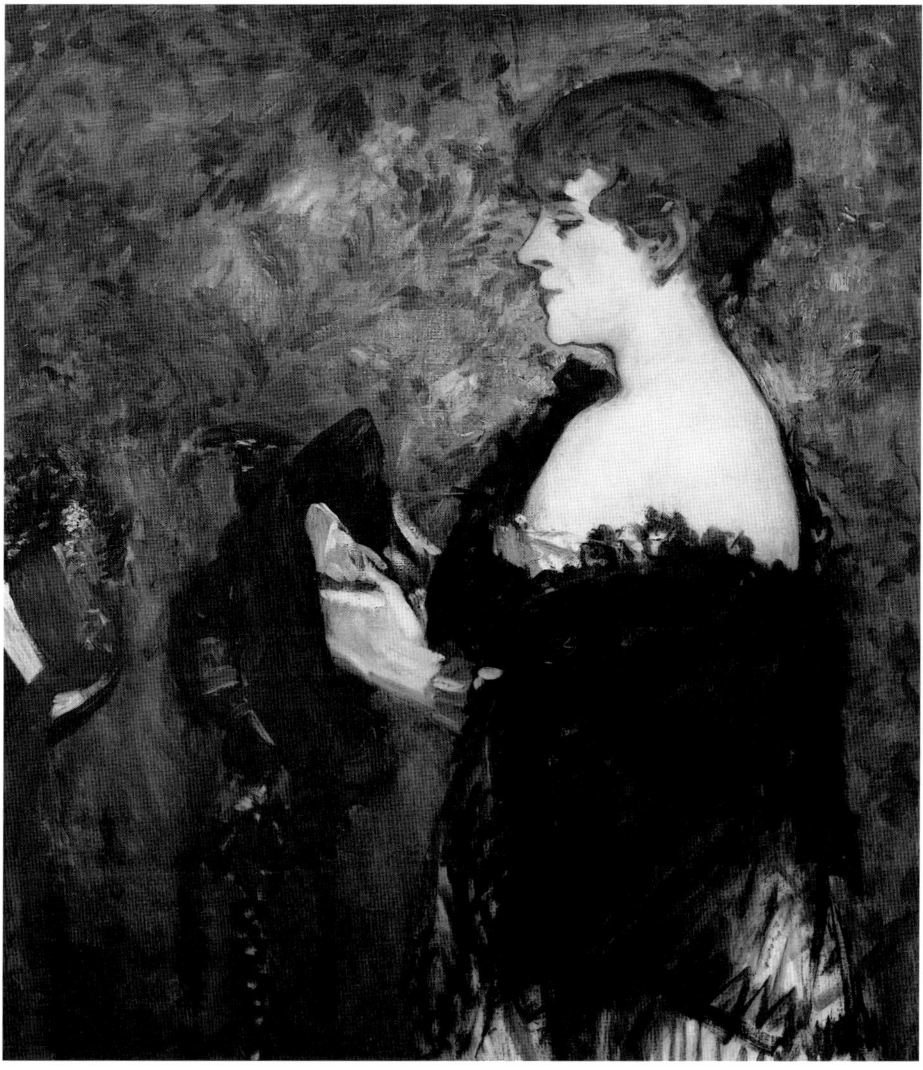

135   Edouard Manet, *At the Milliner's (The Modiste)*, 1881, oil on canvas, 85.1 × 73.7 cm. The Fine Arts Museums of San Francisco, Mildred Anna Williams Collection.

Thus *The Modiste* hesitates between two positions – producer and consumer of female fashion, and of femininity itself. Neither of these positions associated itself with the respectable, bourgeois end of the spectrum promoted by *La Vie Moderne*, to which Morisot adhered. But *The Modiste*'s alternation between those two options complicates her status as an erotic spectacle and a classed object of the gaze, layering together a producer's gesture with a consumer's space in which one finds, not one object of commodified delectation, but two: the woman's body, at once veiled and exposed, and the doubled hats next to her. In a progression running from the black-framed chest with its bit of pink sandwiched between skin and fabric, through the gold bangle on the wrist with its

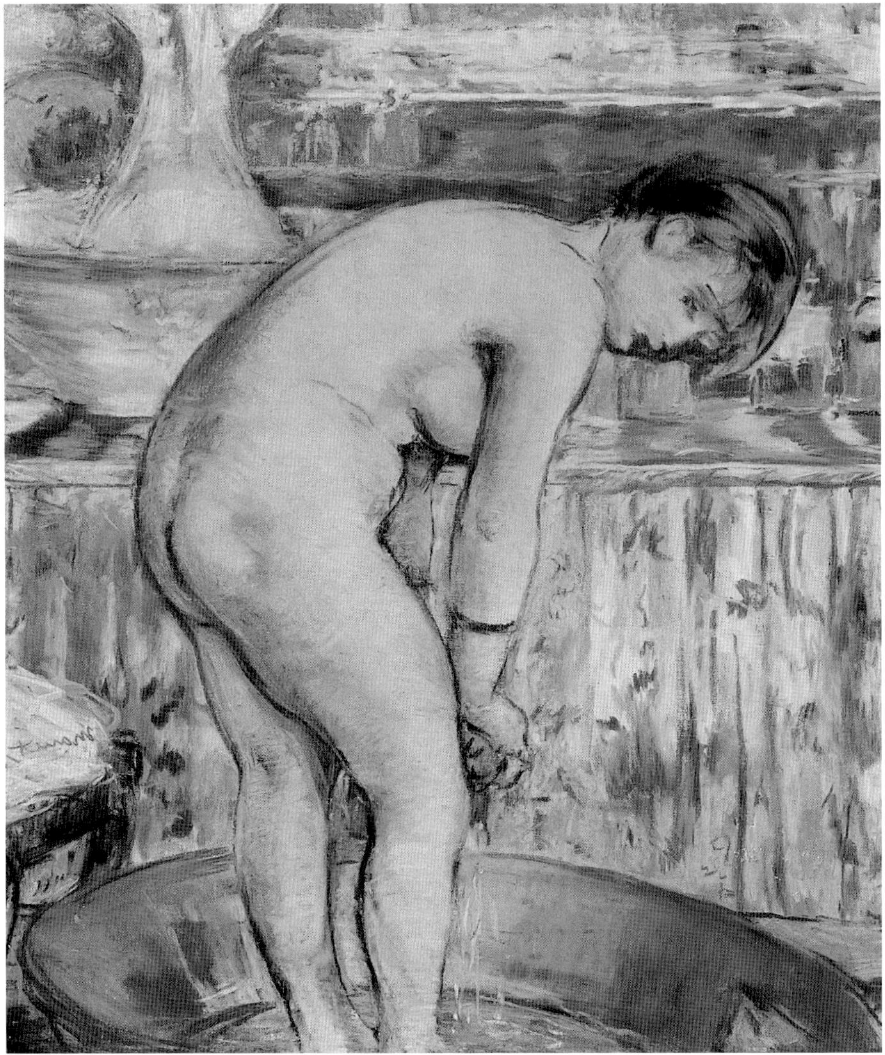

136   Edouard Manet, *Woman in the Tub*, 1878–79, pastel on cardboard, 55 × 45 cm. Musée du Louvre, Cabinet des Dessins, Paris.

prominently factured highlight, to the briefly sketched hand submerged in the black-painted hat, matched by the quick stroke of flesh pigment indicating the thumb of the other hand – together suggesting the erotic symbolism of the hat with marvelous panache – finishing in the sash of red paint that simultaneously marks the flower-decorated straw bonnet at left and the bottom left corner of the painting itself, *The Modiste* lays out its own process of production, along with the choices offered to the consumer of the picture: two confections made of paint, a woman and a hat, a body and an accessory. Suggesting that femininity emerges out of precisely this relay of facture and effect, this circle of production and consumption, *The Modiste* joins the "male gaze" to the pleasures of the feminine supplement.

There is an instructive similarity between the black-outlined rendering of *The Modiste*'s profile and the most naked of Manet's toilette series, the *Woman in the Tub*, whose roughed in contours enclose fleshly contents without much appeal to the eye, or reward for its perusal; as if stripping the female body of its fashionable coverings and accessories inevitably brought with it a withholding of pleasure, if not outright "devenustation." For Manet the naked female body was not the prime locus of painterly or visual pleasure; rather it is found in ornament, in everything around the body, everywhere but the body itself. It is there that Manet disseminates *jouissance*.[53] *The Modiste* is no exception. Pointing back to the show at La Vie Moderne, and with it to Manet's longstanding appropriation of Morisot's signature manner of producing femininity, and forward to the *Bar at the Folies-Bergère*, with its own imbrication of the spaces of consumer and commodity, *The Modiste* is at once a deliberate perplexing of the scopophilic formula and an assertion of Manet's allegiance to the supplemental space of femininity, in which modern painting is matched to the fashioning of modern woman. And it is a fairly direct statement about the double gendering of Manet's facture, its enfolding within itself of the opposite meanings associated with Morisot's scattered-blossom brushwork and Guys's modern painter graphisms, and the positions on femininity assigned to each.

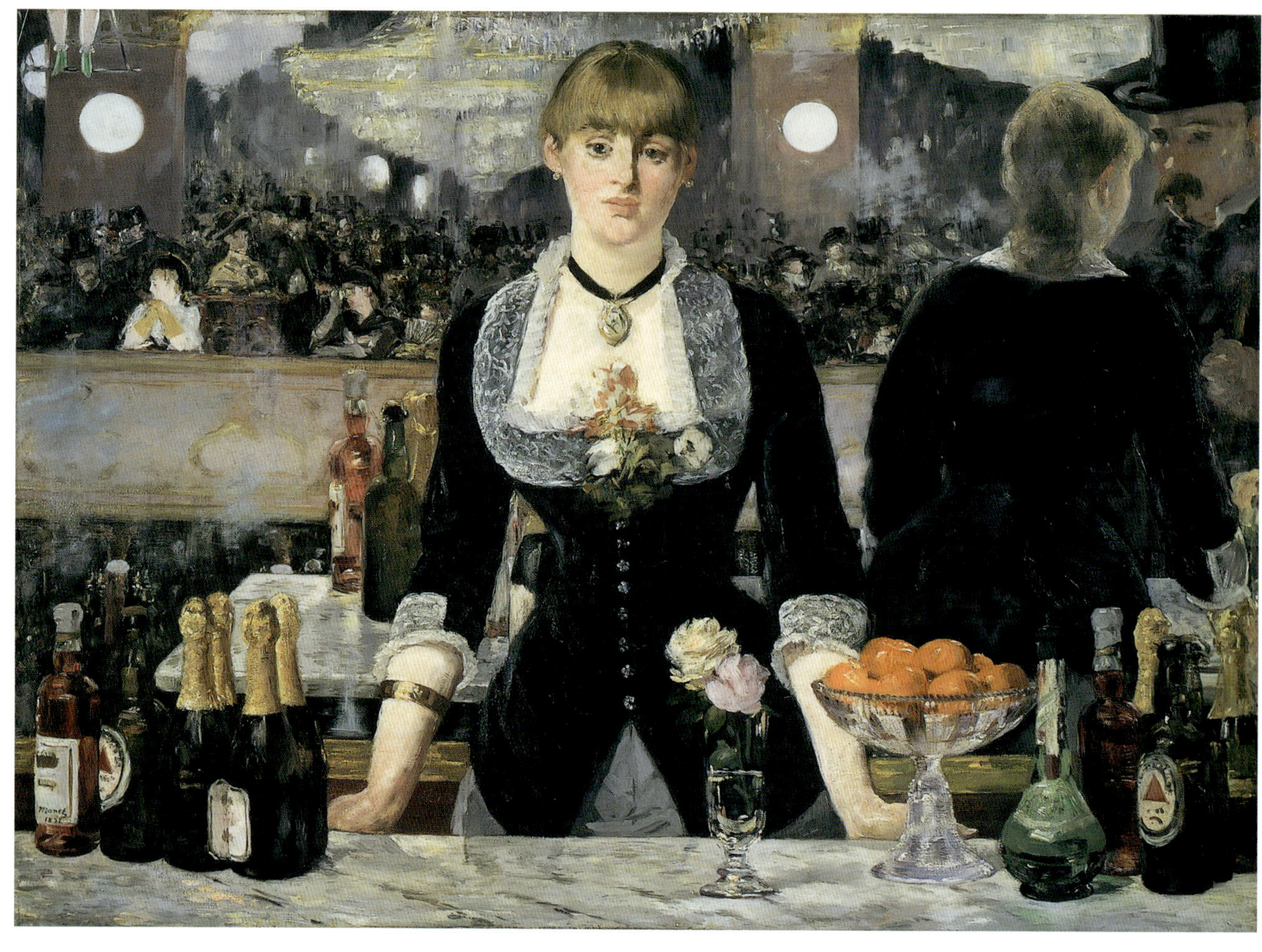

137 Edouard Manet, *Bar at the Folies-Bergère*, 1881–82, oil on canvas, 96 × 130 cm. Courtauld Institute Gallery, London.

Chapter Ten

FINALE:

THE *BAR AT THE FOLIES-BERGÈRE*

Two years after the show at La Vie Moderne, Manet declared he was a "philosopher of the Folies-Bergère": he showed the *Bar at the Folies-Bergère* (fig. 137) at what was to be his last Salon. In that painting, which he exhibited with the fashion-plate profile of Jeanne Demarsy entitled *Spring*, he wove together many of the strands that had run through his work at La Vie Moderne – café culture and its *consommations*, a mirror with a reflection, and the fashion consumerism of the modern woman. Manet also summarized a longstanding preoccupation with the genre of still-life painting, which for him had never been a Salon genre and with a few exceptions had until then remained unexhibited. Moreover, he renewed the force of his earliest fixation on a woman's fixed, perturbing, outwardly gazing face. And finally, he brought together the conflicting signatures, masculine and feminine, Manetian and Morisotian, of his twenty-year-long career in painting. It was almost as if Manet knew his death was approaching, for in the *Bar at the Folies-Bergère* he gathered his strength one last time to paint a triumphant puzzle of a painting with the uncanny presence of a doppelgänger. In the Salon that painting proclaimed Manet's interest in the effects of modern opticality for all to see, but it did so in such a way as to distinguish itself from the naturalized optical unities of Impressionist painting, and indeed to pronounce the difference of painting – the difference of his painting, and the difference of painting from the world it both reflects and manufactures – in the very figure of difference, that of modern woman. Doubled, split, and conjoined with her reflection and her masculine counterpart, who appears in the mirror as a top-hatted, funereally garbed, spookily hollow-eyed stranger – a modern Grim Reaper – she, like the ghost of *Olympia* past, introduces the phantasmatic into the spectacular countertop realm of the commodity.[1] She stands as the specter of Manet's modernity – of the peculiarly doubled, dialogic structure of Manet's different modernism. In short, she was Manet's final Manette.

Back in 1864, Manet had had a particularly intensive brush with several kinds of still-life painting: the kitchen still life, the meal and dessert piece, and flower painting.[2] Only the last showed up unmodified on the counter of the *Bar at the Folies-Bergère*; otherwise, the domestic domains of kitchen and dining room are replaced by the commercial space

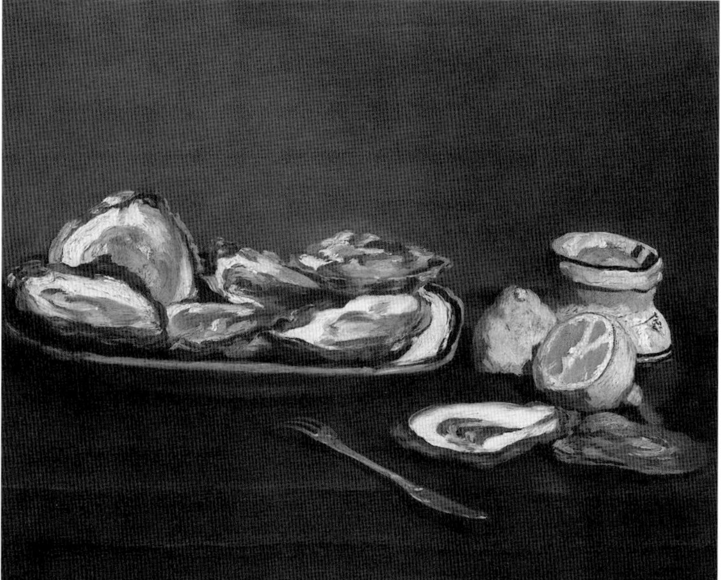

138   Edouard Manet, *Oysters,*
1862, oil on canvas, 39.2 ×
46.8 cm. National Gallery of
Art, Washington, D.C. Gift of
the Adele R. Levy Fund, Inc.

of the refreshment stand, as if Manet sought an appropriate still-life subject for the great markethall that was the Salon.[3] But since the private spaces of food preparation and consumption are the traditional ones of the still-life genre – and the earlier sites of Manet's dialogue with the museum of still-life painting – and since they bear dialectically upon the *Bar*'s zone of the commodity, a consideration of the countertop still-life of the *Bar at the Folies-Bergère* must go back to the beginning, and start with Manet's early inhabiting of the genre's household realm.[4]

Manet's rendering of the scene of preparation of a *pot-au-feu* of fish, with its carp, eel, oysters, and red mullet (fig. 139), is perhaps his most famous. A reinscription of his first still life, the Dutch-referenced *Oysters* (fig. 138) painted in 1862 and given to Suzanne Leenhoff, the *Fish (Still Life with Carp)* closes off the *de rigueur* lemon at right, substitutes a formulaic still life knife (which might be a cook's oyster shucker) for the diner's oyster fork, and resituates the pile of oysters in the kitchen, throwing it together with other pieces of marooned marine life to take different advantage of its combination of matte and glossy, rocky grit and wet viscosity, exterior lumpishness and interior opalescence, enhancing the former to the point of utter amorphousness and redirecting the latter back toward the literal oiliness of oil paint, remaking the crisp white dining-room napkin so beloved of Dutch still-life painting in the unshaped form of dirty kitchen linen complete with fishy stain, and debasing the Chardinian kitchen of such still lifes as the famous *Ray* (see fig. 69), which is not even to mention its reuse of Chardin's favorite copper stockpot, already used repeatedly by Bonvin and others. By these means it materializes the scenario of food production, with which it identifies its own painter's "cuisine."

Chardin's still lifes were themselves debasements of the French still-life tradition of the aristocratic supper, with its elaborate pyramids of fruits and sweets. Manet took that low-

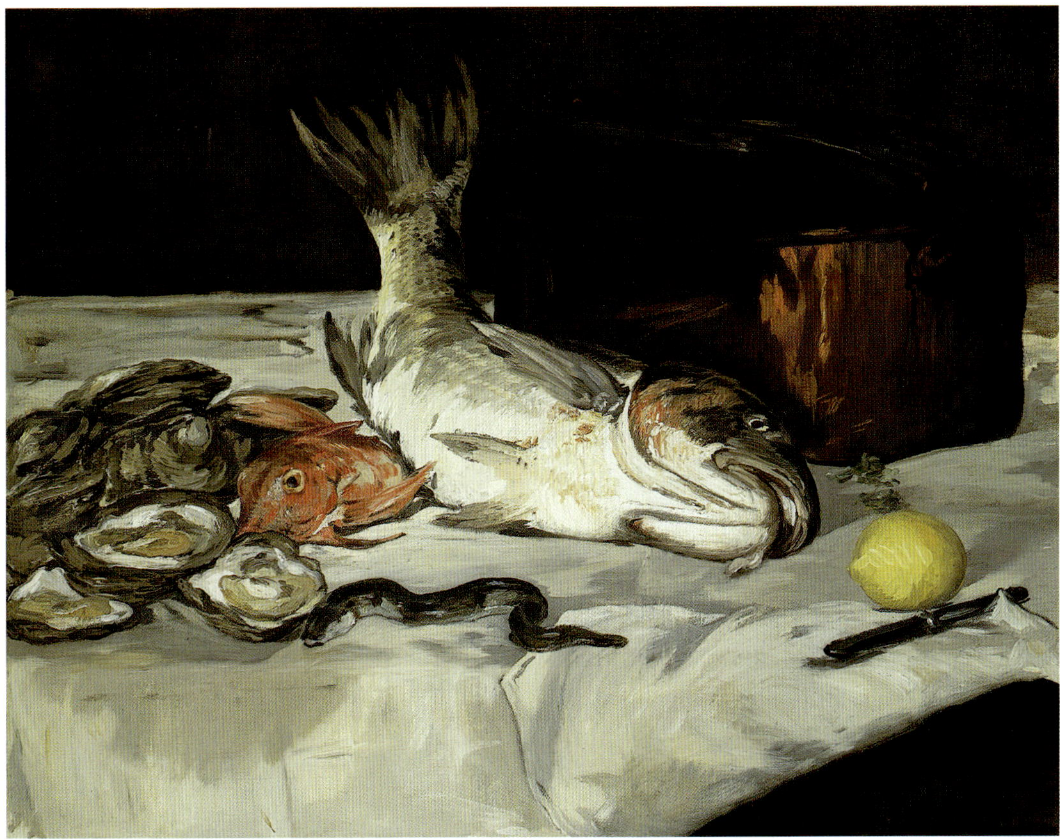

139　Edouard Manet, *Fish (Still Life with Carp)*, 1864, oil on canvas, 73.4 × 92.1 cm. The Art Institute of Chicago. Mr. and Mrs. Lewis Larned Coburn Memorial Collection, 1942.311.

ering one step further, while expanding and complicating the inter-still-life dialogue to include seventeenth-century Dutch painting, the Spanish *bodegone*, and the nineteenth-century Chardin revival, as well as other non-still-life paintings of his own. (*Olympia* comes to mind, with its still life of unclean female flesh displayed upon white bedlinen, like the contemporaneous *The Dead Christ and the Angels*, with its similar *nature morte* disposition of dead meat and off-color skin against pristine white sheet, not to mention the serpent at Christ's feet, recalled in the eel of the *Fish* still life.) Descending to the below-stairs space of the house devoted to female service and bearing witness to the low production that goes into the *haut bourgeois* meal, the *Fish* constitutes a peculiarly literal meditation on the unsublimated materiality of both food and paint. Between the greasy dishwater color rendering the brine-dampened cloth beneath the oysters, to the coagulated build-up of gray, black, buff, and white pigment rendering open oysters swimming in their liquid, the similar brown-tinged black and white of the slimy eel, the broken red marks rendering the scaliness of the mullet, the thick application of white paint yielding the carp's slick underbelly against the grays, taupes, and browns of back and fins, the red traces of blood around its gullet, and the prominent impasto of the copper highlights on the pot, illusionistically different from and yet materially continuous with the pigmented notation of mullet surface and carp blood, the *Fish* links the oil-suspended colors of the paint matter out of which it is produced to the oil and ooze of the raw substances of a seafood dinner in the making. As such, it takes up the challenge of Chardin's *Ray*, with its delicate balance between disgust and desire, the repellent and the appealing, the visceral and the spectacular. But while Chardin's *Ray* is redeemed by its optical play of gleam and glisten, Manet's *Fish* refuses that limpid self-transcendance in its frank display of the lipid base shared by fish and paint. At the same time the *Fish*, with its piled on array of fatty deposits, retains its appeal to the eye, which it still sets in erotic tension with the involuntary distaste induced by the sight (and associated touch, taste, and smell) of abject matter. This it does in order to narrow radically the distance between the literal and the illusionistic, to force and reverse the connection that lies at the root of still-life illusionism between the hungers of the eye and those of nose, mouth, fingertips, skin, and stomach.

The series to which the *Fish (Still Life with Carp)* belongs, which includes an 1864 pair of a *Still Life with Fish and Shrimp* and a *Red Mullet and Eel* and an 1866 *Salmon* (figs. 140, 141), makes explicit the still life's place in the circle of production and consumption, economic exchange, illusionistic equivalence, and bodily appetite. Where the *Fish* belongs to the kitchen's prepatory table, the items in the *Fish and Shrimp* seem fresh from market, still lined with grocer's greenery and a wrapper. Meanwhile the *Salmon* on its platter represents a full-blown meal, replete with decanter, flask and goblet, a reopened, peel-curled lemon in a bowl on one side, on the other a complementary arrangement of cup, corner-curled tablecloth, and projecting knife handle, and finally a second knife handle back on the right, disposed parallel to the horizon line of the table, countering the orthogonal of its left-hand mate and underlining the spatial grid worked out on the painting's flat surface. The *Salmon*, further, cleans up the linen of the *Fish*, substituting its more elegant left-corner curl for the latter's flattened out flip of cloth at the right. Thus the seafood series of the *Fish* situates still-life painting within the

140 Edouard Manet, *Still Life with Fish and Shrimp*, 1864, oil on canvas, 45 × 71 cm. Norton Simon Art Foundation, Pasadena, Calif.

141 Edouard Manet, *Salmon*, 1866, oil on canvas, 73.5 × 94 cm. Shelburne Museum, Vermont.

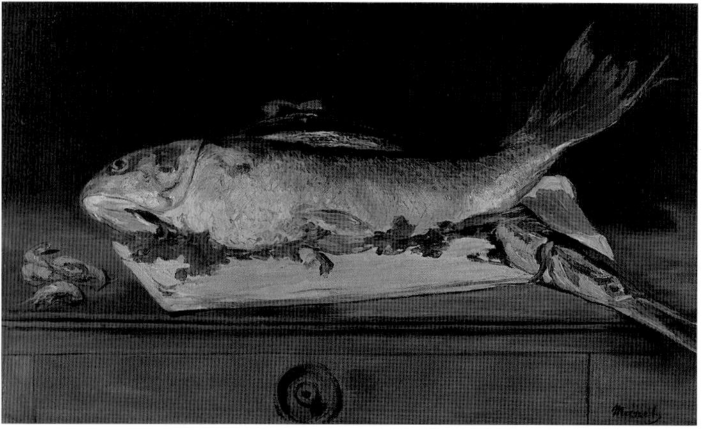

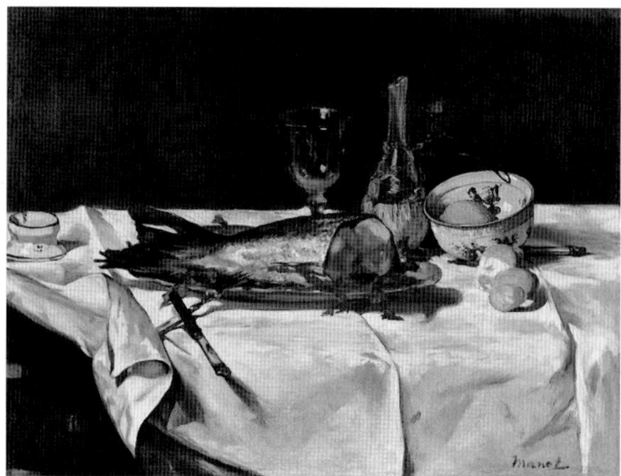

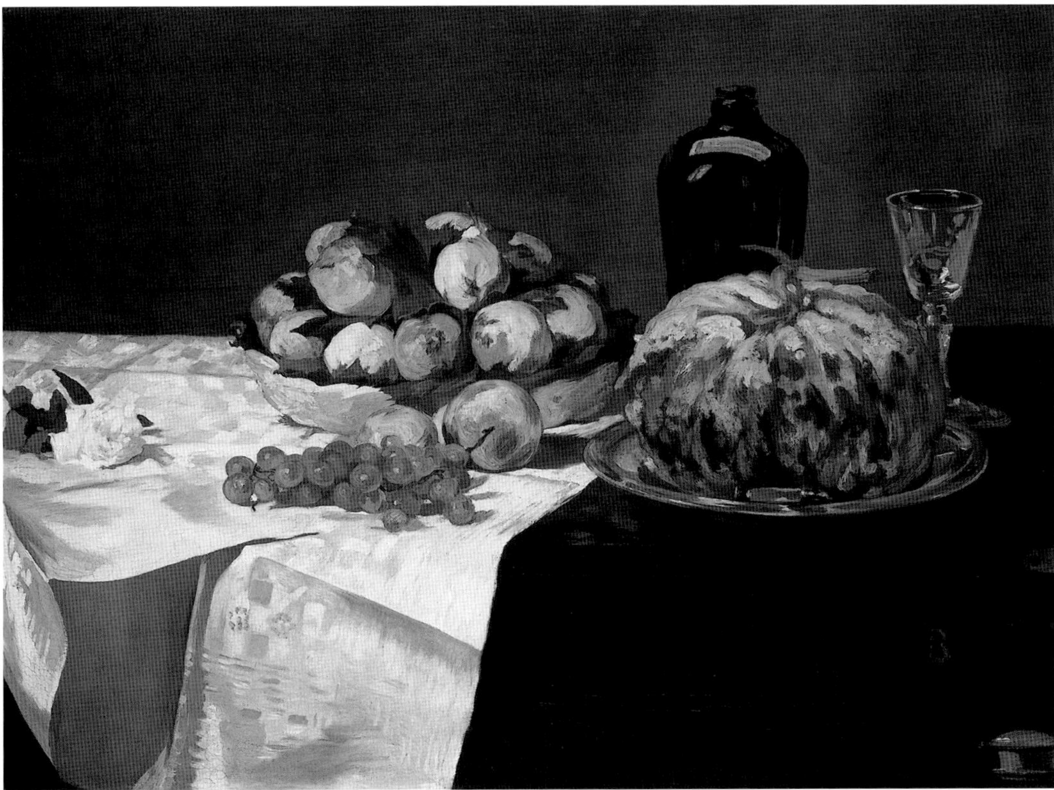

142   Edouard Manet, *Still Life with Melon and Peaches*, c.1866, oil in canvas, 68.3 × 91 cm. National Gallery of Art, Washington, D.C. Gift of Eugene and Agnes E. Meyer.

domestic cycle of buying, cooking, table-setting, and eating that the genre usually either assumes or erases; within that cycle it circles the connection between the material base of its own illusionism and the material acts of transaction and production underpinning the civilization of the meal and its elevation of brute animal ingestion into the refinements of human consumption.

The *ne plus ultra* of the sublimation of food and feeding into decor, delicacy, and supplemental social grace is the dessert. And so, Manet rounds out the seafood meal with a variety of fruit courses, all of them Chardin done in Manet's "handwriting."[5] One of them (fig. 142) picks up the back-from-market pile of another 1864 still life (depicting an unopened melon with almonds and other fruit), while elaborating the arrangement and finishing the meal of that year's *Salmon*, to which it is related in numerous ways. For the *Salmon*'s wine glass, wine bottle, and corked flask, the *Melon and Peaches* substitutes liqueur flask and aperitif glass, rearranged so that the glass closes the composition at right. For the *Salmon*'s bisected fish on a platter, and its two lemons, one closed in a bowl, the other open and outside it, it substitutes an uncut, silver-plattered melon, a ceramic pie-dish of unbroached peaches, and an arrangement of two uneaten peaches and a bunch of grapes outside the dish, two loose and the rest on the stem, continuing

Chardin's habit of pairing contained and massed items with single or twinned specimens outside the bounds of the container and its mass. For the *Salmon*'s two knives, it substitutes one silver knife dug into the silver platter holding the melon, barely differentiated from the encircling rim, hugging the edge of the table. For the *Salmon*'s table covering, it substitutes a check-woven damask cloth that might also be a napkin, whisked off the right side of the table to announce the clearing of the table at the end of the meal, at the same time revealing the Chardinian keyhole situated on the other side of the *Salmon*, and replacing its knife-echoing curl of linen with a larger loop of starched fabric that aligns its crisp crease and cool hollow with the picture's edge and corner – flatness tweaked into depth, volume, and void rather than projection per se. And for the cup that terminates the *Salmon*'s composition at left, the *Melon and Peaches* substitutes the grace note of an elegantly deposited blossom whose blush-tinged cream color vies delicately with the bluish white of the linen. That blossom refers to Manet's florals of 1864, along with Fantin-Latour's signature combinations of fruit and flowers, and as it does so it asserts a further connection – between the supplemental dessert and the decorative flower piece, with its exclusively optical appeal and its utter detachment from the digestive end of consumption. Thus it completes the food chain that begins with buying and cooking and ends with looking and enjoying.

Very much the same blossom is found in the 1864 *Vase of Peonies*, not to mention the *Stem of Peonies with Shears* (see fig. 87). In the *Vase of Peonies* the fallen blossom functions as a kind of signature next to the mound of fallen petals that looks at once like a floral answer to the oysters of the *Fish* and the almonds of *Fruit on a Table*, and a drift of stray facture, brushstrokes detached from their bouquet and discarded beneath it, signifiers come undone from their signified, yet tied more tightly together in the pure equivalence of paint mark to flower petal. For its part, the *Stem of Peonies with Shears* speaks of the round of consumption and production to which the flower piece belongs: the acts of gardening and arranging, pruning and gathering, cutting, choosing, discarding, and composing that go first into the consumption of the garden's products and then into the hand's production of the bouquet for the consumption of the eye.[6] That flowers are removed from their original garden context in order to make first the bouquet and then the painting is pronounced in the stark isolation of the *Stem of Peonies* and the equivalence it suggests between pruning shears and paint brush: once more Manet links the producerly act of painting with feminine gestures and female spaces of production.

Of course, kitchening and gardening are no more the same order of domestic activity than the cook and the lady of the house are the same class of femininity. That is a point about which another 1864 *Peonies with Shears* (fig. 143) seems to have something to say. For this version of the same floral motif, with its pendant stem and fuller rendering of clipping shears projecting like the ubiquitous still-life knife over a Chardinian edge, is in intimate dialogue with another kitchen-invoking motif favored in the French still-life tradition, and that is the hunt piece, with its hanging rabbits and fowl ready for the stew pot (fig. 144). Here, the female act of pruning explicitly replaces the male act of hunting as the material activity with which painting associates itself, while at the same time decor puts itself in place of viscera and venison, the labor of supplementation in lieu of the work of killing, gutting, stewing, and serving, such that once again the civilized delectation of the eye replaces the gutteral nourishment of the

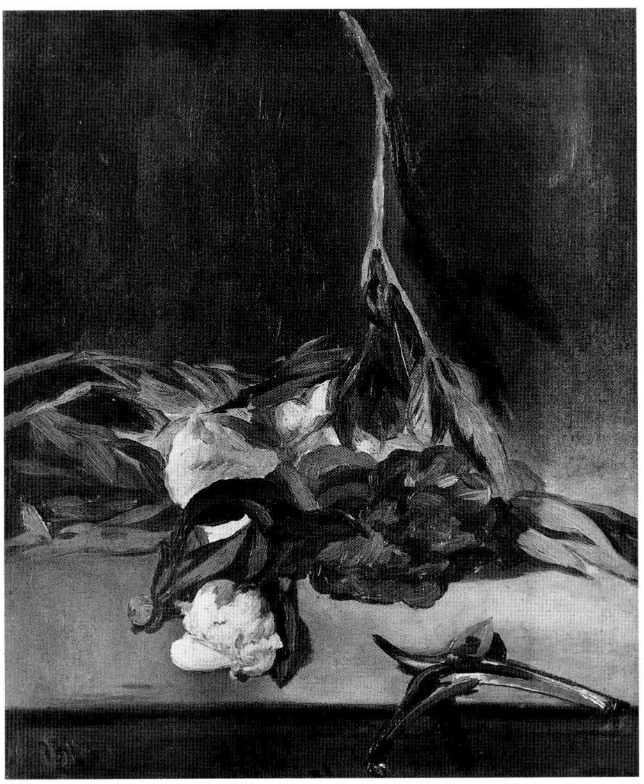

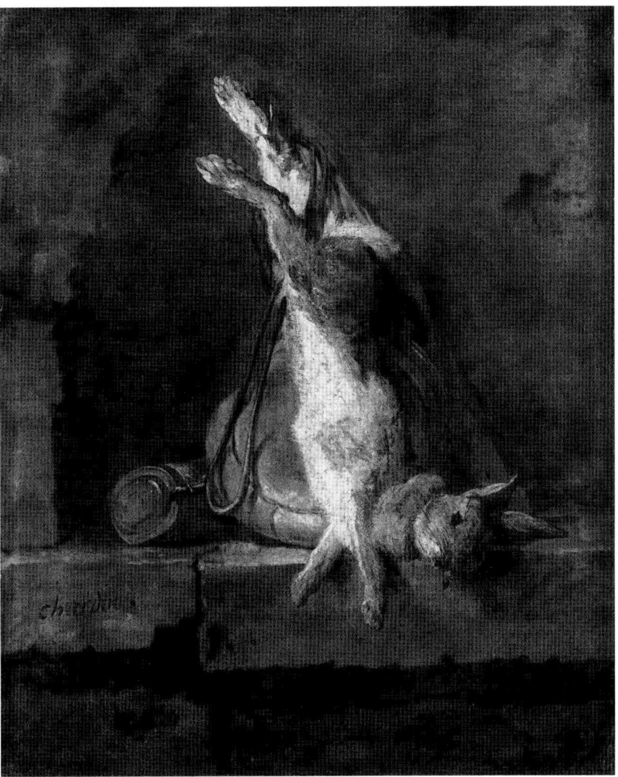

143   Edouard Manet, *Stem of Peonies with Shears*, 1864, oil on canvas, 31 × 46.5 cm. Musée d'Orsay, Paris.

144   Jean Baptiste Siméon Chardin, *Hare with Powder Flask and Game Bag*, c.1727, oil on canvas, 81 × 65 cm. Musée du Louvre, Paris.

body that underpins it. The dead-rabbit palimpsest of the *Peonies* all but states that underpinning – precisely in the dialogic masking of it, such that its repression is overt, structured into Manet's conversation with Chardin.

A half dozen years later, Manet came back to his Chardinian base more insistently and literally than he had before. His *Brioche* of 1870 directly quoted Chardin's *Brioche* (figs. 145, 146), which was part of the La Caze donation to the Louvre the year before. At the same time it is a kind of catalogue of the Chardinian fruit motifs to which Manet kept returning, combined in a single, modern still life and updated to the nineteenth century. It picks up the blossom deposited at the skirt of Eva Gonzalès, makes it into a rose, and poses it atop the brioche of the still life's title. It replaces the silver-handled knife with a dainty bone-handled one, substitutes an elaborate Louis XV ormolu table for Chardin's plain stone surface, and finishes off the composition at left front with a red-lacquer chinoiserie box of candies with its lid atilt to match the grapes and knife at the right. Another half dozen years later, Manet returned to the theme of the brioche, setting it once next to the renewed gustatory motif of the plate of oysters from the beginning of his career.[7] But in the 1870 picture there is no question about the brioche's supplemental rather than digestive function; it is emphatic in its liaison between dessert and

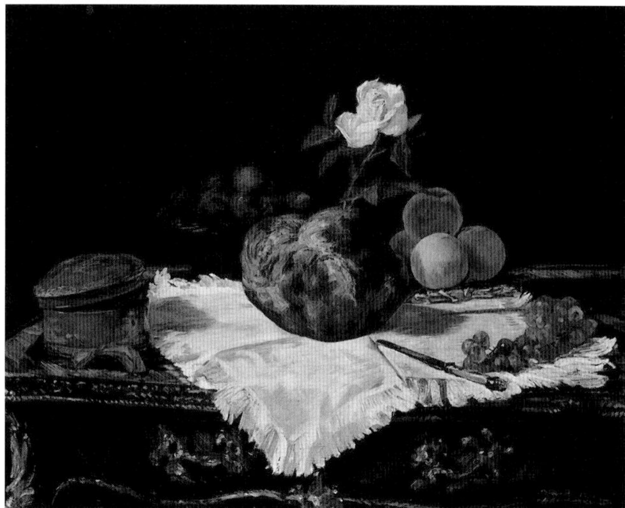

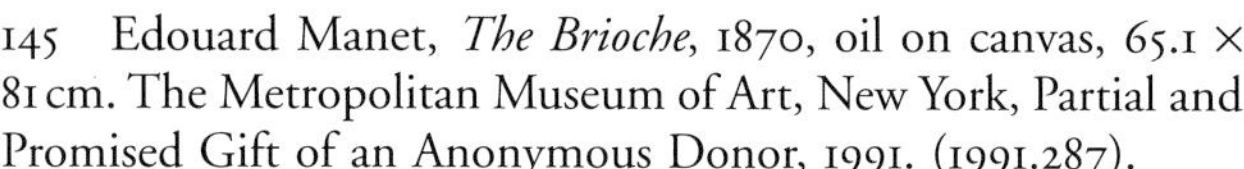

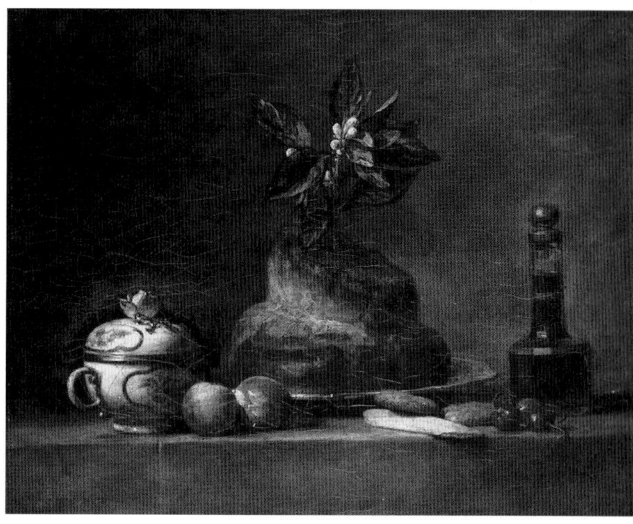

145   Edouard Manet, *The Brioche*, 1870, oil on canvas, 65.1 ×
81 cm. The Metropolitan Museum of Art, New York, Partial and
Promised Gift of an Anonymous Donor, 1991. (1991.287).

146   Jean-Baptiste-Siméon Chardin, *The Brioche* or *A Dessert*,
1763, oil on canvas, 47 × 56 cm. Musée du Louvre, Paris.

decoration, sweets and social graces, which provide the terms of its upmarket Second
Empire response to Chardin.

In 1882, after the completion and exhibition of the *Bar of the Folies-Bergère*, an ill,
house-bound Manet painted more than a dozen marble-topped flower pieces, isolating
what was just one feature of the *Bar*'s still life, varying the vase, goblet, and glass, the
bouquet's composition, and the flowers – red, pink, and white roses, peonies, lilacs, pinks,
and clematis – but always keeping in close, repetitive contact with Chardin's one known
floral piece (figs. 147, 148).[8] Executed under conditions of confinement, visitation, and
gift-receiving, this series completes the dialogism and decorative logic of Manet's still-
life production, the substitution of optical for bodily consumption, the narrowed equation between facture and floral arrangement, and the situation of Manet's painting within
the space of femininity. From two roses in a slender champagne glass; lilacs, lilacs and
roses, and a more varied arrangement including a rose and some violets, all in the same
low crystal vase used repeatedly; a mass of moss roses in a taller, round-bellied, slender-
waisted vase; a bouquet of peonies in an oval, gilt-edged vase used only once; bouquets
of roses and lilacs, pinks and clematis, and sometimes tulips, all in a tall squared vase
etched with a delicate dotted pattern; to a couple of bouquets in a dragon-etched,
octagonal vase, these floral still lifes catalogue the differentiated relationship between
painting and arrangement, and between paint and petal, color and flower, palette and
bouquet. All demonstrate the presentational quality that Manet's work had had since the
beginning, and all state the decorative, artifice-bound status of painting in the simplest
terms possible, punctuating the larger trend away from the corporeal and toward the
optical that marked his still-life practice all the way from 1862 to 1882. And all of them
play with a contrast between transparent (vase) and opaque (flower petals) that opens

onto the larger problematics of the relationship between illusionistic transparency and the colored opacity of paint.[9]

Manet's late florals are tied to two or three series, which went back at least to 1880, involving the still-life representation of single specimens or clusters; the serial rendition of behatted female heads and bodices; and the watercolor alternation between the two in studies and letters to female friends. The first of these series includes a single closed melon, a ham on a plate, one bundle of asparagus, one lone spear of asparagus, a pear and a pair of pears, an unopened lemon on a plate, an apple on a plate, several strewn apples, and more Chardinian fruit baskets, all done between 1880 and 1882. The paintings in this series bear directly on the countertop still life of the *Bar*. Reduced and minimal in their deployment of the means and ends of oil painting, they are all, each one of them, equally unbreached and self-enclosed, and barred from all consumption

147   Edouard Manet, *Roses in a Champagne Glass*, 1882, oil on canvas, 31 × 24 cm. Glasgow Museums: The Burrell Collection.

148   Edouard Manet, *Pinks and Clematis*, 1882, oil on canvas, 56 × 35 cm. Musée d'Orsay, Paris.

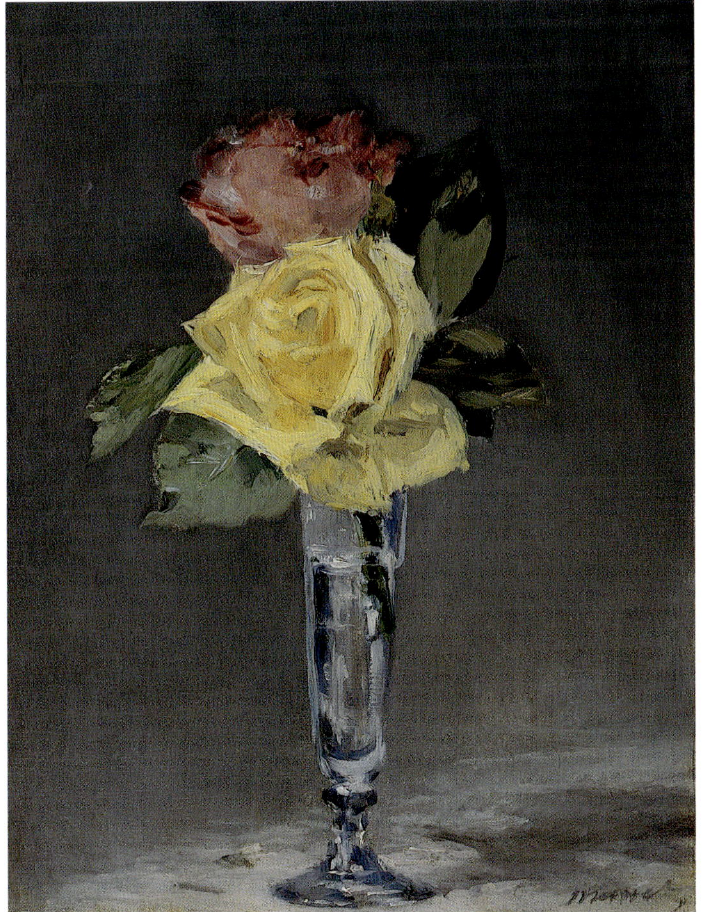

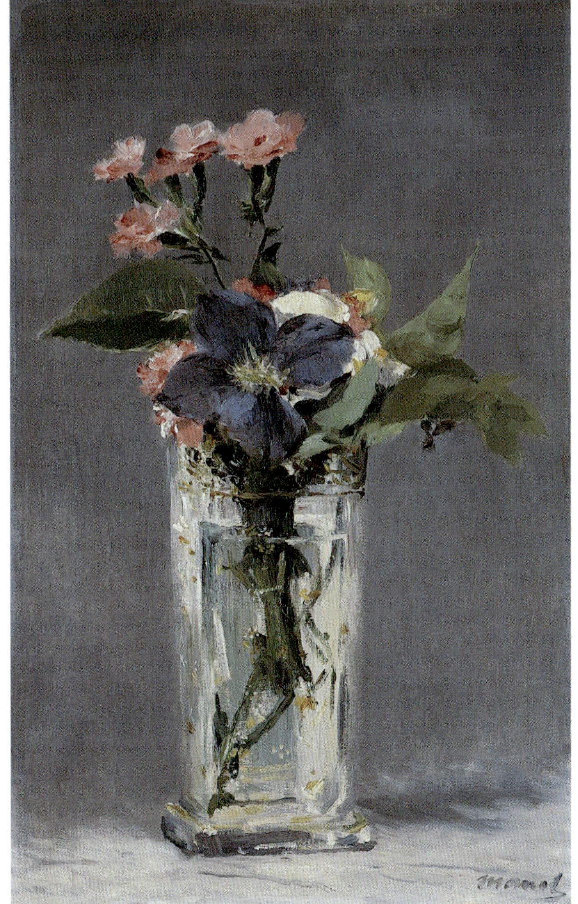

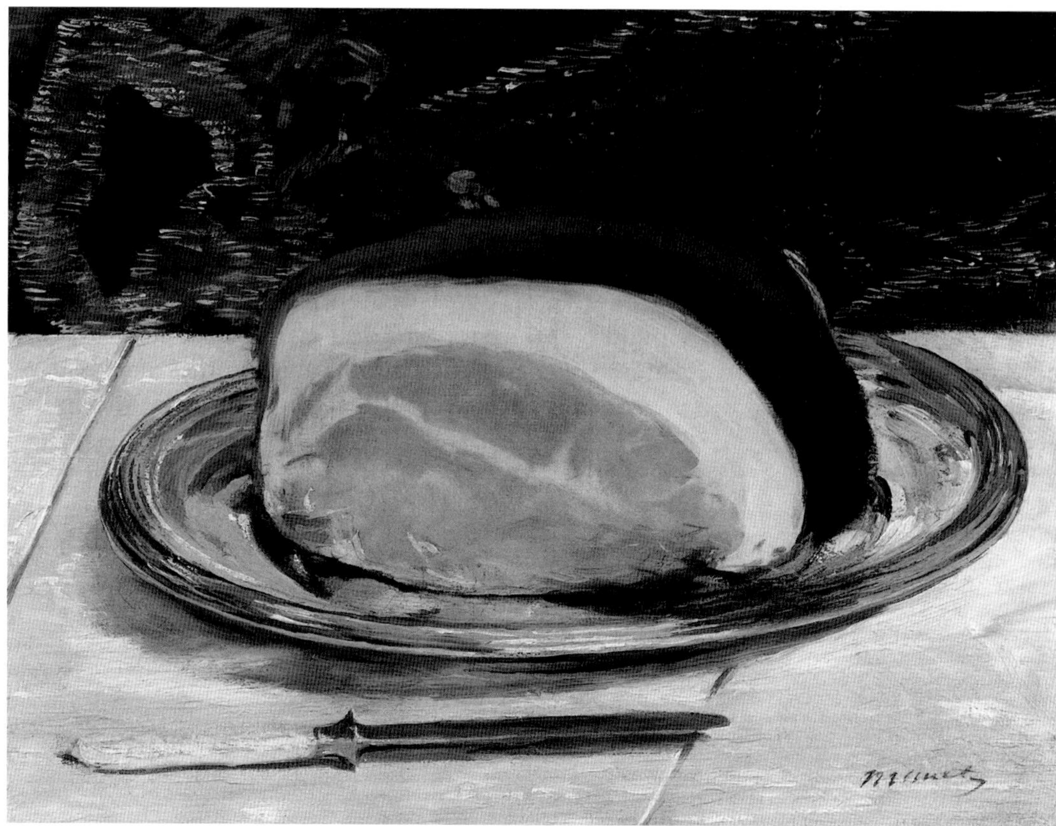

149   Edouard Manet, *Ham*, 1875, oil on canvas, 13 × 16 cm. Glasgow Museums: The Burrell Collection.

but that of the eye; each one proposes a simple, one-to-one equivalence between signifier and signified, painting and item. The *Ham* (fig. 149), for instance, reduces the elaborated scene of the meal found in Chardin-revival still lifes to one knife, one plate, one ham. Although its pink interior is visible, the ham is nevertheless locked away; it is not cut, will never be cut, and the horizontal knife before it can neither be wielded nor do any serious cutting. Instead, the whites that produce the ham's fat, the gleam on the silver platter, the tablecloth, and the bone handle of the knife are set before the eye for comparison, and the meeting between the white-covered horizontal of the table and the gilt-woven vertical plane of the wall is simplified, flattened, and sealed. Most importantly, the veining of the *Ham*'s meat is linked to the ornamental patterning of the screen behind it (the same crane-decorated screen as in *Nana*). Once more with emphasis, the *Ham* stresses the making of bodily sustenance into food for the eye, Nature's organic yield into pure decor, the artifice of interior decoration into the artifice of painting. It is one to one: ham to painting, picture plane to wall plane. And the circuit of signifier to signified is shortened, in the closer relation between brush and loom, oil medium, fat vein, and gilded thread upon which the *Ham* is founded.

For its part, the *Asparagus* (fig. 151) is significant for the role it played in a joke of Manet's concerning the question of value. As the story goes, upon sending the *Bundle*

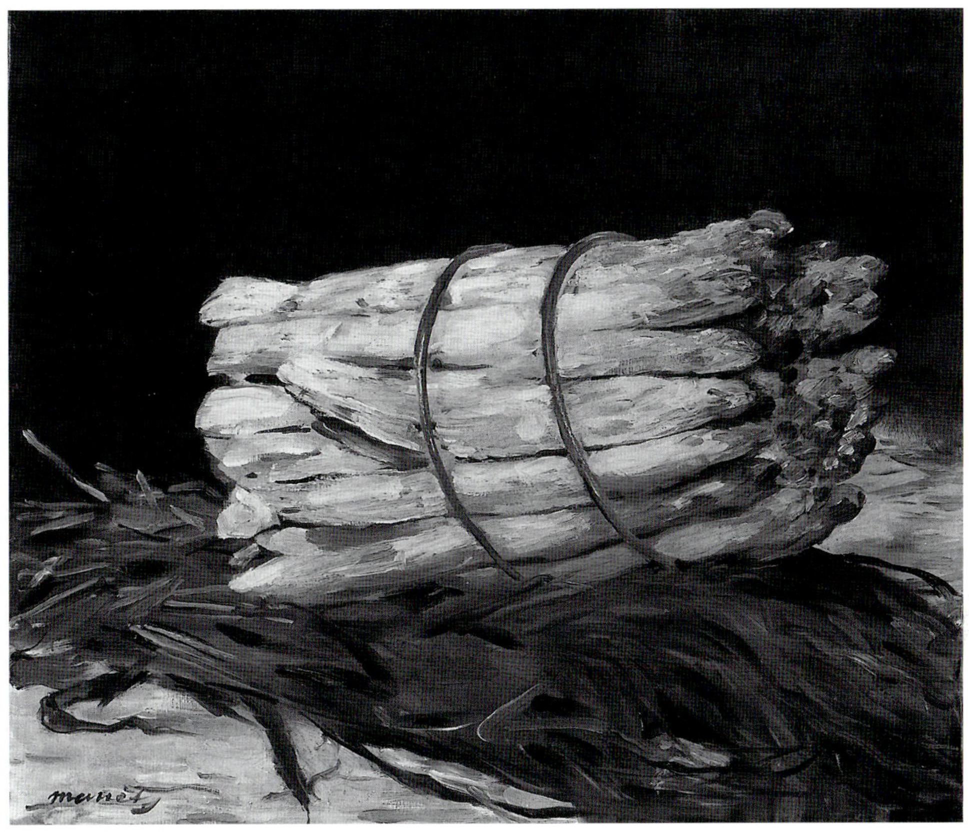

150   Edouard Manet, *Bundle of Asparagus*, 1880, oil on canvas, 46 × 55 cm. Wallraf-Richartz Museum, Cologne.

151   Edouard Manet, *Asparagus*, 1880, oil on canvas, 16.5 × 21.5 cm. Musée d'Orsay, Paris.

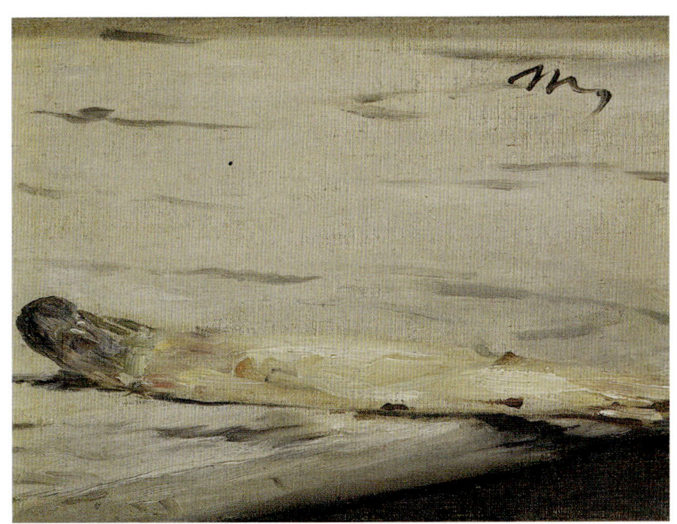

of Asparagus (fig. 150) to Charles Ephrussi, Manet received 200 francs more than the originally agreed price of 800 francs. Whereupon he painted and sent to Ephrussi the image of the single *Asparagus,* noting that there was one missing from the original bundle and thus implying that this little painting made up the difference, and Ephrussi now had his money's worth in painted asparagus.[10] Not unlike Manet's earlier 1872 still life of a bunch of violets sent to Berthe Morisot in lieu of violets themselves, the *Asparagus* plays wittily upon the question of illusionistic substitution, this time as it relates to exchange value. For in suggesting that real and painted asparagus were worth the same amount, and begging the question of whether the *Bundle of Asparagus* represents a single painted item or a plural bundle of countable, weighable, edible items, Manet made a mockery of much more than the relative price of vegetables and paintings. He also spoofed the valuation of the referent in illusionistic painting (particularly acute in the tradition of still-life painting, with its equation of the value of fine painting with that of finely worked luxury objects, and its staging of the painted surface's dialectic of fictive transparency and literal opacity), mounting a tongue-in-cheek demonstration of the interdependence of exchange value and painterly illusionism, and the system of equivalences of which they both partake.

The *Asparagus* interrupts that system, declaring its own paintedness. It tips up the illusionistic marble surface on which the asparagus rests until it is virtually equivalent to the plane of the canvas and the illusion of perpendicularity is almost entirely negated. (That illusion is marginally held onto by the dark lower right-hand corner and its establishment of slight obliquity, doubled in the opposing direction of the asparagus's equally slight oblique angle, its minimal shadow, and its barely broaching of the counter's edge, only to be cut short by the picture's edge.) Thus it shows that the means of creating an asparagus out of paint are not substantially different from those of painting a marble surface, and interferes with the transparency of illusionism and the operations of substitution that underlie its valuation, declaring the object of consumption to be not actually a vegetable but a piece of illusionistic painting. The *Asparagus* thus stands on its head the equation between a painting and an asparagus; it returns us to the worked ground of painterly value, and with it to the moment of painterly production; and it short-circuits the system of substitution, equivalence, and exchange that structures the valuation of illusionistic painting, as well as consumer culture at large. The commodity, after all, is painting – or better, that particular brand of painterly illusionism signed Manet.

Then there is the *Lemon* (fig. 152), which is like the single *Asparagus* both in its singleness and its lack of defining context. The *Lemon* on its pewter plate provides no clues at to whether its context is to be imagined as kitchen, dining room, café, or restaurant. The *Lemon* is a remark about closure. It looks back through a still-life tradition in which lemons figured repeatedly, almost always to signal use and consumption – the preparation, garnishing, and eating of meals.[11] But in its contextlessness and its emphatically unopened and unused state, the *Lemon* puts a period to a still-life tradition that was all about fictive consumption. This lemon is definitely not for actual, bodily consumption. By closing the lemon, the *Lemon* also closes itself off to still-life painting's illusionism of corporeal consumption and announces its own opacity as a piece of painting closed to any other uses but the optical. Thus the *Lemon*'s closure is analogous to the *Asparagus*'s interference with the operations of illusionistic transparency, substitution, and exchange.

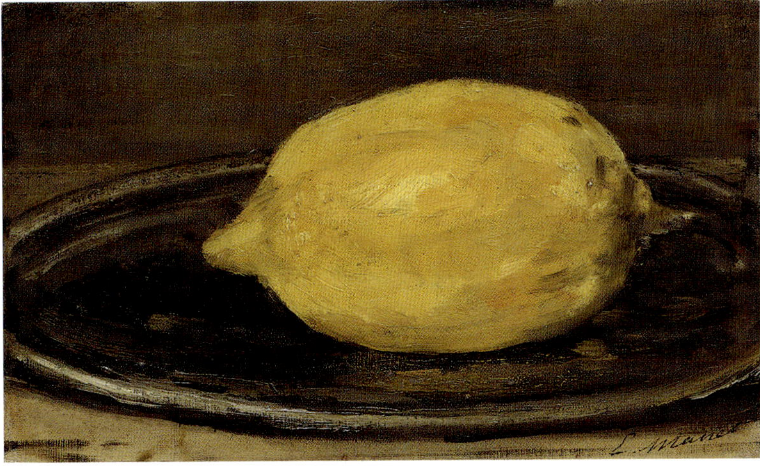

152   Edouard Manet, *Lemon*, 1880, oil on canvas, 14 × 21 cm. Musée d'Orsay, Paris.

For it too announces that still-life painting is the commodity, and that eyeing a painting and opening, squeezing, or eating a lemon are not simultaneous activities and cannot be supported by the same object. The implication of the *Lemon*'s closure too, then, is to distinguish between the bodiliness of use value and the disembodiedness of exchange value – between the physical consumption of material reality and the circulation of equivalences and reality effects that define the ephemera of illusionism and capital.

OBJECTS (COMMODITIES)

As for the *Bar at the Folies-Bergère* itself, finished after the lemon and other single fruits and before the last series of florals, its foreground is occupied by an expanded marble countertop that was probably the same housebound one employed for most of the florals. Along with the bottles of alcohol at either framing edge, that countertop displays two items continuous with the single-article trend in Manet's still-life work of the period: a single glass with two roses floating in it, and a single compotier with a single mass of orange fruit cradled within it, side by side as if to remark on the transition from edibility to decorativity. Yet the context of the *Bar*'s foreground defines its still life as of a kind that Manet had never painted before. Made up of things for sale, the still life on the countertop belongs to the public rather than the private realm of consumption. So in that sense it departs from Manet's kitchen and dining room still lifes of the 1860s and '70s. The labels on the bottles, unreadable though they mostly are, clearly advertise the commodity status of the bottles, while their existence as mass-produced, interchangeable multiples – another defining feature of the commodity – is announced in the duplication of bottles across the counter: the bottle of red aperitif at the left edge is repeated on the right (though it is turned around so that its label is no longer visible), as is the brown bottle of beer with its red triangular logo, and the bottles of champagne with their gold-

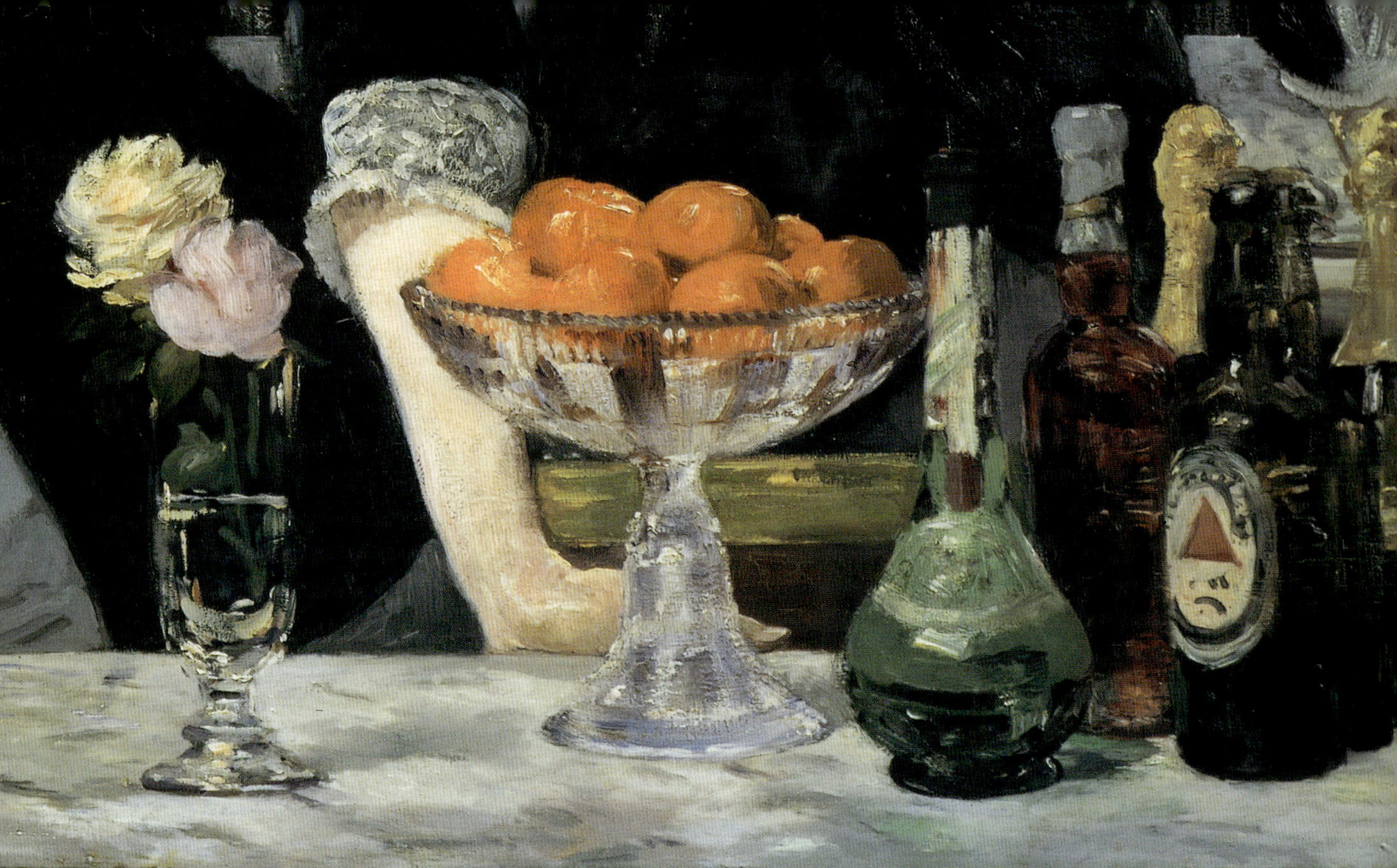

Detail of fig. 137.

foiled necks are multiplied several times. The only bottle not duplicated is the green bottle of cognac; like the glass of roses and the compotier of fruit, it signals some sort of play between single unit and multiple. This play owes a debt to Chardin, but it is also markedly different from the sustained contrast between the singular and the multiple, the individual and the mass, that marks Chardin's still lifes, for it substitutes the logic of commodity surplus and optical spectacle for the social structuring of object "bodies" about which the eighteenth-century painter was so subtle.

Illegible labels notwithstanding, the shapes of the bottles, the colors of glass out of which they are made, and the bits of paper and foil with which they are decorated, all serve clearly signifying functions: reproducing the advertising strategies of product design, they identify the kind of liquor that is being sold. In one way this is markedly different from Manet's earlier preoccupation with consumables: his attention to different kinds of surface effects, ranging from the transparency and translucency of different kinds of glass, to the reflective sheen of marble, the matte white of paper and the glitter of metallic foil, is extricated from its traditional context of enumerating the material comforts of the prosperous bourgeois home and reinserted into the commercial context of the desire-inciting, gaze-confusing space of the shop and its countertop displays. Here illusionism explicitly supports the selling of the commodity; it aligns itself as never before with a type of exhibition that is meant to incite the exchange of money for things (the corporeal satisfactions those things might bring are no longer referred to at all), closely associating modern urban representation and modern urban trade, painterly illusionism and capitalist barter, pictorial spectacle and spectacular capital.[12] Meanwhile, the base materialism of Manet's earliest kitchen still lifes is remade in the image of the commodity.

All of which is to say that Manet's earlier engagement with the confined, at home shelf-space of the Chardinesque still life is here converted into the open-to-the-world shelf-space of the self-advertising, illusion-supported commodity display. Still that shelf-space abuts illusionistically against the literal vertical plane of the *Bar*'s canvas, but now its playful confession of the illusion of perpendicularity pertains to the world of commercial exchange. And so it represents the culmination of a shift from the sorts of marble tabletops that are found in hearth and home and parlor-bound still lifes of Second Empire Chardin revivalists like Philippe Rousseau, such as the marvelously anecdotal teatime of his *Still Life Five O'Clock* (fig. 153), with its hour- and gender-specific arrangement of fan and handkerchief (instead of knife and napkin), ornate copper teapot (instead of copper stockpot), delicate china teacup and Chardinian milk pitcher, and sweet-tooth-satisfying eclairs and creampuffs, to the marble café tables and counters with single servings of brandied plum or beer that delimit the brasserie spaces of the café series that led up to the *Bar at the Folies-Bergère*. In the latter series the single serving indicates the opposite of respectable domestic sociability – namely, the unattached status and potential availability of the female consumer – and the countertop's delimitation of space

153   Philippe Rousseau, *Still Life Five O'Clock*, oil on canvas, 56.8 × 86.7 cm. Musée des Beaux-Arts de la Ville de Reims.

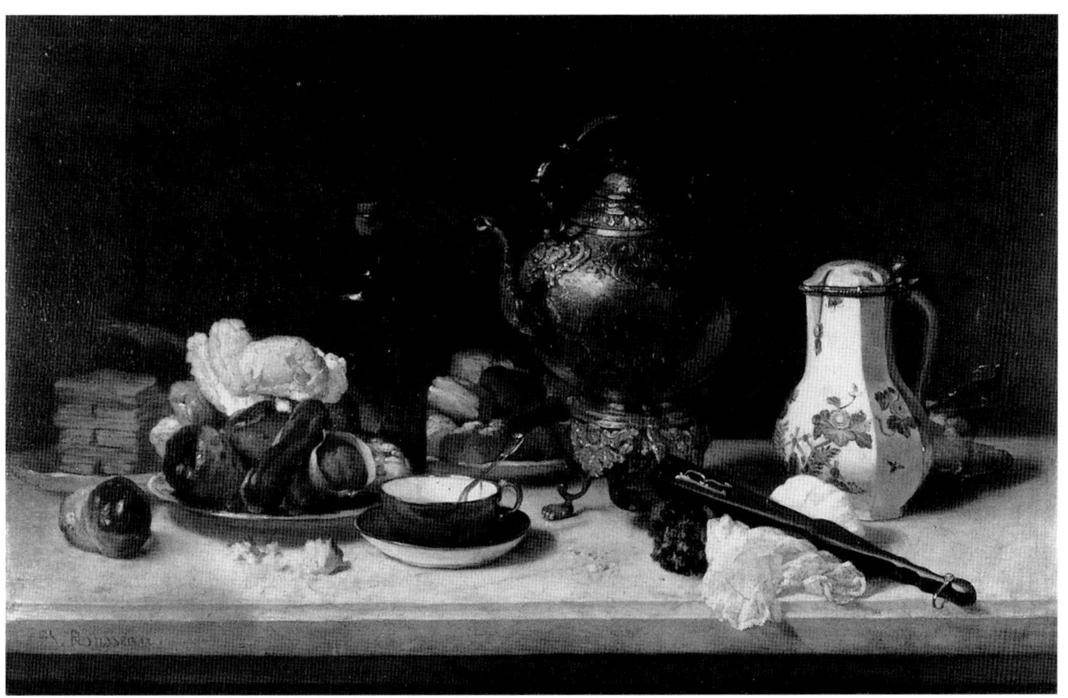

represents, not the closed and confined world of bourgeois femininity with its prescribed afternoon round of social calls, but the threshold of a commercial transaction open to both scintillation and interpretation. In short, the once Chardinian countertop that unfolds so largely in *Bar at the Folies-Bergère* points to its conversion of the site of still life from private into public space, the modification of an illusionism of possessions and utensils into that of advertisement and wares for sale, and the mutation of the thematics of interiority and corporeality into those of exchangeability and opticality.

In its multiplication of objects and expansion of space, the *Bar* seems at the other end of the spectrum from the reduced, single-item still lifes just anterior to it. Nevertheless, the commodity zone of *Bar at the Folies-Bergère* shares something with both the *Asparagus* and the *Lemon*. The marble surface of the *Asparagus*, for instance, and its confounding of the illusion of perpendicularity, is not unlike the countertop of the *Bar*, while the closed surface of the *Lemon* is not unlike the series of unopened items arranged on the marble surface of that countertop. Indeed, it is in the *Bar* that the questions of illusionism, commodity value, and closure raised by those two small still lifes are brought fully and problematically together. For the bottles on the *Bar*'s countertop all appear to be full, their seals unbroken, while the clementines in the *compotier* are all as unbroached as the *Lemon*; indeed, the white highlights upon them could almost be taken as suggesting some sort of transparent outer wrapping, so glossy, finished, and touch-resistant are those orange optical shapes.

The insistently unopened state of the *Bar*'s still-life items pertains to their status as commodities for sale; after all, the appearance of permanently virginal, unused perfection is one of the prime self-advertising features of the commodity on display. The emphasis upon unopenedness announces that this still-life belongs to the public world of commerce rather than the private one of the domicile, and thus to possession – ownership and physical consumption – ever in the future tense. At the same time, the still life of unopened objects on the *Bar*'s countertop multiplies the closed opacity of the *Lemon*'s painted surface. The still life's placement in the front plane of the picture forces an acknowledgment of its identity with the literal plane of the canvas, which refuses to dissolve away into fictive transparency. Thus the still-life zone inverts the referential equivalence of illusionism – it boomerangs to suggest an equation between the depicted commodities and the literal, opaque objecthood of the painting, rather than between the putatively transparent depiction and the commodities to which it outwardly refers. And since the still life's identity with the literal plane of the canvas again proposes the painting as the true object of the consumer's gaze, the state of being ever new, unbroached, and unused, not yet owned and not yet consumed, never to be incorporated by hand or mouth, attaches itself in a self-advertising way to the painting itself – painting as a more purely optical kind of commodity than any other.

Get your vintage Manet here! 1882 was a very good year: as if to reinforce the attention to the painting as a self-advertising luxury commodity, Manet signs his name and dates the painting in miniature at the bottom of the label of the bottle of aperitif at the left edge of the *Bar*. The signature's miniaturization, inscription on the bottle label, and witty mimicking of the printed logo all conspire to suggest another joke of the kind made by the *Asparagus*, where Manet's scribbled "M" in the upper right corner of the image mimics the black marks used to render marble, and thus overtly equates itself with a signature style of illusion painting. The joke, compounded now, is this: Manet's name is a trademark, the logo for a product. The product is not exactly the bottle of aperitif, for in its turn that bottle is simply a kind of logo for the rest. It is a concentrated demonstration of the character of Manet's painting – namely, its characteristic identification with still-life illusionism, the overt paintedness of that illusionism, the equation of that illusionism with the frontality, flatness, and literal objecthood of the painted canvas, and its movement out of the producerly world and abject materiality of the kitchen into the consumerly universe of the capital of capital, with which it identifies itself, which it materializes and spectacularizes, simultaneously celebrating and contravening it. That same illusionism, paradoxically equating itself with painting as a material fact, is the ware that Manet has to offer to his customers, the ware that he advertises here. This is what you see, he seems to say to his Salon customers, when you come to see a Manet; this is what you buy, if you come to buy. The painting itself is a commodity, like those for sale on its countertop, but it is also specific in its materiality and therefore different from the commodities manufactured by its illusionism. In other words, it is very like, but also specifically different from, what you come to see and buy if you are a habitué of the spectacles and *consommations* at the Folies-Bergère. It is also different from the Nature-bound opticality of Impressionism and the naturalist trademarks of Monet and the rest. It is, finally, both similar to and different from Manet himself: at the furthest possible distance from the early years of the *Fish (Still Life with Carp)*, it shares with it Manet's signature preoccupation with the simultaneous narrowing of illusionism to its materialist base and its deft expansion into differentiated effects.

MIRROR (SPECTACLE)

The mirror of the *Bar* compounds what occurs in the still-life zone. It doubles the already multiplied objects in the front plane, confounds the distinction between one kind of duplication and another, and states the attachment of still-life effects to a framed flat plane and the material apparatus of illusionism. Just as the bottles are duplicated and, already like mirror images of one another, turned front to back across the lateral expanse of the first plane of the picture, so they are duplicated and turned front to back in the illusionistic movement back from the front plane into the mirror's "depths": witness, for instance, the reflections of that bottle of red aperitif and of the beer bottle next to it. And, as if to announce the desire-enticing function of optical confusion, as well as the way multiplicity is an effect – an illusion of numerousness, plenty, and surplus supply that underwrites the commodity and helps to sell it to the consumer – the mirror's duplicates are deliberately confounding. There is, for example, the bit of red and white of the fragment of reflection caught between the barmaid's bangled right arm and torso, suggesting a bottle that is nowhere to be found on the countertop. And then there is the way the farthest right champagne bottle appears interpenetrated by the gilt edge of the mirror "behind" it, such that it suggests an impossible reflection at the near edge of the mirror, and makes it fundamentally difficult to tell what is to be taken as in front of, and what within, the confines of the mirror. Finally, returning to the left side of the painting, it is worth noticing the way that bottle of red aperitif appears to have another impossible reflection just the other side of the mirror – the bit of oval white atop a vertical strip of reddish brown which mimics the shape and color of the bottle, only to turn out to be a lit sconce on a distant pillar beneath the reflected balcony, and thus another mirrorly mirage. So the discrepancy between the bar and its reflection, most obviously encountered in the skewed relationship of the barmaid's front to her mirrored back and in the impossible inclusion of the male customer, is multiplied into a series of confusions in the still life's mirror image.

Those multiplied confusions have all to do with the mutual imbrication of illusionism and commodity culture that is one of the painting's large themes.[13] But it is also in the mirror that the difference between Manet's devotion to opticality and that of the Impressionists becomes most distinct and lucid. To see this, one need only note that the confusions instigated by the *Bar*'s mirror recall, but also resituate, the deliberate pseudo-Impressionist perplexities of the suburban *Argenteuil*. Bottle and sconce instead of hat and sailrigging, the *Bar at the Folies-Bergère* explicitly denatures its own opticality, and just as explicitly removes it from the naturalist world of landscape, with its reflecting river, green river banks, sunny day, and clouded sky, to the theatrical scene of urbanity, with its indoor, night-time diversions, artificial light, and manufactured goods. Nowhere is this denaturing more evident than in the mirror's substitution of glittering glass for limpid water, whose reflections it proclaims to be false, different from reality, and whose appearance of transparency it manifests as opacity.

Everywhere across the baffling surface of the *Bar*, the mirror is declared as such: in the white scumbling scattered across its plane, particularly over the top of the painting, where the lights and chandeliers are shown reflected, and streaked across the balcony at left, between the bottles and the barmaid's right arm, and over the reflected interchange between her back and the male customer. In addition to signaling glassiness and glare – the opticality of the mirror glass – that scumbling also draws attention to the paintedness of the mirror zone, as if to announce the identity of painting and opticality, the paintedness of opticality. So in addition to being the illusionistic space of the mirror, this brushmarked surface is also the flat plane of painting, and its depicted gilt edge serves the double function of insinuating that we are looking at a reflection in a mirror and signaling that we are also, simultaneously, looking at a framed painting within a framed painting. And the painting within the painting marks itself as such by being more sketchily painted than the front, still-life zone of the *Bar*, with its harder quality of closed and delimited objecthood.

Clearly, the looser rendering of the mirror image serves the illusionistic function of creating the optical impression of reflected distance, rendering the rustle of a crowd and the glitter of lights, distinguishing between reflected and "real" spaces. But more than the simple pragmatics of illusionism is involved here. For there is a kind of deliberation involved in the contrast between alternative styles of painting that is by no means new to the *Bar*; Manet had engaged in such contrasts before, when no such mirror image was in question. He did so in the *Luncheon on the Grass*, in which just such a contrast between pasty front plane and brushy background is to be found, identified with a contrast between alternative views of woman – one hard, frontal, outward, and still-life associated, the other soft, recessive, and inward, associated more with the process of painting than its products. Where the *Luncheon on the Grass* was a not very veiled evocation of

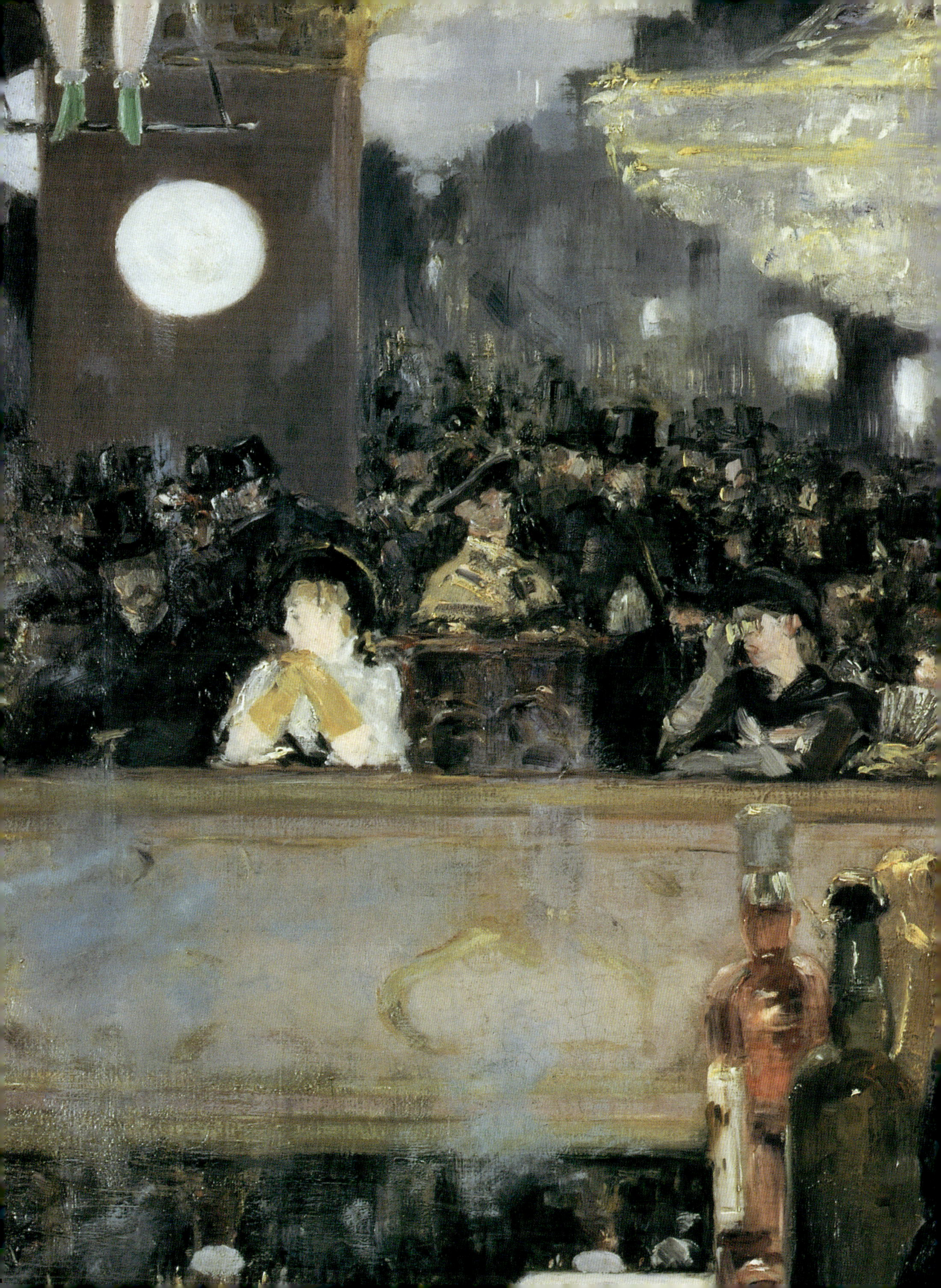

the painter's world of the studio, replete with a faux-picnic still-life arrangement, the *Bar* represents a movement out into the trafficky world beyond the private, producerly confines of the studio. But the *Bar* also turns around and re-presents what happened to Manet's painting when it appeared to move out of that world in the 1870s and tried to take on the open-air domain of Impressionism; its glaring, brightly colored, incident-full mirror substitutes itself for the dark, blank, studio-bound backgrounds of both the figural and the still-life works of the '60s, and introduces a new "inconsistency," a new doubleness into the heart of Manet's painting. That doubleness picks up an old compositional habit of painting in pieces, a longstanding division of Manet's signature into competing factures, and an earlier splitting of the image of woman, identifying painting with a double and divided femininity. But now it brings its pieces together, weaving its factures into a single surface, gives its old fascination a new look, that of the modern *parisienne*, and threads into it the warp of Manet's preoccupation with Morisot's brand of "feminine" painting. And it does so under the sign of the mirror, using the mirror as its optical alibi.

The one other time Manet had been concerned with rendering a mirror image, he did so without any engagement in the mirror's opticality. In *Before the Mirror* (see fig. 126), his reply to the minimal mirror of *Nana*, he had rendered the mirror as a gilt-edged zone, just as spatially discrepant as the mirror in the *Bar*, in which one hardly sees anything at all, but which is no more painterly than the front zone of the image, with its brushy, Rococo-inspired depiction of the back of a woman in her corset, dissolving into a painterly mirage much like Balzac's Catherine Lescault. In the *Bar*, by contrast, the viewer is given the other side of the woman it reflects, less upright and autonomous, less flatly resolved, than her twin behind the counter. So now the mirror provides what it should in the way of another view of the woman it reflects, though it does so to create an enigma. And now the mirror divides the world into separate zones, only to tie them again into an inextricable knot.

All of which is to suggest three things about the mirror image in the *Bar at the Folies-Bergère*, and its identification of opticality with painterliness. First, the zone of the mirror represents a specific fascination with artificial opticality, and instead of an emphasis on its naturalism, a sustained meditation on the uncanniness of the mirror image and its doublings.[14] Second, the mirrored world of the *Bar* mirror, with its alternatively painted alternate view of the barmaid, opens on to some concerns about the relation between modern painting and modern femininity. And third, the differently painted rendering of the mirror zone announces its lack of identity – or more strongly, its refusal of identity – with what it represents, its difference from the world this side of the painting. That is another kind of sense one can make, not only of the difference between the barmaid and her reflection, but also of the spatial inconsistency of the reflection of the counter-top, floating illogically, suspended like the balcony beyond it without apparent support or relation to the ground, like that balcony's flat strip doubling the countertop's play with the illusion of perpendicularity and the tension between the horizontal and vertical. That discrepancy helps to establish the painted difference between the picture and the world it depicts. It is also thus that the *Bar* underlines its difference from itself, and drives home its difference from the naturalized varieties of Impressionist painting, which in the twentieth century came to be generalized as the Nature-based origin of the "unity" of modern painting.[15] In advance of that modernist formulation, the *Bar* states its difference from any such model, and from the polarizing of the literal and illusionistic aspects of painting that goes with it.

It should be said that the difference between the two zones of the *Bar at the Folies-Bergère* is not absolute. For the white scumbling and loose manner of painting of the reflection are also echoed in parts of the front zone of the *Bar*. Both are found in the rendering of bottle surfaces, as if to establish an illusionistic kinship between two kinds of glass, two zones of optical confusion, and two kinds of commodity. The comparison between kinds of painting is most condensed in the meeting between the bottles and their looser reflections; yet it also reveals how very slight the distinction really is. For that comparison is matched to further specular confusions, as in the relationship between the bottles and their reflections, where it is not at all clear which is behind which on the countertop, and which inhabits which zone. As a result of these confusions, the indeterminate distinctions between the painterly styles of mirror and countertop begin to be muddled. In the countertop itself, apparently painted at such variance from the mirror, there are loosely painted suggestions of reflectivity – in the green beneath the cognac bottle, the touches suggesting the beginning of a reflection of the barmaid herself, and the flesh-toned marks beneath the champagne bottles. So the vertical and horizontal surfaces of mirror and countertop turn out to be more alike than different. Then there is the light-handed rendering of the lace edging of the barmaid's decolletage, framing her flesh and face just as the gilt edge frames the mirror, and as the countertop frames her corset-shaped hourglass torso. And there are the brushily rendered blossoms tucked into her bodice, linking the barmaid at once to the flowers in front of her on the countertop, one rendered more loosely than the other, and to the loosely painted zone behind and all around her.

In the end, the painting is more all of a piece than it appears at first: it declares what it is, a painted plane surface, whose differences in painterly manner are scattered laterally across that surface, rather than read through the separate planes of the *Bar*'s fictively mirrored depths. That said, however, its all-of-a-piece-ness is emphatically not given as the product of the natural unity of painting. For like the still-life items on the *Bar*'s countertop, the different kinds of painting in which Manet specialized are presented as multiply artificed offerings gathered and displayed on a single artificed surface. Like the mirror backing them up, they are shown as riven and manufactured, torn asunder and then complexly woven together by the painter's brush. And like the woman inserted between the two, they are presented as the colored yield of painting's difference, its specific materiality, rather than the effect of its essence, considered as an abstract, transcendant unity or an instantaneously perceived, optically rational, automonous totality.

WOMAN (FASHION)

A couple of other things ought to be said about the mirror, as a way of arriving at the barmaid. First, if what the mirror with its many discrepancies suggests is the painting's difference from the world it represents, then that includes the reflected male customer too, as the most dramatic discrepancy of the mirror zone. For the reflected male customer is shown precisely where we as viewers cannot be, from an oblique angle that dislodges the mirrored space from the straight-on world of the counter, so that the painting becomes so deeply fissured between the illusion of obliquity and that of parallel planes of representation that we end up having no idea where to imagine ourselves standing in front of it. The inclusion of the reflection of the male customer dramatizes what we already know, which is that standing in front of *Bar at the Folies-Bergère* is not the same as standing within the eating, drinking, and entertainment establishment called the Folies-Bergère.

In this painting that establishment is pictured as a place in which spectatorship is defined by dislocation: the reflected male customer, fixed at the right side of the painting but opening up a series of spatial discrepancies, dramatizes this imagining of the space of the Folies-Bergère as one in which spectatorial fixture is converted, by a series of dislocations, into spectatorial mobility. This brings me to the second of my remaining comments about the mirror. Within it is represented a plurality of gazes and a multiplicity of vantage-points. From right to left we move from the oblique, estranging vantage-point of the male customer past the barmaid, who intrudes in our scansion of the picture to suggest a head-on confrontation of gazes, to the reflected distance on the other side of the canvas, where we find a series of gazers, one with opera glasses, peering off to the side, suggesting another, detached, differently directed act of glancing, and dangling from the upper corner, the legs of the trapeze artist, bringing us up short against the edge of the canvas and the fact of its status as a hanging thing, cut off from the world it represents, a portable commodity removable from its original context. The difficulty of defining and fixing the place of the spectator which is broached on the right by the reflected male customer is multiplied ad infinitum as we move to the mirrored distance of the left-hand side of the canvas and scan all its instances of floating, hovering dislocation, optical confusion, and spectatorial flotsam and jetsam. In short, the job of the mirror in this painting is specifically to unfix the gaze, to make both the position and identity of the spectator undecidable.

The mirror in the *Bar* also shows how the unfixing of the gaze is part of the solicitation and functioning of consumerly desire. For the domain of the mirror is also that of the consumer – as opposed to the commodity zone of the front-plane countertop. Indeed, various kinds of consumption are alluded to in the space of the mirror, from the overt buying of drinks (and perhaps the covert buying of sex) at the right edge of the picture, to the gazing at the paid-for spectacle at the left edge. Not to mention the gazing at other spectators and their clothing. Sketchily suggested in the small distant figures at the same left edge, such reflexive gazing is an inevitable part of the decor of spectacle consumption like that of the Folies-Bergères. And it is brought up short, condensed, and sharpened in our apprehension of the barmaid, with her store-bought finery, itself the product of her acts of optical and economic consumption as she is now the object of ours. This brings us, finally, to the woman between the counter and the mirror, who stands before us as a kind of pictorial equivalent of the fashion-conscious department-store clerk of Zola's *Au Bonheur des dames*, published the year after the Salon in which the *Bar at the Folies-Bergère* appeared.[16] (It is not without significance, in this regard, that the spectacular space of the Folies-Bergère had once been a department store.[17]) For while the barmaid is presented as a commodity similar in shape and objective appearance to

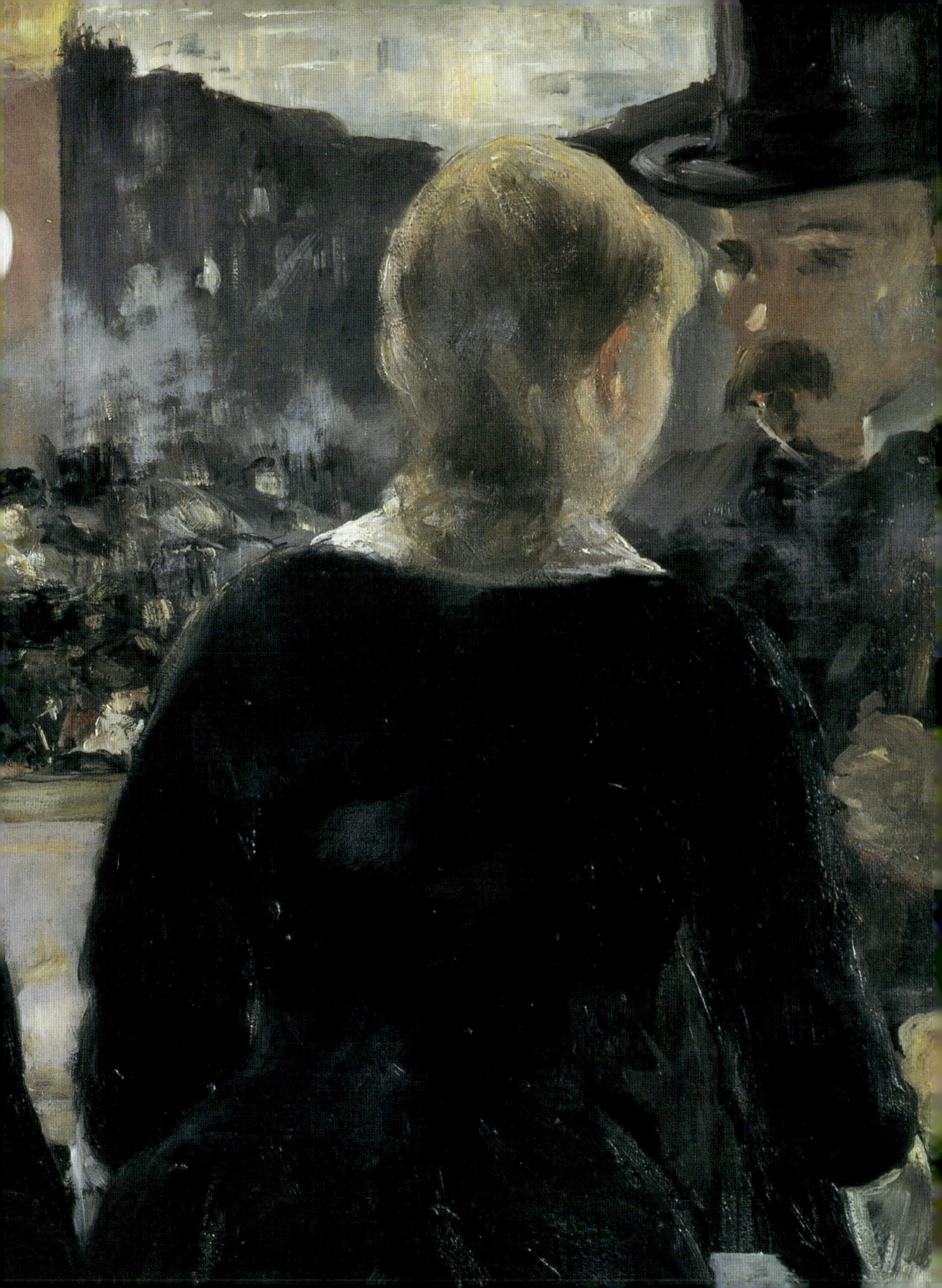

the bottles on the counter, at the same time she is represented as fashion consumer and purveyor of goods. As such, she is a middle term between the worlds of countertop commodities and mirrored consumers.

The barmaid belongs to another of Manet's preoccupations, and that is with women and their clothes. Going back to his depictions of Victorine Meurent in the 1860s, robed

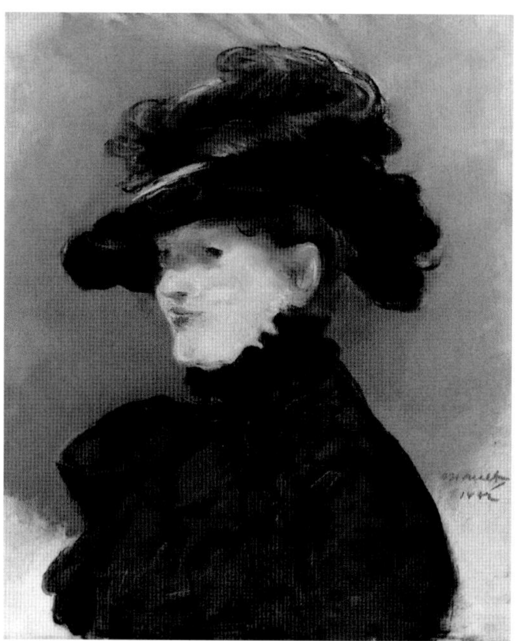

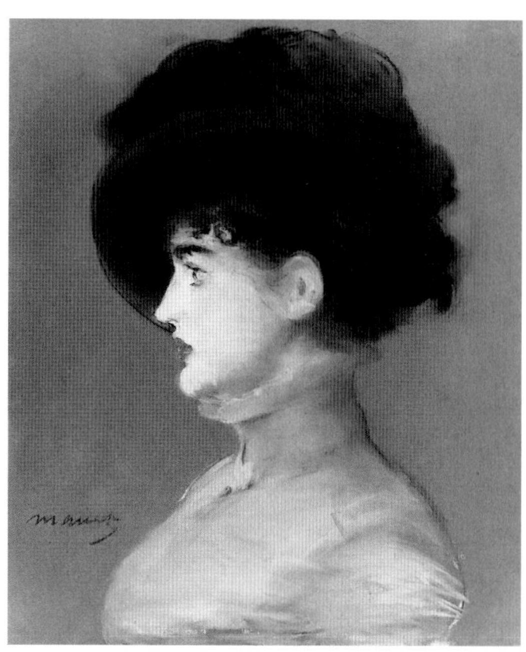

154 (*above left*) Edouard Manet, *Portrait of Méry Laurent*, 1882, pastel on paper, 54 × 44 cm. Musée des Beaux-Arts, Dijon.

155 (*above right*) Edouard Manet, *Portrait of Irma Brunner* or *Woman with a Black Hat* or *La Viennoise*, c.1880, pastel on cardboard, 54 × 46 cm. Musée du Louvre, Paris.

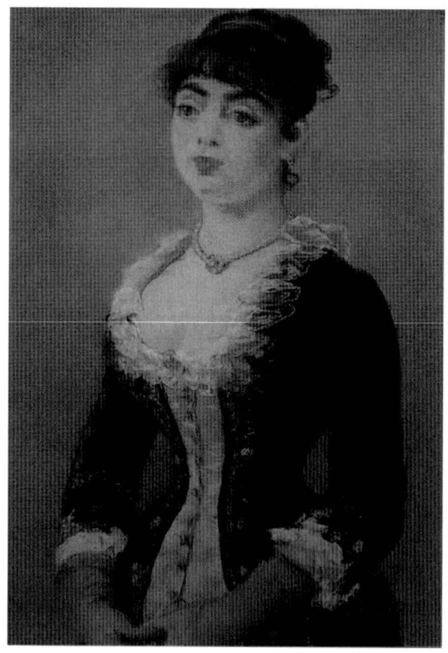

156 Edouard Manet, *Madame Michel-Lévy*, 1882, pastel and oil on canvas, 74.2 × 51 cm. National Gallery of Art, Washington, D.C. Chester Dale Collection.

in a variety of dresses and different apparel, and his paintings of Berthe Morisot at the turn of the decade into the '70s, this fascination manifests itself in an updated, particularly concentrated form in the late '70s and early '80s images of fashionable women such as Méry Laurent and others sporting fashion fetishes like hats and gloves (figs. 154–156). (Méry Laurent is supposed to be one of the sketchily indicated spectators in the reflected distance of the *Bar*: in spite of her quick, diminutive notation, she can be singled out by a pair of yellow gloves similar to those that crop up repeatedly throughout Manet's painting career, as in *Woman Reading* (*Reading the Illustrated Magazine*) (see fig. 122). Her presence there in the mirror as a gazer and consumer also signals a partly feminized zone, contradicting assumptions about the exclusive masculinity of public space.) A portrait of "Suzon" herself, the model for the *Bar*, belongs to this set of paintings and pastels, as do the *Spring* and *Autumn* of the Seasons series (figs. 157, 158). Across his career, Manet's work is marked by its obsession with the complexities of women's clothing, the feminine fashioning of identity through clothing, and female consumerism; it is distinguished

157 Edouard Manet, *Spring: Jeanne*, 1881, photograph of oil painting, with drawing on verso. Courtesy of the Fogg Art Museum, Harvard University Art Museums Cambridge, Mass. Bequest of Grenville L. Winthrop.

158 Edouard Manet, *Autumn* (*Méry Laurent*), 1881, oil on canvas, 73 × 51 cm. Musée des Beaux-Arts, Nancy.

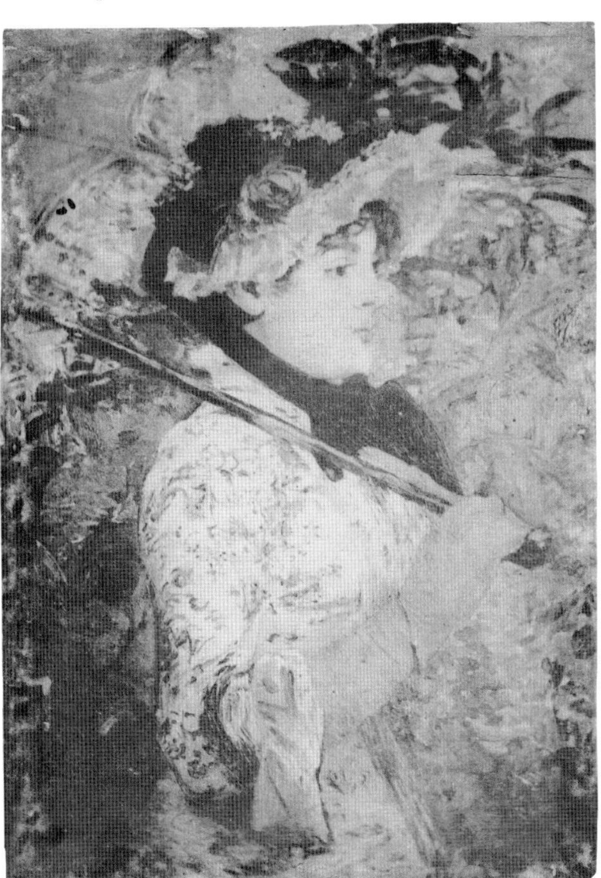

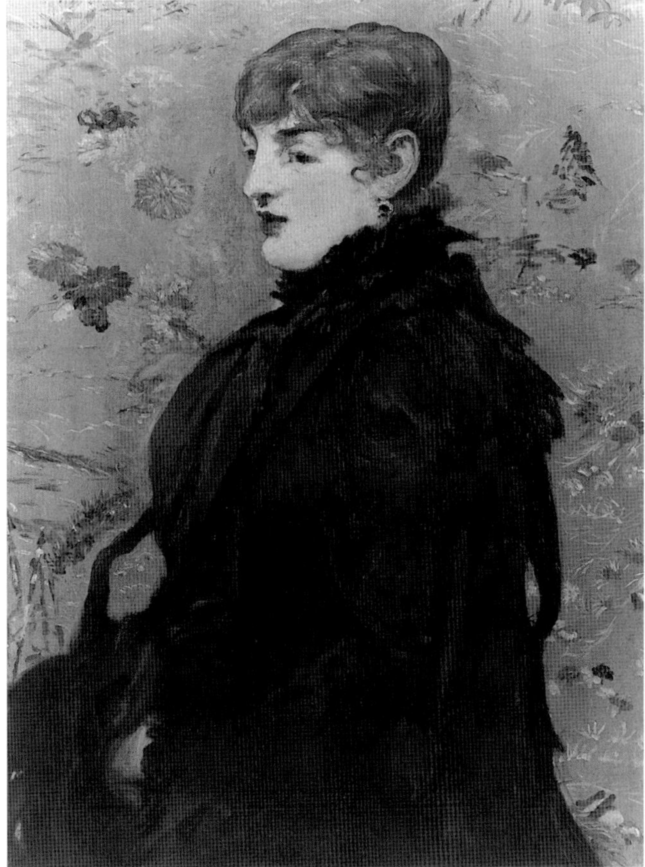

by its repeated attention to the objects and processes by which women attain the commodity of femininity for themselves, and transform themselves into that commodity for others. This was never more true than in the period in which the *Bar* was painted and exhibited: indeed, its exhibiting with the *Spring* fashionplate makes the barmaid's attachment to the image of the fashionable woman explicit. *Spring*'s subject is its Spring-appropriate, Rococo-colored ensemble of hat, dress, glove, and parasol, set against a floral background in Manet's Morisot manner, converting Nature into decor, woman into wallflower, consumer into commodity. As much as it is a portrait of an individual, fashion-consuming woman, *Spring* also represents that woman as a fashion object, to be consumed by both Salon-viewing men and fashion-shopping women, thus picking up one of the dominant themes of *La Vie Moderne* and setting it next to an explicitly "Folies-Bergère" companion.

The larger set of fashionable profiles and three-quarter faces to which *Spring* belongs is linked to the florals and single-object still lifes from the same period both in its often floral decorativeness and in its emphasis upon one thing at a time. It is also tied to yet another series from around 1880 that includes several letters written to Isabelle Lemonnier graced, respectively, with a mirabelle, a peach, and a bonneted head of Isabelle herself, one to Mme Guillemet decorated with a skirt-lifted glimpse of two black slippered and stockinged legs, another to Méry Laurent washed with a transparent rose, a study of almonds, another of three plums, and two hat sketches, one empty of heads, the other with heads supplied (figs. 159–161). These watercolor images are clearly decorative; they are set in a context of social calls, paying court, conversation, and dialogue; and they are overt in their status as female commodity fetishes whose value resides in their exchangeability. In the tradition of the little violets canvas sent to Morisot in 1872, the later epistolary still lifes, at once gifts and ornamental marginalia in letters written to women, index their exchange value with ludic simplicity. At the same time, the watercolor studies of isolated pieces of fruit in and out of these letters articulate the material means of their illusionism precisely in their reduction of those means to a minimum, their attachment to their writing-paper surfaces, written names, and Manet's scrawled signature, and their transparency, which calls up their volumes while also allowing one to see through them to their support. This series, then, brings together the still lifes' questions of exchange value, illusionism, and material literalism, and the one-to-one relationship between painting and represented object, and moves them into the domain of femininity. It also demonstrates the exchangeability of the positions of subject and object, for not only do portrait heads circulate in the same space as still-life objects, they also index recipients of an exchange who are at once subjects and objects of a social transaction, at once persons and things within the rules of the game of human commerce. As such, this series also bears on the *Bar at the Folies-Bergère*, with its mobilization of the same set of issues within the mirrored space of the barmaid: middle woman between the gendered zones of commodity culture, herself at once fashionable subject and fashion object, at once a subjective phantasm and an object among objects who uncannily returns our gaze in its frozen, glassy, lifeless form.

It has been remarked that the barmaid appears radically different from her own reflection.[18] I would like to take another look at the difference between the barmaid and her

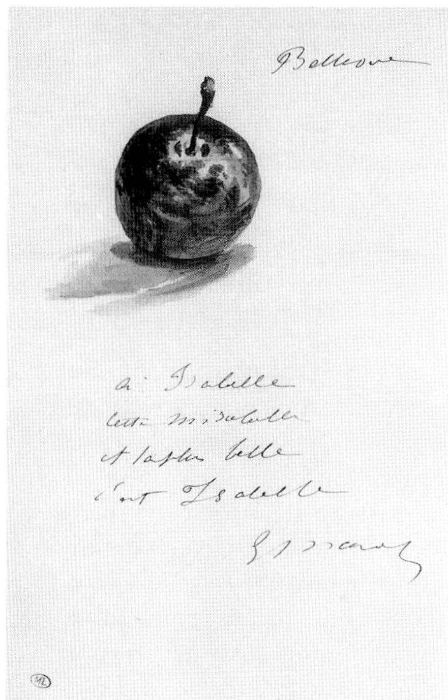 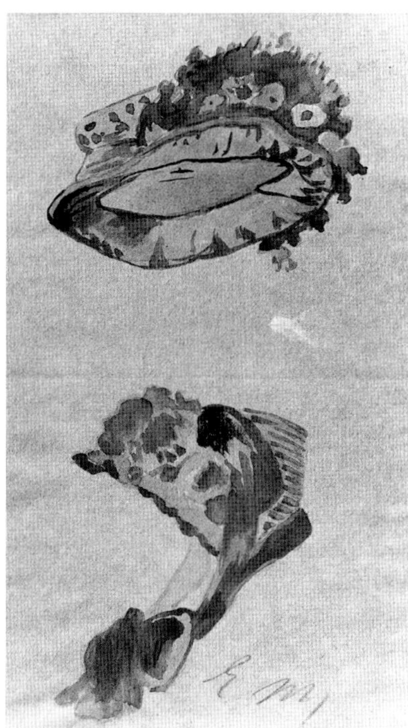 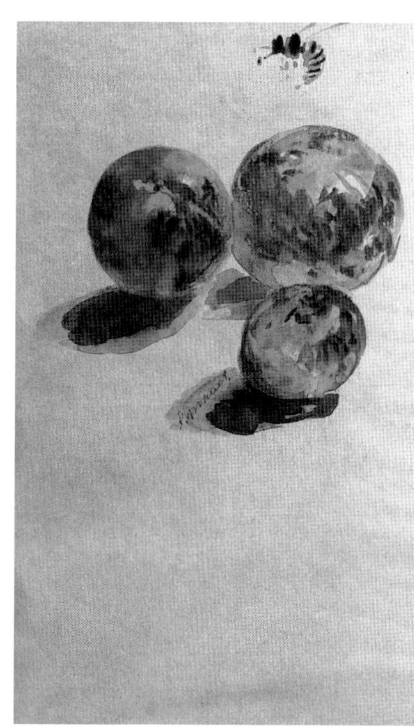

159 (*above left*)   Edouard Manet, *Mirabelle*, 1880, letter with watercolor, 20 × 12.5 cm. Musée du Louvre, Cabinet des Dessins, Paris.

160 (*above center*)   Edouard Manet, *Two Hats*, 1880, watercolor, 19 × 12 cm. Musée des Beaux-Arts, Dijon.

161 (*above right*)   Edouard Manet, *Three Plums*, 1880, watercolor, 19 × 12 cm. Musée des Beaux-Arts, Dijon.

reflection and consider it under the heading of the questions of illusionism, self-advertising commodities, and self-reflexive painting, as well as the unfixed, plural gaze and its double. One might expect the difference between the barmaid and her reflection to follow an illusionistic logic whereby the barmaid would look more "real" than her reflection. But that is not the case: she is rendered more flatly than her reflection. Her harder contours, upright, frontal pose, and closed, finished appearance succeed in likening her to the closed objects in front of her – a likeness furthered by such details as the different views of her two lace cuffs, similar to the views of bottles with labels half showing, fully shown, or shown not at all; the comparison between one white-painted cuff and the working of the *compotier* in white paint; the linking of the blossoms on the counter and those at her bodice; the mimicking of her highlit buttons by the highlights on the glass in which the blossoms on the counter float; the triangulation of a series of blond and gold accents, ranging from her bangs to her locket and bangle, the gilt mirror frame and gold-foiled bottlenecks between which she is sandwiched; and so on. Thus the barmaid appears before us as a kind of signboard advertisement for the *Bar* and its wares, an insert between the counter and mirror, a cut-out, pop-up figure announcing the collapse of the painting's represented layers of mirrored, inverted depth into a collage-like, paper-thin surface, thickened and glutinous with paint, at once single and multiple, literal and illusionist.[19]

The barmaid is part of a series of interruptions, each of which advertises the flatness and paintedness of the whole: the bottles interrupt each other, and the mirror frame; the counter, the flowers in the glass, and the *compotier* interrupt the barmaid; the barmaid interrupts the frame of the mirror as well as the reflection of herself and of the countertop. As a single figure who is also double, she interrupts the unproblematic singleness of the painting too, creating a disturbance both in its illusionist world and in the abstract oneness of its medium. And then, of course, she interrupts our gaze – for she stands where we should be mirrored, if we were standing directly in front of the painted counter and the painted mirror mirrored us correctly. And so the barmaid interrupts as well the *Bar's* own apparently verbatim illustration of the structure of (narrative) identification and (fetishistic) objectification that describes the "male gaze," and the opposition of subject and object that goes with it, in which the subject position, with which the spectator is meant to identify, is always masculine, while the object of the gaze is inevitably feminine. Thus far the readings of the barmaid that bring gender into the field of vision do so to fix it in place – either to illustrate the masculinity of public space or to show how the optical ambiguities of the painting are really sexual ambiguities, which in turn mask and naturalize the certainties of a misogynistic gender ideology.[20] Both readings reiterate the assumption that the subject position is necessarily male and the object position female. That assumption is not wrong as far as late nineteenth-century prostitutional discourse, public space, and gender ideology are concerned. But as far as this painted object is concerned, which is self-declaredly not exactly equivalent to any of those things, that is another question. And while *Bar at the Folies-Bergère* begins by laying out the equation spectator = male, object of vision = female, it ends by so complicating its own equation that it nearly defeats it.

The barmaid's flatly interruptive figure is very much part of the complication. Although she is depicted as an object among other objects, and very much the object of our gaze, at the same time she is just another of those pieces of painting announcing their paintedness and their status as mirages. Her closure, like that of the commodities around her, makes her emphatically unavailable to us – if she is an object of consumption, she is one of those that define its consumption as strictly optical: the buying of her is equated with a cycle of looking that can never be rolled into one of sexual possession and incorporation. And if the reflected interaction between the barmaid and the male customer opens onto a narrative reading of the painting predicated on identification with the customer, the barmaid cuts that narrative reading short and flatly refutes it.[21] One need only compare her to Tissot's slightly later shopgirl flirting with what we can presume to be a male customer buying trinkets for his mistress (fig. 162). Where Tissot's girl serves the opening of the painting from front plane to rear window into layers of transparency, the barmaid is recalcitrantly opaque. Where the other painted girl invites us gamely into her proliferating world of obsequious anecdote, the barmaid is obstinate in her refusal of narrative expansion and resolution. And where the other girl is happy to oblige in the easy identification of picture-viewer with shop customer, and in a lenient reciprocation of glances, repeated and underlined in the glimpsed background exchange through the

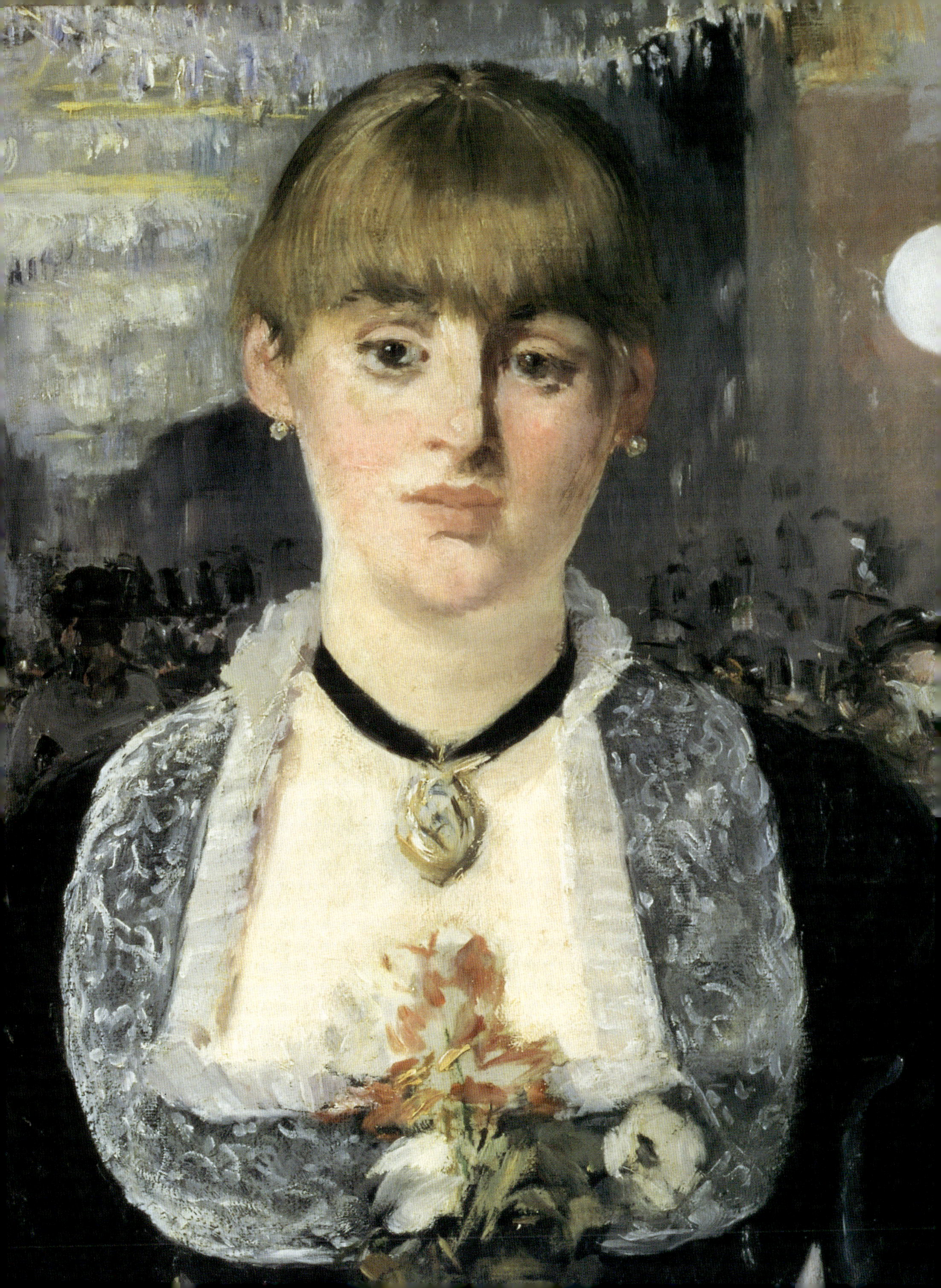

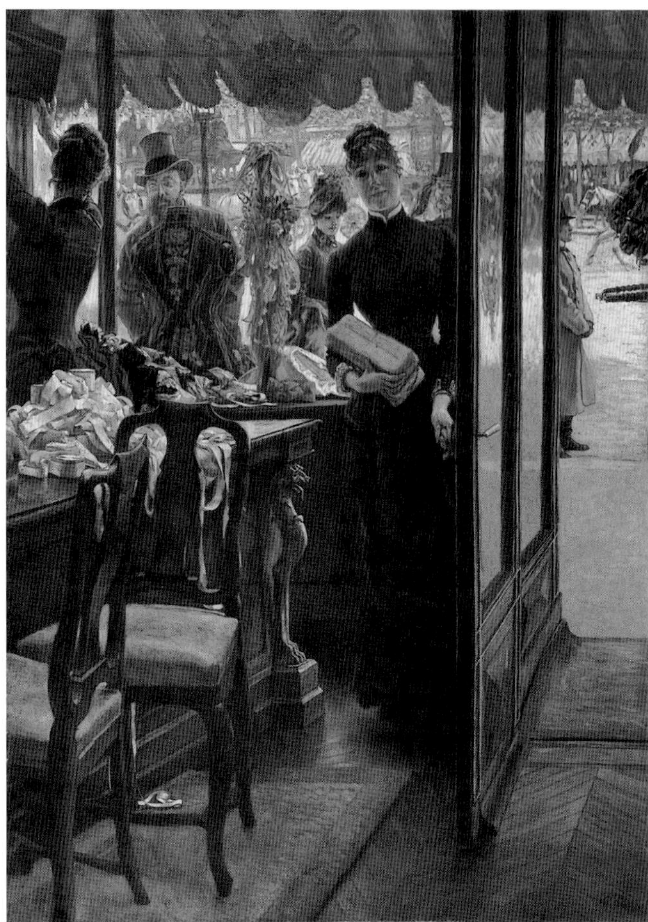

162   James Tissot, *The Shop Girl*,
1883–85, oil on canvas, 146 ×
101.6 cm. Art Gallery of Ontario,
Toronto. Gift from the
Corporations' Subscription Fund,
1968.

shop window, the barmaid stubbornly declines the reciprocity and equation of gazes, his, hers, and ours.[22]

The barmaid is, finally, not exactly what we expect the object of our vision to be: she is not only the object but also the occlusion of our vision. And perhaps what we were waiting to see was not only the painting's dissolve into its illusionistic referent (a dissolve which does not happen), not only a narrative meeting of human gazes (which also does not happen), but some version of ourselves as well. That, too, turns out to be not as we expect: though our implied presence before the picture is directly announced, the barmaid's failure to connect makes us feel we are not there, that we are as much a blind-spot as she is an absence. Instead of ourselves we find the barmaid, who becomes a stand-in for us, not quite our mirror image but our alter ego, as much as the reflected male customer is hers. She folds out twice – to become first her twin and then her mate, her opposite number, so that her difference from and kinship to the subject of vision, the spectator consumer, are so linked and run together as to be indivisible and unopposable. That is, the consumer and the commodity, the subject and object of vision, the spectacle's male and female halves, are sewn together to form a Janus figure.

It is also to say that the barmaid is a sort of doppelgänger for us. She is both a psychic double and a figuration of commodity culture's doubling of consumer and commodity, its structuring of the two as mirror images. The barmaid's insertion between counter and mirror places her in an interstitial no-man's-land between the zone of vision's objects and the visual plane on which identity is mapped in both a psychic and a consumerly sense. Not only does she both divide and bridge the twinned areas of commodity and consumer, showing how interpenetrated they are, she also both divides and bridges the gendered worlds of subject and object, self and other, demonstrating how conjoined they are: how much we are all subjects turning into objects, and objects shifting into subjects, in our commerce with one another. Perhaps, then, the barmaid is something other than simply a fixture of gender ideology, its gendering of the public and private spaces of vision, and its one-way traffic in gender commodities. Instead, she might be Manet's painted imagining of what a subject looks like as an object. She might be an image of the fissure – and elision – between those two aspects of our gendered selves, and of our positioning within the culture of the commodity. To put it another way, she is both a "screen" onto which anything can be projected and an "interval" that interrupts that projection: a "separation [that] has the two senses male and female," as Duchamp suggested somewhat later on.[23] And perhaps, beyond that, she also stands as a figure of the uncanniness of the Other, behind and among objects that turn her into matter, in front of and woven with a mirror that is shown as the site of alienation from the figment that is the self, in a spectacularly commodified world where the objective and phantasmatic meet and intersect like parallel planes at the point of infinity.[24] From the beginning, the figure of Woman had presided over Manet's career; Zola had described her as a phantasm hovering over it like a hungry harpy, disturbing the positivist clarity of the artist's physiologically determined vision. Now, the year before Manet's death, she declares herself the phantasm within his painted world, with its longstanding still-life orientation brought to the fore and capitalized.[25] She is, in all her painted difference, the phantasmatic principle of his painting.

LE TOUT ENSEMBLE

Objects, mirror, woman: these three ingredients of the *Bar at the Folies-Bergère* are brought together in an indivisible ensemble that rivals Manet's earliest paintings in its ambition and complexity, if not its size, and the one-of-a-kind impact of its singularity as a work of art.[26] In its highly wrought, complicatedly optical way it returns to the tradition of the grand composition brought together by drawing and shading, space, gesture, and figural comportment, but in place of such devices it installs the seductions of a new-fangled *coloris*, that old "difference of painting" refashioned in the modern image of the commodity, the spectacle, and, above all, the fashionable woman.[27] And it brings together the disparate manners of Manet's painting and disperses them across its bewildering surface, to both figure and disfigure their distinctions and separations, both resolve and dissolve its own discrepancies, and transform every opposition it renders into an elision, every twofoldness into a singleness and back again, every disintegrative bit and piece of its feminine thesis and masculine antithesis into a masterfully integrative, all-of-a-piece synthesis, which it also undoes when all-at-once scansion narrows to closer inspection.

The *Bar* returns to the single-figure composition of Manet's early days. (In the face of the reflections in the mirror, it is easy to forget that there is really only one person, "Suzon," that the painting stands before us: somehow it manages to combine the effect of a single person's presence with that of several people, not to mention the reflected crowd.) At the same time it cuts its single figure off at the thighs and renders her less than life size. (It is easy to forget this too, because the 96 × 130 centimeter painting is larger than most that Manet produced at this time; at the same time it is smaller than one tends to remember it, and certainly smaller than his early single-figure paintings.) The *Bar* complicates the barmaid's surroundings to such a degree that she hardly dominates her space in the way that Victorine used to do back in the 1860s. And her gaze lacks the insolence and piercingly deadpan quality of Manet's favorite model of the old days; instead it is simply blank and absent. Yet the painting is a sensationally lively one, recalling as well the broken up, vividly colored surface of the *Music at the Tuileries*, with its fanning out of the multicolored skirt of *Lola de Valence* into a modern life crowd. And so, for the illusion of animated personhood, it substitutes the optical vivaciousness of a spectacular specular world, in which liveliness is all optical illusion, indistinguishable from the lifeless gleam and sparkle of *nature morte*, and from the pasty coagulation of paint qua paint, in all its splendidly attractive but ultimately dead materiality.

Most obviously, the *Bar* picks up the double standard of Manet's works of the 1870s, combining the loose, Rococo mode of works like *Before the Mirror* and *Woman Reading* with the harder, flatter, more finished manner of paintings such as *The Conservatory* and *Plum Brandy* to yield its complex doubling of the single figure.[28] And it marries the *faux*-Impressionist busyness of *Argenteuil* to the chock-a-block bric-a-brac of *Nana* to produce its meditation on femininity in the age of capital: its final updating, in the aftermath of the Second Empire's modernization of the city of Paris in the image of the flow of goods and currency, people and pleasures, of Baudelaire's "painting of modern life" in the image of modern woman, and of the old "difference of painting" in the form of the prismatic colors of modern spectacularity. That updating constitutes both modern woman and modern painting as fundamentally twofold.

The figure who stands at the seam of that signature twofoldness is, of course, the barmaid. For it is the barmaid who most of all undoes the apparent opposition, not only between the zones of countertop and mirror, commodities and consumers, but also between Manetian and Morisotian facture. It is on the decorative surface of the barmaid, as well as in her folding out into her reflection, that those zones and factures are most markedly interwoven. As the eye descends her female figure, and then moves laterally to her male-coupled reflection, it shifts across a multiplicity of factured effects – from the chandelier-backed, glossy gold softness of the bangs defining and obscuring her forehead, to the broken marks of her gold locket, and the gleaming gold of her bangle, similar to yet different from her hair; from the pinpointed glints and porcelain whites of her eyes to the pearly globules at her ears and the vertical line of dotted whites rendering rhinestone buttons down her front; from her bluntly brushed straight line of a nose, to the dark shapeliness of her corsetted hourglass torso, and the flatfooted, oddly shapeless horizontal of the heel of her hand, whose gleam parallels the flat white of the marble countertop; from the opaque white of the stiff ruffles edging the décolleté of her bodice to the flecked and filigreed misty grayness of the lace at her neckline and sleeve edges, which move the eye likewise to the marble tabletop and on, across the barrier of bottles, to the rapid inscription of her mirrored cuff, and then back to the foggy white and gray glow, at once edge and blur, delineating her reflection's specular contour, and the quick dry scumble marks found either side of her in the mirrored interstices between her two triangulating arms and single gray-brushed skirt. It is as if the barmaid serves to locate the infinitesimal place of intersection where a boundary becomes a threshold, and a difference unfolds into a collapse of difference.

Last but not least, from the blossoms of her corsage to those before her on the bar, the eye discovers a shift that condenses every other shift across the divide that the barmaid both forms and bridges. The one posy is a study in Impressionist rapidity and abbreviated foliate complexity; the other a demonstration of delicate, two-blossomed – and two-colored – simplicity, simpler than the simplest of the florals that marked the bedridden end of Manet's painting life. The spray at the barmaid's bodice fans up and out into dappled and streaked colors, which include, at the heart of the symmetry that the posy serves to focus, a light blurred pink within the mass just to the left of center and a green-marred splotch of peach that escapes the mass just a little more to the right of center. Those two colors are versions of the two colors of the two blossoms – two roses, perhaps, one tighter and one looser – that dangle asymmetrically in the single, off-center glass on the countertop, apart yet not apart from the figure of the barmaid. The complex corsage and the simple two blossoms are as linked and alike as they are differently handled and divergent from one another. And therein, in Manet's two bouquets to his Other, lies the paradox of his whole career in painting, of which this particular final painting stands as a kind of *summa*: a singularity founded on duality, a self-sameness founded on difference, a single-minded doubleness. A Manet/Manette, in short.

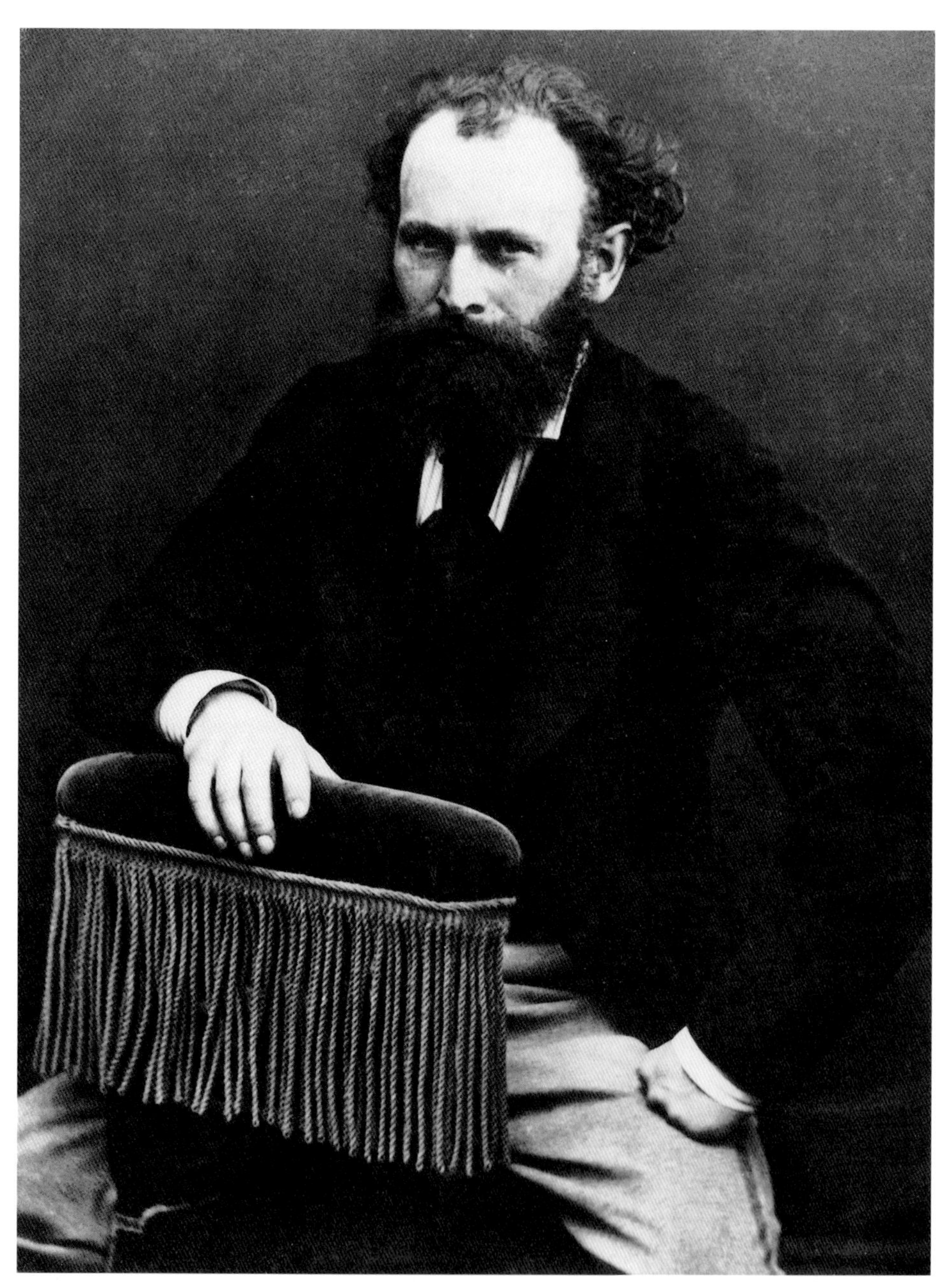

163 Nadar, *Edouard Manet*, c.1865, photograph.

TO YOU, EDOUARD MANET

"Everyone knew how to make the portrait of Manet: he was very well known."[1]
So goes the opening line to one of the most recent of the many biographies of Manet.
And indeed, Manet was a kind of celebrity, a recognizable man about town as well-known
for his Parisian physiognomy and personality as he was for his scandalous paintings,
who turned heads with his handsome features, graceful gait, and elegant clothes, not to
mention his charming manners and sharp wit, who, in short, surprised those who
expected a wild-eyed bohemian with his polished demeanor and gentlemanly exterior. It
was as such that Nadar included him in his *galerie contemporaine* (fig. 163), portraying
him in his prime several times over, as did Degas and others. And from the onset of his
notoriety until the present, writers of note have produced one written portrait after
another of the gentleman painter. As I have noted, Zola described Manet's physical
appearance in the first, biographical part of "Une nouvelle manière en peinture: Edouard
Manet" of 1867. In 1874, Albert Wolff, old and continuing critic of Manet's style of painting, devoted an entire article to Manet in *Le Gaulois*, in which he described his style as
a man appreciatively:

> In front of Tortoni's, in the midst of a bouquet of journalists, from five to six o'clock,
> one could see M. Manet. He is one of the glories of the café . . . A man passing in the
> street with his wife stops, shows her the blond Tortoni patron and says to her, "Look,
> Euphrasie, there is monsieur Manet." To which his wife replies: "Impossible! I had
> imagined him in a red shirt, a beret and a short pipe."
>
> Well no, madame! M. Manet never goes about an in otter cap, like the man in the
> *Bon Bock*; he is indeed the elegant cavalier that you see before you, of medium stature,
> just tall enough so that the painter is neither too big nor too small. Irreproachable
> bearing as you see, specializing in astonishing cravats. His face is at once energetic and
> gentle; his eyes are of a blue as limpid as the Mediterranean in the sun; he has a blond
> beard and hair; his complexion is of that fine tone that colorists love. Velasquez would
> have begged him to pose in his atelier. That, Madame, is M. Manet; and to complete
> this picture of his person, I would add that he is a charming lad, with sweet manners
> beneath a curt exterior, a perfect *gentleman* in a word, whose painting one would love
> to admire . . . without reservation . . . But . . .[2]

Hereafter Manet's portrait was framed by constant contrast to the public's expectations, and his status as a "cavalier" worthy of Velasquez, a "gentleman" up to Beau
Brummel's standards, was articulated in opposition to the bohemian figure that people
expected from his paintings but did not find in his person. Repeatedly, he was described

as a living paradox, a figure made up of dual personae, one the painter and the other the social man, two inconsistent people in one (much as Baudelaire had treated Delacroix in his essay of 1863).[3] But above all, the conversational framework that Wolff establishes for his description of Manet also posits Manet as the object of an audience's gaze (an audience both male and female), quite as much as any of the elegant society women whose company Manet adored.[4] Clearly, Manet cultivated that audience's gaze while appearing not to with careful nonchalance, choosing and arranging his cravats accordingly, like the Restoration dandy that the French Romantics from whom Manet was descended admired.[5]

In 1897, in the decade after Manet's death, Antonin Proust, old studio compatriot and friend of Manet's childhood, painted Manet's likeness in words toward the beginning of his "Souvenirs" of the artist, first published in *La Revue Blanche*. Written as a memoir, in which every anecdotal recollection of the artist is framed within Proust's relationship to him, the "Souvenirs" describe Manet's appearance thus:

> In those days, Edouard Manet was of medium height, and well-muscled. He had an alluring cadence which his hip-swinging gait imprinted with a particularly elegant character. Whatever effort he made to exaggerate that walk and to affect the drawling talk of the Parisian *gamin*, he was never and could never be vulgar. He had the air of a thoroughbred.
>
> Beneath a wide forehead, his nose drew its straight, frank line. His mouth, lifted at the corners, had a teasing look. He had a clear gaze. His eyes were small, but very mobile. When very young, he wore his long, naturally curly hair thrown back. At eighteen years of age, his hairline was already receding, but his beard was well grown in. Because of it, his lower face was softened, while his extremely fine hair harmonized his upper face. Few men have been as seductive as he was . . . .[6]

Proust describes the young Manet from the vantage-point of old-age retrospection, repeating certain key elements from Zola's original description – the mouth lifted at the corners, for instance – and adding to them an evocation of Manet's corporeal and personal allure that is Proust's touch (and very definitely not Zola's). It is signficant that in this account Manet is almost feminine: his face harmonized much as, according to Baudelaire, a woman might unify her complexion with makeup, his walk evoking the swaying of long-skirted female hips, he is soft and fine and elegant, and above all, seductive. Or perhaps it would be better to say that in Proust's account Manet is again a double figure, shuttling between well-muscled, bearded, prematurely balding, frank-featured, thoroughbred masculinity and an undulating Baudelairean femininity. (Whereas in Zola's earlier version of Manet, the role of seducer/seductress was assigned not to the virile Manet himself but to the Great Courtesan presiding greedily and phantasmatically over his painterly imagination.) In any event, the sexy Manet that Proust produces is also a relational one: the Manet who was so seductive (to Proust) was a Manet described in terms of his considerable effect on others, which was as heady as the effect of a Méry Laurent on the gentlemen around her, and which was the reason for everyone wanting to make or take his portrait.

Yet for all the portraits of Manet that others have given us both during his lifetime and after it, Manet rarely made portraits of himself. One might have expected him to, given his attachment to the portrait generally; other artists of his generation who were given to portraiture certainly portrayed themselves. At the beginning of his career, the young, doe-eyed Courbet did, with much evident pleasure in himself, while at the same time portraying his friends, relatives, and patrons. So did the melancholic, sunken-faced and much less appealing Degas in both painting and photograph, at the beginning and at the end of his career, while maintaining a running interest in portraying those around him, in and out of his family circle, as well. And so did the reclusive Cézanne, who also portrayed his intimates repeatedly, both in his early *couillarde* manner and in his later faceted style. And most famously, of course, the tortured Van Gogh, who included portraiture among the genres that preoccupied him, portrayed himself obsessively throughout his brief vocation as a painter, seeming to justify in advance the biographical emphasis of the post-suicide literature on him, and to provide a self-enclosed circle of self-expression to match the advancing self-enclosure and self-definition of modern painting.[7] If I seem to be setting a false problem, then, in asking why Manet did not portray himself more often, it is worth recalling that in this period, when artists were portraitists they also tended to be self-portraitists. Not so Manet, who produced himself for others' consumption, but hardly ever for his own.

A few times Manet portrayed himself marginally: once at the framing edge of a crowd of related figures in the *Music at the Tuileries* (see fig. 13), the many-figured representation of Manet's personal court, which includes at least one of his two brothers, a variety of other artists, writers, and composers, and the three blurred, just identifiable patches rendering Manet's favorite companion of those days, Baudelaire, with Gautier and Baron Taylor. (That they are barely identifiable is germane to Manet's position on the likeness, as is the fact that his own top-hatted face – doubled as it is by that of his erstwhile studio companion Balleroy and then multiplied in all of the other top-hatted faces that fill up the space of the painting – is simultaneously somewhat more easily legible and marginalized almost to the point of being squeezed out: *Music at the Tuileries* offers a range of alternatives as to the "beholder's share" in the differentiation and identification of a series of abbreviated pictorial likenesses that are yet resemblant both of each other, across the series, and of the individuals represented, one to one.) And then there was *Masked Ball at the Opera* of a decade later (fig. 164), in which Manet again hid his top-hatted face among a crowd of similar top-hatted heads, mass-produced yet differentiated enough to solicit a search for individual identities – individual masculine identities, that is, intermingled with masked and thus pictorially more interchangeable female ones.[8] The searching for the identity beneath the mask, after all, is as much the game of the masked ball as the playing of the role assigned by the costume, and thus it is the theme of the 1873 painting, from which Manet looks out, not as a mirrored face confronting himself before the canvas (as the self-portrait so often suggests), but as if to address the viewer in a social relationship, and to question his or her identity within the parallel crowd of spectators of which he or she is one.

Occasionally Manet also represented himself disguised as other people – diminutively, as Rubens, in *Fishing* (see fig. 15) together with Suzanne (and Léon, across the way in a curious limbo); and paradoxically, as the aged Tintoretto, in his youthful copy of the latter's self-portrait, in which a resemblance to Manet's features can be discerned (see fig. 16). Otherwise, we might say that Manet represented himself by representing others

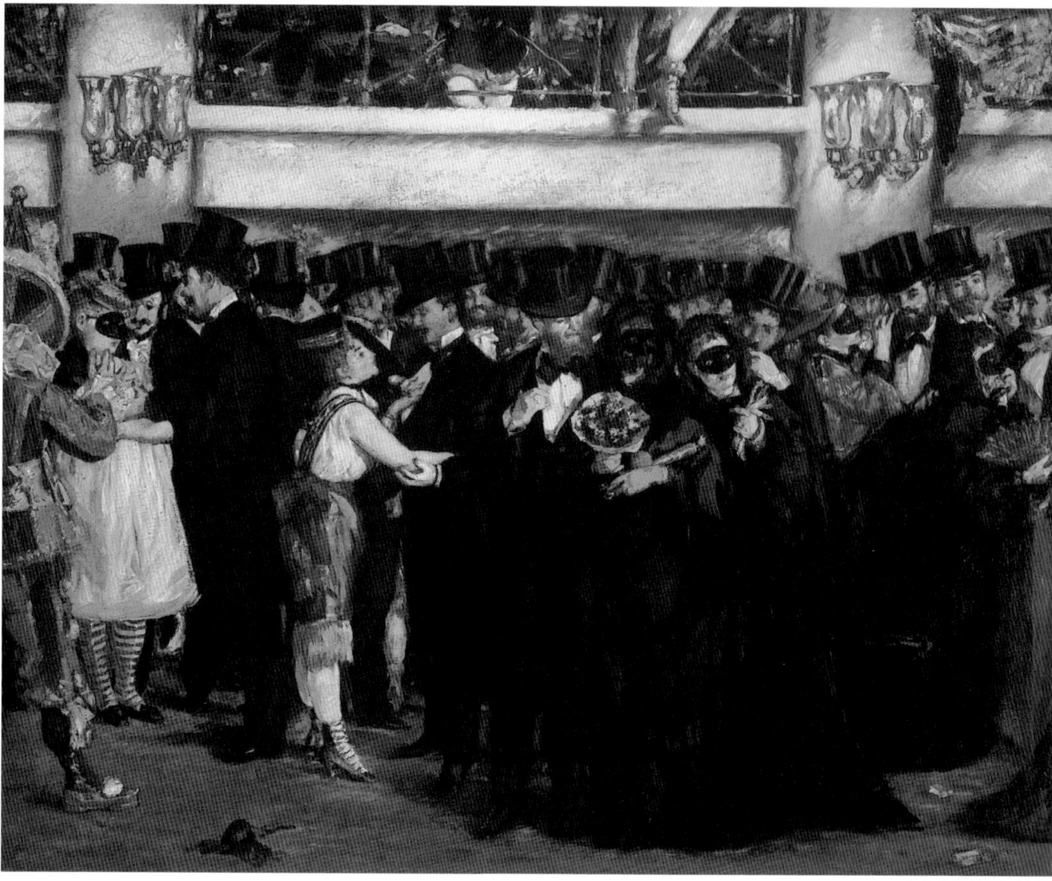

164   Edouard Manet, *Masked Ball at the Opera*, 1873, oil on canvas, 59.1 × 72.5 cm. National Gallery of Art, Washington, D.C. Gift of Mrs. Horace Havemeyer in memory of her mother-in-law, Louisine W. Havemeyer.

who either were related to him or who played signficant roles in his artistic life. At the beginning of his career, he focused on family members such as his parents and brothers, attending especially to the development of the physiognomy and the emergence into manhood of Léon Leenhoff, he of indeterminate paternity who played studio roles and then finally played himself in company with another painter of Manet's circle, in the *Luncheon in the Studio* (see fig. 80). Very rarely he depicted Suzanne, once in dialogue with an 1865 portrait of himself with his wife by Degas, from which, significantly, he excised his own likeness (figs. 165, 166). But in the early 1860s it was his favorite model, Victorine Meurent, on whom Manet leaned the most, using her repeated face and figure to chart the mutability of a single person's identity and likeness through a non-linear series of painting pairs foregrounding her role plays and costume changes – in which both her face and figure, sometimes alone, sometimes grouped with others, and once (in *The Fifer*) collapsed with another likeness, alter and yet remain the same, and somehow recognizable.

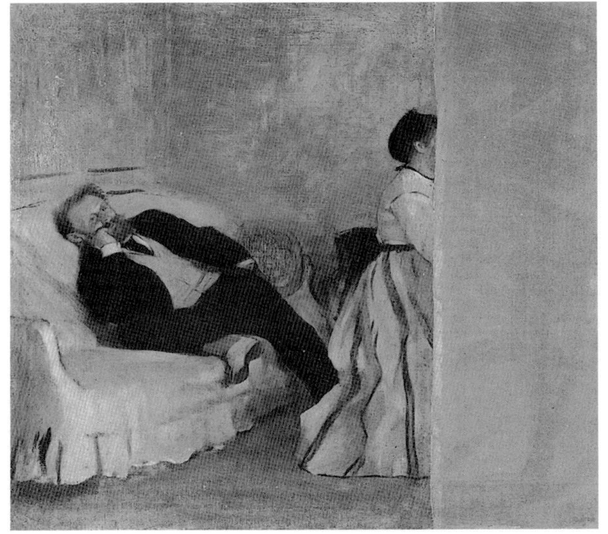

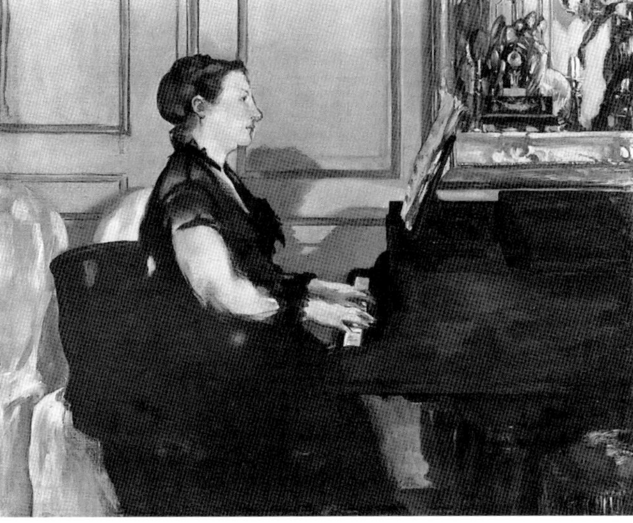

165   Edgar Degas, *M. and Mme Edouard Manet*, c.1868–69, oil on canvas, 65 × 71 cm. Kitakyushi Municipal Museum of Art, Japan.

166   Edouard Manet, *Madame Manet at the Piano*, 1868, oil on canvas, 38 × 46.5 cm. Musée d'Orsay, Paris.

Later, Manet painted portraits of fellow artists with whom he had important relationships: Eva Gonzalès painting under his guidance and with a signature Manet blossom at her skirt – the one painter Manet could truly claim as a student; Berthe Morisot not painting, but looking at once *farouche* and *soignée*, with a casual grace to match Manet's own courtly elegance (as *bourgeois gentilhomme*, Manet clearly identified with Morisot's predicament of painting or propriety, for his doubling of refractoriness and respectability was the masculine version of hers, and hers the feminine variety of his); Claude Monet painting *en plein air*, as Manet was then trying to do, or *en famille* in a property not so far from Manet's own. One might say that Manet represented himself, too, when he painted portraits of writers identified with his project in one way or another – Zacharie Astruc, Théodore Duret, Emile Zola, and later, Stéphane Mallarmé. And sometimes he painted himself into the countenances of people who looked something like him – as, for example, Zola, whose pamphlets are signed with the reciprocal relationship between writer and painter, or Jules Guillemet with his modishly hatted, gowned, and parasoled wife in *The Conservatory*, which might be considered a *sain et sauf* substitute representation of Manet's own married state, in which a man is shown not alone in relation to himself, but in relation to his "other half" (and from which Manet need not go to the trouble of excising his own features). Each of these representations of other people standing in for Manet exist in a different relationship to Manet: in particular, his female counterparts stand in for him rather differently, and certainly less straightforwardly, than his male compatriots, doubling as they all do the roles of subject and object, and making the nature of identity itself ambiguous, as Victorine's features do more specifically. But across them all, it is striking that Manet chose to paint the likenesses of others who were linked to him or like him in one way or another, rather than painting himself.

Toward the end of his life, there was one particular instance of this. In 1880, Manet exhibited a substitute for himself at the Salon, which has some bearing on what I would describe as his dialogic (rather than monologic) model of the likeness, and with it of identity and personal style – his portrait of the man who was the author of the verbal portrait of Manet just cited, Antonin Proust (fig. 167). Proust was a public man, a journalist, critic, and politician, who during his brief tenure as Minister of Fine Arts between 1881 and 1882 awarded Manet a Legion of Honor, finally giving the painter the institutional recognition that he had long sought. His authoritative biography of Manet became one of the most important sources of all later accounts of the artist's life. Who, then, could better "represent" Manet than Proust? Who better to be Manet's public "likeness"?[9] Of course, in any literal sense Manet's portrait of Proust is no self-portrait. But it entered into dialogue with a much earlier portrait of Manet by Fantin-Latour (fig. 168) from the time of the artist's "personal exposition" of 1867, in which Victorine and others wore so many different clothes (other than their own), played so many different roles (other than themselves), and referred to so many different paintings from the history of art (other than Manet's own).[10]

Fantin-Latour's 1867 portrait shows the younger Manet, against a blank ground, as the well-dressed *flâneur* he was reputed to be, decked out in the full regalia of a gleaming top-hat, light brown mustachios, and full, face-softening beard, a blue cravat and white shirt collar, a vest with a precisely rendered watch-fob, an open black coat over buff trousers, two thin glimpses of starched white shirt cuffs, two kid gloves, one off and one on so as to punctuate the lit and shadowed sides of his slightly turned body, and a gilt-headed, silver-tipped cane held horizontally in both gloved, ungloved fists across the front of his thighs, which are cut off and hobbled by the bottom framing edge of the painting. His glance is indeterminately directed, his pose unmoving and without contrapposto, and the slight shadows that his garments cast emphasize the shallow relief and "licked" handling of Fantin-Latour's characteristic manner, signed with a flourish at the lower left edge: "To my friend Manet, Fantin, 1867," so that the signature establishes not just Fantin's authorship of the portrait but his relationship to its subject as well.

Manet's later portrait of Proust retains the blank ground that he and Fantin-Latour often shared, as well as the general haberdashery of Manet's earlier likeness, with the following alterations. The black and buff tonality of Fantin-Latour's painting is given a darker, more forceful cast, and Fantin-Latour's facture is broadened, especially in the face and figure of Proust, particularly in the rendering of the highlit sheen of the top-hat, the hair of Proust's luxurious blond mustache and full gray beard, the sleeves of his coat, and the hand and gloves in which they terminate. The coat that Proust wears is a longer double-breasted frock coat, and rather than being open it is buttoned all the way up to the top, revealing a shirt collar with a black (not blue) cravat and impastoed tie-pin, relieved, not by a gold watch chain, but by a rosebud *boutonnier* and a thin white slash of pocket handerchief, similar to the thicker lines of white making up Proust's shirt cuffs, together showing off Manet's way with facture and that facture's ability to produce such sartorial supplements convincingly. Finally, Proust sports a cane just as Manet did in Fantin-Latour's portrait of him, and he wears one yellow glove on and one off; more than anything else those two loosely treated yellow gloves, together with the one bare, just as loosely treated hand, show off the factural difference between Manet's and Fantin-Latour's handling.

The portrait of Proust also alters the cut-off-at-the-knees stance of the flaneur, so that Fantin-Latour's static, side-turned, close-bodied pose is replaced by a frontal, aggressively open, space-occupying one, with its akimbo right arm and extended left arm, the cane firmly grasped in one fist and this time evidently angled to meet the ground beneath the frame and support Proust's lean into it. Proust's confident gaze, as in so many of Manet's subjects, looks directly out to meet the viewer's. All in all, Manet's portrait of Proust answers Fantin-Latour's portrait of Manet by bringing it alive in the healthy, rosy-complexioned man about town figure of his longtime friend. Indeed, in Manet's portrait Proust is much more robust than Manet himself was at the time. Perhaps this was the way Manet wanted to look then. Certainly Manet's swaggering portrait of Proust is closer to the way Proust later described the young Manet than Manet was at this time. And Manet's signature states his relationship to Proust, for, placed like Fantin's signature at the lower left of the canvas so that it mimics and shifts it, it reads: "To my friend Antonin Proust, 1880, Manet." Thus a triangular relationship of painter, painter, and painted is formed, for that signature serves simultaneously as a tribute to Proust and a doff of the hat to Fantin-Latour, signing and sealing Manet's response both to Fantin-Latour's depiction of him and to Fantin-Latour's "handwriting" while also allying himself to Proust. And so, doubling as autograph and homage, inscription of himself and to another, it points as explicitly as Manet could to his dialogic structuring of his own likeness, to the way his self was to be produced in relay, in the sense of a chain of "persons appointed to relieve [Manet] in the performance of [himself]."[11] It was in that chain of painted persons, in the gaps and correspondences between them, that Manet located himself, rather than in the closed circle and one-to-one equivalence between a man and his mirror, which Manet tended to avoid.

It is worth attending more closely to the yellow gloves, one off and one on, that are worn by both Fantin-Latour's Manet and Manet's Antonin Proust, for they too are emblematic. Those gloves had shown up in more than one portrait by Manet: as noted, they had decorated Mme Guillemet, seated next to her Manet-look-alike husband, in the conservatory painting of 1879 (see fig. 107). Found particularly in portraits of women, they went all the way back to his earliest female portrait of 1860, of Mme Brunet, in which the dangling yellow-gloved hand is answered by a bare, beringed, diagonally posed hand holding its squashed, cupped, half-reversed companion, and thus speaks directly to the supplementarity and reversibility, not to mention the sexual associations, of this particular accessory: its ability to be put on and taken off, to be full and empty, formed and unformed, outside in and inside out, matching and unmatching, the same and different from its partner, not to mention the fact that it declares its constitution out of yellow paint (versus white pigment, for the ungloved hand), while also problematizing the difference between flesh and leather, that which is integral to and that which is detachable from the portrayed individual. One of those yellow gloves showed up again in the fashion-plate profile of Jeanne Demarsy with a springtime bonnet, parasol, and chintz confection of a dress that was exhibited in Manet's last Salon of 1882, together with the *Bar at the Folies-Bergère*. That yellow glove emblematizes Manet's attachment

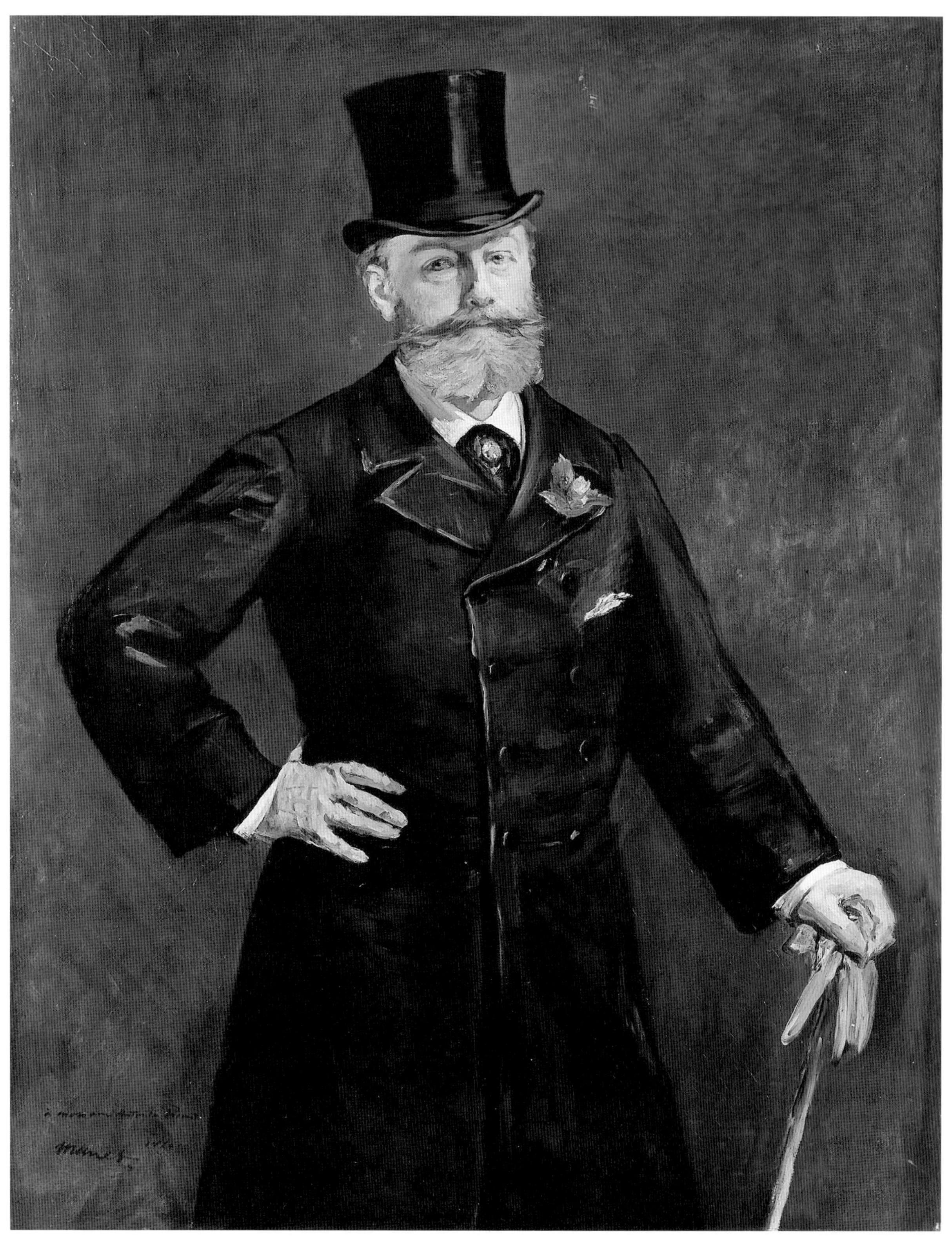

167 Edouard Manet, *Antonin Proust*, 1880, oil on canvas, 129.9 × 95.9 cm. The Toledo Museum of Art. Gift of Edward Drummond Libbey, 1925.108.

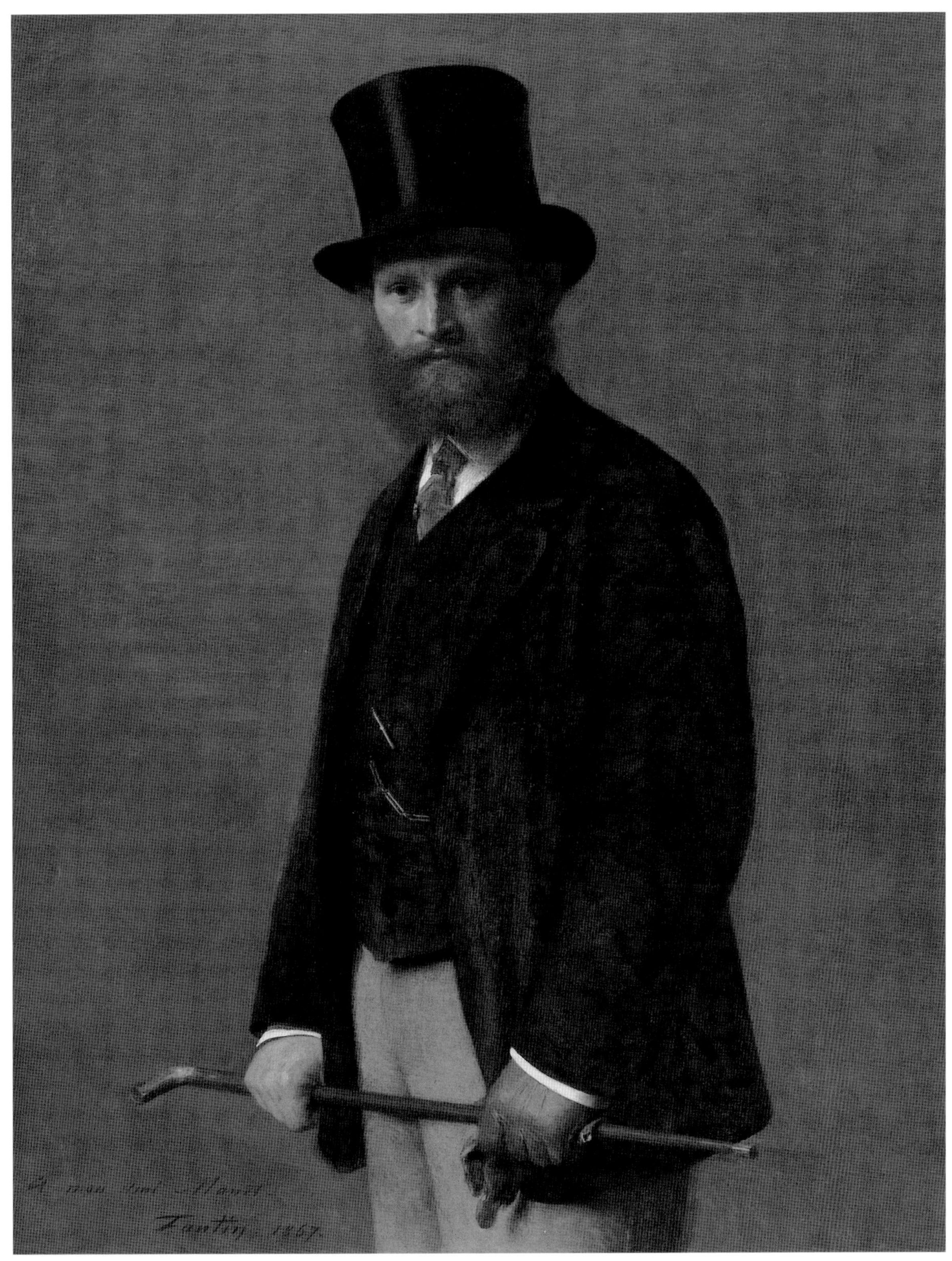

168 Henri Fantin-Latour, *Edouard Manet*, 1867, oil on canvas, 117.5 × 90 cm. The Art Institute of Chicago. Stickney Fund, 1905.207.

to a Baudelairean model of identity: madeup, decentered and dialogic, a cosmetic second skin more often associated with the "feminine," based on the circulation and exchange of supplements, and destabilizing of the transparency of the likeness and the tautological self-identicalness of the self.[12]

In his "Souvenirs," Proust reported on Manet's reactions to the public's reactions to the painter's painting of Proust when it was shown at the Salon.[13] Before going on to quote other remarks concerning the portrait by other friends and critics of Manet's, Proust quotes a letter that Manet wrote to him at the time of the Salon of 1880, which among other things highlights the yellow gloves:

> Manet wrote to me:
>
> "It's been three weeks, my dear friend, since your portrait has been up at the Salon, badly hung in a narrow section near a door, and received even worse than it's hung. But it is my lot to be vilified and I am philosophical about it. Nevertheless, my dear friend, you cannot believe how discomforting it is *to plant a figure alone in a canvas and to invest in this lone and unique figure all one's interest, without its losing its life and presence. To make two figures who draw their attraction from the duality of their personae is child's play in comparison.* . . . Your portrait is the sincerest work there can be. *I remember as if it were yesterday the rapid and summary way in which I handled the glove of the ungloved hand. And when you said to me at that moment: 'I beg you, not another touch,' I felt we were so perfectly in accord that I could not resist the desire to embrace you.* Ah! I trust that later they don't get the idea to stick this portrait in a public collection! I've always had a horror of that mania for piling up art works without letting the light of day between the frames, just as one puts the latest novelties on the shelves of fashionable stores. Anyway, whichever of us lives will see. I leave it in the hands of destiny.
>
> To you,
> Edouard Manet."[14]

Where Manet quotes Fantin in order to portray Proust, Proust quotes Manet remembering himself portraying Proust, in order to portray Manet as Proust remembers him. This passage represents a more restricted, circular dialogue than any that Manet engaged in, but it is emphatically dialogic nonetheless. And it places the yellow gloves, the final "touch" on Manet's canvas representing Proust, at the center of the conversation between the two men: as if to signify a handshake between them, their "embrace," and their exchanging of places. Above all, this letter by Manet to Proust concerning Manet's portrait of Proust, quoted by Proust in his portrait of Manet, confirms the ease with which Manet devoted himself to the "duality of . . . personae," as he put it, relative to the difficulty of painting the single, "lone and unique" person, most particularly himself.[15]

*   *   *

I end with one of the few self-portraits proper that Manet did paint, the *Self-Portrait with Palette* of around 1879 (fig. 169).[16] Never exhibited during Manet's lifetime, this self-portrait was painted toward the end of his career, when he was already ill and his face

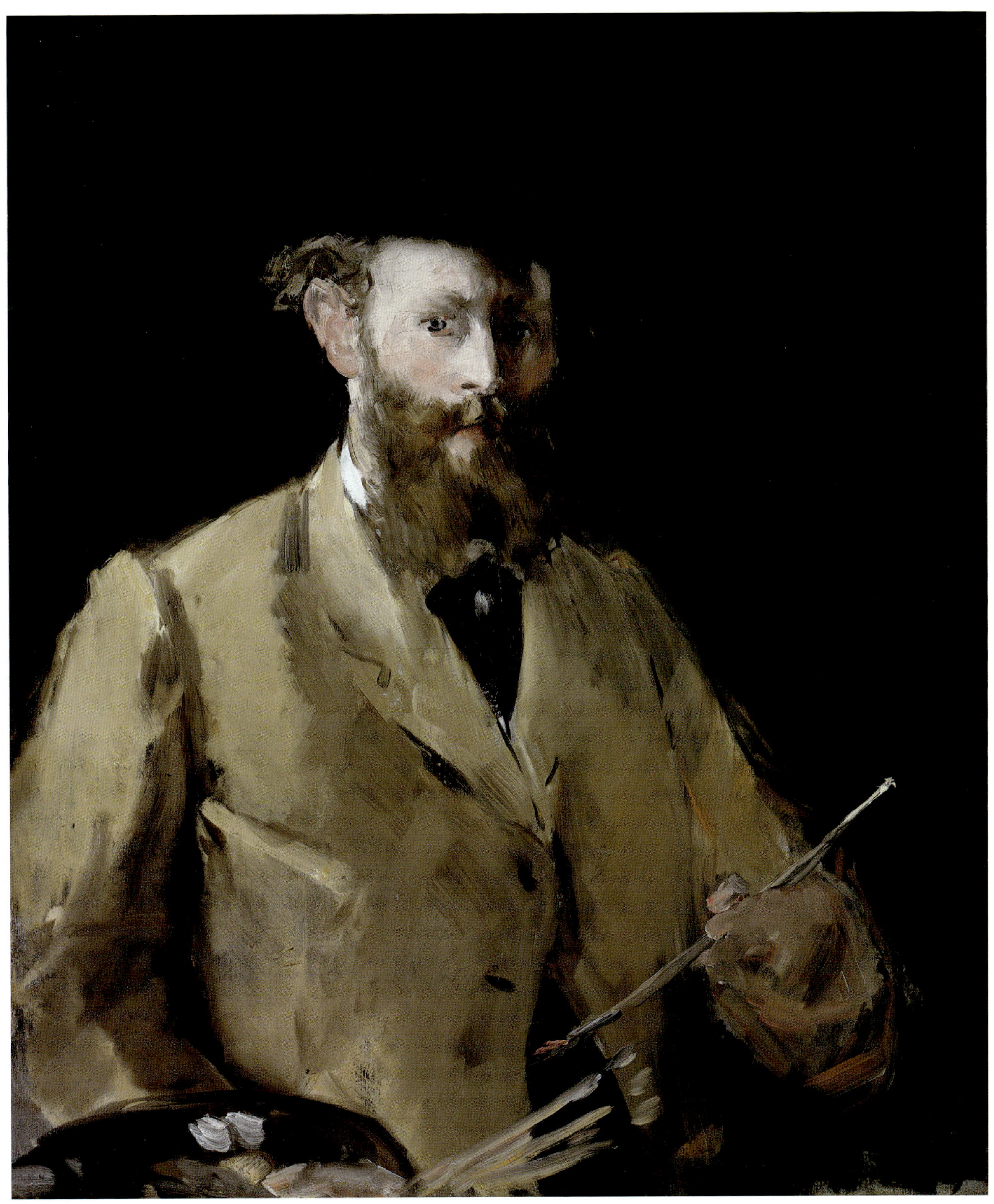

169　Edouard Manet, *Self-Portrait with Palette*, c.1879, oil on canvas, 83 × 67 cm. Stephen A. Wynn, Las Vegas.

was the gaunt ghost of its former attractive self. His diminished, brushily indistinct face has the dotted eyes and blurred aspect of many of his later "Impressionist" studies of women, with the nose more focused than the eyes – one lost to the shadow cast over the left side of the face by the brim of the bowler hat – or the mouth, itself half given over to obscurity and surrendered to the soft smudge of paint that renders the beard that obscures the lower face, or for that matter the outsized right ear, which emerges from beneath hair and hat as a strangely amorphous weal of brick-hued pink – an escutcheon of the *informe* that inserts itself everywhere into the bold singularity of Manet's style, emblazoned on the side of Manet's face. The clothes, too, are inconclusive and contradictory: raffish bowler, loose yellow studio coat with fudged edges, and the briefest indication of cravat and jewel pin, poignant hints at the formality, personal splendor, and care for appearance that were signature traits of Manet's, submerged within a general semblance of casualness that is the combined effect of sartorial choice and paint handling. Meanwhile his trunk has expanded to fill the lower left two-thirds of the canvas, indeterminately bloated so that the status of its mass as body, billowing jacket, or simply undecided facture is irresolute. Overall, the self-portrait has the look of a man standing before his mirror with his paintbrush in hand, ready to paint but not quite able to get himself into focus. (It does not surprise, by the way, that Manet chose Proust to represent him at the Salon, rather than this vacillating likeness of himself.[17])

Then the decision is made: to attend to the hand holding the brush, the pink tip of tensed thumb matched to the livid patch on the pallid cheek, the brush at the end of the diagonal leading down from hand to palette, and the palette itself, with another bit of thumb thrust through it, radiating paint streaks signifying brushes whose tips coincide with the jacket's edge, thumb and palette together lined up with the stabilizing bottom line of the canvas. It is striking that Manet chose to paint himself most fully at the moment when he was decidedly past his best, and to identify his own decline in robustness with the indecisive look of a pseudo-Impressionist facture. But it is also striking that this self-portrait seems to attach itself to the formalist model of the canvas, "hunted back" to itself, emphasizing its own limited opticality, which Greenberg traced back to Impressionist painting.[18]

The *Self-Portrait with Palette* is dialogic too, though it is so in an unusually muted, reduced way: in it Manet adopts the stance of Velasquez before his easel (fig. 170), in reverse as usual (as if still answering to the print-reversal conditions of reproduction), and minus Velasquez's courtly context, which is replaced by the painter's painting relationship with himself, collapsed onto the single plane of the canvas. Indeed, relative to all the slanting away from the canvas found in *Las Meniñas* – in the large, listing canvas on which the royal painter works, in the painter's tilted head and turned body, and in his canted palette – Manet's figure is flattened out to meet and fill the picture surface, and give all of itself to the gaze. But what it gives is somehow both more and less: looking back through Fantin-Latour's group portrait of the *Studio at Batignolles* to Velasquez's *Las Meniñas*, Manet eliminated even more than Fantin-Latour had done. For if Fantin-Latour had replaced the complicated imbrication of prince and painter, power and picture, social and representational relationships in Velasquez's court with a compressed world of artists and artists alone, Manet further contracted Fantin-Latour's social circle

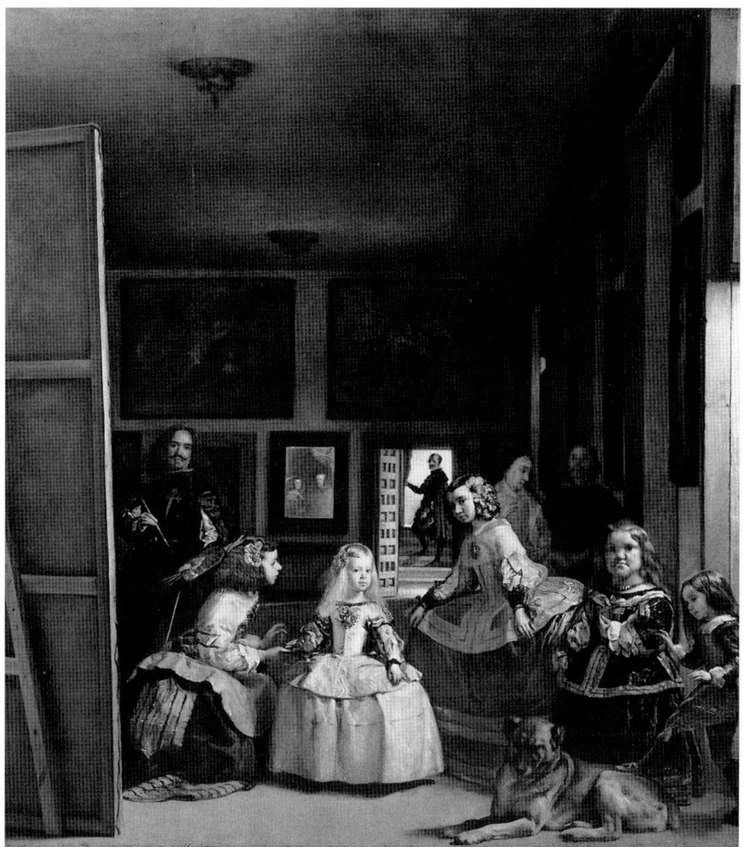

170   Diego Velasquez, *Las Meniñas*, 1656, oil on canvas, 318 × 276 cm. Museo del Prado, Madrid.

of painters and their friends to an attenuated, one-on-one relationship to his own like-ness, from which almost all sense of the social framing of an identity is eradicated.[19] (The glimmer in the cravat notifies us, still, that Manet is a social as well as a painting man, an appearance to others as well as to himself, but it too, like the glint in the uncannily dead eye which it resembles, declares itself a hesitant bit of paint.) Instead, and for once, Manet has painted the tautology of self-identity – I see myself as such, therefore I am. He has, in a sense, given us precisely what Velasquez in his courtly world denied us – the image being painted on the canvas. But that image is himself, and himself alone: the canvas conflates in one figure and one surface the painter painting and the painter painted, the act of painting and the result of that act. The canvas presents itself, that is, as simultaneously a representation of the painter at work (or about to be at work) on a canvas and as, literally, the canvas upon which he works, and upon which his self-representation is produced; it joins its own future, present, and past tenses, too – getting ready to paint, the act of painting, and the fact of having been painted. In short, it suggests that the subject and object of Manet's brush are one and the same, and that no other intrudes, no outside spectator or any differentiation between himself as painter, himself as viewer, and himself as painted and viewed object. This one time, Manet's *Self-Portrait with Palette* conjoins the circular, self-enclosed oneness of the modern identity to the self-reflexive unity of the modernist picture: I am what I am (as man and medium), I am nothing other than myself. It is no wonder, then, that it would serve as a model for other modernist self-portrayers, such as Cézanne, Van Gogh, and Picasso too (figs. 171–73).[20]

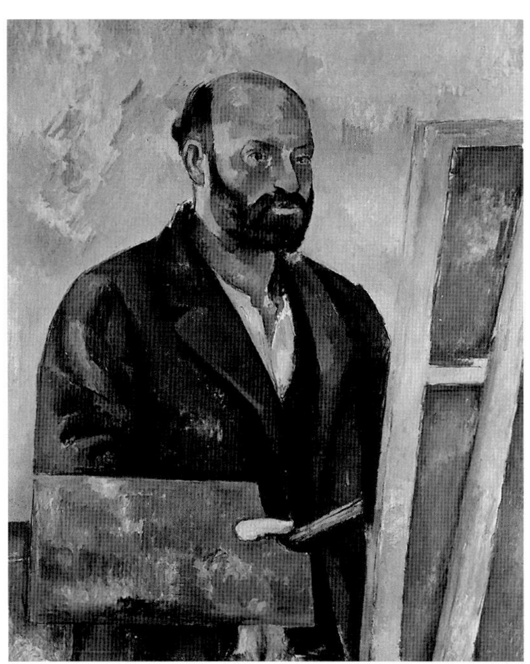

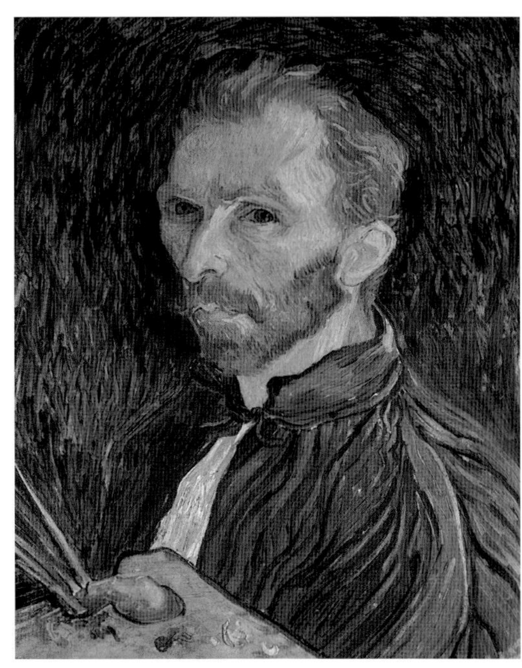

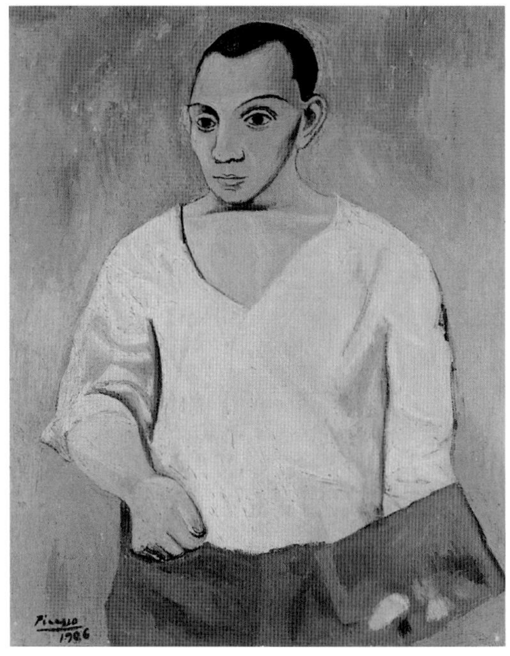

171 (*above left*)   Paul Cézanne, *Self-Portrait with Palette*, 1884, oil on canvas, 92.5 × 73 cm. E. G. Bührle Collection, Zurich.

172 (*above right*)   Vincent Van Gogh, *Self-Portrait*, 1889, oil on canvas, 65.5 × 50.5 cm. Rijksmuseum, Amsterdam.

173   Pablo Ruiz y Picasso, *Self-Portrait*, 1906, oil on canvas, 92 × 73 cm. Philadelphia Museum of Art: A. E. Gallatin Collection.

Yet to focus in this way on the painting's consistency with the modernist models of selfhood and medium specificity is not only to ignore its fundamental undecidedness, not to mention its status as an exception in Manet's oeuvre, the fact that it was the much less traveled of several roads toward the defining of an artistic identity. It is also to miss the poignancy of the self-portrait's reductions and deletions and the cost of what it absents from itself. For indeed, the *Self-Portrait with Palette* is a picture of what, in a sense, Manet had always been: a courtier without a court, a "cavalier" come too late to be painted by Velasquez. It is a picture of a man, "lone and unique," stranded out of time: such is the effect of self-commemoration generally, but in this case that atemporal aloneness is more specific in its negativity; Manet needed the structure of a society for definition, but the society he had was not the society he wanted. Had he worked, like Velasquez, within the confines of a court in which selves were produced in costume, in representation and in relation to others, he would perhaps have been at home, and his portraits of people playing roles, in paintwork that was a coloristic caricature of the seventeenth-century Spanish court painter's work, selected and blown up, might not have seemed so out of place to his peers.[21] But as it was, he worked at a time when the modern, bourgeois sense of the masculine self (and of *puissant* painting too) as a matter of Nature was being solidified once and for all, and where the ultimate values, both given and attained, were to be those of uniqueness, autonomy, and self-consistency. It was Manet's estranged relation to that world that gave his figures "plant[ed] . . . alone in [their] canvases" their existential strangeness: that made them modern, but modern in dialogic and differential relation both to their own time and to the past that went before them. And it was Manet's fascinated relation to women such as Victorine Meurent, Berthe Morisot, and then Méry Laurent and others, who possessed all the lability, the feminine flair for cosmetic and vestimentary artifice, and the Baudelairean *surnaturel* that his gender lacked in the positive age that gave his Manettes their disquieting authority, their weird priority as images of both *autrui* and *lui-même*.

FOREWORD

1   Clement Greenberg, "Manet in Philadelphia," *Artforum*, January 1967, in Clement Greenberg, *The Collected Essays and Criticism*, ed. John O'Brian, 4 vols., University of Chicago Press, 1986–93, vol. 4, p. 240.

2   Greenberg, "The Crisis of the Easel Picture" (1948), *ibid.*, vol. 2, p. 222.

3   The following is a sampling of the occurrence of Manet's name in Greenberg's writing: "And *with Manet and Courbet* Western painting reversed its direction" ("Abstract Art," 1944, *ibid.*, vol. 1, p. 201); "The tradition of painting which runs *from Manet* through impressionism, fauvism, and cubism has created the first original style since the French revolution, and the only original one our bourgeois society has been capable of" ("Surrealist Art," 1945, *ibid.*, vol. 1, p. 230); "Monet worked into the photographic impressionism of atmospheric darks and lights and summary definitions that *Manet was the first* to devise" ("Review of an Exhibition of Claude Monet," 1945, *ibid.*, vol. 2, p. 21); "What characterized painting *in the line Manet to Mondrian*" ("Review of Exhibitions of Hyman Bloom, David Smith, and Robert Motherwell," 1946, *ibid.*, vol. 2, p. 51); "In his epoch-making *Déjeuner sur l'Herbe Manet anticipates* what Gauguin only isolates and emphasizes: the large, sharply silhouetted areas of flat, uniform color" ("Review of Exhibitions of Paul Gauguin and Arshile Gorky," 1946, *ibid.*, vol. 2, p. 77); "the character of painting *since Manet*" ("Review of an Exhibition of Giorgio de Chirico," 1947, *ibid.*, vol. 2, p. 135); "One thing that painting *since Manet* has emphasized is that a picture has to have a 'back'" ("Review of the Whitney Annual and Exhibitions of Picasso and Henri Cartier-Bresson," 1947, *ibid.*, vol. 2, p. 139); "Matisse . . . uses black better than anyone else *since Manet*, not excepting Braque" ("Review of Exhibitions of Henri Matisse, Eugène Boudin, John Piper, and Misha Reznikoff," 1948, *ibid.*, vol. 2, p. 209); "When, as *Manet and the impressionists* began doing, the artist flattens this cavity out . . . The evolution of modern painting *from Manet on* has subjected the traditional cabinet picture to an interrupted process of attrition . . . (It is significant that the most radical steps taken in painting *since Manet's time* have . . . been accompanied by the tendency to atomize the picture surface into separate brush-strokes.)" ("The Crisis of the Easel Picture," 1948, *ibid.*, vol. 2, pp. 221, 222, 223); "what painting has been about *since Manet* first laid his shapes in flat . . . the central premise of painting *since Manet* . . . has been its progressive surrender to, its increasing acknowledgement of, the physical nature of the medium . . ." ("Review of the Exhibition *Collage*," 1948, *ibid.*, vol. 2, pp. 259, 262); "The apostles of the modern movement on, *from Manet on* . . . Completing *Manet's* involuntary break with Renaissance tradition, he [Cézanne] fell upon a new principle of painting that carried further into the future. Like *Manet* . . . he changed the course of art . . ." ("Cézanne and the Unity of Modern Art," 1951, *ibid.*, vol. 3, pp. 82, 84); "*Edouard Manet* (1832–1883) was the first painter in our tradition to flatten . . . a tendency towards flatness in painting . . . that *goes back to Manet* . . ." ("Cézanne: Gateway to Contemporary Painting," 1952, *ibid.*, vol. 3, pp. 114, 118); "Every fresh and productive impulse in painting *since*

Manet..." ("Symposium: Is the French Avant-Garde Overrated?," 1953, *ibid.*, vol. 3, p. 156); "But *Manet* began to pull the backdrop of this stage forward..." ("Abstract and Representational," 1954, *ibid.*, vol. 3, p. 190); "Modern art, *dating from Manet...*" ("The Later Monet," 1957, *ibid.*, vol. 4, p. 11); "*Manet's* became the first Modernist pictures by virtue of the frankness with which they declared the flat surfaces on which they were painted. The Impressionists, *in Manet's wake... With Manet and the Impressionists* the question... became one of purely optical experience against optical experience as revised or modified by tactile associations" ("Modernist Painting," 1960, *ibid.*, vol. 4, pp. 86, 89); "the evolution of Western art (at progressively shorter intervals *since Manet*)" ("After Abstract Expressionism," 1962, *ibid.*, vol. 4, p. 123); "*Since Manet* every step in the evolution of modernist art..." ("How Art Writing Earns Its Bad Name," 1962, *ibid.*, vol. 4, p. 143); "In the early 1860s *Manet's* flat and rapid version of naturalism led the way" ("Avant-Garde Attitudes: New Art in the Sixties," 1969, *ibid.*, vol. 4, p. 295). My emphasis.

4 Greenberg's use of the name Manet as synonomous with the modernist teleology is linked, often implicitly and sometimes explicitly, to the Kantian and Hegelian traditions of aesthetic thought. In "Abstract Art" (1944), *ibid.*, vol. 1, p. 201, the reference to the names "Courbet" and "Manet" follows immediately on a mention of the name "Hegel" and the end of "world systems" such as Hegel's, which were to be replaced by an "age of specialization." In "Modernist Painting" (1960), *ibid.*, vol. 4, Greenberg deploys the terms of Wölfflinian formalism while also identifying "Modernism" with "Kantian self-criticism" (pp. 85, 90): "I identify Modernism with the intensification, almost the exacerbation, of this self-critical tendency that began with the philosopher Kant. Because he was the first to criticize the means itself of criticism, I conceive of Kant as the first real Modernist" (p. 85). Elsewhere he calls on Kant to support his view that all (good) art is "one," and that as such quality in art transcends discourse: "This is what all the serious philosophers of art since Immanuel Kant have concluded" ("The Identity of Art," *ibid.*, vol. 4, pp. 117–18). Mentions of Kant abound in Greenberg's earlier criticism as well; it is clear that Greenberg thought that Immanuel Kant's *Critique of Aesthetic Judgement* (1790), (J. H. Bernard, trans.), New York, Hafner Press, 1951,

was foundational to his formalism. At the same time, the 1960 essay "Modernist Painting" is the most concerted statement regarding the Kantianism of Greenbergian modernism, and in general the emphasis on the transcendental aspect of Kant's notion of aesthetic judgment is stepped up in the later criticism. On the vexed subject of Greenberg's Kantianism, see Stephen Melville, "Kant after Greenberg," *Journal of Aesthetics and Art Criticism* 51, Winter 1998, pp. 67–74; Paul Crowther, "Greenberg's Kant and the Problems of Modernist Painting," *British Journal of Aesthetics* 25, Autumn 1985, pp. 317–25; Thierry de Duve, *Kant after Duchamp*, Cambridge, Mass., MIT Press, 1996. See also de Duve, *Clement Greenberg Between the Lines* (Brian Holmes, trans.), Paris, Editions Dis Voir, 1996.

5 On this, see my *Odd Man Out: Readings of the Work and Reputation of Edgar Degas*, University of Chicago Press, 1991, esp. pp. 40–43.

6 See Christopher Reed, ed., *A Roger Fry Reader*, Chicago and London, University of Chicago Press, 1996, pp. 83, 87, 106, 403.

7 This view is repeated by Robert Hughes, for example, in *The Shock of the New*, New York, Alfred A. Knopf, 1982, p. 373.

8 T. J. Clark, *The Painting of Modern Life: Paris in the Art of Manet and his Followers*, New York, Alfred A. Knopf, 1985.

9 Michael Fried, *Manet's Modernism or, The Face of Painting in the 1860s*, Chicago and London, University of Chicago Press, 1996.

10 Clark, *Painting of Modern Life*, pp. 10–11; he cites Greenberg, "Modernist Painting," *Art and Literature* 4, Spring 1965, p. 194 (first given in 1960 as a "Forum Lecture" on Voice of America; rev. and repr. in *The Collected Essays and Criticism*, vol. 4, pp. 85–93; cited above). Clark, *The Painting of Modern Life*, pp. 3–5, 9, 16, also cites Meyer Schapiro, "The Nature of Abstract Art," *Marxist Quarterly*, January–March 1937, repr. in *Modern Art: 19th and 20th Centuries*, New York, George Braziller, 1978, pp. 185–211. In addition, he assimilates Mallarmé's view of Manet to that of Greenberg (Stéphane Mallarmé, "The Impressionists and Edouard Manet," *Art Monthly Review*, September 30, 1876). This engagement with the formalist account of modernism also constitutes the strength and interest of Clark's account – its difference from other socio-historical accounts, such as Robert Herbert's *Impressionism: Art, Leisure, and Parisian Society*, New Haven and London, Yale University Press, 1988. (See in addition Hollis Clayson, *Painted Love:*

Prostitution in French Art of the Impressionist Era, New Haven and London, Yale University Press, 1991, p. 27, for its address to the Greenbergian account of modernism.) Clark's commitment to a heroic modernism – whose very failure is a mark of its tragic greatness – is nowhere more evident than in *Farewell to an Idea: Episodes from a History of Modernism*, New Haven and London, Yale University Press, 1999, which traces a (broken) line from David, through Pissarro and Cézanne, Picasso and Malevich, to Pollock. See also Clark, "Clement Greenberg's Theory of Art," *Critical Inquiry* 9, September 1980, pp. 139–56.

11   Fried, *Manet's Modernism*, pp. 13–16. *Manet's Modernism* (pp. xxv, 23–184) begins with a republication, updating, and vindication of "Manet's Sources: Aspects of his Art, 1859–1865," *Artforum*, March 1969 (published two years after Greenberg's review).

12   See Fried on looking back to the eighteenth century: *Manet's Modernism*, p. xxv. On the theatricality of Minimalism, see Michael Fried, "Art and Objecthood" (*Artforum*, 1967), in Gregory Battcock, ed., *Minimal Art: A Critical Anthology*, New York, Dutton, 1968, pp. 116–47; and in *Art and Objecthood: Essays and Reviews*, Chicago and London, University of Chicago Press, 1998, pp. 148–172.

13   Greenberg understood that single-painting inconsistency, as so many before him had, as evidence of compositional difficulties and, as was his wont, recommended radical surgery as a retrospective cure for the problem – "Manet in Philadelphia," p. 243.

14   The repression – and the irrepressible return of the repressed – of the ruptural effects of body parts and other elements on the aesthetic plane that is characteristic of formalist aesthetics is exemplified in several notable passages in Roger Fry, *Cézanne, A Study of His Development* (1927), Chicago and London, University of Chicago Press, 1989, as in his discussion of "the foot sticking into the picture" and "growing from the edge of the frame" of Cézanne's *Banquet*, the disturbance created by the shadow cast by the open drawer in the book's centerpiece, the *Compotier* – Fry is tempted "to cover this part of the canvas with an indiscreet finger" – and the discourse on the disruptive effect of the image of Woman (in *La Femme*) on the coherence of Cézanne's "internal stimulus," etc. (pp. 11, 47, 80–81). See Hubert Damisch, *The Judgment of Paris* (John Goodman, trans.), Chicago and London, University of Chicago Press, 1996, on the sublimation of the sexual in Western aesthetics. In *The Judgment of Paris*, Manet's *Déjeuner sur l'herbe* is both emblematic and the object of a chapter of sustained analysis ("A Woman, Then: *Le Déjeuner sur l'herbe*," pp. 61–76).

15   See Heinrich Wölfflin, *Principles of Art History: The Problem of the Development of Style in Later Art* (1915) (M. D. Hottinger, trans.), New York, Dover, 1950; and Aloïs Riegl, "Das Holländische Gruppenporträt," *Jahrbuch der Kunsthistorischen Sammlungen des Allerhöchsten Kaiserhauses* 23 (1902), pp. 71–278, excerpts of which, translated by Benjamin Binstock, are to be found in *October* 74, Fall 1995, pp. 3–35.

16   Or, among others, the 1884 retrospective held the year after Manet's death at the Ecole Nationale des Beaux-Arts in Paris; the retrospective held at the Orangerie in 1932, the centennial of Manet's birth; and the 1983 show held at the Grand Palais in Paris and the Metropolitan Museum of Art in New York at the time of the centennial of Manet's death.

17   For an equally, though differently ambivalent relationship to formalist models of unity, totality, and teleology, and to the Kantian/Hegelian tradition that underwrites them, see Theodor Adorno's *Aesthetic Theory* (1970) (C. Lenhardt, trans.), London and New York: Routledge & Kegan Paul, 1984.

18   See Andrew McClellan, *Inventing the Louvre: Art, Politics, and the Origins of the Modern Museum in 18th-Century Paris*, Cambridge University Press, 1994, pp. 3–48, on the application of Roger de Piles's comparative, dialogic principles to the hanging of the first modern museum, the Luxembourg.

19   On the series, see my *Odd Man Out*, esp. pp. 157–209; and Steven Z. Levine, "Monet's Series: Repetition, Obsession," *October* 37, Summer 1986, pp. 65–75.

20   On Manet's "exhibition strategy," see Kathleen Adler, *Manet*, Oxford, Phaidon, 1986, pp. 95–105: Adler finds Manet's "exhibition strategy" "diverse," experimental, and without a "formula," with which I agree, although I think its experimental diversity stands in need of more sustained analysis than that.

21   For a dialogic model of painting – both as a polyvocal structure in and of itself and as a process of conversation between pictures – I rely on M. M. Bahktin, *The Dialogic Imagination* (Caryl Emerson and Michael Holquist, trans.), Austin, University of Texas Press, 1981, who developed that model in relation to the nineteenth-century European novel. In general, I prefer the Russian formalist model of

criticism, predicated on critical concepts, like "impeded form" and "making strange," quite other than the transcendental values of autonomy and unity found in German, English, and American aesthetics: see Ladislav Matejka and Krystyna Pomorska, eds., *Readings in Russian Poetics: Formalist and Structuralist Views*, Cambridge, Mass., MIT Press, 1959; and Roman Jakobson, *Language and Literature* (Krystyna Pomorska and Stephen Rudy, trans. and ed.), Cambridge and London, Belknap Press of Harvard University Press, 1987, esp. "On Realism in Art," and "Linguistics and Poetics," pp. 19–27, 62–94. See also Ferdinand de Saussure, *Course in General Linguistics* (Wade Baskin, trans.), New York, McGraw-Hill, 1966, for its articulation of the divided structure of the sign – fundamentally distinguishing formalisms predicated on structural linguistics from those based on transcendental aesthetics.

22 See Greenberg, "Towards a Newer Laocoon" (1940), *Collected Essays and Criticism*, vol. 1, p. 32: "The arts, then, have been hunted back to their mediums, and there they have been isolated, concentrated and defined."

23 See G. W. F. Hegel, *Aesthetics: Lectures on Fine Art* (1828) (T. M. Knox, trans.), Oxford, Clarendon Press, 1975. Hegel's "romantic form of art," in which "art falls to pieces, on the one hand into the imitation of external objectivity in all its contingent shapes; on the other hand, however, into the liberation of subjectivity . . ." (vol. 1, p. 608), dividing itself between subject and object, form and content, matter and spirit, fragmenting into a multitudinous array of appearances and subject matters, and ultimately dissolving into obsolescence, applies to everything after ancient art; the history of painting to which it refers centers on the period from the Renaissance to the seventeenth century; it extends to the nineteenth century in the forms of literature and music. There is a medium-specific logic to this account; whereas according to Hegel sculpture, the medium of "the classical form of art," joins subject and object, form and content in one autonomous, self-sufficient, spirit-inhering body, it is the destiny of the medium of painting, the romantic (and therefore modern) form of visual art, to divide and be divided. This view of modern painting and its history resonates with the divided signifier/signified structure of the linguistic sign. And although it takes its cue in part from the Kantian distinction between the beautiful and the sublime as different modalities of self-reflexive subjectivity and

subject–object relations, and although its model of dialectical historical progression is taken up by Greenberg, this nevertheless marks a point of potential divergence between Hegel's story of "modernism" and that of Greenberg's Kantian-based formalism. See also Michael Podro, *The Critical Historians of Art*, New Haven and London, Yale University Press, 1982, pp. 17–30.

24 "le Coloris est non seulement une partie essentielle de la Peinture; mais encore qu'il est la différence . . . le Dessein soit le genre de la Peinture, et la Couleur sa différence"; "la Peinture n'est qu'un fard . . ." – Roger de Piles, *Dialogue sur le coloris*, pp. 25–26, 67, 68. See Jacqueline Lichtenstein, *La Couleur éloquente: Rhétorique et peinture à l'âge classique*, Paris, Flammarion, 1989; and "Making up Representation: The Risks of Femininity," *Representations* 20, Fall 1987, pp. 77–87. On de Piles, see Thomas Puttfarken, *Roger de Piles' Theory of Art*, New Haven and London, Yale University Press, 1985. There are, of course, some two hundred years between de Piles's *Dialogue* and Manet's two decades of painting. But the views espoused in the *Dialogue* had an afterlife: first, in the Rococo, and particularly in those painters like Watteau, Boucher, and Fragonard who in the eighteenth century took up the Rubensian strand of painting championed by de Piles in lieu of the Poussinian "line," but who were decried by critics of the Enlightenment such as Diderot. The Rococo was celebrated in the latter half of the nineteenth century by writers including the Goncourt brothers, and had its own afterlife in painting – in the Rubensian excesses and coloristic epiphanies of Delacroix, for example, in the nudes and suburban *fêtes-galantes* of painters such as Renoir, and in the early Watteau inspirations and the late florals and female portraits by Manet (which Greenberg surely would have described as kitsch – brushy and "illustrative").

25 For the classic articulation of the "male gaze," see Laura Mulvey, "Visual Pleasure and Narrative Cinema" (1975), *Visual and Other Pleasures*, Bloomington and Indianapolis, Indiana University Press, 1989, pp. 14–26. See also E. Ann Kaplan, "Is the Gaze Male?," in *Women and Film: Both Sides of the Camera*, New York and London, Methuen, 1983, pp. 23–35; Edward Snow, "Theorizing the Male Gaze: Some Problems," *Representations* 25, 1989, pp. 30–41; and Abigail Solomon-Godeau, "The Other Side of Venus: The Visual Economy of Feminine Display," in Victoria de Grazia and

Ellen Furlough, *The Sex of Things: Gender and Consumption in Historical Perspective*, Berkeley, University of California Press, 1996.

26 I include Baudelaire's *Le Peintre de la vie moderne*, published in 1863, within the literary genre of the story of the artist-*célibataire* that includes Balzac's novella, the Goncourts' and Zola's novels, among others, even though its protagonist, "M. G.," is putatively nonfictional. (At the time of the first publication of *Le Peintre de la vie moderne*, it was not known that "M. G." referred to Constantin Guys.)

27 There are many ways in which I depend upon Luce Irigaray's *This Sex Which Is Not One* (1977) (Catherine Porter, trans.), Ithaca, Cornell University Press, 1985. Although most of them are oblique, they are nonetheless crucial to my argument. I understand *This Sex Which Is Not One* not as an essentialist tract but as a strategic intervention into the structure of mainstream Western metaphysics and aesthetics as well as psychoanalysis, which, Irigaray claims, rests upon a (phallic, or "phallo-logocentric") model of unity, totality, and singularity, and which in aesthetics translates into the classical value of the visually rationalized and contained form or the transcendental One of the sublime instant. As with the "sex which is not one," so with Manet's painting: my claim will be that it defies and undermines such a structure from within.

ONE TWO RETROSPECTIVES

1 The brochure was reprinted again in 1879, in Zola's *Mes Haines*, as *Edouard Manet*. I refer to the reprint of the essay found in F. W. J. Hemmings and Robert J. Niess, *Emile Zola Salons*, Ann Arbor, University of Michigan, 1959, pp. 83–103.

2 Edmond and Jules de Goncourt, *Manette Salomon*, Paris, 1867; all of my references are to the 1979 edition, Fin de Siècle series, Paris, Union Générale d'Editions.

3 Courbet's first Salon was that of 1844, into which his *Self-Portrait with Black Dog* was accepted.

4 In 1822, Horace Vernet had exhibited forty-five of his own paintings in his studio: this was one of the few existing precedents for Courbet's maneuver. See Patricia Mainardi, "Courbet's Exhibitionism," *Gazette des Beaux-Arts* CXVIII, no. 1475, Dec. 1991, p. 264, n. 12; and Mainardi, *Art and Politics of the Second Empire: The Universal Expositions of 1855 and 1867*, New Haven

and London, Yale University Press, 1987, pp. 141–42. On the device of the retrospective, see Robert Jensen, *Marketing Modernism in Fin-de-Siècle Europe*, Princeton University Press, 1994, ch. 4, "The Retrospective," pp. 107–37. And on Courbet's retrospective specifically, see Yve-Alain Bois, "Exposition: esthétique de la distraction, espace de démonstration," *Cahiers du Musée national d'art moderne* 29, Automne 1989, pp. 57–79.

5 See Mainardi, *Art and Politics of the Second Empire*, pp. 57–61, 92–96. See also *L'Art en France sous le Second Empire*, Paris, Grand Palais, Réunion des musées nationaux, 1979.

6 See Hélène Toussaint, *Gustave Courbet 1819–1877*, Paris, Grand Palais, Réunion des musées nationaux, 1977, pp. 31–32.

7 There were 38 paintings originally listed, with 4 drawings and 2 other miscellaneous works added and 1 final addition handwritten at the end of the catalogue's list of works. See "Exhibition et vente de 40 tableaux et 4 dessins de l'oeuvre de M. Gustave Courbet" (copy in Paris, Bibliothèque Nationale, Cabinet des Estampes), in Theodore Reff, ed., *Exhibitions of Realist Art I* (*Modern Art in Paris: 200 Catalogues of the Major Exhibitions Reproduced in Facsimile in 47 Volumes*), New York and London, Garland, 1981.

8 In addition to the 4 works included in the Exposition of that year, there were 115 works listed in the catalogue to the 1867 retrospective – with 4–25 works gathered under each of the genre headings. (These works were no more chronologically ordered than those in the 1855 show.) Some 20 works beyond those listed were also shown. See Toussaint, *Gustave Courbet 1819–1877*, pp. 41–44; and Reff, *Exhibitions of Realist Art I*.

9 On Courbet's early Baroque-Romantic works, see T. J. Clark, *Image of the People: Gustave Courbet and the 1848 Revolution*, Princeton University Press, 1982, pp. 36–46. On his developing practice in landscape painting, see Anne Wagner, "Courbet's Landscapes and their Market," *Art History* 4, 1981, pp. 410–31. On Courbet's career more generally, see among others James H. Rubin, *Courbet*, London, Phaidon, 1997; Sarah Faunce and Linda Nochlin, *Courbet Reconsidered*, The Brooklyn Museum, Yale University Press, 1988; Michael Fried, *Courbet's Realism*, Chicago and London, University of Chicago Press, 1990; Klaus Herding, *Courbet: To Venture Independence* (John William Gabriel, trans.), New Haven and London, Yale University Press, 1991; Jack

Lindsay, *Gustave Courbet, His Life and Art*, Bath, Adams & Dart, 1973; and Linda Nochlin, *Gustave Courbet: A Study of Style and Society*, New York, Garland, 1976.

10 On David's studio exhibition of *The Oath of the Horatii* in Rome, for example, see Elizabeth Holt, *The Triumph of Art for the Public: The Emerging Role of Exhibitions and Critics*, Garden City, N.Y.: Anchor Books, 1979, pp. 12–28.

11 Courbet, "le sentiment raisonné et indépendant de ma propre individualité" – "Le Réalisme," "Exhibition et vente de 40 tableaux," Reff, *Exhibitions of Realist Art I*.

12 The story of Delacroix's *Liberty Leading the People*, taken out of storage, where it had lain since 1848, to appear in Delacroix's retrospective at the petition of the artist and the urging of Napoleon III but against the will of Nieuwerkerke – the latter thought its politics inappropriate, while Napoleon III thought its aesthetic quality and its representativity of Delacroix's oeuvre merited its inclusion – was a particularly acute example of this situation. See Mainardi, *Art and Politics of the Second Empire*, pp. 52–54; and T. J. Clark, *The Absolute Bourgeois: Artists and Politics in France, 1848–51*, London and New York, Thames and Hudson, 1973, pp. 17–20.

13 On the resolution of nationalist trends in a modern drive toward universalism, both in Manet's art and in contemporary criticism, see Fried, "Manet's Sources"; and *Manet's Modernism*, esp. pp. 124–28, 140–41, 342, 403. See also Mainardi, *Art and Politics of the Second Empire*, pp. 66–96, on a related but opposed notion of the "eclecticism" championed in the criticism of the era of the Universal Expositions.

14 On the "real allegory," see Toussaint's "Le dossier de 'l'Atelier' de Courbet," in *Gustave Courbet 1819–1877*, pp. 241–71. See also Nochlin, "Courbet's Real Allegory: Rereading 'The Painter's Studio,'" in *Courbet Reconsidered*, pp. 17–41; Rubin, *Courbet*, pp. 133–74; Herding, "*The Painter's Studio*: Focus on World Events, Site of Reconciliation," *Courbet: To Venture Independence*, pp. 45–61; Lindsay, *Gustave Courbet, His Life and Art*, pp. 126–44.

15 On the later depoliticization of Courbet, see Linda Nochlin, "The De-Politicization of Gustave Courbet: Transformation and Rehabilitation under the Third Republic," *October* 22, 1986, pp. 65–77.

16 See Clark, *Image of the People*, pp. 47–154, on the relation between Courbet's art and revolutionary politics during the Second Republic. See also James H. Rubin, *Realism and Social Vision in Courbet and Proudhon*, Princeton University Press, 1980.

17 Moreover, the veiled political references of the left side of *The Painter's Studio*, whatever one makes them add up to, pick up another thread in Courbet's oeuvre: an artistic commitment to the political that had always been obliquely represented, as in the Second Republic triad of the *Stonebreakers*, the *Burial at Ornans*, and *The Return from the Fair*, none of which represents the revolutionary Republic directly or iconographically but implicates it by association and provocation. See Clark, *Image of the People*.

18 See Fried on this painting, *Courbet's Realism*, pp. 155–64.

19 Bruyas funded the exhibition, and indeed Courbet was said to have described his pavilion as the "Bruyas Gallery." On the relation between Courbet and Bruyas in 1855, see Mainardi, *Art and Politics of the Second Empire*, pp. 57–61.

20 On the relation between production and consumption, labor, commodity, and exchange under capitalism, see Karl Marx, selections from *Capital*, vol. 1, in Robert C. Tucker, ed., *The Marx–Engels Reader*, New York, W. W. Norton, 1978, especially pp. 302–61, 388–417.

21 On the decision to hold a Salon for recent works separate from the arts survey of the Universal Exposition, and on the Ingres retrospective, see Mainardi, *Art and Politics of the Second Empire*, pp. 135–40, 151–53. (As Mainardi points out, until his untimely death in 1867, Ingres was the only one remaining of the four who had been celebrated with official retrospectives in 1855. Thus his show at the Ecole des Beaux-Arts, which included almost 600 works, was the only "official" retrospective with which the privately sponsored installations of Courbet and Manet had to compete in 1867.)

22 "Il a cherché simplement à être lui-même et non un autre" – Edouard Manet, "Motifs d'une exposition particulière," in Theodore Reff, ed., *Exhibitions of Impressionist Art II* (*Modern Art in Paris: 200 Catalogues of the Major Exhibitions Reproduced in Facsimile in 47 Volumes*), New York and London, Garland, 1981. The "Motifs d'une exposition particulière" has been attributed to Zacharie Astruc, although Hamilton speculates that it might have been a collaboration between Manet and Zola: see George Heard Hamilton, *Manet and his Critics*, New York, W. W. Norton, 1969, pp. 105–7. See also Alan Krell, "Manet, Zola and the 'Motifs d'une Exposition Particulière' 1867," *Gazette*

des Beaux-Arts VIe période, tome 99, March 1982, pp. 109–15.

23 See Reff, *Exhibitions of Impressionist Art II*; also Etienne Moreau-Nélaton, *Manet raconté par lui-même*, 2 vols., Paris, Henri Laurens, 1926, vol. 1, p. 86.

24 As there are no photographs of the installation at the Place de l'Alma, we do not know how the order of the catalogue list of the works in Manet's retrospective corresponded to the physical arrangement of the installation. But in *Le Journal Amusant* of June 29, 1867 (no. 600, pp. 6–8), the caricaturist G. Randon provides a three-page visual report on the exhibition, which possibly conforms to some portions of its layout, and which suggests that the numbering of the list was not followed consecutively in the hanging. On page 6, a fictitious "Temple of Taste" hangs next to no. 31, *The Philosopher*, which in turn hangs next to no. 17, *Lola de Valence*, and above a row containing nos. 45, 49, and 34 – *Fishing Boat arriving with the wind behind it, The Smoker*, and *The Steamboat*. On the facing page, nos. 20, 2, and 9, *Portrait of Mme. B., Olympia*, and *The Gypsies*, are shown together in the top row, and in the bottom row are lined up the *Portrait of Tintoretto* from the copies at the end of the list, together with nos. 1 and 39, the *Luncheon on the Grass* and *Woman at her window (study)*. (On this page, at least nos. 1 and 2, the *Luncheon on the Grass* and *Olympia*, hang together, one above the other, in the center of the page, and no doubt of the wall in the exhibition.) Finally, on page 8, nos. 32, 15, and 29 – the second *Philosopher*, the *Young Woman in 1866*, and *The Absinthe Drinker* – are grouped together above, and below are found a *Fruit Still-Life* (either no. 37 or no. 47), *The Battle of the Kearsarge and the Alabama* (no. 22), a fictitious entry representing the "author," and the "Registry of observations." Obviously the numbering and hanging of exhibitions at that time did not correspond as we might expect them to now. But in any case, Randon's three-page spread confirms the principle of disorder that underwrites the catalogue list, retaining, as does that list, only the singling out and pairing of the *Luncheon on the Grass* and *Olympia* as the most important works in the show, and the basic distinction between large and small, high and low genres, in its representation of the exhibition wall and the order of its hanging. And in his captions, Randon makes some connections of his own: beneath the *Young Woman in 1866*, for example, he

writes "Manque de tenue et de distinction; mais si vous l'aviez vue ce matin déjeunant sur l'herbe, sans chemise et sans façons, avec des camarades, vous diriez comme moi que c'est une bonne fille, et surtout pas bégueule." In other words, he ties one picture of Victorine Meurent back to another, the *Luncheon on the Grass*, caricatured on the previous page, and notices that they represent the same woman, with and without clothes.

25 For a rare, and overall sympathetic contemporary review of the exhibition, see Hippolyte Babou, "Les Dissidents de l'exposition," *Revue libérale* 2, 1867, pp. 284–89. Babou compares three "expositions particulières," those of Clésinger, Courbet, and Manet. He calls Courbet's exhibition (of 1867) a "second universal exposition" (p. 285), questions the authenticity of some of the works signed with Courbet's name, and remarks that there is nothing new to be seen in it. By contrast, he describes the intimacy and elegance – the "perfume of gallantry" – that characterizes Manet's show, and remarks that it has the quality of both a boudoir and a chapel, in which "a young Spanishwoman" could find a retreat for love and prayer (p. 286). (He also notes the paucity of visitors to the show.) Quoting the "Motifs d'une exposition particulière" almost in full, he finds that Manet's claims to sincerity are borne out, and that he has the "soul of an artist." In short, Babou seems to reiterate Manet's own emphasis on his "individuality" – in contrast to both Courbet's contemporaneous pavilion and the Universal Exposition – and implies that it is merely Manet's relative youth that accounts for some of the oddities in his work and that prevents him from being recognized as he should be. Théodore Duret, in *Les Peintres français en 1867*, Paris, E. Dentu, 1867, offers a much larger, and very different view of both Manet and Courbet in 1867. His is an encyclopedic overview which holds to the positivist understanding both of the progress of modern art and of its determination by and reflection of its epoch and milieu. Within that context, he describes Courbet as a natural painter, painting by instinct as a tree yields fruit, who does not change or develop, but who represents himself completely – he emptied his studio, says Duret, to put everything he ever made on view – and in a remarkably consistent and naturally unified way. He also finds Manet to be a powerful "individuality," but one that has not yet had

time to realize itself properly. Although Manet's works are not nearly as shocking, in his view, as all the hubbub would suggest, the dominant note struck by Duret's judgment with regard to Manet is: too young, too soon. This, Duret emphasizes, was simply contrary to the Salon jury's emphasis on maturity. (At the same time, it aligns with a progressivist understanding of modernity as that which is young, particularized, and unfinished, awaiting realization, generalization, and completion in the future.) What links Babou's and Duret's reactions to Manet's exhibition is their shared sense of an unripe, and somehow uncategorizable, irreducibly idiosyncratic "individuality," and of the smallness and partialness – the "particularity" – of his "exposition" in contrast to the largeness and "universality" of Courbet's in 1867. Otherwise, there was not enough critical reaction to Manet's "exposition particulière" to get a very good impression of how his audience understood the strangeness of the "particularity" put on display at the Place de l'Alma.

26 In Courbet's case, the references were to the Florentine and the Flemish, as indicated in the titles of his "pastiches."

27 After the retrospective exhibition of 1867, *The Gypsies* was cut down and then destroyed by Manet himself. On this painting, see Fried, *Manet's Modernism*, pp. 64ff. See also Anne C. Hanson, "Edouard Manet, 'Les gitanos', and the cut canvas," *Burlington Magazine* CXII, 1970, pp. 158–66.

28 See Fried on *The Old Musician*'s variety of sources in "Manet's Sources," and *Manet's Modernism*, pp. 28–37, 66–88. For the reaction to the original article and its claims, see Theodore Reff, "'Manet's Sources': A Critical Evaluation," *Artforum* 8, Sept. 1969, pp. 40–48. Although I disagree with the conclusions he draws, and with his understanding of history, I remain convinced by Fried's account of Manet's "sources," rather than by Reff's: it is visually acute, often brilliant, and on target about the strangeness of Manet's practice of quoting. Even its excesses are germane to that practice, and it is to be reckoned with and relied upon, as I have done here, by anyone wishing to confront Manet's quotational paintings.

29 See Fried, *Manet's Modernism*, esp. pp. 40–46, 55–58, 66–78, on the critical resuscitation of the Le Nains and Watteau in this period. Fried understands those references as unifying Manet's practice, as essential to it (as opposed to the superficiality of his citations from Spanish art, which "mask" the more important, underlying relationship to Watteau), and as conducive eventually to a universalist reading of Manet's realism.

30 See Nils Gösta Sandblad, *Manet: Three Studies in Artistic Conception*, Publications of the New Society of Letters at Lund, Sweden, Hakan Ohlsson Lund, 1954, for another, earlier, account of Manet's work of the 1860s that takes his borrowings from past art seriously and intelligently – rather than accounting for them as weaknesses, or simply denying or disregarding them. Particularly in the chapter dedicated to *Olympia* and related works (pp. 69–107), Sandblad resolves whatever "inconsistencies" he finds in Manet's works by recourse to what he sees as the *japoniste* cast of the flattened space of Manet's compositions.

31 On the concept of the supplement, see Jacques Derrida, *Of Grammatology* (Gayatri Chakravorty Spivak, trans.), Baltimore and London, Johns Hopkins University Press, 1976, esp. pp. 7, 141–64, 269–316. Traditionally a derogated, secondary term in Western thinking about the relationship between spoken and written language, the signified and the signifier, the supplement becomes, for Derrida, the very principle of the exteriority, alterity, artificiality, and materiality, the not-Nature and "specular dispossession" of language upon which both the sign and the subject are constituted.

32 On the "museum without walls," see André Malraux, *The Voices of Silence* (Stuart Gilbert, trans.), Princeton University Press, Bollingen Series, no. 24, 1978. On the relation between Manet and the "museum without walls," see Douglas Crimp, *On the Museum's Ruins*, Cambridge, Mass., MIT Press, 1993, pp. 48–54, and the passage on Manet cited from Michel Foucault, "Fantasia of the Library," in *Language, Counter-Memory, Practice* (Donald F. Bouchard and Sherry Simon, trans.), Ithaca, Cornell University Press, 1977, pp. 87–109 (p. 92). For the application of the discourse of the museum to Manet's work, see Jean Clay, "Ointments, Makeup, Pollen," *October* 27, Winter 1983, pp. 3–44; much of what I have to say about Manet in this book proceeds from Clay's essay.

33 Manet, of course, was by no means the first to insert his features into the margins of a larger figural composition; the practice has a long history, and includes such canonical works from the High Renaissance as Raphael's *School of Athens*. Manet's painting also relies on references to more recent, and much less populated

works, such as Courbet's *Bonjour M. Courbet* of 1854, picked up contemporaneously in Degas's self-portrait of 1862, *Degas Saluting*. From one to the other, the hat-doffing gesture migrates from patron to artist to crowd enframing the artist.

34 It is entirely possible that this is a connoisseurial fantasy. It is, nonetheless, one of the effects produced by Manet's work, especially in comparison with *pompier* painting, or the still-life production of painters like Fantin-Latour, or even the Impressionists. It strikes me, however, that the effect of singularity produced by Manet's paintings is mysterious, and hard to pin to a particular gestural language: rather it is an effect of pasty materiality which is, for instance, related to but substantially different from Courbet's mortar-like facture. For a relevant example of the notion of "handwriting" shared by Berenson, Wölfflin, and Fry, and derived from Morelli – the artist's signature handling conceived of as a consistent form of unconscious deformation best represented in the subsidiary details of a composition – see Fry, *Cézanne*, esp. pp. 42ff. See Richard Wollheim, "Giovanni Morelli and the Origins of Scientific Connoisseurship," in *On Art and the Mind*, Cambridge, Mass., Harvard University Press, 1974, pp. 177–201.

35 Just prior to *Fishing* on the list is Manet's version of Chardin's repeated dead-rabbit motif, and *The Smoker*, neither of which have I reproduced – the latter was an updating of another of Manet's Northern copies, his 1858 imitation of Adrian Brouwer's *Smoker* in the Louvre.

36 On the question of Léon Leenhoff's paternity, see Nancy Locke, "Manet's *Le Déjeuner sur l'herbe* as a Family Romance," in Paul Tucker, ed., *Manet's Déjeuner sur l'herbe*, Cambridge University Press, 1998, pp. 119–51; and *Manet and the Family Romance*, Princeton University Press, 2000. Locke surmises, rightly, I think, that Leenhoff must not have been Manet's son but rather his half-brother – the son of Manet's father – since Manet never officially recognized him as his own offspring, for all that he married Léon's mother. There is nonetheless enough ambiguity surrounding the matter, enough irregularity in the Manet household, and enough mythologizing of the bastard son in artist novels that had something to do with Manet, such as the Goncourts' *Manette Salomon* and Zola's *L'Oeuvre*, to warrant leaving the question of his paternity open.

37 Manet, "Motifs d'une exposition particulière," in Reff, *Exhibitions of Impressionist Art II*.

TWO   A NEW MANNER IN PAINTING

1 "sa chair et son sang"; "il s'était trouvé lui-même"; "me conte l'histoire d'un coeur et d'une chair, elle me parle d'une civilisation et d'un contrée"; "une vaste boutique de confiserie"; "L'art s'est . . . fragmenté; le grand royaume, en se morcelant, a formé une foule de petites républiques" – Zola, "Une nouvelle manière en peinture: Edouard Manet," *Revue du dix-neuvième siècle*, Jan. 1, 1867, republished as *Ed. Manet, Etude biographique et critique*, Paris, Dentu, 1867; repr. in Hemmings and Niess, *Emile Zola Salons*, pp. 83–103; see esp. pp. 87–89, 102. On Zola's art criticism and his relation to the modern painters of his time, see Hélène and Jean Adhémar, "Zola et la peinture," *Arts*, Dec. 12–18, 1952; J. Berg, *The Visual Novel: Emile Zola and the Art of His Times*, University Park, Pennsylvania State University Press, 1992; Henri Mitterand, *Zola Journaliste, de l'affaire Manet à l'affaire Dreyfus*, Paris, Armand Colin, 1962; and Robert J. Niess, *Zola, Cézanne, and Manet: A Study of L'Oeuvre*, Ann Arbor, University of Michigan Press, 1968.

2 In 1866, Zola constantly referred to Manet as "fort," "solide," "puissant," and as an "homme" in a crowd of mannequins and boudoir painters with the tastes of women and children in a bonbon shop: "Mon Salon," 1866, repr. in Hemmings and Niess, *Emile Zola Salons*, pp. 64–68, 70.

3 "Il les a réunies là pour juger de l'ensemble qu'elles feraient à l'Exposition universelle." Zola, "Une nouvelle manière en peinture," p. 93.

4 See Hamilton, *Manet and His Critics*, p. 105.

5 That is the part of Zola's essay most often cited; of the three sections it is the one that is least relevant to the discussion at hand, and therefore I shall not discuss it.

6 "Ce que je demande à l'artiste . . . c'est de se livrer lui-même, coeur et chair, c'est d'affirmer hautement un esprit puissant et particulier, une nature âpre et forte . . . il s'agit d'être soi, de montrer son coeur à nu, de formuler énergiquement une individualité . . . Ce que je cherche avant tout dans un tableau, c'est un homme et non pas un tableau" – Zola, "Mon Salon," *L'Evénement*, Apr. 27, 1866, repr. in Hemmings and Niess, *Emile Zola Salons*, p. 61.

7 "la personnalité d'un artiste"; "L'analyse s'exerce alors sur un ensemble complet; on étudie sous toutes ses faces un génie entier, on trace un portrait exact et précis, sans craindre de laisser

échapper quelques traits" – Zola, "Une nouvelle maniere en peinture," p. 83.

8 "Et il y a, pour le critique, une joie pénétrante à se dire qu'il peut disséquer un être, qu'il a à faire l'anatomie d'un organisme parfait, et qu'il reconstruira ensuite, dans sa réalité vivante, un homme avec tous ses membres, tous ses nerfs et tout son coeur, toutes ses rêveries et toute sa chair" – *ibid.*

9 See *The Positive Philosophy of Auguste Comte* (Harriet Martineau, trans.), London, John Chapman, 1853, vol. 1: "In order to understand the true value and character of the Positive Philosophy, we must take a brief general view of the progressive course of the human mind, regarded as a whole; for no conception can be understood otherwise than through its history" (p. 1); "It would be absurd to pretend to offer this new science [Social physics] at once in a complete state . . . the philosophical system of the moderns will be in fact complete, as there will then be no phenomenon which does not naturally enter into some one of the five great categories [Astronomy, Chemistry, Physics, Physiology, Social physics]. All our fundamental conceptions having become homogeneous, the Positive state will be fully established. It can never again change its character, though it will be for ever in course of development by additions of new knowledge. Having acquired the character of universality which has hitherto been the only advantage resting with the two preceding systems [the Theological and the Metaphysical], it will supersede them by its natural superiority, and leave to them only an historical existence" (pp. 8–9).

10 "qu'un coin de sa personnalité" – Zola, "Une nouvelle manière en peinture," p. 83.

11 "c'est notre mouvement artistique lui-même, ce sont les opinions contemporaines en matière d'esthétique" – *ibid.*

12 "qu'un curieux indépendant comme moi" – *ibid.*, p. 84.

13 On modern specialization, see *Positive Philosophy of Auguste Comte*, vol. 1, p. 9: "In the primitive state of human knowledge there is no regular division of intellectual labour. Every student cultivates all the sciences. As knowledge accrues, the sciences part off; and students devote themselves each to some one branch."

14 "La race chevelue de 1830 a même, Dieu merci! complètement disparu" – Zola, "Une nouvelle manière en peinture," p. 84.

15 "Mais les arts, la peinture est pour eux la grande Impure, la Courtisane toujours affamée de chair fraîche, qui doit boire le sang de leurs enfants et les tordre tout pantelants sur sa gorge insatiable" – *ibid.*, p. 85.

16 "peu de détails biographiques" – *ibid.*, p. 84.

17 "Sans doute la grande Impure, la Courtisane toujours affamée de chair fraîche s'embarqua avec lui et acheva de le séduire au milieu des solitudes lumineuses de l'Océan et du ciel; elle parla à sa chair, elle balança amoureusement devant ses yeux les lignes éclatantes des horizons, elle lui parla de passion avec le langage doux et vigoureux des couleurs. Au retour, Edouard Manet appartenait tout entier à l'Infâme" – *ibid.*, p. 85.

18 "Il y avait en lui un tempérament particulier qui ne put se plier à . . . cette éducation artistique contraire à sa nature"; "qui contient déja en germe la manière personnelle de l'artiste" – *ibid.*

19 "Edouard Manet est de taille moyenne, plutôt petite que grande. Les cheveux et la barbe sont d'un châtain pâle; les yeux, étroits et profonds, ont une vivacité et une flamme juvéniles; la bouche est caractéristique, mince, mobile, un peu moqueuse dans les coins. Le visage entier, d'une irrégularité fine et intelligente, annonce la souplesse et l'audace, le mépris de la sottise et de la banalité. Et si du visage nous descendons à la personne, nous trouvons dans Edouard Manet un homme d'une amabilité et d'une politesse exquises, d'allures distinguées et d'apparence sympathique" – *ibid.*, pp. 85–86.

20 "esquisser la physionomie"; "montrer le personnage réel" – *ibid.*

21 "Il m'a avoué qu'il adorait le monde et qu'il trouvait des voluptés secrètes dans les délicatesses parfumées et lumineuses des soirées. Il y est entraîné sans doute par son amour des couleurs larges et vives; mail il y a aussi, au fond de lui, un besoin inné de distinction et d'élégance que je me fait fort de retrouver dans ses oeuvres" – *ibid.*, p. 86.

22 "marchant droit devant lui, obéissant à sa nature"; "les joies calmes de la bourgeoisie moderne" – *ibid.*

23 "dans son intérieur" – *ibid.*

24 "Ce fut donc au sortir des préceptes d'une nature autre que la sienne, qu'Edouard Manet essaya de chercher et de voir par lui-même" – *ibid.*

25 "ceux que les maîtres ne reconnaissent pas pour leurs enfants; ils sont d'une race à part, ils apportent chacun leur mot dans la grande phrase que l'humanité écrit et qui ne sera jamais complète, ils ont pour destinées d'être des

maîtres à leur tour, des égoïstes, des personnal-
ités nettes et tranchées" – *ibid.*, p. 87.

26 "Il parla un language plein de rudesse et de
grâce . . . Je n'affirme point . . . qu'il ne contînt
pas quelques tournures espagnoles"; "Celui-là
parlait une langue qu'il avait fait sienne" –
ibid.

27 "Sentant qu'il n'arrivait à rien en copiant les
maîtres, en peignant la nature vue au travers des
individualités différentes de la sienne, il aura
compris, tout naïvement, un beau matin, qu'il
lui restait à essayer de voir la nature telle qu'elle
est, sans la regarder à travers les oeuvres et les
opinions des autres. . . . il . . . se mit à le reproduire sur une toile, selon ses facultés de vision
. . . Il fit effort pour oublier tout ce qu'il avait
étudié dans les musées; il tâche de ne plus se
rappeler . . . les oeuvres peintes qu'il avait
regardé. Il n'y eut plus là qu'une intelligence
particulière, servie par des organes doués d'une
certaine façon, mise en face de la nature et la
traduisant à sa manière.

L'artiste obtint ainsi une oeuvre qui était sa
chair et son sang . . . d'une saveur nouvelle et
d'un aspect particulier . . . [qui] était une face
encore inconnue du génie humain . . . il s'était
trouvé lui-même: il voyait de ses yeux, il devait
nous donner dans chacune de ses toiles une traduction de la nature en cette langue originale
qu'il venait de découvrir au fond de lui." –
"Une nouvelle manière en peinture," pp. 87–88.

28 "Mon esthétique, ou plutôt la science que
j'appelerai l'esthétique moderne"; "l'opinion
de la foule sur l'art" – *ibid.*, p. 88.

29 "Il faut procéder comme l'artiste a procédé
lui-même: oublier les richesses des musées . . .
chasser le souvenir des tableaux entassés par les
peintres morts; ne plus voir que la nature face
à face, telle qu'elle est; ne chercher enfin dans
les oeuvres d'Edouard Manet qu'une traduction
de la nature, particulière à un tempérament,
belle d'un intérêt humain" – *ibid.*

30 Sarcastically, Zola describes the classical view of
the arts this way: "Ainsi, voilà la large production du génie humain . . . réduite à la simple
éclosion du génie grec . . . Pendant plus de
deux mille ans, le monde se transforme, les
civilisations s'élèvent et s'écroulent, les sociétés
se précipitent ou languissent, au milieu de
moeurs toujours changeantes; et, d'autre part,
les artistes naissent ici et là, dans les matinées
pâles et froides de la Hollande, dans les soirées
chaudes et voluptueuses de l'Italie et de
l'Espagne. Qu'importe! le beau absolu est
là, immuable, dominant les âges" – *ibid.*,
pp. 88–89.

31 "Voici maintenant quelles sont mes croyances
en matière artistique. J'embrasse d'un regard
l'humanité qui a vécu et qui, devant la nature,
à toute heure, sous tous les climats, dans toutes
les circonstances, s'est senti l'impérieux besoin
de créer humainement, de reproduire par les
arts les objets et les êtres. J'ai ainsi un vaste spectacle dont chaque partie m'intéresse et m'émeut
profondément. Chaque grand artiste est venu
nous donner une traduction nouvelle et personnelle de la nature . . . Je voudrais que les
toiles de tous les peintres du monde fussent
réunies dans une immense salle, où nous pour-
rions aller lire page à page l'épopée de la création humaine. Et le thème serait toujours la
même nature, la même réalité, et les variations
seraient les façons particulières et originales à
l'aide desquelles les artistes auraient rendu la
grande création de Dieu . . . Ce qui m'intéresse,
moi homme, c'est l'humanité, ma grande
mère; ce qui me touche, ce qui me ravit dans
les créations humaines, dans les oeuvres d'art,
c'est de retrouver au fond de chacune d'elles un
artiste, un frère, qui me présente la nature sous
une face nouvelle, avec toute la puissance ou
toute la douceur de sa personnalité. Cette
oeuvre, ainsi envisagée, me conte l'histoire d'un
coeur et d'une chair, elle me parle d'une civilisation et d'une contrée. Et lorsque, au centre de
l'immense salle où sont pendus les tableaux de
tous les peintres du monde, je jette un coup
d'oeil sur ce vaste ensemble, j'ai là le même
poème en mille langues différentes, et je me
lasse pas de le relire dans chaque tableau,
charmé des délicatesses et des vigueurs de
chaque dialecte.

. . . Et notre création s'étend du passé à
l'infini de l'avenir; chaque société apportera
ses artistes qui apporteront leur personnalité"
– *ibid.*, pp. 89–90.

32 Greenberg followed Zola's positivist model in a
number of regards, emphasizing the positivity
of modernity as well as its tendency toward specialization: see Greenberg, *Collected Essays and
Criticism*, "Abstract Art," vol. 1, pp. 199–204;
"Review of an Exhibition by Claude Monet,"
"The Role of Nature in Modern Painting," and
"Review of an Exhibition of Gustave Courbet,"
vol. 2, pp. 20–23, 271–75, 275–79; and "Sculpture in Our Time," vol. 4, pp. 55–61.

33 "Je vois en lui un peintre analyste . . . Je le
répète, c'est un simple analyste" – Zola, "Une
nouvelle manière en peinture," p. 92.

34 "Je ne veux analyser que des faits, et les oeuvres
d'art sont de simples faits. /Donc . . . je me
place devant les tableaux d'Edouard Manet

comme devant des faits nouveaux que je désire expliquer" – *ibid.*, p. 90.

35 "Des fruits sont posés sur une table et se détachent contre un fond gris; il y a entre les fruits . . . des valeurs de coloration formant toute une gamme de teintes" – *ibid.*

36 "d'une saveur amère et forte" – *ibid.*, p. 84.

37 "Edouard Manet d'ordinaire part d'une note plus claire que la note existant dans la nature. Ses peintures sont blondes et lumineuses, d'une pâleur solide et ferme. La lumière tombe blanche et large, éclairant les objets d'une façon douce" – *ibid.*, p. 90, my emphasis and in the following quotations.

38 "L'artiste . . . se laisse guider par ses yeux qui aperçoivent . . . en larges teintes . . . Une tête posée contre un mur, n'est plus qu'une tache plus ou moins blanche sur un fond plus ou moins gris; et le vêtement juxtaposé à la figure devient par exemple une tache plus ou moins bleue mis à côté de la tache plus ou moins blanche . . . Toute la personnalité de l'artiste consiste dans la manière dont son oeil est organisé: il voit blond, et il voit par masses" – *ibid.*, pp. 90–91.

39 "L'aspect général . . . est d'un blond lumineux"; "La note nouvelle qu'il apporte, est cette note blonde emplissant la toile de lumière" – *ibid.*, pp. 91, 92.

40 "L'impression première qui produit une toile d'Edouard Manet est un peu dure et âpre . . . qui rend la nature avec une brutalité douce, si je puis m'exprimer ainsi" – *ibid.*

41 "Il y a de l'âpreté et de la douceur dans le premier regard . . . et toutes les couleurs claires, ces formes élégantes . . . ont . . . une douceur d'un simplicité et d'une énergie extrêmes" – *ibid.*, p. 94.

42 "les raideurs franches, les taches justes et puissantes d'*Olympia*" – *ibid.*

43 "Mais la toile que je préfère . . . est la *Chanteuse des rues*. Une jeune femme, bien connue sur les hauteurs du Panthéon, sort d'une brasserie en mangeant des cerises qu'elle tient dans une feuille de papier. L'oeuvre entière est d'un gris doux et blond, et la nature m'y a semblé analysée avec une sympathie et une exactitude extrêmes. Un pareil tableau a, en dehors du sujet, une austerité . . . on y sent la recherche âpre de la vérité . . . d'un homme qui veut, avant tout, dire franchement ce qu'il voit" – *ibid.*, p. 95.

44 In describing *Lola de Valence* in his section "Les oeuvres," Zola quotes in full the infamous four-liner by Baudelaire, a variation on one of the *Fleurs du mal* associated with the poet's obscen-

ity trial in 1857, which was attached to both the painting and the etching when they were exhibited at Martinet's and the Salon des Refusés in 1863. I shall return to that verse in Chapter Five; here it is worth remarking that though Zola admits the relevance of the quoted quatrain to Manet's painting, his own reading of the poem erases the sly genital reference contained in it – the notorious "*bijou rose et noir*" – in favor of his own trademark understanding of its colorism: "It is perfectly true that *Lola de Valence* is a pink and black jewel; already the painter proceeds only by *patches*, and his Spanish-woman is painted broadly, in vivid oppositions; the entire canvas is covered in two tones" ("Il est parfaitement vrai que *Lola de Valence* est un bijou rose et noir; le peintre ne procède déjà plus que par taches, et son Espagnole est peinte largement, par vives oppositions; la toile entière est couverte de deux teintes" – *ibid.*, p. 91.).

45 "une à une" – *ibid.*, p. 96.

46 *Ibid.*, p. 103.

47 *Ibid.*, pp. 95–96.

48 "le peintre y a été plus coloriste qu'il n'a coutume de l'être. La peinture est toujours blonde, mais d'un blond fauve et éclatant" – *ibid.*, p. 96.

49 "Ce qu'il faut voir dans le tableau, ce n'est pas un déjeuner sur l'herbe, c'est le paysage entier"; "les éléments particuliers et rares qui étaient en lui" – *ibid.*

50 "je retrouve là Edouard Manet tout entier, avec les partis-pris de son oeil et les audaces de sa main" – *ibid.*, p. 97.

51 "Je prétends que cette toile est véritablement la chair et le sang du peintre . . . Elle est l'expression complète de son tempérament; elle le contient tout entier et ne contient que lui. Elle restera comme l'oeuvre caractéristique de son talent, comme la marque la plus haute de sa puissance, comme la mesure de sa force. J'ai lu en elle la personnalité d'Edouard Manet, et lorsque j'ai analysé l'artiste lui-même, j'avais uniquement devant les yeux cette toile qui renferme toutes les autres" – *ibid.*

52 "Je préfère d'ailleurs le *Joueur de fifre*, un petit bonhomme, un enfant de troupe musicien qui souffle dans son instrument de toute son haleine et de tout son coeur . . . Le jaune des galons, le bleu noir de la tunique, le rouge des culottes ne sont encore ici que de larges taches. Et cette simplification produite par l'oeil clair et juste de l'artiste a fait de la toile une oeuvre toute blonde et toute naïve, charmante jusqu'à la grâce et réelle jusqu'à l'âpreté" – *ibid.*, p. 98.

53 "En terminant, je trouve, nettement caractérisée dans *La femme en rose*, cette élégance native qu'Edouard Manet, homme du monde, a au fond de lui. Une jeune femme, vêtue d'un long peignoir rose, est debout, la tête gracieusement penchée, et respirant le parfum d'un bouquet de violettes qu'elle tient dans sa main droite; à sa gauche, un perroquet se courbe sur son perchoir. Le peignoir est d'une grâce infinie, doux à l'oeil, très ample et très riche; le mouvement de la jeune femme a un charme indicible. Cela serait même trop joli, si le tempérament du peintre ne venait mettre sur cet ensemble l'empreinte de son austérité" – *ibid.*, pp. 98–99.

54 "une jeune fille de seize ans, sans doute un modèle qu'Edouard Manet a tranquillement copié tel qu'elle était" – *ibid.*, p. 97.

55 See Hippolyte Taine, *Philosophie de l'art dans les Pays-Bas*, Paris, Germer Baillère, 1869, p. 2: "nous étudions l'histoire de l'art moderne chez ses représentants les plus grands et les plus opposés." (Taine lists the "Italiens, Français, Espagnols et Portugais" under Latin or Southern peoples, and the "Belges, Hollandais, Allemands, Danois, Suédois, Norvégiens, Anglais, Ecossais, Américains" under Germanic or Northern peoples, but selects the Italians and Dutch as the purest embodiments of the two opposed racial spirits in their respective schools of art – p. 1.) See the sections on "national characteristics" under each of the headings – "Linear and Painterly," "Plane and Recession," "Closed and Open Form," "Multiplicity and Unity," and "Clearness and Unclearness" – in Wölfflin, *Principles of Art History*. See also Svetlana Alpers, *The Art of Describing: Dutch Art in the Seventeenth Century*, Chicago and London, University of Chicago Press, 1983.

56 This is very evident later in the '70s, in the writings on modern art of Edmond Duranty and others. See my *Odd Man Out*, pp. 82–83, 88–96, 99, 123, 172.

57 See Wilhelm Bürger (Théophile Thoré), *Trésors d'art exposés à Manchester en 1857, et provenant des collections royales, des collections publiques et des collections particulières de la Grande Bretagne*, Paris, 1857; Charles Blanc, *Ecole hollandaise* (1861), *Histoire des peintres de toutes les écoles*, Paris, 1860–76; Taine, *Philosophie de l'art dans les Pays-Bas*, 1869. On the later reaction, on the part of writers like Joris-Karl Huysmans and Sâr Péladan, to this school of art historical thought – dubbed the "theory of the milieu" – for which Taine's name came to stand, see my

Odd Man Out, pp. 82, 168, 172–77, 180–82, 186, 191, 196, 213.

58 These writers included modern literature in their positivist accounts of the history of human culture. Some, like Thoré and Blanc, wrote also on modern developments separately from their discussions of Dutch painting or their nation-by-nation surveys of the history of art. See Théophile Thoré, *Salons de W. Bürger, 1861–1868*, 2 vols., Paris, 1870; Charles Blanc, *Les Artistes de Mon Temps*, Paris, Firmin-Didot, 1876.

59 Both of Taine's *Philosophie de l'art* publications were based on lectures previously given at the Ecole des Beaux-Arts, beginning in 1864, after Taine's writings on English literature, his discovery of English positivism, and his publication of *Le Positivisme anglais, étude sur Stuart Mill* (1864). On Taine's brand of positivist criticism, see Jean-Thomas Nordmann, *Taine et la critique scientifique*, Paris, Presses Universitaires de France, 1992.

60 "Je vous montrerai d'abord le graine, c'est-à-dire la race avec ses qualités fondamentales et indélébiles . . . ensuite la plante, c'est-à-dire le peuple lui-même avec ses qualités . . . transformées par son milieu et son histoire; enfin la fleur, c'est-à-dire l'art et notamment la peinture, à laquelle tout ce développment aboutit." – Taine, *Philosophie de l'art dans les Pays-Bas*, p. 2.

61 This is consistent with Comte's procedure of beginning with an articulation of the "positive method" as it applies to each of the sciences laid out in encyclopedic order in *The Positive Philosophy of Auguste Comte*; see esp. vol. 2, ch. 3, "Characteristics of the Positive Method in its Application to Social Phenomena," pp. 67–110, with its emphasis on the "Historical Method" as the fourth and final "means" of positivism.

62 "Au physique, nous trouvons une chair plus blanche et plus molle, ordinairement des yeux bleus, souvent d'un bleu de faïence, ou pâles, plus pâles à mesure qu'on avance vers le nord . . . Le teint est d'un rose charmant, infiniment délicat, chez les jeunes filles, vif et teinté de vermillon chez les jeunes hommes, et quelquefois même ches les gens âgés." – Taine, *Philosophie de l'art dans les Pays-Bas*, pp. 3–4.

63 "les canaux de la sensation et de l'expression semblent obstrués" – *Ibid.*, p. 9.

64 *Ibid.*, pp. 30–31.

65 Fashion, wit, courtliness, and the love of shock are all associated with the less modern Latin temperament rather than with the more modern Northern character – *ibid.*, p. 12. These

are the same traits associated with modernity by Baudelaire.

66 *Ibid.*, pp. 13, 20, 22. This follows Hegel's description of Dutch painting; see Hegel, *Aesthetics*, vol. 1, pp. 597–600: "A tree, or a landscape, is something already fixed, independent, and permanent. But the lustre of metal, the shimmer of a bunch of grapes by candlelight, a vanishing glimpse of the moon or the sun, a smile, the expression of a swiftly passing emotion, ludicrous movements, postures, facial expressions – to grasp this most transitory and fugitive material, and to give it permanence for our contemplation in the fulness of its life, is the hard task of art at this stage. While classical art essentially gave shape in its ideal figures only to what is substantial, here we have, riveted and brought before our eyes, changing nature in its fleeting expressions, a burn, a waterfall, the foaming waves of the ocean, still-life with casual flashes of glass, cutlery, etc., the external shape of spiritual reality in the most detailed situations, a woman threading a needle by candlelight, a halt of robbers in a casual foray, the most momentary aspect of a look which quickly changes again, the laughing and jeering of a peasant; in all this Ostade, Teniers, and Steen are masters. It is a triumph of art over the transitory, a triumph in which the substantial is as it were cheated of its power over the contingent and the fleeting" (p. 599). Hegel's emphasis is upon subject matter, and upon the temporality of Dutch painting (again, Baudelaire's emphasis on modern contingency resonates with this discussion), but his contrast between the substantial and the superficial is not far from Taine's opposition between "la forme" and "le fond." Moreover, he also describes Dutch painting as coloristic and "painterly": "The older Dutch painters made a most thorough study of the physical effects of colour; van Eyck, Hemling, and Scorel could imitate in a most deceptive way the sheen of gold and silver, the lustre of jewels, silk, velvet, furs, etc. This mastery in the production of the most striking effects through the magic of colour and the secrets of its spell has now an independent justification . . . This is as it were an objective music, a peal in colour. In other words, just as in music the single note is nothing by itself but produces its effect only in its relation to another, in its counterpoint, concord, modulation, and harmony, so here it is just the same with colour. If we look closely at the play of colour, which glints like gold and glitters like braid under the light, we see perhaps only white or yellow strokes, points of colour, coloured surfaces; the single colour as such does not have this gleam which it produces; it is the juxtaposition *alone* which makes this glistening and gleaming. If we take, e.g., Terburg's satin, each spot of colour by itself is a subdued gray, more or less whitish, bluish, yellowish, but when it is looked at from a certain distance there comes out through its position beside another colour the beautiful soft sheen proper to actual satin" (pp. 599–600). In vol. 2, under "The Romantic Arts," Hegel's more detailed discussion of the opticality and coloristic medium specificity of painting elaborates on the distinction between sculptural form and painterly color, and mentions Goethe and Diderot along the way (pp. 837–50). Thus Hegel situates the advent of modern opticality, modern color practice and theory, and even modern abstraction and the modern musical paradigm for visual art, within Dutch realism. Baudelaire took much from this as well, as did Greenberg. But Greenberg, of course, prefers a positive narrative of narrowing, specialization, and advance to Hegel's emphasis on the "Dissolution of the Romantic Form of Art," and dispenses with Hegel's focus on the internal division, fundamental to coloristic painting and exemplified in the above passages, between signifier and signified, in favor of a more unified model of self-reflexivity.

67 "Un des principaux mérites de cette peinture est l'excellence et la délicatesse du coloris. C'est que l'éducation de l'oeil, en Flandre et en Hollande, a été particulière. Le pays est un delta humide . . . Ici comme à Venise, la nature a fait l'homme coloriste . . . Dans la contrée sèche, la ligne prédomine et attire d'abord l'attention . . . Ici l'horizon plat n'a pas d'intérêt, et les contours des choses sont amolllis, estompés, brouillés par la vapeur imperceptible qui nage éternellement dans l'air; ce qui prédomine c'est la tache" – Taine, *Philosophie de l'art dans les Pays-Bas*, pp. 56–57.

68 "cette subordination de la ligne à la tache"; "la tache fauve des bestiaux accroupis"; "Et ces taches ne sont point amorties par la clarté trop forte du ciel" – *ibid.*, pp. 58, 60–61.

69 "l'art a suivi la nature, et la main était forcément conduite par la sensation que l'oeil recevait" – *ibid.*, p. 62.

70 "par une structure d'oeil particulière . . . ont poussé au-delà de leur nation et de leur siècle jusqu'aux instincts communs qui relient les races germaniques et conduisent aux sentiments

modernes . . . il a compris et suivi dans toutes ses conséquences cette vérité, que pour l'oeil toute l'essence d'une chose visible est dans la tache, que la plus simple couleur est infiniment complexe, que toute sensation visuelle est un produit de ses éléments et en outre de ses alentours, que chaque objet dans le champ visuel n'est qu'une tache modifiée par d'autres taches" – *ibid.*, pp. 162–63.

71 On the relation between nineteenth-century art and the Dutch masters, and on the myth of Rembrandt, see Petra Ten Doesschate Chu, *French Realism and the Dutch Masters*, Utrecht, 1974. See also Svetlana Alpers, *Rembrandt's Enterprise: The Studio and the Market*, Chicago and London, University of Chicago Press, 1988.

72 "Olympia, couchée sur des linges blancs, fait une grande tache pâle sur le fond noir; dans ce fond noir se trouve la tête de la négresse qui apporte un bouquet, et ce fameux chat qui a tant égayé le public. Au premier regard, on ne distingue ainsi que deux teintes dans le tableau, deux teintes violentes, s'enlevant l'une sur l'autre. D'ailleurs, les détails ont disparu. Regardez la tête de la jeune fille: les lèvres sont deux minces lignes roses, les yeux se réduisent à quelques traits noirs. Voyez maintenant le bouquet, et de près, je vous prie: des plaques jaunes, des plaques bleues, des plaques vertes. Tout se simplifie, et si vous voulez reconstruire la réalité, il faut que vous reculiez de quelques pas. Alors il arrive une étrange histoire: chaque objet se met à son plan, la tête d'Olympia se détache du fond avec un relief saisissant, le bouquet devient une merveille d'éclat et de fraîcheur. . . . le peintre a procédé comme la nature procède elle-même, par masses claires, par larges pans de lumière, et son oeuvre a l'aspect un peu rude et austère de la nature. Il y a d'ailleurs des partis-pris . . . [qui] sont cette sécheresse élégante, cette violence des transitions que j'ai signalées. C'est l'accent personnel, la saveur particulière de l'oeuvre." – Zola, "Une nouvelle manière en peinture," p. 97.

73 On the reception of *Olympia* in light of the discourse on prostitution, see Clark, "Olympia's Choice," *The Painting of Modern Life*, pp. 79–146.

74 "L'avenir est à lui" – Zola, "Une nouvelle manière en peinture," p. 99.

75 "Edouard Manet est homme du monde, et il y a dans ses tableaux certaines lignes exquises, certaines attitudes grêles et jolies qui témoignent de son amour pour les élégances des salons. C'est là l'élément inconscient, la nature même du peintre. Et je profite de l'oc-casion pour protester contre la parenté qu'on a voulu établir entre les tableaux de Manet et les vers de Charles Baudelaire. . . . s'il assemble plusieurs objets ou plusieurs figures, il est seulement guidé dans son choix par le désir d'obtenir de belles taches, de belles oppositions. Il est ridicule de vouloir faire un rêveur mystique d'un artiste obéissant à un pareil tempérament" – *ibid.*, p. 91.

76 On the "optical unconscious" of the modernist tradition, see Rosalind Krauss, *The Optical Unconscious*, Cambridge, Mass., MIT Press, 1993.

77 "qu'un bâtard de Vélasquez et de Goya" – Zola, "Une nouvelle manière en peinture," p. 93.

78 Moreover, the prints themselves (as, for example, the print on Zola's wall) were modern, from the eighteenth and nineteenth centuries. See Gabriel P. Weisberg, *Japonisme: Japanese Influence on French Art 1854–1910*, Ohio, Cleveland Museum of Art, 1980; and B. Dorival, *Japon et Occident: Deux siècles d'échanges artistiques*, Paris, 1976.

79 "Il serait beaucoup plus intéressant de comparer cette peinture simplifiée avec les gravures japonaises qui lui ressemblent par leur élégance étrange et leurs taches magnifiques" – Zola, "Une nouvelle manière en peinture," p. 91.

80 Instead, Zola asserts that Manet simply had Spanish costumes hanging around in his studio, and that he actually went to Spain only in 1865.

81 "on est toujours fils de quelqu'un" – *ibid.*, p. 93.

THREE   MANETTE SALOMON

1 See Reff, *Exhibitions of Impressionist Art II*, 1981: "Exposition rétrospective" held at the Ecole Nationale des Beaux-Arts in 1884. For an account of this exhibition, see Michael R. Orwicz, "Reinventing Edouard Manet: Rewriting the Face of National Art in the Early Third Republic," in Michael R. Orwicz, ed., *Art Criticism and Its Institutions in Nineteenth-Century France*, Manchester and New York, Manchester University Press, 1994, pp. 122–45.

2 Taine's books on Italian and Dutch art were published on either side of the Universal Exposition of 1867 (in 1866 and 1869, respectively), and in the latter Taine speaks directly about the Universal Exposition of the "year before" – *Philosophie de l'art dans les Pays-Bas*, p. 52. Charles Blanc, for his part, addressed himself to all the modern variants of the European schools of art that were on view in the Univer-

sal Exposition of 1867 in *Les Artistes de mon temps.*

3 Goncourt, *Manette Salomon. Manette Salomon* came out in November 1867, after the close of the Universal Exposition. On the Goncourts, see Pierre Sabatier, *L'Esthetique des Goncourt,* Paris, Hachette, 1920; Enzo Caramaschi, *Réalisme et impressionnisme dans l'oeuvre des frères Goncourt,* Pisa, Libreria Goliardica, 1971; and Wanda Bannour, *Edmond et Jules de Goncourt, ou, le génie androgyne,* Paris, Persona, 1985.

4 Edmond de Goncourt's first mention of Manet occurs on Nov. 22, 1873: see Edmond and Jules de Goncourt, *Journal: Mémoires de la vie littéraire,* Monaco, Farquelle et Flammarion, 1956, vol. 10, p. 147. After that he is mentioned a few times during the '70s and '80s but not with much approbation. Manet's friend Alfred Stevens, by contrast, is frequently mentioned (though not in the '60s either) from the '70s through to the '90s, and the Goncourts call him "Le peintre de grand talent, le coloriste de l'intimité moderne" – *Journal,* vol. 11, pp. 7–8.

By contrast, this is how Goncourt later spoke of Manet: "With Manet, whose procedures are borrowed from Goya, with Manet and the painters coming after him, oil painting is dead, that's to say painting of the sort characterized by a lovely, ambered and crystallized transparency, of which Rubens's woman in the straw hat is the representative type. Now we have opaque painting, matte painting, plastery painting, painting with all the characteristics of paint bound with glue." ("Avec Manet, dont les procédés sont empruntés à Goya, avec Manet et les peintres à sa suite, est morte la peinture à l'huile, c'est-à-dire la peinture à la jolie transparence ambrée et cristallisé, dont la femme au chapeau de paille de Rubens est le type. C'est maintenant de la peinture opaque, de la peinture mate, de la peinture plâtreuse, de la peinture ayant tous les caractères de la peinture à la colle.") *Journal,* May 18, 1889 (vol. 14, p. 7). Later, however, he admired one of Manet's watercolors: "a masterpiece by Manet, a letter by the painter at the bottom of which are three plums, washed in watercolor, which are marvels of artistic wash drawing and coloring." ("un chef d'oeuvre de Manet, une lettre du peintre au bas de laquelle sont trois prunes, lavées à l'aquarelle, qui sont de merveilles de lavis et de coloriage artiste.") *Journal,* Aug. 21, 1893 (vol. 19, p. 163).

5 Antonin Proust, "L'Art d'Edouard Manet," *Le Studio* 21, Jan. 15, 1901, p. 75.

6 Thus *Manette Salomon* took up the Hegelian master narrative of modern art in its disintegrative aspect, following its emphasis on dissolution and indeed on "The End of the Romantic Form of Art."

7 Goncourt, *Journal,* Aug. 5, 1886 (vol. 14, pp. 109–10).

8 "'suite d'aquarelles et d'eaux fortes'"; "une psychologie très fouillé"; "Va, va, mon gigantesque Zola, fais simplement une psychologie comme celle du ménage de Coriolis et de Manette!", Goncourt, *Journal,* vol. 14, p. 28.

9 This is Bahktin's analysis of the novel's form, and its difference from earlier forms such as the epic, in *The Dialogic Imagination.*

10 On realism and the novel, see Georg Lukács, *The Theory of the Novel* (1920) (Anna Bostock, trans.), Cambridge, Mass., MIT Press, 1971; and *Problèmes du Réalisme* (Claude Prévost and Jean Guégan, trans.), Paris, L'Arche Editeur, 1975.

11 On Balzac's novella, see Dore Ashton, *A Fable of Modern Art,* New York and London, Thames and Hudson, 1980; *Autour de Chef d'oeuvre inconnu du Balzac,* Paris, Ecole Nationale Supérieure des Art Décoratifs, 1985; and Françoise Pitt-Rivers, *Balzac et l'art,* Paris, Chêne, 1993. See also Hubert Damisch, *Fenêtre jaune cadmium, ou le dessous de la peinture,* Paris, Seuil, 1984. Following Ashton, who treats the novelette in relation to Cézanne ("Frenhofer c'est moi"), Rilke, Picasso, and Schoenberg, Damisch is primarily concerned with the model that *Le Chef-d'oeuvre inconnu* provides for understanding twentieth-century art. In that context, he associates the mysterious painting that is featured in *Le Chef-d'oeuvre inconnu* with Manet's paintings of Victorine Meurent – see p. 26.

12 "Eh! bien, le voilà, leur dit le vieillard dont les cheveux étaient en désordre, dont le visage était enflammé par une exaltation surnaturelle, dont les yeux pétillaient, et qui haletait comme un jeune homme ivre d'amour. Vous êtes devant une femme et vous cherchez un tableau. Il y a tant de profondeur sur cette toile, l'air y est si vrai, que vous ne pouvez plus le distinguer de l'air qui nous environne. Où est l'art? perdu, disparu! Voilà les formes mêmes d'une jeune fille. N'ai-je pas bien saisi le couleur, le vif de la ligne qui paraît terminer le corps? N'est-ce pas le même phénomène que nous présentent les objets qui sont dans l'atmosphère comme les poissons dans l'eau? Admirez comme les contours se détachent du fond? Ne semble-t-il pas que vous puissiez passer la main sur ce dos? Aussi,

pendant sept années, ai-je étudié les effets de l'accouplement du jour et des objets. Et ces cheveux, la lumière les inonde-t-elle pas? . . . Mais elle a respiré, je crois! . . . Ce sein, voyez? Ah! qui ne voudrait l'adorer à genoux? Les chairs palpitent. Elle va se lever, attendez." – Honoré de Balzac, "Le Chef-d'oeuvre inconnu" (1831/37), in *Le Chef-d'oeuvre inconnu/Gambara/Massimilla Doni*, Paris, Flammarion, 1981, pp. 68–69, my translation.

13 "En s'approchant, ils aperçurent dans un coin de la toile le bout d'un pied nu qui sortait de ce chaos de couleurs, de tons, de nuances indécises, espèce de brouillard sans forme; mais un pied délicieux, un pied vivant! Ils restèrent pétrifiés d'admiration devant ce fragment échappé à une incroyable, à une lent et progressive destruction. Ce pied apparaissait là comme le torse de quelque Vénus en marbre de Paros qui surgirait parmi les décombres d'une ville incendiée.

"– Il y a une femme là-dessous! s'écria Porbus en faisant remarquer à Poussin les couches de couleurs que le vieux peintre avait successivement superposées en croyant perfectionner sa peinture" – *Le Chef-d'oeuvre inconnu*, pp. 69–70.

14 "– Oui, mon ami, répondit le vieillard en se réveillant, il faut de la foi, de la foi dans l'art, et vivre pendant longtemps avec son oeuvre pour produire une semblable création. Quelques-unes de ces ombres m'ont coûté bien des travaux. Tenez, il y a là sur sa joue, au-dessous des yeux, une légère pénombre qui, si vous l'observez dans la nature, vous paraîtra presque intraduisible. Eh! bien, croyez-vous qu'elle ne m'ait pas coûté des peines inouïes à reproduire? Mais aussi, mon cher Porbus, regarde attentivement mon travail, et tu comprendras mieux ce que je te disais sur la manière de traiter le modelé et les contours. Regarde la lumière du sein, et vois comme, par une suite de touches et de rehauts fortement empâtés, je suis parvenu à accrocher la véritable lumière et à la combiner avec la blancheur luisante des tons éclairés; et comme, par un travail contraire, en effaçant les saillies et le grain de la pâte, j'ai pu, à force de caresser le contour de ma figure, noyé dans la demi-teinte, ôter jusqu'à l'idée de dessin et de moyens artificiels, et lui donner l'aspect et la rondeur même de la nature. Approchez, vous verrez la rondeur même de la nature. De loin, il disparaît. Tenez? Là il est, je crois, très remarquable.

Et du bout de sa brosse, il désignait aux deux peintres un pâté de couleur claire" – *Le Chef d'oeuvre inconnu*, p. 70.

15 By contrast, the two young painters are petrified – turned to stone, like the statuary evoked in the painting. This introduces a thematic dialectics of petrification and vaporization, and an erotics oscillating between frozen form and formlessness, almost always articulated in some relation to the female body, that is carried through the poetics of Baudelaire and the artist stories of the Goncourts, Zola, and Huysmans, to which I shall return in the chapters that follow.

16 Thus Hegel's view of Romantic art as falling to pieces becomes a literary topos: it is significant that this should happen in literature, for the literary (which, not coincidentally, Greenberg opposes to modernist painting) is predicated on the divided structure of the verbal sign, as opposed to the unity of the aesthetic plane.

17 In an entry of Jan. 20, 1896 (*Journal*, vol. 20, pp. 170–72), Edmond de Goncourt discusses a theatrical production of *Manette Salomon* and remarks on the power of the absence of Manette.

18 Indeed, the Goncourts raise the stakes of the multiplicitous, unstable world of eclecticism, by having their separate artists share attributes, characteristics, and references: for instance, the monkey belongs first to Coriolis and then to Anatole, the two artists share the reference to Decamps, and Decamps himself, with his different genre specialties, was already a fairly eclectic figure. See also Dewey F. Mosby, *Alexandre-Gabriel Decamps 1803–1860*, New York and London, Garland, 1977 (Harvard University Ph.D. diss., 1973).

19 Decamps, the likely source for Coriolis, was an Orientalist and a declared favorite of the Goncourts in 1855 – see Edmond and Jules de Goncourt, *Etudes d'art: Le Salon de 1852, La peinture à l'Exposition de 1855*, Paris, E. Flammarion, 1893. The Goncourts devote eight pages of their 1855 remarks to Decamps (pp. 202–09); their only mention of Chassériau is a few unrevealing lines in their *Salon* of 1852, suggesting that his works are like, but come off a little better than, those of Delacroix (p. 99). Delacroix, Chassériau, and Chassériau's *Bain turc* are mentioned together, in the context of an Exposition of 1853, in *Manette Salomon*, p. 215.

20 See Marc Sandoz, *Théodore Chassériau 1819–1856: Catalogue raisonné des peintures et estampes*, Paris, Art et Métiers Graphiques, 1974, pp. 354–56.

21 "pêle-mêle étrange de talents et de nullités" – Goncourt, *Manette Salomon*, p. 38.

22 "du fond de l'homme et de catholique, des instincts du créole, de ce sang orgueilleux que font les colonies" – *ibid.*, p. 202.

23 *Ibid.*, p. 150.

24 *Ibid.*, p. 21.

25 The situation described by the Goncourts is a reflexive variation on the discourse of Orientalism, in which the function of the Oriental is to define, delimit, and prop up the Western subject, and to disavow that subject's own internal alterity. *Manette Salomon*, and in general the antisemitic discourse on the figure of the Jew, represents the anxious underside, not to say the pathology, of Orientalism, in which that normative function breaks down, the Orient is here, and the Other is within. See Reina Lewis, *Gendering Orientalism: Race, Femininity and Representation*, New York, Routledge, 1996; Sander Gilman, *Difference and Pathology: Stereotypes of Sexuality, Race, and Madness*, Ithaca, Cornell University Press, 1985; *Inscribing the Other*, Lincoln, University of Nebraska Press, 1991; and *The Visibility of the Jew in the Diaspora: Body Imagery and Its Cultural Context*, Syracuse University Press, 1992; and Klaus Theweleit, *Male Fantasies* (1978) (Erica Carter and Chris Turner, trans.), Minneapolis, University of Minnesota Press), 1989.

26 "Du monde allait dans le Jardin des Plantes, montait au labyrinthe, un monde particulier, mêlé, cosmopolite, composé de toutes les sortes de gens de Paris, de la province et de l'étranger, que rassemble ce rendez-vous populaire.

C'était d'abord un groupe classique d'Anglais et d'Anglaises à voiles bruns, à lunettes bleues.

. . .

Venaient ensuite: un sapeur . . . un prince jaune, tout frais habillé de Dusautoy, accompagné d'une espèce d'heiduque à figure de Turc, à dolman d'Albanais – un apprenti maçon, un petit gâcheur débarqué du Limousin . . .

Un peu plus loin, grimpait un interne de la Pitié . . . Et presque à côté de lui, sur la même ligne, un ouvrier en redingote . . .

Un père, à rudes moustaches grises, regardait courir devant lui un bel enfant, en robe russe de velours bleu, à boutons d'argent, à manches de toile blanche, au cou duquel battait un collier d'ambre.

. . .

Et, fermant la marche, une femme de chambre tirait et traînait par la main un petit négrillon, embarrassé dans sa culotte, et qui semblait tout triste d'avoir vu des singes en cage" – Goncourt, *Manette Salomon*, pp. 17–18 (my emphases).

27 "Paris était sous eux, à gauche, à droite, partout.

Entre les pointes des arbres verts, là où s'ouvrait un peu le rideau des pins, des morceaux de la grande ville s'étendait d'abord des toits pressés, aux tuiles brunes, faisant des masses d'un ton brûlé, s'assombrissaient et s'enfonçaient dans du noir-roux en allant vers le quai. Sur le quai, les carrés des maisons blanches, avec les petites raies noires de leurs milliers de fenêtres, formaient et développaient comme un front de caserne d'une blancheur effacée et jaunâtre, sur laquelle reculait, de loin en loin, dans le rouillé de la pierre, une construction plus vieille. Au-delà de cette ligne nette et claire, on ne voyait plus qu'une espèce de chaos perdu dans un nuit d'ardoise, un fouillis de toits, des milliers de toits d'où des tuyaux noirs se dressaient avec une finesse d'aiguille, une mêlée de faîtes et de têtes de maisons enveloppées par l'obscurité grise de l'éloignement, brouillées dans le fond du jour baissant; un fourmillement de demeures, un gâchis de lignes et d'architectures, un amas de pierres pareil à l'ébauche et à l'encombrement d'une carrière, sur lequel dominaient et planaient le chevet et le dôme d'une église, dont la nuageuse solidité ressemblait à une vapeur condensé" – *ibid.*, pp. 18–19 (my emphases).

28 For a reading of this painting, see Mainardi, *Art and Politics of the Second Empire*, pp. 141–50, esp. p. 147; see also Clark, *Painting of Modern Life*, pp. 60–66, for an acute rendering of the *Exposition* in terms of its range of social classes, its stress on viewing, and its emphasis on "spectacle."

29 "Peu à peu, il s'abandonne à toutes ces choses. Il s'oublie, il se perd à voir, à écouter, à aspirer. Ce qui est autour de lui le pénètre par tous les pores, et la Nature l'embrassant par tous les sens, il se laisse couler en elle, et reste à s'y tremper. . . . Il glisse dans l'être des êtres qui sont là. Il lui semble qu'il est un peu dans tout ce qui vole, dans tout ce qui croît, dans tout ce qui court. . . . la créature commence à se dissoudre dans le Tout vivant de la création.

Et parfois, dans ce jour du commencement . . . l'ancien Bohême revit des joies d'Eden, et il s'élève en lui, presque célestement, comme un peu de la félicité du premier homme en face de la Nature vierge" – Goncourt, *Manette Salomon*, pp. 425–26.

30 "Anatole présentait le curieux phenomène psychologique d'un homme qui n'a pas la possession de son individualité" – *ibid.*, p. 356.

31   "Ce fut comme une longue dépossession de lui-même, à la fin de laquelle il ne s'appartint presque plus" – *ibid.*, p. 392.

32   "Au Louvre même, dans le Salon carré, ces quatre murs de chefs-d'oeuvres ne lui semblaient plus rayonner. Le Salon s'assombrissait, et arrivait à ne plus lui montrer qu'une sorte de momification des couleurs sous la patine et le jaunissement du temps . . .

 La lumière, il était arrivé à ne plus la concevoir, la voir, que dans l'intensité, la gloire flamboyante, la diffusion, l'aveuglement de rayonnement, les électricités de l'orage, le flamboiement des apothéoses de théâtre, le feu d'artifice du grésil, le blanc incendie du magnésium. De jour, il n'essayait plus de peindre que l'éblouissement. A l'exemple de certains coloristes qui, la maturité de leur talent franchie, perdent dans l'excès la dominante de leur talent, Coriolis . . . était revenu, dans ces derniers temps, à sa première manière, et peu à peu . . . il descendait un peu de cette hallucination du grand Turner qui, sur la fin de sa vie, blessé par l'ombre des tableaux, mécontent même du jour de son temps, essayait de s'élever, dans une toile, avec le rêve des couleurs, à un jour vierge et primordial, à la Lumière avant le Déluge.

 Il cherchait partout de quoi monter sa palette, chauffer ses tons, les enflammer, les brillanter. Devant les vitrines de minéralogie, essayant de voler la Nature, de ravir et d'emporter les feux multicolores de ces pétrifications et de ces cristallisations d'éclairs, il s'arrêtait à ces bleus d'azurité, d'un bleu d'émail chinois, à ces bleus défaillants des cuivres oxydés, au bleu céleste de la lazulite allant du bleu de roi au bleu de l'eau. Il suivait toute la gamme du rouge, des mercures sulfurés, carmins et saignants, jusqu'au rouge noir de l'hématite, et rêvait à l'amatito, la couleur perdue du XVIe siècle, la couleur cardinale, la vraie pourpre de Rome. Il suivait les ors et les verts queue de paon des poudingues diluviens, les verts de velours, les verts changeants et bleuissants des cuivres arséniatés, le vert de lézard du feldspath; l'infinie variété des jaunes, du jaune-serin au jaune miellé des orpiments cristallisés et des fluorines; les couleurs embrasées des cuivres pyriteux, les couleurs de pierres roses ou violettes, qui font penser à des fleurs de cristal.

 Des minéraux, il passait aux coquilles, aux colorations mères de la tendresse et de l'idéal du ton, à toutes ces variations du rose dans une fonte de porcelaine, depuis la pourpre ténébreuse jusqu'au rose mourant, à la nacre noyant le prisme dans son lait. Il allait à toutes les irisations, aux opalisations d'arc-en-ciel, miroitantes sur le verre antique sortie de terre comme avec du ciel enterré. Il se mettait dans les yeux l'azur du saphir, le sang du rubis, l'orient de la perle, l'eau du diamant. Pour peindre, le peintre croyait avoir maintenant besoin de tout ce qui brille, de tout ce qui brûle dans le Ciel, dans la Terre, dans la Mer" – *ibid.*, pp. 411–13.

 The Goncourts' description of Coriolis' confrontation with the colors of brilliance bears a strong resemblance to their discussion elsewhere of Decamps's Orientalist use of color: "Et de ce kaléidoscope, et de cet arc-en-ciel, et de ce royal vestiaire d'Arlequin – l'Orient – comme il a fait son bien et son douaire! Ce ne sont pas ces toiles, que tendres, vives et gaies couleurs, que fanfares et pétillements de vermillon, de jaune d'or, de cendre verte, riant dans l'harmonie jaune de l'ensemble. Les beaux éclairs de ton, ramenés au ton général par les blancs jaunes, reliés entre eux par les contours et les ombres brûlées de terre de Sienne! Et de cette palette, un jour, s'échappe tout un écrin, ces ânes d'Asie, brillants, étincelants d'une poudre de perle, de topaz, de rubis et de diamant, le chef d'oeuvre de cette peinture agatisée que tous cherchaient alors: Delacroix et Bonington, et Isabey, – et de cette palette reposée, un jour s'envole une merveille de merveilles: le Boucher Turc!" – *Etudes d'art*, pp. 207–8; "A Decamps, les mers bleuissantes, ourlées de diamants; les campagnes embrasées, craquantes et dartreuses! A Decamps, le paradis torride, fleuri, emperlé, éblouissant, l'eden incendiée! A Decamps, la lumière ivre./ A Decamps seul, – le soleil!" – *ibid.*, p. 209.

33   For a marvelous treatment of the alchemy of painting, see James Elkins, *What Painting Is: How to Think about Oil Painting, Using the Language of Alchemy*, New York and London: Routledge, 1999.

34   "Sous la paleur chaude de son teint, transparaissait ce rose du sang qui paraît fleurir et pasteller de carmin la joue des juives, cette lueur de rouge en haut des pommettes pareil au reste essuyé de fard qu'une actrice s'est posé sous l'oeil. Tout ce visage, le front creusant à la racine du nez, le nez délicatement busqué, les narines découpées et un peu remontantes, montrait un modelage ciselé des traits. La bouche . . . rappelait la bouche . . . des jeunes garçons dans les beaux portraits italiens" – Goncourts, *Manette Salomon*, p. 207.

35   "Par-dessus l'Orientale, il y avait, dans sa personne, une Parisienne . . . il passait . . . sur la pure et tranquille sculpture de sa figure . . . le

mauvais sourire des méchantes petites têtes dans les quartiers pauvres: on êut dit . . . que la rue montait . . . dans son visage" – *ibid.*

36 "une petite casquette sur la tête, le bourgeon aux épaules, le doigt sur la gachette d'un fusil de chasse" –*ibid.*, p. 206.

37 "Alors elle commençait à chercher les beautés, les voluptés, la grâce nue de la femme . . . Et à la fin, comme sous un long modelage d'une volonté artiste, se levait de la forme ondulante et assouplie, une admirable statue d'un moment . . . Un minute, Manette se contemplait et se possédait dans cette victoire de sa pose: elle s'aimait . . . Et sur le bord de ses lèvres . . . les compliments qu'une femme murmure tout bas à sa beauté, paraissaient monter et mourir . . . dans le dessin parlant de sa bouche. '. . . il n'y a que la glace qui me voit!'" – *ibid.*, pp. 214–15.

Again in the context of his worries about the play production of *Manette Salomon*, Goncourt stresses the importance of this passage on Manette's self-creation and self-love: *Journal*, Feb. 10, 11, 14, 1896 (vol. 20, pp. 183–4, 187).

38 *L'Oeuvre*, published two years after *A Rebours*, that critical tract disguised as a novel by Zola's erstwhile disciple Joris-Karl Huysmans, may also be taken as a response to the latter book's departure from the Naturalist principle of the novel, as well as its championing of figures like Moreau and Redon and others. On Zola and Huysmans, see my *Odd Man Out*, pp. 168–72.

39 "cette folie tout bonnement esthétique . . . chez moi"; "la note cochonne, obscène qu'il y ajoute"; "des rubis dans le nombril et les parties génitales de son modèle" – Goncourt, *Journal*, vol. 14, p. 109.

40 "Claude, obéissant au geste dominateur dont elle lui montrait le tableau, s'était levé et regardait . . . Il s'éveillait enfin de son rêve, et *la Femme*, vue ainsi d'en bas, avec quelques pas de recul, l'emplissait de stupeur. Qui donc venait de peindre *cette idole* d'une religion inconnue? qui l'avait *faite de métaux, de marbres et de gemmes, épanouissant la rose mystique de son sexe, entre les colonnes précieuses des cuisses, sous la voûte sacrée du ventre?* Etait-ce lui qui, sans le savoir, était l'ouvrier de ce symbole du désir insatiable, de *cette image extra-humaine de la chair, devenue de l'or et du diamant entre ses doigts, dans son vain effort d'en faire de la vie?* Et, béant, il avait peur de son oeuvre, tremblant de ce brusque saut dans l'au-delà, comprenant bien que la réalité elle-même ne lui était possible, au bout de sa longue lutte pour la vaincre et la repétrir plus réelle, de ses mains d'homme" – Emile Zola, *L'Oeuvre* (1886), Paris, Fasquelle, 1985, pp. 416–17 (my emphases).

41 Indeed, Zola seems very aware of, and even competes with, the bejeweled description of Moreau's *Salomé* given in Joris-Karl Huysmans, *A Rebours* (1884), Paris, Garnier-Flammarion, 1978, pp. 104–10.

42 "les hanches élargissaient leur rondeur soyeuse, la gorge ferme se redressait, gonflée du sang de son désir" – Zola, *L'Oeuvre*, p. 418.

43 "une chaire dorée, une finesse de soie" – *ibid.*, p. 20.

44 The specifics of deconstructive tendencies in the nineteenth century would be this: that they coincide with the post-Revolution formation and solidification of modern bourgeois models of transparency, positivity, and naturalized ideology, as opposed to both the Ancien Régime acceptance of artifice and performativity, which had no such models to militate against, and postmodernist deconstruction, which takes those models as *a priori* structures already formed, in place, and in need of dismantling. In such a scenario, then (which presupposes a dialogical rather than a teleological model of historical progression), deconstruction emerges with rather than subsequent to modernism.

FOUR   REPRODUCING ORIGINALITY

1 On Martinet's gallery, which opened in 1859, was rebuilt in 1862, and closed in 1865, which had concerts on its premises, and to which *Le Courrier artistique* and the short-lived Société Nationale des Beaux-Arts were connected, see Adler, *Manet*, p. 97; Fried, *Manet's Modernism*, pp. 139–40, 509 n. 9; Nicholas Green, "Circuits of Production, Circuits of Consumption: The Case of Mid-Nineteenth-Century French Art Dealing," *Art Journal* 48:1, Spring 1989, pp. 40–45; Nicholas Green, "Dealing in Temperaments: Economic Transformation of the Artistic Field in France During the Second Half of the Nineteenth Century," *Art History* March 1987, pp. 59–78; Hamilton, *Manet and His Critics*, p. 28; Lorne Huston, "Le Salon et les exposition d'art: Réflexions à partir de l'expérience de Louis Martinet (1861–65)," *Gazette des Beaux-Arts* 6th ser., 116 (July–Aug. 1990), pp. 45–50; Patricia Mainardi, *The End of the Salon: Art and the State in the Early Third Republic*, Cambridge University Press, 1993, p. 129; and Gustave Ribeaucourt, *Une Figure d'artiste: Louis Martinet (1814–1894)*, Paris, 1894. In the first number of *Le Courrier artistique*, Martinet's periodical, Martinet declared a commitment to the encyclopedic coverage of the modern schools of Europe, as if his gallery were

a mini Universal Exposition of its own: "une indication sommaire des mouvements des arts dans les départements et à l'étranger, principalement en Belgique, en Hollande, en Allemagne et en Angleterre . . . nos expositions, qui comprennent toutes les écoles" – "Aux Artistes et aux amateurs," *Le Courrier artistique* 1e année, no. 1, July 15, 1861, p. 1. In succeeding issues of the periodical, lists are given of Martinet's exhibitions of French artists of the modern school, of the "Ecole française" going back to the seventeenth and eighteenth centuries, of "Ecoles diverses" comprising Italian Renaissance as well as Dutch and Flemish sixteenth and seventeenth-century painters, and so on. There are also articles on the Le Nain brothers, David's *Marat*, and other painters and paintings from the French and other schools.

2 The formation of the Société Nationale des Beaux-Arts was announced in the March 15, 1862 issue of *Le Courrier artistique* (no. 19, p. 73), at which point Martinet indicated that the prime function of the Société was to protect and support the "droits d'auteur" of the contemporary artist. Manet's name does not appear on the list of the society's founders in either that issue or in no. 24 (June 1, 1862), when another fuller list (of artists who had works exhibited in the Society's first exhibition) was published; it does appear on the list of the "Cercle artistique de la Société Nationale des Beaux-Arts" in the August 9, 1863 (III:8) issue of *Le Courrier artistique*, pp. 29–30. (This was after Martinet's gallery closed for reconstruction at the end of 1862, and opened again on March 1, 1863, just in time for Manet's exhibition, which helped inaugurate the new space.) The only other time that Manet's name was mentioned in the journal was in Edouard Lockroy's review of "L'Exposition des Refusés," *Le Courrier artistique* II:24, May 16, 1863, p. 93, in which Manet was declared a talent for the future, but misunderstood and somewhat unripe at the present. Manet had works in group shows at Martinet's in 1864 and 1865 as well.

3 "Nous nous addressons autant aux artistes qui commencent qu'aux artistes en renom" – Louis Martinet, "L'Exposition permanente du Boulevard des Italiens," *Le Courrier artistique* no. 4, Aug. 1, 1861, p. 14.

4 "On a senti sérieusement la nécessité de tenir toujours ouvert au coeur de Paris, un local où un certain nombre de toiles choisies . . . fussent toujours offertes au public. Le Salon doit être le complément, le couronnement d'une série d'expositions préalables . . . l'artiste qui débute par un envoi de palais de l'Industrie ignore tout d'abord l'effet que produiront ses oeuvres . . . / Des peintres éminents ont bien des fois exprimé devant nous le désir qu'il leur fût permis de faire subir à leurs oeuvres une épreuve préliminaire, de les exposer une première fois pour les retirer ensuite, les retoucher et en modifier certain détails." – Louis Martinet, "Aux Artistes et aux amateurs," p. 1. While Martinet proclaimed that his goal was not to put only "masterpieces" on view – that was impossible with beginning artists – another writer in *Le Courrier artistique* argued against "peindre au premier coup" and the tendency to improvisation that he saw in current French oil painting, and which he contrasted to the slow and painstaking acquisition and demonstration of methodic skill, thus implicitly arguing against the valuation of the new artist and especially against the kind of "fast" painting that Manet produced and displayed: L. St-François, "Causeries d'art – des procédés de la peinture à l'huile," *Le Courrier artistique* no. 4, Aug. 1, 1861, p. 4. Moreover, such was the negative reaction to Manet's exhibition at Martinet's that, far from serving as an anteroom to the Salon, it resulted in the artist's relegation to the category of the "refusé."

5 "En vérité, on s'habitue trop, en France, à compter sur l'appui du gouvernement et l'on songe trop peu à reposer sur soi-même . . . on lui demande [le gouvernement] un concours si universel, on l'intéresse dans tant de questions, on invoque de sa part un soutien si continu, que l'individu finit par s'anéantir lui-même" – Martinet, "L'Exposition permanente du Boulevard des Italiens," p. 13.

6 "Il est presque impossible qu'un débutant soit remarqué au Salon . . . Dans une exposition où le catalogue comprend quatre mille numéros, et à laquelle chacun n'accorde, le plus souvent, qu'une seule visite, l'artiste a dix-neuf fois moins de chances d'être vu que dans une galerie de deux cent tableaux" – Martinet, "Aux Artistes et aux amateurs," p. 1.

7 "Ce que l'individu isolé serait impuissant à produire, une société . . . l'amènerait forcément. Dans les arts surtout, l'esprit d'association peut tout changer: alors les éléments les plus hétérogènes se soutiendront les uns les autres; ces tempéraments opposés, ces tendances diverses et ces traditions hostiles se confondrent en un tout indestructible, et, tous animés d'une seule pensée, mettant leurs facultés multiples au service d'une idée vraiment grande et utile pour l'art, sauront anéantir des répugnances dictées

par la prévention seule" – Martinet, "De l'association dans les arts," *Le Courrier artistique* no. 12, Dec. 1, 1861, p. 46.

8 The other images at Martinet's include the following possibilities: the print after *The Gypsies*, the print and/or painting of Mario Camprubi, *The Spanish Singer*, the *Portrait of Mme Brunet*, the *Boy with the Cherries*, *The Reader* (*Old Man Reading*), and/or *The Students of Salamanca*.

9 The two works in the Louvre were believed to be by Velasquez but actually were not. The latter is now believed to be by his studio assistant Mazo.

10 A painted copy of *Little Cavaliers* (1855–60) exists (Chrysler Museum of Art, Norfolk, Va.).

11 See Jean Harris, "Manet's Graphic Work of the Sixties," in Joel Isaacson, ed., *Manet and Spain: Prints and Drawings*, Ann Arbor, University of Michigan Museum of Art, 1969, pp. 1–7; as well as Marcel Guerin, *L'Oeuvre gravé de Manet*, Paris, Floury, 1944; Jean Harris, *The Graphic Work of Edouard Manet*, Ph.D. dissertation, Radcliffe University, 1961, reissued as *Edouard Manet: The Graphic Work: A Catalogue Raisonné*, San Francisco, A. Wofsky Fine Arts, 1990; Jean Leymarie and Michel Melot, *The Graphic Work of the Impressionists: Manet, Pissarro, Renoir, Cézanne, Sisley* (Jane Brenton, trans.), London, Thames and Hudson, 1972; Michel Melot, *L'Estampe impressionniste*, Paris, Bibliothèque Nationale, 1974; E. Moreau-Nélaton, *Manet graveur et lithographe*, Paris, 1906; and Léon Rosenthal, *Manet aquafortiste et lithographe*, Paris, 1925.

12 "le *Courrier Artistique* . . . veut surtout tenir les peintres et les amateurs au courant de toutes les reproductions remarquables qui surgissent dans le domaine des arts et en particulier de celles dont s'enrichit chaque jour l'Exposition du boulevard des Italiens" – Martinet, "Aux Artistes et aux amateurs," p. 1.

13 "La vente, au profit des artistes, des reproductions de leurs ouvrages, constituant ainsi un comptoir spécial de reproduction auquel pourra se rattacher par la suite tout ce qui a rapport à la propriété artistique" – *Le Courrier artistique* 23, May 15, 1862, p. 89.

14 "qu'elle suive davantage les traditions des maîtres" – Martinet, "De la gravure actuelle," *Le Courrier artistique* II:8, Oct. 1, 1862, p. 30.

15 This figure would have been even higher had Manet included the four additional works he had once envisioned for the portfolio.

16 "Spanishicity" is a play on the concept of "Italianicity" in Roland Barthes, "The Rhetoric of the Image" (1964), *The Responsibility of Forms: Critical Essays on Music, Art, and Representation* (Richard Howard, trans.), Berkeley and Los Angeles, University of California Press, 1985, pp. 21–40.

17 On the etching revival see Isabelle Auffret, *Du Réalisme à l'impressionnisme: L'eau-forte en France 1850–1890*, Courbevoie, Musée Roybet-Fould, 1994; Michel Melot, *Graphic Art of the Pre-Impressionists*, New York, Abrams, 1980/1; Janine Bailly-Herzberg, *L'Eau-forte de peintre au dix-neuvième siècle: La Société des Acquafortistes 1862–1867*, 2 vols., Paris, Léonce Laget, 1972; and Gabriel P. Weisberg, *The Etching Renaissance in France: 1850–1880*, Salt Lake City, University of Utah, 1971. Harris addresses Manet's use of reproductive etching as a cheap means of making copies and advertising his own images, in "Manet's Graphic Work of the Sixties," p. 2.

18 Here it is worth noting once again the images painted onto the bulletin board in Manet's later portrait of Zola, for of course it is there that Manet's painted copy after Goya's etched copy after Velasquez's *The Drinkers* speaks directly to the Velasquez–Goya–Manet lineage and to Manet's fashioning of his own originality through the double copy screen of the two Spanish masters.

19 On Goya, see Alfonso E. Perez Sanchez and Julian Gallego, *Goya, The Complete Etchings and Lithographs* (David Robinson Edwards and Jenifer Wakelyn, trans.), Munich and New York, Prestel, 1995; Janis Tomlinson, *Goya in the Twilight of the Enlightenment*, New Haven and London, Yale University Press, 1992; Verna Posever Custer, *La Tauromaquia: Goya, Picasso, and the Bullfight*, Milwaukee Art Museum, 1986; and C. Yriarte, *Goya*, Paris, 1867. On Baudelaire and Goya, see Isaacson, "Manet and Spain," *Manet and Spain*, p. 10.

20 On "originality" and mechanical reproduction in modernism, see Krauss, *Originality of the Avant-Garde*, pp. 151–70.

21 According to Proust, a visitor to Manet's studio pointed out the left-handedness of the painting of the *Spanish Singer* – Antonin Proust, "Edouard Manet: Souvenirs," *La Revue Blanche*, Feb.–May 1897, p. 170. According to Tabarant, however, it was not remarked until long afterward – A. Tabarant, *La Vie artistique au temps de Baudelaire*, Paris, Mercure de France, 1942, p. 42. See Cachin, *Manet*, p. 64.

22 Charles Baudelaire, "Peintres et aquafortistes," *Le Boulevard* no. 37, Sept. 14, 1862, cited in Hamilton, *Manet and His Critics*, p. 31; reproduced in *Ecrits esthétiques par Charles*

Baudelaire (Jean-Christophe Bailly, ed.), Paris, Union Générale d'Editions, 1986, pp. 414–19.

23 Théophile Gautier, *Moniteur universel*, July 3, 1861; cited in Hamilton, *Manet and His Critics*, p. 25. On Gautier, see Robert Snell, *Théophile Gautier, A Romantic Critic of the Visual Arts*, Oxford, Clarendon Press, 1982.

24 On the related but quite different problem of mirror reversal in the art (particularly the self-portraits) of Manet and his cohorts, see Fried, *Manet's Modernism*, pp. 365–98.

25 Goya's *Duchess of Alba* had been in the Galerie Espagnole, then went into the Pereire collection in Paris after 1848. See Cachin, *Manet*, p. 146. On the Galerie Espagnole, see J. Baticle and C. Marinas, *La Galerie espagnole de Louis-Philippe, 1838–1848*, Paris, 1981. On photographs of Spanish dancers and on Manet's use of carte-de-visite photographs more generally, see Anne McCauley, *A. A. E. Disdéri and the Carte de Visite Portrait Photograph*, New Haven and London, Yale University Press, 1985, pp. 172–95.

26 On the ambiguous identity and history of the *Portrait of Mme Brunet*, see Cachin, *Manet*, pp. 53–54.

27 On Astruc's song and the lithograph, see *ibid.*, pp. 154–56.

28 The Hippodrome at which the real Lola performed with her troupe was an open-air theater.

29 "cette imagination vive et ample, sensible, audacieuse"; "qui exprime si bien le caractère personnel de l'artiste" – Baudelaire, "Peintres et aquafortistes." Here Baudelaire speaks of Manet and Legros together; Michael Fried links the two as well – see *Manet's Modernism*, esp. pp. 186–97. (See also Baudelaire, "L'eau-forte est à la mode," *Revue anecdotique*, April 2, 1862; reproduced in *Ecrits esthétiques*, pp. 412–13.)

30 "la traduction la plus nette possible du caractère de l'artiste" – Baudelaire, "Peintres et aquafortistes."

31 "une méthode expéditive . . . et peu couteuse; chose importante, dans un temps où chacun considère le bon marché comme la qualité dominante, et ne voudrait pas payer à leur prix les lentes operations du burin" – *ibid.*

32 "de promener l'aiguille sur cette planche noire qui reproduira trop fidèlement toutes les arabesques de la fantaisie, toutes les hachures de la caprice!"; "Non seulement l'eau-forte sert à glorifier l'individualité de l'artiste, mais il serait même difficile à l'artiste de ne pas décrire sur la planche sa personnalité la plus intime" – *ibid.* Here in the context of *Le Boulevard*, the word "promener" suggests a kind of flaneurism of the aquatint needle, as if the boulevardier mode of

the "painter of modern life," along with his "lightning" style of visual attention, was integral to the very means and physical procedures of the medium.

33 "il y a eu autant de manières de le cultiver qu'il y a eu d'aquafortistes" – *ibid.*

34 "De tous les procédés utilisés pour reproduire et multiplier par l'impression les oeuvres d'art, il n'en est pas de plus vif, de plus spontané, surtout de plus sincère que la gravure à l'eau-forte. . . .

Accessible à tous ceux qui savent se servir de la plume ou de crayon, elle offre le précieux avantage de conserver le caractère intime de la manière du peintre qui l'emploie – soit pour reproduire son propre tableau, soit pour improviser une composition sur le cuivre même.

Une épreuve à l'eau-forte est toujours, au même degré qu'un dessin, une oeuvre originale. De là vient la valeur que certaines planches célèbres ont atteint, valeur souvent égale à celle d'un tableau unique, car elles portent en elles le cachet indélible du maître, et conservent aux yeux de l'amateur éclairé les vraies qualités picturales où la pensée de l'auteur jaillit sous le tranchant de l'outil, où son intention s'exprime . . .

Il n'est pas nécessaire de chercher un nom ou un titre inscrit au bas d'une estampe pour savoir attribuer à tout maître d'un tempérament vigoureusement individuel l'eau-forte qu'il aiera traitée dans la complète expression de son indépendance et de son talent" – Albert de la Fizelière, "La Société des Eau-fortistes," *Le Boulevard*, Sept. 7, 1862.

35 "Ainsi peut-on dire que l'eau-forte, dans l'estime de quiconque s'attache à l'analyse des oeuvres d'art et cherche à se rendre compte du principe comme des moyens d'éxécution de telle ou telle école, de tel ou tel maître, est la gravure par excellence, l'agent de vulgarisation le plus intelligent et le plus véridique" – *ibid.*

36 "Aux deux derniers siècles, l'eau-forte était le caprice et la recréation des maîtres, ils jetaient toute vive sur la planche l'idée ou la conception que le pinceau devrait ralentir; ils dessinaient sur le vernis comme sur le papier. Leurs plus intimes confidences sont écrites sous cette forme libre et rapide, car l'eau-forte d'un grand peintre suppose toujours un éclair de verve qu'il n'a pas voulu laisser refroidir. Il était en train, l'inspiration lui venait, le démon de la verve lui poussait le coude, lorsqu'au lieu du pinceau il prenait la pointe . . . Il avait hâte de fixer cette vision fugace, de faire mordre et retenir sur le cuivre l'image qui traversait son cerveau. Sa

main courait sur le vernis et découvrait le métal à peine effleuré; il versait l'acide . . . l'eau-forte était enlevée. – L'eau-forte, c'est l'éponge de Zeuxis tombant sur la toile, et d'un jet, y formant l'écume que son pinceau n'avait pas su rendre" – Paul de St. Victor, "Beaux-arts: Société des Aquafortistes: Eaux-fortes modernes, publication d'oeuvres originales et inédites (1)," *La Presse*, 28e année, April 27, 1863. De St. Victor, who succeeded Gautier as the art journalist for *La Presse* in 1855, was a conservative critic who fought against Manet's inclusion in the Salon for years. See Hamilton, *Manet and His Critics*, p. 39.

37   "La gravure à la manière noire commençait à ralentir le zèle des graveurs au burin; la photographie semble avoir paralysé leurs efforts, non pas que cette dernière remplace la gravure, mais elle envahit tout.

Nous sommes loin de méconnaître les services de la photographie; mais tout le monde sent la nécessité d'une réaction contre ses envahissements. De cette idée est née la Société des aqua-fortistes" – Martinet, "De la gravure actuelle," p. 30.

38   Walter Benjamin, "The Work of Art in the Age of Mechanical Reproduction," *Illuminations* (Harry Zohn, trans.), New York, Schocken Books, 1969, pp. 217–51.

39   "En ce temps où la photographie charme le vulgaire par la fidélité mécanique de ses reproductions, il devait se déclarer dans l'art une tendance au libre caprice et à la fantaisie pittoresque. Le besoin de réagir contre le positivisme de l'instrument-miroir a fait prendre à plus d'un peintre la pointe du graveur à l'eau-forte, et de la réunion de ces talents, ennuyés de voir les murs tapissés de monotones images d'où l'âme est absente, est née la *Société des Aquafortistes*" – Théophile Gautier, "Un mot sur l'eau-forte," *La Société des Aquafortistes*, 1e année, Aug. 1863; cited in Bailly-Herzberg, *L'Eau-forte de peintre au dix-neuvième siècle*, vol. 1, p. 266.

40   Gautier's and others' discussions of the invasion of photography, its deleterious effects on the artist's imagination, the vulgarization of the public, and the necessity of combatting it with the arts of originality and temperament resound with Baudelaire's famous pronouncements on the matter in the "Salon de 1859" – reproduced in *Ecrits esthétiques par Charles Baudelaire*, pp. 285–91.

41   "Nul moyen, en effet, n'est plus simple, plus direct, plus personnel que l'eau-forte" – Gautier, "Un mot sur l'eau-forte," p. 266.

42   "La moisure réussie, la planche est faite; on peut la tirer, et l'on a l'idée même du maître, toute pétillante de vie et de spontanéité, sans l'intermédiaire d'aucune traduction. Chaque eau-forte est un dessin original; que de motifs charmants, que d'intentions exquises, que de mouvements primesautiers a conservé cette rapide et facile gravure, qui sait immortaliser des croquis dont le papier ne garderait pas trace! Mais, pour y réussir, il faut une décision de main, une sûreté de trait, une préscience de l'effet, que ne possèdent pas toujours des talents honnêtes et soigneux; elle ne souffre pas les tâtonnements, les retouches, les repentirs. Le fini, le rendu extrême ne lui vont pas. Mais elle ne trahit jamais la naïveté de l'esprit; elle comprend à demi-mot; il lui suffit de quelques brusques hachures pour entendre et exprimer votre rêve secret" – *ibid.*

43   "Cette Société n'a d'autre code que l'individualisme"; "Elle a l'authenticité d'un parafe, car le talent de celui qui la pratique se signe dans chaque taille" – *ibid.*

44   "combattre la photographie, la lithographie, l'aqua-tinta, la gravure dont les hachures recroisées ont une point au milieu; en un mot le travail régulier, automatique, sans inspiration qui dénature l'idée même de l'artiste" – *ibid.*, p. 267.

45   "parler directement au public" – *ibid.*

46   "Chacun doit inventer et graver lui-même le sujet qu'il apporte à l'oeuvre collective. Aucun genre ne prévaut, aucune manière n'est recommandée; on est libre de montrer tout l'originalité qu'on a, et personne ne s'en fait faute. Celui-ci raye brutalement son cuivre à coups de sabre et se contente de quelques traits rudes et sommaires, n'écrivant sa pensée que pour les yeux qui savent lire; celui-là pousse à l'effet, recroise ses hachures, accumule les travaux; cet autre cherche l'aspect blond; un quatrième risque les brusques oppositions de noir et de blanc" – *ibid.*

47   "très hostiles à la machine et remplis de respect pour la main pleine d'éclairs et de génie. Ils ont résolu de conjurer de toutes leurs forces la photographie envahissante et se défendre . . . le domaine enchanté des grands maîtres. . . . ils ont opposés le burin, qui grave sur le cuivre et l'acier des oeuvres impérissables, au collodion qu'un souffle emporte . . . les plus fanatiques de la photographie ont salué la gravure" – Jules Janin, "L'eau-forte, le soleil et le crayon," *La Société des Aquafortistes*, cited in Bailly-Herzberg, *L'Eau-forte de peintre au dix-neuvième siècle*, p. 268.

48   "L'eau-forte est aussi prompte que la photographie" – *ibid.*

49   "Relativement au dessin, l'eau-forte est l'analogue de l'imprimerie et de la presse, qui multiplient la pensée écrite" – W. Bürger, preface to *La Société des Aquafortistes*, 3e année, 1865, cited in *ibid.*, p. 271.

50   "l'expression de la pensée individuelle"; "Dans la main, cette science consommée qui arrive à la suppression même du métier; dans l'esprit, ce tour original et hardi qui n'est autre que la personnalité même" – Jules Castagnary, preface to La Société des Aquafortistes, 4e année, 1864, cited in *ibid.*, pp. 273–74.

51   "un passe-temps plein de charme pour quelques femme du monde" – *ibid.* In the same preface, Castagnary also speaks of aquatint as "une spécialité originale et curieuse de l'art français."

52   "une habileté d'outil qui ne peut s'acquérir du premier coup" – Philippe Burty, "La Gravure, le bois et la lithographie au Salon de 1868," *Gazette des Beaux-Arts* XXV, 10e année, Aug. 1, 1868, p. 110.

53   "[il est] capable, plus qu'aucun autre procédé, d'exprimer la coloration, l'épiderme des objets . . . Alors que le burin . . . moderne, ne tend qu'à reproduire a coloration discrète de la fresque, les détails généraux du tableau, ou l'expression recueillie du portrait, la pointe, plus vive, plus alerte, plus passionnée, creuse les ombres, fouille les rides, fait saillir les angles, miroiter les plans, étinceler les facettes; elle allume le regard, elle crispe le geste, elle brode d'or le vêtement du prince et taille en lambeaux le haillon du pauvre" – Philippe Burty, "La Gravure au Salon de 1866," *Gazette des Beaux-Arts* XXI, ser. 1, Aug. 1, 1866, p. 184.

54   This is, more generally, one of the two central paradoxes of the *coloris* equation – which not only conflates literal and illusionistic color but also integrates the subjective and objective dimensions of art. Here, not coincidentally, the represented surfaces of the world which combine subjective aspect and objective fact are those of costume.

55   "Manet! ses eaux-fortes espagnoles créent l'illusion d'une peinture, tant les taches en sont coloriées; mais pourquoi ne nous grave-t-il pas ses jolies Parisiennes?" – Théodore de Banville, "La Société des Aquafortistes," *L'Union des Arts* no. 36, Oct. 1, 1864, cited in Bailly-Herzberg, *L'Eau-forte de peintre au dix-neuvième siècle*, p. 129.

56   See Hamilton, *Manet and His Critics*, p. 24.

57   Charles Blanc, "Velasquez à Madrid," *Gazette des Beaux-Arts* année 5, XV, July 1863, pp. 65–74; Charles Blanc (with W. Bürger, Paul Mantz, L. Viardot, and Paul Lefort), *Histoire des peintres de toutes les écoles: Ecole Espagnole*, Paris, Jules Renouard, 1869. For earlier accounts, see Louis Viardot, *Etudes sur l'histoire des institutions, de la littérature, et des beaux-arts en Espagne*, Paris, 1835; *Notice sur M. le Baron Taylor et sur les tableaux espagnols achetés par lui d'après les ordres du roi*, Paris, 1837; Musée National du Louvre, *Notice des tableaux de la Galerie Espagnole*, Paris, 1838; and Paul Mantz, "La Galerie Pourtalès," *Gazette des Beaux-Arts* année 7, XVIII, Feb. 1, 1865, pp. 97–117.

58   "une physionomie fortement marquée, un caractère, de conserver constamment la couleur et la vérité locales, d'être, en un mot, avant tout et toujours espagnole"; "suivre une marche tout à fait contraire aux tendances des autres peuples de l'Europe" – Charles Blanc, *Ecole Espagnole*, Introduction, pp. 2, 11.

59   The Galerie Espagnole was open between 1838 and 1848. With the Second Republic, most of the Napoleonic spoils contained in it were sent back to Spain.

60   "Le plus grand et le plus espagnol de tous les peintres de l'Espagne"; "Velazquez ne paye jamais qu'en monnaie d'Espagne"; "Velazquez revint d'Italie aussi Espagnol, aussi Velazquez qu'auparavant" – Blanc, *Ecole Espagnole*, "Histoire, Portraits: Don Diégo Velazquez," pp. 1, 7, 8.

61   "Sa palette, très peu chargée, se compose de deux ou trois tons avec lesquels il combine toutes les variantes du gris, qui est la base constante de sa couleur. Voyez ses portraits en pied; il sont tous colorés sur ce thème: le ton de chair et l'habit noir s'enlèvant sur un fond gris; les bas gris s'enlèvant sur un fond noir. Mais les noirs ne sont pas noirs, pas plus que les blancs ne sont blancs. Chez Vélasquez . . . le blanc est écru; le noir n'est jamais mat . . . Le mérite de Vélasquez . . . consiste à réunir le charme d'un coloriste à une extrême sobriété de couleur. C'est un gourmet . . . c'est un virtuose qui exécute une excellente musique avec deux ou trois notes, là ou un Rubens, un Véronèse prendraient l'occasion de jouer un morceau à grand orchestre" – Charles Blanc, "Vélasquez à Madrid," *Gazette des Beaux-Arts* XV, July 1, 1863, p. 67.

62   "Toutes les variétés du rouge s'y jouent et y sont opposées à des nuances de bleu, il est vrai que ce bleu, très légèrement glacé de jaune dans le jupon de la fileuse, tourne au vert; mais les bleus, plus ou moins rompus, sont tous d'un côté et tous les rouges d'un autre" – *ibid.*, p. 69.

63 "Rien n'est donc plus embarrassant pour un graveur que d'avoir à transposer sur sa planche les peintures d'un coloration semblable à Teniers, à Vélasquez, parce que là où le peintre a su distinguer deux tons de même valeur, le graveur est amené à les confondre. Il est donc forcé de prendre une interprétation libre. Aussi Vélasquez n'a-t-il pas été bien gravé que par un peintre, peu savant sans doute, mais plein de tempérament, d'intuition, d'extravagance et de génie, par Goya. Ne craignant pas d'intervertir l'ordre des valeurs, Goya repeint à l'eau-forte les portraits du maître, et il parvient même, par le ménagement du papier et par la franchise de sa moisure, à leur donner un ressort, un montant, une saveur épicée qui ne se trouvent pas dans l'original" – *ibid.*, p. 67.

64 "M. Manet est l'auteur du *Guitariste*, qui a produit une vive sensation au Salon dernier. On verra au prochain Salon plusieurs tableaux de lui empreints de la saveur espagnole la plus forte, et qui donnent à croire que la génie espagnole s'est réfugiée en France. . . . un gout décidé pour la . . . réalité moderne" – Baudelaire, "Peintres et aquafortistes."

65 "ce petit musée personnel"; "Une jeune Espagnole" – Jules Claretie, *L'Indépendance belge*, June 15, 1867, cited by Hamilton, *Manet and His Critics*, p. 107; and Babou, "Les Dissidents de l'Exposition," pp. 286, 288.

66 "M. Manet adore l'Espagne, et son maître d'affection parait être Goya, dont il imite les tons vifs et heurté, la touche libre et fougueuse." – Théophile Thoré, "Salon de 1863," *Salons de W. Bürger, 1861 à 1868*, Paris: Le Renouard, 1870, vol. 1, p. 424.

67 "M. Manet, qui est un espagnol de Paris, et qu'une parenté mystérieuse rattache à la tradition de Goya"; "la caricature de la couleur et non la couleur elle-même" – Paul Mantz, "Exposition du Boulevard des Italiens," *Gazette des Beaux-Arts* XV, April 1, 1863, p. 383.

68 Paul de St. Victor accompanied Charles Blanc to Spain in September 1862 (Blanc, "Vélasquez à Madrid, p. 62). For his part Manet did not actually go to Spain until 1865; his enthusiasm for Spain was a museum-mediated one, and remained such even during and after his trip to Spain. During his 1865 visit to Madrid, he wrote a letter to Fantin-Latour describing his encounter with Velasquez at the Prado, remarking that the Louvre *Philip IV* that he himself had copied in his aquatint was not actually by Velasquez, expressing his admiration for the *Portrait of Pablo de Valladolid* and *Las Meninas* which he saw in the Madrid museum, and

underlining his preference for Velasquez over Goya, whom he described as a "spirited" but inferior imitation of the seventeenth-century master; see Pierre Courthion, *Manet raconté par lui-même et par ses amis*, Geneva, Pierre Cailler, 1945, pp. 42–44.

69 "Imaginez Goya passé au Mexique, devenu sauvage au milieu des *pampas*, et barbouillant des toiles avec de la cochenille écrasée, vous avez M. Manet, le réaliste de la dernière heure. Ses tableaux de l'Exposition des Italiens sont des charivaris de palette; jamais on ne fait plus éffroyablement grimacer les lignes et hurler les tons. Ses *Toréros* feraient peur aux vaches espagnoles . . . Il y a pourtant un certain talent dans ces pochades indigestes, mais nous doutons que M. Manet s'applique jamais à les dégrossir. L'eau-forte lui réussit mieux que la toile: ses *Gitanos* ont de la race et de la tournure. J'aime surtout celui qui, la tête penchée en arrière, renverse une cruche sur sa bouche ouverte: les *Bevidores* de Vélasquez l'admetteraient dans leur confrérie" – de St. Victor, "Beaux-arts: Société des Aquafortistes."

70 On gypsies, see Sir Richard Burton, *The Jew, the Gypsy and El Islam*, Chicago and New York, H. S. Stone and Co., 1898; Françoise de Vaux de Foletier, *Les Bohémiens en France au dix-neuvième siècle*, Paris, J. C. Lattès, 1981; Marilyn R. Brown, *Gypsies and Other Bohemians: The Myth of the Artist in Nineteenth Century France*, Ann Arbor, UMI Research Press, 1985; Bernard Leblon, *Les Gitans d'Espagne*, Paris, Presses Universitaires de France, 1985; David Mayall, *Gypsy Travellers in Nineteenth Century Society*, Cambridge University Press, 1988; Wim Willems, *In Search of the True Gypsy: From Enlightenment to Final Solution*, London and Portland, F. Cass, 1997; and Leo Lucassen, Wim Willems, and Annemarie Cottaar, *Gypsies and Other Itinerant Groups: A Socio-historical Approach*, New York, St. Martin's Press, 1998.

FIVE   BETWEEN GAUTIER'S SPAIN AND BAUDELAIRE'S MODERN LIFE

1 See Cachin, *Manet*, pp. 196–97. It was in response to the charges of plagiarism and pastiche that Baudelaire also denied Manet's direct recourse to Spanish art, saying that he had never been to the Pourtalès collection; see Etienne Moreau-Nélaton, *Manet raconté par lui-même*, Paris, 1926, vol. 1, p. 59. Manet painted one more *Bullfight* in 1865–66.

2   *Mlle V.* was titled simply "Espada" when it appeared in print in the Cadart portofolio.

3   This painting also refers to Goya's paintings of children, such as *Manuel Osorio* and *Pepito Costa*; see Cachin, *Manet*, p. 76.

4   And here, as in the *Majo* of 1863, Manet returned to the baroque excesses of color and decoration that characterize the masculine costume of the matador (as opposed to the relative sobriety of color that marked Victorine as an *espada* and Nadar's mistress as a Spanishwoman in male drag), characterized in detail by Zacharie Astruc in an 1867 piece on the Spanish bullfight: "Ils ont dépouillé leurs grands manteaux de couleur; on les dirait prêts pour le bal, les bas de soie bien tirés sur leurs jambes élégants, pointant leurs jolis souliers découverts. Leur coulotte courte, pailletée d'or, étincelle; la veste, poudrée d'argent, se joue au corps ainsi qu'une nuée changeante. La petite cravate, retenue au cou par un anneau d'or, les enjolive étrangement, la toque noire ornée de glands, de boules de jais, de chenilles, couvre à peine leur chignon noir qui les fait ressembler à des femmes maigres. Celui-ci est rose, brodé d'argent, celui-là, pourpre et or; un autre, couleur du plus bel azur; un autre jonquille-ou lilas, ou vert. Je ne dis rien de gris-perle, les plus ravissants! . . . Ah! l'intéressante galerie à peindre. Véronèse, quittez pour un instant votre tombe" – Astruc, "Madrid L'Hiver: Courses de jeunes taureux," *Revue libérale: politique, littéraire, scientifique, financière*, t. II, June–July 1867, pp. 548–49. (Astruc goes on to remark that only the *espada* has a cape "*couleur de sang*" – p. 550.)

5   Both of these retain some of the theatricality of Manet's earlier Spanishizing works – the *Execution of Emperor Maximilian* in the bullfight-like group of spectators in the background, *The Balcony* in its air of a theatrical loge.

6   On the femininity of masquerade, see Joan Rivière, "Womanliness as Masquerade," in Victor Burgin, James Donald, and Cora Kaplan, eds., *Formations of Fantasy*, London, Methuen, 1981; and Mary Anne Doane, "Film and the Masquerade: Theorizing the Female Spectator," *Screen* 23, no. 3–4, 1982, pp. 74–88. See also Judith Butler, *Gender Trouble: Feminism and the Subversion of Identity*, New York, Routledge, 1990.

7   See Beatrice Farwell, *Manet and the Nude: A Study in the Iconology of the Second Empire*, New York, Garland, 1981; and Marcia Pointon, *Naked Authority: The Body in Western Painting 1830–1906*, Cambridge University Press, 1990.

8   The painting was shown in St. Petersburg in 1861; see Cachin, *Manet*, pp. 83–86.

9   It is remarkable how close Manet came to being an Orientalist painter in the 1860s, while at the same time positioning himself at the margins of Orientalist discourse. With his focus on Spanish themes, he broached Orientalism at a tangent, rather than embracing it from the center of its discursive field. See Edward Said, *Orientalism*, New York, Random House, 1978.

10 For Astruc's song, see Cachin, *Manet*, p. 154. (These were years in which Manet seemed particularly ready to have his painting associated with poetry – Astruc's lines attached to *Olympia* when she was shown in the Salon of 1865 are a prime example, perhaps modeled on the example set by *Lola de Valence*.) Astruc wrote more expansively about Spain, underlining the Orientalist aspect of the Spanishwoman – indeed, her phanstasmatic function as a nearly nude *odalisque* – as well as her role as a Baudelairean figure of art, decor, and desire, and her enframing in the scenes and settings of (Frenchified Spanish) modern life: "Vive le ciel! vive la femme! salut à elle, nonne parée du rosaire ou danseuse portant la mandoline au bras, musulmane et chrétienne, beauté voilée, mieux encore: ravissante enfant plus nue que Vénus dans ses déshabillés de soie, d'argent; elle séduisit les poètes, les artistes . . . Elle a fécondé les deux mondes. L'Afrique fait surgir l'Amerique du fond des eaux . . . / L'Espagnole est mon délice et mes peines. L'Espagnole fut créé pour le désir. Elle enchante, elle éblouit . . . Mettez-la dans sa litière, derrière les courtines roses aux franges d'argent, derrière la vitre claire d'une voiture qui passe, dans une loge de théâtre, dans le cirque où les taureaux agonisent, à la promenade, au café, dans les allées des parcs édifiés par les Bourbons charmants, dans ces retraites où sourit l'ombre de Watteau, au bord des fenêtres cloîtrées de grilles, cages de fer pour ces oiseaux ramageurs; supposez-la penchée sur les balcons où flottent les rideaux de couleurs qui défendent les ardents soleils et facilitent la curiosité, donnez-lui ces cadres différents, l'Espagnole est sans rivale, tant est puissant l'impérieux caprice qu'elle excite" – Zacharie Astruc, *Espagne: Le Généralife, Sérénades et Songes*, Paris, Société Française d'Editions d'Art, 1897, pp. 272–73.

11 This painting refers also to one of Goya's *Tauromaquia*, as does the etched *La Posada*, which Cachin sees as a kind of pendant to *The Spanish Ballet*; see Cachin, *Manet*, p. 145.

12 "Ni homme, ni femme; mais qu'est-ce que ce peut-être?" – Charles Randon, *Le Journal amusant*, June 29, 1867.

13 "l'un est resté immobile à l'Orient et l'autre s'est transplanté à l'Occident" – Baron Isidore Taylor, *Voyage pittoresque en Espagne*, Paris, Plon, 1826, p. 27. Baron Taylor made a trip to Spain in 1835–36 to collect works for Louis-Philippe's Galerie Espagnol. Taylor's emphasis on Velasquez is clearly aligned with Charles Blanc's electing of the seventeenth-century court painter as the representative of Spanish art history.

14 "Ces filles sont grandes, leur taille est fine, le teint brun, les dents admirables, les cheveux noirs et lustrés comme du jais . . . elles ont sur la tête une espèce de petit voile de mousseline brodée de fleurs d'or et de soie qui voltige et qui couvre la gorge; elles portent des pendants d'oreille d'or et de perles et des colliers de corail, elles ont les espèces de juste-au-corps comme nos bohémiennes" – *Voyage pittoresque en Espagne*, pp. 36–37. Taylor quotes from Mme D'Aulnoy, *Relation du Voyage d'Espagne*, La Haye, 1691.

15 "Cette description du dix-septième siècle est encore vraie à notre époque" – *ibid.*, p. 37.

16 Spain had been a romantic site at least since Mérimée's stories began to come out in the late 1820s and he took his trip to Spain in 1830, at which point the idea for *Carmen* was hatched, though the story was not published until 1845. In 1875 it yielded the famous opera of the same name by Bizet (with libretto by Ludovic Halévy and Henri Meilhac). The eponymous central character of the novella and opera, who figures the bohemian, the gypsy, and the *Espagnole* all at once, lurks beneath the *Espagnoles* of Gautier and Astruc, not to mention Manet's *Lola* (if not his *Gypsy with a Cigarette* of 1862 as well). See Dominique Maingueneau, *Carmen: Les racines d'un mythe*, Paris, Editions du Sorbier, 1984; Susan McClary, ed., *Georges Bizet: Carmen*, New York, Cambridge University Press, 1996; and Evelyn Gould, *The Fate of Carmen*, Baltimore, Johns Hopkins University Press, 1996. On romantic travels to Spain, see Paul Guinard, "Romantiques français en Espagne," *Art de France* no. 2, 1962, pp. 179–206.

17 "On nous avait beaucoup vanté les *manolas* de Madrid: la manola est un type disparu comme la grisette de Paris, comme les Trastéverins de Rome; elle existe bien encore, mais dépouillée de son caractère primitif; elle n'a plus son costume si hardi et si pittoresque; l'ignoble indienne a remplacé les jupes de couleurs éclatantes brodées de ramages exorbitants; l'affreux soulier de peau a chassé le chausson de satin, et, chose horrible à penser, la robe s'est allongée de deux bons doigts. Autrefois elles variaient l'aspect du Prado par leurs vives allures et leur costume singulier: aujourd'hui on a peine à les distinguer des petites bourgeoises et des femmes de marchands. J'ai cherché la manola pur sang dans tous les coins de Madrid . . . je me trouvais dans une petite ruelle déserte, et là je vis, pour la première et la dernière fois, la manola demandée. C'était une grande fille bien découplée, de vingt-quatre ans environ, la plus haute vieillesse où puissent arriver les *manolas* et les grisettes. Elle avait le taint basané, le regard ferme et triste, la bouche un peu épaisse, et je ne sais quoi d'africain dans la construction du masque. Une énorme tresse de cheveux bleus à force d'être noirs, nattée comme le jonc d'une corbeille, lui faisait le tour de la tête et venait se rattacher à un grand peigne à galerie; des paquets de grains de corail pendaient à ses oreilles; son cou fauve était orné d'un collier de même matière; une mantille de velours noir encadrait sa tête et ses épaules; sa robe, aussi courte que celle des Suissesses du canton de Berne, était de drap brodé, et laissait voir des jambes fines et nerveuses enfermées dans un bas de soie noire bien tiré; le soulier était de satin, selon l'ancienne mode; un éventail rouge tremblait comme un papillon de cinabre dans ses doigts chargés de bagues d'argent" – Théophile Gautier, *Voyage en Espagne (Tra los Montes)*, Paris, Bibliothèque Charpentier, 1843, pp. 93–94.

18 See Jay McKean Fisher, *The Prints of Edouard Manet*, Washington, D.C., International Exhibitions Foundation, 1985, pp. 58–59; Harris, *Edouard Manet: Graphic Works*, p. 128.

19 See Gautier, *Voyage en Espagne*, pp. 235–37.

20 "Les paysans valenciens ont un costume d'une étrangeté caractéristique, qui ne doit pas avoir varié beaucoup depuis l'invasion des Arabes, et qui ne diffère que très-peu du costume actuel des Mores d'Afrique"; "il a vraiment l'air d'un Bédouin . . . cet air féroce"; "les femmes de ces Kabiles européens sont pâles, blondes, *bionde e grassote*, comme les Vénitiennes"; "cet effroyable costume anglo-français . . . les robes manches à la gigot et autres abominations pareilles" – *ibid.*, pp. 371–73.

21 The painting was based on the ragpicker Colardet, but also on the Baudelairean literary figure of the *chiffonnier*.

22 Zacharie Astruc, too, another Spanish enthusiast and the celebrator of Lola Melea in song, shows up seated beneath the trees.

23 Babou, "Les dissidents de l'exposition": "la manie de *voir par taches*"; "la *tache-Baudelaire*, la *tache-Gautier*, la *tache-Manet*."

24 Zola quoted in full Baudelaire's four lines (see next note), which he said "fut sifflé et maltraité autant que le tableau lui-même" – Zola, "Une nouvelle manière en peinture," p. 95. Already cited in Chapter Two above.

25 "Entre tant de beautés que partout on peut voir/Je comprends bien, amis, que le Désir balance;/Mais on voit scintiller dans Lola de Valence/Le charme inattendu d'un bijou rose et noir." – Charles Baudelaire, *Oeuvres complètes* (Claude Pichois, ed.), Paris, 1975–76, vol. 1, p. 168; cited in Françoise Cachin, *Manet 1832–1883*, Paris, Grand Palais, 1983, p. 148. The original poem of which the quatrain is a version, a five-line "fleur du mal" written for Mme. Sabatier in 1857, went, a bit more explicitly, this way:

> Parmi toutes les belles choses
> Dont est fait son enchantement,
> Parmi les objects noirs ou roses
> Qui composent son corps chantant
> Quel est le plus doux?
>> (Baudelaire, *Oeuvres complètes*, vol. 1, p. 42; cited in *ibid.*, p. 148.)

26 *Ibid.* In the racialist subtext hovering around the reception of Lola's gender indeterminacy then and now she is treated as a Spanish *hommasse* – a woman both mannish and Spanish, with too much black in her face for French standards of femininity. Cachin *et al* find Manet's "fierce," "terrible" portrait of Baudelaire's mistress Jeanne Duval equally ugly, describing her as neither "black nor mulatto but no doubt simply creole" – *ibid.*, p. 87.

27 The genital reference was picked up later, in 1914, by Gertrude Stein in a piece in *Tender Buttons* called "Petticoat": "A light white, a disgrace, an ink spot, a rosy charm" – *Tender Buttons* (1914), Mineola, N.Y., Dover Publications, 1997, "Objects," p. 22.

28 He was, after all, the poet who had written: "La très-chère était nue, et, connaissant mon coeur,/Elle n'avait gardé que ses bijoux sonores,/Dont le riche attirail lui donnait l'air vainqueur/Qu'ont dans leurs jours heureux les esclaves des Mores. – Charles Baudelaire, "Les Bijoux," *Flowers of Evil: A Selection* (Marthiel and Jackson Mathews, eds.,), New York, New Directions, 1958, pp. 22–23; my translation. On

the erotics of Baudelaire's poetry, its shifting between the fluid and the frozen, see Leo Bersani, *Baudelaire and Freud*, Berkeley, University of California Press, 1977.

29 Later, Valéry picked up that phrase and used it to describe Manet's paintings of Berthe Morisot: see Paul Valéry, *Degas Manet Morisot* (David Paul, trans.), New York, Pantheon, Bollingen Series XLV, 12, 1960, pp. 105–14. On this, see Chapter Seven below.

30 Letter of May 11, 1865 (reply to letter from Manet, regarding the reception of *Olympia*); cited in Hamilton, *Manet and His Critics*, pp. 34–35. For other discussions of Manet and Baudelaire, see James H. Rubin, *Manet's Silence and the Poetics of Bouquets*, London, Reaktion, 1994, esp. pp. 101–09; and Michael Fried, "Painting Memories: On the Containment of the Past in Baudelaire and Manet," *Critical Inquiry* 10, March 1984, pp. 510–42; and *Manet's Modernism*, esp. pp. 8–9, 15, 62, 132, 164–67. On Baudelaire's aesthetics, see Susan Blood, *Baudelaire and the Aesthetics of Bad Faith*, Stanford University Press, 1997; David Carrier, *High Art: Charles Baudelaire and the Origins of Modernist Painting*, University Park, Pennsylvania State University Press, 1996; Isabel Valverde, *Moderne/modernité: deux notions dans la critique d'art française de Stendhal à Baudelaire, 1824–1863*, Frankfurt-am-Main and New York, P. Lang, 1994; Timothy Bell Raser, *A Poetics of Art Criticism: The Case of Baudelaire*, Chapel Hill, University of North Carolina, 1989; Margaret Gilman, *Baudelaire, the Critic*, New York, Columbia University Press, 1943; and Dario Gamboni, "Propositions pour l'étude de la critique d'art du XIXe siècle," in "Critique d'art," *Romantisme* 21, no. 71, 1991, pp. 9–17. See also Michele Hannoosh, *Baudelaire and Caricature: From the Comic to an Art of Modernity*, University Park, Pennsylvania State University Press, 1992.

31 "J'ignore s'il est fier de sa qualité de romantique; mais sa place est ici, parce que la majorité du public l'a depuis longtemps, et de sa première oeuvre, constitué le chef de l'école moderne." – Baudelaire, "Salon de 1846: IV. Eugène Delacroix," in *Ecrits esthétiques*, pp. 112–13. All translations of the "Salon de 1846" are from *Art in Paris 1845–1862, Salons and Other Exhibitions Reviewed by Charles Baudelaire* (Jonathan Mayne, trans.), Oxford, Phaidon, 1965, pp. 41–120.

32 "Le Peintre de la vie moderne" was published in *Le Figaro* on November 26 and 29, and December 3, 1863. According to Baudelaire's

correspondence, however, it was written between the end of 1859 and the beginning of 1860, just as Manet was beginning his painting career – editor's note, Baudelaire, *Curiosités esthétiques: L'Art romantique et autres oeuvres critiques de Baudelaire* (Henri Lemaitre, ed.), Paris, 1962, p. 453.

33 The following year Théophile Thoré directly associated Manet's situation to Delacroix's: "Rappelons-nous les débuts d'Eugène Delacroix, son triomphe à l'exposition universelle et sa vente – après décès!" – Thoré, "Salon de 1864," *Salons de W. Bürger*, vol. 2, p. 100.

34 Baudelaire's comment about Manet's being the "first in the decrepitude of [his] art" suggests something of the same idea, namely that Manet represented the end of a line as much as the beginning of one.

35 See Hamilton, *Manet and His Critics*, p. 18.

36 On Baudelaire and Delacroix, see Armand Moss, *Baudelaire et Delacroix*, Paris, A. G. Nizet, 1973. See also Anne Larue, "Delacroix and his Critics: The Stakes and Strategies," in Orwicz, ed. *Art Criticism and its Institutions in Nineteenth-Century France*, pp. 63–87.

37 "Qui dit romantisme dit art moderne, – c'est-à-dire intimité, spiritualité, couleur, aspiration vers l'infini, exprimées par tous les moyens que contiennent les arts." – Baudelaire, "Salon de 1846: II. Qu'est-ce que le romantisme?," p. 106.

38 "Le romantisme est fils du Nord, et le Nord est coloriste"; "En revanche le Midi est naturaliste . . . Le Midi est brutal et positif comme un sculpteur" – *ibid.*, pp. 106–07.

39 "le rouge chante la gloire du vert"; "divisible à l'infini"; "un toton"; "la gamme des tons"; "La couleur est donc l'accord de deux tons. Le ton chaud et le ton froid, dans l'opposition desquels consiste toute la théorie, ne peuvent se définir d'une manière absolue: ils n'existent que relativement" – Baudelaire, "Salon de 1846": "De la couleur," pp. 107–12.

40 "le détail dans le détail . . . la main d'une femme"; on verra qu'il y a harmonie parfaite entre le vert des fortes veines qui la sillonnent et les tons sanguinolents qui marquent les jointures; les ongles roses tranchent sur la première phalange qui possède quelques tons gris et bruns. Quant à la paume, les lignes de vie, plus roses et plus vineuses, sont séparées les unes des autres par le système des veines vertes ou bleues qui les traversent. L'étude du même objet, faite avec une loupe, fournira dans n'importe quel espace, si petit qu'il soit, une

harmonie parfaite de tons gris, bleus, bruns, verts, orangés et blancs réchauffés par un peu de jaune – harmonie qui, combinée avec les ombres, produit le modelé des coloristes, essentiellement différent du modelé des dessinateurs, dont les difficultés se réduisent à peu près à copier un plâtre" – *ibid.*, p. 109.

41 "de rouges fanfares . . . une sanglante harmonie . . . le vert s'empourpre richement" – *ibid.*

42 "un cabaret mi-parti de vert et de rouge crus" – *ibid.*, p. 111.

43 "cette sanglante et farouche désolation, à peine compensée par le vert sombre de l'espérance" – *ibid:* "Eugène Delacroix," p. 123.

44 "pour les coloristes . . . les lignes ne sont jamais, comme dans l'arc-en-ciel, que la fusion intime de deux couleurs" – *ibid.*, p. 121.

45 See Paul Signac, *D'Eugène Delacroix au néo-impressionnisme* (1899), Paris, H. Floury, 1911. Like Signac and others before and after him, of course, Baudelaire picks up and contributes to a long line of modern color theory in both science and aesthetics going back at least to J. W. Goethe's *Farbenlehre* of 1810; he was not the inventor of the discourse, by any means, but he did twist its terms to his own ends. See John Gage, *Color and Culture: Practice and Meaning from Antiquity to Abstraction*, London, Thames and Hudson, and Berkeley and Los Angeles, University of California Press, 1993; Janine Bourriau and Trevor Lamb, *Colour: Art and Science*, Cambridge University Press, 1995; and Charles A. Riley II, *Color Codes: Modern Theories of Color in Philosophy, Painting and Architecture, Literature, Music and Psychology*, Hanover and London, University Press of New England, 1995.

46 "La loupe, c'est l'oeil du coloriste" – Baudelaire, "Salon de 1846," p. 109.

47 "un espace d'air bien moindre entre le spectateur et le tableau qu'entre le spectateur et la nature"; "tout différent de la nature" – *ibid.*, p. 110.

48 "physionomiques et imaginés"; "la troisième . . . en représente une autre, analogue à l'ésprit et au tempérament de l'auteur" – *ibid.*, p. 121.

49 "Les mensonges sont continuellement nécessaires" – *ibid.*, p. 110.

50 "encombré des riches étoffes et de brimborions de toilette, exhale je ne sais quel haut parfum de mauvais lieu" – *ibid.*, p. 127.

51 "Les folâtres et élégantes princesses de Watteau, à côté des Vénus sérieuses et reposées de M. Ingres; les splendides blancheurs de Rubens et de Jordaens et les mornes beautés de Delacroix, telles qu'on peut se le figurer: de grandes

femmes pâles, noyées dans le satin" – *ibid.*, pp. 130–31.

52 This aligns Baudelaire's combined theory of color, modernism, and femininity with the theory of the feminine articulated by Luce Irigaray in *This Sex Which Is Not One*: "She is neither one nor two"; "She has at least two . . . Her sexuality, always at least double . . . is plural" – pp. 26, 28.

53 "Eugène Delacroix était un curieux mélange de scepticisme, de politesse, de dandyisme, de volonté ardente, de ruse, de despotisme, et enfin d'une espèce de bonté particulière et de tendresse modérée qui accompagne toujours le génie . . .

Eugène Delacroix a toujours gardé les traces de cette origine révolutionnaire . . . Sceptique et aristocrate . . . Haïsseur des multitudes . . . Eugène Delacroix apparaissait simplement comme un homme *éclairé*, dans le sens honorable du mot, comme un parfait *gentleman* sans préjugés et sans passions . . .

Il y avait dans Eugène Delacroix beaucoup du *sauvage*, c'était là la plus précieuse partie de son âme, la partie vouée tout entière à la peinture de ses rêves et au culte de son art. Il y avait en lui beaucoup de l'homme du monde; cette partie-là était destinée à voiler la première . . .

. . . Il tirait aussi de lui-même, bien plus qu'il ne les empruntait à sa longue fréquentation du monde . . . une certitude, une aisance de manières merveilleuse, avec une politesse qui admettait, comme un prisme, toutes les nuances, depuis la bonhomie la plus cordiale jusqu'à l'impertinence la plus irréprochable" – Baudelaire, "La Vie et l'oeuvre d'Eugène Delacroix," in *Ecrits esthétiques*, pp. 436–39. The translation comes from "The Life and Work of Eugène Delacroix," *Charles Baudelaire: Selected Writings on Art and Literature* (P. E. Charvet, ed., trans.), Harmondsworth, England, Penguin, 1992 (2nd edition), pp. 359–89, esp. pp. 374–77.

54 "La biographie d'Eugène Delacroix est peu accidentée" – Baudelaire, "Le Salon de 1846," p. 115.

55 "l'élégant, le raffiné, l'érudit" – Baudelaire, "La Vie et l'oeuvre d'Eugène Delacroix," p. 443.

56 "un objet d'art" – *ibid.*, p. 447.

57 "Supposons un enfant destiné à perfectionner la partie de l'art qui s'appelle couleur: c'est du choc ou de l'accord heureux de deux tons et du plaisir qui en résulte pour lui, qu'il tirera la science infinie des combinaisons de tons" – *ibid.*, p. 432.

58 Dictionary definition of "perverse" (OED): turned the wrong way, awry, turned away from the right way, not in accordance with the accepted standard or practice, obstinate or persistent in what is wrong; disposed to go counter to what is reasonable or required, hence wayward, cross-grained, ill-tempered, etc. Also: (Geom.) a figure or image in which the right and left directions of the original are reversed: such are the impressions taken from any figured surface, and the image of anything seen in a plane mirror.

59 See Baudelaire on Horace Vernet in the "Salon de 1846," in *Ecrits esthétiques*, pp. 157–61.

60 "avoir passé de longues heures à feuilleter des estampes libertines" – Baudelaire, "Salon de 1846," p. 130. This section of the "Salon de 1846" makes one wonder about the sincerity of Baudelaire's much vaunted dualism of the universal and the historical.

61 "le pastel, l'eau-forte, l'acqua-tinte . . . cet immense dictionnaire de la vie moderne disséminé dans les bibliothèques, dans les cartons des amateurs et derrière les vitres des plus vulgaires boutiques" – Charles Baudelaire, "Le Peintre de la vie moderne," *Ecrits esthétiques*, p. 364. The "amateur," for Baudelaire, designates a collector of obscene and fashion prints.

62 "Dans cette immense exposition, je me figure la beauté et l'amour de tous les climats exprimés par les premiers artistes; depuis les folles, évaporées et merveilleuses créatures que nous a laissées Watteau fils dans ses gravures de mode, jusqu'à ces Vénus de Rembrandt qui se font faire les ongles, comme de simples mortelles, et peigner avec un gros peigne de buis" – Baudelaire, "Salon de 1846," p. 131.

63 "l'unité qui s'appelle nation"; "Il y a dans le monde, et même dans le monde des artistes, des gens qui vont au musée du Louvre, passent rapidement devant une foule de tableaux très intéressants, quoique de *second ordre*, et se plantent rêveurs devant un Titien ou un Raphaël, un de ceux que la gravure a le plus popularisés; puis sortent satisfaits, plus d'un se disant: 'Je connais mon musée.' " – Baudelaire, "Le Peintre de la vie moderne": "Le Beau, la mode et le bonheur," p. 360.

64 "ces créatures que le dictionnaire de la mode a successivement classées sous les titres grossiers ou badins *d'impures*, de *filles entretenues*, de *lorettes* et de *biches*", rather than "Titien et Raphael" (those two names are reiterated) – *ibid.*, "La Modernité," p. 374. It is in this context, too, that Baudelaire makes light of the

concept of "inspiration": "Si un peintre . . . ayant à peindre une courtisane du temps présent, *s'inspire* (c'est le mot consacré) d'une courtisane de Titien ou de Raphael" (p. 468).

65 "je vis tout d'abord que je n'avais pas affaire précisément à un *artiste*, mais plutôt à un *homme du monde . . . Homme du monde*, c'est-à-dire homme du monde entier, homme qui comprend le monde et les raisons mystérieuses et légitimes de tous ses usages; *artiste*, c'est-à-dire spécialiste, homme attaché à sa palette comme le serf à la glèbe. M. G. n'aime pas être appelé artiste" – *ibid.*, "L'Artiste, homme du monde, homme des foules et enfant," pp. 366–67.

66 "La modernité, c'est le transitoire, le fugitif, le contingent, la moitié de l'art, dont l'autre moitié est l'éternel et l'ummuable" – *ibid.*, "La Modernité," pp. 372–73.

67 "Derrière la vitre d'un café, un convalescent, contemplant la foule avec jouissance, se mêle par la pensé, à toutes les pensées qui s'agitent autour de lui. . . . Finalement, il se précipite à travers cette foule à la recherche d'un inconnu dont la physionomie entrevue l'a, en un clin d'oeil, fasciné" – *ibid.*, p. 367.

68 See Bersani on "Le Peintre de la vie moderne" in *Baudelaire and Freud*, pp. 9–15. Bersani's brief discussion of the "painter of modern life" as one who "loses his virile identity *through* an obscene openness to external reality which makes him an artist but which also makes him – a woman" (p. 14) is a view that I wish to extend in my own argument about "Le Peintre de la vie moderne."

69 "Sa passion et sa profession, c' est d'épouser la foule. Pour le parfait flâneur, pour l'observateur passionné, c'est une immense jouissance que d'élire domicile dans le nombre, dans l'ondoyant, dans le mouvement, dans le fugitif et l'infini. *Etre hors de chez soi, et pourtant se sentir partout chez soi; voir le monde, être au centre du monde et rester caché au monde . . .* L'observateur est un prince qui jouit partout de son incognito. L'amateur de la vie fait du monde sa famille, comme l'amateur du beau sexe compose sa famille de toutes les beautés . . . comme l'amateur de tableaux vit dans une société enchantée de rêves peints sur toile. . . . *On peut aussi le comparer, lui, à un miroir aussi immense que cette foule; à un kaléidoscope doué de conscience*, qui, à chacun de ses mouvements, représente la vie multiple et la grâce mouvante de tous les éléments de la vie. *C'est un* moi *insatiable du* non-moi, qui, à chaque instant, le rend et l'exprime en images plus vivantes que

la vie elle-même, toujours instable et fugitive. 'Tout homme', disait un jour M. G. . . . 'qui s'ennuie au sein de la multitude, est un sot!' " –Baudelaire, "Le Peintre de la vie moderne," pp. 369–70.

70 "Si une mode, une coupe de vêtement a été légèrement transformée, si les noeuds de rubans, les boucles ont été détronés par les cocardes, si le bavolet s'est élargi et si le chignon est descendu d'un cran sur la nuque, si la ceinture a été exhaussée et la jupe amplifiée, croyez qu'à une distance énorme son oeil d'aigle l'a déjà deviné" – *ibid.*, p. 370.

71 "Harnachements, scintillements, musique, regards décidés, moustaches lourdes et sérieuses, tout cela entre pêle-mêle en lui" – *ibid.*, p. 371. See Sandblad, *Manet: Three Studies in Artistic Conception*, pp. 17–68, on this painting, including its relation to the *Little Cavaliers* and to Baudelaire's "Le Peintre de la vie moderne." Sandblad was the first to work out the Baudelairean aspect of *Music at the Tuileries*, which he did fairly thoroughly. Thus, it is by no means new to state the relationship between Manet and Baudelaire or novel to remark on the affinities, more specifically, between the painting of the Tuileries garden and "the painter of modern life." What I wish to highlight, however, is twofold: 1) the continuities between Baudelaire's earlier "Romantic" criticism and his treatise on the modern painter; and 2) the discontinuities between a Baudelairean reading of Manet's painting and the naturalist/positivist strain of criticism, running from Zola to Greenberg, that came to dominate the understanding of Impressionism and its abstractionist aftermath – the ways in which a Baudelairean understanding of Manet's art runs directly counter to the latter tradition. Of course, there are myriad ways in which Baudelaire's ideas predict Impressionist opticality, sketchiness, and modern-life subject matter; but those ideas are enframed within a larger emphasis on the artifices of color, a commitment to perversity, and an argument against positivist thought that together undermine their suitability for a naturalist theory of art – and that, I think, has not been understood sufficiently.

72 E.g., "à une distance énorme"; "au centre du monde"; "caché au monde"; "un miroir aussi immense" – *ibid.*

73 "C'est une espèce de culte de soi-même, qui peut survivre à la recherche du bonheur à trouver *dans autrui, dans la femme*" – *ibid.*, p. 389 (my emphases).

74   Baudelaire's pluralizing of femininity, both in his discussion of the crowd and in his later transition from "La Femme" to "Les femmes et les filles" is, particularly in the latter case, strongly suggestive of the Orientalist harem. But it also brings to mind Irigaray's *This Sex Which Is Not One* once again, with its view of femininity as essentially plural and polymorphous.

75   "C'est à cette curiosité profonde et joyeuse qu'il faut attribuer l'oeil fixe et animalement extatique des enfants devant le *nouveau*, quel qu'il soit, visage ou paysage, lumière, dorure, couleurs, étoffes chatoyantes, enchantement de la beauté embellié par la toilette. Un de mes amis me disait un jour qu'étant fort petit, il assistait à la toilette de son père, et qu'alors il contemplait, avec une stupeur mêlée de délices, les muscles des bras, les dégradations de couleurs de la peau nuancée de rose et de jaune, et le réseau bleuâtre des veines. Le tableau de la vie extérieure le pénétrait déjà… Déjà la forme l'obsédait et le possédait… La *damnation* était faite. Ai-je besoin de dire que cet enfant est aujourd'hui un peintre célèbre?" – Baudelaire, "Le Peintre de la vie moderne," p. 368.

76   For one thing, *Music at the Tuileries* was painted in the studio on the basis of Guysian sketches on the spot, thus maintaining academic distinctions and procedures. The term "Impressionist," although coined later, is used here and throughout this book to mean optical painting, the landscape emphasis of the Impressionist group to be, and in general the Naturist/naturalist tendencies of the new school of painting. This is what the term "impression" suggested at the time, and it is what it signifies in Greenberg's modernist context as well.

77   Monet's interest in fashion in these years, together with the size of *Luncheon on the Grass* ("a mirror as large as that crowd"), aligns it with Baudelaire's ideas. But Monet's painting twists Baudelaire, as much as Manet, around in a naturalist direction.

78   See Sandblad, *Manet: Three Studies in Artistic Conception*, p. 57, and Fried, *Manet's Modernism*, pp. 62, 476–77, both on the trio of figures in the *Music at the Tuileries* and on Baudelaire's close relation to Gautier, to whom he dedicated his *Fleurs du mal*. Fried disagrees with Sandblad about the "conservative" status of Gautier and Taylor, asserting their roles as "heroes of romanticism" instead. Given the context of the exhibition at Martinet's, I understand the meaning of the relationship between the three figures a little differently from either Sandblad or Fried – and I also find both homage to Gautier and disagreement with his views in the attitudes to modern female fashion expressed in "Le Peintre de la vie moderne."

79   "la guerre d'Orient" – Baudelaire, "Le Peintre de la vie moderne": "Les annales de la guerre," "Pompes et solennités," pp. 379–85.

80   Already cited. On the "lorette" and the "fille entretenue," see Baudelaire, "Quelques caricaturistes français" (1857–58), *Écrits ésthetiques*, pp. 226–27: "Gavarni a crée la Lorette. Elle existait bien un peu avant lui, mail il l'a complétée. Je crois même que c'est lui qui a inventé le mot. La Lorette, on l'a déjà dit, n'est pas la fille entretenue, cette chose de l'Empire, condamnée à vivre en tête-à-tête funèbre avec le cadavre métallique dont elle vivait, général ou banquier. La Lorette est une personne libre. Elle va et elle vient. Elle tient maison ouverte. Elle n'a pas de maître; elle fréquente les artistes et les journalistes." The mobility of the *demimondaine* (or in Baudelaire's word, the *lorette*) is of a different order from the "ambiguities" of prostitutional physiognomics, as described, for example, by Hollis Clayson in *Painted Love: Prostitution in French Art of the Impressionist Era*, New Haven and London, Yale University Press, 1991: quite apart from providing a cover for the ideological practice of misogyny – for firmly othering, defining the place of, and fixing blame upon the feminine – the *demimondaine* seems to have been a figurative alternative to the social and sexual fixity of the *femme honnête*, a form for figuring a kind of mobility within the feminine with which it was possible to identify. This is not to say that Baudelaire's feminine is without its misogyny; it would be absurd to claim that, for the disparaging nastiness of the tone of his writing about women is one of its most apparent characteristics. But Baudelaire's is a misogyny that is typically double-edged, and strategic: a device for making Woman figure everything that departs from "Nature" and its norms, and from "Man." For the best discussion of the psychic structure of Baudelaire's poetry, including his conflicted identification with the feminine, see Bersani, *Baudelaire and Freud*.

81   "des femmes très parées et embellies par toutes les pompes artificielles, à quelque ordre de la société qu'elles appartiennent"; "dans la loge qui leur sert de cadre"; "dans les allées des jardins publiques" – Baudelaire, "Le Peintre de la vie moderne": "Les femmes et les filles," pp. 397–98.

82 "Voici, maintenant . . . ces Valentinos, ces Casinos, ces *Prados* (autrefois des Tivolis, des Idalies, des Folies, des Paphos), ces capharnaüms . . . Des femmes qui ont exagéré la mode jusqu'à altérer la grâce et en détruire l'intention, balayent fastueusement les parquets avec la queue de leurs robes et la pointe de leurs châles . . .

Sur un fond d'une lumière infernale ou sur un fond d'aurore boréale, rouge, orangé, sulfureux, rose . . . quelquesfois violet . . . sur ces fonds magiques, imitant diversement les feux de Bengale, s'enlève l'image variée de la beauté interlope. Ici majestueuse, là légère, tantôt svelte, grêle même, tantôt cyclopéenne; tantôt petite et pétillante, tantôt lourde et monumentale. Elle a inventé une élégance provoquante et barbare . . . Elle s'avance, glisse, danse, roule avec son poids de jupons brodés qui lui sert à la fois de piédestal et de balancier; elle darde son regard sous son chapeau, comme un portrait dans son cadre. Elle représente bien la sauvagerie dans la civilisation" – Baudelaire, "Le Peintre de la vie moderne": "Les femmes et les filles," p. 399.

83 See Clark, "Olympia's Choice," *Manet and the Painting of Modern Life*, and Clayson, *Painted Love* on the nineteenth-century discourse on prostitution.

84 "la peinture du visage": "maquillage . . . si niaisement anathématisé par les philosophes candides, a pour but et pour résultat de fair disparaître du teint toutes les taches que la nature y a outrageusement semées, et de créer une unité abstraite dans le grain et la couleur de la peau . . . Quant au *noir* artificiel qui cerne l'oeil et au *rouge* qui marque la partie supérieure de la joue . . . le résultat est fait pour satisfaire à une besoin tout opposé. *Le rouge et le noir* représentent la vie, une vie surnaturelle et excessive; *ce cadre noir* rend le regard plus profond et plus singulier . . . *le rouge*, qui enflamme la pommette, augmente encore la clarté de la prunelle . . ." – Baudelaire, "Le Peintre de la vie moderne": "Eloge du maquillage," pp. 396–97 (my emphases).

85 On the frame and the Western aesthetic tradition, see Jacques Derrida, "Parergon," *The Truth in Painting* (Geoff Bennington and Ian McLeod, trans.), University of Chicago Press, 1987.

86 See Walter Benjamin, *Charles Baudelaire: A Lyric Poet in the Era of High Capitalism*, London, Verso, 1983.

87 L'être . . . pour qui, mais surtout *par qui* les artistes et les poètes composent leurs plus déli-

cats bijoux . . . la femme, en un mot, n'est pas seulement pour l'artiste en général, et pour M. G. en particulier, la femelle de l'homme . . . C'est une espèce d'idole . . . Ce n'est pas . . . un animal dont les membres, correctement assemblés, fournissent un parfait exemple d'harmonie; ce n'est même pas le type de beauté pure, tel que peut le rêver le sculpteur dans ses plus sévères méditations . . . Nous n'avons que faire ici de Winckelmann et de Raphaël; et je suis bien sûr que M. G. . . . négligerait un morceau de la statuaire antique, s'il lui fallait ainsi perdre l'occasion de savourer un portrait de Reynolds ou de Lawrence. Tout ce qui orne la femme . . . fait partie d'elle-même . . . La femme . . . est surtout une harmonie générale, non seulement dans son allure et le mouvement de ses membres, mais aussi dans les mousselines, les gazes, les vastes et chatoyantes nuées d'étoffes dont elle s'enveloppe, et qui sont comme les attributs et le piédestal de sa divinité; dans le métal et le minéral qui serpentent autour de ses bras et de son cou, qui ajoutent leurs étincelles au feu de ses regards, ou qui jasent doucement à ses oreilles. Quel poète oserait, dans la peinture du plaisir causé par l'apparition d'une beauté, séparer la femme de son costume? Quel est l'homme qui, dans la rue, au théâtre, au bois, n'a pas joui . . . d'une toilette savamment composée, et n'en a pas emporté une image inséparable de la beauté . . . faisant ainsi des deux, de la femme et de la robe, une totalité indivisible? C'est ici le lieu, ce me semble . . . de revenir sur certaines questions relatives à la mode et à la parure . . . et de venger l'art de la toilette des ineptes calomnies dont l'accablent certains amants très équivoques de la nature." – Baudelaire, "Le Peintre de la vie moderne": "La Femme," pp. 392–93.

88 "des deux"; "le métal et le minéral qui serpentent"; "les vastes et chatoyantes nuées" – *ibid*. Here the theme of the fixity and fluidity of desire in Baudelaire's poetics, as Bersani develops it in *Baudelaire and Freud*, translates into the painting- and sculpture-specific thematics of petrification and vaporization, which can be traced back to Balzac and forward to the Goncourts, reaching its apogee in Huysmans – a topic for another study.

89 What I regard as one of the most compelling of the existing readings of Manet's art – Jean Clay's "Ointments, Makeup, Pollen" – might be criticized on the grounds that it is written from a postmodernist, and therefore necessarily anachronistic, perspective. (See Fried, *Manet's Modernism*, pp. 181–84.) It is true that

Clay's set of concerns are identified with the historical category named "postmodernism." But postmodernism is a rubric put in place by culture critics and historians in order to group together a set of disparate, contemporaneous phenomena in the arts and in the arenas of politics, economics, and culture. And it is a rubric whose logic derives from its dialectical relationship to that which is said to precede it historically, the era designated as "modernism," itself a rubric invented to cover another set of disparate phenomena and used retrospectively to describe a "line" of a hundred years' duration. So it is only if one accepts as a given the historical truth of this periodization and its linear, dialectical sequencing, as well as the internal unity of each of the periods that punctuate the "line" from modernism to postmodernism, that notions covered by the latter category rather than the former will come to seem so indisputably ahistorical.

But no cross-section of the history of cultural discourse was ever as total a shape as that. Like stylistic categories such as "Romanticism," "Realism," and "Impressionism" (into none of which does Manet's art fit very neatly), often treated as chronological sequences describing more or less fixed blocks of historical time, both "modernism" and "postmodernism" are unifying constructs which paper over the divergence of voices, opinions, and cultural products that marks any cut in time and socio-cultural space. It is true, I think, that the discursive configuration that we label "postmodernist" is what allows us to gain some purchase on concerns with which "modernist" criticism either has no truck or that it suppresses; at the same time, however, it is possible to see the seeds of that discursive configuration in any number of cultural statements exceptional in but contemporaneous with what has been defined as early modernism. In the field of contestation that was nineteenth-century French art criticism and aesthetic discourse, one finds not only Hippolyte Taine, Théophile Thoré, Théodore Duret, Emile Zola, and others on the positivist side, but also Baudelaire (and the Goncourt brothers and Stéphane Mallarmé), whose deliberate perversity as an art writer describes a view of the "modern" much at odds with the positivist model, and which, rather than containing the embryo of "modernist" formalism, as positivist art history and criticism does, predicts many of the ingredients of the "postmodernist" attitude – though, within the more dialogical model of historical progression that I am

proposing, the "post" in "postmodernist" ultimately makes little sense.

SIX   "MLLE V. . . . IN THE COSTUME OF . . ."

1 Zola, "Une nouvelle manière en peinture," p. 95, cited in Chapter Two above.

2 "Une femme sortit d'un cabaret louche, relevant sa robe, retenant sa guitare. Il alla droit à elle et lui demanda de venir poser chez lui. Elle se prit à rire. 'Je la repincerai, dit-il, et puis, si elle ne veut pas, j'ai Victorine.' Victorine Meurend, dont il a fait le portrait, était son modèle de prédilection. Nous montâmes à l'atelier" – Antonin Proust, *Edouard Manet, Souvenirs*, Paris, Librairie Renouard, 1913, pp. 39–40.

3 " L'atelier vit arriver quelque temps après, pour créer la *Chanteuse des rues*, une jeune femme qui va tenir dans cette histoire une place considérable, car elle sera jusqu'en 1875, non sans de longues éclipses, le modèle attitré de Manet: Victorine-Louise Meurent. Elle ne comptait guère vingt ans, en cette année 62, mais on lui en eût donné vint-cinq, tant ses trait se marquaient de gravité. Il est vrai que si le profil était plutôt dur, la face entière démentait cette impression de dureté, une face où vivaient de beaux yeux et qu'animait une bouche fraîche et souriante. Avec cela, le corps nerveux de la Parisienne, délicat en chacun de ses détails, remarquable par la ligne harmonieuse des hanches et la souplesse gracieuse du buste. La poitrine était d'une pâte ferme et fine. D'où venait cette blonde fille? Nous doutons que Manet l'ait rencontrée, comme le veut Théodore Duret, au Palais de Justice, où il aurait été 'frappé de son aspect original et de sa manière d'être tranchée'. Elle n'était pas une inconnue sur la rive gauche. Sur son Carnet de notes et d'adresses, que nous avons, Manet a tracé cette mention: 'Louise Meuran, rue Maître-Albert, 17'. Il s'agit certainement d'elle, qui se faisait appeler tantôt Louise et tantôt Victorine, et c'est précisement rue Maître-Albert, près de la place Maubert, que Manet venait faire mordre les cuivres de ses premières eaux-fortes. Tres fantâsque, elle se piquait d'être artiste et grattait de la guitare. Même, elle dessinait et, plus tard, elle peindra.

Manet la représenta – toile de 1m.74 × 1m. 18 – telle qu'elle était, ouvrant de grands yeux hardis dans une face fatiguée. Chapeau toque, mantelet, robe grise. Tenant en main sa guitare, elle serre sous le bras des cerises enveloppées dans du papier, et qu'elle porte à sa bouche. Mais ce n'aurait été là qu'un portrait de genre entre tant d'autres, si Manet ne s'était avisé de donner comme fond à son tableau une salle de cabaret où s'entrevoient des buveurs attablés, l'un de ceux-ci coiffant un chapeau de haute forme, et dos tourné, un garçon en tablier blanc. Signé en bas, à gauche: ed. Manet." – A. Tabarant, *Manet et ses oeuvres*, Paris, Gallimard, 1947, pp. 47–48. See also A. Tabarant, "La fin douloureuse de celle qui fut l'Olympia," *L'Oeuvre*, July 10, 1932; Margaret Seibert, *A Biography of Victorine-Louise Meurent and Her Role in the Art of Edouard Manet*, Ph.D. dissertation, Ohio State University, 1986; and Eunice Lipton, *Alias Olympia: A Woman's Search for Manet's Notorious Model and Her Own Desire*, London, Thames and Hudson, 1992.

4 Only once did he show a straight portrait at the Salon, and that had not been particularly successful: the portrait of his parents in 1861.

5 "Une jeune femme, bien connue sur les hauteurs du Panthéon" – Zola, "Une nouvelle manière en peinture," p. 95, cited in Chapter Two above.

6 See E. H. Gombrich, *Art and Illusion: A Study in the Psychology of Pictorial Representation*, Princeton University Press, Bollingen Series XXXV:5, 1960, esp. p. 39 on the "beholder's share."

7 "Toute forme se perd dans ses grands portraits de femmes, et notamment dans celui de la *Chanteuse*, où, par une singularité qui nous trouble profondément, les sourcils renoncent à leur position horizontale pour venir se placer verticalement le long du nez, comme deux virgules d'ombre; il n'y a plus là que la lutte criarde de tons plâtreux avec des tons noirs." – Paul Mantz, "L'Exposition du blvd. des Italiens," *Gazette des Beaux-Arts*, April 15, 1863, p. 383, cited in Cachin, 1983, p. 106.

8 There is, for example, the later *Argenteuil*, with the "wild twist of tulle" on the woman's hat, "piped onto the oval like cream on a cake, smeared on like a great flourishing brushmark, blown up to impossible size" – Clark, *Painting of Modern Life*, p. 164: I find it difficult to improve on that description, or to substitute other terms for its pastry-chef vocabulary and its summoning up of Roy Lichtenstein's jokey brushstroke paintings.

9 "à droite, une demoiselle de Paris en costume d' *Espada*, agitant son manteau pourpre dans le cirque d'un combat de taureaux . . . Il y a des étoffes étonnantes . . . mais, sous ces brillantes

costumes, manque un peu la personne elle-même; les têtes devraient être peintes autrement que les draperies" – Thoré, "Salon de 1863," *Salons de W. Bürger 1861 à 1868*, vol. 1, pp. 424–25, quoted in Cachin, *Manet 1832–1883*, pp. 111–12. Thoré directly linked the three paintings that were shown together in the Salon des Refusés: "Au milieu, une scène de *Bain*; à gauche, un *Majo* espagnol; à droite, une demoiselle de Paris en costume *d'Espada*" (this is the same quote in which he spoke of Manet adoring Spain, cited in Chapter Four above).

10 This is T. J. Clark's observation: see *Painting of Modern Life*, p. 137: "There are *two* faces, one produced by the hardness of the face's edge and the closed look of its mouth and eyes; the other less clearly demarcated, opening out into hair let down." Clark attaches the doubleness of *Olympia's* face to the discourse on prostitution that ran rampant through the critical and caricatural reception of her when she was shown in 1865; I wish, instead, to reinsert *Olympia* into the Victorine series to which she belongs, and to treat her doubleness as an aspect of Manet's probing of the problem of rendering the model's person in paint. My understanding of Manet's *Olympia* depends on Clark's reading of the painting at many points, but it shifts the slant away from the reception of *Olympia* and the question of class, and changes the object of interpretation, from the battle of representations that constituted French culture in 1865, to the painting per se and the logic of the production to which it belongs. That is, my rereading of the *Olympia* is predicated at least in part on the principle of looking at the artist's larger oeuvre – not for its unified, developmental logic or for its expression of the psychology of Manet but rather for its particular series of pictorial fascinations and recurrences. See also T. J. Clark, "Preliminaries to a Possible Treatment of 'Olympia' in 1865," *Screen* Spring 1980, pp. 18–41.

11 Clark has argued that the subversiveness of *Olympia* resides largely in the naked rendering of the body, which he sees as "a strong sign of class" (*Painting of Modern Life*, p. 146), and that the painting's refusal to fit that body to its accouterments and its art-historical references in large part accounts for the critics' reading of *Olympia* as a painting of a low-rung prostitute (rather than the courtesan that her adornment and surroundings suggest), and for their missing the obvious reference to Titian's *Venus of Urbino* (pp. 93–96). But rather than an account according to class – rather than

discovering a proletarian corporeality in Victorine's bluntly painted, discrepant body – I wish to offer a reading of her body, as it is rendered in both paintings, as participating in Manet's serial questioning of the problem of painting personhood.

12 See John Berger, *Ways of Seeing*, London, British Broadcasting Corporation, and Harmondsworth, Penguin, 1977, esp. p. 63, for a succinct version of the classic view of *Olympia* as confronting and questioning the role of woman as the object of the male "spectator-owner." On the *Luncheon*, see Anne McCauley, "Sex and the Salon: Defining Art and Immorality in 1863," in Tucker, *Manet's Déjeuner sur l'herbe*, pp. 38–74.

13 On the black servant in *Olympia*, see Sander Gilman, "Black Bodies, White Bodies: Towards an Iconography of Female Sexuality in Late Nineteenth Century Art, Medicine, and Literature," in Henry Louis Gates Jr., ed., 'Race', *Writing and Difference*, University of Chicago Press, 1989, pp. 223–61; Griselda Pollock, *Differencing the Canon: Feminist Desire and the Writing of Art's Histories*, London, Routledge, 1999, esp. pp. 277–306; and Theodore Reff, *Manet: Olympia*, New York, Viking, and Harmondsworth, Allen Lane, 1976, pp. 91–95. See also Griselda Pollock, *Avant-garde Gambits: Gender and the Colour of Art History*, London, Thames and Hudson, 1992.

14 If I were given to biographical speculation, here I would wonder about Manet's painting of these pictures around the time he married Suzanne Leenhoff (the marriage occurred in October 1863, after the couple had lived together since 1860, when Manet, Suzanne, and Léon moved into an apartment in the Batignolles together). I would also be inclined to speculate about his use of Suzanne's brother as well as his own next to a *fille entretenue*, and particularly about his use of Léon as a model, over and over again. Obviously convenience was an issue – these were the people most available to Manet, whose modeling came cheap. But it seems likely that other considerations may have been at work as well – that Manet may have been, albeit elliptically, working out such things as the ordering of his domestic life, its relationship to his vocational life, the intrusion into the French high-bourgeois home of those alien to it, the exact nature of paternity, and so on.

15 *The Ray* was part of the La Caze bequest to the Louvre in 1869. See John McCoubrey, "The Revival of Chardin in French Still-Life Painting, 1850–1870," *Art Bulletin* XLVI:1, March 1964, pp. 39–53. Fried notes the similarity among the cats in *The Ray*, *Young Woman Reclining in Spanish Costume*, and *Olympia* – *Manet's Modernism*, p. 62, no. 85.

16 On the *Luncheon* as a compendium of the genres, see Fried, *Manet's Modernism*, p. 403. See also Norman Bryson, *Looking at the Overlooked: Four Essays on Still Life Painting*, Cambridge, Mass., Harvard University Press, 1990, pp. 136–78, on the "femininity" of the genre of still-life painting.

17 Baudelaire, "Le Peintre de la vie moderne," pp. 487–89, cited in Chapter Five above.

18 See *ibid.*, pp. 360, 374, cited in Chapter Five above. The references to "Titian and Raphael" also resonate with the *Luncheon* by itself, with its quotations of a painting by Giorgione/Titian and of a print after Raphael. Twenty pages later ("Le Peintre de la vie moderne, p. 393), Baudelaire returns to the same theme, this time with a comment about "Winckelmann and Raphael."

19 Anyway, Baudelaire's ideas on femininity were everywhere mediated through the gravure – the pornographic print, the fashion plate, Guys's reportorial images, opposed yet at the same time perversely linked to the high-art museum reproduction. Although the balance of museum reproduction and modern-life rendering was not the same for Manet as it was for Baudelaire in 1863, his presentation of modern femininity was similarly mediated.

20 Moreover, the missing half of Manet's quotation of the *Venus of Urbino* – the background handmaiden – makes her way into the left background of Manet's portrait of Zacharie Astruc of 1866, as if to reinforce the reference to the *Venus of Urbino* ignored by the critics when *Olympia* was shown in 1865, and to index Manet's relationship with Astruc, whose Baudelairean five-line verse had been appended to *Olympia's* title in the 1865 Salon booklet, just as Baudelaire's quatrain had decorated the frame of *Lola de Valence* in 1863.

21 See my essay, "To Paint, to Point, to Pose: Manet's *Le Déjeuner sur l'herbe*," in Tucker, *Manet's Le Déjeuner sur l'herbe*, pp. 90–118, in which I treat the *Luncheon on the Grass*, with Manet's other Victorine paintings, as a picture exhibiting the presence and processes of the studio. Svetlana Alpers has remarked, in *Rembrandt's Enterprise*, p. 56, on the similarity between Manet's staging of Victorine Meurent and Rembrandt's theatrical uses of the model. There are many other overlaps, too, between

the practices of the two painters, and between Alpers's and my treatments of them: in both, the studio looms large. However, my approach to the studio is much less anthropological than Alpers's: I have not attempted to reconstruct the social structures embodied in Manet's studio or the conditions surrounding and informing it; rather, I have simply attempted to read the studio's presence in the paintings themselves.

22 See Clark, *Painting of Modern Life*, pp. 93–96, on the fact that all but two of the critics who responded to the *Olympia* either missed or ignored the connection to the *Venus of Urbino*.

23 In 1864, Thoré wrote about the pastiche effects of *The Bullfight* (*The Dead Toreador*) and *The Dead Christ and the Angels*, remarking on the Hispanicism of both paintings, declaring that for the former Manet had directly copied a work by Velasquez in the Pourtalès collection while also recalling Goya, and that the latter was marked with the more general influence of El Greco. At the same time he compared the *Dead Christ* with a range of other old masters that included Rubens and Carracci – Thoré, "Salon de 1864," *Salons de W. Bürger*, vol. 2, pp. 99–100. In 1865, Thoré returned to the same themes, emphasizing *The Mocking of Christ* of that year over *Olympia*, underlining pastiche as the retrograde logic of Manet's practice, and straining to see if pastiche and "original" modernity could thrive together: "Il arrive aussi que pastichant une vieille idée vous êtes entraînés à imiter de vieilles formes et de vieilles pratiques. Si vous peignez Vénus, Diane, Galatée, des nymphes ou des naïades, comment ne pas songer à la statuaire grecque et à la renaissance italienne qui en ressuscitait le style? Si vous peignez des martyrs chrétiens, qui donc a plus cruellement dramatisé la torture et la douleur que les Espagnols mystiques et surtout que Ribera . . . ? /C'est fatal, irrésistible: il ne paraît pas que Manet veuille être pris pour un routinier de l'art pensif; néanmois, ayant eu la malheureuse idée de peindre un Christ dans le prétoir, bon! voilà que cet original copie presque la célèbre composition de Van Dyck! L'autre année, faisant un sujet espagnol qu'il n'avait jamais vu, bon! voilà qu'il copiait le Velazquez de la galerie Pourtalès!" – Thoré, "Salon de 1865," *Salons de W. Bürger*, vol. 2, p. 193.

24 See Cachin, *Manet*, p. 243. The hypothesis that Victorine modeled for *The Fifer* was first made by Paul Jamot, "Manet, 'Le fifre' et Victorine Meurend," *Revue de l'art ancien et moderne* LI

(May 1927), pp. 31–41; while the suggestion that Léon Leenhoff also modeled was made by Tabarant, in *Manet et ses oeuvres*, p. 119. Supposedly, a young boy from the Imperial Guard was also sent to pose for Manet by Commandant Lejosne.

25 Zola, "Une nouvelle manière en peinture," p. 94, cited in Chapter Two above.

26 See Goncourt, *Manette Salomon*, pp. 206, 207, cited in Chapter Three above.

27 Zola, "Une nouvelle manière en peinture," p. 98, cited in Chapter Two above. Zola contrasts *The Fifer* to *The Tragic Actor*, but then immediately segues into the *Young Woman in 1866*, with which he concludes.

28 "En 1866, la note grise sert de fond à diverses figures, au *Fifre* par exemple, qui, pendant quelques années a passé pour un type définitif et un classique. C'est un jeune musicien d'un dessin quelconque, enluminé de couleurs vives parmi lesquelles le rouge du pantalon parle avec audace. Il est appliqué sur un fond gris monochrome: pas de terrain, pas d'air, pas de perspective: l'infortuné est collé contre un mur chimérique. L'idée qu'il y a positivement une atmosphère qui passe derrière les corps et les entoure ne peut pas entrer dans la tête de Manet: il reste fidèle au système de la découpure; il s'incline devant les hardis faiseurs de jeux de cartes. Le *Fifre*, amusant spécimen d'un imagerie encore barbare, est un valet de carreau placardé sur une porte." – Paul Mantz, "Les Oeuvres de Manet," *Le Temps* Jan. 16, 1884; cited in Cachin, *Manet 1832–1883*, p. 246.

29 There are similar shadows cast in *The Tragic Actor*, the *Philosopher*s, *Saluting Matador* – all of them referring to Velasquez and all from the same period.

30 See Jacques Lacan, "Qu'est-ce qu'un tableau," *Les Quatres Concepts fondamentaux de la psychanalyse (Le Séminaire, livre XI)*, Paris, Seuil, 1973, pp. 97–109, on the psychoanalytic interest of pictorial illusionism. See also Richard Wollheim, "The Spectator in the Picture: Friedrich, Manet, Hals," *Painting as an Art*, London, Thames and Hudson, and Princeton University Press, Bollingen Series XXXV:33, 1987, on Manet's blank backgrounds as spaces of projection.

31 Zola, "Une nouvelle manière en peinture," p. 94.

32 *Ibid.*, pp. 98–99, cited in Chapter Two above.

33 "Il y avait . . . une étude de jeune fille en robe rose, qui sera peut-être refusée au prochain Salon. Ces tons rosés sur fond gris défieraient les plus fins coloristes. Ebauche, c'est vrai,

comme est, au Louvre, l'Ile de Cythère, par Watteau. Watteau aurait pu pousser son ébauche à la perfection. Manet se débat encore contre cette difficulté extrême de la peinture, qui est de finir certaines parties d'un tableau pour donner à l'ensemble sa valeur effective. Mais on peut prédire qu'il aura son tour de succès, comme tous les persécutés du Salon. ... La tête, bien qu'elle soit de face et dans la même lumière que l'étoffe rose, on n'y fait guère attention; elle se perd dans la modulation du coloris" – Thoré, "Salon de 1868," *Salons de W. Bürger 1861 à 1868*, vol. 2, p. 318; cited in Cachin, *Manet 1832–1883*, p. 256.

34 "Cette jeune femme a, dit-on, été peinte d'après un modèle dont la tête est fine, jolie et spirituelle, et ornée de la plus riche chevelure vénitienne qu'un coloriste puisse souhaiter ... La tête qu'il nous montre est, à coup sûr, flattée en laid." – T. Gautier, "Le Salon de 1868," *Le Moniteur Universel*, May 11, 1868; cited in Cachin, *ibid.*, p. 256.

35 "L'intention de M. Manet était, on doit le supposer, d'engager un dialogue symphonique, une sorte de duo, entre la robe rose de la jeune femme et les teintes rosées de son visage. Il n'y est nullement parvenu, car il ne sait pas peindre la chair." – Paul Mantz, "Le Salon de 1868," *L'Illustration*, June 6, 1868; cited in Cachin, *ibid.*, p. 256.

36 The term is Leo Steinberg's in "The Algerian Women and Picasso at Large," *Other Criteria: Confrontations with Twentieth Century Art*, Oxford and New York, Oxford University Press, 1975, p. 189.

37 See Balzac, *Le Chef d'oeuvre inconnu*, pp. 69–70; already cited in the Introduction above. See also Damisch, *Fenêtre jaune cadmium*, p. 26, who ties Balzac's image of the foot emerging from the chaos of the "unknown masterpiece" to Manet's paintings of Victorine: "ce fragment ... ce pied fasse ainsi retour, *sous la peinture*, à travers les décombres du tableau, là où Manet fera bientôt surgir sous la robe de ses modèles la pointe incongrue d'un soulier."

38 See Jennifer L. Shaw, "The Figure of Venus: Rhetoric of the Ideal and the Salon of 1863," *Art History* 14:4, December 1991, pp. 540–57, on the nineteenth-century maintenance of the opposition of drawing, the fixed ideal, and men's mastery of women, versus color, effeminacy, and the fluctuant, out-of-control bodies of women. Shaw cites Charles Blanc's *Grammaire des arts du dessin* on the association between color and femininity.

39 In his 1867 essay on bullfights in Spain, Zacharie Astruc mentioned the orange as a kind of coloristic emblem of Spanishness: "Des marchands d'oranges trottent dans l'arène, offrant leurs produits ... Les oranges arrivent, décrivant leurs paraboles dorées ... Madrid, du reste, est friand d'oranges ..." – Astruc, "Madrid l'hiver: Courses de jeunes taureux," pp. 547–48.

40 "On attaqua beaucoup la *Femme au perroquet*: M. Manet, qui n'aurait pas dû oublier la panique causée, il y a quelques années, par son chat noir du tableau d'*Ophélie* [sic], a emprunté le perroquet de son ami Courbet, et l'a placé sur un perchoir à coté d'une jeune femme en peignoir rose. Ces réalistes sont capables de tout! Le malheur est que ce perroquet n'est pas empaillé comme les portraits de M. Cabanel, et que le peignoir rose est d'un ton assez riche. Les accessoires empêchent même qu'on remarque la figure; mais on n'y perd rien." – M. Chaumelin, "Le Salon de 1868," *La Presse*, June 23, 1868, cited in Cachin, *Manet 1832–1883*, p. 256.

41 See also M. Hadler, "Manet's 'Woman with a Parrot' of 1866," *Metropolitan Museum Journal* VII, 1973, pp. 115–22.

42 See Peter Mitchell, *Alfred Emile Léopold Stevens 1823–1906*, London, John Mitchell and Sons, 1973, p. 10; William A. Coles, *Alfred Stevens*, Ann Arbor, University of Michigan Museum of Art, 1977, pp. xvi, 12; and Mainardi, *Art and Politics of the Second Empire*, pp. 97–99, 112, 168, 184. Stevens had also been a success in the 1855 Exposition, where his art, like that of the rest of the Belgians, was seen as a subdivision of the French school.

43 "La *Dame en rose* est encore une jeune femme, debout, dans un intérieur élégant. Les cheveux, d'un blond châtain, sont épais, rebelles au peigne, avec ces frisures légères qui distinguent les belles Vénitiennes de Paul Véronèse; le visage plein, avec des formes délicates et spirituelles, respire cette grâce familière à laquelle la Parisienne se reconnaît; les mains longues, grasses et effilées sont des merveilles; la toilette est un déshabillé du goût le plus fantasque et le plus charmant. Une robe rose, lâche et pourtant coquette, comme celle des femmes de Watteau; là-dessus des flots de gaze et de dentelles ... Le type est si rendu, qu'il arrive à être l'expression d'un caractère. On perçoit, comme sous un eau transparente, la situation, les habitudes, les goûts, la vie du personnage représenté; on discerne toutes les recherches d'un siècle affolé de luxe, toute la liberté inhérente

aux sphères élevées, toute l'amabilité naturelle à un pays où la femme est reine. Chaque trait remue un petit monde de pensées." – Théophile Thoré, "Salon de 1866," *Salons de W. Bürger*, vol. 2, p. 299.

44 "Vous voyez bien que tout ce qu'elles font est assez indifférent. Elles font la vie des "femmes de qualité." Sentir des fleurs, s'amuser avec des bibelots, mettre ses gants ou ôter ses bijoux, lire ou écrire un billet, s'étendre sur un divan, regarder la couleur du ciel, s'impatienter ou rêver, c'est l'existence des belles dames. L' insignifiance des sujets dans ces tableaux d'Alfred Stevens a donc sa signification, parfaitement expressive des moeurs de la société aristocratique et même bourgeoise"; "personne ne peint mieux que lui les fraîches et riches étoffes, les cachemires, les tapis et les menus objets des demeures luxueuses" – Thoré, "Exposition Universelle de 1867," *Salons de W. Bürger*, vol. 2, pp. 378–81.

45 See Philippe Perrot, *Fashioning the Bourgeoisie: A History of Clothing in the Nineteenth Century* (Richard Bienvenu, trans.), Princeton University Press, 1994, pp. 91–31, on morning *peignoirs*.

46 See Chapter One above, pp. 11–13, 324, n. 24.

47 That year, Thoré stressed the connection between the two portraits, suggesting that what linked them was a way of seeing, a vividness, and an illusion of air circulating through the interior space of each, and a levelling of face, figure, and accouterments, of portrait and still-life functions. He looked back to *Olympia* (identifying her by one of her accessories, as the *Black Cat*), and announced his partisanship with Zola: "Je me risque à dire que M. Edouard Manet voit très bien . . . Manet voit la couleur et la lumière, après quoi il ne s'inquiète plus du reste. Quand il a fait sur sa toile 'la tache de couleur' qui font sur la nature ambiante un personnage ou un objet, il se tient quitte . . . Son vice actuel est une sorte de panthéisme, qui n'estime pas plus une tête qu'une pantoufle; qui parfois accorde même plus d'importance à un bouquet de fleurs qu'à la physiognomie d'une femme, par exemple, dans son fameux tableau du *Chat noir*; qui peint tout presque uniformément, les meubles, les tapis, les livres, les costumes, les chairs, les accents du visage, par exemple dans son portrait de M. Emile Zola, exposé au présent Salon./ Ce portrait de notre confrère Zola, qui écrit sur les arts et la littérature avec une vive indépendance, et néanmoins triomphe de l'animosité des âmes délicates! On

ne l'a pas trouvé trop inconvenant ni trop excentrique. On a concédé que les livres, surtout un livre à gravures, grand ouvert, et d'autres objets encombrant la table ou accrochés au lambris, étaient d'une réalité étonnante. Mais le mérite principal du portrait de M. Zola, comme des autres oeuvres d'Edouard Manet, c'est la lumière qui circule dans cet intérieur et qui distribue partout le modelé et le relief./ L'air impalpable, comme nous disions tout à l'heure, il est aussi dans le portrait de jeune femme en robe rose" – Thoré, "Salon de 1868," *Salons de W. Bürger*, vol. 2, pp. 531–32.

48 In the interim between the *Young Woman in 1866* and *The Railway*, the last painting by Manet in which Victorine's features appeared, Victorine had been away in the United States. See Juliet Wilson-Bareau, *Manet, Monet, and the Gare Saint-Lazare*, Washington, D.C., National Gallery of Art, and New Haven and London, Yale University Press, 1998, pp. 41–42.

SEVEN   MANET, MORISOT, AND THE GONZALÈS AFFAIR

1 Paul Valéry, "The Triumph of Manet (Manet et Manebit)," *Degas Manet Morisot* (David Paul, trans.), New York, Pantheon, Bollingen Series XLV:12, 1960, pp. 112–14. The original French essay, "Triomphe de Manet," in *Manet*, Paris, Orangerie, 1932, pp. XIV–XVI, is quoted extensively in Cachin, *Manet, 1832–1883*, pp. 334–36:

"Avant toute chose, le *Noir*, le noir absolu, le noir d'un chapeau de deuil et des brides de ce petit chapeau mêlées de mèches de cheveux châtains à reflets roses, le noir qui n'appartient qu'à Manet, m'a saisi.

"Il s'y rattache un enrubannement large et noir, qui déborde l'oreille gauche, entoure et engonce le cou; et le noir mantelet qui couvre les épaules, laisse paraître un peu de claire chair, dans l'échancrure d'un col de linge blanc.

"Ces places éclatantes de noir intense encadrent et proposent un visage aux trop grands yeux noirs, d'expression distraite et comme lointaine. La peinture en est fluide, et venue facile, et obéissante à la souplesse de la brosse . . .

"Mais ici, l'éxécution semble plus prompte, plus libre, plus immédiate. Le moderne va vite, et veut agir avant la mort de l'impression.

"La toute puissance de ces noirs, la froideur simple du fond, les clartés pâles ou rosées de la chair, la bizarre silhouette du chapeau qui fut 'à la dernière mode' et 'jeune'; le désordre des mèches, des brides, du ruban, qui encombrent les abords du visage; ce visage aux grands yeux, dont la fixité vague est d'une distraction profonde, et offre, en quelque sorte, *une présence d'absence*, – tout ceci se concerte et m'impose une sensation singulière . . . de *Poésie* . . .

"Je puis dire à présent que le portrait dont je parle est poème. Par l'harmonie étrange des couleurs, par la dissonance de leurs forces; par l'opposition du détail futile et éphémère d'une coiffure de jadis avec je ne sais quoi d'assez tragique dans l'expression de la figure, Manet fait résonner son oeuvre . . . Il combine à la ressemblance physique du modèle, l'accord unique qui convient à une personne singulière, et fixe fortement le charme distinct et abstrait de Berthe Morisot."

2   Valéry, "Triumph of Manet," p. 107.
3   *Ibid.*, pp. 107–08.
4   Beginning with the *Battle of the Kearsarge and Alabama*, Manet occasionally tried history painting. But apart from the *Execution of Emperor Maximilian*, these efforts were often conducted in minor media or genres, and were frequently repetitions of his own earlier work: this was the case of the *Barricade* sketches, which were updated redoings of the *Execution of Emperor Maximilian*, and *The Escape of Rochefort*, which suggests a return to the *Battle of the Kearsarge and Alabama*. (The *Execution* itself not only restages Goya's *Third of May* but also seems to refer to Manet's own slightly earlier, rejected *Fifer*.) One might also understand the *Masked Ball at the Opera*, rejected from the Salon of 1874, as an updating of the *Execution*'s spectatorial aspect: the *Execution* is recalled in the *Masked Ball* in the relationship between mass of figures below and glimpse of balconied spectators above. I have neglected this aspect of Manet's career because, even though the *Execution* in particular evidences ambition on Manet's part, if not a desire to situate himself in the lineage of great, reportorial modern history painting going back to Géricault, nonetheless it was intermittent and unsuccessful – in my view, a desire against which his actual production (in the domain of the female figure and ladies' wear) was measured but which remained essentially unrealized. But most others have found the *Execution of Emperor Maximilian* to be central enough to Manet's enterprise to devote considerable space to it: see Oskar Bätschmann, *Edouard Manet:* *Der Tod des Maximilian*, Frankfurt-am-Main and Leipzig, Insel, 1993; Albert Boime, "New Light on Manet's *Execution of Emperor Maximilian*," *Art Quarterly* 35, Autumn 1973, pp. 172–208; *Edouard Manet and the "Execution of Maximilian*, Providence, R. I., Brown University, 1981; Manfred Fath and Stefan Germer, *Edouard Manet: Augenblicke der Geschichte*, Mannheim, Städtischen Kunsthalle, 1993; Fried, *Manet's Modernism*, pp. 354–60; John House, "Manet's Maximilian: Censorship and the Salon," in Elizabeth C. Childs, ed., *Suspended License: Censorship and the Visual Arts*, Seattle, University of Washington Press, 1997, pp. 185–209; Sandblad, *Manet: Three Studies in Artistic Conception*, pp. 109–61; and Juliet Wilson-Bareau, *The Execution of Maximilian: Painting, Politics and Censorship*, London, National Gallery, 1992.

5   This, of course, is Walter Benjamin's famous nickname for Paris: see *Paris, Capitale du XIXe Siècle: Le Livre des Passages*, Paris, Editions du Cerf, 1997 (3rd ed.).

6   On Morisot, see Kathleen Adler and Tamar Garb, *Berthe Morisot*, Oxford, Phaidon, 1987; T. J. Edestein, ed., *Perspectives on Morisot*, New York, Hudson Hills, in association with Mount Holyoke College of Art Museum, 1990, esp. Beatrice Farwell, "Manet, Morisot and Propriety," pp. 45–56, and Tamar Garb, "Berthe Morisot and the Feminizing of Impressionism," pp. 57–66; Anne Higonnet, *Berthe Morisot*, New York, Harper and Row, 1990; Anne Higonnet, *Berthe Morisot's Images of Women*, Cambridge, Mass., Harvard University Press, 1992; and Charles F. Stuckey and William P. Scott, *Berthe Morisot, Impressionist*, New York, Hudson Hills (Mount Holyoke College Art Museum and the National Gallery of Art), 1987. On Manet's depictions of Morisot, see Marnie Kessler, "Unmasking Manet's Morisot," *Art Bulletin*, September 1999, pp. 473–89. In addition, see Tamar Garb, "Framing Femininity in Manet's Portrait of Mlle E. G.," in Aruna D'Souza, ed., *Self and History: A Tribute to Linda Nochlin*, London, Thames and Hudson, 1999, pp. 77–89.

7   On the relationship between Manet and Emilie Ambre, the Comtesse d'Amboise, who asked Manet to portray her as Carmen (she had not yet played the part), and who took Manet's *Execution of Emperor Maximilian* with her to the United States to show it there, see Beth Archer Brombert, *Edouard Manet: Rebel in a Frock Coat*, University of Chicago Press, 1996, pp. 378–79.

8   "Close the window," cried Cham in the caption to his caricature, indicating the painting's proximity to the street. ("*Fermez donc cette fenêtre!*" – Cham, *Charivari*, 1869, p. 365; cited in Cachin, *Manet 1832–1883*, p. 307.) Meanwhile both Wolff and Leroy spoke of housepainting with regard to the green shutters (Albert Wolff, *Le Figaro* May 20, 1869, and Louis Leroy, *Charivari* May 6, 1869; cited in Hamilton, *Manet and His Critics*, pp. 133, 139); and Castagnary questioned the relationship between the women, while suggesting that Morisot was "placed solely to enjoy the spectacle of the street" (and Fanny Claus "put on her gloves as if she was about to go out [into that street]"). "That contradictory attitude stopped me in my tracks," he added. ("Sur ce balcon, j'aperçois deux femmes, dont une toute jeune. Sont-ce les deux soeurs? Est-ce la mère et la fille? Je ne sais. Et puis, l'une est assise et semble s'être placée uniquement pour jouir du spectacle de la rue; l'autre se gante comme si elle allait sortir. Cette attitude contradictoire me déroute." – *Le Siècle* June 11, 1869; cited in Cachin, *ibid.*, p. 307, and Hamilton, *ibid.*, pp. 137–38.) Paul Mantz found the two figures' motivation and relation to each other equally confusing – *Gazette des Beaux-Arts*, July 1869; cited in Hamilton, *ibid.*, pp. 135–36. On the critical response to *The Balcony*, see Fried, *Manet's Modernism*, pp. 297–302.

9   On the sources for the *Luncheon in the Studio* and *The Balcony*, see Fried, *ibid.*, pp. 105, 109, 111–12, 160–61. (Fried also sees *The Balcony* as belonging to a turning-point in Manet's career.)

10   It is curious that the disappearance of Léon from Manet's painting, when he had appeared in it repeatedly in the earlier 1860s, coincides with the sudden absence of Victorine Meurent, who had likewise been important to the scene of Manet's painting.

11   On morning and walking dresses, cravats, and gloves, see Philippe Perrot, *Fashioning the Bourgeoisie: A History of Clothing in the Nineteenth Century* (Richard Bienvenu, trans.), Princeton University Press, 1994. See also Higonnet, *Berthe Morisot's Images of Women*, pp. 69–70.

12   See Cachin, *Manet 1832–1883*, pp. 292, 302.

13   See *ibid.*, pp. 290–94 on *Luncheon on the Grass*. In addition to noting the connection to Renoir's painting, the catalogue remarks on the similarity between the lighting of Léon's face and that of Victorine's in the small 1862 portrait, the facts of Léon's adolescence – he was sixteen years old – and current employment by Degas's banker father, and the interpretations of the painting as an image of a boy's entrance into manhood, which include the suggestion (which the catalogue refutes) that the female servant and male diner behind him should be taken as representations of Manet and his wife Suzanne and of their domestic arrangement. See S. Kovacs, "Manet and his son in *Déjeuner dans l'atelier*," *Connoisseur* CLXXXI, Nov. 1972, pp. 196–202. I find that proposition more plausible than the catalogue does; given Manet's characteristic use of models, his diffidence about representing himself and his habit of using others (who often looked like him) to stand in for him, and the need for discretion in the treatment of his relationship to Léon, the fact that Auguste Rousselin posed for the picture does not mean that it is a picture of or about Rousselin, nor does it argue against the view of the painting as a kind of allegory concerning Manet's domesticity in particular or the relation between domesticity and manhood in general. (On the latter, see Jeannene Pryslbyski, *Le Parti Pris des Choses: French Still Life and Modern Painting, 1848–1876*, Ph.D. dissertation, University of California, Berkeley, 1995, esp. ch. 3: "Modern Interiors and Masculine Subjects: The Still Life Paintings of Fantin-Latour and Manet," pp. 161–227.) Indeed, that the *Luncheon in the Studio* was the last painting to feature Léon is perhaps best explained by the painting itself, according to such a view: effectively, it shows Léon leaving the home/studio for the wider world, shedding his role as private studio property (like the items on the chair next to him) to take up his position in the *plein air* public domain of masculine *affaires*.

14   "Je suis plus étrange que laide; il paraît que l'épithète de *femme fatale* a circulé parmi les curieux." See Denis Rouart, ed., *The Correspondence of Berthe Morisot with her Family and her Friends* (*Manet, Puvis de Chavannes, Degas, Monet, Renoir and Mallarmé*) (Betty W. Hubbard, trans.), London, Camden Press, 1986, p. 36; letter from Berthe to Edma of May 2, 1869. For the original French version of the letters, see Denis Rouart, ed., *Correspondance de Berthe Morisot avec sa famille et ses amis Manet, Puvis de Chavannes, Degas, Monet, Renoir et Mallarmé*, Paris, Quatre Chemins Editart, 1950, p. 27.

15   *Ibid.*, May 11, 1869, p. 38.

16   "j'ai trouvé [Manet] jubilant de plus en plus devant le modèle Gonzalès; la mère m'a fait toucher les mains de sa belle-fille me disant qu'elle avait la fièvre; la fille rit du bout des lèvres et m'a rappelé que tu devais lui écrire. Quant à Manet il n'a pas bougé de son

tabouret. Il m'a demandé de tes nouvelles et je lui ai répondu que j'allais te signaler sa froideur. Tu es hors de son cerveau pour le quart d'heure, Mlle G. a toutes les vertus, tous les charmes; c'est une femme accomplie" – *ibid.*, p. 43/p. 32.

17 "Manet me fait de la morale et m'offre cette éternelle Mlle Gonzalès comme modèle; elle a de la tenue, de la persévérance, elle sait mener une chose à bien, tandis que moi, je ne suis capable de rien. En attendant, il recommmence son portrait pour la vingt-cinquième fois; elle pose tous les jours et le soir, sa tête est lavée au savon noir. Voilà qui est encourageant pour demander aux gens de poser" – *ibid.*, August 13, p. 44/pp. 33–34.

18 "Mlle Gonzalès me produit un effet d'agacement, je ne sais pourquoi: je m'imagine que Manet l'a prise bien au-dessus de sa valeur et que nous avons, ou plutôt que tu as, autant de talent qu'elle" – *ibid.*, undated, p. 44/p. 34.

19 He showed it with *The Music Lesson*, featuring another female model and Zacharie Astruc playing the guitar.

20 "Nous avons passé la soirée de jeudi ensemble chez Manet; ce dernier était d'une gaieté folle; il débitait cent extravagances plus drôles les unes que les autres. Pour le quart d'heure, toutes ses admirations sont concentrées sur Mlle Gonzalès, mais son portrait n'avance toujours pas; il me dit être à la quarantième séance et la tête est de nouveau effacée" – *ibid.*

21 "Les Manet sont venus nous voir mardi soir, on a visité l'atelier; à mon grand étonnement et contentement, j'ai recueilli les plus grands éloges; il paraît que c'est décidement mieux qu'Eva Gonzalès." – *ibid.*, undated, p. 45/p. 35.

22 Unlike Morisot, Gonzalès had had some official training before she accepted Manet's tutelage: she had been enrolled in the studio of Charles Chaplin (who also taught Cassatt for a while) and had then set up her own studio. These facts also help to account for Manet's representation of her as a painter rather than a society lady – he evidently took her more seriously than Morisot, at least for a brief time.

23 "Manet m'a tant recommandé de retoucher un peu à ce que j'ai fait de toi, qu'a ton arrivée ici, je te prierai de me laisser redessiner les mains et ajouter quelques finesses au bas de la robe et voilà tout. Il me dit que mon exposition est faite et que je n'ai pas besoin de me tourmenter, puis, immédiatement, il ajoute que je serai refusée; de tout cela, je voudrais ne pas me soucier" – *ibid.*, p. 46/p. 35.

24 "Fatiguée, énervée, je vais le samedi visiter l'atelier de Manet; il me demande où j'en suis et me voyant indécise il me dit avec entrain: 'J'irai demain après mon envoi voir votre tableau et fiez-vous à moi; je vous dirai ce qu'il faut faire.'

Le lendemain, qui était hier, il arrive vers une heure, il trouve cela très bien, moins le bas de la robe; il prend les pinceaux, y met quelques accents qui font très bien; ma mère s'extasie. Voilà où commencent mes malheurs; une fois en train, rien ne peut l'arrêter; il passe du jupon au corsage, du corsage à la tête, de la tête au fond; il fait mille plaisanteries, rit comme un fou, me donne la palette, la reprend, enfin à cinq heures du soir, nous avions fait la plus jolie caricature qu'il puisse se voir. On attendait pour l'emporter; bon gré, mal gré, il me le fait mettre sur le brancard et je reste confondue; mon seul espoir est d'être refusée, ma mère trouve l'aventure drôle, moi je la trouve navrante.

J'ai mis avec ce que j'ai fait de toi à Lorient. Je voudrais bien qu'on me le gardât tout seul" – *ibid.*, Winter of 1869/1870, undated, p. 48/p. 37.

25 "Jamais Manet n'a rien fait d'aussi bien que le portrait de Mlle Gonzalès; il a peut-être encore plus de charme que lorsque tu l'as vu" – *ibid.*, p. 49/p. 37.

26 ". . . je trouvais atroces les améliorations que Manet avait fait subir à ma tête . . . vos organizations nerveuses et fébriles" – *ibid.*, March 22, 1870, p. 49/p. 38.

27 *Ibid.*, May 5, p. 50.

28 "Je ne puis dire que Manet ait abîmé ses tableaux, puisque je les ai vus à l'atelier la veille de l'exposition et que j'en ai été enchantée; mais je ne sais à quoi attribuer l'effet décoloré du portrait de Mlle Gonzalès; le voisinage de l'autre peinture, qui est pourtant exécrable, lui fait perdre énormément; il y a des finesses de ton, des délicatesses qui m'avaient charmée à l'atelier et qui disparaissent à ce grand jour. La tête est toujours restée faible et pas jolie du tout . . ." – *ibid.*, pp. 51–52/p. 40.

29 There is general agreement about which painting was worked on by Manet – its facture seems to suggest the double portrait as the one that Manet retouched. But there are some references to the painting of Edma alone – titled *Woman at the Window* rather than *Reading* – being in the Salon too: see Monique Angoulvent, *Berthe Morisot*, Paris, Morancé, 1933, p. 36, cited in Higonnet, *Berthe Morisot's Images of Women*, p. 116; and Rouart, *Correspondance de Berthe Morisot*, p. 37, cited in Eric Darragon, *Manet*, Paris, Fayard, 1989, pp. 181–82. It is very possible, then, that it was *Woman at the Window (Portrait of Edma Pontillon)* that accompanied

Reading at the Salon, rather than the *Harbor at Lorient*, as has been usually understood, following Berthe's own remark about "the painting I did of you at Lorient."

30 See Berger, *Ways of Seeing*, pp. 45–64, on this double awareness.

31 I suggest also that this period was as crucial for Morisot as it was for Manet, and that in fact she produced her best paintings when she was in dialogue with him, both during this time and later. This is not, however, to argue for Morisot's one-way dependence on Manet, quite the contrary: it is to argue for a two-way exchange between the two painters in which the dependence was entirely mutual, and in which sometimes Manet, sometimes Morisot took the lead.

32 On the place of women in the public spaces of the new city, and the habit of the female Impressionists Morisot and Cassatt of carving out a private zone in their pictures of women confronting the city, see Griselda Pollock, "Modernity and the Spaces of Femininity," *Vision and Difference: Femininity, Feminism, and Histories of Art*, London and New York, Routledge, 1988, pp. 50–90. Manet's painting of Morisot on the balcony effectively calls into question the boundary between women's private sphere and the public zone of the street (and the gazes that go with it).

33 Morisot's portrait of her sister and mother together in the parlor also responded to Degas's 1869 indoor portrait of the eldest Morisot daughter Yves – see Higonnet, *Berthe Morisot's Images of Women*, pp. 67–68. Berthe Morisot had two older sisters, Yves Gobillard and Edma Pontillon (who were three and two years older than Berthe), and one younger brother, Tiburce. Yves had married in 1866 and Edma, who, like her younger sister, had set out to be a painter, married in 1869, just before *The Balcony* was exhibited at the Salon and the Manet–Morisot saga began. Both Edma and Berthe had studied unofficially with Corot.

34 On Morisot and fashion plates, see Higonnet, *Berthe Morisot's Images of Women*, pp. 84–122; and Anne Schirrmeister, "La Dernière Mode: Berthe Morisot and Costume," in Edestein, *Perspectives on Morisot*, pp. 103–15.

35 On women and flower painting in particular, and on the "femininity" of still-life painting in general, see Norman Bryson, "Still Life and 'Feminine' Space," *Looking at the Overlooked: Four Essays on Still Life Painting*, Cambridge, Mass., Harvard University Press, 1990, pp. 136–78, esp. pp. 174–75. See also Germaine

Greer, *The Obstacle Race: The Fortunes of Women Painters and their Work*, New York, Farrar, Straus, & Giroux, 1979, pp. 227–49.

36 Manet returned to the epistolary witticism of the 1872 painting of violets, in a series of letters written to female friends in the early 1880s which he decorated with watercolors of single pieces of fruit or flower – as, for example, the letter to Méry Laurent with a flower inscribed upon the written sheet. At this later date he also turned back to still-life painting, and from his sickbed concentrated on a series of flowerpieces of his own; see Robert Gordon and Andrew Forge, *The Last Flowers of Manet*, New York, Abradale Press (Abrams), 1986; and Rubin, *Manet's Silence and the Poetics of Bouquets*, pp. 192–97. See Chapter Ten below.

37 Just as Manet attached his gallant, jokey painting of violets to his imaging of Morisot, so the *Bon Bock* had a painterly gag attached to it, in the more robust form of the *Palette au Bock* of 1873, in which Manet painted a glass of beer directly onto the palette with which he had painted the *Bon Bock*, thereby inverting the jest of the *Bunch of Violets*: where the *Bunch of Violets* purports to stand in for a real posy and a real letter delivered to a female friend, the *Palette au Bock* returns the representation of the glass of beer to the material ground out of which it was produced in the masculine space of the studio; the one is part of an outward exchange and transitive relationship, the other turns back intransitively on itself.

38 On the portrait of Duval, see Thérèse Dolan, "Skirting the Issue: Manet's *Portrait of Baudelaire's Mistress, Reclining*," *Art Bulletin* 76:4, December 1997, pp. 611–29. See also Pollock, *Differencing the Canon*, pp. 261–77, on Jeanne Duval.

39 As Farwell notes in "Manet, Morisot, and Propriety" (Edestein, *Perspectives on Morisot*, pp. 45–56), *Repose* was related to a series of pictures of semi-reclining women of different repute, including not only the portrait of Baudelaire's mistress (and the *Young Woman Reclining in Spanish Costume*, not to mention *Olympia*) but also the later portrait of the popular *demi-monde* salon hostess Nina de Callias in exotic costume (*La Femme aux Eventails* of 1874) and another, darker portrait of Morisot from around 1873, which, though cut off at the waist, contains enough of Morisot's diagonally arranged torso to suggest a more fully reclining position, and thus to connect her obliquely to the *odalisque* and its anything but proper bourgeois connotations

(as well as to associations of *nervrosité* and the sickbed).

40 See Cachin, *Manet 1832–1883*, pp. 258–60, on the dating of *Reading*: Cachin proposes that the majority of the composition, including the youthful looking figure of Suzanne, was painted in 1865, while the dark, cornered figure of Léon, possibly as an adolescent, was added later, some time around 1873 perhaps.

41 Morisot clearly felt some rivalry with Suzanne as well, disparaging her as "fat" much as she had Valentine Carré – see *Correspondence of Berthe Morisot*, p. 89/p. 72 (1872–74).

42 One critic said Berthe was "ni debout, ni assise" – Francion, *L'Illustration*, June 14, 1873; cited in Cachin, *Manet 1832–1883*, p. 317.

43 In the same letter in which Berthe described her promenade at the Salon with the "fat" Valentine Carré, and in which she rendered her final negative judgment about the effect of Manet's painting of Gonzalès at the Salon, she also gave an account of Manet's attempts to arrange for Carré to sit for him in Morisot's studio, and again her jealousy at Manet's passing fancy for Carré is evident. Rouart fills in the details, telling the rest of the story about the garden placement of Carré, Tiburce's position next to her, Mme Carré's intervention and removal of her daughter, Edma's sitting in for her, and the resulting face, which was neither the one woman's nor the other's – *Correspondence of Berthe Morisot*, pp. 51–52/p. 40 (May 1870).

EIGHT MODERNITY ACCORDING TO MANET

1 Fantin-Latour's *A Studio at the Batignolles* served as the curtain opener to the 1994–95 exhibition at the Grand Palais and the Metropolitan Museum of Art called "Origins of Impressionism," thus emphasizing the idea that the painting itself proposes, that Manet be considered the father and leader of Impressionism: see Gary Tinterow and Henri Loyrette, *Origins of Impressionism*, New York, The Metropolitan Museum of Art and Abrams, 1994. I thank Margaret Doyle, a graduate student at the Graduate Center of the City University of New York, where I taught on Manet and Impressionism, for her insights about this painting. The representation of members of the group as insiders and outsiders might perhaps have something to do with their relationship to the Salon at the time – with Renoir, framed at the center, the most successful Salon exhibitor, and Monet, at the edges of the composition, the

least. (Renoir, for all intents and purposes, remained the Salon painter of the group, while Monet sought to set himself apart from the Salon most assiduously.) Other members of the future group were simply excluded from the painting, such as Degas, Pissarro, Sisley, and Cézanne. See also Fried, *Manet's Modernism*, pp. 340–44.

2 That Manet was understood to be the sire of the new school is made very clear by the fact that Cézanne marked his involvement with the group in the first exhibition of 1874 with a direct gesture in Manet's direction – *A Modern Olympia* – which was received in kind. Louis Leroy remarked, in *Le Charivari* of April 25, that this was the "republic" of the "great Manet," and that Cézanne's *Modern Olympia* was a kind of caricature of the original *Olympia*. See John Rewald, *The History of Impressionism*, New York, The Museum of Modern Art, 1961, pp. 318–24; and Linda Nochlin, *Impressionism and Post-Impressionism 1874–1904* (Sources & Documents in the History of Art Series, ed. H. W. Janson), Englewood Cliffs, Prentice-Hall, 1966, pp. 10–14.

3 On the importance of the siege and the civil war to the "new painting," see Hollis Clayson, "A Wintry Masculinity: Art, Soldiering, and Gendered Space in Paris under Siege," *Nineteenth Century Contexts*, Boston, Northeastern University, 1998, vol. 20, pp. 385–408; Jane Roos, *Early Impressionism and the French State*, Cambridge University Press, 1996; Paul Tucker, "The First Impressionist Exhibition in Context," in Charles S. Moffett, *The New Painting: Impressionism 1874–1886*, San Francisco, The Fine Arts Museums of San Francisco, 1986, pp. 93–117; and Wilson-Bareau, *Manet, Monet, and the Gare Saint-Lazare*, pp. 25–41. See also Edouard Manet, *Lettres du siège de Paris*, Paris, Editions de l'Amateur, 1996.

4 The early 1870s seem to have marked a moment of doubt for Manet, with regard to what kind of painting he should be undertaking, and what he should be exhibiting at the Salon and elsewhere. In addition to his hesitation over paintings like the *Portrait of Eva Gonzalès*, he also showed old and miscellaneous works: in 1870, for instance, he showed one of his *Philosopher*s and a watercolor version of *The Dead Christ and the Angels* at the Cercle de l'Union Artistique; and, as we have seen, in 1872 he showed the *Battle of the Kearsarge and Alabama* at the Salon. His submissions to the Salon of 1874 – *The Railway*, the watercolor *Punchinello*, the *Swallows*, and the *Masked Ball*

at the Opera, the last two of which were refused – were miscellaneous in both medium and subject matter. In 1875 and '76, he continued a series of illustration ventures begun the year before – eight etchings illustrating Charles Cros's poem *Le Fleuve*, his collaboration with Mallarmé on the French translation of Edgar Allen Poe's *The Raven*, and wood-engraved illustrations for Mallarmé's *L'Après-midi d'un faune* – while exhibiting *Argenteuil* at the Salon of 1875, sending *Washing* and *The Artist* to the Salon of 1876, from which they were refused, submitting *Faure in the Role of Hamlet* and *Nana* to the Salon of 1877, and when the latter was refused, exhibiting it in a knick-knack shop, and so on.

5 Just as the beginning of Manet's and Morisot's relationship coincided with Léon's growing up and moving out of the studio/home, and with Edma's retiring from the scene of painting due to her marriage, so the end of Manet's painting of Morisot, marked by his peculiarly screened and almost disfigured picture of her in mourning garb (almost a caricature of the "rose et noir" painting of her with a bouquet of violets from two years before), corresponded to the death of her father, the beginning of her activities as an Impressionist painter, and then her marriage to Manet's brother. One event marked her departure from the regime of the father; another what Manet may have felt as her betrayal of him, and the final event the end of his gallantry, because of the substitution of his brother for him as the object of her romantic regard. This was a chain of events that had meaning for both painters; it also underlines the intermediate position that the interlude with Morisot occupied between Manet's painting of the '60s and the "new painting" of the next generation.

6 On this painting, see Harry Rand, *Manet's Contemplation at the Gare Saint-Lazare*, Berkeley, University of California Press, 1987.

7 Stuckey and Scott, *Berthe Morisot, Impressionist*, p. 44, identify the figures of Yves and Bichette in this painting, and also speak to its looking back to Manet's *The Garden*, as well as Manet's looking back to it for his *Railway*.

8 See, for example, Ann Sutherland Harris and Linda Nochlin, *Women Artists 1550–1950*, Los Angeles County Museum of Art, and New York, Knopf, 1977, p. 234.

9 See Louis Prosper Ernest Duvergier de Hauranne, *Revue des deux mondes*, 1874; cited in Hamilton, *Manet and His Critics*, p. 179.

10 In this painting, then, Manet returns to the domestic fidelity of the lapdog of the *Venus of Urbino* that the *Olympia* had replaced with its hissing black cat and salacious overtones.

11 In fact, the fashion of Victorine's dress was slightly passé – as evidenced in Philippe Burty's comment in "Les Ateliers," *La Renaissance littéraire et artistique*, Nov. 2, 1874, pp. 220–21, that the dress was fashioned of "the blue twill that was all the fashion until this autumn" – see Wilson-Bareau, *Manet, Monet, and the Gare St. Lazare*, pp. 47–48. (Burty identifies the picture as a "double portrait," and speaks of the two figures as mother and daughter.) The figure of Victorine in *The Gare Saint-Lazare* conforms to current fashion illustrations in its detail, but Victorine's pose, like that of Morisot in *The Balcony*, complicates a clear reading of the dress.

12 The term *punctum* comes from Roland Barthes, *La Chambre claire*, Paris, Gallimard Seuil, Cahiers du Cinéma, 1980, where it refers to the ruptural detail of the photograph, which punctures the photograph's objective or aesthetic *studium* and affects the viewer with its subjective, temporal poignance. Gazes that look outward from photographs are central to Barthes's sense of the *punctum*, and even though Manet's paintings of Victorine are not photographs, some of the same quality of the photograph adheres to them. Not only is their tonality similar to that of the photograph but also the gazes and poses found in them are related to those of the photograph. See McCauley, *A. A. E. Disdéri and the Carte de Visite Portrait Photograph*. It is therefore not merely coincidental that Barthes's favorite photograph in *La Chambre claire*, Nadar's photograph of his ailing wife (which Barthes prefers to identify as Nadar's mother), resembles – perhaps even quotes – one of Manet's pictures of Victorine, *The Streetsinger*, with its hand held up to the face half obscuring the mouth.

13 Manet's image of the back of a child with a large sash comes right out of fashion prints; see Higonnet, *Berthe Morisot's Images of Women*, esp. p. 119; and Anne Schirrmeister, "La Dernière Mode," in Edestein, *Perspectives on Morisot*, sep. p. 109. As for the child's tightly coiffed hair, which contrasts to Victorine's long mane, it picks up the opposition between the sleek and hair-loosened sides of *Olympia*.

14 On the "femininity" of Morisot's manner, see Tamar Garb, "Berthe Morisot and the Feminizing of Impressionism," in Edestein,

Perspectives on Morisot; and "'L'Art Féminin': The formation of a critical category in late nineteenth-century France," *Art History* 12, no. 1, March 1989, pp. 39–65. See also Anne Higonnet, "Imaging Gender," in Orwicz, *Art Criticism and its Institutions in Nineteenth-Century France*, pp. 146–61.

15   Not all of the Impressionists were landscapists by any means, which is easy to see from any of the catalogue listings of artists and works in the Impressionist exhibitions. For example, in addition to the landscapes and other works by the painters who gained lasting renown as so-called "Impressionist" painters, the first exhibition included still lifes, portraits, and miscellaneous figural works by artists such as Zacharie Astruc, Antoine-Ferdinand Attendu, Félix Bracquemond (etchings), Edouard Brandon, Adolphe-Félix Cals, Alfred Meyer, and Auguste-Louis-Marie Ottin. The landscape emphasis of certain members and factions of the group was stressed later on, particularly after the Impressionist shows themselves, with Monet's one-man exhibits featuring landscape series. Landscape was not one of Manet's specialties, and the few examples of the genre that he submitted to the Salon did not meet with success – *The Battle of the Kearsarge and Alabama*, a cross between battle painting and seascape, was not highly regarded and, as noted earlier, *The Swallows*, effectively a landscape painting, was rejected.

16   Wilson-Bareau identifies the glimpsed facade as part of Manet's own studio; see *Manet, Monet, and the Gare St. Lazare*, p. 47.

17   Where the critics and caricaturists responding to *The Railway* emphasized the unreadable expression on Victorine's face, the inexplicable relationship between the two figures, and the effect of prison bars produced by the railing behind them (see *ibid.*, pp. 47–55), the reactions to Caillebotte's and Monet's contributions to the 1877 Impressionist show representing the area of the railway station were quite different. Some identified the Parisian locale of Caillebotte's Place de l'Europe series, or stressed the anecdotal relationships contained in them, or debated about whether Caillebotte ought to be considered an Impressionist or not. With regard to Monet's set of Gare St. Lazare paintings, all addressed them as a coherent series, treating Monet as "the customary painter of the Gare Saint-Lazare" (Baron Schop, alias Théodore de Banville, *Le National*, April 8, 1877). One remarked on "the black, pink, gray,

and purple smoke" (Léon de Lora, alias Louis de Fourcaud, *Le Gaulois*, 10 April 1877), while Bertall (alias Charles-Albert d'Arnoux) declared that "Manet's scepter is now held by Monet," and also remarked on the smoke that screened the trains (*Paris-Journal*, April 9, 1877). See Moffett, *The New Painting*, pp. 208–10, 222–24; and Richard Brettell, "The 'First' Exhibition of Impressionist Painters," pp. 189–202. Despite the habitual identification of the group with Manet, it is clear that the understandings of these works as "modernist" representations of modernity were quite divergent, and that the context in which they were viewed – the Salon versus the exhibition at the rue Le Peletier – mattered. And where Monet may have been understood as a follower of Manet, it is fairly evident that in the context of the Salon, few thought to identify the painter of the *Gare Saint-Lazare* as an Impressionist.

18   On Caillebotte, see Michael Fried, "Caillebotte's Impressionism," *Representations* 66, Spring 1999, pp. 1–51; Julia Sagraves, *Gustave Caillebotte: Urban Impressionist*, New York, London, and Paris, Abbeville, 1995; and Kirk Varnedoe, *Gustave Caillebotte*, New Haven and London, Yale University Press, 1987.

19   On capitalist production, see Karl Marx, *Capital*, vol. 1, in Tucker, *The Marx–Engels Reader* (2nd ed.), esp. "Division of Labor and Manufacture," pp. 388–403. On the situationist Marxist theory of "spectacle," see Guy Debord, *The Society of the Spectacle* (Donald Nicholson-Smith, trans.), New York, Zone Books, 1994. Debord's claim that "The spectacle is *capital* accumulated until it becomes an image" (p. 24) is one of the main metaphors of Clark's *Painting of Modern Life* (pp. 9–10).

20   See Derrida, "Parergon," *The Truth in Painting*, pp. 14–147, esp. pp. 52ff, where the *parergon* is defined, in relation to Kant's *Critique of Judgment* (and Western aesthetic and methaphysical thought in general), as a "hinge" between what is intrinsic and extrinsic to the work of art, as ornamentation, as the "supplement" as opposed to essence: "The Greek here confers a quasi-conceptual dignity to the notion of this *hors-d'oeuvre* which however does not simply stand outside the work [*hors d'oeuvre*], also acting alongside, right up against the work [*ergon*]. Dictionaries most often give 'hors-d'oeuvre,' which is the strictest translation, but also 'accessory, foreign or secondary object,' 'supplement,' 'aside,' 'remainder.' . . . Philosophical discourse will always be *against* the *parergon*" (p. 54). The

concept of the *parergon* thus applies to Manet's work not only in the sense of this painting's importing the principle of the frame into the interior of the work, or in the sense of his pre-occupation with clothing, fashion, and femininity, but also in the sense of his general emphasis, not on content or the essence of the subject (matter), but on that which divides painting from world as the very "difference" of painting itself.

21 This is the point made by Greenberg in "Manet in Philadelphia," about Manet's difference from the others of his generation, his devotion to the "'machine'," and the necessity of taking his paintings in as "single works" – see the Introduction above.

22 Cited in Hamilton, *Manet and His Critics*, p. 188.

23 See Paul Tucker, *Monet at Argenteuil*, New Haven and London, Yale University Press, 1982. Monet lived in Argenteuil between 1871 and 1877. Manet's family had a house in Gennevilliers, across the Seine from Argenteuil, but like many Manet did not live there continuously. Caillebotte, Sisley, and Renoir also painted in the area, but none lived there so exclusively or represented it so repeatedly. And Manet responded to Monet's involvement with Argenteuil, not to Renoir's, even though the latter's paintings were close to Monet's. (Manet is said to have made disparaging remarks about Renoir as a painter – see Brombert, *Edouard Manet, Rebel in a Frock Coat*, p. 224.) See also Richard Brettell et al, *A Day in the Country: Impressionism and the French Landscape*, Los Angeles County Museum of Art, The Art Institute of Chicago, Paris, Réunion des Musées Nationaux, and New York, Abrams, 1984.

24 The shoe protruding from Suzanne Manet's skirt recalls the glimpsed slippers of the portraits of Jeanne Duval, Victorine Meurent, and Berthe Morisot, but possesses little of the subtle erotics of the motif in those paintings, which calls up the fetishization of the foot in nineteenth-century culture.

25 This painting also refers to Monet and in a broader way Boudin, whose Normandy beach scenes are specifically indicated in Manet's 1868 *On the Beach at Boulogne* (Virginia Museum of Fine Arts, Richmond).

26 Cachin, following Rewald, claims that *Argenteuil* was the first of Manet's paintings to be painted at least partly outdoors, while also admitting that "no document proves it" – *Manet 1832–1883*, p. 353. The evidence of the

painting itself, it seems to me, is otherwise: that the figures were models from Paris posed at least in part indoors, and that their background was cobbled together in a very piecemeal way from indoor props and outdoor atmosphere.

27 On the methods and ethos of Impressionism, see Michel Butor, "Monet, or the World Upside Down," in T. B. Hess and John Ashbery, eds., *The Avant-Garde: Art News Annual* 34, 1968, pp. 20–33; Robert L. Herbert, "Method and Meaning in Monet," *Art in America* 67, September 1979, pp. 901–08; John House, *Monet, Nature into Art*, New Haven and London, Yale University Press, 1986; and Rosalind Krauss, "Impressionism: The Narcissism of Light," *Partisan Review* XLIII:1, 1976, pp. 102–12. I am indebted to Thomas Crow's undergraduate lectures at Princeton for the observation about the relationship between the top and bottom halves of the *Regatta at Argenteuil*.

28 In his discussion of Chardin's still lifes, Diderot oscillated between wondering at their "handling" and marveling at the "air circulat[ing] around . . . objects" – see for example Denis Diderot, "Salon of 1765," in John Goodman, ed., *Diderot on Art I*, New Haven and London, Yale University Press, 1995, pp. 60–64.

29 Not all naturalist painters asserted this equation between facture, optical surface, and reflection: Courbet, by contrast, equated painting with the material, if not sculptural work of Nature, as in water carving out stone in *The Source of the Loue* series, or the emphasis on rock and earth, and the imbuing of Nature with a kind of fleshly substance throughout his landscape work.

30 See Clark, *Painting of Modern Life*, pp. 164–70, on *Argenteuil*. I am indebted to Clark's thick description and thorough reading of this painting – his remarks about the flatness of the hat, the joke of the rope/reflection, and the indigo of the background landscape, but also his sense of it being "a picture for the salon" and of the models posing "as people might for a photograph." But, once again, though I believe that the class analysis that Clark produces works for the reception of the picture, I do not think it is adequate to the oddity of the painting itself or its parting of company with Monet *et al* on the Impressionist subject of the suburbs.

31 "Code vestimentaire" is Roland Barthes's term, from *Système de la Mode*, Paris, Seuil, 1967.

32 On *In the Conservatory* and related paintings by Manet, see Jonathan Crary, *Suspensions of*

Perception: Attention, Spectacle, and Modern Culture, Cambridge, Mass., MIT Press (October Books), 1999, pp. 81–127; and the earlier "Unbinding Vision," *October* 68, Spring 1994, pp. 21–44. See also Bradford Collins, "Manet's 'In the Conservatory' and 'Chez le Père Lathuille'," *Art Journal* 45, 1985, pp. 59–66; and Jed Perl, "Art and Urbanity: The Manet Retrospective," *New Criterion*, November 1983, pp. 43–54.

33 Cachin, *Manet 1832–1883*, p. 434, remarks on the relationship of *In the Conservatory* to *The Balcony* and says that Jules and Antoine Guillemet were not related.

34 Jules Castagnary, "Le Salon de 1879," *Le Siècle*, June 28, 1879; cited in Hamilton, *Manet and His Critics*, p. 215. Cachin, Manet 1832–1883, p. 436, cited some of Castagnary's review: "Rien n'est plus simple que la composition, ni plus naturel que les attitudes. Une chose cependant mérite d'être louée davantage, c'est la fraîcheur des tons et l'harmonie de la coloration général . . . Les visages et les mains sont dessinés avec plus de soin que d'ordinaire: Manet ferait-il des concessions?"

35 "*Dans la serre* représente une femme assise sur un banc vert, écoutant un monsieur penché sur le dossier de ce banc. De tous côtés, des grandes plantes, et à gauche des fleurs rouges. La femme, un peu engoncée et rêvante, vêtue d'une robe qui semble faite à grands coups, au galop, . . . et qui est superbe d'exécution; l'homme, nu-tête, avec des coups de lumière se jouant sur le front, frisant çà et là, touchant aux mains enlevées en quelques traits et tenant un cigare. Ainsi posée, dans un abandon de causerie, cette figure est vraiment belle: elle flirte et vit" – Joris-Karl Huysmans, "Le Salon de 1879," *L'Art Moderne*, pp. 51–52; cited in Hamilton, *Manet and His Critics*, p. 216.

36 See Stéphane Mallarmé, "The Impressionists and Edouard Manet," *The Art Monthly Review and Photographic Portfolio*, Sept. 30, 1876, reprinted in Moffett, *The New Painting*, pp. 28–34. See Jean Harris, "A Little-known Essay on Manet by Stéphane Mallarmé," *Art Bulletin* XLVI, December 1964, pp. 559–63.

37 Mallarmé, "The Impressionists and Edouard Manet," p. 33.

38 In 1874 (April 12) Mallarmé had published "Jury de peinture pour 1874 et Edouard Manet" in *La Renaissance littéraire et artistique*, part of which he recycled in the 1876 English essay.

39 Mallarmé, "The Impressionists and Edouard Manet," p. 34.

40 *Ibid.*, p. 28.

41 Little known though it may have been at the time, Mallarmé's essay on Manet is now canonical. It is crucial to Stephen Eisenman's discussion of the term "Intransigent" in "The Intransigent Artist *or* How the Impressionists Got Their Name," in Moffett, *The New Painting*, pp. 51–59. Clark gives it pride of place at the outset of *Painting of Modern Life*, pp. 10–12, and for good reason equates its views with the Greenbergian definition of modernist painting. (As for Greenberg himself, he repeatedly included Mallarmé in his canon of literary modernists, describing him as the true originator of "pure poetry" – see esp. "Towards a Newer Laocoon," p. 33.) It is mentioned in passing by Fried, *Manet's Modernism*, pp. 408–09, in a discussion of Manet as one of several founders of the "formalist-modernist" line. My views of Mallarmé's essay align best with those of Clay, in "Ointments, Makeup, Pollen."

42 Mallarmé, "Manet and the Impressionists," pp. 28, 29.

43 *Ibid.*, p. 32.

44 *Ibid.*, p. 29.

45 *Ibid.*, p. 30.

NINE   FACTURING FEMININITY

1 In 1873 Manet had sold five paintings, including *The Spanish Singer*, to the baritone Jean-Baptiste Faure, whose theatrical portrait is reminiscent of that of Rouvière (also in the role of Hamlet) of twelve years before.

2 At the same time, he showed his modern history painting the *Execution of Emperor Maximilian* in New York, and in late 1880 he also showed a few scattered works in Besançon and Marseilles. In 1883, before his death, he showed the *Corner of the Café-concert* that he had already shown at La Vie Moderne in Lyon.

3 Proust commissioned a series of four portraits of women in modish, seasonally appropriate clothes, each representing an allegory of one of the four seasons. Only two of the four, *Spring* (Jeanne Demarsy) and *Autumn* (Méry Laurent) were finished. See Cachin, *Manet 1832–1883*, pp. 486–91. These paintings continue the dialogue with Morisot, who was also painting her own seasonally garbed portraits during this period: thus the duality of the *Bar's* facture is supported by Manet's continuing fascination with Morisot's way of painting, as it is inscribed in the other painting shown with the *Bar* at the Salon of 1882.

4 See Robida, *La Vie Parisienne*, May 12, 1877; reproduced in Cachin, *Manet*, p. 394.

5 On the department store, advertising and display, women's shopping, and the incitement to consumer desire, see Rachel Bowlby, *Just Looking: Consumer Culture in Dreiser, Gissing, and Zola*, New York, Methuen, 1985; Michael Miller, *The Bon Marché: Bourgeois Culture and the Department Store, 1869–1920*, Princeton University Press, 1981; and Rosalind H. Williams, *Dream Worlds: Mass Consumption in Late Nineteenth Century France*, Berkeley, University of California Press, 1982.

6 Here it is appropriate to remember that a decade earlier, Zola had described the Salon as a giant bonbon shop.

7 Huysmans's review, "La Nana de Manet," in *L'Artiste* (Brussels), May 13, 1877, speaks to this when he addresses the crowd of scandalized viewers, inured to what the Salon offered in the way of nudities, who came to gawk at Giroux's window: "Le tableau de Manet que le jury du Salon de 1877 a refusé d'admettre, à l'unanimité, vient d'être exposé aux vitrines de la maison Giroux. Inutile d'ajouter que, matin et soir, l'on s'entasse devant cette toile, et qu'elle soulève les cris indignés et les rires d'une foule abêtie par la contemplation des stores que les Cabanel, Bouguereau, Toulmouche et autres croient nécessaire de barbouiller et d'exposer sur la cimaise, au printemps de chaque année." Cited in Tabarant, *Manet et ses oeuvres*, p. 305. For the classic account of Manet's *Nana*, see Werner Hofmann, *Nana: Mythos und Wirklichkeit*, Cologne, DuMont, 1973/1987.

8 Huysmans published *Marthe, histoire d'une fille* in Brussels in 1876 (and then in Paris in 1879); to be followed by the Goncourts in 1877 (*La Fille Elisa*), Zola in 1879–1880 (*Nana*), Paul Alexis in 1880 (*La Fin de Lucie Pellegrin*), and Guy de Maupassant in 1880 and 1881 ("Boule de suif," "La Maison Tellier").

9 "L'aristocratie du vice se reconnaît aujourd'hui au linge . . . – La soie, c'est la marque de fabrique des courtisanes qui se louent cher." "Nana est donc arrivée, dans le tableau du peintre, au sommet envié par ses semblables et, intelligente et corrompue comme elle est, elle a compris que l'élégance des bas et des mules était, à coup sûr, l'un des adjuvants les plus précieux que les filles de joie aient inventés pour culbuter les hommes." – Huysmans, "La Nana de Manet," pp. 148–49; cited in Clayson, *Painted Love*, p. 78; see also Hofmann, *Nana: Mythos und Wirklichkeit*, p. 19.

10 "la Nana de l'*Assommoir* se poudre le visage d'une fleur de riz. Un monsieur la regarde." "Manet a eu absolument raison de nous présenter dans sa Nana l'un des plus parfaits échantillons de ce type de filles que son ami et notre cher maître, Emile Zola, va nous dépeindre dans l'un de ses prochains romans. Manet l'a fait voir telle que forcément elle sera avec son vice compliqué et savant, son extravagance et son luxe des paillardises." – Huysmans, "La Nana de Manet." Slightly later, one other contemporary writer who was a friend of Manet's noted the connection to Zola's Nana – Félicien Champsaur, *Les Contemporains*, June 16, 1881, p. 29; cited in Cachin, *Manet 1832–1883*, p. 394.

11 On the problem of description in text and image, see Svetlana Alpers, "Describe or Narrate?: A Problem in Realistic Representation," *New Literary History* 8 (1976–77), pp. 15–41; Norman Bryson, "Discourse, figure," *Word and Image: French Painting of the Ancien Regime*, Cambridge University Press, 1981, pp. 1–28; George Lukács, "Raconter ou décrire?: Contribution à la discussion sur le naturalisme et le formalisme," *Problèmes du réalisme* (Claude Prévost and Jean Guégan, trans.), Paris, L'Arche Editeur, 1975, pp. 130–75; and "Towards a Theory of Description," *Yale French Studies* 61 (1981).

12 "Blonde, rose, figure parisienne, très éveillée, le nez légèrement retroussé, la bouche petite et rieuse, un petit trou au menton, les yeux bleus très clairs, avec des cils d'or. Quelques taches de son qui reviennent l'été, mais très rares, cinq ou six sur chaque tempe comme de parcelles d'or. La nuque ambrée, avec un fouillis de petits cheveux. Sentant la femme, très femme. Un duvet sur les joues.

"Il faudra raconter sa vie antérieure. Voir *L'Assommoir* pour toute la première période: a roulé enfant dans le quartier de la Goutte-d'Or, a fait son apprentissage de fleuriste chez Titreville, rue du Caire, s'est sauvée pour se mettre avec un vieux . . . a quitté son vieux pour rouler; des bas et des hauts; est revenue chez ses parents plusieurs fois, s'est sauvée encore, enfin n'est plus reparue. C'est là où je l'ai laissée . . .

" . . . Dans les premiers temps, très lâchée, grossière; puis, faisant la dame et s'observant beaucoup. Avec cela, finissant par considérer l'homme comme une matière à exploiter, *devenant une force de la nature, un ferment de destruction, mais cela sans le vouloir, par son sexe seul et par sa puissante odeur de femme*, détruisant tous ce qu'elle approche, faisant tourner la société comme les femmes qui ont leurs règles font tourner le lait. Le *cul* dans toute sa puissance; le *cul* sur un autel et tous sacrifiant devant. Il faut que le livre soit le poème du *cul*, et la moralité sera le *cul* faisant tout tourner. Dès le premier chapitre, je montre toute la salle prise et adorant: étudier les femmes, étudier les hommes devant cette apparition souveraine du cul. – En outre, Nana est la mangeuse d'or, l'avaleuse de toute richesse; les goûts les plus dispendieux, le gaspillage le plus effroyable. Elle se rue aux jouissances, à la possession, par instinct. Tout ce qu'elle dévore; elle mange ce qu'on gagne autour d'elle dans *l'industrie, dans l'agio, dans les hautes situations,* dans tout ce qui rapporte. Et elle ne laisse que de la cendre. En un mot, la *vraie fille.* – Ne pas la faire spirituelle, ce qui serait une faute; elle n'est que la chair, mais la chair avec toute sa grâce. Et bonne fille, je le répète.

"Des hauts et des bas. A la fin, il faut qu'elle meure en pleine jeunesse, en plein triomphe.

"La question d'hérédité chez Nana. Une expression extrême des Rougon-Macquarts. Le produit de Gervaise et d'un alcoolisé, Coupeau." – Zola, documentary note on *Nana* from the summer of 1878, quoted in the introduction to Emile Zola, *Nana* (George Holden, trans.), Harmondsworth, England, Penguin, 1972/1977, pp. 11–13. French edition Emile Zola, *Nana,* Paris, Dunod, Classiques Garnier, 1994, "Dossier Documentaire: Fiches-Personnages (Folios 191–193)," pp. 569–71 (emphasis in original).

13   The story of Nana thus irresistibly suggests the conjunction of the commodity fetish and the sexual fetish. See Emily Apter, *Feminizing the Fetish: Psychoanalysis and Narrative Obsession in Turn-of-the-Century France,* Ithaca and London, Cornell University Press, 1991, esp. chs. 1, 3, 4, and 9; and Peter Brooks, *Body Work: Objects of Desire in Modern Narrative,* Cambridge, Mass., Harvard University Press, 1993, esp. ch. 5, "Nana at Last Unveil'd? Problems of the Modern Nude," pp. 123–61. See also Rémy Saisselin, *The Bourgeois and the Bibelot,* New Brunswick, Rutgers University Press, 1984.

14   On the problem of the prostitute, scapegoating, and the regulation of sexuality, see Clayson, *Painted Love*; Charles Bernheimer, *Figures of Ill Repute,* Cambridge, Mass., Harvard University Press, 1989; Clark, "Olympia's Choice," *Painting of Modern Life,* pp. 79–146; Alain Corbin, *Les Filles de noce: Misère sexuelle et prostitution aux dix-neuvième et vingtième siècles,* Paris,

Aubier Montaigne, 1978; Jill Harsin, *Policing Prostitution in Nineteenth-Century Paris,* Princeton University Press, 1985; James McMillan, *Housewife or Harlot: The Place of Women in French Society, 1870–1940,* New York, St. Martin's Press, 1981; A. J. B. Parent-Duchâtelet, *De la prostitution dans la ville de Paris: considérée sous le rapport de l'hygiène publique, de la morale et de l'administration: ouvrage appuyé de documents statistiques puisés dans les Archives de la Préfecture de Paris* (1836), 2 vols., Paris, 1857 (3rd ed.). See also Jean-Michel Charles Lanskin, *Le "scénario sans amour" d'une fille de joie: Analyse transactionnelle de Nana,* Paris, Lettres Modernes, 1996.

15   Zola, *Nana,* pp. 154–57.

16   "Nana . . . vivait au premier étage, dans ses trois pièces, la chambre, le cabinet et le petit salon. Deux foix déjà, elle avait refait la chambre, la première en satin mauve, la seconde en application de dentelle sur soie bleue; et elle n'était pas satisfaite, elle trouvait ça fade, cherchant encore, sans pouvoir trouver. Il y avait pour vingt mille francs de point de Venise au lit capitonné, bas comme un sofa. Les meubles étaient de laque blanche et bleue, incrustée de filets d'argent; partout, des peaux d'ours blancs traînaient, si nombreuses, qu'elles couvraient le tapis; un caprice, un raffinement de Nana, qui n'avait pu se déshabituer de s'asseoir à terre pour ôter ses bas. A côté de la chambre, le petit salon offrait un pêle-mêle amusant, d'un art exquis; contre la tenture de soie rose pâle, un rose turc fané, broché de fils d'or, se détachaient un monde d'objets de tous les pays et de tous les styles, des cabinets italiens, des coffres espagnols et portugais, des pagodes chinoises, un paravent japonais d'un fini précieux, puis des faïences, des bronzes, des soies brodées, des tapisseries au petit point; tandis que des fauteuils larges comme des lits, et des canapés profonds comme des alcoves, mettaient là une paresse molle, une vie somnolente de sérail. La pièce gardait le ton du vieil or, fondu de vert et de rouge, sans que rien marquât trop la fille, en dehors de la volupté des sièges; seules, deux statuettes de biscuit, une femme en chemise cherchant des puces, et une autre absolument nue, marchant sur les mains, les jambes en l'air, suffisaient à salir le salon d'une tache de bêtise originelle. Et, par une porte presque toujours ouverte, on apercevait le cabinet de toilette, tout en marbre et en glace, avec la vasque blanche de sa baignoire, ses pots et ses cuvettes d'argent, ses garnitures de cristal et d'ivoire.

Un rideau fermé y faisait un petit jour blanc, qui semblait dormir, comme chauffé d'un parfum de violette, ce parfum troublant de Nana dont l'hôtel entier, jusqu'à la cour, était pénétré." – Zola, *Nana*, Paris, Bibliothèque-Charpentier, 1925, t. II, pp. 82–83. (All the French citations are from this edition.) English ed., pp. 312–13.

17   "les fauteuils larges comme des lits et les canapés profonds comme des alcôves invitaient à des somnolences oublieuses de l'heure, à des tendresses rieuses, chuchotées dans l'ombre des coins." "Deux lampes éclairaient d'une lueur molle les tentures roses, les bibelots aux tons de laque et de vieil or . . . au milieu des coffres, des bronzes, des faïences, un jeu de lumière discret allumant une incrustation d'argent ou d'ivoire, détachant le luisant d'une baguette sculptée, moirant un panneau d'un reflet de soie . . . Et, dans cette pièce toute pleine de la vie intime de Nana, où traînaient ses gants, un mouchoir tombé, un livre ouvert, on la retrouvait au déshabillé, avec son odeur de violette, son désordre de bonne fille, d'un effet charmant parmi ces richesses" – *Nana*, pp. 336–37/II, pp. 108–9.

18   On items that might have been sold at shops like Giroux's, see writers such as Octave Uzanne, who devoted a whole treatise to the fan: *L'Eventail*, Paris, A. Quantin, 1882. On Giroux's shop (Alphonse père et fils), which sold cameras and photography equipment, stationery, paintings, dolls, and fans from the 1840s on, see E. Anne McCauley, *Industrial Madness: Commerical Photography in Paris 1848–1871*, New Haven and London, Yale University Press, 1994, pp. 48, 376, n. 7.

19   On Zola's themes and procedures in the Rougon-Macquarts series, see John A. Frey, *The Aesthetics of the Rougon-Macquarts*, Madrid, Studia Humanitatis, 1978; Lewis Kamm, *The Object in Zola's Rougon-Macquarts*, Madrid, Studia Humanitatis, 1978; and Brian Nelson, *Zola and the Bourgeoisie: A Study of the Themes and Techniques in Les Rougon-Macquarts*, Totowa, N. J., Barnes & Noble Books, 1983. See also Chantal Bertrand-Jennings, *L'éros et la femme chez Zola*, Paris, Klincksieck, 1977. See also F. W. J. Hemmings, *Emile Zola*, Oxford, Clarendon Press, 1966; and Joanna Richardson, *Zola*, London, Weidenfeld and Nicolson, 1978.

20   Zola's interest in female consumerism in the period is best represented by his novel of three years later, about life in a department store modeled on the Bon Marché, *Au Bonheur des Dames* (1883). But that interest is unlike Manet's in being subsumed in a larger project of providing an encyclopedic diagnosis of modern French society that is at once patrilineal in its emphasis and critical in its outlook. (The critique that Zola mounts, however, is significantly undercut by his own seduction by the spectacle of the capitalist system that he seeks to analyze and by the fact that his naturalist procedures require that seduction, and the eroticized surplus of commodities which it both reflects and constructs.)

21   "Elle portait les couleurs de l'écure Vandeuvres, bleu et blanc, dans une toilette extraordinaire: le petit corsage et la tunique de soie bleue collant sur le corps, relevés derrière les reins en un pouf énorme, ce qui dessinait les cuisses d'une façon hardie, par ces temps de jupes ballonnées; puis, la robe de satin blanc, les manches de satin blanc, une écharpe de satin blanc en sautoir, le tout orné d'un guipure d'argent que le soleil allumait. Avec ça, crânement, pour ressembler davantage à un jockey, elle s'était posé une toque bleue à plume blanche sur son chignon, dont les mèches jaunes lui coulaient au milieu du dos, pareilles à une énorme queue de poils roux." – *Nana*, pp. 345–46/II, p. 120.

22   "Après s'être passé du cold-cream avec la main sur les bras et sur la figure, elle étalait le blanc gras, à l'aide d'un coin de serviette. Un instant, elle cessa de se regarder dans la glace, elle sourit en glissant un regard vers le prince, sans lâcher le blanc gras.

. . .

"Cette fois, Nana ne se retourna point. Elle avait pris la patte de lièvre, elle la promenait légèrement, très attentive, si cambrée au-dessus de la toilette, que la rondeur blanche de son pantalon saillait et se tendait, avec le petit bout de chemise . . .

". . . elle eut un rire aimable, elle se tourna une seconde, la joue gauche très blanche, au milieu d'un nuage de poudre. Puis, elle devint subitement sérieuse; il s'agissait de mettre le rouge. De nouveau, le visage près de la glace, elle trempait son doigt dans un pot, elle appliquait le rouge sous les yeux, l'étalait doucement, jusqu'à la temple. Ces messieurs se taisaient, respectueux.

"Le comte Muffat n'avait pas encore ouvert les lèvres. Il songeait invinciblement à sa jeunesse. Sa chambre d'enfant . . . Et, brusquement, on le jetait dans cette loge d'actrice, devant cette fille nue. Lui qui n'avait jamais vu la comtesse Muffat mettre ses jarretières, il assistait aux détails intimes d'une toilette de femme, dans la débandade des pots et des cuvettes, au milieu de cette odeur si forte et si douce . . .

. . .

"Elle avait trempé le pinceau dans un pot de noir; puis, le nez sur la glace, fermant l'oeil gauche, elle le passa délicatement entre les cils. Muffat, derrière elle, regardait. Il la voyait dans la glace, avec ses épaules rondes et sa gorge noyée d'une ombre rose. . . . Lorsqu'elle ferma l'oeil droit et qu'elle passa le pinceau, il comprit qu'il lui appartenait.

. . .

"Maintenant, sa figure et ses bras étaient faits. Elle ajouta, avec le doigt, deux larges traits de carmin sur ses lèvres. Le comte Muffat se sentait plus troublé encore, séduit par la perversion des poudres et des fards, pris du désir déreglé de cette jeunesse peinte, la bouche trop rouge dans la face trop blanche, les yeux agrandis, cerclés de noir . . . Cependant, Nana passa un instant derrière le rideau pour enfiler le maillot de Vénus, après avoir ôté son pantalon. Puis, tranquille d'impudeur, elle vint déboutonner son petit corsage de percale, entendant les bras à madame Jules, qui lui passa les courtes manches de la tunique" – *Nana*, pp. 154–57/1, pp. 159–63.

23 There were those who ranked Manet with the literary naturalists, such as Jules de Marthold, who compared him to Balzac and Flaubert in *La Vie Moderne*, April 15, 1879; cited in Cachin, *Manet 1832–1883*, p. 394.

24 In the twenty-eighth issue of *La Vie Moderne*, there was a great fanfare about the serialized appearance of Zola's *Nana* in *Le Voltaire*: "*Nana* sera et doit être un énorme succès. Le roman a pour lui d'être attendu depuis deux ans et annoncé par les prophètes . . . du naturalisme. Jamais livre ne fut plus désiré, plus demandé, plus surveillé" – Jean Sapan, "Nana," *La Vie Moderne* 28, October 18, 1879. Surely Manet was one such "prophet of naturalism," having exhibited his *Nana* exactly two years before. On Manet's exhibition at La Vie Moderne, see my "Facturing Femininity: Manet's Before the Mirror," *October* 74, Fall 1995, pp. 74–104. A complete list of the works, ten oils and fifteen pastels, that Manet showed at La Vie Moderne appears in the April 10, 1880 issue of the journal, p. 239:

PEINTURE A L'HUILE

1   Portrait de M. D.***, avocat.
2   Café-Concert.
3   Coin de Café-Concert.
4   La Prune.
5   Le peintre Claude Monet dans son atelier.
6   Un Skating.
7   Portrait de M. B***.
8   Devant la glace.
9   Fleurs (étude décorative).
10 La Lecture.

PASTELS

11 Portrait de Mme E. Z***.
12 ″   de Mme du P***.
13 ″   de Mlle L.
14 ″   de M. C. G.
15 ″   de M. G. M.
16 La Toilette.
17 Le Tricot.
18 Etude.
19 Tête de femme.
20 Tête de femme.
21 Etudes.
22 Le Buveur.
23 Les Buveurs de bocks.
24 Le Skating.
25 Etude de femme.

25 La Vie Moderne was also Renoir's gallery and briefly set itself up as an alternative exhibition space for members of the Impressionist group. See Michel Robida, *Le Salon Charpentier et les impressionnistes*, Paris, Bibliothèque des Arts, 1958. Georges Charpentier, the son of Gautier's publisher Gervais Charpentier, tied to the world of *haut-monde* salons through his wife, and experienced in the publication of journals as well as of the novels of Zola, Maupassant, Daudet, and others, first became interested in the Impressionists through Renoir, from whom he bought a painting in 1875. Both the journal *La Vie Moderne* and the gallery attached to it (in the entrance to the Passage des Princes, near the Boulevard des Italiens) were created to provide more substantial support for Renoir and his friends than simply buying a picture here and there. Manet's exhibition in the Spring of 1880 was preceded by one-man shows by Giuseppe de Nittis and Renoir, and followed by shows of Monet's and Sisley's works. See also Rewald, *History of Impressionism*, pp. 382–84, 440.

26 "Un journal qui par ce double renseignement, texte et dessins, fasse assister à tous les évènements de la vie moderne, l'initie à tous les progrès de l'art, l'intéresse à toutes les phases de son evolution, lui donne dans son fauteuil le spectacle de toutes les découvertes de la science, celui des fluctuations des usages et des moeurs,

et qui ne néglige dans son exploration universelle que le monde discordant de la politique" – Emile Bergerat, "Notre programme," *La Vie Moderne*, April 10, 1879, no. 1.

27 "si quelque philosophe des Folies-Bergère vient encore nous dire que la famille est morte"; "Peut-être est-il temps aussi de démontrer que toutes les femmes élégantes ne sont pas nécessairement des aventurières, toutes les grandes dames des gourgandines, et que l'amour de l'intérieur n'est pas l'apanage exclusif des classes pauvres" – *ibid.*

28 "Je sais des gens qui voudraient que l'on pût exposer au Salon une robe, un tapis, un meuble, et qu'un jury leur affectât des médailles. Donc, nous en agirons sur cette donnée, et nous suivrons fidèlement le mouvement de l'art industriel sur la route du progrès où l'Exposition universelle semble l'avoir lancé.

"*La Vie Moderne* mentirait à son nom si elle négligeait, j'imagine, d'entretenir régulièrement ses lecteurs de l'extension de cette passion caractéristique pour les bibelots qui est un des signes du temps" – *ibid.*

29 *La Vie Moderne*, April 24, 1880, no. 17.

30 On June 12, 1880, no. 24, d'Orsay's "Gazette du Chic" addressed itself to new editions of Barbey d'Aurevilly's "Du Dandyisme et de G. Brummel."

31 "C'est le temps des soirées intimes et des sauteries en familles, préludes des grandes fêtes de l'hiver. On est entre soi et la toilette de bal est rigoureusement proscrit; tout au plus une demi-toilette est-elle tolérée. Je vous conseille, Mesdames, pour ces réunions, un habillement d'un goût charmant, d'une grâce parfaite et qui participe à la fois de l'été qui nous quitte et de l'hiver qui nous menace. C'est une robe en mousseline de l'Inde, souple, solide et légère en même temps, relevée par des noeuds en ruban de satin blanc. C'est avec cette étoffe d'ailleurs que se confectionnent en ce moment les plus jolies toilettes de mariées. – La mousseline de l'Inde blanche s'associe merveilleusement à la dentelle et sert à faire valoir sa transparence et sa légèrté; quelques noeuds de satin, jetant leur éclat vif de ci de là sur le ton mat de cette toilette, la complètent admirablement.

"Pour vos emplettes d'hiver, Mesdames, je vous signale *le Comptoir des Indes*, maison Bizé, 45, ave. de l'Opéra, une série de nouveaux tissus qui sont ce qu'on peut imaginer de plus charmant: le *Drap du Thibet*, par exemple, tissé en cinq nuances diverses, et dont l'assemblage donne une étoffe d'une curieuse et séduisante fantaisie, forte, souple et chaude; le *Pastou*, à carreaux grecs en soie sur fond de laine, dont les broderies claires et brillantes, s'enlevant sur le ton mat de la laine, ont un incomparable éclat; des tissus lamés d'or, d'une grande richesse, couverts de dessins chinois en soie avec or ou argent, dont on peut faire à son gré des corsages, des garnitures de robes et des sorties de bal; des variétés innombrables et nouvelles de *Cachemires de l'Inde* unis, et un tissu d'un nouveau genre, dit *Peluche hongroise*, qui rappelle la loutre à s'y méprendre et qu'on pourra employer comme la fourrure pour corsage, veste et manteau et comme garniture de costume" – *La Vie Moderne*, 1880, p. 639.

32 "Cette année, comme les précédentes, on a fait dans les magasins du *Printemps* provision de merveilles, et je vous annonce pour le lundi 8 novembre prochain une exposition de robes et de manteaux pour dames et enfants qui dépassera dans le genre tout ce qu'on a vu jusqu'ici de plus attirant, et réunira les spécimens les plus variés et les plus charmants que la mode ait imaginé.

"On sait que, pour l'élégance de ses modèles, la richesse, la variété, la solidité de ses tissus, le *Printemps* est depuis longtemps à peu près sans rival. J'ai vu hier dans ses rayons des étoffes de soie et de velours dont la qualité et le bon marché m'ont paru défier toute concurrence. Nos charmantes lectrices trouveront là de quoi s'achalender de tout ce que leur imagination a pu rêver de plus séduisant, à un prix qui satisfera certainement les plus parcimonieuses et les plus sages" – "Gazette du Chic," *La Vie Moderne* 45, Nov. 6, 1880, p. 719.

33 A good representative of the discourse on women's spending is Octave Uzanne's pseudosociological, Rococo-*galant* tome, *Parisiennes de ce temps en leurs divers milieux, états et conditions: études pour servir à l'histoire des femmes, de la société, de la galanterie française, des moeurs contemporaines et de l'égoisme masculin: ménagères, ouvrières et courtisanes, bourgeoises et mondaines, artistes et comédiennes*, Paris, Mercure de France, 1910. (This book summarizes earlier work done in the 1880s and '90s, such as *La Française du siècle: modes, moeurs, usages*, Paris, A. Quantin, 1886; and *Les Modes de Paris. Fashion in Paris: the various phases of feminine taste and aesthetics from 1797 to 1897*, Lady Mary Loyd, trans., London, W. Heinemann, and New York, C. Scribner's Sons, 1898.)

34 Gustave Goetschy, "Edouard Manet," *La Vie Moderne*, April 17, 1880, no. 16.

35 On graphic codes, see William Ivins, *Prints and Visual Communication*, London, Routledge and Kegan Paul, 1953; and Estelle Jussim, *Visual Communication and the Graphic Arts: Photographic Technologies in the Nineteenth Century*, New York, R. R. Bowker, 1974. See also Higonnet, "Feminine Visual Culture in the Age of Mechanical Reproduction," *Berthe Morisot's Images of Women*, pp. 84–122.

36 From the 1860s to the 1880s a caricatured version of the style of Baudelaire's modern artist, with its loose, quick notation and its exaggeration of dress and bodily features, was the standard graphic code of journals with a satirical or libertine edge to them, such as *La Vie Parisienne*, which was clearly aimed at men as much as, if not more than, women. Despite its devotion to a variety of print styles, *La Vie Moderne* tended to stay clear of the graphic exaggeration that characterized such magazines. For Baudelaire's views on the art of modern caricature, see his essays, "De L'Essence de Rire," "Quelques Caricaturistes Français," and "Quelques Caricaturistes Etrangers," in *Ecrits esthétiques*, pp. 188–242.

37 On November 20, 1880, no. 47, *La Vie Moderne* began an international "Revue des journaux illustrés" that continued in several issues thereafter.

38 It has been assumed that *The Reader* (*La Lecture*) that was shown at La Vie Moderne was the earlier portrait of Manet's wife Suzanne being read to by her son. I am inclined to think that it must have been *Woman Reading (Reading the Illustrated Magazine)* instead, because that was a more recent work (and it was all recent works that Manet showed otherwise), because it was part of the larger café thematics that Manet put on display at the gallery, and because of its focus on an illustrated magazine. Its loose facture might disqualify it – except that Manet showed at least one other painting done in the same manner at La Vie Moderne, along with a variety of pastels. Manet clearly felt that a much greater factural license was warranted in such a setting than at the Salon. Cachin, *Manet 1832–1883*, includes *Woman Reading* as one of the works shown at La Vie Moderne in its list of exhibitions at the end of the catalogue (p. 534), though it does not mention it in its entry on the painting (pp. 423–24).

39 On the *consommations* (coffee, beer, cigarettes, brandy, absinthe, and so on) bought and consumed in cafés and brasseries such as the ones represented by Manet, see Herbert, *Impressionism*, pp. 65–76. On Manet's paintings of the *brasseries à femmes* shown at La Vie Moderne, see Clayson, *Painted Love*, pp. 142–47.

40 See Cachin, *Manet 1832–1883*, p. 424, for a summary of the different views of the background of *The Reader*. Tabarant, *Manet et ses oeuvres*, p. 327, sees a mirror; Anne Coffin Hanson, *Edouard Manet 1832–1883*, Philadelphia Museum of Art, 1966, p. 173, sees a window opening onto a garden; and Theodore Reff, *Manet and Modern Paris*, Washington, D.C., National Gallery of Art, 1982, no. 22, sees a painting or wallpaper.

41 It is noteworthy that Manet was interested in the illusionism of marble and newspaper, given the later exploration of the boundary lines between the illusionisms and literalisms of exactly those materials in Cubist collage, with its established place in the lineage of modernism: as in Cubist collage, Manet's address to still-life illusionism in these and slightly later paintings is more complicated than the flattening and literalizing trajectory that Greenberg's modernism would suggest. But, typically, in his own more specific address to Cubist collage, Greenberg himself proposed a more complex reading than was his wont in his overarching articulations of the modernist teleology: see Greenberg, "The Pasted-Paper Revolution" (1958), in *Collected Essays and Criticism*, vol. 4, pp. 61–66; revised, simplified, and reissued as "Collage" in Clement Greenberg, *Art and Culture: Critical Essays*, Boston, Beacon Press, 1961, pp. 70–83.

42 The model for the figure in *Woman Reading* is supposed to have been a well-known café and brasserie habituée named Trognette, while it has been speculated (and denied) that the model for *Plum Brandy* was Ellen Andrée (who also modeled for Degas's similar *Absinthe Drinker*), and that the decor might or might not suggest the setting of the Nouvelle-Athènes, frequented by the Impressionist group – see Moreau-Nélaton, *Manet raconté par lui-même*, vol. 2, p. 53; Reff, *Manet and Modern Paris*, no. 18; and A. Tabarant, *Manet: Histoire catalographique*, Paris, Editions Montaigne, 1931, p. 341; cited in Cachin, *Manet 1832–1883*, pp. 407–09; 423–24.

43 On the reviews of *Before the Mirror* and *Woman Fastening Her Garter*, see Clayson, *Painted Love*, pp. 75–79.

44 "L'une, la *Toilette*, représentant une femme décolletée, avançant sur la sortie de sa poitraille,

un sommet de chignon et un bout de pif, tandis qu'elle attache une jarretière sur un bas bleu, fleure à plein nez la prostituée qui nous est chère. Envelopper ses personnages de la senteur de monde auquel ils appartient, telle a été une des plus constantes préoccupations de M. Manet.

Son oeuvre claire, débarbouillée des terres de momie et des jus de pipes qui ont crassé si longtemps les toiles, a une touche souvent câline, sous son apparence bravache, un dessin concisé mais titubant, un bouquet de taches vives dans une peinture argentine et blonde." – J. K. Huysmans, "Salon de 1880," *L'Art moderne* (1883), in *L'Art Moderne/Certains*, ed. Hubert Juin, Paris, Union Générale d'Editions, 1973, p. 150; second paragraph cited in Cachin, *Manet*, p. 391.

45 On the theme of visual possession, see Leo Steinberg, "The Algerian Women and Picasso at Large," *Other Criteria*, Oxford University Press, 1972, pp. 125–234, esp. "Drawing as if to Possess," pp. 174–92.

46 This suggests the options of "visual pleasure" versus "narrative" articulated by Mulvey in "Visual Pleasure and Narrative Cinema."

47 See Gombrich, *Art and Illusion*, p. 5, on the impossibility of simultaneously perceiving two illusions, or an illusion and its literal support, at once, which he illustrates with the example of the rabbit–duck drawing.

48 Both *Nana* and *Before the Mirror* remained in Manet's studio until his death and the posthumous sale of his works, at which time they were acquired by the same man, Dr. Albert Robin, who lived in Manet's apartment building, so that for a time they existed as companion pieces.

49 On the "bachelor"'s cooptation and deconstruction of "the term 'woman'," see my "Warriors, Bachelors, Artists, and Other Women," in *Raritan* 19 : 4, Spring 2000, pp. 123–47, where I argue that such deconstruction was only possible for the male artist, and not for the female artist, in the nineteenth century. Aside from deeming "identification" with femininity a psychic impossibility for the male subject (a view that I do not share), many feminists will have difficulty with precisely this limitation in the historical field of gender: with the male subject's power – and the female subject's powerlessness – to determine, appropriate, play with, and even disrupt the discursive value of femininity, with no real consequences for either sex. That is, in my view, simply an historical fact with which there is no arguing, but for

me it does not negate or undermine the interest of practices like Manet's (or Baudelaire's, for example) that suggest a complex and indeterminate relationship between the values of masculinity and femininity, and therefore a destabilizing, denaturalizing, and opening up of the discursive structure of gender difference, which permit modes of identification impossible in more fixed (i.e. Freudian) gender scenarios.

50 See Higonnet, "Painting Women," and "Mirrored Bodies," in *Berthe Morisot's Images of Women*, pp. 123–94, on *Woman at Her Toilette* and the suite of paintings related to it. Other (male) painters with whom Manet was in contact who painted the subject of the woman at her toilette in the same period include Degas and Alfred Stevens: Manet entered into dialogue with their variations as well.

51 "Mme Berthe Morisot est Française par la distinction, l'élégance, la gaieté, l'insousiance; elle aime la peinture réjouissante et remuante; elle broie sur sa palette des pétales de fleurs, pour les étaler ensuite sur la toile en touches spirituelles, soufflées, jetées un peu au hasard, qui s'accordent, se combinent et finissent par produire quelque chose de fin, de vif et de charmant qu'on devine plutôt qu'on ne le voit . . . De jeunes femmes bercées dans une barque . . . celle-là à sa toilette sont vues toutes à travers des tons gris fins, blancs mats et rose clair sans aucune ombre, relevées de petites taches multicolores, l'ensemble donnant l'impression de teintes opalines vagues et incertaines. Cette légèreté fugitive, cette vivacité aimable, pétillante et frivole rappellent Fragonard, moins la science profonde, la solidité de la pâte et cette lumière diffuse qui donne au tableau du maître tant d'homogénéité." – Charles Ephrussi, "Exposition des artistes indépendantes," *Gazette des Beaux-Arts*, May 1, 1880, p. 487; cited in Moffett, *The New Painting*, p. 327. On gender as a critical category used to classify women's art, see Anne Higonnet, "Imaging Gender," in Orwicz, *Art Criticism and Its Institutions*, pp. 146–61; and Tamar Garb, " 'L'Art Féminin'," pp. 39–65.

52 This picture might have involved a visit to the shop of a specific milliner, one Mme Virot on the Rue de la Paix, to which Manet went to complete an outfit for Jeanne Demarsy, for the painting *Spring* – see Cachin, *Manet 1832–1883*, pp. 484–86.

53 See Jacques Lacan, "Dieu et la jouissance de la femme," *Le Seminaire XX Encore*, Paris, Seuil,

1975, pp. 61–71, for his discussion of femininity and feminine "jouissance" as an excess ("*au-delà du phallus* – p. 69) rather than the opposite of masculinity.

TEN   FINALE

1   That Grim Reaper in a top hat picks up a long attraction to the uncanny (found most particularly in the *punctum* of his female figures' gazes) and gives it a new resonance. In this sense, the figure that intrudes in the reflection of the *Bar at the Folies-Bergère* may be understood as a making visible of the invisible presences that Wollheim detects in the blank backgrounds of Manet's early works ("The spectator in the picture: Friedrich, Manet, Hals"). At the same time, the death's-head look of that figure also may be said to allegorize the "necromancy" of commodity culture, its freezing of life and congealing of human desire in the image of the dead thing, and conversely, its phantasmatic animation of the inanimate object. See Marx, "Commodities and Money," *Capital* I, in *The Marx-Engels Reader*, 302–29, esp. p. 324; and Debord, *Society of the Spectacle*, p. 12: "The spectacle in its generality is a concrete inversion of life, and, as such, the autonomous movement of non-life."

2   Manet showed these still lifes in an 1865 show at Martinet's, as well as in the 1867 retrospective, and then at La Vie Moderne he included a few florals. For the most part, however, his still lifes were not made for exhibition, though unlike much of the work that Manet did do for exhibition (such as the *Olympia*), they found admirers and sometimes purchasers fairly readily. See Ernest Chesneau, "Salon de 1865: Les excentriques," *Le Constitutionnel*, 16 May 1865, cited in Eric Darragon, *Manet*, Paris, Fayard, 1989, pp. 106–07: "Il est tels ouvrages de M. Manet aperçus à une exposition du boulevard des Italiens . . . des tableaux de nature inanimées où l'artiste avait jeté des fruits et des poissons sur des nappes d'un blanc éclatant, des études de pivoines encore, qui révélaient des qualités pittoresques incontestables."

3   One other painter was interested in market and shop still lifes during the period in which Manet was at work on the *Bar at the Folies-Bergère*: Caillebotte's still lifes of 1880–82 represent produce at a fruit stall (*Fruits à l'étalage*, Boston Museum of Fine Arts) and a butcher's display of poultry and game (*Nature morte –*

poulets, gibiers à l'étalage, Paris, private collection), among other things, and suggest an even more sustained attention to the commodification and marketplace context of still-life objects, if not a direct dialogue with Manet's work, borne out by Caillebotte's *Melon and Compotier of Figs* (Paris, private collection), which looks back to Manet's 1864 fruit pieces and sideways to his closed melon(s) of 1880. (That dialogue appears to have been a two-way street, as evidenced by Manet's reference to Caillebotte's *In a Café* of 1880 – Musée des Beaux Arts, Rouen – in the *Bar at the Folies-Bergère*, which picks up on the mirror, countertop, and frontal figure of the former painting; for its part *In a Café* had already taken up the theme and pose of Manet's *Luncheon in the Studio* and set it in a public café context. Both the fruit-vendor still life and *In a Café* were shown in Impressionist shows, those of 1880 and 1882, respectively.) But unlike Manet's painting, Caillebotte's still lifes of these years represent a familiar, far from modern marketplace (going back at least to sixteenth- and seventeenth-century Northern painting) and remain tied to the corporeality of consumption in their adherence to the round of butchery and buying, the preparing and eating of food. These still lifes by Caillebotte do suggest a tie to Zola's *Le Ventre de Paris* of the previous decade (1872), with its vivid descriptions of butcher shops and vegetable stands in the larger context of *Les Halles* and its painterly rendition of the character Claude's coloristic perception of those displays. (Evidently, Manet was interested in that novel as well, given his desire at the end of the '70s to paint the subject of Les Halles.)

4   I am indebted to Jeannene Pryzlbyski, *The Art of the Table: French Still-life Painting 1850–1880*, Ph.D. dissertation, University of California, Berkeley, 1994: many of my ideas about the still-life zone of the *Bar at the Folies-Bergère* were developed and expanded in the discussions and consultation that surrounded the genesis of this dissertation. See also Rubin, *Manet's Silence and the Poetics of Bouquets*; Bryson, *Looking at the Overlooked*; Gabriel Weisberg, *Chardin and the Still-life Tradition in France*, Cleveland Museum of Art, 1979; and John McCoubrey, "The Revival of Chardin in French Still-Life Painting, 1850–1870," *Art Bulletin*, March 1964, pp. 39–53.

5   In 1864 Manet painted a whole series of fruit studies, which together move between the poles of reduced simplicity – two apples, two pears –

and expansive bounty, as in the *Still Life with Melon and Almonds* (private collection). In these works, Manet returns repeatedly to the Chardinian basket of fruit, making him one of the prime participants in the "Chardin revival" of this era. On "handwriting" and the "purely plastic significance of still-life," see Fry, *Cézanne*, pp. 38–54, in which nine pages are devoted to a single still life, Cézanne's 1880 *Compotier, Glass, and Apples*: "In still life the ideas and emotions associated with the objects represented are, for the most part so utterly commonplace and insignificant that neither artist nor spectator need consider them. It is this fact that makes the still-life so valuable to the critic as a gauge of the artist's personality" (p. 41).

6 Manet returned to this theme in his late floral series, which includes a few paintings of pairs of strewn blossoms.

7 Another time he set it on a tablecloth with some pears against a decorative, wallpapered plane of wall. There is also another brioche still life, whose date and attribution are uncertain, in which the brioche is cut open on a plate atop a tablecloth with a projecting knife and a lemon unfurling a spiral of rind and peel, suggesting the eating of the still life with unusual forthrightness.

8 On Manet's late florals, see Gordon and Forge, *Last Flowers of Manet*.

9 That problematics was part of the heritage of still-life painting and its reception. And it is specific in its attachment to the Chardin revival, for ever since the eighteenth century Chardin's still lifes have been treated in terms of precisely this dialectic between transparency and frank handling, as exemplified in Diderot's "Salons" of 1761, 1763, and 1765 particularly, which move between inventorial lists of objects, as if the depicted things were there before the critic's eyes, with the air circulating about them, and a formalist appreciation of Chardin's colorist "faire." See Pierre Rosenberg, *Chardin* (Grand Palais, Royal Academy of Arts, Metropolitan Museum), London, Royal Academy, and Paris, Réunion des Musées Nationaux, 2000.

10 See Tabarant, *Manet, histoire catalographique*, p. 381; cited in Cachin, *Manet 1832–1883*, pp. 450–51.

11 See Roland Barthes, "World as Object," *Critical Essays* (Richard Howard, trans.), Evanston, Northwestern University Press, 1972, pp. 3–12. While in the beginning the lemon's status as a privileged item in still-life painting was conferred by the luxury value of real lemons, by the time Manet himself displayed it and other citrus in his own paintings, the lemon had become more commonplace: one of the things that this downsized painting of a single lemon announces is that the lemon is now a small affair. (Significantly, like the other single items, the lemon in the 14 × 21 cm *Lemon* is close to life size.)

12 My reading of the front zone of the *Bar at the Folies-Bergère* (as well as of its mirror) is entirely consistent with Meyer Schapiro's Marxist understanding of Impressionism as a reflection of the ideology of capital, in "The Nature of Abstract Art," pp. 192–93. I depart from that classic essay, on which I have depended, only in my pictorially specific sense of the painting's particularity about its own status as a commodity and its own difference from the world it represents. For the socio-cultural context of the *Bar at the Folies-Bergère's* treatment of commodity culture and use of contemporaneous advertisement strategies, see Ruth E. Iskin, "Selling, Seduction, and Soliciting the Eye: Manet's *Bar at the Folies-Bergère*," *Art Bulletin* LXXVII: 1, March 1995, pp. 25–44, which was not yet published when I first wrote the essay that led to this chapter, "Counter, Mirror, Maid: Some Infra-thin Notes on *A Bar at the Folies-Bergère*," in Bradford R. Collins, ed., *12 Views of Manet's Bar*, Princeton University Press, 1996.

13 I do not think these confusions have much pictorially to do with the thematics of class and prostitution that others have seen there, such as Clark, *Painting of Modern Life*, pp. 205–258, and Clayson, *Painted Love*, pp. 151–52. However, it does seem to me that Cachin's (*Manet 1832–1883*, p. 478) and Herbert's (*Impressionism*, p. 80) objections to the reading of the barmaid as a possible clandestine prostitute on the grounds that the Folies-Bergère was not such an establishment are easily answered by the libertine connotations of the phrase "philosopher of the Folies-Bergère," cited in the previous chapter, and by remembering the differences among actuality, perception, and representation to which the painting itself seems to point.

14 This was by no means Manet's only specular option, for as we have seen, he had taken up the problem of the mirror before in different ways. (Indeed, in *Before the Mirror* he might possibly have been suggesting a tilted mirror: that would account for its specular enigma, namely the high, upper left-hand corner

placement of the reflection.) It is true that Manet went to great lengths to set up the mirror in his studio, and it is on that basis that Thierry de Duve claims to have solved the famous riddle of the *Bar's* mirror in "How Manet's *Bar at the Folies-Bergère* Is Constructed," *Critical Inquiry* 25, Autumn 1998, pp. 136–68. It is also true that the sketch for the painting shows how deliberately the discrepancy between front plane and reflection must have been painted, and that the audience of the 1882 Salon noticed it, as witnessed in the caricature by Stop in *Le Journal Amusant*, which posits the missing gentleman to whom the reflection belongs directly between us the picture's spectators and the counter behind which the barmaid stands: "Son dos se reflet dans une glace; mais sans doute par suite d'une distraction du peintre, un monsieur avec lequel elle cause et dont on voit l'image dans la glace n'existe pas dans le tableau. – Nous croyons devoir réparer cette omission" – cited in Cachin, *Manet 1832–1883*, p. 481. None of these facts speaks interpretively to Manet's reasons for choosing to paint the mirror the way he did this time, however, or to the specular logic that is everywhere expressed in the canvas as the result of that decision, or, finally, to its relation to the commodity zone of the painting or to the figuration of femininity that interposes itself between mirror and counter.

15   See Greenberg, "The Role of Nature in Modern Painting" (1949), *Collected Essays and Criticism*, vol. 2, pp. 271–75, according to which "The paradox of French painting between Courbet and Cézanne is that . . . the medium['s] . . . claims – the limitations imposed by the flat surface, the canvas's shape, and the nature of the pigments – had to be accommodated to those of nature" (p. 272).

16   It is in this way that "Suzon" really does appear to be the "calicot" that Clark makes her out to be in *Painting of Modern Life*: that is, in resembling Denise and the others in *Au Bonheur des dames*, published in 1883, the year of Manet's death. Just as Zola's *Nana* was in preparation during the painting of *Nana*, so *Au Bonheur des dames* was in the offing while Manet was painting his picture.

17   See Herbert, *Impressionism*, p. 79: "Its evolution is another capsule history of Second Empire speculation. It began as a department store devoted to bedding, opened in 1860, one of the newer urban forms of commerce. Perhaps because of its favorable location on the rue Richer, just above the *grands boulevards*, it added a 'salle des spectacles' to the rear of the store in 1863. This was so successful . . . that in 1869 the whole enterprise shifted to variety shows in emulation of London music halls. In November 1871, the talented entrepreneur Léon Sari took it over. He remodeled it inside and out, refurbishing two large spaces. One was the 'Garden,' an impressive hall with balconies . . . The other, where Manet places us, was the horseshoe-shaped theater with fixed seats in the orchestra and a balcony above, supported on columns . . ." Of course, the painting is not actually an on-the-spot reflection of this space; Manet constructed his own false version of it in his studio. Still, the Folies-Bergère seems to have attracted Manet at least partly on account of the modernity of its form of commercial space. See Siegfried Giedion, *Space, Time, and Architecture*, 5th ed., Cambridge, Mass., Harvard University Press, 1967, pp. 234–43, for a relevant account of the open, interpenetrated spatiality of the department store and its functioning in the display of commodities. See also David Van Zanten, "Architectural Composition at the Ecole des Beaux-Arts from Charles Percier to Charles Garnier," in Arthur Drexler, ed., *The Architecture of the Ecole des Beaux-Arts*, New York, Museum of Modern Art, 1977, pp. 254–73 – on Charles Garnier's theorization of such spatiality in *Le Théâtre* (Paris, Hachette, 1871). The terms of that discussion are remarkably resonant for Manet's *Bar at the Folies-Bergère*.

18   See Clark, *Painting of Modern Life*, pp. 249–55, on the problem of the mirror and the relation between its "uncertainties" and the barmaid as "the face of the popular."

19   Indeed, the *Bar* coincides neatly with Greenberg's marvelous description of the duality of Cubist collage, some three decades after Manet's painting, in "The Pasted Paper Revolution" (1958), *Collected Essays and Criticism*, vol. 4, pp. 61–66: "The flatness of the surface permeates the illusion, and the illusion itself re-asserts the flatness. The effect is to fuse the illusion with the picture plane without derogation of either – in principle" (p. 63).

20   See Pollock, *Vision and Difference*, pp. 51–55, for whom the *Bar* embodies the masculinity of public space; and Clayson, *Painted Love*, pp. 151–52: "The familiar history of modernism emphasizes and admires ambiguity. In the argument I present here I opposed that pattern of admiration. Rather than serving to avoid the inscription of sexual attitudes, modernist indeterminacy has a vivid and pronounced sexual

politics, especially when prostitution is thematized. Rather than beclouding moral and sexual issues, illegibility helps to fix the morality and character of the women portrayed . . . Ambiguity constituted, then, a male sexual politics . . ."

21 The structure of the filmic gaze as described by Mulvey ("Visual Pleasure and Narrative Cinema") appears to be illustrated almost verbatim in the *Bar*; at the same time, I believe that one of the things the *Bar* does is to show how the very terms of that structure can exceed and disturb it – how, for instance, the fetishistic object of the gaze is potentially also a disturbance of the field of the gaze, particularly if it is not mastered, decided, and resolved in an identificatory narrative, as it is not in the *Bar*, whose flat frozenness and narrative ambiguity differentiate it from the narrative determinacy of classic cinema.

22 On Tissot, see Nancy Rose Marshall, *James Tissot: Victorian Life, Modern Love*, New Haven and London, Yale Center for British Art and Yale University Press, 1999. Whether the implied customer is male or female is, perhaps, a more open question than I have presented it here: the buying of feminine items might seem to suggest a female client; however, the come-hither quality of the shopgirl's glance together with the background echo of the flirtation between the girl at the window with her back to us and the male passerby in the street seem to implicate a masculine viewer. What that might suggest is a kind of double viewing situation, a picture which addresses itself, slightly differently, to both male and female spectators, but does so complicitously and easily rather than in the contrary, difficult manner of the equally double *Bar*.

23 See Paul Matisse, ed., *Marcel Duchamp Notes* (Anne d'Harnancourt, trans.), Boston, G. K. Hall, 1983, p. 9: these phrases describe Duchamp's elliptical "infra-thin." One might, in fact, associate the *Bar at Folies-Bergère* with Duchamp's "Large Glass," the famous *Bride Stripped Bare by her Bachelors, Even*, which like the *Bar* thematizes a relationship between male and female zones but does so in terms that refute the opticality shared by the *Bar* and Impressionist painting.

24 In this, the barmaid also opens up aspects of the gaze and the mirror, and onto questions of identification that are not specifically gendered – see Jacques Lacan, "The Mirror Stage as Formative of the Function of the I as Revealed in Psychoanalytic Experience," *Ecrits* (Alan Sheridan, trans.), New York, Norton, 1982, pp. 1–7.

25 Like many others, Zola had also emphasized the still-life aspect of Manet's work, as a way of talking about both its objective orientation and its subjective opticality. What the barmaid does, then, is to put together the two opposed terms – the phantasmatic and the positivistic – of Zola's description of Manet's character as a painter and show how one structures and disturbs the other.

26 When I saw it again at the Courtauld in London recently, I was struck by how relatively small the *Bar at the Folies-Bergère* seemed to be, for all its splendor and complexity; certainly its 96 × 130 cm dimensions give its front plane figure much less than the life-size effect of many of Manet's larger canvases, particularly of his single-figure paintings.

27 On "le tout ensemble," and with it the values of the instantaneous "coup d'oeil" and the autonomy of the "fully realized tableau," which link classical art theory to that of transcendental formalism, see Puttfarken, *Roger de Piles' Theory of Art*, pp. 80–105; and Fried, *Absorption and Theatricality*, pp. 82–104. In a sense, the aim of this book has been to show how Manet's peculiar modernism represents a fundamental fissuring of those values.

28 I am inclined to think that it is that division of an essentially double manner into two separate, single ones, rather than the quality of either style per se, that accounts for the uncertain quality of Manet's production during the 1870s, which Greenberg judged so severely in "Manet in Philadelphia." Thus, while I concur with the judgment that the work of the 1870s is of lesser quality, I find myself fundamentally at odds with the reasons for that judgment, which for Greenberg have to do with the failure of the paintings of that period to achieve what he sees as the powerful singularity and unity of the best '60s work. The proof of the pudding for me lies in the fact that it is precisely the *Bar's* duality that allows it to re-attain the compelling (yet estranging) effect of Manet's first decade.

AFTERWORD   TO YOU, EDOUARD MANET

1 "Tout le monde a su faire le portrait de Manet: il était très connu" – Darragon, *Manet*, i. Darragon's comprehensive biography is superb, the best of the recent contributions to the already long list of Manet biographies dating back to Zola, which includes: E. Bazire, *Manet*,

Paris, 1884; Théodore Duret, *Histoire d'Edouard Manet et de son oeuvre*, Paris, 1902; Antonin Proust, *Edouard Manet, souvenirs*, Paris, 1913; Jacques-Emile Blanche, *Manet*, Paris, 1924; E. Moreau-Nélaton, *Manet raconté par lui-même*, Paris, 1926, 2 vols; A. Tabarant, *Manet et ses oeuvres*, Paris, 1947; P. Courthion and P. Cailler, *Manet raconté par lui-même et par ses amis*, Geneva, 1953, 2 vols; Georges Bataille, *Manet*, Lausanne, 1955; Henri Perruchot, *La vie de Manet*, Paris, Hachette, 1959; Pierre Daix, *La vie de peintre d'Edouard Manet*, Paris, 1983; Beth Archer Brombert, *Edouard Manet, Rebel in a Frock Coat*, University of Chicago Press, 1996. But of all of those Darragon's is the most intelligent in its understanding of the critical relationship between Manet's painting and social life, brilliantly sketching out what might be the aesthetic consequences of his narrative, which is moving about Manet's predicament without being maudlin or clichéd, and which gathers a host of documents without merely parroting the old myths and anecdotes. And rather than seeing the painting as a reflection of the life, Darragon treats painting and life as involved in a complex dialogue with each other. It happens that I did not discover this biography until the end of writing this book, but its sense of Manet the gentleman painter who never intended to be and never got over being the *refusé* of 1863, who confronted his entrance into "history" reluctantly, and who despite his reputation as the head of the school of Impressionism and the father of modernism, had no real artistic progeny, tallies with my interpretive sense of the paintings on almost all counts: Manet as late-coming Romantic; Manet as the indicator of the *surréal* within the real; Manet as the painter of pairs and groups of pictures in complex, often antipathetic conversation with each other; Manet's "sense de l'antithèse" (p. 410) and "démon du contraste" (p. 431); the importance of women to Manet; and so on.

2   "Devant Tortoni, au milieu d'un bouquet de journalistes, de 5 à 6 heures, on peut voir M. Manet. C'est une des gloires du café . . . Le monsieur qui passe avec sa femme s'arrête, lui montre le comsommateur blond de Tortoni et lui dit: 'Tiens, Euphrasie, voilà monsieur Manet.' Ce à quoi la femme répond: 'Pas possible! je me l'étais figuré avec une vareuse rouge, un béret et une pipe culottée.'

"Eh bien! non, madame! M. Manet ne se promène point avec une casquette de loutre, comme l'homme du *Bon Bock*; c'est bien l'élégant cavalier que vous avez sous les yeux, d'une taille juste, assez élevée pour que le peintre ne soit ni trop grand ni trop petit. Tenue irréprochable comme vous voyez; spécialité de cravates étonnantes. La tête est à la fois énergique et douce; les yeux d'un bleu limpide comme la Méditerranée quand il fait du soleil; barbe et chevelure blondes; le teint d'une tonalité fine qui tenterait un coloriste. Vélasquez l'eût prié de poser dans son atelier. Tel, Madame, est M. Manet; et pour vous édifier complètement sur sa personne, j'ajouterai que c'est un charmant garçon, de moeurs très douces sous des dehors cassants, un parfait *gentleman* en un mot, dont on aimerait à admirer la peinture . . . sans réserve . . . Mais . . ." – Albert Wolff, *Le Gaulois*, 15 April 1874; cited in Darragon, *Manet*, pp. 279–80. In 1877, Manet attempted to solidify his relationship with Wolff by painting his portrait (Guggenheim). Wolff disliked the portrait and discontinued sittings, so Manet never completed it.

3   Two years later, at the time of Manet's studio exhibition of 1876, another description of him (and his studio) appeared in *Le Gaulois*: "Connaissez-vous Édouard Manet? C'est le paradoxe incarné lui-même. Je ne sais à Paris ni un homme de plus d'esprit, ni un plus galant homme . . . Dandy de réalisme plutôt que réaliste, rien, hors son esprit délié et ses manières excellentes, ne le distingue de ses confrères de la palette ou de ses anciens camarades du collège Rollin où il fit ses études. Il est de taille moyenne, carré d'épaules, la figure pâle, incorrecte et trouée de deux yeux ronds fort vifs, avec une barbe fauve et des cheveux ardents qui jettent des rayons tout autour. D'ailleurs point de révolte en sa démarche, d'extravagance dans sa mise, de sacerdoce en son allure" – Junius, M. Édouard Manet," *Le Gaulois*, 25 April 1876; cited in Darragon, Manet, p. 264.

Because of his studio exhibition in 1876, many were able to picture his atelier at this time too, and did so in terms remarkably similar to those in which his appearance was described, emphasizing the disconnection between the radicalism of his paintings and the propriety of his person. Thus the *pompier* painter Gérôme wrote: "Je suis allé chez M. Manet. Son atelier est grand, bien éclairé, le plafond est à poutres en saillie, comme dans les loges du Moyen Age ou de la Renaissance; les poutres, peintes en brun, sont relevées de légers ornements en or. C'est l'atelier le plus propre et le mieux rangé qu'on puisse voir. Il ne sent pas du tout la révolution. Il est doux et tranquille à l'oeil comme

M. Manet lui-même, qui est des peintres les moins rébarbatifs dans leur extérieur et les plus corrects dans leur tenue que je connaisse. Quoi! ce monsieur aux traits fins, au regard pacifique, à la barbe blonde et soignée, ce monsieur vêtu de noir, bien brossé, bien chaussée, bien ganté, c'est l'auteur des *Canotiers*. Mon Dieu, oui; vous ne pouvez le croire, eh bien! je vous assure que c'est lui, lui et point un autre!" – Gérôme, "Courrier de Paris," *L'Univers illustré*, 13 May 1876; cited in Darragon, *Manet*, p. 263.

4   In 1879, Paul Alexis remembered Manet enframed by women: "Les élégances dont il est entouré donnent à ses yeux vifs et profonds plus de flamme juvénile. Sa lèvre, mobile et moqueuse, a des bonheurs d'attitude en confessant des Parisiennes. Les deux longues pointes effilées de sa barbe châtain clair battent l'atmosphère embaumée comme deux rames. Et les narines de son nez finement irrégulier se dilatent: il sourit! il est heureux! C'est qu'il vient de décocher quelque pénétrante malice. Amabilité, esprit, politesse, le tout pimenté d'un originalité né dans l'air libre de l'atelier, voilà l'homme. Une personne qui l'aime et lui touche de près me le dépaignait l'autre soir en trois mots: 'Un grand enfant!'" – Paul Alexis, *Le Voltaire*, 25 July, 1879; cited in Darragon, Manet, p. 319.

5   On this subject, see Amelia Jones, "'Clothes Make the Man': The Male Artist as a Performative Function," *Oxford Art Journal* 18, no. 2 (1995), pp. 18–32.

6   "A cette époque Edouard Manet était de taille moyenne, fortement musclé. Il avait une allure rythmée à laquelle le déhanchement de sa démarche imprimait un caractère de particulière élégance. Quelque effort qu'il fît en exagérant ce déhanchement et en affectant le parler traînant du gamin de Paris, il ne pouvait parvenir à être vulgaire. On le sentait de race.

"Sous un front large, le nez dessinait franchement sa ligne droite. La bouche, relevée aux extrémités, était railleuse. Il avait le regard clair. L'oeil était petit, mais d'une grande mobilité. Très jeune, il rejetait en arrière une chevelure longue qui frisait naturellement. A dix-huit ans, le front s'etait déjà dégarni, mais la barbe avait poussé. Par elle, le bas de la figure s'était fait plus doux, tandis que les cheveux d'une finesse extrême harmonisaient le haut du visage. Peu d'hommes ont été aussi séduisants" – Proust, *Manet, souvenirs*, p. 15.

7   It is worth remarking here on the changes in the function and definition of the portrait. Where portraiture of the Ancien Régime in France and elsewhere was more often than not a commissioned, public affair involving the commonly recognized likenesses of public individuals, proving their social and cultural status, advertising their attributes and contributing to the maintenance, circulation, and reproduction of power – in other words, the portrait was literally public currency – portraiture in the bourgeois age was as much a matter of the private as the public person, and tended more and more to isolate the individual qua individual, as a private, biologically and psychologically defined self: hence the artist's portraits of intimates either unknown to others (and often unnamed and anonymous when exhibited) or known only to a relatively restricted and specialized circle; hence also the tendency for portraitists to be self-portraitists as well. The fact that Manet declined to represent himself much, then, is only peculiar in the post-revolutionary age; it would not have been remarkable in Velasquez's time, for example. Nor would it have been remarkable had Manet not been so interested in portraits of private (as well as public) people, and in interrogating and undermining the internal unity of personhood and continuity of identity upon which the private portrait rests, as if to stress the definitional instability that actually lies at the heart of tautological concepts like "identity," which the Oxford English Dictionary defines in the following somewhat contradictory ways: "That which in a person is really and intrinsically *he*"; "a permanent subject of successive and varying states of consciousness"; "What one is at a particular time or in a particular aspect or relation"; "one's nature, character, or physical constitution or appearance, considered as different at different times"; and "An assemblage of characteristics or dispositions which may be conceived as constituting one of various conflicting personalities within a human being." On the modern portrait, see Tony Halliday, *Portraiture in the Aftermath of the French Revolution*, Manchester University Press, 2000; Melissa McQuillan, *Impressionist Portraits*, London, Thames and Hudson, 1986; and George Shackleford, *A Magic Mirror: The Portrait in France, 1700–1900*, Houston, The Museum of Fine Arts, 1986.

8   It is relevant to note that there is a certain gender logic to the masquerade, as presented in the *Masked Ball at the Opera*, in which the women are characterized through the brightly colored costumes that they wear – that which

9 With regard to Proust's portrait and its public function for Manet, it was painted in a period in which Manet painted several portraits of public men, notably Georges Clemenceau (1879–80) and Henri Rochefort (1881), no doubt hoping thereby to position himself anew as a Salon painter with a public reputation (which he sought, inconsistently, now to modify and now to exacerbate).

10 In April of 1880, before the Salon, when Manet put on his one-man show of recent works at the galleries of *La Vie Moderne*, that likeness had appeared as an advertisement for the show in the pages of the illustrated magazine in the form of a lithograph after the painting.

11 This is one of the O.E.D.'s definitions of "relay."

12 Portraits, especially female portraits, of people with one glove off and one glove on have a history going back to Renaissance court portraits. During his time, they were not idiosyncratic to Manet: to see that it is a conventional motif, one need think only of Carolus-Duran's 1869 portrait of his wife in an elaborate black gown taking one glove off in a flirtatious, delicate-fingered gesture while the other glove lies discarded at her feet near her husband's scarlet signature (as if to signify the relationship between painter and painted as reciprocal, private as well as public, intimate as well as professional, indeed subtly sexual – for she performs a little striptease, and the placement of his signature beneath her glove suggests the gallant, prostrate position of glove-retrieving, hem-kissing dalliance). In Manet's case, however, the one-glove-off-one-glove-on motif is never so narrative, and never so directly suggestive in its hinted connotations. But it is tied to a running painterly theme in his pictures of people, especially of women, in which there is often a peculiar discrepancy between one hand and the other, both in their posing and in their manner of painting, such that the two-handedness of the body is used to disturb its symmetry and unity, to articulate a fundamental doubleness, and to index, more particularly, the doubleness and internal difference of Manet's way of painting, as well as of *coloris* more generally.

13 The portrait of Proust was received in relation to the much criticized *Chez la Père Lathuille*, with which it was shown at the Salon of 1880

– as if Proust had just emerged from the establishment pictured in the latter painting (thus suggesting that the Salon was a spectator event in which viewers looked at pictures in narrative relation to one another, and also providing evidence that people saw Manet's submissions as dialogic pairs, even if they did not read those pairs in the way that Manet might have wanted them to: as contrasting alternatives to one another). Others, who liked the portrait, described the personality of Proust that they felt was pictured in it, in a shorthand manner that was very like the descriptions of Manet as gentleman: "M. Proust est debout, sanglé dans sa redingote, la main sur la hanche, la face en pleine lumière, non pas avec une grave physionomie de rapporteur, mais avec le sourire qui va en s'éteignant de l'homme de l'esprit qui vient de décocher une ironie" – Philippe Burty, *La République Française*, 4 May, 1880; see Darragon, *Manet*, pp. 320–32.

14 "Manet m'écrivit:

'Voici, mon cher ami, trois semaines, que ton portrait est au Salon, mal exposé sur un pan coupé près d'une porte et encore plus mal jugé. Mais c'est mon lot d'être vilipendé et je prends la chose avec philosophie. On ne saurait cependant croire, mon cher ami, combien il est malaisé de *camper une figure seule sur une toile et de concentrer sur cette seule et unique figure tout l'intérêt, sans qu'elle cesse d'être vivante et pleine. Faire deux figures qui puisent leur attraction dans la dualité des personnages est à côté de cela un jeu d'enfant . . .* Ton portrait est une oeuvre sincère par excellence. *Je me souviens si c'était hier de la façon rapide et sommaire dont j'ai traité le gant de la main dégantée. Et quand tu m'as dit à ce moment: 'Je t'en prie, pas un trait de plus,' je sentais que nous étions si parfaitement d'accord que je n'ai pu résister au désir de t'embrasser.* Ah! pourvu que plus tard on n'ait pas la fantaisie de coller ce portrait dans une collection publique! J'ai toujours eu en horreur cette manie d'entasser les oeuvres d'art sans laisser de jour entre les cadres, comme on met les dernières nouveautés sur les rayons des magasins à la mode. Enfin, qui vivra verra. A la fortune du destin.

A toi,
Edouard Manet"

– Proust, *Manet, souvenirs*, pp. 102–03, my emphasis.

15 In fact, a good portion of Manet's output consists of paintings of "lone and unique" persons, each of whom, however, seems invested with

16 the "duality of . . . personae" that seems to have come easily to Manet.

16 Around the same time, Manet painted another self-portrait showing himself standing, full length, in studio apparel: uncompleted, this portrait (Tokyo, Bridgestone Museum of Art) stands, as was Manet's habit, as a kind of alternative to the *Self-Portrait with Palette*, and shows himself posing not as if before a mirror but as if he were a fellow artist come to pose, much like Marcelin Desboutin four years ealier, in the portrait otherwise known as *The Artist* (now in São Paolo). The two self-portraits hung together, on either side of his portait of Faure in the role of Hamlet (another substitute for himself), in his studio – see Darragon, *Manet*, p. 435.

17 In fact, self-portraits tend to be private business anyway; Manet also did not exhibit the other self-portrait painted at the same time but kept it in his studio (along with so much of the rest of his production that went back to his studio after being shown either at the Salon or at one of his other exhibition venues).

18 On the self-portrait and its opticality, see Gregory Galligan, "The Self Pictured: Manet, the Mirror, and the Occupation of Realist Painting," *Art Bulletin* LXXX:1, March 1998, pp. 139–71. See also Fried, *Manet's Modernism*, pp. 395–98.

19 On *Las Meninas*, see Michel Foucault, *The Order of Things: An Archaeology of the Human Sciences* (*Les Mots et les Choses*, 1966), New York, Vintage, 1973, pp. 3–16.

20 There seems to be a chain of references, sometimes dialogic and sometimes simply a matter of borrowing, linking the Manet, Cézanne, Van Gogh, and Picasso self-portraits: Cézanne lifts the painter's palette up above the bottom line of the canvas so that all of its tipped forward, flattened out surface can be seen and he adds back in Velasquez's turned canvas within a canvas (still reversed); Van Gogh repeats Cézanne's self-portrait almost verbatim, though with a different facture and a slightly closer, more tightly cropped presentation; and then Picasso reverses all three self-portraits to return to the orientation of his Spanish predecessor, still minus the larger context, and this time the brush in the painting hand has been omitted, so that an empty fist partners the palette-bearing hand, with its palette simultaneously flattened to meet the canvas and corner-up to ape the tilt of Velasquez's palette. Thus Manet's self-portrait (and with it Velasquez's self-image minus his court) has a substantial modernist afterlife, from which all of its poignant hesitations have been erased in favor of the artist's particular "handwriting" and its emphasis upon a pictorial confidence in the autonomous, self-reflexive self, whether sternly hermetic (Cézanne), troubled (Van Gogh), or simply ephebic (Picasso).

21 See Stephen Greenblatt, *Renaissance Self-Fashioning: From More to Shakespeare*, Chicago University Press, 1980.

Index